Leveraging Lean in Healthcare

Transforming Your Enterprise into a High Quality Patient Care Delivery System

" I never knew that four letters – L E A N – could be so powerful! Of particular interest to me were the productive principles and techniques of selected Lean applications in a healthcare setting. I'll never walk onto a hospital floor again without assessing for waste! Thank you for a thought provoking read that has caused me to assess my effectiveness in the healthcare environment."

— **Mary Jo Kirkpatrick,** MSN, RN Chair of the Associate of Science in Nursing Program, Mississippi University for Women, Chairman of the Quality Committee of the Board of Directors, Methodist/LeBonheur Healthcare System

"Lean methodologies, as profiled so succinctly in Protzman's book, offer an avenue towards improved patient safety and marked increases in efficiency for healthcare. The science and technology of healthcare, along with recent legislative and payment reforms, continue forcing the industry through a period of profound and unsettling change. This instructive book is well-timed and highly informative for those committed to creating deep levels of sustainable change in healthcare."

— **Peter B. Angood,** MD, FACS, FCCM Senior Advisor – Patient Safety, National Quality Forum (NQF)

"Having derived tremendous value through the application of PDSA/PDCA rapid cycle process improvement methods over the past decade to support discrete improvement initiatives, I now look forward to using *Leveraging Lean in Healthcare* as an essential reference as we pursue larger scale efforts to reduce waste and improve clinical effectiveness and safety across our organization."

— **David J. Ballard,** MD, PhD, FACP Chair, 2006-2010, AHRQ's Health Care Quality and Effectiveness Research Study Section, Chief Quality Officer, Baylor Health Care System, Recipient of the 2007 Leapfrog Patient-Centered Care Award, 2008 National Quality Healthcare Award of the National Quality Form, 2010 Preeminence Award of the American Medical Group Association

"In today's healthcare environment we must work to improve outcomes and reduce cost. It is a matter of survival. *Leveraging Lean in Healthcare: Transforming Your Enterprise into a High Quality Patient Care Delivery System* is the most practical and healthcare applicable book I have ever read on LEAN thinking and concepts. A must read for CEOs, managers and supervisors as it has all the tools needed to get the results we must achieve."

— **Gary Shorb,** CEO, Methodist Le Bonheur Healthcare

Over the years, ValuMetrix® Services has successfully partnered with Charlie Protzman and Business Improvement Group numerous times as we all worked toward a common goal – enabling healthcare organizations to begin their Lean journeys as an integral part of overall efforts to improve healthcare. The insights provided in this book will be invaluable to anyone trying to get a clearer understanding of what that Lean journey entails. To those wondering what Lean can do for them, Charlie and his colleagues provide case studies gleaned from many years of experience to illustrate Lean at work in the real world. We believe Charlie has succeeded in his goal to have this book play a role in the "quest to provide high quality, affordable healthcare to everyone in the years to come."

— **Rick Malik,** Worldwide Director, ValuMetrix® Services

"From the C-Suite to the frontline supervisor who desire to decrease waste, focus on patient-centered care and improve quality *Leveraging Lean in Healthcare* is a fundamental read. The authors' skillfully point out that successful outcomes depend on organizational will and an integrated, systematic approach using Lean methodology. In this book, Lean manufacturing principles were aptly translated into useful healthcare examples and tools based upon the authors' extensive clinical experiences. I can recommend this well written book as an essential reference in the library of all healthcare leaders interested in performance improvement."

— **Lee M. Adler,** DO Vice President, Quality and Safety Innovation & Research, Florida Hospital, Associate Professor of Internal Medicine, University of Central Florida College of Medicine

"It is a must read for all Leadership involved in healthcare. I think you would have a market for this book in the Masters of Nursing Leadership and Management realm as well as Masters Programs in Health Care Administration. I can see reading this book over and over."

— **Brigit Zamora,** BSN, RN, CPAN, CAPA Administrative Nurse Manager, Surigical RIO, Peds RIO, PTEC, Florida Hospital, Orlando

"The authors' hands-on experience shines through in this book. The understanding of Lean transformation principles coupled with practical examples delivers a powerful message to those striving for excellence in healthcare. This book does both!"

— **Thomas Chickerella,** CPM, Vice President and Program Management Officer, Vanguard Health Systems

Leveraging Lean in Healthcare

Transforming Your Enterprise into a High Quality Patient Care Delivery System

Charles Protzman • George Mayzell, MD • Joyce Kerpchar

CRC Press
Taylor & Francis Group
Boca Raton   London   New York

CRC Press is an imprint of the
Taylor & Francis Group, an **informa** business

A PRODUCTIVITY PRESS BOOK

Productivity Press
Taylor & Francis Group
270 Madison Avenue
New York, NY 10016

Printed in the United States of America on acid-free paper
10 9 8 7 6 5 4 3 2 1

International Standard Book Number: 978-1-4398-1385-0 (Paperback)

Visit the Taylor & Francis Web site at
http://www.taylorandfrancis.com

and the Productivity Press Web site at
http://www.productivitypress.com

This book is dedicated to the memory of David O'Koren. Dave was a business associate and a true friend as we worked and grew up in the challenging world of Lean.

Forty percent of the authors' profits from this book will be donated to help the homeless in their struggle for healthcare, shelter, hope in breaking the devastating cycle of drug addiction, and spiritual recovery through two local Baltimore charities: Helping Up Mission and Healthcare for the Homeless.

Contents

SECTION I Lean Overview and History

SECTION II Lean Tools, Methodology and Application

SECTION III Selected Lean Implementation Case Studies

SECTION IV Appendices

Preface

This book is intended to be a reference guide for healthcare executives and leaders, managers, process improvement team members, and inquisitive frontline workers who want to implement and leverage Lean to transform their enterprise into a *High-Quality Patient Care Business Delivery System*. Each word is key. Lean is a different way of thinking about processes. *High-Quality Patient Care* is imperative in healthcare. We always strive for the highest quality care systems. We do not encourage working faster or harder, as "haste makes wastes" and when we rush we make mistakes. *Business* means that Lean applies to anything that is a process, whether it is part of the physical patient care, information systems, or business systems (i.e., accounting, billing, marketing, etc.). All business processes should flow in order to reduce time throughout the whole system. *Delivery* refers to what it takes to deliver your product or service to the customer. The focus is on what value is added to the customer. *System* means every process we try to improve is linked or integrated with other processes. In most cases, healthcare is provided through an integrated delivery network or system. It is difficult to change one process without impacting several others. When you put all these words together, it leads to a culture change that is very powerful for any organization. The culture change is such that if you REALLY apply the concepts and tools, you become a world-class leader. If you have started or are considering Baldrige, or Shingo Prize, Lean Six Sigma positively impacts virtually all the criteria. Baldrige and Lean are about never-ending, continuous iterations of improvement.

The book is divided into parts and chapters by design. The chapters are designed, in most cases, to stand alone. Therefore, you will find some repetition throughout the book. There is also some repetition of concepts or even similarities among some lessons learned because we felt that these were important to the reader. This book is divided into three parts:

Part 1, Chapters 1 through 4, defines what Lean is, along with some unique history on the journey of the Lean maturity level that exists today. We also want to point out linkages between the Toyota Production System (TPS) and scientific management and the linkages between Frank and Lillian Gilbreth and Frederick Taylor. There are also links with a little-known organization called the Civil Communications Section (CCS), which was made up of Frank Polkinghorn, Homer Sarasohn, and my grandfather Charles W. Protzman Sr.

Between the authors, we have read more than 300 books on Lean, Six Sigma, and total quality, many of them from Productivity Press, to which we owe a debt to Norman Bodek, a pioneer in this field. We have been a customer of Productivity Press for many years; leveraging their expertise, we reference books from Productivity as well as other publishers. Many of these books are given out during our Lean training sessions, teaching students from all over the world. This book focuses primarily on Lean. It is our experience that the majority of initial productivity improvements in healthcare come from implementing Lean. We recommend using Lean concepts and tools first to streamline process and eliminate waste, then applying Six Sigma tools to reduce variation in process. Because the first four chapters focus more on the introduction and history of Lean, there are many manufacturing examples.

Part 2, which begins with Chapter 5, starts with descriptions of each of the Lean tools and concepts and how to apply them. They are organized in typical order of use and hierarchical priority; however, it should be noted that not all the tools are used all the time. We use the tools when appropriate to solve the problems at hand. We have put the tools in a format we call BASICS. Many organizations have standardized their own Lean problem-solving model while some have standardized on Six Sigma's DMAIC (design, measure, analyze, implement, control) model, or PDCA. The Lean tools can be worked into DMAIC or any other model; however, the Lean tools tend to cross categories within the DMAIC model. It does not matter what model you use as long as everyone understands that they are "tools" within the toolbox to use when implementing Lean Six Sigma to make improvements.

Part 3, which includes Chapters 15 through 23, is the final section and is a detailed look at how to implement Lean in various healthcare processes. We have spent many years studying and implementing Lean in small, medium, and large healthcare systems and organizations, and we have found that sharing lessons learned can be extremely valuable. The format for the chapters begins with the normal operation of each area from a traditional standpoint and where the typical problems occur. Then we walk through various Lean initiatives and show how we have used value stream mapping and other Lean tools. We introduce actionable blueprints so results can be duplicated or modified for use at other institutions. We also include examples, stories and case studies/results, and lessons learned.

This book promotes a philosophy based on measurable results with clear measurable improvements in quality and efficiency. We point out the tangible and intangible challenges around measuring return on investment (ROI).

Lean is not just an operations initiative. If implemented properly, the Lean philosophy will encourage changes in all aspects and areas of your organization. There are too few pages here to contain all the knowledge and techniques of implementing a Lean business delivery system. Instead, this book strives to include the most basic information that will be common to most business processes. The reader is encouraged to seek more information through reading the many good books on this subject and through interacting with others that are in pursuit of establishing a Lean enterprise. Additional reference books will be noted as we progress through each chapter.

Adopting a Lean culture is discussed, which includes implementing continuous improvement and scientific management principles to enable one to make decisions based on data vs. subjective opinions. The tools and implementation tips in this guide are designed to take you out of your comfort zone and provide you with facts to base decisions on who and what is ultimately value-added to your customer.

The book drives home the importance of the Lean Six Sigma journey. The pursuit of continuous improvement has no end. There is always more waste to be found and eliminated.

The reader should find encouragement and excitement on their journey with each success, and pay attention to and learn from the lessons taught by each setback. Your joy must be found in the quest to becoming Lean, because there is no end to what you and your organization can accomplish. Good luck on your Lean journey!

*A journey of a thousand miles begins by taking the initial step.**

Charles Protzman III, MBA, CPM,
George Mayzell, MD, MBA, FACP,
Joyce Kerpchar, PA-C

---

* Laozi, http://acc6.its.brooklyn.cuny.edu/~phalsall/texts/taote-v3.html, http://www.religiousworlds.com/taoism/ttcstan3.html Lao-Tzu, Tao Te Ching ch. 64.

Acknowledgments

This book includes many of our own firsthand experiences over the years and also references the work and experiences of many other reputable individuals who have worked in the world of Lean. We have been influenced by a great many who have chronicled their own Lean experiences, some of which we have incorporated into this work. We would like to thank all of those, too numerous to mention here, who have worked with us on Lean teams in the past and the senior leadership whose support made them successful. This book would not have been possible without your hard work, perseverance, and courage during our Lean journey together. Again, it would be impossible to cite all of them and, if we overlooked anyone, we truly apologize, but we hope each recognizes that this book wouldn't have come to fruition without their influence and expertise.

We would like to thank the following for their contributions to voluntarily co-author or contribute to the chapters below:

1. Chapter 2—History of Lean—Kenneth Hopper, international consultant and writer on management and industrial management history; co-author of book, *The Puritan Gift*

2. Chapter 13—Finance, Marketing, and our Hospitals—Brian Maskell, president of BMA Associates, who read several drafts of this chapter and provided content, editing advice, and text on the "Lean accounting" part of the chapter

3. Chapter 16—Nutritional Services—Shawn Noseworthy, RD, LD, MSA, director of Food and Nutrition Services, Florida Hospital Memorial Medical System

4. Chapter 18—Emergency Departments—Jody Lazarus, RN, CMAS, CCTC, MBA, BS, manager Nurse Auditing, Patient Financial Services, Adventist Health Systems

5. Chapter 20—Inpatient Floors—Douglas C. Johnson, RN, Lean Six Sigma Black

6. Chapter 22—Primary Care Clinics—Steve Stenberg, president, Continuous Progress

7. Michael Hogan of Progressive Business Solutions, LLC, whose partnership on many of these hospital projects has been invaluable. Mike's project work and resulting ideas have indirectly contributed to many parts of this book.

8. Special thanks to Rick Malik, Audrey Knable, and JoAnn Hegarty of ValuMetrix® Services for their help and guidance. Business Improvement Group has had a very successful and long-standing strategic partnership with ValuMetrix® Services, the division of Ortho-Clinical Diagnostics that provides expert Lean consulting to hospitals. Working together, we have been able to help healthcare organizations take the first steps along the path of their Lean journeys as we work toward improving healthcare for all. Without ValuMetrix® Services, this book would not have been possible.

9. Presbyterian Hospital in Albuquerque for their help and support: Alison B. Stanley, Director of Process Excellence, Beth Smith, MBA, Director, Perioperative Services for CNM, and Steve Griego, Master Black Belt.

10. Russ Scaffede for his insight into the Toyota System and for his contributions through numerous e-mail correspondence and edits with various parts of the book. He is owner of Lean Manufacturing Systems Group, LLC and Management Consulting Consultant, vice president of manufacturing at Toyota Boshoku America, past general manager/vice president of Toyota Motor Manufacturing Power Train, and past senior vice president, senior vice president of Global Manufacturing at Donnelly Corporation. Russ is co-author of the book, *The Leadership Roadmap: People, Lean & Innovation*, along with Dwane Baumgardner.

11. Many thanks to Kenneth Hopper and William Hopper for their assistance and input into this book. Kenneth and William are the authors of *The Puritan Gift: Reclaiming the American Dream amidst Global Financial Chaos*; their bios can be found at www.puritangift.com. It was Kenneth who brought the Civil Communications Section's (CCS) existence, mission, and contributions to light. Kenneth interviewed Charles Protzman Sr. in the early 1970s, which resulted in several articles on the CCS.

12. Joel Barker for his permission in referencing the paradigm material so important and integral to Lean implementations.

13. Thanks to Amy Evers, PhD, vice president of Type Resources, Myers-Briggs Type Indicator® certified, for her help and editing suggestions on the MBTI section

14. Thanks to our Productivity Press editor, Kris Medansky, who has been terrific at guiding us through our first writing project.

15. Many thanks to Cheryl Fenske, Fenske Communications, LLC, for the initial professional edit of the book.

16. Tim Schindele, Lewis Lefteroff and Brigit Zamora for taking valuable time out of their schedules to provide insightful thoughts, edits, and critiques of the initial drafts.

17. MaryBeth Protzman for her help in typing, editing, and reading over the many drafts of this text. We could not have done this project without the many hours she has devoted to this project. We are a good team.

18. MaryBeth Protzman, Lauren Protzman, and J.C. Protzman for their transcription support.

19. Daniel Protzman, Tim Schindele, Donna Fox, Jack Protzman, and Jon Banks for their editing assistance.

20. The AlliedSignal Bendix Communications Division "Hats" team for all their assistance and support, which resulted in our initial successful Lean culture changes in manufacturing.

21. The families of all the authors for their support and contributions throughout the process of this project.

22. There are many more individuals who contributed to this book, both directly and indirectly. We have worked with a great many dedicated individuals—too many to list here—who have shared their knowledge and experiences with us. While it is impossible to cite them all, we hope they see this book as the culmination of our respect and appreciation for all they have done.

23. William M. Tsutsui, associate dean for International Studies, professor of History, College of Liberal Arts & Sciences, University of Kansas, for his assistance in Japanese Kanji translation.

Charlie states, "My grandfather started me down this path and has influenced my life in the past and continues to do so to this day. My grandfather made four trips to Japan from 1948 to the 1960s. He loved the Japanese people and culture and was passionate and determined to see Japanese manufacturing recover from World War II and become economically viable." Charles W. Protzman Sr., who worked at Western Electric Hawthorne Works (during the Hawthorne Experiments) was asked by General MacArthur to join Frank Polkinghorn and Homer Sarasohn as part of the Civil Communication Section during the occupation of Japan after World War II.

Lean Is a Matter of Survival

What hospitals must realize is that cost reduction (not cost cutting) and the ability to maintain customer service and delivery of quality care through continuous process improvement is not an option but a necessity if they are to survive. This book is an attempt to show that while not easy to implement, Lean is a very powerful system and is applicable to the entire healthcare value stream. While all hospitals and departments are somewhat unique, Lean principles and thinking can be applied to everyone, everywhere, throughout the world. We hope this book is helpful in providing a catalyst for healthcare systems to change and thrive, making healthcare an affordable and efficient proposition for all of us who eventually become patients. In addition, that it will provide some insight to a key piece of the puzzle in the quest to provide high quality, affordable healthcare to everyone in the years to come.

Authors

CHARLES W. PROTZMAN, III, MBA, CPM

In November 1997, Charlie Protzman formed Business Improvement Group, LLC (BIG). BIG is located in Baltimore, MD, and specializes in implementing Lean thinking principles and the Lean business delivery system (LBDS).

Charlie has over 26 years experience in materials and operations management. He spent over 13 years with AlliedSignal, now Honeywell, where he was an aerospace strategic operations manager and the first AlliedSignal Lean master. He has received numerous special-recognition and cost-reduction awards. Charlie was an external consultant for DBED's Maryland Consortium while he was with AlliedSignal. He had input into the resulting World Class Criteria document and assisted in the first three initial DBED World Class Company Assessments. Charlie has taught students in Lean principles and total quality from all over the world.

Charlie has spent the last 16 years implementing successful Lean product line conversions, Kaizen events, administrative business system improvements (transactional Lean) across the United States. He specializes in hospital/healthcare implementations in addition to manufacturing.

Charlie has a BA and MBA from Loyola University in Maryland. He is currently a member of SME, SAE, IIE, and the Association for Psychological Type. He is a charter certified MBTI instructor. He was a past member of APICS, AME Champions Club, and NAPM organizations.

GEORGE MAYZELL, MD, MBA, FACP

Dr. George Mayzell is a board certified internist and geriatrician with over 10 years of patient care experience and over 15 years of administrative health industry experience.

Dr. Mayzell assumed the role of senior vice president and chief patient care officer in December 2008 at Methodist Le Bonheur Healthcare. Methodist is a seven hospital system with over 1600 licensed beds in Memphis, TN. He is responsible for patient care operations and oversight of regulatory readiness for the system. Previously, he served as chief medical officer (CMO) for Methodist Germantown Hospital.

In addition to being a past faculty member at the University of Florida, Dr. Mayzell also worked at Blue Cross Blue Shield of Florida where he was directly involved with medical management activities, including disease management, utilization review, appeals and grievances, case management, pharmacy benefits, pay for performance, and Medicare risk.

JOYCE KERPCHAR, PA-C

Joyce Kerpchar has over twenty-eight years of healthcare industry experience and currently serves as the Director of the Institute for Surgical Advancement at Florida Hospital Orlando, which is part of the Adventist Health System, an acute-care, tertiary hospital caring for more than 1.5 million patients a year. She joined Florida Hospital in 2001 and spent over five years as a senior consultant implementing Lean across the eight campuses in a variety of clinical departments, is a Six Sigma Black Belt and is a certified MBTI instructor.

She began her career as a board certified physician's assistant in cardiovascular and thoracic surgery and primary care medicine. Prior to joining Florida Hospital, she held a variety of administrative positions in healthcare-related industries, which included managed care operations and contracting for a PruCare/Prudential Healthcare who served 200,000 members in nine counties in Central Florida, Product Management for Avio Corporation, a provider of information technology for ambulatory healthcare organization, and was a partner in a consulting firm which specialized in business and market entry strategy for high tech start-ups.

Ms. Kerpchar is passionate about leveraging Lean in healthcare processes, to eliminate waste and reduce errors, to improve the overall quality and reduce the cost of providing healthcare.

Author's Notes

BACKGROUND—NOTES FROM THE AUTHORS

Our approach is based on the traditional plan-do-study-act (PDSA) Shewhart model and later changed by the Japanese to plan-do-check-act (PDCA) normally associated with Deming. We have assigned our initial implementation and problem-solving model the acronym BASICS, which stands for Baseline, Analyze, Suggest Recommend, Implement, Create, and Sustain. We then follow up on this model with never-ending PDSA cycles.

There is a linkage and synergy between Six Sigma and Lean. Six Sigma was popularized by Motorola and GE and is basically a re-packaging of total quality, Deming, and Juran tools. Six Sigma and Lean attack similar problems but how they approach the problem differs. Six Sigma approaches problems by focusing on the reduction variation and defects, Lean approaches problems through the elimination of non-value added activities or waste, and improves process flow. We believe they are complementary approaches and both are needed in order to have a complete continuous improvement program.

Note: Toyota does not have Six Sigma Green or Black Belts.[*] The Toyota production system incorporates Six Sigma tools, but they are utilized as part of a total company-wide quality control culture. Toyota's system is based on using mistake proofing to eliminate defects vs. Six Sigma, which denotes 3.4 defects per million opportunities in order for companies to "measure" defects. Both strive to achieve zero defects.

PARADOXES

How did we get so far away from the great American company culture models of the past since the time of the Industrial Revolution? Too many companies want too much from too few, and they want it right away with a total focus on the next quarter's stock analysts meetings. What a paradox that American companies outsource so much now, yet many other countries' companies now manufacture in the United States. We have managers who are business and health administration school trained, but have never done the work of their employees and finance people driving operational decisions in our hospital and clinical environments. This creates a challenge in credibility with staff if their supervisors and managers cannot even train them in how to do the job. As a country, we have abandoned the techniques and philosophies that we created and made us great. We have since taught these principles to the Japanese, who listened to our teachers, the CCS, Deming, Drucker, Juran, etc., while the United States would not listen.

We need to get back to basics where company loyalty, promotion from within, job flexibility, and cross-training participation on cross-functional improvement teams with a focus on the long term becomes the way of life. This is the embodiment of the Lean culture. We need to get back to a culture where continuous improvement is expected and employee participation is not only encouraged, but also becomes part of their job. In the 1960s, the Japanese were known for making cheap toys and copying everything.[†] Now it is the Japanese who are teaching us what we taught them and which they have continuously improved on.

CHARLIE PROTZMAN

Lean principles are based primarily on what has come to be known as the Toyota Production System. The Honda Production System was introduced to me by a former Honda employee and later hospital executive, Tom Chickerella, who gave me a copy of the book, *Powered by Honda*. Tom explained how the Honda system is different from Toyota and has influenced many of their American supply chain companies, and hospitals so it is mentioned in this book as well.

Toyota has been working on implementing Lean principles with the automobile since the late 1950s, but one could argue it started back with Toyoda Loom Works in 1924 with the automatic spinning loom.[‡] Toyota's success came to light after the oil shocks in the 1970s. Toyota outsold Ford worldwide for the first time in September 2003[§] while posting a $4.8 billion profit and then surpassed Ford as number 2 in 2007.[¶] They outsold GM for the first time during the first quarter of 2007 worldwide[**] and hit a profit record in May 2007.[††] They assumed the number one position in 2008, ending GM's 77-year reign by selling 8.9 million vehicles vs. GM's 8.36 million;[‡‡] however, even the Toyota system has been challenged by a series of recent recalls showing the journey toward perfection is never ending.

---

[*] Talk to MWCMC by Gary Convis, April 2008; Yoshio Kondo, *Company Wide Quality Control* (Zenshateki Hinshitsu Kanri) (JUSE Press) 1993; Jeffrey Liker, *Toyota Way* (New York: McGraw Hill) 2005.

[†] Joel Barker, *Business of Paradigms,* 2001. http://www.joelbarker.com/nvideos.php.

[‡] http://www.toyota-industries.com/corporateinfo/history; Sakichi Toyoda invents Toyoda automatic loom, Type G, with non-stop shuttle-change motion.

[§] "Toyota Outsells Ford Worldwide," *USA Today*, November 1, 2003; "Toyota's 6-month profit jumps to 4.8 billion," USA Today, November 6, 2003.

[¶] *Baltimore Sun Papers*, January 4, 2008.

[**] "Toyota Outsells GM for the First Time," *USA Today*, April 25, 2007.

[††] "Toyota's Annual Profit Hits Record," *USA Today*, May 10, 2007.

[‡‡] *Baltimore Sun Papers*, *Bloomberg News*, *Associated Press* and the *Washington Post* contributed to the article, January 23, 2009.

My formal training in Lean started with demand flow technology (DFT) provided by the World Wide Consulting Group in Denver and described in a book called *Quantum Leap*.[*] I was then taught by a group called TBM and Shingijitsu, who implemented Lean using a tool called "Point Kaizen events." We implemented Point Kaizen events at AlliedSignal (now Honeywell) for nearly two years, which included a trip to Japan in 1996 where I was involved in a Point Kaizen event with Hitachi. All our events were initially successful, but many had trouble sustaining themselves. We found pros and cons to this implementation method.

Prior to Lean, we rolled out total quality management (TQM) and incorporated various pieces of what came to be known as Lean. We were also rolling out a program called Six Sigma. At Bendix Communications Division of AlliedSignal, we were launching so many different initiatives that many became "flavors of the month." There was a constant political battle between Six Sigma and Lean within AlliedSignal, with total quality being the framework for both.

Fortunately, our vice president of Lean introduced me to a Lean consultant, Mark Jamrog of SMC Group, and told me to help him with whatever he needed. Mark sat me down and asked if I had an open mind and was willing to learn. I said yes. In the first hour with Mark, I learned more about Lean than from all the other consultants put together.

Our first Lean system implementation, notice I say *implementation* vs. Point Kaizen event, was on a secure communications product for the military. We went from 27 operators to 13 with a 205% increase in output for an 82% improvement in productivity on the line—and that was after it had been hit with three one-week Point Kaizen events over the course of a year, one of which was led by a leading Japanese consulting firm. No one was laid off! Everyone was redeployed to another project or to new improvement teams.

I worked with Mark for nine months and, gradually, I really started learning Lean thinking. The Lean system implementation approach that Mark had developed was what we might now refer to as a combination of the Ohno and Shingo approach. Mark then told me to read two books: *Toyota Production System From an Engineering Viewpoint* and *Today and Tomorrow* by Henry Ford. I have since read more than 300 books on Lean (most from Productivity Press), with some dating back to 1911 and one back to the 1700s. Mark taught me how little I really knew. Mark's approach based on the Shingo and Ohno methodology has never failed us. This approach has always worked, and most of my clients are still sustaining and improving as we write this book. We have now taken this approach and adopted it for hospitals.

I use both Six Sigma and Total Quality tools in addition to the Lean tools. They should all co-exist in the continuous improvement tool chest. Since I am not a Six Sigma Black Belt, I refer my manufacturing companies to a good friend of mine and Master Black Belt, Cory Liffrig, president of Six Sigma Solutions. Cory is a practitioner who has a unique approach, focusing the training on the practical application of the Six Sigma tools rather than focusing just on the eloquent use of statistics.

Lessons Learned: *When you think you know it all, it's time to quit. Even today, I am still learning with every Lean implementation.*

JOYCE KERPCHAR, PA-C.

I was introduced to Lean more than five years ago as a seasoned healthcare expert leveraging traditional quality improvement methods to improve processes, working directly for Integrated Delivery Networks/Systems (IDN/IDS), for companies who paid for the services provided by IDNs and/or developing and selling products to IDNs. In 2004, I was given the opportunity to embark on leading out the Lean journey in a large healthcare organization at a time when Lean was just being introduced to healthcare organizations and they were beginning to "test" the application of Lean in healthcare and service-related environments. Throughout the initial Lean project, the concepts were put to the test in one of the most challenging healthcare environments—the emergency room—and there was an immediate recognition that the application of Lean concepts and tools, if coupled with appropriate change management techniques, could transform how healthcare is delivered within the United States and throughout the world. By shifting the paradigm of healthcare workers to look at the value stream and leverage the "voice of the customer" to identify and drive waste out of the system, it was quickly determined that both the quality and how healthcare is delivered could be dramatically improved. After spending the next four years utilizing Lean concepts and tools in a variety of clinical and support service settings, I saw how Lean became key in solving quality and safety concerns by reducing errors and improving productivity, thereby enabling organizations to do more with less, providing techniques to better predict customer demand, and optimizing the utilization of space, all contributing to dramatic improvements in financial performance. I recognized that the dissemination of Lean concepts and culture and the application of Lean tools are crucial to help the country to transform healthcare and assist in producing the savings needed to extend healthcare coverage to all.

I would like to thank my fellow co-author, Charles Protzman, who subcontracted for ValuMetrix Services® as my original "Lean sensei"; Charles Morris, who mentored my Six Sigma Black Belt; and Florida Hospital (Adventist Health System), who gave me the opportunity to learn and apply and train others in Lean/Six Sigma. After years of engaging in a blended Lean/Six Sigma approach, I believe that the combination of Lean concepts and tools, and the analytical rigor, variation reduction, and change management of Six Sigma provides a comprehensive methodology of how to revolutionize healthcare. I hope this book it helps you to advance to the next level of understanding of how the application of Lean can transform the delivery of healthcare and play a pivotal role in the healthcare reform effort.

---

[*] Costanza, Quantum Leap (Costanza Institute of Technology) 1996.

GEORGE MAYZELL, MD

Compared to my co-authors, I am relatively new to Lean. My focus and experience is primarily in healthcare, first running a large physician practice, and then ultimately working for a known managed care company and now for a hospital system. As I have had a chance to survey the healthcare industry from multiple different viewpoints, I have learned to appreciate the inefficiencies that are inherent in this complex and often incomprehensible system. Clearly, I am not alone in this observation, with the push for healthcare reform imminent.

As I learned about Lean over the years, I quickly realized that in some ways, this is what I have been doing every day. Most of my jobs have centered on looking at complex medical processes and helping to simplify them. While I have been doing this for many years, I have to confess that I have not always been aware that the disciplined science and system of Lean was what I was trying to do. It would have been nice to be able to name such activities many, many years ago as I started on my process improvement journeys.

I have greatly enjoyed writing this book and, hopefully, I have added a healthcare focus as well as macro-economic views of healthcare. Clearly, efficiency is going to become increasingly important in healthcare as the healthcare delivery system becomes more ROI focused.

The healthcare system is still currently a patchwork of cottage industry physician practices, third-party payers, and volunteer hospital medical staff, healthcare workers (who may or may not be unionized), as well as myriad medico legal complexities. The dramatic expansion of healthcare and medical knowledge and evidence-based care adds to an ever expanding landscape. In this mix and match of healthcare delivery, it is very difficult sometimes to remember who the customer is. For many years, we have been confused into making the customer the physician, or the payer and even sometimes the patient. Lean makes the voice of the customer a paramount focus and an important baseline in understanding and focus.

I think many of us would agree that the current healthcare system is unsustainable and must be changed. As the improvements are made, many will focus on expanding coverage and decreasing reimbursement. They will focus on utilization as well as unit cost controls. These adjustments will push healthcare providers (I mean all healthcare providers) to increase efficiency and provide a Lean and efficient healthcare system. An efficient healthcare system is not only important for the near term; it is critical to long-term survival.

I believe that without a much more efficient healthcare system, we cannot continue to deliver the same quality of healthcare that we know and cherish. The economics just will not work. While many people believe that America has the best healthcare in the world, many people also believe that we have some of the worst healthcare in the world for the dollars that we spend. Creating a more efficient healthcare system that keeps sight of the quality that the customer wants and deserves is critical. I hope that this book helps other healthcare executives accomplish this.

Section I

Lean Overview and History

1 Introduction to Lean

EXECUTIVE SUMMARY

Because Lean started in manufacturing and is being adapted to healthcare, this chapter begins with several manufacturing examples. It is only in this environment that Lean principles can be truly understood in their purest form. All of the lessons that have been learned readily apply to Lean in healthcare and examples are provided. Discussions related to "big company disease" are also included.

The results that one can expect from implementing Lean in most hospital/healthcare-related areas are outlined. These results are functionally based, since most hospitals are still functionally based. Some hospitals are moving to the service line concept. These results will translate to the service lines as well. Many companies will try Lean. Based on previous experience, it seems that of the companies that try it:

- 40% are either not exposed to it, dabble with it, or choose not to try it.
- 40% will try it and struggle with it.
- 20% will try it with some level of success (and of these, 5% will take Lean further).

Typical Lean results, when given sufficient time to work, can result in:

- 20–80% productivity improvement
- 50–90% reduction in inven∆tory
- 50–99% throughput time reduction
- 30–50% reduction in space requirements
- 10–30% reduction in overheads

KEY LEARNINGS

- Hospitals can leverage Lean to improve their processes.
- Lessons learned can help hospitals to implement Lean successfully in order to improve the overall adoption.
- Lean can achieve results which will drive customer-focused, high-quality, and cost-effective care.

INTRODUCTION – WHAT IS LEAN?

No one has more trouble than the person who claims to have no trouble.

—Taiichi Ohno
Father of the Toyota Production System

There are hundreds of books that address Lean thinking and the Toyota Production System (TPS). Lean is a term that originated in manufacturing to describe a way of thinking about or running companies as an enterprise. Becoming Lean requires the continual pursuit to identify and eliminate waste and establish efficient flow within the overall organization. The term "value stream" is used today to describe what is involved in producing a product or service from raw material, manufacturing, distributing, wholesaling, and retailing to recycling. Even though healthcare and service organizations may not begin with raw material or even manufacture a product, they still have value streams related to providing healthcare services to their customers.

The purpose of this book is to give the reader an overview of Lean thinking and principles and how it has been and can be applied to healthcare. This book is primarily directed toward healthcare leadership, from the CEO to the frontline supervisor; however, it can also be helpful to anyone who wishes to learn more about Lean thinking. The book is designed for those who have had some introduction to Lean principles or Point Kaizen events. Lean concepts were originally developed around manufacturing, so we have used some manufacturing terms and examples throughout the book in order to best explain the underlying meanings to the reader. Lean principles have been adapted to healthcare, and as such, the reader needs to be able to stretch and convert referenced manufacturing examples to apply them in their healthcare environment.

"Lean" is a term used to describe a philosophy and way of thinking. Lean has its roots in the United States, but what we know today as Lean was taken to another level and expanded company-wide by Toyota. Lean, if implemented properly, is an enterprise-wide initiative that requires a significant cultural change. It will not be successful if it is directed only at the frontline staff. This means if Lean or Lean/Sigma (the combination of Lean and Six Sigma) is to be truly successful it must include all functional areas (i.e., finance, marketing, information systems, etc.), all levels, from the board of directors to the patient, and all value streams within the enterprise. Lean principles are based on what is known today as the Toyota Production System. Toyota Motor Company has been working on implementing and improving the application of Lean principles since Taiichi Ohno started in their machine shop in Japan in 1945.[*]

---

[*] Art Smalley, "A Brief History of Setup Reduction," www.artoflean.com; also Taiichi Ohno, *Toyota Production System* (New York: Productivity Press) 1988.

MY INTRODUCTION TO LEAN THINKING—BY CHARLIE PROTZMAN

We are all introduced to Lean in a different way, sometimes by a friend, article, book, or simply by visiting a company where Lean has been implemented. I want to share my initial entry into Lean, so you can see how my experiences in manufacturing may be similar to what you have or what you are experiencing in implementing Lean in your company or healthcare environment. Many of us are exposed to Lean principles and some of us naturally think Lean, yet we don't realize it.

The following are several manufacturing stories that reveal important lessons I learned as I was introduced to and grew up in the Lean world. Each can be tied in some way to the healthcare world. Whether you are new to Lean or well down the Lean maturity path, as you read through the stories, I encourage you to reflect on your own experiences with Lean. I am sure you will find some similarities.

While I didn't know it at the time, my history with Lean began with a new general manager (GM) of our plant. At the time, I had been promoted to "dock-to-stock" manager, managing all supplies and materials shipped to the plant. I was responsible for receiving and stocking, as well as issuing parts kits to the manufacturing floor. At the time, our manufacturing floor was experiencing significant shortages (lack of parts), and we could not ship our product. When I first toured the receiving area, I found boxes of materials that had been sitting in a large store room prior to inspection for months and couldn't get through the inspection and stocking process.

My general manager gave me specific instructions to issue only one box at a time to the Inspection Department. At the point, I didn't understand how this would help our severe backlog. I worked with another new manager of inspection (QA), Curtis McTeer, and others to barcode and create a Microsoft Access® database to log every item in the dock-to-stock process. We took every item out of inspection and into a holding area, issuing one box at a time to each inspector and logging each into the database. Once they completed the work, inspectors could come back for another box. Suddenly, something amazing happened: over a 2-week period, we cut our backlog from 12 weeks to 6 weeks! In addition, we found that, without the excess inventory, there was plenty of room in the Inspection Department. We also found that we had double-ordered much of the material that was assumed to be lost. Within 4 weeks, we were down to a 2-week backlog and within 6 weeks we had caught up. We freed up a tremendous amount of space and everything now flowed smoothly through the dock-to-stock process. This is when we first learned the true power of one-piece flow (Lean), even though we didn't understand it at the time.

When we went back to analyze the root cause of the problem, we discovered the reason we got so far behind was that we were batching the inspection of items. Batching, in this case, meant the inspectors would go into the dock storage area and grab four or five lots of material, usually choosing the easiest things to do. When we cleaned out the inspection area, we found each station was full of material that the inspectors were "working on." Instead of finishing one lot, they would take each lot and run it through the first inspection operation, then run all the lots through the second operation, etc., until they were all completed. This means each lot was stuck and could not be completed until the last operation was done on every lot. A great deal of time was lost moving and searching, and our management staff had been turned into day-to-day firefighters and high-paid expediters.

Lesson Learned: *Batching environments are fraught with waste, inventory, lack of space, and delays. One-piece flow works better than batch. Batch environments create the perception of the need for more space and more people. People always take the easiest things to work on first in a batch environment. Once you "Lean out" an area, it makes supervision of the area much easier, provides time to work on improvements, and makes identification of what needs to be worked on more visually apparent. Results can be obtained quickly within a specific area or process. Root cause analysis solves the problem so it never comes back.*

Note: *Technically, since Lean is continuous improvement it is never "Leaned out." This term is used occasionally throughout the book referencing the first time Lean principles have been applied or implemented in an area.*

My next experience with Lean dealt with something called slide lines. Our division manufactured electronic circuit boards and systems equipment primarily for the military. We invested significant capital in machines that sequenced transistors and diodes so they could be put onto another machine, which put those parts into circuit boards. The boards would then move to another set of functionally laid out equipment ("like" machines placed together) that would put integrated circuit chips into the circuit boards. We would issue parts kits pulled from the first and second floors of our stockroom (sometimes for hundreds of boards), which were transported across a parking lot to the manufacturing building. The kits would slowly make their way from machine to machine. We were doing major league "batching." We had an army of material, inventory, and production control people to track all the material being batch processed through the factory. When notified that there was a parts shortage in the kits, we found the problem was that we regularly released up to a week's worth of kits to the floor at a time. If an operator had a problem with a part or lost a part, he would simply "steal" it from the next kit, creating a shortage.

Note: *We have found similar problems in surgery in hospitals. If a supply item is missing and it just so happens to be on the next case cart, it would find its way into the current case and create a shortage for the next case. There is no hesitation in opening the next surgical pack to solve the current crisis, even at the expense of delaying the next case.*

The longer it took to change a machine over from one lot to the next, the larger the batch of boards we would run through it. There were so many carts of material on the floor in various unfinished stages that it was difficult to find a particular customer order. As the batches got larger, the time it took to get the boards through the factory grew, putting us behind on our delivery dates and requiring us to pick and choose lots we had to expedite (often based on the most vocally upset customers).

Note: *This process is similar to the triage process in an Emergency Department (ED), when patients are not seen in first in, first out order (FIFO), but are seen based on level of complaint. If they are asked to wait so patients who require more urgent attention can be evaluated first, over time, "the waiting" patients become dissatisfied and the most vocal often get the next priority, thus "the squeaky wheel." This is also true of clinics. In general, the longer a patient has to wait, the longer the physician or nurse needs to spend with them to appease them. This increases the delays for the next patient.*

After all the parts were inserted, the boards were wave soldered on a huge machine and inspected by several people to fix all the problems the machines created. Ironically, some boards were so bad that we sent them to what we called the "hospital" to be fixed. Many manufacturers have specially designated areas where parts or products are reworked; these virtual rework cells are often built into the processes and factory layouts. We create these "hospital" areas because we assume we can't fix the design or root cause problem in the process, so we actually *plan for rework*.

Once, when things got really bad, the production manager said, "Let's set up a slide line!" This was a temporary line put together that had stand-up workstations with two adjustable tracks running down the length of the line. The circuit board would fit in these tracks and slide from person to person. Each person had three or four parts that they would assemble into the board before passing it on. The fascinating part of this story is that we could produce boards so much faster this way that we would catch up our past due customer orders within 1–3 weeks. This line also had virtually no rework and thus did not need the "hospital" areas. We didn't know it at the time, but we were utilizing what we now know as a "Lean" line.

Of course, once we had caught up our production schedule, we would go back to batching all the parts through the machines until someone would suggest we set the slide line up again. Why didn't it occur to us to just keep the slide lines set up? It was because we had all this money and time invested in the old equipment and systems. Previous managers had spent a lot of time putting together return on investments (ROIs) to justify all the capital equipment we purchased and we weren't about to just abandon it. After all, people's job descriptions, training, and reporting had been built around these batch processes. It was our investment in these "systems" that got in our way of standardizing the slide line type of assembly.

During this time, a new book came out called *The Machine That Changed the World*, by Jim Womack and Dan Jones. It was a 5-year MIT study of the automotive industry. In addition, a new video called *Business of Paradigms* by Joel Barker was released. The managers read this book, watched the video and we started to realize we could make changes to our processes and obtain significant improvements. In the end, we created a model Lean site that was benchmarked by other companies for high-performance work teams and Lean systems.

Lessons Learned: *We don't always realize when we are doing Lean things and if we do, it doesn't always occur to us to standardize it. Large batch sizes result in longer lead times and increased inventory. One-piece flow works better than batch. One-piece flow resulted in eliminating hundreds of carts we no longer needed to store inventory and freed up more than 50% of our space in manufacturing. We also eliminated the stockroom building, stopped issuing kits, and had room to put all the materials on the floor, reducing searching, firefighting, and expediting. Old batch systems and financial systems and philosophy get in the way of implementing Lean systems. Building rework into the process removes the need to fix the underlying root cause of the problem, thus accepting it as a part of the process and lowering the overall standard for the operation.*

The next story involves a "counter bagger" machine, which counted out the screws for the kits we issued to the floor. A year or so prior to my arrival, the previous director convinced upper management of the need to purchase this equipment. It was supposed to free up a person and speed up operations. However, when I took over the department I found no one ever used it and only one person even knew how to run it. It was already in need of maintenance (with no money in the budget to fix it) and the person whose time it was supposed to save had to stand and run/watch the machine in case it broke down or jammed. The machine wasted a lot of valuable space and went against the normal flow of the stockroom. All the parts were stored and counted upstairs, but the counter bagger was put downstairs because that was where it fit. When we analyzed the process and realized the number of mistakes the machine made and how often it was "down" (not working), we discovered that we could actually count the parts out faster by hand. Being a young, somewhat naïve manager, I decided to submit a request to scrap the machine. The previous director got wind of it and confronted me. Then, finance said we couldn't get rid of it because it wasn't written off yet and my job was literally threatened if I continued down this course. Since the first rule of a change agent is "to survive," I kept the machine… but we were never able to use it! Over time, as we shifted the factory into a Lean environment, the whole stockroom went away, and we eventually scrapped the machine.

Lesson Learned: *Automation and the introduction of new software do not always solve the problem. Automation does not always free up people and, in some cases, results in* *more people. If you purchase a machine, it should free up a person's time. They should not have to watch the machine in case it might stop or breakdown.*

DEALING DIRECTLY WITH TOYOTA

During a company training session, I was told the following story from someone in our automotive group. There was a company that wanted to sell their spark plugs to Toyota. Toyota insisted on receiving samples prior to deciding whether to utilize them as a supplier. The company pulled the best samples out of its production lot and sent them to Toyota. Toyota analyzed the samples and told the company they would not purchase their product because the quality was poor. The company asked if any of the spark plugs did not meet the specs. Toyota said they all met the specs. So what was the problem? Toyota responded that the problem was that when they completed testing the random sample of spark plugs, they were actually able to determine the order in which they were processed. They also noticed that the process was not under control owing to the variations in the specs. This means the spark plugs would have gone out of spec and, at some point, would be bad. This indicated that the company did not have enough process controls in place nor did it have what is known as the Six Sigma term—process capability.

Lesson Learned: *Batch systems, not always, but generally have little control over their processes. The emphasis is placed on meeting a specification using inspection, "experience," or statistical process control (SPC) vs. developing a capable process with a combination of people, material, and machines designed to make good parts all the time with zero defects.*

PLACING ORDERS WITH A JAPANESE SUPPLIER

In another instance, parts were ordered from a Japanese supplier. One of the normal purchase order clauses imposed quality criteria, which stated that "lots" of parts shipped had to be 97% good parts. So the Japanese supplier shipped 3% of the parts in a bag labeled "bad" parts. When asked why, the Japanese supplier said they did this to meet our 97% acceptable parts criteria.

Lesson Learned: *Be careful what you ask for. Insist on a 100% defect-free product.*

UNITED STATES VS. JAPAN—DEALING WITH QUALITY

Company X, a tier two automotive supplier, was experiencing problems with its production line. The problem turned into delinquent deliveries and broken promises to their customers. One of the customers was a US company and one was Honda. Both customers scheduled visits with the company to find out first hand what the problem was and how they were going to

resolve it. Several of Company X's people were charged by senior management with preparing a first class PowerPoint presentation designed to get them out of this mess. The US customer arrived and was taken to a conference room filled with delicious assorted breakfast items. Company X presented the PowerPoint to the US customer, describing the problems with late deliveries and the corrective actions that were to be taken. The customer was given lunch followed by a quick tour of the line and returned home satisfied with the explanation. Honda visited the next day. Company X took them to the conference room filled with delicious goodies and stated their intentions to go through the same thoroughly re-scrubbed PowerPoint presentation. Honda told them to forget the presentation and take them to the floor to show them the problem. Honda asked Company X for the root causes, which Honda found to be symptoms rather than the root causes of the problem. Honda worked with Company X for 3 days to discover the true root cause, countermeasures and corrective actions.

Lesson Learned: *You can't fix problems with PowerPoint presentations, reviewing reports in your office, or by listening to what someone else thinks is the problem. If you really want to know what is going on as a manager or leader, you must experience the problem first hand on the floor (at the Gemba).*

LEAN AND HOSPITALS

So How can we make a Comparison in what Occurs on the Manufacturing Floor to How a Hospital Provides Services?

First of all, we can all agree that hospitals are not factories. Factories deal with products while hospitals deal with people. While our products in factories cannot talk to us, patients do talk to us before, during, and after they go through our processes.

The stories outlined above show that, prior to implementing Lean, manufacturing entities were ignorant about their processes. In many cases, the processes were poorly documented, if documented at all. They also show that when Lean solutions are applied, they result in significant improvement. We have found that organizations and processes within the healthcare environment are not all that different from organizations and processes within factories. Most departments are organized in silos, while executive leadership is located sometimes on the top floor or even in another building miles away, and they spend the majority of their time in meetings. They have no time left to get out to the floor (*Gemba*) "actual place" to see what is happening first hand. Most healthcare leadership teams we have seen do not have a clear understanding of their value streams or the interconnectivity of their processes. In today's literature, this is referred to as "big company disease." It is somewhat ironic that this manufacturing terminology has the healthcare connotation "disease."

Listed below are the worst symptoms of this disease.[*]

1. People can't get anything done because they are always at a meeting. Meetings are not run effectively, people show up late, don't come to any conclusions, actions aren't recorded, and there is no follow up.
2. Your employees do not think of the customer as the number one priority and are more concerned with internal politics.
3. The company has more than five layers from the front-line to the president and is slow to respond to any type of challenge, leadership initiative, or customer feedback. It takes more than an hour to make a decision.
4. The company hires consultants to do their strategic planning.
5. The company tends to emphasize consensus at the expense of professional insight.
6. The budgeting process takes over a week and, in some cases, 3–6 months, and then finance dictates the budget.
7. The company reacts to people's opinions and makes "knee-jerk" decisions vs. discovering and acting on data and facts.
8. Talk about past glories increases at the expense of future dreams, resulting in general complacency and stagnation.
9. Authority, loyalty, and respect are replaced by the desire for power at the expense of your employees.
10. You pay a service to water your plants.

We hypothesize that big company disease starts at the point where leaders switch from wearing many hats to when they are assigned one hat for a specific department and are not responsible for the value stream. This begins the "that's not our job" or the territorial "they are doing our job" discussions. The goal with Lean is to get back to basic fundamentals in management. We need to restore the ideals of company loyalty, gain domain knowledge of the business, have supervisors able to train employees in the job, develop our leaders by promoting from within, and insourcing vs. outsourcing our products and services.

The concept of batching initially seems counterintuitive until you understand the Lean paradigm. The stories above show that batching took up significant amounts of valuable resources, time, space, and "stored" cash, as well as a lack of overall process controls and resulting rework. This behavior or mindset is what we have recently coined the politically incorrect noun "Batchards." The stories above show that we all start off with similar paradigms we have learned from school or work. Why should we change when

"we have always done it this way for the last 20–30 years?" We fail to see opportunities for improvement, and when we do finally see them, our expensive equipment and inventory-based batched systems, finance, and cultures get in our way of moving forward. Prior to Lean, we literally sat in meetings and listened while managers lied outright to executives about how things were going on the factory floor. If the manager never leaves his/her office, how will he/she ever know about the actual problems, lack of progress being made, or if what is reported is the truth? How reliable is the information transferred from layer to layer up to the CFO, CEO or Board of Directors?

This is the case for hospitals as well. When we initially tour hospitals, we see materials everywhere, from the stash the nurses keep in pockets or desk drawers, to closets, shelves, and rooms full of inventory. Much of this is what we call "just-in-case" inventory. We constantly hear, "we need more space," "we don't have enough room," "our workstations are too small," or "our area layouts are poorly designed." We see lots of batching everywhere in the hospital. Hopefully, at some point, we see and begin to recognize the need to start our improvement journey and our continuous pursuit of waste elimination.

When you do make the decision to embark on a Lean journey, you must realize and admit how little you know about your processes or how to improve those processes. Remember, all the problems you have today are the result of changes you or someone prior to you made in the past. You must abandon the old way of doing things, along with brute force results-based management style (i.e., telling your managers that they must improve customer satisfaction within a month), which drives wild and crazy behaviors. This reactive management approach creates a "shoot-from-the-hip" mentality, adds variation, and results in endless workarounds, ultimately creating metrics telling you what you want to hear vs. what you need to know.

Once we start to understand Lean Six Sigma tools and that Lean is a philosophy and a different way of thinking, we can start to see applications to remove waste, create flow, and increase velocity in the healthcare world.

In manufacturing, most factories make things, while other factories repair things. If you think about it, hospitals are more in the repair business. Whether we work in a hospital, stand-alone emergency room, urgent care center, or any type of clinic, we tend to be in the business of diagnosing what is wrong with someone, developing a treatment plan of care, and then implementing the plan and monitoring the results. If we are in the rehab business, hospice, nursing home, or long term care facility, we are generally involved in some portion of carrying out the plan of care and monitoring the patient. It is in this notion that one can find many similarities between the healthcare world and factories. Healthcare businesses, just like factories, have "systems" based on and designed with many processes. We all have government and outside regulatory bodies to deal with that create an uncertain political and economic future. We all have formal and informal SYSTEMS at work, and anything that is a Process can be improved and thus Leaned out.

---

[*] Influenced by Tsuyoshi Kawanishi, legendary former CEO of Toshiba Semiconductor, *Chip Management, Ten Symptoms of Big Company Disease,* as compiled by Professor Yoshiya Teramoto of Meiji Gakuin University, and influenced by Bob Norton, "Big Company Disease is Most Often Fatal for Startup Companies. The Top Ten Signs a Company has 'Big Company Disease'," http://www.clevelenterprises.com/articles/big_company_disease.html.

Some areas of hospitals and healthcare institutions function almost exactly like factories. Nutritional services, engineering/maintenance, laundry service, laboratory, and pharmacy are very similar to their counterparts in manufacturing. Factories and hospitals, while very different and unique, share many of the same issues around implementing continuous improvement. The acceptance of Lean principles, concepts, and tools is often easier to implement in these areas, but remember, waste elimination and Lean tools can be applied across the continuum of healthcare.

WHAT RESULTS CAN YOU EXPECT?

We have been implementing Lean in hospitals for many years now. We have clients that have dramatically improved their hospital and clinic delivery systems. Reductions in labor of 50% or more have been experienced in nutritional areas and many other hospital processes. We have increased productivity in most areas, from 30% to 50% or more. We have reduced length of stay (LOS), which we also call throughput time, by up to 80%. We have reduced emergency room waits to see a doctor from 14 hrs down to less than 30 min, resulting in declines in "left without seeing doctor" (LWSD) and have seen dramatic increases in physician productivity. Laboratory turnaround times have been reduced by 50% and inventory in surgery and pharmacy reduced by millions of dollars. We have also been able to increase the number of surgeries performed within the current scheduled time frames by up to 20% or more per surgeon. The results one receives from implementing Lean Six Sigma strategies are directly proportional to the investment the business puts into them. If you have a CEO and board that are knowledgeable in Lean Six Sigma principles and the best people are dedicated and supported to implementing the initial improvements, that business will see excellent results. If you have a CEO and board that support Lean and put some of their best people into the effort, they will see good results but may not sustain them. If you have a CEO and board that don't understand Lean or support it properly and put the people on it that are easiest to free up, they will see spotty results and will not sustain it. In addition, the best results are recognized in organizations that develop a standard process of monitoring gains to ensure sustainment and adopt a culture of continuous improvement.

THE CEO AND LEAN

This book will emphasize many times over that Lean is a journey. Some hospitals and clinics have tried Lean or Six Sigma and had bad experiences. This is unfortunate as it tends to hurt their overall improvement efforts. Many hospitals have started with Six Sigma tools and while getting good results they have had difficulty reducing variation in a complex system with few standardized processes. Our experience in the United States is that:

- 40% of companies are either not exposed to Lean, dabble with it, or choose not to try it.

- 40% will make ongoing attempts and struggle with it and may have pockets of excellence where several projects have improved and some have sustained.
- 20% will try it with some level of success (and of these, 5% will take Lean further).

Although these statistics may leave some asking why even attempt the Lean journey, we have found that organizations who engage in Lean achieve results that exceed traditional process improvement initiatives. We believe that providing an advanced discussion as to what organizations encounter as they engage in a Lean journey, sharing lessons learned, and helping organizations to understand what can help make a Lean implementation successful will improve the success and sustain the rate of Lean. We will explore this observation later in the book. The bottom line is that implementing Lean is not easy; however, if implemented correctly, it has worked extremely well. The proliferation of Lean in healthcare will help achieve a customer-focused, high-quality, cost-effective healthcare system.

Over the first few years of implementing Lean Six Sigma, we generally start with implementing Lean and following up with a Six Sigma effort. Generally, the CEOs "support" the Lean initiative rather than lead it until they see the outcomes for themselves. So the initial part of the journey generally results in "pockets of excellence" from various events or implementations throughout the organization. If the CEO does not recognize the gains obtained while learning the value of Lean and start leading by example with Lean principles, the organization will have a difficult time sustaining it because even the best-intentioned CEO will be driving the wrong behaviors.

If the CEO gets on board and drives Lean as part of the strategic plan, and then incorporates "Hoshin" or "bottom-up" planning, they will see excellent results in bottom-line improvement. Results will be direct cost savings and significant cost avoidance. We define cost savings as those that directly hit the bottom line, whereas cost avoidance refers to items that would have increased costs had we not alleviated the need for them. In addition, the elimination of waste in a process will decrease the process steps and reduce the opportunities for errors, thereby improving customer satisfaction and, ultimately, quality.

We have had hospital clients that, over the first 5 years, have saved millions of dollars, avoided hiring significantly more labor, and avoided construction projects. Notice that we quantified these results over the first 5 years. Many times, hospitals don't see huge bottom-line improvements immediately, as it takes time to Lean out the overall system: however, some projects can quickly result in large gains. Quality and service can be improved substantially. Customer satisfaction as well as physician, surgeon, and staff satisfaction improve as well. There is an investment that is required to implement Lean properly, but it should be more than offset (sometimes 10 × paybacks) by the benefits.

Lean is not a venture that should be entered into lightly. It takes a tremendous amount of training and perseverance and sometimes brute force to implement.

Unfortunately, there will be "casualties," as not everyone will buy in; therefore, there may be a need to place people on a different "seat on the bus" (or a different bus altogether); however, the benefits are extremely rewarding. We honestly believe that, with all the uncertainty in healthcare today, if healthcare institutions are to survive, they will *have* to implement Lean. The auto industry is a good example. You can see what has happened to the companies that did not or were late to adopt Lean. Very early adopting hospitals started implementing Lean Six Sigma back in the late 1990s. The healthcare business is way behind the curve, but can still catch up. With the ongoing pressure from insurance companies and government to cut costs, the decision to implement continuous improvement will eventually not be a choice but a necessity for a hospital's survival.

TYPICAL LEAN METRICS AND OUTCOMES

The results and metrics discussed in the following sections are "typical" but not guaranteed. Results are highly dependent on the culture, equipment, layout, training, and ability to sustain all Lean system implementation guidelines. Results may vary depending on the department and data required for sustaining the new Lean processing methods. In all areas, cycle time of key individual operations and processes need to be measured and monitored; normally these data types are not available or currently measured. It is developed through the Lean implementation.

There are typical results we see in Lean implementations, but they don't happen without dedication, monitoring, and buy-in. Lean is a culture change and should be part of your business strategic plan. It is not unusual to take 2–3 years to see results start to impact the bottom line, even though you will see the results immediately in the areas you are improving. Lean is not a quick-fix solution. Lean should be considered a commitment that once started, never ends.

Hospitals that truly embrace this culture change will overtake their competition and will improve their patients' experiences. Hospitals that don't embrace this eventually, may not survive. The Joint Commission on Accreditation of Healthcare (JCAHO), the Agency for Healthcare Administration (ACHA), and other regulatory bodies are starting to embrace Lean. Truly Lean institutions don't fear audits, but embrace them as opportunities. If our processes were really all standardized, would we ever fear an audit? We should look forward to these audits as exposing waste and opportunities for us to improve.

The Institute for Healthcare Improvement (IHI) and other organizations are also embracing Lean and publishing books and articles. Five years ago, there were very few Internet hits on hospitals and Lean; today you get 1,370,000 of them and more every day. The goal of Lean is for you to be able to see waste and get rid of it; however, most of us don't truly recognize waste when we see it.

POTENTIAL LEAN RETURNS BY DEPARTMENT

The following section describes the results one can expect by hospital department; there can be both tangible ("hard") and intangible ("soft") benefits defined for a Lean initiative. We have put these in terms of ROI for those readers who deem it necessary (Table 1.1).

TYPICAL RESULTS/RETURN ON INVESTMENTS (ROI) AND IMPLEMENTING LEAN

There is no denying it, ROI is very important and can be an important metric to gauge the success of your Lean implementation; however, ROI in and of itself can be a very misleading metric and is not the true goal of any Lean practitioner.

In today's manufacturing and healthcare organizations, the ROI tends to equate to only one thing—eliminating full-time employees (FTEs). No one wants to admit it, but in many organizations quality, safety, and inventory all take a backseat, or a rumble seat, to the almighty FTE savings. Many times, as Lean consultants, we are asked up front by CEOs and CFOs to stipulate how many FTEs we are going to take out, even before the first meeting.

A colleague made the all-too-common consultant mistake, on completing a plant tour: he stated that it appeared to him that this plant could run with 50% fewer employees. The next noise we heard was the company stone mason selecting a slab and banging the 50% target on it for all to live by. At the same time, the vice president (then known by his nickname of Attila) broke out that shiny leather case with the blue velvet interior and that all-too-familiar club to beat his subordinates with if they each didn't get a 50% reduction in FTEs!

For the past several years, it has become extremely frustrating for Lean consultants to go into organization after organization and be asked to stand behind an upfront-quoted ROI for implementing Lean. Everyone is interested in implementing Lean and really thinks they want to do it. They know they need it, they are aware that they have broken processes, escalating internal costs, skyrocketing inventories, and a goal of survival in the face of declining reimbursement; however, understanding the ROI often becomes front and center.

Executives must understand that the ROI can come in the form of clinical improvements, financial performance, increase in market share, and improved service. Generally, most Lean initiatives provide benefits in more than one area. ROI comes in the form of hard dollar savings such as FTE savings (productivity improvements, decrease in the use of contract or travelers), operational savings such as a reduction in LOS, waste in medications, reductions in over processing patients, and supply savings. Soft dollar savings such as cost avoidance (avoiding new construction, doing more in the same or less space, capital dollars) and revenue increases (backfill or capacity opportunity) are only recognized if the organization has a plan in conjunction with Lean to grow their business. Improvement in first case starts and turnover reduction enable an increase in capacity with the same or less staff in the same number of hours. If ROI is going to be your main objective, it is recommended that all projects engage a financial analyst (at least part-time) to assist in calculating the financial ROI that will be accepted by the organization. If the initiative is anticipated to provide the opportunity to increase capacity, marketing must be engaged to develop and

TABLE 1.1
ROI Summary by Area

Emergency Department (Outpatient)	Surgery	Laboratory	Pharmacy	Radiology/Ultrasound	Inpatient Throughput	Nutritional
Tangible ROI						
Increase volume due directly to Lean initiative not just LWSD. (May require some layout changes. Lean gives ability to predict capacity)	Pre-admitting test improvements—ability to handle more patients with same staff. (May require some layout changes. Lean gives ability to predict capacity—point of use testing laboratory)	Ability to do more testing during the same amount of time (increase in volume opportunity)	Ability to fill more requests in less time and with less space	Ability to increase volumes (capacity) with same staffing	Ability to expand capacity but does not necessarily reduce headcount	Reduced headcount
Cycle time improvement door to MD (critical productivity metric) resulting in lower LWSD%	The ability to do more cases in the same amount of time with improved outcomes	Potential for reduced headcount	Potential headcount reduction (FTEs) in pharmacy	Reduced backlog in some areas (time request to appointment availability)	Can free space in ED and other areas (decrease patients holding for beds)	Reduced inventory
Increased volume (with same staffing) and less over time	Potential for reduced staffing in Sterile Processing Department, staffing scheduling changes in OR (staff to demand)	Space savings	Savings of waste from over-producing and wasting IV solutions	Possible reductions in staff or staff over time or ability to expand hours with same staff	Increased staff satisfaction and retention	Reduced space
Inventory reduction in material supplies	Potential large returns in inventory and reduced need for instrument sets and reduction in excess and obsolete materials	Reduced inventory	Reductions in inventory		Reduction in LOS	Potential to eliminate need for cook chill process
Increase in physician productivity	Turnaround time reduction with reductions in case cancellations and delays	Reduced excess and obsolete materials	Quicker turnaround of stat and regular orders		Can free space in ED, PACU, and other areas	
Outpatient LOS reduction	Increase in surgical volumes (if marketing plan is a component of Lean initiative)	Typically better quality and tracking of specimens	Increased capacity		Reduce or eliminate diversions	
Potential for reduction of inpatient LOS	Improvement in patient readiness resulting in higher percentage of first cases that start on time	Increased capacity	Significantly reduce or eliminate expired materials			
Increased physician and staff satisfaction and morale resulting in potential staff retention benefits	Quicker case build times, decrease in equipment replacement and sharpening, with resulting decrease in defects by count (overall)	Quicker turnaround of results—patient safety				
	Increased physician and staff satisfaction and morale resulting in potential staff retention benefits	Improved staff and physician retention				
Non-Tangible ROIs						
Less searching by staff	Standard work leads to compliance in universal protocols resulting in improved third party audit results	Increased patient and staff satisfaction	Increased patient and staff satisfaction	Increased patient and staff satisfaction	Increased patient and staff satisfaction	Increased patient and staff satisfaction
	Quicker patient throughput and resulting reduced need for Pre-Op and PACU beds		Less stat orders			

		Challenges				
Initial high resistance to change based on implementation of new system model	May require physician scheduling changes and investment in scheduling software and patient contact software for appointment reminders	Major layout changes normally required	Potential for more frequent deliveries	May require changes to registration	May require staff scheduling changes (staff to demand)	May require renegotiation of supplier contracts
When selecting metrics or Big "Y"s such as patient satisfaction, or LOS, these may require programs (or sequential Lean initiatives) as there are many "x"s that drive patient satisfaction to obtain the desired results	Level loading may result in block time policy changes—standardization of drop off times and release of blocks, add on/ emergency cases review. May require changes in surgery service line room assignments, introduction of day of surgery scheduling rules	Can save investments in new automated type equipment	May have ability to use third shift tech and or nursing resources for re-stocking	May require changes to scheduling process	Cultural shift (patients accepted to units during shift change)	May require capital for layout changes and removal of or different equipment
Data gathering to support ROI	Will require physician collaboration on standard order sets and agreement on common definitions for cycle and turnover times, surgeons council creation or participation and development of enforcement rules, i.e., cancel case, lose block time, etc., and escalation process, and standardizing of instruments sets and equipment	Will require staff scheduling changes for Phlebotomy laboratory	Resistance to point of use pharmacy floor locaitons	May require marketing efforts to backfill excess capacity to show additional revenue	Needs support from physicians and/or hospitalists to break batch "rounding" habits and changes to discharge process	May require changes ro menu offerings
	May require labor expense to revise preference cards and real-time updating of preference cards, and ongoing (after the project) par level adjustments	May require changes to skill sets and job descriptions	Data gathering to support ROI	Data gathering to support ROI	Hospitalists will resist move to "unit-based" care	Data gathering to support ROI
	May require investment in some inventory tracking (RFID) and may require negotiation of supply chain contracts	Requires stand up vs. sit down operations			Decentralizing some departments and realignment of some departments in the organization	
	Changes to flip rooms or readiness rooms—determination and communication related to use of flip rooms, induction rooms, and priority of "rules" surrounding use of flip rooms if indicated					
	May require changes to anesthesia contract, will require review and standardization of anesthesia guidelines. Standardization of floor preparation of patients. Mandatory pre-testing by acuity level 72 hrs prior or case canceled/future loss of block time with anesthesia review 24 hrs prior to surgery					

execute a plan to drive more business to backfill the time that has been "freed up" because of the elimination of waste, otherwise real value will not be achieved.

One of the most challenging facets is coming to an agreement on what the ROI should be. Generally, the Financial Department of the organization is only interested in the "bottom line," in other words, "when can they adjust the department's budget and show reductions?" Executives must keep an open mind and be willing to challenge those who believe each initiative must yield hard dollar savings. Hard dollar savings can and will be achieved, but may not be an immediate return on every project and may have a longer time horizon.

As organizational proponents begin to engage in Lean deployments, all "eyes" will be on the Lean initiative. We believe that one reason the ROI is emphasized is that everyone has heard of the potential improvements and successes in other industries and other healthcare organizations. Executives want to make sure the initiatives they are sponsoring yield success. If they are hiring consultants, they want to justify the price they are paying for their services. Organizations must realize that there will, and should be successes on each Lean initiative; however, the correct infrastructure must be in place to train, implement, and sustain the gains. The most successful ROIs are recognized when there is a cultural shift and the entire organization, both vertically and horizontally, "buys" into Lean. Seeing and eliminating waste is how the organization does business, leveraging tools, such as *Gemba* walks (go to the place and see) and top (leader) to bottom (frontline) standard work, are implemented. We are often asked how long it takes to see results. There should be immediate results in flow and productivity, while financial results may lag behind. Sustainability will need to be proven.

Lesson Learned: *You will know you are further down the Lean culture path when building a culture of ongoing continuous improvement every day outweighs the insistence on implementing only those perceived large ROI projects first!*

The United States is currently driven by a "short-term focus." We are always worried about the next quarter results. While the short term is important, we must convert our decision making to a long-term focus if we are going to survive. ROIs tend to be short-term focused. Paybacks within a year are normally prescribed. Toyota has a long-term focus; some companies, among them Toyota, SC Johnson, Medtronic, and Unigen Pharmaceuticals, are rumored to have 100-year business plans.[*]

Lesson Learned: *The solution to this sole ROI focus is simple yet takes great patience to achieve. Ultimately, it is the efficiency of the "process" and layout that dictate how many FTEs are required. Once waste is removed, the process and the layout, designed for "flexing," spell out what one needs to effectively run that particular operation. If one focuses on improving the process, the ROI will take care of itself.*

At Hospital X, we applied Lean in one operation with only 11 employees in a batch nutritional environment. The Lean tools proved we only needed six people to run the process in half the time, with 100% better quality in order to support the current demand. Freeing up five people is a great ROI. Still, management didn't believe it and kept eight to nine employees there, just to make sure. In their eyes, this gave them a two-person buffer. In essence, the area ran worse because they kept the extra people in place. This meant there was two to three people's worth of idle time across the eight to nine left. Six months later, we were told the area wasn't running well, and we didn't meet the ROI target for the area. So what good was putting the ROI together when management wasn't going to listen or be held accountable to follow through on freeing up the additional people?

Lesson Learned: *Once reductions are identified, management must have the fortitude to act on facts and make the changes without laying people off.*

In Hospital X, food production Lean lines went from eight people, 8 hrs per day to three people for 4 hrs per day of running time. In this case, management was accountable and worked hard to continuously improve the system after it was installed. It took more than a year to get there and became more productive than even Lean predicted.

So patience and perseverance is the key. What is really required is upper level "executive" leadership to drive culture change, adoption, and deployment. Toyota did not get there in a month. It took many years to implement the TPS system and they are still working on perfecting it today. As healthcare organizations embark on their multiyear Lean journey, they will need to determine what they will accept as their ROI and how to articulate the benefits of Lean across the enterprise in order to sustain ongoing cycles of continuous improvement.

Lesson Learned: *Companies that are truly Lean no longer keep track of ROIs. They implement Lean because focusing on continuous process improvement is the right thing to do for their patients and their organization's survival.*

MBAs, Return on Investments, and Lean

What is the true benefit of ROIs? We are all taught to use them, but we seldom use them correctly or follow up to see if we received the benefits. The Lean philosophy is *It is better to do what is "right for the process" than utilizing an ROI approach.* As Yoda said, "We must unlearn what we have learned."[†] While there is much benefit to obtaining an MBA, it is argued in the bestselling book, *The Puritan Gift*[‡] by Kenneth and Will Hopper, that MBA schools have been creating "professional managers" since the 1970s. We believe,

[*] Brian Gongol, "100-Year Business Plans," http://www.gongol.com/research/economics/100yearplans/, http://www.nutraingredients-usa.com/Industry/Unigen-pens-100-year-plan.

[†] Star Wars, Return of the Jedi.

[‡] Kenneth Hopper and William Hopper. Kenneth Hopper is an engineer, and William Hopper is an investment banker. They are the authors of *The Puritan Gift: Reclaiming the American Dream amidst Global Financial Chaos.* You can read their bios at: www.puritangift.com.

as this book hypothesizes, that MBA curriculums are a root cause that has hurt many of our manufacturing and healthcare institutions as well as the ability of the United States to maintain and grow the manufacturing base.

We would estimate that we have had to "unlearn" 30%–50% of what we learned in MBA class to be successful at implementing Lean systems. In fact, one of our operations theory and management book(s)[*] in MBA class in 1984 had eight pages stating that there is another system called "Just In Time" (JIT) and Kanban being used in Japan and that it would be very difficult to implement in the United States because our culture and practices are so different from the Japanese. The authors profiled JIT at John Deere but in the end were heavily MRP biased. This is slowly changing, as several prominent business schools are now teaching Lean, and later versions of this same text book are more JIT oriented.

Lesson Learned: *Traditional MBA learnings fostering financially ROI-driven cultures and business get in the way of implementing the transition to Lean systems.*

LEAN AND SYSTEMS THINKING

BOILED FROG SYNDROME

If a frog is thrown into a pot of boiling water, it will jump out. If the frog is placed into a pot of water and you slowly turn up the heat to a boil, we will have "frog legs" for dinner.

The point of this story is that after several months to a year of being in the same job most of us don't really recognize much of the waste that surrounds us. After all, it has become part of the familiar landscape. Sometimes this waste can only be seen by "outsiders" unless we train ourselves to see it again. When we identify waste and ask why it is there, we often encounter answers like, "I don't know" and "because we have always done it that way" or "this is the way I do it but everyone else does it differently" or "I thought it was stupid to do it that way when I arrived, but no one would listen to my suggestion, and told me just do it, so I just gave up."

Homework: *Think back to your first day at your current job. Was there something you were shown or told and you said to yourself, "Wow! I can't believe they do it this way!" Then ask yourself, "Are you still doing it that way today?" This is the boiled frog test.*

SYSTEMS THINKING PRINCIPLES

Lean fosters systems thinking. Lean tools are designed to help one see the value stream from the beginning or starting point of the service or product to the end of the service or product delivery to the customer, thereby making the system more transparent. Most inherent inefficiencies are caused by flaws within the overall hospital system. Because most organizations are segmented into silos, people may not be trained, organized, or incentivized to see how the system as a whole is working.

This creates challenges in identifying the true root cause of problems. In our experience, we have found that hospitals and all healthcare integrated delivery systems have similar challenges. It is generally not the individual or worker who causes the problem or waste, but the wastes inherent within the system that drive the staff person to work inefficiently. Therefore, the only way to fix problems is to change the systems. We have found the following challenges related to systems[†]:

- The system controls us more than we control it.
- The world works through systems, but we are not trained to understand or manage them.
- The inventory contained in the system is directly proportional to the amount of inherent risk that is in the system.
- System structure determines managerial behavior and organizational performance.
- Most of us make decisions in a vacuum; we only look at our piece of the system, our department, not the larger whole.
- To change the system you must change the structure, not the symptoms.
- Small events trigger large reactions creating chaos.
- Today's problems come from yesterday's solutions.
- The easier it is to see the whole system, the easier it is to fix the elements of the system.
- Small changes in the system structure can yield great change in behavior.

The statements above represent the challenges with systems. As we gain a better understanding of Lean systems and learn more about why and how to implement Lean in healthcare, we will begin to understand how Lean helps break down barriers found in most systems. As the barriers are broken, we create better workflow and communication and we better understand the value stream or the service we are delivering to our customer. In summary, implementing Lean principles within the context of "systems thinking" provides a foundation for businesses to eliminate waste and ultimately survive. Lean can provide extraordinary results if implemented properly, given time, and if the method of accounting for Lean savings is revised.

Lesson Learned: *The Lean business delivery system is an ongoing journey in the pursuit of waste elimination and error reduction. By understanding and utilizing "systems thinking," it should enable more healthcare organizations to provide affordable healthcare and ultimately facilitate true healthcare reform in the form of coverage, quality, and cost in the future.*

Homework: *Analyze your organization from a systems thinking perspective. Who is accountable for the overall system or processes that span several departments today? What changes in the organization would help to assign owners to the overall system vs. the individual departments or processes? How does your current organization structure discourage systems thinking?*

---

[*] Evans, James, *Applied Production & Operations Management* (West Publishing) 1984.

[†] Peter Senge, *The Fifth Discipline* (New York: Doubleday) 1994.

Patient Throughput Process

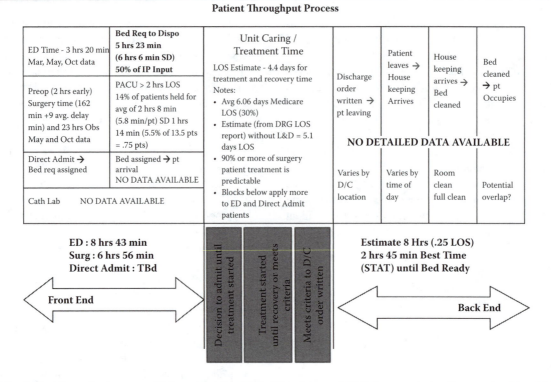

FIGURE 1.1 Patient throughput process. Notice where it is labeled "no data available". Lean projects often require data which does not currently exist and must be manually captured via reports, employee handwritten notes, or direct observation. Chart was first created by Kia Loo, Lean practitioner, Business Excellence Consulting.

Viewing the Hospital with Systems Thinking

The TPS or Toyota Production System, sometimes called the "Thinking Production System," is an integrated system developed by Toyota that combines its management philosophy and standard operations into the optimal production of products that sell with a high-value-added proposition for the customer.

Providing healthcare products and services also requires an integrated delivery model that starts with the customer requiring a service, which sets off a series of integrated activities to produce the desired results (Figure 1.1). Healthcare institutions need a management philosophy, standardized operations and processes, supplier participation, and refined logistics to deliver the highest quality product to their customers.

When viewing the hospital as a system, we identify inputs and outputs, but the system as a whole is very interdependent on all of its parts. If one part fails, it impacts the entire system. For example, if the ED is over capacity and waiting on inpatient beds, the post-operative recovery unit may also be competing for the same beds, both vying for the same support resources, such as transportation or maybe even a CT slot (Figure 1.2). In addition, we find floor units waiting for pharmacy to complete medication orders, while all areas of the hospital await laboratory results.

For instance, a physician needs a laboratory result in order to discharge a patient. If the phlebotomist does not draw the patient's blood in time or there is a delay in the laboratory getting the result to the physician, the physician may not be

able to discharge the patient at the time he/she is rounding. This could result in further delays, up to another day in many cases, for the patient, as it is more difficult to reach the physician once he/she is out of the hospital or occupied doing a procedure. The delay also impacts the hospital's ability to get the bed cleaned and turned over for the next patient, which, in turn, may impede overall flow and create bottlenecks in the ED or surgery. These delays are mostly hidden within their LOS and are very costly to the hospital.

Lesson Learned: *The hospital is a complex system generating systemic-type problems. Each part is dependent on the others. These problems need to be approached with systems thinking tools; yet, most of us are never trained in systems thinking.*

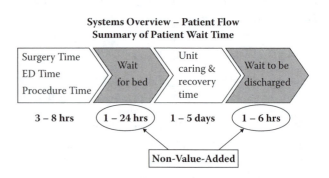

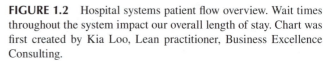

FIGURE 1.2 Hospital systems patient flow overview. Wait times throughout the system impact our overall length of stay. Chart was first created by Kia Loo, Lean practitioner, Business Excellence Consulting.

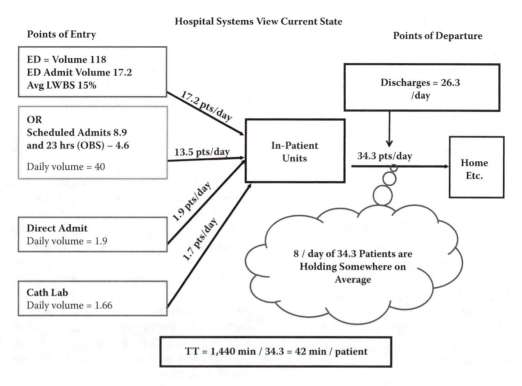

FIGURE 1.3 Hospital systems current state view inflows vs. outflows. First created by Kia Loo, Lean practitioner, Business Excellence Consulting.

To further highlight the inter-relationships within the hospital at a system level, we can look at the suppliers to the system in relation to bed availability (Figure 1.3). Hospital primary feeders (inputs) or suppliers consist of patients who enter through the ED, surgery, both in and outpatients, and scheduled admissions for inpatients. Minor feeders or suppliers include procedural areas such as the Cardiac Catheterization Laboratory, Electrophysiology Laboratory (EP), Radiology, and transfers from other hospitals, nursing homes, etc. Outputs occur in the system when patients leave the hospital or clinic (Figure 1.4). They leave the system as outpatients or through the discharge process from inpatient units to home, skilled nursing facilities (SNFs), or other extended care facilities (rehabilitation, etc.). Outpatients can be sent home on the same day from the ED or surgery. Constraints on the overall process include:

- Improper match of bed demand to the supply beds available (includes SNFs, etc.)

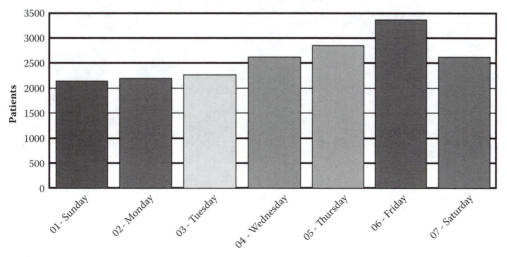

FIGURE 1.4 Hospital discharges by day of week.

- Lack of understanding of supply (patients coming in) and demand needed (timing issue)
- Long turnover times throughout the hospital (surgery, bed cleaning, etc.)
- Midnight census resulting in the holding of patients in order to bill for their stays
- Mismatch of staffing and demand (created by staffing to demand, traditional shift assignments and lack of monitoring)
- Support processes, many often centralized, can also impede flow:
  - Transportation
  - Registration
  - Scheduling
  - Pharmacy
  - Core and non-core laboratory
  - Nutritional services
  - Catering
  - Housekeeping
  - Radiology
  - Billing
  - Insurance verification
  - Central scheduling
- Pre-admission testing
- Engineering/maintenance

Then there are other departments like marketing, finance, and information systems. All these areas play a role in the integrated delivery system and have processes that can be improved significantly.

Because Lean principles are geared toward culture and process improvement, one can conclude that the TPS model can, and has been, applied to healthcare. In addition, if Lean is implemented properly, one may find some major changes in how these areas interact within the new system. The TPS cannot be applied the exact same way as in the Toyota car factory, but all the principles and techniques can be applied to any hospital process or functional area.

Interestingly enough, most hospitals across the country have similar delivery systems. Therefore, solutions for a business problem at one facility can often be transferred to the rest. However, because every hospital is organized differently, we cannot "cookie cutter" the solutions. Even though the solutions may be able to be deployed, the solution is only one piece of the equation.

2 History of Lean

EXECUTIVE SUMMARY

Chapter 2 provides an overview of the history and evolution of Lean and its migration to healthcare. Lean has its roots in the United States as an American initiative that was subsequently perfected by the Japanese. The transformation of hospitals from poor-houses to their current complex system-driven entities is discussed. A number of different historical references are also discussed, including:

- The Taylor System
- The Gilbreth System
- The Henry Ford and Edison Systems
- The Shingo System

KEY LEARNING

- The historical journey of Lean

BRIEF HISTORY OF LEAN

As you read, reflect on the journey that your healthcare organization has taken throughout the years reflecting on the implementation of the past quality improvement initiatives and what initiatives in various states have been adopted and are still in use today. Think about the initiatives that worked and which were not as successful and what the contributing factors were to those successes and failures.

ADAM SMITH—THE START OF SINGLE PIECE FLOW AND STANDARD WORK

In Adam Smith's eighteenth century book, *The Wealth of Nations*, he speculates that the first modern writer who described division of labor was Sir William Petty. Petty wrote, "Those who have the command of the sea trade may Work at easier Freight with more profit, than others at greater: For as cloth must be cheaper made, when one Cards, another Spins, another Weaves, another Draws, another Dresses, another Presses, and Packs; than when all the operations above mentioned, were clumsily performed by the same hand."[*] Adam Smith describes a pin factory where they experimented with dividing the jobs up into small manageable tasks among all the workers. In this experiment, he was able to rapidly expand his production output. He divided up the making of a pin into eighteen different operations across ten people. "One draws out the wire, another straights it, a third cuts it, a fourth points

it, a fifth grinds it at the top for receiving the head, and so on. They could when they exerted themselves make 12 pounds a day or 48,000 pins per day."[†‡] He found a side benefit in that it was easier to train workers in subdivided tasks vs. trying to train each worker in every task from the beginning. If all the parts of the pin were to be made by one uneducated man, he would be lucky to make twenty pins a day.

Since this concept of division of labor was introduced, it has been a threat to the true craftsman who specializes in one-of-a-kind production because each item was crafted differently in order to make it fit. This was how automobiles were made in the early 1900s and still today, many U.S. companies make products this way. Think about how complicated it is to support equipment in the field in which all the equipment is made slightly differently. It requires drawings for each piece of equipment, additionally it requires the equipment be returned to the factory in order to be repaired because there are no standard parts to repair it.

In 1777, George Washington ordered the creation of the Springfield Armory[§] to manufacture gun cartridges and gun carriages to support the Revolutionary War. The armory made its first musket in 1794. In 1819, Thomas Blanchard developed a specialized lathe to manufacture consistent stocks. Historians credit the French military with the first attempt to manufacture small arms from interchangeable (i.e., standardized) parts as early as 1765 when the watchmaker, Honore Le Blanc was appointed to supervise three arsenals. In 1785, Le Blanc was able to show a selection of disassembled musket locks to Thomas Jefferson, then American minister in Paris. Jefferson found he could reassemble the locks from parts chosen at random. His report argued that when arms needed repair, the advantages "are obvious". It would not, however, be possible to take advantage of interchangeable parts until the English and New England machine tool makers had built their revolutionary new machine tools.[¶]

TAYLOR SYSTEM—EVOLVING BATCH PRODUCTION

Many of the systems we have today can be traced to Frederick W. Taylor, who is known as the "Father of Time Study." Taylor's approach to improvement was, "You do and I will think." His mission was to develop "first-class men" and help

---

[*] Sir William Petty, *Political Arithmetick* (London) 1690.

[†] Adam Smith, *An Inquiry into the Nature and Causes of the Wealth of Nations* (Liberty Fund) 1976.

[‡] Adam Smith, *An Inquiry into the Nature and Causes of the Wealth of Nations* (Liberty Fund) 1976.

[§] http://www.springfield-armory.com/aboutus.php.

[¶] Kenneth Hopper and William Hopper, *The Puritan Gift,* 2009, pg 43.

them earn more money from "piece-rate" production. Taylor was optimizing batch production.

CHARLES BEDAUX—ADVANCING THE CAUSE OF TAYLORISM IN THE UNITED STATES[*]

Discovering the importance of work study, Charles Bedaux set up a management consultancy in Cleveland, Ohio, in 1918, introducing a technique of rating separate elements of work done by timed operators and publishing tables of fatigue allowances that would influence all future work study. He conferred his own name on his version of Taylor's work units; they became "Bedaux units." By the 1930s, about 200 American companies had adopted his system, including General Electric, Campbell Soup, and Goodrich Rubber. His industrial legacy lives on in workplaces throughout the world.

Time Study

Time study is essentially holding a stopwatch over someone's head and figuring out how long each step should take. It is not a "people friendly technique". The problem with the way time study is normally carried out is it creates the perception that people are like robots. An example of a traditional time study involves consultants following nurses around for several days or weeks and then telling the leadership, with no input from the nurses they followed, how many bodies they should lay off. We think this type of time study activity is unilateral and demeaning. Nursing and healthcare support tasks within a hospital are not exact sciences, as they involve people who are interactive and have feelings, and are not cars or machinery.

GILBRETH SYSTEM—ELIMINATING THE WASTE OF MOTION

In his book, *Motion Study*, Frank Gilbreth shows how he applies these techniques to bricklayers; he is known as the "Father of Motion Study." Motion study is worker-friendly, while time study is not. The worker was not given much say in Taylor's drive to create "first-class men."[†] Gilbreth and Taylor lived in the same time period, and Gilbreth used to substitute for Taylor at his Sunday lectures; however, they had a falling out and each went his own way. It was Frank's wife, Lillian Gilbreth, who carried on his work after his death.

Motion Study

Frank Gilbreth discovered eighteen fundamental motions that he named *Therbligs* (a variation of Gilbreth spelled backward). The big advantage to motion study is the identification and elimination of wasted motions, which is one of the seven fundamental wastes in Lean thinking. Like time study, motion study still has an element of time associated with each step; however, it is done in a context where the operators share their ideas on how the job can be done better. Therefore, it becomes a win/win for the workers as well as management. As we reduce wasted motions, the workers' jobs become easier, they like it better, and the work gets done faster.

Gilbreth's motion study concepts were made famous in the book and the movie entitled *Cheaper by the Dozen*. The story chronicles how Frank Gilbreth took these same exacting work standards and tried to apply them to raising his family of twelve children and run the household. This story is humorous, as it included things like the best way to take a shower, brush teeth, and button a shirt.

LEAN CONCEPTS BEGAN IN THE UNITED STATES

In 1926, Sakichi started Toyoda Automatic Loom Works. Sakichi and his son Kiichiro had invented a shuttle loom that would stop automatically if a thread broke. This was the beginning of the concept of *Jidoka*. In 1929, Kiichiro Toyoda traveled to Platt Brothers, a textile firm in the United States, to study American manufacturing methods and to try to find licensees for his patents on the spinning looms. When he saw all the automobiles in the United States, he decided to venture into that business. At the time, GM and Ford had 84% of the Japanese markets. During 1934 and 1935, within Toyota Loom Works, Toyoda developed the first Toyota car models, the A1 and the G1. In 1937, Toyoda Automatic Loom Works spun off Toyota Motor Company.[‡] After visiting Ford, Kiichiro Toyoda, who would become the president of Toyota between 1941 and 1950, came up with the idea of "Just In Time" (JIT). At that time, the United States was eight times more productive than Toyota. After World War II, Kiichiro told his cousin Eiji Toyoda to bring Toyota up to U.S. technological standards within 3 years. Eiji tasked Taiichi Ohno, manager of the machine shop, to work with him to develop a new production system. The two worked together to combine Sakichi's *Jidoka* with Kiichiro's JIT to improve production. Toyota came up with the idea of JIT by applying the supermarket concepts in the United States to the material replenishment system for automobiles. In the 1940s, Ohno began implementing these concepts in their machine shop; however, it was not all easy going and he met a lot of resistance. In some cases, he had to "brute force" his system in place.[§] We will explore this later in the book. It was Ohno who implemented Kiichiro's vision for JIT and in 1956, when Taiichi Ohno benchmarked Ford,[¶] he states he was able "to see an American supermarket first-hand." Ohno is now considered the "Father of the Toyota

---

[*] Kenneth Hopper and William Hopper, *The Puritan Gift* (New York: I.B. Tauris) 2009.

[†] Frederick Taylor, *Principles of Scientific Management* (New York: Dover Publishing) 1998.

[‡] http://www.yamasa.org/japan/english/destinations/aichi/toyota.html also attached article kiichiro bio.pdf is a reference.

[§] Correspondence with Russ Scaffede, senior vice president of Global Manufacturing, Donnelly Corporation, past general manager/vice president of Toyota Motor Manufacturing Power Train and consultant: "I fully agree, Toyota did not Kaizen the team Lean. If you listen to the leaders such as Mr. Cho and my executive coordinator Bud Sato, both of whom worked directly with Ohno, there was first a system developing and yes with lots of direct command and control."

[¶] Taiichi Ohno, *Toyota Production System: Beyond Large Scale Production* (New York: Productivity Press) 1978.

Production System." For a more detailed history on the Toyota system, read *How Toyota Became Number One*.[*]

Shigeo Shingo was a consultant hired by Taiichi Ohno to help implement the process improvement piece of Toyota's system.[†] Shingo trained more than 3,000 Toyota employees in the "P" (production) course; however, this course did not cover process flow, JIT, Kanban, supermarkets, multiprocess handling, stop the line, or other concepts associated with the TPS.

It is interesting to note the linkage to scientific management between the United States and Japan. Shingo was a student of Kenichi Horigome, who studied under Lt. Jiro Kakuda, who studied under Frank Gilbreth.[‡]

Shingo stated, "I was so impressed by reading Taylor's *The Principles of Scientific Management* that I decided to enter the field of production."[§] Shingo also stated, "In 1937, Ken'ichi Horigome, managing director of the Japan Management Association, provided me with a thorough grounding in Gilbreth's philosophy during a 2-month seminar in Tokyo. Ever since, production improvement has been my life's work… he (Horigome) had me make one improvement every day during the seminar."

Fortunately, Shingo's teachings seem to be 90% based on Gilbreth's motion study and 10% based on Taylor's time study. While motion study incorporates time study, it is much more worker-friendly.

The way Shingo described the Toyota system was to divide the product and the operator and look at each one separately and then together as a "network" of processes and operations. This was a revolutionary way of looking at work.

Prior to Shingo's discovery, both processes and operations had been considered on the same axis. For years, we have only looked at the operator and tried to improve his/her job, but we never looked at what the product was doing. Some of the biggest opportunities lay in improving the product flow. In healthcare, the product is usually the patient. If we eliminate a product step, we have also eliminated the operator steps that go with it. In addition, every step we can remove or simplify eliminates the opportunity for a defect and improves quality. Therefore, it is possible to do a job quicker and have better quality. One cannot express how important it is to separate the product flow from the operator when analyzing or assessing a process or an area. While simple in understanding, it is truly a remarkable discovery and when we teach people this, they find it extremely difficult to do at first. In addition, while Shingo doesn't necessarily indicate this, there is a definite priority to the network. The priority starts with looking at the product flow (or patient), then the operator (healthcare providers), and then setup reduction in that order.

There are many examples of setups that are sometimes referred to as changeovers or turnovers in healthcare. Some of these are turnovers of patient rooms, operating and CT/MRI rooms, reagent changeovers in the laboratory or from breakfast to lunch in nutritional services. Shingo spent 19 years refining and developing the thought process and steps behind this system. It is not known whom to give credit for the idea of setup reduction. We know Henry Ford was implementing it at Ford[¶] and we know Frank Gilbreth was using it back in the early 1900s. We also know Toyota was implementing setup reduction prior to Shingo's arrival[**] to work on the setup he describes in his white SMED book on setup reduction. Setup reduction is a key component of Lean.

HENRY FORD

Henry Ford's assembly line is the first known example of bringing the work to the men, using skilled personnel to make unskilled jobs. Henry Ford's growth strategy was to make cars his employees could afford and to supply 95% of the population. Ford's goal was to continually increase the workers' wages, which would force management to continue to improve their processes. How many companies today have a goal to continually increase their worker's wages?

UNITED STATES TEACHES POST-WAR JAPAN

According to Kenneth Hopper, co-author of *The Puritan Gift*,

In my view it is of the greatest importance for future East West relations that the United States make a comprehensive collection of material relating to the vital knowledge about manufacturing factory management that it made available to the Japanese during and after the Occupation. That the United States should share that information may have been decided at the highest level in Washington in order to counteract the destructive behavior of the Soviet Union but I can testify that at lower levels the motivation was much more to help cure the desperate poverty that so many Americans had been forced to witness through the world as they served in their countries military. I found that a quarter of a century after the final conclusion of the Second World War, when I was presenting my seminars for Industrial Education Institute in the late 1960s, I had only to phone most U.S. manufacturing operations and mention that I needed some information to help the developing world, to have simple questions about how they managed their factories. I was looking for the kind of information they shared with their most vigorous competitors so sharing with the Third World did not worry them. The formal Factory Tours organized by the Japan Productivity Organization were still running and let Japanese managers actually see the operation of American factories. It was as if, as my brother Will commented, every American factory manager was running his own low cost Marshall Plan. It was nevertheless generous teaching that the European Colonial Powers had never provided. When the Japanese took American advice and in

[*] David Magee, *How Toyota Became Number One* (New York: Penguin Group) 2007.
[†] Art Smalley, "A Brief History of Setup Reduction," www.artoflean.com.
[‡] Shigeo Shingo, *The Shingo Production Management System, Improving Process Functions* (New York: Productivity Press) 2002.
[§] Shigeo Shingo, *The Shingo Non Stock Production: The Shingo System for Continuous Improvement* (New York: Productivity Press) 1988.

[¶] William Levinson, *Henry Ford's Lean Vision* (New York: Productivity Press) 2002. Also, Smalley, "A Brief History of Setup Reduction," www.artoflean.com.
[**] Smalley, "A Brief History of Setup Reduction," www.artoflean.com.

turn shared basic manufacturing advice with the rest of Asia, we saw the beginning of the now massive Asian Economic Miracle. Already, we read that China which has learned so much may be giving all credit to themselves and to their national culture of centuries past.[*]

THE CIVIL COMMUNICATIONS SECTION ENGINEERS OF GHQ TOKYO

Kenneth Hopper remembers,

Thanks to Peter Drucker, in 1968, I met Takeo Kato, an older Mitsubishi industrial engineer who in turn introduced me to Frank Polkinghorn, the Director of the Research and Industry Divisions of General MacArthur's Civil Communications Section (CCS). I have already written substantially about the work of the Industry Division and will not repeat myself here other than to say that there may have been as many as 60 highly qualified civilian technical specialists, mostly from the great AT&T and its subsidiaries working in Japan to improve the Japanese communications system from the winter of 1945/46 till 1950. They provided sector wide, in depth advice and assistance to the Japanese communications system and its suppliers. These were know-how people, not economists. Indeed, the many economists who worked for MacArthur's Headquarters seem to have been kept in the dark about much of the work of CCS. It did not seem to be done deliberately but as a result of MacArthur's engineering, military mind: they did not qualify as 'having need to know.'

We must credit the three CCS engineers, Homer Sarasohn, Charles Protzman, (Figure 2.1) and Frank Polkinghorn (in order of their arrival in Japan) with having been the vehicle that brought manufacturing know-how to the Japanese Electrical Communications Equipment Manufacturers (as they like to be called in English before they became known as the world stunning Japanese Consumer Electronics industry) (Figure 2.2). However, we must give credit to the Japanese managers for having learned, even though few spoke competent English and few American companies wanted to set up plants or affiliates in Japan. As a result, there were no well-run factories to serve as models with staff to be poached, closer than some 5000 miles away. Also, it is not what is taught that matters, but what is learned. The British, with their continuing class traditions, had no trouble not learning how to manufacture from those upstarts, the Yanks, for over a century.[†]

U.S. TOTAL QUALITY CONTROL VS. JAPANESE TOTAL COMPANY-WIDE QUALITY CONTROL

In the 1960s, the Japanese took the concepts of Total Quality much more seriously than people in the United States. They took the teaching of CCS, Deming and others and launched total company-wide quality control (CWQC).[‡] This distinction, though simple in title, was far-reaching in the workplace.

FIGURE 2.1 Charles Protzman Sr., teaching Japanese managers at Waseda University.

"Company-wide" meant that it was not just a shop floor initiative, but impacted the whole company including the office staff. The Japanese have two notions of Total Quality. One is meeting the customer's specifications and the second is meeting what the customer desires, which may be different from the specification. It is a small but important differentiator between the Japanese and the United States approach to quality.

QUALITY CIRCLES

Starting in 1949, quality circles were taught to the Japanese by the Americans.[§] The American QC experts advocated a "do things right the first time" philosophy. In Professor Yoshio Kondo's book, *Company Wide Quality Control*, he explains that quality circles began to emerge in Japan. In 1956, there was a 13-week shortwave radio series entitled "Dai-Issen Kantokusha No Tame No QC" (QC for frontline supervisors), which was subsequently taken over by the Japan Broadcasting Corporation (NHK) and shown on television until 1962. Another weekly series on QC started in 1959, and the book *QC Text for Foremen*, edited by Ishikawa, sold more than 200,000 copies in the 8 years after it was published. In 1962, the Japanese Union of Scientists and Engineers (JUSE) launched the monthly journal, *Genba to QC*, as a sister publication to the monthly, *Hinshitsu Kanri* (SQC). The goals of these shows and publications were to:

1. Inform supervisors and workers about statistical techniques.
2. Encourage the formation of QC circles.

---

[*] Personal correspondence from Kenneth Hopper, CWP article, January 2010.

[†] Kenneth Hopper and William Hopper, *The Puritan Gift* (New York: I.B. Tauris) 2009.

[‡] Yoshio Kondo, translated by J. H. Loftus, *Company Wide Quality Control* (Zenshateki Hinshitsu Kanri) (Tokyo: JUSE Press) 1993.

[§] *CCS Training Manual*, Charles Protzman Sr. and Homer Sarasohn, 1949–1950. An e-book transcription of the version presented at the 1949 Tokyo seminar has been prepared by Nick Fisher and Suzanne Lavery of ValueMetrics, Australia, and is widely available on the internet. The documents that formed the final English version, which was translated by Bunzaemon Inoue and others and published in 1952 in Japanese by Diamond Press, are in the Civil Communications Section Archive, Hopper, Hackettstown, NJ.

FIGURE 2.2   Protzman and Sarasohn.

3. Encourage workers to use their knowledge in their daily work, to achieve objectives, and to keep improving their own abilities.

It was realized that, without the unremitting day-to-day efforts of rank-and-file employees, it would be impossible to secure product quality. May 1962 saw the first registration of quality circles with the JUSE. As of October 1994, there were almost three million registered QC circles in Japan.

A quality circle was originally where the supervisor met voluntarily with his/her group of workers to undertake various activities with the aim of solving quality problems relating to the circle members' work. Efforts are made to link these activities closely with the company's overall CWQC program.

The purposes behind quality circles were:

1. To allow people to exercise their full capabilities and develop their unlimited potential
2. To practice respect for the individual and create cheerful, positive, and purposeful workplaces
3. To contribute to the improvement and development of the enterprise

The quality circles developed over time into the following:

1. Division of QC circles into sub-circles and mini-circles
2. Formation of joint QC circles
3. Leading of QC circles by shop floor workers
4. Self-organization
5. Expansion of QC circle topics
6. Development of techniques
7. Introduction of QC off the production floor
8. Extension to suppliers and affiliates

The most notable benefit from QC circles is the empowerment that the frontline has in ensuring the quality of the product they deliver. This has benefited the hospitality industry as well as the production floor. It has also given the responsibility for quality to those that have direct control instead of pushing it back to the manager or engineers.

Quality circles were re-exported to the United States in the 1970s and 1980s with the Total Quality movement; however, they have met a lot of resistance in the U.S. workplace. One of the failure modes in the United States is that leadership of quality circle teams was delegated to human resources (HR) instead of the supervisor of the group. When layoffs were looming, these quality circle HR personnel became easy targets for the first layer of reductions.

Lesson Learned: *While it is certainly effective to use QC circle consultants and facilitators, problems arise when they become the ongoing leaders of the quality circle. Ongoing leadership of the quality circle must be left to the supervisor of the area or it makes it vulnerable to cancellation.*

HISTORICAL PERSPECTIVE OF HOSPITALS

The indifference to patients' needs for information, comfort, and humane contact is a common complaint about hospitals today. These issues are rooted in the historical evolution of our hospital system. It is helpful to understand how hospitals were formed in order to understand the current structure and its current individual systematic approach to healthcare. This is in direct contrast to a more integrated and Lean (run) hospital system.

Initially, hospitals were founded as shelters for older Americans, orphans, vagrants, and the contagious to keep them isolated from other community members. They then evolved to becoming poor houses for both the insane as well as for sailors who could not be treated at home. The wealthy were treated for medical afflictions at home. There was no such thing as a hospital setting at that time other than these "poor houses."

Later on, religious orders took this as a calling, and hospitals evolved closer to their current model. In 1503 the Spanish built a hospital in Santo Domingo in Hispaniola (present-day Dominican Republic). More than a century later, in 1639, the first hospital on the mainland of North America was built in Quebec, Canada. In 1751 statesman and inventor Benjamin

Franklin (1706–1790) was instrumental in founding the first U.S. hospital, which was built in Philadelphia, Pennsylvania.* They initially started as more charitable institutions and have evolved to their current private healthcare insurance and Medicare payer sources.

Will and Kenneth Hoppers book, *The Puritan Gift*, sheds light on this time period.

To describe the well-managed 'blue-chip' American manufacturing companies of the mid-twentieth century, we coined the term, 'Great Engines of Growth and Prosperity'. An appropriate name for the equivalent institution in the field of medicine would be 'the Nightingale Hospital', so-called because it was organized along lines first laid down by the Lady with the Lamp in London a 100 years before. The backbone of these hospitals was a 'line-and-staff' system, the principal, largely male, line-of-command consisting of physicians and surgeons and headed by the Registrar or Senior Physician. These gentlemen were supported by two 'staff' departments, one largely female and headed by the Matron, which was responsible for nursing care in the widest sense; and the other headed by the Almoner or Treasurer, which collected the income and paid the bills. Each of these departments contained its own, mini-line-of-command. The Matron's line was simple; it led down to the Ward Sisters (the term 'Sister' being borrowed from religious orders), each of whom managed, as the name implied, one or more hospital wards. In Toyota-speak, the wards were, collectively, the *Gemba*, the real place, the place where value was created. It was of the essence of the Nightingale system that every task was assigned to one person so that, if something went wrong, it was possible to pinpoint responsibility. As the Lady liked to say, "someone had to be *in charge*." Conceptually simple but subtle in its *modus operandi*, the system would be imported wholesale into the American hospitals. It is not entirely a coincidence that this occurred in the 1860s and 1870s, after the doctrine of line-and-staff had been formally promulgated by the mighty Pennsylvania Railroad.

In the Nightingale Hospital, the management of what is now called the 'core competences' was strictly in the hands of medically qualified men and women – both physicians and nurses.

Since the 1960s and 1970s, hospitals have organized themselves for their own self-interests and economic livelihood. This new model was designed around the needs of the physicians and hospital staff. Even today, there is not a patient-centric approach in most hospitals.

From this model evolved the department-centered world of hospitalization that we see today. The hospitals today are made up of multiple departments, comprised of administrative departments and a medical departments. Physicians receive hospital privileges but they may not be actually employed by the hospital. In many instances the incentives are not aligned making the efficient operation of the entire

organization, which should be patient-centric, a considerable challenge.

THE HOSPITAL BUSINESS MODEL

Imagine setting up a manufacturing operation where the company furnished the labor and materials and provided all the training and services. Then someone else, who worked for another firm, came in to run the line. Each person demanded his/her own team of workers and whatever supplies or tools they wanted. Then, to top it off, an insurance company or the government paid both the manufacturing company and the firm that ran the line.

Imagine each operator on the Toyota lines wanting to use different tools or doing the job differently than other operators because they thought their way was better. Imagine that all materials used on each version of the same car were different or that the battery was in a different place in each car.

Hospitals have this interesting business model described above. They supply the majority of the staff, rooms, and supplies, but typically not the physicians. The physicians normally work for an outside group, and then insurance companies, the government, or sometimes the patients pay for it. Because of the Emergency Medical Treatment & Labor Act (EMTALA), the rule that mandates hospitals to treat all patients coming into the Emergency Department (ED), which was never funded, hospitals pay out billions in unfunded "charitable" medical care.[†] Manufacturing companies could never run under this type of model and expect to stay in business.

As you reflect on the challenges that healthcare organizations face each day and read the following chapters, consider what components of the TPS, Lean concepts, and tools could be leveraged to improve quality, cost, and service as we work toward reforming the U.S. healthcare system.

---

* Saari, Peggy. "Medicine And Disease - When Was The First North American Hospital Built?." History Fact Finder. Ed. Julie L. Carnagie. UXL-GALE, 2001. eNotes.com. 2006. 25 Jul, 2010 <http://www.enotes.com/history-fact-finder/medicine-disease/when-was-first-north-american-hospital-built>.

[†] http://www.cms.hhs.gov/emtala/. In 1986, Congress enacted the EMTALA to ensure public access to emergency services regardless of ability to pay. Section 1867 of the Social Security Act imposes specific obligations on Medicare-participating hospitals that offer emergency services to provide a medical screening examination (MSE) when a request is made for examination or treatment for an emergency medical condition (EMC), including active labor, regardless of an individual's ability to pay. Hospitals are then required to provide stabilizing treatment for patients with EMCs. If a hospital is unable to stabilize a patient within its capability, or if the patient requests, an appropriate transfer should be implemented.

[10.a b] *The Uninsured: Access to Medical Care*, American College of Emergency Physicians, accessed October 5, 2007. Cost pressures on hospitals. According to the Centers for Medicare & Medicaid Services, 55% of U.S. emergency care now goes uncompensated. When medical bills go unpaid, healthcare providers must either shift the costs onto those who can pay or go uncompensated. In the first decade of EMTALA, such cost shifting amounted to a hidden tax levied by providers. For example, it has been estimated that this cost shifting amounts to $455 per individual or $1186 per family in California each year. However, because of the recent influence of managed care and other cost control initiatives by insurance companies, hospitals are less able to shift costs, and end up writing off more in uncompensated care. The amount of uncompensated care delivered by non-federal community hospitals grew from $6.1 billion in 1983 to $40.7 billion in 2004, according to a 2004 report from the Kaiser Commission on Medicaid and the Uninsured, but it is unclear what percentage of this was emergency care and therefore attributable to EMTALA. [11.a b] (Peter Harbage and Len M. Nichols, PhD, "A Premium Price: The Hidden Costs All Californians Pay In Our Fragmented Health Care System," New America Foundation, 12/2006).

3 Batching vs. Lean Thinking and Flow

EXECUTIVE SUMMARY

Chapter 3 emphasizes one of the main tenants of Lean—it requires a new thought process which leverages single-process flow. It discusses the problems with batching, using both case studies and examples. It discusses the different types of batching and emphasizes the advantage of one-piece or single-piece flow. Examples of this in healthcare include centralized registration and physician rounding, among others. It defines "value-added" in relation to a product or (as in the present case) patients, and discusses the problems of overproduction and waiting as significant wastes in healthcare. The different types of batching are identified and explained.

To be value-added[*] an item must:

- Be desired by the customer;
- Be done correctly the first time; and
- Physically change the product.

Six things that require you to batch:

1. Set-up
2. Transportation
3. Equipment, i.e., centrifuge which hold 50 tubes
4. Processes
5. Idle time
6. Space— either too little or too much

KEY LEARNINGS

- Understanding that single-piece flow is always more efficient than batch flow; however, sometimes it cannot be implemented for specific reasons.
- Understanding of the six things that require you to batch.
- Understanding the definition of "value-added."
- Identifying the critical wastes in healthcare.

BATCHING VS. LEAN THINKING AND FLOW

"The current cost and quality pressures that hospitals are facing provide a natural burning platform for Lean introduction. 10 years ago, I had to convince the leadership teams that change was necessary, and that the opportunities existed. This is no longer the case... the 'pull' for Lean is evident".[†]

— **Tom Chickerella Corporate VP &**
Program Management Officer
Vanguard Health Systems, Nashville, Tennessee

Lean thinking is the continual and relentless pursuit of eliminating waste in our systems and processes. To think Lean is to think of how we can eliminate waste in every activity we do. The term "Lean thinking" was coined by Jim Womack and Dan Jones in the book, *Lean Thinking,*[‡] and expanded on in the sequel, *Lean Solutions.*[§] The book most influential to the Lean movement was *The Machine That Changed the World,*[¶] a 5 year MIT study of the automotive companies that profiled Toyota in setting the benchmarks for the rest of the industry. Learning to develop how to "think Lean" is easier than it sounds. One must learn to recognize waste in order to clearly see it. In order to see it we must first understand how waste is defined.[**]

As you walk around the workplace, do you see any waste? Waste surrounds us every day and results in lost time and frustration. But lost time is very difficult to see or track. Once trained in Lean, we are actually able to see the lost time and the lost output, as it occurs. In addition, there are different levels of waste that we will explore later as we dive deeper into the Lean tools and how to analyze it; we have to train ourselves to see waste.

Lean is a different way of thinking and philosophically approaching how we work in and manage our organizations. By eliminating waste, we increase the percentage of added valued to our processes. To be value-added,[††] an item must:

- Be desired by the customer
- Be done correctly the first time
- Physically change the product

If it does not meet all three criteria, the item is not considered value-added. Some items may be required by the customer but do not physically change the product.

---

[*] As defined in the AMA video "Time: The Next Dimension of Quality" by the American Management Association; featuring John Guaspari and Edward Hay.

[†] Personal correspondence from Tom Chickerella, Corporate VP & Program Management Officer, Vanguard Health Systems, Nashville, TN.

[‡] James P. Womack and Daniel T. Jones, *Lean Thinking* (New York: Simon & Schuster) 2003.

[§] James P. Womack and Daniel T. Jones, *Lean Solutions* (New York: Simon and Schuster) 2005.

[¶] James P. Womack, Daniel T. Jones, and Daniel Roos, *The Machine that Changed the World* (New York: Harper Collins) 1991.

[**] Influenced by Mark Jamrog, principal, The SMC Group.

[††] As defined in the AMA video, *Time: The Next Dimension of Quality*, by the American Management Association.

Lesson Learned: *Our analysis shows that we typically spend only 5%–30% of time doing value-added steps for our patients/customers.*

BATCHING VS. FLOW IN A HEALTHCARE ENVIRONMENT

What is batching? The word batch* comes from Old English and originally meant "to bake" or "something that is baked." Even today we tend to bake things which are mostly made in batches (i.e., batch of cookies or making a triple batch of cupcakes). A batch system is where one step is done to multiple items or things at a time before the next step is started or before the next process begins. This process is repeated until all steps are completed for each process, so one doesn't see the first piece completed until the entire lot or batch is done.

Six Things that Force You to Batch

1. *Setups/changeovers*: The amount of time it takes to set up or change-over an area or piece of equipment may require large batches of products (e.g., test tubes, laboratory equipment). The reason is that it takes too much time to changeover for each single person or piece. Therefore, we must reduce setup times before going to one-piece flow.
2. *Transportation*: How long it takes or the distance traveled from one area to another area may force us to batch. We may carry multiple patients medicines at one time to a distant unit from the pharmacy for the day. How often would we go to the store and purchase only one day's worth of groceries at a time?
3. *Equipment*: Equipment can force us to batch. If you have a centrifuge that holds fifty tubes of blood, would it make sense to load it with only one test tube?
4. *Processes*: Making slides from a specimen in the histology department, mixing IV medicines (for multiple patients), and making cookies are all examples of batch processing. This would also include centralization of processes as well as processes containing significant amounts of variation.
5. *Idle time*: If someone is idle, they will find things to do (batch) to try and keep busy.
6. *Space*: Too little or too much—when we don't have enough space we tend to batch in the space we have simply because we don't have room to flow the process. When we have too much space we tend to batch because we have plenty of room to put the extra inventory.

---

* From Middle English *bache* (or *bacche*) < Old English *bæcce* ("something baked") < *bacan* ("to bake"). Compare German *Gebäck* and Dutch *baksel.*

ONE-PIECE/PATIENT FLOW

One of the key concepts in Lean is "one-piece flow" or small-lot processing. One-piece flow or single-piece flow refers to the processing or servicing of each thing or patient, one at a time. One-piece flow or a small-lot system, if possible to create, is always faster and results in a decreased opportunity for errors in comparison to processing things or patients in batches. In order to *flow* we must eliminate the reason or need for the batching. Converting from batch to one-piece flow reduces cycle times by reducing delays in the process, hence reducing the inventory needed within that process. As we implement one-piece flow, waste and variation immediately surface, showing clearly opportunities to improve at each step in the process.

By reducing the steps in the process, we also reduce the opportunity for defects in the process. Consider the common example of folding and stuffing one hundred envelopes in a batch mode:

Step 1: Fold the letters. The first letter is picked up off the stack of copies and folded. Once it is folded, it needs to be stored or placed somewhere, which requires space… and space costs money! The next letter is then picked up, folded, and placed on top of the first folded letter. In the process of folding the letters, some may fall off the pile or off the table, requiring the process to stop. We may have to recount the stack of letters to validate how many we folded. The process continues until all one hundred letters are folded.

Individual tasks for Step 1 are: reach for letter, grasp and pick up letter, fold letter, move letter to table, put down letter, recount if necessary.

Step 2: Stuff the envelopes. The first folded letter is picked up and stuffed into the envelope. Remove the adhesive strip and seal the envelope. The envelope is now placed in a new location, which requires even more space! Once again, space costs money. (When this concept is expanded to consider the entire inventory in an area or system, it results in the need for some type of computerized inventory tracking system.)

Individual tasks for Step 2 are: reach for letter, grasp and pick up letter, move letter, reach for envelope, grasp and pick up envelope, move envelope into position, stuff letter in envelope, seal envelope, move envelope back to table, put down envelope.

Step 3: Placing stamps and mailing labels. Each of the envelopes is picked up again and a stamp and mailing label is placed on the front of the envelope. Once again, they are placed on the table in a third location, requiring additional space!

Individual tasks for Step 3 are: reach for envelope, grasp and pick up envelope, move envelope, reach for labels, grasp and pick up labels, move labels into position, apply labels to envelope, move to table, put down envelope.

There were a total of twenty-four individual tasks across all three steps. If we considered the need to complete a batch of 100 envelopes and each of the three major steps (i.e., fold, stuff, place labels) took 1 min for each piece, the entire batch would be completed in 300 min (100 envelopes × 3 tasks × 1 min each = 300 min); however, the first envelope would be completed and ready to be mailed in 201 min, but we wouldn't normally see it until the entire batch of three hundred were completed. This does not include the time it took to pick up and put down the envelopes each time.

Now let's explore defects and errors. First, with batching, when do we find the defect? The answer is normally once the batch is completed or in the last step. In Six Sigma and Lean, we learn that each step is an opportunity for a defect. There were twenty-four total steps in this process. It can be postulated that each of these steps, particularly in the hospital world, is an opportunity for defects to occur. For example: Can something or someone get damaged during transportation? Can things get damaged in storage? Have you ever seen equipment get damaged in storage in an operating room, hallways, or equipment storage area?

Lesson Learned: *If we can eliminate the steps, we also eliminate the opportunity for the defect, thus improving quality.*

ONE-PIECE FLOW EXAMPLE

Let's revisit the envelope example (Figure 3.1). If we revise our process to one-piece flow, it would look like this:

1. Reach for the letter.
2. Grasp and pick up the letter.
3. Move the letter.
4. Fold the letter.
5. Reach for and grasp the envelope.
6. Pick up the envelope.

7. While holding the envelope, stuff with the letter already in your other hand.
8. Seal the envelope.
9. Reach for and grasp the stamp and mailing labels.
10. Put stamp and address labels on envelope.
11. Move the envelope.
12. Put the envelope down.

When do we get our first piece? The answer should be 3 min, i.e., fold, stuff, and label. Using single piece or one-piece flow, the process went from twenty-four steps to twelve steps or a 50% reduction in individual tasks! So batching doesn't really save us anything; in fact, it only costs us in the long run. Therefore, batching is not truly efficient.

With one-piece flow, the first envelope was completed in 3 mins compared to 201 min when batching. The entire process was completed in 300 min equal to the batch processing but not including the extra time to pick up and put down each envelope throughout the process. However, we don't see the first piece in the batch model until the entire batch is completed.

In our one-piece flow scenario, if the number of resources performing the work was increased to three staff members, then all the work would have been completed in 102 min (3 + 99 min). The first piece would have been completed in 3 min, with the remaining envelopes being completed with a cycle time of every minute vs. the 300 min in the batching environment.

In addition, twelve steps were reduced, thus reducing twelve opportunities for defects times 100 pieces, for a total reduction of twelve hundred defect opportunities. While Lean may not always yield an increase in quality, it will certainly not cause a degradation. It is not unusual to get an increase in quality, and many times, it is unexpected. In addition, if a defect occurs in our one-piece flow scenario, we find it right away, and our rework is minimal and limited to one

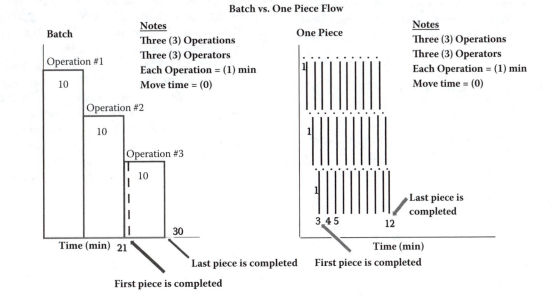

Batch vs. One Piece Flow

FIGURE 3.1   Courtesy of Mark Jamrog, Principal The SMC Group.

piece, instead of at the end of a batch where the entire batch may be defective.

We have a Lean saying: "When you work on something you don't need, you can't work on something you do need!" This is extremely important. This is the premise behind the waste of overproduction, and while this saying sounds simple, it is violated all the time. Toyota differentiates this by highlighting the difference between apparent vs. true efficiency. True efficiency occurs only when we increase efficiency without overproducing. A common example of overproduction in the hospital pre-operative (Pre-Op) area is having every outpatient arrive at 5:00 a.m. for the 7:30 a.m. cases. Think of the behavior this batching drives. The practice of bringing patients in "batches" at the same time of the morning ultimately requires that we have more staff and more space to handle all the patients throughout the system, i.e., registration, surgery waiting or admitting, Pre-Op, etc. They end up processing patients prior to the time they would be required to be ready for their surgical procedure, due to the fact patients are all arriving at the same time regardless of their surgical time. Often they are processed in the wrong order and the OR finds they still wait for patients to be ready. This results in excess labor not only to process the patients, monitor the patients, installing tracking system to keep track of all the patients, but also a larger Pre-Op area with more beds required to hold the patients. In addition, this creates challenges in being able to "pull" inpatients from the floors to the Pre-Op area in time for surgery. This process can result in a Pre-Op area full of patients waiting for surgery, but the surgery area is not ready for them. Then, all of a sudden, we have an emergency patient who needs to go to surgery immediately, but there is no room in Pre-Op to process the patient. What do we do?

Lesson Learned: *A product or patient in a batch process spends most of its time (greater than 80%) in waiting (storage) and typically less than 10% in a value-added process. Queues in the process result in longer throughput times, requiring more inventory, rooms, staff, and larger waiting rooms to fill the demand. This also creates unhappy patients.*

DIFFERENT TYPES OF BATCHING

Pure Batch

Pure batching is working with a "lot" or "group" of patients and doing each task to each patient or product as a "group." For example, consider a morning run in the laboratory. Thirty blood specimens in tubes are collected on a unit at one time and then sent to the laboratory. All specimens are received in the laboratory at the same time and then moved to the centrifuge area. The centrifuge (or several large centrifuges) can hold the entire batch. Once the specimens are spun, they are moved in a rack to the chemistry department. They are all logged into the system together and then placed into a batch processor. In essence, they move through the overall system as a large batch of tubes.

Segmented Batch

Segmented batching is processing a batch of products one piece at a time. For example, this would be like building all Camrys in the morning using one-piece flow, then building all Corollas in the afternoon, one-piece flow. In a hospital laboratory, it would be like processing all the chemistry tubes one-piece flow then processing all the hematology tubes one-piece flow, and then working on all the urine specimens.

Period Batch*

Period batching is working on a batch of patients or things on each task for a specified time period. An example of this might be in the Emergency Department, where the department secretary might choose to work on all the documentation and validation at the end of the shift for all the discharges that occurred for that particular shift.

Group Technology†

Group technology is dividing up patients or products into families or similar/like "groups" or service lines and then working on them using one-piece flow or small lot. Group technology falls somewhere between batching and one-piece flow. An example would be having cardiac surgery and vascular surgery—"like or similar services"—share the same surgical suites or patient care areas, as they use similar supplies and surgical instruments.

True Mixed Model Sequencing

This is working true one-piece flow regardless of the type of patient or product. An example in the automotive industry is producing any model type one behind the other on the same line. This requires the line to be level loaded. "Even the production of large numbers of Coronas is leveled, for example, suppose we make 10,000 Coronas working 20 days a month. Assume that this breaks down to 5000 sedans, 2500 hardtops and 2500 wagons. This means that 250 sedans, 125 hardtops and 125 wagons are made daily. These are arranged on the production line as follows: one sedan, one hardtop then a sedan then a wagon and so on."‡ This example shows how the production line at Toyota is finely tuned. Each day they are planning not only the next day's, but for the next week's, and next month's production. This can be applied to a surgical schedule: How far ahead do we typically plan for surgery at hospitals? It has been our experience that relatively little planning takes place and most of the day-to-day management of the surgery schedule is reactive.

---

* Jan Riezebos, *Design of a Period Batch Control Planning System for Cellular Manufacturing* (The Netherlands: Print Partners) 2001.
† John L. Burbidge, *Group Technology* (London: Mechanical Engineering Publications) 1975.
‡ Taiichi Ohno, *Toyota Production System* (New York: Productivity Press) 1988.

Lesson Learned: *We need to establish level loaded pull systems and advanced planning in order to better manage the day-to-day flow through surgery.*

So why do people batch? Whether you are 10 or 80 years old, our minds are programmed that batching is better. We don't know why this is; maybe it is in our genes. Most people believe it is more efficient and, hence, more productive that if we are working on one piece, we should continue to do the same operation to all the other pieces. It is this belief that batching is better that is always working against us when implementing Lean and makes Lean so difficult to sustain.

What is productivity? What does it mean to be more efficient? Efficiency or being more productive is doing the same or more output with fewer resources and more efficiently by utilizing all resources—man (labor), method (process), machine (equipment), and materials (supplies)—in the best way possible.

BATCHING IN DAILY PATIENT ROUNDS

How does a physician conduct patient rounds? Typically, physicians round first thing in the morning, and there may be several physicians rounding on a large unit within a short period of time. Depending on the layout of the unit, the physician may take several patient charts and head off to see their patients. We call this the beginning of "domino effect batching." The batching occurs in large part because of the travel distance that would be incurred if the doctor had to walk back to get a chart each time he/she needed to see the next patient. In essence, the waste of excess travel distance is forcing the batch process.

The physician proceeds to see the first patient, for example, who may be in a significant amount of pain. The doctor writes an order for pain medicine and makes notes or in some cases completes the chart documentation; however, because of the distance to the unit desk, the doctor continues on to see the remainder of patients for which he/she has charts. Each time a patient is seen, the doctor documents the visit and writes orders that will go to the pharmacy, laboratory, and radiology. *Meanwhile, our first patient is still in a lot of pain.*

Once all the patients are evaluated, the doctor completes any unfinished or additional orders and documentation. The doctor then takes the charts to the unit floor clerk. Generally, these patient charts are not handed to the clerk in the order that each patient was seen. The unit clerk enters all the orders not only from this doctor, but also several other physicians who were rounding. What is the chance that the unit clerk is going to enter the orders in the sequence that the patients were seen by the doctor? *Meanwhile, our first patient is still in a lot of pain and has not yet received any medication.*

Then the domino effect continues. Within a short period of time, batches of orders are sent to the laboratory, pharmacy, radiology, discharge, and other service providers that the patients need. This creates spikes in demand for all these services every time the unit clerk batches the orders received from each doctor. *Eventually, our patient receives pain medicine. What if that first patient was you?*

Homework: *Go and view the rounding process for yourself. Mark the first chart and follow it to see how long it takes to get medication to the first patient.*

So let's look at one of these departments. Pharmacy receives a large batch of orders from the unit clerk all at the same time (and potentially from several other units in the same time period, with the same rounding processes). When this occurs, we refer to this as "peak demand." Peak demand is the point where demand spikes in the process due to the "domino effect."

Since one person can't handle the workload during peak demand, more staff is allocated during these periods. But in the off-peak demand times, the staff are left with little or nothing to do (idle). In some cases, it is difficult to staff for peak demand, so it is handled with less people. As demand fluctuates, the system is stressed, bottlenecks are created, and staff members become frustrated. Because the orders bottleneck, the pharmacy can get behind, which further inhibits orders being processed in first in, first out (FIFO) order. What is interesting is if you ask the staff how their day went, they don't think about their idle times, but they dwell on the times they were stressed!

The nursing staff typically has little or no visibility into the status of their patient's orders in the pharmacy queue. This creates the need for many phone calls by the frustrated clerical and nursing staff to follow up on their patient's orders with the pharmacy. Because these queues develop as a result of the batching, we have to design *STAT* processes to handle those orders that are critical in order to ensure the pharmacy fills them first during peak demand periods. We thus create *STATS* not for patient needs, but for staff and process needs. This further bottlenecks the system and leads to more *STATS*, further adding to the problem.

Peak demand is a phenomenon that also happens outside healthcare. For example, restaurants refer to this as being "slammed." In non-Lean manufacturing companies it is referred to as "end of the month."

What is the problem here? The problem statement would be, "there are numerous spikes in demand throughout the hospital, creating bottlenecks, staff frustration, and customer dissatisfaction," impacting timely order or service fulfillment. In order to begin to identify the root cause of the problem, we would chart the demand and map the process. Then, with further probing, we would go to the actual place (*Gemba*) on the unit and use the five why's to determine the causes or what we call Xs in the Six Sigma equation: $Y = f(x)$, which are driving the problem(s).

We would find physician rounding is filled with activities that contributed to the batch process. We would also find that the doctor rounding system is the root cause of the spikes in demand and the need for *STAT* orders in not just the pharmacy but throughout the entire hospital.

Underlying factors that play a role in physician rounding might be the travel distance to the central location where the charts are stored vs. at the bedside, manual ordering and charting, missing charts, and "this is the way we have always done rounding," as well as how the unit clerk has always processed the orders.

All this occurs with little understanding or a lack of awareness by the doctors as to how their activities might be impacting the process downstream. What could be done to fix root causes? In essence, one needs to consider changing the entire system.

Improvements could include level loading and eliminating batch processing, where possible. If the systems were level loaded, this would require less staffing, since peak demands would diminish and the need for *STAT* orders would be minimized if not eliminated as bottlenecks shrink or disappear. Additionally staff would feel less frustrated and stressed at the end of the day. What if there was an orderly way to process the orders in FIFO by the unit clerk? What if the charts could be accessed through a computer or PDA? What if the doctor could enter the orders at the time of the patient visit, i.e., computerized physician order entry (CPOE), similar to a restaurant touch screen? CPOE drives one-piece flow. This example is just a simple representation of batching and some of the causes and potential solutions, which may impact the healthcare system in the near future.

OTHER EXAMPLES OF BATCHING IN HEALTHCARE

CHART PREPARATION

Hospital X had a process called "chart preparation." Charts were prepared in advance for patients who were scheduled for surgery. As faxes and other paperwork were received, the information was placed into patient named manila folders. Two or three days prior to surgery, each secretary would go through and organize the manila folders again, placing the information contained in the folders in order. Manila folders were everywhere. The day prior to surgery, the secretary would pull out the hard charts and stack them up. She would take the manila folders and place each one into a hard chart. Then she would go back and reorganize what was in the manila chart again into the hard chart, occasionally having to punch holes in the paperwork.

Problem: There was the perception among the workers that they didn't have enough clerical staff to keep up with all the paperwork and charts. The unit was considering hiring another full-time secretary to assist in the chart preparation process. To determine whether or not this was actually a problem, a series of questions related to the process were asked (ask "why" five times) to determine if the root of the problem was the need for additional staff.

During video analysis, the first question put to the clerk was if she had placed the contents of the chart (in the manila folder) in the correct order the previous day and, "if so, why was the second clerk putting it into a different order in the hard chart today?" The response was, "Because that is the way we have always done it." What was observed was that these charts were handled over and over and over again, essentially adding no value.

A staff member, department manager and the acting supervisor were engaged during the Lean implementation to help analyze and change the process. Several process changes occurred. First, the manila folders were eliminated and the paperwork was placed in the proper order, directly into the hard charts. Each chart was only handled once and the batching was eliminated. An assembly line model for the charts was constructed utilizing one-piece flow. This resulted in freeing up space where batch processing of charts used to occur. If new paperwork came in, the chart was pulled and the paperwork put into the right spot in the hard chart.

Prior to the improvement, the secretaries had trouble keeping up with the charts for the day of surgery and couldn't even get a day ahead. After the improvement, the chart completion rate increased from 40% to more than 80% the day prior to surgery. In addition, 50% of the charts were completed three or more days prior to surgery, which had never been accomplished before. One final improvement was to add EFAX* to eliminate all the lost orders faxed in from the doctors' offices. This improved surgeon satisfaction and eliminated many phone calls back and forth to the doctor's offices each day.

APPLICATION OF ONE-PIECE FLOW TO HEALTHCARE

How can the concept of single-piece flow apply in the healthcare setting? Let's look at how routine blood tests are drawn and completed in time for physicians to round on their patients. Generally, laboratory tests are drawn between 2 a.m. and 5 a.m. each morning. This is normally a batch process in which the phlebotomists go from room to room to collect blood. Each patient may have one or several test tubes of blood drawn, depending on the number and type of tests ordered by the physician. In most cases, phlebotomists draw half of the patients on the unit, depending on the location of the "tube" system station (which is utilized to transport specimens to the laboratory). The specimens are sent in batch mode via a tube system to the laboratory, where they all drop in the bottom of the tube station at once. Sending multiple patients specimens down to the laboratory in large batches can create difficulties for laboratories that are trying to meet turnaround time metrics, e.g., lab tests draw to result times (Table 3.1).

The phlebotomist arrived on the unit and began the first patient at 2:58 a.m., and was able to complete a routine patient's blood draw within a 4–6 min time period, she then proceeded and had 2 patients that were difficult to draw, taking 9 and 12 min. The phlebotomist took 59 min to complete 7 patients and all the blood was sent to the laboratory at the same time.

What if the laboratory was trying to achieve an average turnaround time of 60 min? Table 3.2 shows the actual time by patient in minutes from the time the first patient was drawn to the time the phlebotomist reached the tube system.

TABLE 3.1
Phlebotomist Times of the Patient Draw Process

Patient	#1		#2		#3		#4		#5		#6		#7		At Tube Station
In room	2:58		3:03		3:08		3:21		3:28		3:38		3:46		
Out room	3:01		3:07		3:20		3:26		3:32		3:44		3:55		3:57
Travel (min)		2		1		1		2		6		2		2	
Draw time	0:03		0:04		0:12		0:05		0:04		0:06		0:09		
Delays					Difficult blood draw				Delayed by RN				Difficult blood draw		
Total process time from drawing first patient to tube station on unit															0:59

If we assume (for this example) that it would take a minimum of 20 min for each specimen to reach the laboratory by tube, be received, checked in, and have the test performed (result) in the laboratory, then the first two specimens could not possibly meet the target of 60 min (patient blood draw to result). The next two specimens would more than likely be at risk of not meeting the goal as well. Therefore, it would be a challenge for the laboratory to meet the 60 min turnaround time.

Let's apply the concepts of single-piece flow to the scenario above. If all specimens were drawn one at a time and then immediately sent to the laboratory, the goal of a 60 min turnaround would be achieved; however, it probably does not make sense to expect a phlebotomist to perform a blood draw on a single patient and then travel to the tube station after each blood draw. Remember, travel distance forces us to batch! One can still apply the concept of single-piece or small-lot batching to this scenario and have the phlebotomist only draw 2–4 patients (Table 3.3).

This would not only make the probability of achieving the turnaround time goal, but it would also level load the work in the laboratory (Table 3.4).

We can conclude that one-piece or one-patient flow is "true efficiency" vs. "apparent efficiency." Productivity equals paid hours per unit (both direct and indirect). It is only efficient if we do it better than or within the standard and without overproducing. If we raise only the output without looking at our true demand then this is considered apparent efficiency. If we add workers or machines to raise the output but the demand is not there, then we overproduce, which is the number one waste in the Toyota system. One-piece flow (or small-lot production) results in shorter throughput times, reduced inventories, increased responsiveness to customers, reduced cost, and reduced opportunities for defects. Other examples of batching in hospitals are surgery or catheterization laboratory start times, all at 7:00 or 7:30 a.m. (all the cases beginning at the same time), requiring all the resources to prepare and transport at the same time, creating an artificial peak demand instead of potentially staggering or level loading the work at intervals; this also creates the domino effect throughout the hospital to support services.

Even though we have provided these examples, which show that one-piece flow is more efficient than batching, many readers will still think batching is better or, for some reason, there is no way you can flow your processes.

We have never run into a process that we could not improve by applying the Lean principles of flow and waste elimination. There may be good reasons to batch; if there is a long distance to travel to put something away, batching may be necessary and more efficient. The key is to eliminate the need or reason behind the batching. It is not always easy, but if one believes it can be done, then it is normally possible to find the answer. It may mean altering the layout or process to come up with the right solution and flow. As Joel Barker states in the video, *The Business of Paradigms*,[*] "Those who say it cannot be done should get out of the way of those who are doing it."[†]

FLOW—ONE-PIECE FLOW OR SMALL LOT

One-piece flow will always get the first piece completed significantly quicker than batching. One-piece flow reduces cycle times, inventory and storage time, as well as highlighting waste in the process.

We were staying in a hotel in Columbia, SC, when a bellhop saw me waiting for the elevators at around 11

TABLE 3.2
Morning Run Blood Draw Process—7 Patients

Patient	Draw Complete to Tube*		Tube to Result (est)		Estimated TAT
1	0:56	+	20	=	76
2	0:50	+	20	=	70
3	0:37	+	20	=	57
4	0:31	+	20	=	51
5	0:25	+	20	=	45
6	0:13	+	20	=	33
7	0:02	+	20	=	22

Drawing all 7 patients in one "batch" impacts the ability to meet 60 min TAT.

*Note may vary slightly pending travel distances to tube.

[*] Joel Barker, *The Business of Paradigms* video.
[†] Joel Barker, *The Business of Paradigms* video.

TABLE 3.3
Morning Blood Draw—4 Patients

Patient	#1		#2		#3		#4			At Tube Station
In room	2:58		3:03		3:08		3:21			
Out room	3:01		3:07		3:20		3:26			3:32
Travel (min)		2		1		1			6	
Draw time	0:03		0:04		0:12		0:05			
Delays					Difficult blood draw				Delayed by RN	
Total process time from drawing first patient to tube station on unit										0:39

a.m.—check-out *time. Much to the chagrin of his front desk supervisor, he said to me, "You know, if they would just stagger the checkout, the waits for the elevator wouldn't be so long." I told the person he was absolutely correct and saw the front desk supervisor look at him with an angry smirk.*

Many hospitals have the same challenges and flaws with their overall hospital throughput. We find the majority of patients tend to be discharged around the same time of the day. In fact, many hospitals are trying to model hotels and discharge their patients all at the same time. We think this approach is fundamentally flawed. When discharges from the hospital are batched, all the problems that go with batch-type systems are created, leading to more chaos and requiring more staff to transport patients out of the hospital (or delays in discharges). This is because all the resources are being pulled at the same time. In addition, just like the hotel, everyone is trying to use the elevators at the same time. The idea should be what Toyota calls *Heijunka*, or to level load your discharges as they occur throughout the day. Demand for rooms is not all at the same time. In fact, post-operative care units will start needing beds around 9 a.m. and demand diminishes by mid-afternoon as surgeons complete the peak case demand for the day. The goal should be to match availability to demand. In addition, when all the patients are ready for discharge at the same time it leads to challenges in cleaning or turning around unit beds.

TABLE 3.4
Morning Run Blood Draw Process—4 Patients

Patient	Draw Complete to Tube*		Tube to Result (est)		Estimated TAT
1	0:31	+	20	=	51
2	0:25	+	20	=	45
3	0:12	+	20	=	32
4	0:06	+	20	=	26

Sending to lab after drawing 4 patients will enable the process targets of 60 min to be achived.

*Note may vary slightly pending travel distances to tube.

Homework: *Take a look at your discharge process. Do you batch the process? If so, check out the elevators! Also, time how long it takes your elevator doors to close. Imagine if all the elevators in the hospital closed (safely) even 1 sec faster. Could this help your overall productivity?*

4 Can the Toyota Model Be Applied to Hospitals?

EXECUTIVE SUMMARY

This chapter emphasizes the Toyota business model and its relevance to American healthcare.

The Toyota model, in summary, is made up of the following:

1. A modified Assembly Line concept
2. The American Supermarket
3. Changeover Reduction
4. Participative Management

The importance of Lean in the future healthcare environment is discussed along with the important concept of fixed reimbursements and the criticality of minimizing costs. There are two ways of making a profit: The first is to make the product for a cost less than the price at which it is to be sold.

$$Selling\ Price - Cost = Profit.$$

The other option is to sell the product for a price higher than it costs to make.

$$Cost + Profit = Selling\ Price.$$

With fixed reimbursement, the selling price is fixed.

The Lean Business Delivery model begins with understanding customer expectations and the Pillars of the TPS model;

1. Just In Time (JIT)
2. JIDOKA—automating with a human touch

LEAN IS A JOURNEY

Lean is a multi-year journey and—depending on the improvement needed and waste identified—a multi-year plan or program will need to be established to determine sequential initiatives which will drive the desired results. Lean works best with a clearly stated policy, up front, which ensures that no one will be laid off as a result of Lean.

KEY LEARNINGS

- Understanding the basics of the Toyota production system.
- Understanding how to translate the Toyota Lean principals to the American Healthcare system.
- Understanding the importance of increased productivity and efficiency in a fixed reimbursement model.
- Understanding the necessity of a multi-year commitment to Lean.

THE NEED FOR CHANGE

Just do an Internet search on Lean hospitals and within 0.28 sec there are 2,040,000 hits.[*]

A recent ASQ study shows

53 percent of hospitals report some level (minor, moderate, or full) of Lean deployment, and 42 percent of hospitals report some level of Six Sigma deployment. Few hospitals participating in the study report "full deployment" of either Lean (four percent of hospitals) or Six Sigma (eight percent). The reasons that neither method has been deployed in hospitals include: the need for resources (59 percent of hospitals), lack of information (41 percent), and leadership buy-in (30 percent). Eleven percent of hospitals surveyed were not familiar with either method.[†]

Lean is not a quick-fix solution; it takes time. We must be patient with the process, but impatient with the results.[‡] It is critical to get everyone trained in Lean and involved in the projects, whether they are Point Kaizen events or Lean implementations.

THE TOYOTA PRODUCTION SYSTEM MODEL HAD ITS ROOTS IN THE UNITED STATES

As discussed earlier, the Toyota Production System (TPS) model had its roots in the United States. In actuality it is an American system which Toyota has been working on perfecting. In it's simplest form it is based on the following four parts which we will explore:[§]

1. A modified Assembly Line concept
2. The American Supermarket
3. Changeover Reduction
4. Participative Management

---

[*] Internet Google search on September 13, 2009.
[†] "Hospitals See Benefits of Lean and Six Sigma," *ASQ Releases Benchmark Study Results*, March 17, 2009.
[‡] *Speed is Life*, Tom Peters, a co-production of Video Publishing House and KERA, 1991.
[§] William Levinson, *Henry Ford's Lean Vision* (New York: Productivity Press), 2002.

A Modified Assembly Line Concept based on Henry Ford's Production System

While Henry Ford introduced the concept of single-piece flow, it was actually Charles Sorenson[*] who figured out how to implement the assembly line. Ford also introduced job rotation, machines to do boring or dangerous work, the concept of Kaizen, and the idea that there is an advantage to constantly working to reduce your pricing while increasing wages, the suggestions system, and much more.

The U.S. Supermarket Replenishment System

In his book, *Toyota Production System*, Taiichi Ohno states,

> In 1956, I toured U.S. production plants at GM and Ford, and other machinery companies. But my strongest impression was the extent of the supermarket's prevalence in America... Combining automobiles and supermarkets may seem odd. But for a long time, since learning about the setup of supermarkets in America, we made a connection between supermarkets and the just-in-time system... Our biggest problem was how to avoid throwing the earlier process into confusion when a later process picked up large quantities at a time. Eventually, after trial and error, we came up with production leveling.[†]

Changeover Reduction

The concept of setup reduction goes back to at least 1911, when Frank Gilbreth provided an example of setup reduction: "Two horse carts with horses changed from the empty to the full carts will require fewer and cheaper motions than any other methods of transportation." This method is used today with tractor trailers. Because Toyota was forced to manufacture "low volume high mix," they decided to revise and improve on the Ford system. In order to produce one-piece flow or Just in Time (JIT), they had to implement fool proofing or *Jidoka* (automation), and reduce setup times to make the system work. They then combined this with the U.S. Training Within Industry systems, which was the basis for what has become known as standard work, i.e., the "Toyota Way."

Participative Management

In the *Civil Communications Section (CSS) manual* from 1949, Charles Protzman Sr. writes,

> Some may think that this factor (Employee Participation) is merely a part of recognition but it means more. It actually means doing things together – giving the worker a chance to get into the act. There is a feeling in the mind of every person no matter how lowly or how high that he would like to be a part of things. Just analyze that aspect of human nature. The average person who has enough money for food, clothing and shelter will spend his next few dollars in joining some club, society or other organization. He will go to endless time and trouble to participate in such outside activities. If we who are paying these people for working with us could foster that desire to participate, what a profitable undertaking it would be. What an increase in efficiency and output we would experience if we could get people to feel they are participating on the job as in outside activities. The factor of participation has been overlooked to a considerable extent by management men everywhere.[‡]

In a speech to the Japan JITVA, Charles Protzman Sr. states the following, which still has much applicability today:

> Perhaps it would be quite true to say that we do not entirely know how to encourage people to think in new ways or how to convert training into potential economic power. An executive the other day said to me, 'I want to think in new ways. I want to have practical ideas and encourage them in other people. But how do I learn to think in new ways?'
>
> This is a general problem and it emphasizes the need to get away from the traditional concept that training, of any sort, is for the primary purpose of acquiring theoretical knowledge. Industrial training must have the objective of making us able to reason, to translate this knowledge into useful economic power.
>
> At present I believe it is safe to say that most workers do not want to think! For one thing practically no one has ever encouraged them to. The few who do think become union leaders, and by observing what is happening in other parts of the company and comparing with their own conditions they make demands that force management to take a minimum of very reluctant action.
>
> Also, the worker wants to protect his position and that of his fellow workers. If he has ideas that might increase productivity or make a job easier, he believes he or one of his fellows might lose his job.
>
> It is necessary now to take advantage of the potential ability and the excellent brains in all levels of business or industry, and to dramatically reduce the long time interval that would be required merely by following the steps of other people.
>
> I believe the two basic things that must be done... The first and most important is for the executives at policy making levels to overcome closed mind or traditional ways of thinking... Productivity is not merely a matter of training management and engineers in ways of accomplishing more. The

---

[*] Charles Sorenson, *My 40 Years With Ford* (New York: Norton) 1956.

[†] Taiichi Ohno, *Toyota Production System*, *Beyond Large Scale Production* (New York: Productivity Press) 1978.

[‡] *CCS Training Manual*, Charles Protzman Sr. and Homer Sarasohn, 1949–1950. An e-book transcription of the version presented at the 1949 Tokyo seminar has been prepared by Nick Fisher and Suzanne Lavery of ValueMetrics Australia and is widely available on the Internet. The documents, which formed a final English version that was translated by Bunzaemon Inoue and others and published in 1952 in Japanese by Diamond Press, are in the Civil Communications Section Archive, Hackettstown, NJ.

first and most important thing is for management, engineers and workers to have the desire to do more.

The second thing that must be done is to overcome the traditional concepts that are the result of our past educational system. This is the phase where we must encourage and help people to make practical use of the theoretical things they have learned. This practical use is to find easier or better or less expensive ways to do things.[*]

A quote from Kenneth Hopper

Arthur Spinanger (Industrial Engineer) and I met at a rest stop on Route 80, near the Delaware Water Gap. He presented me with a copy of a fascinating book, 'The Amazing Oversight: Total Participation for Productivity'.[†] I found this near forgotten book had articles by Mogensen, Graham who was Mogensen's principal disciple, Lillian Gilbreth, Arthur Spinanger, M. Scott Myers of Texas Instruments and others. Mogensen describes himself as having concluded (in the early 1930s?) that *the person doing the job knows far more than anyone else about the best way of doing that job, and therefore is the one best fitted to improve it.* (pg 20) Spinanger (pg 163) quotes the Chairman of P&G as praising its Deliberate Methods Change program as having provided a 1 year savings in 1970–1971 of $90,000,000. Spinanger concluded (pg 166) that for every dollar spent on the program there was a return of five to ten dollars, adding 'I know of no other portion of management type effort that can match that rate of return'.

COST EQUATIONS

The United States taught the Japanese, after World War II, in the CCS American Management Training course the following:

Why do companies exist? … Many people would answer by saying the purpose of a company is to make a profit. But such a statement is not a complete idea, nor is it a satisfactory answer because it does not clearly state the objective of the company or the principal goal that the company management is striving towards. A company's objective should be stated in a way which will not permit any uncertainty as to its real fundamental purpose. For example there are two ways of looking at the statement about profit. The first is to make the product for a cost which is less than the price at which it is to be sold.

Selling Price – Cost = Profit

The other is to sell the product for a price higher than it costs to make.

Cost + Profit = Selling Price

These two views are similar yet still quite different. The first implies a cost conscious attitude on the part of the company. The second seems to say whatever the product costs, it will be sold at a higher prices.

The other problem with the statement above is that it is entirely selfish and one sided. It ignores entirely the sociologic aspects which need to be part of successful company's thinking. A business enterprise should be based on its responsibility to the public, service to its customers as well as the realization that it can and does exert some influence on the life of the community in which it is located. These things are just as important to consider as the profit motive.[‡]

It is interesting to note how often these equations appear in Japanese Lean books. In many respects, it seems we in the United States have forgotten the teachings that we shared with the Japanese so long ago.

After WWII, there were few options for goods and services, so U.S. businesses could increase their profit by simply raising their price. If the cost of labor went up, they could raise their price. If the cost of material went up, they would raise their price, thus capitalizing on the second equation above.

Some readers may be old enough to remember when companies would actually tell their customers, "We will get your parts there when we get your parts there! If you don't like it, go somewhere else." This strategy worked fine when customers did not have a choice in the products they purchased or from whom they purchased them, or before the Internet when customers did not have the ability to seek out the best price for the item and have it shipped directly to their home for little cost.

Healthcare organizations have seen their customers shop for services, with access to information at their fingertips. Customers today seek out treatment and provider options and soon will be able to seek out services that offer the most value. Quality information is also starting to be available and understandable. Pay for performance (perceived customer value) and healthcare reform will reinforce the need for healthcare organizations to offer customer value, yielding high quality and a high service at low cost.

Today, we live in a competitive global economy. The global market drives the selling price as customers seek to find the best value at the lowest cost. Today, the value of our healthcare in service, quality, and cost is being compared to healthcare around the world; therefore, the global market, in

---

[*] BIG Archives—personal papers, speech in 1956 by Charles Protzman Sr. to Japanese JITVA—Japanese Industrial Training. JIVTA stands for Japan Industrial and Vocational Training Associations, a group that is associated with Nikkeiren, the Japanese Federation of Industrial Associations. For a period it was called JITA, the Japan Industrial Training Association. The other big industrial group, Keidanren, is more famous and deals with relationship with government, etc.

[†] Edited by Ben S. Graham, Jr. and Parvin S. Titus (American Management Association, 1979).

[‡] *CCS Training Manual*, Charles Protzman Sr. and Homer Sarasohn, 1949–1950. An e-book transcription of the version presented at the 1949 Tokyo seminar has been prepared by Nick Fisher and Suzanne Lavery of ValueMetrics, Australia and is widely available on the Internet. The documents, which formed a final English version that was translated by Bunzaemon Inoue and others and published in 1952 in Japanese by Diamond Press, are in the Civil Communications Section Archive, Hopper, Hackettstown, NJ.

turn, will impact the customer's (patient's) value proposition of healthcare. The worldwide system impacts our ability to increase or maintain our profits; we can no longer just raise our prices! The only way to stay competitive is to reduce costs. Global competition today is as close as your Internet screen; therefore, companies have to abide by the first equation listed above.

Today, if companies want to raise their profit, their only option is to *reduce* costs. This means that companies have to be able to manufacture or provide the best and most services they can, in as little space as possible, with the least amount of inventory, with the fewest number of people, and the least number of errors. This is a challenge. But companies that can delight their customers with the lowest cost will survive in the upcoming decade of increased global competition. Nowhere is this truer than in healthcare. Hospitals have experienced this with the current Medicare reimbursement model, and have been shifting the cost of providing services for Medicare patients and the uninsured to the insured. Hospital reimbursements have always had a "fixed" component with contracted fee payments. They often manage profits by cutting costs and full-time employees (FTEs). This is not a sustainable strategy. Eventually they will have to move to a more efficient care delivery model to be successful. With healthcare reform and increasing healthcare costs always on the horizon, it appears that the only way to survive will be for organizations to become Lean.

If healthcare organizations can reduce costs and set predictable delivery systems in place that can meet or exceed customer expectations, they can position themselves to grow their businesses. As they better understand the customer value stream, they will identify opportunities to streamline or expand services and grow both horizontally and vertically through partnering or the acquisition of other companies. They will be able to gain market share by providing improved customer value and satisfaction, expand service lines and product offerings, i.e., add outpatient radiology services or set up urgent care or outpatient clinics adjacent or aligned to their facilities.

In summary, implementing Lean principles provides a foundation for healthcare-related businesses and the opportunity for hospitals to eliminate waste. The waste is then converted into value-added services that lower labor costs in the product while increasing the output of the product. This makes the organization more efficient and provides a firm foundation for growth.

GLOBAL COMPETITION

In this world of truly global competition, there is an ever-changing landscape in the world of healthcare. Not so long ago, very few hospitals were adopting Lean principles as a way to eliminate waste, improve processes, and become more competitive. Today, there are an increasing number of healthcare systems showing interest in learning about, and deploying Lean. It is no longer used solely to provide a competitive

edge; it is practiced to help these organizations grow and stay in business. With yearly reductions in reimbursement and healthcare reform on the horizon, hospitals must determine how they will stay in business and what practices they will adopt to survive in the years to come.

Systems are at work all around us. Lean does not guarantee your business will grow, but it is an *enabler* to grow your business. Truly Lean companies have much fewer employees but they pay them 20%–30% more than the market.

Lesson Learned: *As the price of healthcare continues to climb and reimbursement continues to decline, the only way hospitals will survive in the future is to reduce costs. Lean thinking is all about reducing costs through a culture of ongoing continuous improvement.*

CHALLENGES FOR THE HEALTHCARE WORKER

Hospitals and healthcare organizations are not the only ones facing competition. U.S. workers are faced with and have been losing their jobs to offshore labor in an alarmingly increasing fashion. With the exception of companies like Toyota, it seems the days of employee loyalty or even companies that encourage employee loyalty are virtually gone. We feel companies have gone too far. Companies should value, respect, and listen to their employees.

Emerging entities are trying to drive healthcare services to the global marketplace, offering high-end surgeries in Bangkok, Dubai, and other foreign nations (see Figure 4.1). American insurance companies are also beginning to include some foreign healthcare facilities in their networks. Although the real value in moving healthcare services out of the United States is controversial, it further demonstrates the importance to begin to identify ways to provide high quality, affordable options.

In the world we live in today, we must consider the possibility that few jobs are immune from offshore labor. If an offshore worker gets paid ten times less, then we need to be ten times more efficient to keep jobs onshore. By implementing Lean principles, we can reduce waste and increase the value-added, which is then converted to lower labor costs and increased output. Implementing Lean principles are designed, over time, to increase job security.

Lean and Layoffs

Most workers feel Lean is designed to eliminate their jobs. When we ask staff who are exposed to Lean what they think of when they hear the word, we get feedback that the word "Lean" or "becoming Lean" conjures up ideas related to cutting costs and eliminating staff. This is not the impression we would like to make as we embark on a cultural revolution. We have to admit, however, that this is not an unfounded concern. Implementing Lean principles will free up people from their jobs because we can now get more output or productivity with less labor. Attrition and invoking hiring freezes on new staff or positions can normally mitigate this risk, especially

Medical Tourism or Health care travel to India

Medical tourism- also know as medical outsourcing, **medical travel**, health value travel, health tourism or health care tourism is the concept of traveling abroad to a particular destination to avail the opportunity of the World-Class **Healthcare services** offered by the best experienced Healthcare professionals at the technologically most advanced **medical facilities overseas** at **affordable** costs. The low-cost offshore healthcare procedure is usually combined with family holidays so the concept is also called medical vacation travel, health vacation travel, medical value travel, health care value travel abroad, health value tour etc. Medical tourism to India means availing World-Class Healthcare services in India at just a small fraction of the cost of the same Healthcare procedure in the home country thereby managing a big saving on health care costs. The medical surgery treatments in India facilitated by Life Smile health care is an easy access to advanced Health Care Technology, World-Class medical health care services, **board certified surgeons / doctors**, JCI (JCAHO) / ISO accredited hospitals, affordable low-cost medicare and immediate treatment- no wait list.

Affordable, Low-Cost Health Services, Medical Treatments & Patient Care with Life Smile

World-Class, advanced, **high quality** healthcare in India is 60% to 90% cheaper in comparison to developed economies due to: extremely favorable currency exchange rates with USD, GBP, EURO and other major currencies, lowest medical malpractice insurance coverage cost for medical professionals, India is a developing economy so services sector costs are low, India is also one of the world's largest producer and exporter of bulk drugs so high quality medicines are cheap.

FIGURE 4.1   Medical tourism example. From http://www.healthoursindia.com/. With permission.

if the hospital is proactive. There is generally a shortage of qualified nursing personnel and technical staff in hospitals; therefore, layoffs tend to be less of an issue. Most hospitals do not go into Lean with the desire to lay off people and it has been our experience that layoffs are rarely related to process improvements; however, businesses engaging in Lean generally do so because they have a "compelling need to change" and, at times, this may be related to a business condition that forces a reduction in growth or loss of a service line. Lean was not the driving force that caused their need to reduce their workforce.

Lesson Learned: *To truly make Lean successful there must be a written management commitment not to lay anyone off as a result of continuous improvement otherwise people will not work to eliminate their jobs.*

TRADITIONAL HEALTHCARE MODEL

The traditional hospital (since the 1970s or so) and healthcare business model would never work in the manufacturing world. In the current healthcare model:

1. The hospital provides the staff, materials, equipment, and billing.
2. Depending on the healthcare system, physicians may be part of an employed physician group, a contracted group by the hospital, a private community-based physician group, or solo practitioners. In most instances, hospitals are composed of components of each, with a large component often being volunteer independent medical staff.
3. Private insurance companies and government-funded Medicare and Medicaid pay the bills. There are few "self-pays." Most of the time this is a nice way of saying "no pays."

4. Government and other state and industry bodies regulate it.

While some may argue that the U.S. healthcare system is the best in the world, many would argue the contrary, that it still has much room for improvement and that there may be other countries' healthcare systems from which we can learn.

The British National Health Service provides free universal coverage for all citizens. The principal hospitals are nationalized, with managers, doctors, and nurses effectively being public servants. The standard of care varies from exceptionally high, particularly in the great teaching hospitals, to mediocre, with occasional complaints about poor care.[*]

In the French system, 65% of the medical cost is paid for by the government, with the balance picked up by private insurers. French Emergency Department (ED) doctors are paid one-third to two-thirds of their U.S. counterparts ($50K to $100K per year).[†] The French have a unique approach to Emergency Care. Emergency calls are screened by a physician who decides whether to respond and what type of team

---

[*] Kenneth Hopper and William Hopper, *The Puritan Gift: Reclaiming the American Dream amidst Global Financial Chaos* (New York: I.B. Tauris) 2009.

[†] CBS video, *Sunday Morning, A Votre Santé, CBS Sunday Morning: Why The French Can Afford To Get Sick*, Paris, October 26, 2008 (CBS). 8 years ago, the World Health Organization released a study ranking France as having the best healthcare system in the world. Yet the study's methodology is questionable. From Euro Health 2006, previously ranked by WHO as the best performer, the French health system is not without problems. It has traditionally operated with little regard for efficiency or cost containment. It has the highest rate of pharmaceutical use in the EU, while, until recently at least, there has been little attempt to incorporate cost effectiveness into policy making. The health workforce is aging; geographical inequalities in access to services exist, moreover, promotion and prevention have not been high priorities. http://www.euro.who.int/observatory/publications/20020524_26.

to respond, or to tell the patient to come into the emergency room. Ten percent of calls to which they respond are handled by a full team, including a physician to diagnose the problem and stabilize the patient on the scene, then take the patient to the hospital that specializes in their needed care. The French system costs approximately $3400 per capita (person) with no uninsured vs. almost double per capita in the United States with millions uninsured.

In the Canadian model, the government appoints the CEO who is responsible to run the hospital and meet budget. The business model is different, yet the hospitals run similarly to U.S. hospitals. We have found that much of what we discuss in this book is applicable internationally. The main difference we have witnessed is that, while operational challenges are similar, there are different incentives to improve government-run health systems. This is in large part because the systems tend to work on budgets that do not always reimburse the hospitals by the number of patients treated. Where this is the case, continuous improvement may provide more capacity but no financial incentive to physicians to see those patients and, in fact, increased patient volume can actually hurt compliance to a fixed budget. In the Canadian system, we have witnessed surgeons who left at 4.00 p.m. with patients waiting. These patients were told there was no time to get them in, and they need to be rescheduled. This is simply explained: it was time for the surgeon to go home. Since they are not paid by the patient operation, there is no financial incentive to stay. The system wants increased capacity (shorter wait lists), the hospital must minimize costs, and adding capacity may only increase costs for consumables or other fixed per-patient expenses, and the physicians' only incentive may be their compassion for the patient. Of course, much of this same struggle can be similar in inner-city U.S. hospitals that primarily treat Medicaid patients and, in fact, may lose money for each patient they treat. Despite the funding model, we can all come back to the common need to decrease costs while simultaneously improving quality and access to care.

Regardless of your business model or incentive for improving, this book can help you on your journey, as the basic elements of all hospital systems, all over the world, are based on evaluate, test, result, diagnose, treat, and monitor. Our intent is not to condemn or criticize any other country's healthcare system. We believe all countries could benefit by examining the best practices of everyone and applying Lean principles to their existing systems. We don't think any one country to date has completely stumbled on the right Lean answer, although we have found pieces of Lean internationally, like the French ED response.

Once the United States instituted EMTALA* in 1986, essentially, and to many unknowingly, U.S. national health-care was launched. EMTALA mandated hospitals treat anyone who arrives at the ED the same, regardless of their ability to pay. This was a totally unfunded mandate; however, for those who can't be turned away from an ED, presenting to the emergency room for a minor sore throat or earache is a very expensive national solution.

While some hospitals have found themselves entrenched in their complacent cultures, the world has changed around them. In the past several years, we have seen the development of "Minute Clinics," outpatient surgery centers (i.e., "Doc in the Box"), stand-alone ED centers, and the adoption of electronic records. A search on the Internet for "international elective services"† resulted in 1.8 million hits.‡

WHAT IS A LEAN BUSINESS DELIVERY SYSTEM?

The goal of the Lean Enterprise is to supply the best value to the customer, at the right time, with the highest quality at the lowest cost. This means creating a culture of continuous improvement and an environment where everyone in the organization participates in eliminating waste and streamlining processes in order to supply the best value to the customer. Best value means meeting or exceeding the customer's expectations for delivery and service for both product quality and customer-desired quality before and after their visit. Any company's primary mission is not solely to satisfy its customers, but exceed expectations the customers and promote customer loyalty. In doing so, it is important to remember that the company must make a profit so it can stay in business.

LEAN BUSINESS DELIVERY SYSTEM VISION

The vision for a Lean Business Delivery system is to have an organization without any waste. Imagine any business process today with zero waste. Lean initially started as a process improvement method for manufacturing, but a Lean Business Delivery system is not only a manufacturing shop floor initiative. Lean is now used for all business models and, if Lean principles are implemented properly, they will prompt changes from all parts of the organization, including finance, accounting, marketing, sales, HR, engineering, etc. Eliminating waste, also known as *Muda* in Japan, can be applied to any business process, including information systems, bed management administration, registration, transport, laboratory, pharmacy, ED, radiology, surgery, clinic, general physician offices, or other service areas.

A true Lean system, sometimes referred to as operational excellence, integrates or is simply an extension of past initiatives, including: Total Quality, Deming's 14 principles, Just in Time, Six Sigma, Kanbans, and Kaizen, to name a few.

---

* http://www.cms.hhs.gov/emtala/. In 1986, Congress enacted the Emergency Medical Treatment & Labor Act (EMTALA) to ensure public access to emergency services regardless of ability to pay. Section 1867 of the Social Security Act.

† http://www.google.com/search?q=elective+healthcare+overseas &rls=com.microsoft:en-us:IE-SearchBox&ie=UTF-8&oe=UTF-8&sourceid=ie7&rlz=1I7GGLL_en.

‡ http://medicalhealthcareindia.com/.

The tools in this book are designed to help you find waste in your organization. We have seen the Lean tools applied from shop floors to offices, hospitals to home builders, and even PTA volunteers to Moms and Dads at home.

If utilized properly, Lean tools will expose waste but do not guarantee the elimination of waste. That job will be up to each organization. When your organization becomes literally obsessed with the total elimination of waste in everything it does and is never satisfied with the current state, then your organization will be well on its way into its Lean journey. Lean should be viewed as a competitive business strategy and must be implemented in combination with a strategy to grow the business.

UNDERSTANDING THE VALUE OF THE LEAN BUSINESS DELIVERY SYSTEM

The Lean Business Delivery model begins with understanding customer expectations. Let's start with a basic example of going out to a restaurant. What kind of demands or expectations do you have when you walk into a restaurant? Most of us expect good service. We expect the waiter or waitress to be attentive to our needs, recognize us if we go there frequently, and address us by our name. We expect the food to be delivered on time, to our order specifications in the quantity promised on the menu, and served at the appropriate temperature. We expect the meal to be manufactured in a clean and orderly environment and prepared correctly or in essence "done right the first time".

Related to speed, the restaurant would need to understand if the customers who frequent their restaurant view speed of service as value, or is the expectation of food delivery an even-paced, slower atmosphere. It is critical to understand what your customers want and value. Most of us just expect good value for our money. Sometimes we are willing to pay a little more if we know we are getting superior service. Examples of superior service might be the 1 hr photo store, 1 hr dry cleaner, or overnight delivery.

It is difficult, if not impossible, to achieve or exceed customer expectations if we don't have a good understanding of what the customer views as value-added. If there is waste in the process then there will always be opportunities for variability and inconsistency thus leading to opportunities for customer dissatisfaction. We find healthcare organizations don't routinely survey "customer value." Today's healthcare customer does not necessarily pay fully or directly for the majority of care received. At a minimum, the customer would expect a positive outcome (high quality, error- or mistake-free), in a courteous (caring) environment, and in a timely manner. This is rapidly changing as the consumer is becoming more attuned to healthcare reform and may be directly paying for a higher percentage of his or her healthcare costs to one that is more value-based, which would include high quality, cost effective, timely, and provided in a courteous (caring) environment. One of the challenges is that, until recently, patients assumed quality and wanted service. Now they demand both in the value equation.

Business System from a Leadership Perspective

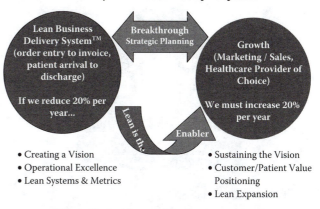

- Creating a Vision
- Operational Excellence
- Lean Systems & Metrics

- Sustaining the Vision
- Customer/Patient Value Positioning
- Lean Expansion

We must look at the overall business as a system!

FIGURE 4.2 Business systems overview model.

We describe the Lean system at a high level in the model pictured in Figure 4.2. On the left side are the Lean tools. Lean tools can be applied to anything that is a process. On the right is the marketing and growth piece. The goal is to grow the business at the same rate that we are improving the business. The model works as follows: Lean is an enabler for growth but does not guarantee growth. Growth must be part of the overall Lean initiative in order to succeed. When a company can produce its products with less waste than its competition, it has a distinct advantage. The increased profits can be invested in research and development, capital equipment, higher wages, or passed on to customers to undercut the competitor's price. Organizations must understand that *waste threatens all our jobs*[*] and the health of the business. Remember that once the organization achieves a competitive advantage through Lean, it must communicate its benefits and "key differentiators" to the consumer in order to recognize the full growth potential.

JUST IN TIME: THE FIRST PILLAR OF THE TOYOTA PRODUCTION SYSTEM MODEL

Companies need to be more responsive to customers, provide what the customer orders, in the quantity and quality the customer orders, at just the right time that the customer wants it. This is called Just in Time. JIT is one of the two pillars of the Toyota system (Figure 4.3). The goal behind JIT is to use the minimum amount of inventory, equipment, time, labor, and space necessary to deliver JUST IN TIME TO THE CUSTOMER!

Our healthcare definition of JIT developed by nurses is: "Giving the Right patient, the Right care, the Right way, while providing a Great Patient Experience." It includes providing the staff with the necessary and proper tools and supplies in the right locations, when they need them, and in the right amount with shortest nurse travel distances within efficient layouts.

* Mark Jamrog, principal, The SMC Group LLC.

FIGURE 4.3 Toyota house.

The goal is to create an efficient system with the same or better quality and safety than exists today. It doesn't do any good to create the most efficient or quickest system if we don't have the same or better patient and staff safety, ergonomics, and quality.

The true purpose behind JIT is to reduce the inventory in order to make problems more visible. Excess inventory and idle time are always signs of problems. Excess inventory hides problems. The analogy for this is to think of water rushing down the river (Figure 4.4). When the water level is high, the rocks in the river create "rapids." If you are white water rafting, kayaking, or canoeing, you look for the open "Vs" in order to traverse the rocks, but mostly you move swiftly over the rocks. As you lower the water level of the river, the rapids disappear and the rocks rise to the surface. This is the same with inventory. When we have lots of inventory (high water), we never see all the waste (rocks) because we are too busy rushing around and over it. Waste hides other waste. The rocks represent waste that was "hidden" by either inventory or other wastes or "work arounds" created within a process, otherwise known as "hidden wastes" (which will be discussed later in the book). As one lowers the water (inventory), which in healthcare can be reducing patients waiting

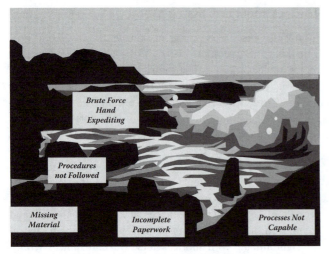

As You Lower Inventory You Quickly Expose The Rocks

FIGURE 4.4 JIT (just in time) reveals the rocks (problems) analogy.

times, overflowing charts, or excess operating room (OR) or hall supplies surface, one starts to expose the problems or rocks (other hidden wastes) underneath along with all the variations that exist in the system. One must make sure there is a continual pursuit to drive down waste.

JIT does not mean zero inventories. All systems need some inventory to function. JIT means there is a small amount of inventory available at point of use before it is needed. It means that the nurses don't have to go to the supply area or closet to get what they need; it should be right there where they need it. We call this at "point of use" inventory. The goal is to work with the minimum amount of inventory necessary but still be safe for the patient.

An Example of One of the Rocks—Short-Staffed

Restaurants can provide another analogy for hospitals. Have you ever walked into a restaurant and had to wait, even though you could see several open tables? This can create a frustrating feeling. Normally, this means the restaurant did not schedule enough staff or is short-staffed, perhaps due to someone calling in sick, so they don't want to seat the customer without being able to provide quality customer service.

Hospitals face a similar problem. Many hospitals today run "short-staffed" in order to try to save money or they simply can't find enough nurses. If the hospital is short-staffed, even though they may have beds available, they will not be able to open the beds for use as there is not enough staff to care for patients. Therefore, the hospital cannot accommodate the total patient demand. As a result, patients experience waits and delays, and other departments (i.e., ED and OR) dependent on the floors may back up.

In Hospital X's post-anesthesia care unit (PACU), the administration chose to staff to average demand. This resulted in closing four to six beds in PACU (22 to 16). This meant, on average, there were enough nurses but whenever they exceeded the average surgery demand per day or per hour or had an influx of pediatric patients (which require one-to-one care), the PACU would back up the OR rooms and pre-operative area (Pre-Op). This would delay surgeries, present safety issues for any emergency cases that may arise, and frustrate staff and physicians, resulting in extending the workday, overtime pay for many nurses, technicians, and housekeepers, and low morale. The ability to extend the workday and pay overtime hid the initial problem of the conscious decision to run short-staffed in PACU. Did the money saved by cutting two or three PACU nurses justify the cost of the overtime and frustration and eventual loss of surgeons?

JIDOKA—THE SECOND PILLAR OF THE TOYOTA PRODUCTION SYSTEM

The closest English translation of *Jidoka*, 自働化,[*] is autonomation or automating with a human touch. The

---

[*] Translation provided by Professor William Tsutsui, Associate Dean for International Studies, Professor of History, College of Liberal Arts & Sciences, The University of Kansas.

Japanese term "is ji-do-ka," which consists of three Chinese characters. The first character, ji—"自" means the worker him or her "self," do— "動" means "movement," and ka—"化" means "to change." In the TPS, the second character was replaced by 働—which translates to "work or to labor." It added a character (radical) in the front representing "human" to the original 動.[*] This idea is credited to Sakichi Toyoda,[†] who developed a spinning loom that would automatically shut off if a thread snapped. Creating "smart machines" or machines that can stop themselves if they make a mistake is a central principle to the Lean system. This links to the idea of mistake proofing at the source. The goal is to prevent the error so that a defect does not result. With *Jidoka*, machines are designed to detect a defect prior to passing it on to the next process. Machines should check items before they work on them and after they work on them. An example of a *Jidoka* machine in healthcare is the smart IV pumps. The pump uses bar codes on the drug to make sure it is delivered to the right patient, at the correct rate. Another example would be an IV pump that stops and signals when it is empty vs. letting air enter the patient when the solution runs out. This same idea transcends to safety with the philosophy that the machine should protect the human. Many times in the laboratory setting, one laboratory specimen can be used for more than one test. "Splitting" a laboratory sample in two is called aliquoting. This used to be a manual process that posed a safety risk to laboratory technicians who had to perform this task. With the new automated technology, this can now be performed by a machine, eliminating the "human" intervention.

The second idea of *Jidoka* is that machines and equipment should be designed so that humans do not need safety glasses or protective gear. Protected cages and laser curtains should prevent injuries to workers. One of the principles of Lean is to be able to separate man from machine. Machines should do heavy, repetitive, or dangerous work. This concept translates to the worker in kanji with "ji" added to "do" or self-work. This idea of self-work means that if the worker feels that "this is not right" or "I am creating a defective product," he/she must immediately stop the conveyor.[‡] Stopping the line or the process is a difficult concept to get across in manufacturing and can also be difficult in healthcare. In the United States, our short term "make the quarterly numbers" strategically conflicts with this concept.

The third idea associated with *Jidoka* is mistake proofing or "poka yoke," meaning never pass on a bad part. A few examples of *Jidoka* or mistake-proofing techniques in healthcare include the Broselow® Tape for Pediatric Trauma. The tape measure is color-coded according to height, and appropriately sized medical devices and doses of medications are contained in packets of the same color to facilitate rapid treatment, and reduce calculations and dosing errors; orange-colored oral syringes are designed so they will not fit onto any IV tubing, providing a visual alert and design, so oral medication cannot be accidentally administered intravenously, and the sponge-counter bag assists in keeping track of sponges removed from a patient.[§]

JIDOKA MEANS: NEVER PASS ON A BAD PART OR PATIENT

In the book, *The Nun and the Bureaucrat*,[¶] the authors cite several hospitals that encouraged their nurses to admit mistakes. This is an application of *Jidoka* in healthcare and is one of the keys to Lean systems. Mistake-proofing examples in hospitals are numerous. But errors and mistakes cost all of us money and, more important, the reputation of our hospitals. We must take caution, as humans are at best two or three Sigma. Consider that three Sigma is approximately 66,000 mistakes per million opportunities. As long as the process depends on a human, the system will probably never get better than two or three Sigma because humans make mistakes. In order to mistake proof or foolproof processes, we need a way to take the humans out of the equation. Mistakes and errors not only cause human tragedy, but also add expense to an already overburdened healthcare system.

APPLYING JIDOKA TO HEALTHCARE

We may not realize it but we have machines and equipment all over the hospital. They are in the laboratory, radiology, the ORs, and in the patient rooms on the floors. How do we know the equipment is working correctly, measuring correctly, or notifying us when it should? If you expand the concept to mistake proofing, how do we eliminate errors in hospitals? We constantly encounter articles, news reports, and journals highlighting all the errors made in hospitals. In many cases, patients' lives are put on the line because our processes and machines are not mistake proofed. In the book, *The Nun and the Bureaucrat: How They Found an Unlikely Cure for America's Sick Hospitals* and the subsequent video, *Good News: How Hospitals Heal Themselves*. These preventable mistakes are exposed with, in some cases, simple solutions.[**] At the end of the documentary the following interim results were reported at various hospitals after the implementation of the continual improvement philosophy, elimination of blame, and the creation of a management vision and application of Lean:

- An 85% reduction in hospital-acquired infections that were often fatal and cost $30,000–$90,000 each
- A 63% reduction in central line infections since 2001, half of which are fatal and each cost $30,000 to treat

[*] Video, *A Passion for Manufacturing, the Essence of the Toyota Production System*, www.saiga-jp.com, kanji to English dictionary, http://dict.regex.info Japanese to English dictionary.

[†] Taiichi Ohno, *Toyota Production System* (New York: Productivity Press) 1988.

[‡] Japanese Management Association, *Kanban Just in Time at Toyota* (New York: Productivity Press) 1986.

[§] http://www.ahrq.gov/qual/mistakeproof/.

[¶] Louis M. Savary and Clare Crawford-Mason, *The Nun and The Bureaucrat* (Washington, D. C.: CC-M Productions) 2006, 40–41.

[**] Louis M. Savary and Clare Crawford-Mason, *The Nun and The Bureaucrat* (Washington, D. C.: CC-M Productions) 2006.

- Lowering of staph infections from 26 per 1000 patients to 8 per 1000
- Decreasing intensive care unit mortality from 5.5% to 3.3%
- Lowering acute diabetic complications from 13.5% to 5%

THE TOP OF THE TOYOTA HOUSE— RESPECT FOR HUMANITY

Companies that are successful in Lean grow their businesses and provide jobs for people. Over time (typically, a couple of years), as hospitals improve their bottom line, we encourage them to share a portion of the extra profits with their employees. Some companies increase employee benefits, set up gain sharing plans, provide cash bonuses or incentive reward programs to help drive results and desired behaviors. After several years of implementing Lean, our goal should be to share bonuses monthly up to 20%–30% or more of an employee's annual pay in monthly, quarterly, or yearly payments. We encourage companies to share the wealth. Companies can attract and keep the best talent in what is a very tight labor market because reducing their costs makes them not only more flexible with their customers' pricing, but also more flexible with employees' paychecks.

Lesson Learned: *Lean works best with a clearly stated policy, up front, which ensures no one will be laid off as a result of Lean or continuous improvement activities. Most people will not contribute to a team if they think they will be laid off as a result. Tying Lean to layoffs or FTE cutbacks won't prevent you from getting results, but it will keep you from getting the additional results that evolve from creating a Lean culture where employees contribute ideas every day. Many companies unknowingly have limited their improvements because this communication was not handled properly. The improvements they get are only those that the management dictates to their employees. This is not a Lean culture.*

A good Lean system implementation, or what some may term System Kaizen, provides staff with the opportunity to suggest improvements within their work areas, which improves the flow of communication and ideas. Listening to staff and implementing their suggestions always yields an improvement in morale and is part of the "Respect for Humanity" concept. Everyone works together as a team and has the opportunity to learn additional jobs and skills; this is referred to as cross-training. The more skills learned, the more marketable and valuable the employee becomes to any company. The opportunity will also exist for you to lead your team in daily production activities and coach others in the skills you have learned. This provides the foundation to build leadership skills.

Implementing Lean does not only impact each person on the unit or clinical area, but everyone in the hospital or clinic will also be affected in some way. Eliminating waste in administrative processes will free up people, and the need for middle management personnel will also be reduced over time. Moving to value streams or service line organizations will provide better "line of sight" to the patient. Overheads should be reduced by 30% or more after several years. Some of this will involve converting staff positions into line positions. Those in administrative positions or middle management positions need to constantly expand their skill sets and stay current with training if they are to add value to the company.

As organizations embark on their Lean journey, they need to understand that every department within the enterprise can benefit from becoming "Lean." If every area is not actively engaged in the "pursuit of waste elimination" (or becoming "Lean"), then you have not crossed the cultural chasm of "Lean thinking." One main reason why so many companies fail in this cultural transformation is that organizations implement pieces of the Lean system but not the whole system. Lean thinking is a cultural change. If it stays in the realm of multiple projects, then it will run out of steam when resources and budgets get tight. That is why it must be leadership-driven, but staff-level-implemented.

It is a very challenging and difficult journey that ultimately requires understanding and commitment to be successful. The book, *The Leadership Road Map,** explains in detail what is necessary to create a Lean culture and how to begin and sustain the Lean journey from a CEO's point of view. It starts with the culture piece, i.e., creating your vision and values and provides templates or blueprints to create your Lean road map.

Lesson Learned: *It is imperative that everyone be relentless in the elimination of waste, by analyzing all components affecting the value stream. A culture of continuous improvement must be created from the top down and from the bottom up. We must create and nurture a learning organization that will cause us to un-learn some of the things we currently practice. The organization must be willing to expand the tool-kit to be able to address any challenge, by utilizing Lean Tools, Six Sigma Tools, and other innovative techniques. By constantly lowering operating costs, we increase the opportunity to reward and improve our processes.*

LEAN IS A JOURNEY

Depending on the improvement needed and waste identified, a multi-year program may need to be established to determine sequential initiatives that will drive the desired results. Remember, the healthcare delivery system is comprised of many interrelated parts; many "x's" (or causes) will impact a Big "Y" (goal). For example, there are many little x's which

---

* Dwane Baumgardner, former CEO of Donnelly Corporation, and Russ Scafede, senior vice president of Global Manufacturing, Donnelly Corporation, past general manager/vice president of Toyota Motor Manufacturing Power Train, and consultant.

drive an OR room turnover time (BIG Y). It may start with the staff understanding what it means to have a room ready, and when is the room ready to bring the patient in, anesthesia must be ready for the patient, the room must be cleaned, supplies and instruments readied for the case as well as "picked" accurately. The staff must be available, and each must understand what his/her role is, or what we call their "standard work." If you have the patient ready at the time the OR calls, and yet the supplies or anesthesia are not available, turnover will take longer. Therefore, there may need to be several Lean initiatives in order to effectively tackle room turnover. The overarching goal of Lean thinking is to get everyone in your organization focused on improving the process. The difference between Toyota and American companies is that Toyota makes thousands of improvements every month as a result of every employee working with his/her group leaders and managers. Every once in a while, one might get a big return on investment (ROI) improvement, but that is not the main focus. In the United States, we tend to only focus on the largest ROI projects first and miss the opportunity to get everyone involved in the improvement process.

Lesson Learned: *You will know you are further down the Lean culture path when building a culture of ongoing continuous improvement every day outweighs the insistence on implementing only those perceived large ROI projects first. Thousands of small improvements turn into large overall returns. Sometimes, a project with a lower ROI can lead to a project with a higher ROI. Many times, jumping to the highest ROI project is not the best strategy.*

In summary, although there may be some differences between manufacturing and providing patient care, the Lean Business Delivery system has been shown to have application within healthcare organizations, such as hospitals, clinics, surgery centers, free-standing laboratories as well as other support areas, and will continue to grow as more organizations realize the benefits gained through the Integrated Delivery System/Network (IDS/IDN).

Section II

Lean Tools, Methodology and Application

5 Lean and Change Management

EXECUTIVE SUMMARY

Chapter 5 discusses the challenges in implementing Lean and the change in culture that must occur in order to create a Lean environment. It explains the need to understand how foreign this culture can seem to many companies. Major indicators of potential success for change estimates are described and highlight the fact that there is approximately 30 to 50% or more MUDA (waste) in healthcare.

The change equation is discussed: $C \times V \times N \times S > R$ (resistance to change)

C = compelling need to change

V = vision

N = next step

S = sustain

Change Acceleration Process (CAP)[*] is also discussed:

Quality × Acceptance = Effectiveness or $Q \times A = E$.

This model looks at the Quality (content) of your message and the Acceptance of your message (soft skills) while creating a shared need for the change.

Emphasis is placed on the fact that waste is not just simply "administrative waste" but can be seen in all aspects of healthcare. It discusses many of the issues of resistance to change, including the terminology of "Concrete Heads" and lists warning signs that will help illustrate that change will be extremely difficult.

Finally, the various personality types using the Myers Briggs Type Indicator® (MBTI®) model are described, as is how an understanding of our differences can help with change management.

The appropriate use and success of meetings is also noted.

KEY LEARNINGS:

- Change can be difficult and one must be persistent in order to overcome the resistance to change.
- Change is cultural and there must be both a compelling need to change and some advantage for staff members if they are to accept it.
- Some of the barriers one runs into are individuals' personalities and paradigms.

- Most organizations talk Lean (operational excellence) but are not truly implementing it.
- Lean is tough to implement and very difficult to sustain.
- Top management's attitude and drive can "make or break" Lean implementations.
- Leadership must walk the walk.
- Changing the reward system can be critical to success.

CHANGE MANAGEMENT AND LEAN

All progress comes from change, but not all change is progress.

—**Unknown**

It was difficult to know where in the book to discuss change management. The difficulty is that change management is not only a large part of Lean, it also occurs before, during, and after any Lean implementation. One should not underestimate the importance of this component to successfully disseminate, deploy, and sustain Lean.

We have a saying that Lean is 50/50 task vs. people. Fifty percent of Lean is implementing Lean tools. This is the scientific management part of Lean. The other 50% of Lean is what we call the "people" piece or what others call change management. There must be a balance between these two pieces. If the Lean balance scale swings too much to the scientific management side, we can end up with low morale and discontent with the ultimate result being unionization. If we swing too far on the people side, then we end up with no discipline on the floor and no chain of command. People do whatever they want to do, are not accountable, hoard their knowledge (to protect their job), and are out of control. That is why striking this balance before, during, and after the ongoing improvement phase of Lean is so important.

There are many books and videos that explore this topic. In *Training Within Industry*,[†] the people piece is referred to as job relations. While learning and implementing Lean tools is not easy, implementing the people piece or what Toyota calls "Respect for Humanity" is much more difficult. The people piece includes getting people not only to buy-in and accept Lean, but also to embrace and sustain the changes. Anyone who has implemented Lean knows this to be true. The real goal of Lean is to create a continuous improvement

---

* See Footnote '†' on page 53.

* Donald Dinero, *Training Within Industry* (New York: Productivity Press) 2005.

culture where employees are contributing and supervisors or team leaders are budgeted 50% or more time to implement small improvements on a daily basis.

This is a very difficult culture to create. In discussing this with Jerry Solomon, multiple Shingo Prize winner,[*] Jerry said, "Why would you want to embark on the Lean journey when over 90% of companies fail in their quest to truly become Lean? What will your company do differently to be successful?"

Lesson Learned: *It is extremely important if you are starting a Lean journey that you answer the question above. We ask this of any healthcare institution or department even thinking about going down the Lean path. Think through it, plan and map it out, get the right people on board, don't waiver, and never look back. Hopefully, we can reverse this to 90% of companies are successful in implementing Lean and Six Sigma.*

Homework: *Answer the following question: What are you going to do differently that will make you one of the 10% of healthcare companies in the United States or the world that is successful in implementing Lean?*

This chapter explores various change models and topics to consider in your Lean quest. Since every company is different, it is difficult to throw out a "cookie cutter" solution for implementing culture change. Suffice it to say, that to be successful and truly sustain, the change must start and be driven with a "pull" from the top level and driven (and at times "pushed") through the line leadership. A roadmap for Lean implementation is depicted in a book called *The Leadership Roadmap.*[†] This chapter will also explore different change management tools. There are many tools out there to choose from[‡] and we have selected a few that we use across virtually all implementations. The first concept of change management we explore is paradigms.

PARADIGMS

How many times have you had a great idea for improving a process? How many of you had trouble implementing your new idea? This is the concept Joel Barker explores in his video series, *Business of Paradigms.* He describes paradigms as "a set of rules or regulations we use to filter data." Data that meet our expectations passes through our filters easily. Data that doesn't meet our expectations is sometimes rejected out of hand or is very difficult for us to see. "Sometimes we simply ignore the data that doesn't fit our paradigms." We all have paradigms and they are easy to slip into without realizing it. Barker goes on to say that paradigms are good because they help us filter out unneeded data, but they can be bad when our paradigm

becomes "the" paradigm, or the only way to see things. The real challenge lies in recognizing and dealing with them.

We are all full of great ideas on how to improve and all great ideas tend to meet some resistance. Many times, those great ideas come from outsiders because they are not vested in your paradigms. The first step we take in change management is to educate those participating in the change about the trap of paradigms. This serves two purposes:

1. It helps to open up their minds to the changes we will be making with them.
2. It lets them know that people are not so open-minded to the changes we will be making. There will be resistance.

CHANGE EQUATION

$$C \times V \times N \times S > R_{\text{Change}}$$

FIGURE 5.1 Change equation.

The next tool is called the change equation (Figure 5.1). Again, this is a critical tool that we use with every company. It was originally developed by Gleicher, Beckard, and Harris. Their equation was $D \times V \times F > R_{\text{change}}$,[§] which stood for Dissatisfaction × Vision × First steps has to be greater than the Resistance to change.

We have slightly modified the change equation by Gleicher, Beckhard, and Harris.[¶] The modified equation is $C \times V \times N \times S > R_{\text{change}}$. Over many years of implementing Lean, we have found we always come back to this equation with every implementation or Point Kaizen.

C = COMPELLING NEED TO CHANGE

We have traded the *D* for dissatisfaction for *C* the compelling need to change (Figure 5.2). While we agree that dissatisfaction is important and that Shingo said, "Dissatisfaction was the Mother (relationship) of all improvement,"[**] we feel it is not by itself a strong enough statement. People can be dissatisfied but never change. Change is hard. People constantly complain but they are so used to the old way that they don't want to change. If we don't have a compelling need to change, then all efforts are futile as, ultimately, nothing

$$\textcircled{C} \times V \times N \times S > R_{\text{Change}}$$

FIGURE 5.2 Change equation—Compelling Need to Change.

---

[*] Jerrold Solomon, *Accounting for World Class Operation* (Fort Wayne, IN: WCM Associates) 2007, *Who's Counting* (Fort Wayne, IN: WCM Associates) 2003. Both books won the Shingo Prize.

[†] Baumgardner and Scaffede, *The Leadership Roadmap* (Great Barrington, MA: North River Press) 2008.

[‡] www.12manage.com and many books on change management—see suggested reading list in the Appendix.

[§] This equation was taught to Charlie Protzman by Coopers and Lybrand as part of the AlliedSignal TQ training.

[¶] http://ezinearticles.com/?Change-Guided-By-A-Mathematical-Formula&id=260182, April 21, 2009. Gleicher, Beckhard, and Harris have found an equation that shows the relation to overcome resistance to change. The formula is modeled in the following way: $D \times V \times F > R$.

[**] Shigeo Shingo, *Non Stock Production* (New York: Productivity Press) 1988.

will change. If change does occur and it is not driven or supported, it will have no chance of sustaining the process.

To be successful with Lean, we need more than dissatisfaction. We have to literally have so much passion that we need to live and breathe waste reduction. There are two ways to incentivize change. One is to have an actual "crisis" or business case that, without change, the organization will not survive. The crisis dictates a true compelling need to change. The other way is to invent a crisis or to set very high goals for the organization that can't be achieved by doing it the way it has always been done. This creates a healthy "fear" or paranoia that keeps the organization changing/improving. While this can be done at a department level, it is most successful when started at the senior executive level.

Why Change?

When faced with this question, our answer is "What is the option?" Can we afford to continue to work with the level of waste in our current processes? Have past improvements worked? All the solutions put in place over the years have gotten us to where we are today! Is your department or company world class? (Figure 5.3) Do you want to be world class? Are other departments you impact satisfied with your performance? How many of you are satisfied with your current processes? Can your company or department survive in the future? Healthcare is a dynamic industry; not to change is the equivalent of moving backward.

Lesson Learned: *Did you create that process? Remember, most of us tend to be most resistant to new process changes than changes we have previously implemented.*

The cost of all waste goes to your bottom line. For example, if you are idle, who is paying for that waste? If you have to search for something, who is paying for that waste? The answer is: the patient who is our customer, and in healthcare, if it is not the patient, it is you, the taxpayer, as the customer who is ultimately paying for the waste in the form of higher costs. The waste adds cost to the bottom line because

the hospital is paying you while you are idle or searching. This cost makes organizations less profitable and when organizations we work for become less profitable, financial managers start looking for bodies to layoff. Hence, the cost of the waste threatens our jobs.[*]

Dr. Berwick, president and CEO of IHI,[†] said he recognizes the central irony of U.S. healthcare: "While a great many Americans don't receive the care they need, another large segment of the population receives unnecessary care in a system that is bloated by its emphasis on growth and profit—rather than on better health." Berwick has estimated that "up to half of the more than $2 trillion that the U.S. spends on healthcare does nothing to relieve suffering." To the contrary, "much of it adds to suffering."[‡]

> The same study estimated that another $210 billion is wasted each year on medical paperwork… At the [Cleveland] clinic's patients' accounts office, rows of cubicles are piled high with file folders and printouts, testimony to its dealings with thousands of different health plans from hundreds of insurance companies all over the country. Thousands of times a day, clerks pick up the phone and get put on hold like anyone else who calls an insurance company. Industry estimates put the average cost of handling a phone call at $3, to each party… in which the clinic's 2,000 doctors require 1,400 clerks to handle their billing.[§]

An estimated 40% of U.S. healthcare spending is wasted on inefficiency, duplicative or unnecessary tests and treatment, error and complications that result from lapses of quality.[¶]

Cindy Jimmerson,[**] a nurse who has also been pursuing Lean healthcare methods, states, "The national numbers for waste in healthcare are between 30–40%, but the reality of what we have observed by doing minute-by-minute observation over the last 3 years is closer to *60%!* That's waste of time, waste of money, and a waste of material resources. It's nasty! The waste is not limited to administrative costs, which most research on healthcare has documented. It's everywhere: patient care and non-patient care alike."

$$C \times \boxed{V} \times N \times S > R_{\text{Change}}$$

FIGURE 5.4 Change equation—*V.*

---

[*] Mark Jamrog, principal, The SMC Group—original quote "Waste threatens all our jobs."

[†] http://www.ihi.org/ihi/aboutus/people.aspx, Donald M. Berwick, MD, MPP, FRCP, president and chief executive officer.

[‡] http://www.healthbeatblog.org/2008/02/how-do-we-fund.html, February 1, 2008, "How Do We Fund National Health Reform?" Health Beat Blog, Maggie Mahar.

[§] Jerry Adler and Jeneen Interlandi, "The Hospital That Could Cure Health Care," *Newsweek,* Published November 27, 2009. From the magazine issued December 7, 2009, The evidence was in the 2008 *Dartmouth Atlas of Health Care.*

[¶] http://www.prhi.org/docs/ROOT Celebrating 10 Years of the Pittsburgh Regional Health Initiative.pdf.

[**] Cindy Jimmerson, *A3 Problem Solving For Healthcare* (New York: Productivity Press) 2007.

FIGURE 5.3 OR room used as storage.

V = Vision

The next letter in the change equation is *V* for vision (Figure 5.4). A good example of a vision statement comes from the Civil Communications Section (CCS) Management Training Course[*] for Newport News Ship Building Company, whose vision statement went like this:

> We will build good ships here
> At a profit if we can—at a loss if we must—
> But; always build good ships!

"This is the guiding principle of this company. And it is a good one, too, because it's concise, but it tells the whole reason for the existence of the enterprise. And yet inherent in these few words there is a wealth of meaning:

- The determination to put quality ahead of profit,
- A promise to stay in business in spite of adversity, and
- A determination to find the best production methods.

Every business enterprise should have as its very basic policy a simple clear statement, something of this nature, which will set forth its reason for being. In fact, it is imperative that it should have such a fundamental pronouncement because there are some very definite and important uses to which it can be put. The most important use of basic policy is to aim the entire resources and efforts of the company toward a well-defined target. In a general way, it charts the course that the activity of the company will follow.[†]

Vision is important in the change equation because if people understand the vision and the change that is required supports the vision, then the change will be easier to "sell" and become accepted/adopted, reducing the resistance to change.

$$C \times V \times \boxed{N} \times S > R_{\text{Change}}$$

FIGURE 5.5   Change equation—*N*.

N = Next Steps

N stands for next steps (Figure 5.5). Once we know we have a compelling need to change and know and understand the vision, we need to determine the next steps (not just the first) to get to the vision. These steps come from assessing where we currently are relative to the vision. If the "roadmap" of how we are going to achieve the vision is communicated and people gain an understanding of it, this will help diminish the resistance to change. There are many Lean tools that help with this letter of the equation.

[*] *CCS Training Manual*, Charles Protzman Sr. and Homer Sarasohn, 1949–1950. An e-book transcription of the version presented at the 1949 Tokyo seminar has been prepared by *Nick Fisher* and Suzanne Lavery of ValueMetrics, Australia, and is widely available on the Internet. The documents that formed the final English version, which was translated by Bunzaemon Inoue and others and published in 1952 in Japanese by Diamond Press, are in the Civil Communications Section Archive, Hackettstown, NJ.
[†] Ibid.

$$C \times V \times N \times \boxed{S} > R_{\text{Change}}$$

FIGURE 5.6   Change equation—*S*.

S = Sustain

The final letter, *S*, stands for sustain, which we have added to the original equation (Figure 5.6). Once we have implemented our next steps, we must sustain ongoing improvement. This is the most difficult step of all. Sustaining is the true test of whether there was a compelling enough reason to change and a sign if the other letters were implemented properly. Once again, the only way to truly sustain is with top management leadership and drive (not just support). The leadership must be unwavering and totally committed to sustain and continually foster the compelling need to change and ongoing improvement.

Notice there is a multiplication sign between each letter. This is because if any of the letters are zero or are not addressed, we will not overcome the R_{change}, which stands for resistance to change, thus effective change will *not* occur. In addition, each step needs to be followed in order. When you stop and think about it, this is really a problem-solving model for change.

CHANGE AND WHAT'S IN IT FOR ME

We developed this tool knowing each employee is going to ask "What's In It For Me" (WIFM) when challenged with a new initiative. It is important that when we begin to answer this question, it is addressed from multiple perspectives. For example, an Operating Room director is in the middle of a Lean initiative that will reduce turnover times between cases and, if successfully implemented, can shorten the surgery day by 1 hr. This means that employees will no longer have to stay past their normal working hours to finish routine surgical cases.

Let's look at this from different perspectives: Employee #1 is silently concerned that she will no longer receive the five to ten overtime hours per week she is accustomed to; therefore the project will potentially impact her current lifestyle and is perceived negatively. Employee #2 is a working parent who has struggled over the past year to pick up her children at daycare; from her perspective, the project is a positive one. We find the WIFM question applies to changes even in our personal lives. Management has to be ready with the answers that will address both positive and negative impacts from the employees' perspective. If we do not answer this question, employees are left in the dark, they will fill in the gaps or blanks of information which is not clearly communicated, think the worst, and rumors will run rampant.

Think about the proverbial call from the school nurse. The nurse leaves a message on your voice mail asking you to call her back. What starts going through your mind? You start to think the worst things that could possibly happen.

People mainly fear changes they perceive as negative in some way. After all, none of us resist changes that we perceive as truly positive. Would any of you object to the change of increasing your pay by 10%? Even if I made the change without telling you ahead of time, it would probably be viewed as positive. Positive changes or changes that fit our paradigms pass through our filters easily. It is the negative changes that meet resistance. It is crucial not only to know the answers to the questions below, but also to be able to frame them in a positive fashion. This should not be difficult if there is a truly compelling need to change. The key to WIFM is to answer the questions below from the point of view of the employee each time they are impacted by the change. What do they really want to know and why? These questions will help communicate to the organization the compelling need to change.

We generally suggest scripting answers to the following questions prior to starting the Lean journey:

1. What is the change we are making?
2. Why are we making the change?
3. How will it affect the employee? Now and in the future?
4. How will it affect the company? Now and in the future?
5. What's in it for the employee if we make the change?
6. What's in it for the company if we make the change?

Once scripted, it is important to communicate the answers with the staff in each department prior to rolling out the Lean implementation. This tool forces the leadership to think through each of these questions. The answers must be compelling enough to support the big *C* in the change equation.

Homework: *Script out your answers to the questions prior to implementing your Lean initiative.*

"RIGHT SEAT ON THE RIGHT BUS"*

The next tool we call "the right seat on the right bus." This concept from the book, *Good To Great*,[†] which we have found invaluable in our change management toolset. The goal is to find out if your employees are on the right bus or, in other words, supporting our change initiative and then assess if they are in the right seat on the bus (in the organization chart) to help us get to the next level of change. To implement this tool, we take the organization chart and review the persons in each position. This is a very difficult process and should be taken very seriously from an extremely critical and realistic point of view.

The other dimension in this tool is time. It is possible for a person to be in the right seat on the right bus during one time frame but not for the next. One may not have the necessary

skills required to implement the next phase. Do not underestimate the importance of having the right people in the right seat on the bus as it will impact the success of your organization, especially as you go through a Lean journey.

*We had a director at Clinic X that supported the necessary Lean changes during our implementation phase and we got great results. But the director did not have the willingness and drive to sustain and continue improving the area. Two of the director's staff members were fighting the Lean changes at every opportunity but covertly, behind the scenes. The director, after much coaching and counseling, refused to confront these individuals and make the necessary changes to coach and mentor them. Therefore, the director was not in the right seat or even **on** the right bus after the implementation. The director eventually left the company.*

One has to decide what time frame to use, but generally it pays to review the organization every 6 months to a year. If we determine someone is not going to be in the right seat but is on the right bus, there are a couple of options. This means either the person needs to be moved to another area of the organization where they can be successful or they need a clear plan to receive coaching, mentoring and skills to stay in the same seat. Sometimes, they're just not the right fit for where the organization is going.

The goal of the evaluation is to determine the development needs required to keep the person in the same role. This should be a collaborative process. The persons being evaluated should also be given the opportunity to determine if they have the skills to take them to the next level. They should be asked to write down what they think are their strengths and weaknesses. These should be compared with the evaluator's perception of their strengths and weaknesses. Differences should be discussed. The end result should be either to agree on a move or on what steps should be taken to raise the level of skills for the individuals to stay in the same roles.

Lesson Learned: *During any culture change there are some individuals (sometimes at high levels) that after coaching and mentoring honestly believe the changes will never work. The longer you hold on to these individuals the more adverse it will become for the change for the organization.*

SUCCESSION PLANNING

As a leader (whether supervisor or executive manager), it is important to have a succession plan. We find that many healthcare organizations do not have succession plans in place. We need to be prepared in the event someone leaves or is unable to continue on in that position. As leaders, part of our duty should be to develop our people to be able to take our place. This is also part of Toyota's Respect for Humanity principle.

It is a general rule of thumb that we can't be promoted if there is no one to take our place. Therefore, it is in our own best interest to make sure we are constantly developing a successor(s). This also helps to prove if people are truly in

---

* Jim Collins, *Good to Great* (New York: Harper Business Press) 2001.
† Ibid.

TABLE 5.1
"A" Player Grid

Ability to embrace change	Continuous learning
Leadership	Coach
Manager	Diligence
Trust / Credibility	Communicator
Initiative	Listener
Team Focus	Customer Focus
Flexibility	Business Acumen
Speed	Judgment
Sense of Urgency	

Source: BIG Archive - AlliedSignal TQ Training Materials.

the right seats. If your successor does not have the ability to take over your job or cannot either physically or mentally do the job, then we need to re-evaluate the future and what role that person will be playing. Not everyone can be the boss and not everyone can be "A" players (Table 5.1). We need people to get the work done every day and some people reach their limit or don't want to move further in the organization. We call these folks "seasoned professionals", who we need as they provide a significant contribution to the organization.

Lesson Learned: *It is difficult to do, but we need to constantly assess our bench strength to get our work done each day and develop those who are going to take us to the next levels of continuous improvement.*

RESISTANCE TO CHANGE

We all fall into the guilty category when it comes to our resistance to change, some of us more than others; however, it is important to realize that we can view change not only as a threat, but also as an opportunity. Staff members who look at it as a threat, resist the change and focus only on the negative. Many times, it results in a self-fulfilling prophecy, where the person ends up being moved, or let go, because they couldn't adjust to the change. Everything that happened fit their paradigm, making them believe, "the change would not succeed; therefore, I will not succeed."

Those who embrace change and see it as a positive not only succeed but also have fun doing it. They also tend to advance in their organizations. Some people are just naturally early adopters for change while others wait and sit back to see what will happen. We need to remember that, in any given area of the organization, you will find all types of people, at all levels, who respond to change differently and we must be prepared and have a plan in place to deal with each of them.

Homework: *Take the Complacency Test*

- *When was the last time you made an improvement to your process? What are your average implemented suggestions per month from your employees?*
- *How often do you say:*
  - *"It can't be done"*

- *"Management won't let me…"*
- *"I can't get money…"*
- *"We tried that before…"*
- *"We don't need to get any better…"*
- *"My department's metrics look great… What does it matter that we impacted the other department… That's their problem!"*
- *"I'm tired of hearing about customer satisfaction issues. We know we have problems… we will fix them when we get that new facility with more beds and space."*
- *"We can wait on that improvement… the new software we are installing will solve all our problems!"*
- *"I can't make any changes because…"*
- *Are you complacent?*

EXPECTATIONS… HIGHS AND LOWS

As we implement the recommended changes, the teams as well as individuals and process owners tend to go through highs and lows. This is normal. It is important to try to manage people's expectations and to minimize the highs and lows they experience. If the team cannot recover from the low, then the implementation can fail. If expectations get too high, the team cannot meet them and will feel like they failed.

RULE OF UNINTENDED CONSEQUENCES AND BUMPS IN THE ROAD

Part of systems thinking is the rule of unintended consequences. No matter how much we plan, we still run into unexpected problems or situations. This is not unusual and is, in fact, normal. As long as there is not a safety-related issue, it is very important not to overreact to these unintended consequences or how people initially react to change. Change is difficult and people react in different ways and say things that sometimes might be out of character. If we overreact and make "on the fly" adjustments, without a fact-based problem-solving approach, it can have disastrous effects and even kill the implementation. In addition, if we keep changing things, people get confused and frustrated. So we need to analyze these situations as they occur as opposed to reacting to them and see what we can learn going forward. We need to look at these as "bumps in the road" and move on and persevere with the change. When communicating expectations for change everyone should recognize process changes will not roll-out "perfectly". Team members and staff should realize that most changes in process as they are implemented will require some adjustment initially as they are fully operationalized into real life settings post-pilot. These revisions should be expected and not viewed as failures. In addition, the processes that are implemented today should NOT remain the same for months or years. A continuous improvement plan should be in place so processes are revised based upon changes to the business that occur over time.

CHANGE IS A FUNNY THING

Change is part of the very fabric of our everyday lives. It is ironic that, in some respects, the only constant in our lives is change. Everyday something or someone we know has changed. Each day we get 1 day older! Often, when we go on vacation for a week, we come back home only to notice something has changed somewhere on the way home.

There are different parts to this equation. We have to deal with the change itself, the rate of change, and the repercussions of the change. In order to be successful, we need to give people as much control over the change as possible. We need to over-communicate "why change," train people in the "changes," and show how the changes will help them and the organization. We need to be sensitive to the fact that change is uncomfortable for most of us and deploying Lean can literally turn people's worlds upside down. We may not necessarily change what they do, but we may change when or how they do it, with the added expectation that everyone does it the same way. We need to create an environment that is "change friendly" and train and coach people on how to deal with change and practice the new change until we can meet the objective of the change.

WE ARE ALL INTERCONNECTED BUT NOT TYPICALLY MEASURED THAT WAY

We are all interconnected, so it is important that if we change a process, we ascertain its impact on other inter-related processes. This is especially true and critical in healthcare. It does no good to make our area better at the expense of another area. How can we work together to improve the overall system? It is critical that changes are not made in silos and that the cross-departmental views and/or value streams are evaluated and the appropriate stakeholders are engaged in process changes. Any proposed changes should be performed through collaboration, agreed upon and then communicated to all staff involved.

HORSE ANALOGY

During our Lean system implementations, we find people at all levels who resist change. Some people just seem physically incapable of changing their paradigms. As stated in Thomas Kuhn's *The Structure of Scientific Revolutions*,[*] "It is as though some scientists, particularly the older and more experienced ones, may resist indefinitely, most of them (eventually) can be reached in one way or another". Our analogy is: We lead the horse to water. The horse drinks the water. The horse likes the water but then refuses to drink it again. We find it odd that we implement the new process and people like it! They get great results but, if allowed, will go back to the old way of doing it. How can this be? How often have you experienced this in your organization?

---

[*] Thomas Kuhn, *The Structure of Scientific Revolutions* (Chicago, IL: University of Chicago Press) 1996 p.162.

COMPARISON TO WHERE WE ARE TODAY

Many times, as we introduce new Lean concepts, people will dismiss them out of hand. This is because they are comparing what we are saying to the current work environment. In most cases, the transition to Lean thinking and Lean practices is so different that it is impossible to imagine what is possible when compared to the current work environment.

At Hospital X we were discussing a level-loaded schedule for a clinic that wasn't possible with the current way they were scheduling. The root cause was how the scheduling software was being utilized. Once we changed the paradigm and made minor modifications to the software they were able to level load the schedule.

Lesson Learned: *Even though we try to help people see the vision, sometimes it is difficult for them to see it or "get it" until we actually implement the changes and they experience it.*

CHANGE ACCELERATION PROCESS[†]

The Change Acceleration Process (CAP) model was popularized by GE. The model is Quality × Acceptance = Effectiveness or $Q \times A = E$.

This model looks at the quality (content) of the change and message and the acceptance of the change (soft skills) while creating a shared need for the change. If the change you are trying to deploy is not accepted, then you will not achieve an effective result. You must understand (leverage

---

[†] http://bvonderlinn.wordpress.com/2009/01/25/overview-of-ges-change-acceleration-process-cap/. In 1989–1990, under the direction of Jack Welch, GE launched "Work-Out"—a team-based problem solving and employee empowerment program modeled after the Japanese quality circles model that was in vogue at the time. Work-Out was a huge success and Welch was frustrated by the rate of adoption through the business. Welch, the visionary, realized that GE (and everyone else!) was entering an era of constant change, and that those who adapted to change the fastest would be the survivors. He commissioned a team of consultants (including Steve Kerr, who was to become GE's first chief learning officer) to scour industry and academia to study the best practices in change management and come back to GE with a tool kit that Welch's managers could easily implement. The result was the change acceleration process, commonly referred to within GE simply as "CAP." The team studied hundreds of projects and business initiatives. One of their insights was that a high-quality technical strategy solution is insufficient to guarantee success. An astonishingly high percentage of failed projects had excellent technical plans. As an example of such a project, consider a business adopting the Siebel Customer Relationship Management (CRM) system enterprise-wide. Typically a great deal of effort is put into the technical strategy—to deploy the hardware and software, train the employees, etc. The team found that it is lack of attention to the cultural factors that derail the project when there is a failure—not the technical strategy. Failure, for our purposes, is defined as failing to achieve the anticipated benefits of the project (i.e., the benefits that justified the project in the first place). The team created the change effectiveness equation, $Q \times A = E$, as a simple way to describe the phenomena. Translated into English, it reads: the Effectiveness (E) of any initiative is equal to the product of the Quality (Q) of the technical strategy and the Acceptance (A) of that strategy. In other words, paying attention to the people side of the equation is as important to success as the technical side. It is interesting to note that they used a multiplicative relationship; if there is a zero for the Acceptance factor, the total effectiveness of the initiative will be zero, regardless of the strength of the technical strategy. I'm sure we can all cite examples from our own experience when this was observed.

TABLE 5.2

Toyota Suggestion System

Year	Number of Suggestions	Number of Suggestions/ person	Participation Rate (%)	Adoption Rate (%)
1976	463,442	10.6	83	83
1977	454,552	10.6	86	86
1978	527,718	12.2	89	88
1979	575,861	13.3	91	92
1980	859,039	19.2	92	93
1981	1,412,565	31.2	93	93
1982	1,905,642	38.8	94	95
1983	1,655,868	31.5	94	95
1984	2,149,744	40.2	95	96
1985	2,453,105	45.6	95	96
1986	2,648,710	47.7	95	96
1987	1,831,560	–	–	96
1988	1,903,858	–	–	96

Source: Yasuda, Y., *40 Years, 20 Million Ideas: The Toyota Suggestion System,* Productivity Press, Cambridge, MA, 1990. With permission.

Stakeholders Analysis tools) and deal with resistance from key stakeholders, build an effective influence strategy and communication plan for the change, and determine its effectiveness. Again, the relationship in the equation is multiplicative, which suggests if any of the components are zero, the change will not be effective. For example, if you have a great process in quality "10" and can not articulate the message and have it accepted "0" the result is that the change will not occur. There are many great tools that can be leveraged to facilitate change management in the GE CAP model.

EMPLOYEE SUGGESTION SYSTEMS

In 1988, the Toyota suggestion rate was four suggestions per month per employee with a 96% implementation rate, resulting in 20 million ideas over a 40-year period (Table 5.2). In comparison, the typical U.S. company averages about one-sixth of a suggestion per month per employee.[*] Toyota's is not a normal type of suggestion system. There is no "suggestion box" that gets reviewed by management prior to implementation. Suggestion box systems normally use up significant amounts of time in the review, return on investment (ROI) analysis, and approval cycles. The employee may or may not hear back on their suggestion which can negatively impact the employees perception of the solicitation of request or actual suggestion. Toyota, on the other hand, budgets 50% of the team leader's time to implementing and encouraging employee suggestions. They try out the suggestion prior to submitting it for approval. This is how their implementation rate is so high. The Toyota system is explained in detail in the book, *40 Years, 20 Million Ideas: The Toyota Suggestion System.*

TOYOTA IMPROVEMENT SOURCE BREAKDOWN

Based on all the reading we have done, it is estimated that

- 80% of Toyota's improvements suggestions come from line personnel and are implemented by team leaders and managers.[†]
- 10% come from Point Kaizen events.
- 10% come from the GI (good idea) club,[‡] an elite chartered invitation-only Toyota group.

This estimate was confirmed by Russ Scaffede,[§] who stated, "I would certainly state without question 80% is low. Once a product is in production, between 85–90% of all suggestions for process improvement and cost reduction come from the plant floor and their team member engagement processes. That is still a very big issue and the reasons for most companies not getting Toyota type results. Most companies lack the understanding of the participation process utilizing all the Toyota tools."

BARRIERS TO CHANGE

The biggest barrier to change is YOUR MIND! Words like *I can't… It won't work… I already know… It won't work here… I tried that before… I don't want to run it that way… It's not our way… We need more data… How do you know it will work?*

These words should raise a big red flag. We have a saying, "When you say 'I can't' you admit your own ignorance!"[¶] Our other saying is "if you tell me you CAN'T, I will agree with you that you CAN'T and then I will go find someone who can!"

MOST LOVED WORDS

A favorite story growing up was *The Little Engine that Could.*[**] The Little Engine kept saying, "I think I can, I think I can." The most loved words with Lean are: *What if we could… What if we tried… How can we… I know we can… I saw someone else doing it…Why didn't it work the last time… When was the last time we tried… Maybe the manufacturer can help us… Let's benchmark a company that is doing it that way… Let's take the best from YOUR WAY and MY WAY and make it OUR WAY…*

---

[*] Yuzo Yasuda, *40 Years, 20 Million Ideas: The Toyota Suggestion System* (New York: Productivity Press) 1990.

[†] Toyota Kata, Mike Rother, McGraw Hill, 2009, 40 million ideas in 20 years book, Yasuda, Productivity Press, ©1990, www.artoflean.com, Understanding A3 Thinking: A Critical Component of Toyota's PDCA Management System, Sobek, Productivity Press ©2008, Managing to Learn, John Shook, ©2008.

[‡] Yuzo Yasuda, *40 Years, 20 Million Ideas: The Toyota Suggestion System* (New York: Productivity Press) 1990.

[§] Russ Scaffede, owner, Lean Manufacturing Systems Group, LLC and Management Consulting Consultant, vice president of manufacturing at Toyota Boshoku America. Past general manager/vice President of Toyota Motor Manufacturing Power Train, Past senior vice president, senior vice president of Global Manufacturing at Donnelly Corporation, co-author with Dwane Baumgardner and Russ Scaffede, *The Leadership Roadmap: People, Lean & Innovation* (Great Barrington, MA: North River Press) 2008.

[¶] Source: Kanban/JIT at *Toyota/Management Begins at The Workplace,* Japan Management Association.

[**] Watty Piper and Loren Long, *The Little Engine That Could* (New York: Philomel Books) 2005.

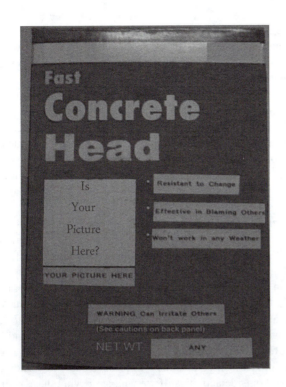

FIGURE 5.7   Concrete head.

FIGURE 5.8   Sacred cow. From Yasuda, Y, *40 Years, 20 Million Ideas: The Toyota Suggestion System,* Productivity Press, Cambridge, MA, 1990. With permission.

You will find that a subset of individuals will resist change and, in fact, may not be able to make the transition to work within a Lean environment. "Concrete Heads" is the Japanese term for someone who does not accept that the organization must be focused on the elimination of waste.[*]

Top Ten Signs that People don't get it (Concrete Heads)
(Figure 5.7)

1. Just wait until it breaks, then we can replace it.
2. We are too busy to implement Lean now. We have to make the end of the month.
3. We need to cut indirect labor!
4. We need more inventory and more space.
5. Tell me what I need to do. When will you get to us?
6. We have improved enough already. Why should we improve anymore? Is there any return (ROI)?
7. We don't want to invest in teams or training; we would rather lay them off as soon as we eliminate jobs!
8. We don't need to benchmark other companies; besides, the travel budget has been cut again.
9. We have to make double-digit return on sales. We can't get there with Lean!
10. What does "get-it" mean? Do I have it?

DOES YOUR ORGANIZATION HAVE SACRED COWS?[†]

As organizations begin to implement change, they often encounter "Sacred Cows" (Figure 5.8). Sacred Cows are an out-moded belief, assumption, practice, system, or strategy, generally invisible, that inhibit change and prevent responsiveness to new opportunities. If not recognized and addressed, the transition to a Lean organization may be challenging.

Homework: *List four Sacred Cows at your company.*

How would you change them?
Complete the following sentences:

- *This job would be great if I didn't have to…*
- *What a pain it is to…*
- *It's a waste of time to….*
- *I could be more productive if I didn't have to…*
- *We could save a lot of money if we stopped…*

Leadership: The Softer Side of Lean

When considering the area of change management, we need to consider how effective we are as leaders and how we roll out the change to our team members. As we implement Lean changes, consider the following.

FIVE FACTORS OF JOB SUPERVISION[‡]

1. We must be sure that we are not looking at their job from the standpoint of trying to find something wrong. This is entirely different from making a critical analysis with the idea of trying to do it better. When analyzing the team's jobs, the concept of teamwork should be the basic approach of each supervisor.

---

[*] www.gembutsu.com/articles/leanmanufacturingglossary.html.
[†] Robert Kriegel, *Sacred Cows Make The Best Burgers* (New York: Warner Books) 1996.

[‡] *CCS Training Manual*, Charles Protzman Sr. and Homer Sarasohn, 1949–1950.

2. We must make sure that every person understands that when we question anything or make suggestions, we are part of a team that is working together to get the best results.

3. We must remember that the person is a human being who feels just the same as we do. If a reprimand is necessary (which is seldom, if you are a leader), it should be given in private.

4. No one likes to be short-circuited, that is, passed by with instructions given to their subordinates.

5. If you are a good enough leader, you can usually find ways of encouraging your team to see what is needed without telling them. When you have done this, you have helped them to develop their own ability to think and analyze, and you have boosted their morale by making them feel that they have contributed something and that they had an idea of their own.

Earlier we discussed the change equation and the questions that must be answered when implementing major changes. When we consider the answer to "What's In It For Me?" consider the following.

FIVE FACTORS OF JOB SATISFACTION*

(a) Fair Pay

The wish to survive is a basic instinct and pay is a factor of importance in that connection so it is being put first. From the standpoint of job satisfaction, however, the fairness of pay is just as significant as the amount of pay. The question in the worker's mind is not so much how good his pay is, but how fair it is. A janitor is rather well satisfied that his pay is less than a vice president's. He recognizes that this is equitable. But he does want fair pay for the particular job he is doing. He becomes upset when a neighbour down the street who is also a janitor receives more than he. What matters most (assuming a living wage) is that the scale of pay differential by skills is as it should be.

(b) Security

There are three kinds of security in which the worker is interested. These are:

1. Security by the day – Suppose he became ill. What about pay?

2. Security by the year – What are his chances of keeping his job? How will he do on an average annual earning basis?

3. Security for life – What happens when he retires? Is there a pension? Is there something to see to it that security is not a factor that stops when he stops working?

(c) Opportunity

This factor is especially important to the younger employees. They are a natural desire to get ahead, and want to know that there is opportunity for advancement. Good merit rating and promotional planning are necessary to insure that a worker will have a chance to advance as his abilities develop and openings occur.

(d) Recognition

This factor costs the least and yet is so often missed. The value of a pat on the back for a job well done is frequently overlooked by supervisors. They pass by and fail to give the praise that would improve morale and production without costing anyone anything.

(e) Participation

Some may think that this factor is merely a part of recognition but it means more. It actually means doing things together – giving the worker a chance to get into the act. There is a feeling in the mind of every person, no matter how lowly or how high, that he would like to be a part of things. Just analyze that aspect of human nature. The average person who has enough money for food, clothing and shelter will spend his next few dollars in joining some club, society, or other organization. He will go to endless time and trouble to participate in such outside activities. If we who are paying these people for working with us could foster that desire to participate, what a profitable undertaking it would be. What an increase in efficiency and output we would experience if we could get people to feel they are participating on the job as in outside activities. The factor of participation has been overlooked to a considerable extent by management men everywhere.

These, then, are the 5 factors that tend to bring about job satisfaction. The analysis of these factors must be followed by careful planning and skilful practice. No intelligent supervisor today can get by just by being a good fellow. More and more, the art of dealing with people gives way to the greater emphasis and improved results of the science of dealing with people.

STYLES AND LEAN—LEVERAGING THE MYERS BRIGGS TYPE INDICATOR®†

Change management is very difficult and how people react to change is related to a variety of factors. We have found that knowing a person's type can be valuable in helping to understand how a person may respond in different situations. In our experience, we have found the MBTI® instrument very helpful in gaining insight into people's personalities, which has been very beneficial with change management and Lean.

The MBTI® instrument is utilized for leadership, improving team dynamics, and change management and this is, by far, not an inclusive list. We can't emphasize enough how important the MBTI® tool can be when implementing Lean.

We will not go into too much detail since it is beyond the scope of this book; however, exposing co-workers and team

---

* Ibid.

† Isabel Briggs Myers, revised by Kinda K. Kirby and Katharine D. Myers, *Introduction to Type* (Washington, DC: Consulting Psychologists Press) 1998.

members to MBTI® allows them to recognize that people have different preferences and there is power in knowing that any change, recognition, or consequence will need to be communicated or implemented in more than one way to reach every type. This is critical in order to foster buy-in and achieve acceptance.

ABOUT THE MYERS BRIGGS TYPE INDICATOR®*

Katharine Cook Briggs and her daughter Isabelle Briggs Myers developed the MBTI® based on their observations and the work and writings of Swiss psychiatrist Carl Jung. They studied and elaborated on the ideas of Jung and developed the MBTI® to help people understand *type* and appreciate the gifts and benefits within each of us. The indicator results come in various forms, including self-assessment and a very detailed computer report. More than two million indicators are administered each year and they are used in a wide variety of ways:

- Self-understanding
- Career counseling
- Marriage counseling
- Education and academic counseling
- Problem solving and team building
- Management and leadership development

Jung's theory says we are born with our psychological styles and we continue to develop them throughout our lives. As one gets more into the theory, one finds we are all set up for conflict. This model is the base for several other personality models as well and is still being studied and scientifically validated.

Amy Evers of Type Resources states: "There are 16 type codes, and thus 16 combinations of preferences, but how developed each of the eight functions is for each individual makes for an infinite combination."†

The model looks for our preferences, as opposed to trait models, and we all share pieces of all the styles, yet "when push comes to shove," we prefer our style just as you prefer your right hand or left hand.

The model has four scales and each scale is a dichotomy (opposite).

Scale	Type		Type	Scale Explanation
1	Introvert	vs.	Extrovert	Where you get your energy
2	Sensing	vs.	Intuitive	How you take in information
3	Thinking	vs.	Feeling	How you make decisions
4	Judging	vs.	Perceiving	How you live and deal with the outside world

* Note: One must be certified to deliver the MBTI® instrument and training. Significant contributions to this section were received in correspondence from Amy Evers, Type Resources Inc.
† Amy Evers Type Resources, www.Type-Resources.com.

What does this have to do with Lean, you ask? The MBTI® helps in many ways, but most importantly, when dealing with teams and change management, knowing a person's type can help you to interact with them in the manner in which they are most comfortable (their preference), especially when interacting with a person or group who possesses different types. We use it within a team framework to find out the team composition and which preferences are strong (i.e., several people with the same type) or weak. It is possible to have many of the same style on the team, and while this is perceived as a strength, it can actually be a weakness for the team, as they may all view and communicate things from a similar perspective. In teams where we are weak in a style, we look for ways to offset it. Even after working with the model for more than 11 years, we have found that having team members and even co-workers know and understand types does not prevent disagreements, but at least you understand why there *are* disagreements. Let's review the four scales; note as you go through each scale, there are no absolutes and there are "grades" within each scale.

Introvert vs. Extrovert

The first scale identifies the source of your energy. People with a preference for introversion get their energy from within and enjoy their alone time to get re-energized. People with a preference for extraversion get their energy from other people and like to be more social. People with a preference for extraversion can easily over run the meeting, making it difficult for introverts to interject. People with a preference for introversion can sit in a meeting and never open their mouths yet felt they totally participated. After the meeting, you might hear comments from introverts that they knew the answer all along. When asked incredulously, "why didn't you speak up?" their answer was "nobody asked me!"

Sensing vs. Intuitive

This scale looks at how we take in information. Those who prefer sensing tend to see and remember details and facts. Those who prefer intuition remember facts when they relate to a trend or problem. If you are not clear when giving direction to any style, you can have a problem. The sensing preference needs very specific direction relating to a project or task or they will become frustrated. They take in information by using either their five senses or based on their past experiences. They are very realistic and practical people. Those who prefer intuition take in information based on the big picture. They remember facts when they relate to a pattern or trend. Those who prefer sensing trust their experience while those who prefer intuition trust their "gut" and use hunches. Those who prefer sensing tend to prefer focusing on the current reality or how this situation relates to the past rather than generating ideas for the future.

During a value stream mapping exercise working on the ideal state, we had one person who asked if he could be excused. When asked why, he said we were so far off reality he couldn't stand it anymore. If we had not under-stood styles, we would have thought he was negative and not a team player. Since we knew he had a preference for sensing, we told him we understood why he needed to leave and told him we would call him back when we were done. We called him back in and he was able to give us some very practical suggestions to help us implement some of the ideas we brainstormed.

Thinking vs. Feeling

The next scale seems to create the most conflict in organizations and marriages. This scale looks at how we make decisions. People who prefer thinking tend to make very objective decisions, and they normally don't take into account people's feelings nor do they look at decision making from an individual's point of view. They are energized by critiquing, and their definition of fairness is to treat everyone equally. These tend to be your "drivers" in other personality models. Keep in mind that the MBTI® measures preferences and is neither a "trait" model nor does it measure strength.

Those who prefer feeling tend to make decisions by taking into consideration the individuals and their values and morals developed over their lifetime. They tend to be more compassionate than thinkers. They prefer harmony and their definition of fair is to treat everyone as an individual.

With Lean, this scale is very important because we make many decisions that impact people. We recommend training classes in MBTI® for everyone in the organization. We instruct our class participants that it is important to seek out people who have opposite preferences from yourself so they can help "coach" you on decision making, as it may make your decision more balanced, providing a different perspective.

Judging vs. Perceiving

The next scale looks at how we live in the outer world. People who prefer the judging process (not judgmental or emotional, which clouds all styles) like to live in a planned and organized way vs. people who prefer to live in a flexible and spontaneous way, not seeking to control life but to enjoy the moment (perceiving). This scale impacts our Lean teams as well.

People who prefer judging tend to like keeping lists (although to different degrees), tend to procrastinate when they are over-tasked, tend to work before play, have a difficult time relaxing until all their work is done, prefer to work to a schedule, and tend to plan out their day's work.

People who prefer perceiving don't generally like to keep lists, but may keep them when they have to or to remind them of things they have to do, tend to procrastinate in order to keep their options open until the last minute, prefer to play before work, tend to work in bursts of energy and if they like their work then work becomes play, and don't like to have their day fully scheduled.

As one gets into the MBTI® model, one finds that it goes down several levels. The combination of the letters or preferences gives a four-letter type code, i.e., INTJ, which is actually just the beginning of the theory. When you break the type code down, you learn which mental processes each type prefers (extroverted sensing, introverted sensing, extroverted intuition, introverted intuition, extroverted thinking, introverted thinking, extroverted feeling, and introverted feeling), and why two type codes, such as ESTJ and ESTP, which appear to have so much in common, actually prefer very different mental processes and, thus, may experience much conflict. Although we have only touched the surface on describing MBTI® we recommend developing a solid understanding of the MBTI® model as we have found it to be extremely beneficial when dealing with teams and change management communication.

EFFECTIVE MEETING TECHNIQUES*

One area we focus early on with Lean is meetings. While we agree that meetings are necessary for communication and problem solving, we also know that poorly run meetings cost organizations significantly, probably millions of dollars, each year.

According to the Wall Street Journal report on Wharton Centre for Applied Research, the average CEO in the United States spends 17 hrs a week in meetings that costs the company $42,500 per year. Senior executives spend 23 hrs a week in meetings and cost up to $46,000 per year each. Middle managers spend 11 hrs a week in meetings that cost up to $20,000 a year each.[†]

According to the Ayers Report Newsletter, some 25 million meetings take place in corporate America daily. Roughly half that time is wasted.[‡]

Despite the cost and lost productivity, most organizations still believe that meetings play a crucial role in disseminating information and providing a venue to discuss topics requiring decisions. Additionally, understanding MBTI® can help cultivate techniques for effective meetings, as personality types of participants will impact the outcome and perceived value of the meeting. Meetings, however, need to be used for the right reason. At Toyota and Honda, going to the *Gemba, Genchi Genbutsu,* "actual place," seeing the "actual thing" stresses the importance of understanding what is occurring through first-hand experience, and all levels of employees are expected to go and see the problems for themselves rather than calling a meeting to receive a report on a problem.[§] The "meeting" is expected to take place where the problem surfaced. Meetings need to have perceived value for both the participants and the organization.

Have you ever been to a bad meeting? But why was the meeting bad? When we brainstorm this in our training classes, we find most people know what a good meeting is and how to have one but for some reason we just don't do it.

---

* Coopers and Lybrand AlliedSignal TQ training classes, 1995.
† Jon Jenkins and Gerrit Visser, "Meetings Bloody Meetings" *Global Flipchart*, Nov. 2004.
‡ Gene Moncrief, "Meetings: time wasted or well spent?" *Ayers Report*, Vol. 5, fall 2005, issue 11.
§ Jeffery Liker, *Toyota Way* (New York: McGraw Hill) 2004, 223.

There are a variety of effective meeting techniques, one of which is Spacer (Figure 5.9). We are not going to delve deeply into the model, but it is one that we have found helpful over the years. SPACER is an acronym for

- Safety
- Purpose
- Agenda
- Code of conduct
- Expectations
- Roles

SPACER is a great way to kick off each meeting. It is the team leader's responsibility and it generally only takes a minute or two to walk through the tool.

MEETING METRICS

How do you know if you ran a good meeting? One way is to collect data from those who attended. In 1 min or less, you can ask each person to rate the meeting on a scale of 1–5, what went well and what could be improved for the next meeting. Even if the meeting didn't go as well as it could have, those in attendance will appreciate knowing you think their time is valuable and that you are working on constantly improving the meetings they attend. Consider building meeting metrics into your agenda.

WHY ARE MEETINGS ALWAYS IN SCHEDULED HALF HOUR OR HOUR INCREMENTS?

When scheduling your meeting, ask yourself how long the meeting really needs to be. Many times, we tend to round off meeting times to the nearest 15 min or 1 hr. If your agenda says you need 37 min, then schedule it for 37 min. One thing for sure, we tend to fill up the meeting time we have scheduled. If you schedule a meeting for an hour it will probably run at least that long whether it needs to or not.

The following list is a pre-meeting checklist for the meeting leader designed to help the meeting go smoother.

Effective Team Pre-Meetings Checklist

- ❑ What is the purpose of the meeting and what kind of meeting it is?
- ❑ What do you expect to accomplish? Is a meeting the best way to accomplish it?
- ❑ Is your purpose ultimately value-added to the Customer?
- ❑ Create an agenda and distribute prior to meeting. Let people know what they need to bring or think about in advance to be prepared.
- ❑ Use SPACER
- ❑ Use Roles
- ❑ Agree ahead of time how decisions will be reached. Majority, Unanimous etc.
- ❑ Use TQ Tools as appropriate, brainstorming, pareto, affinity, histograms, decision matrix, drivers/barriers, problem solving etc.
- ❑ Be considerate of peoples styles
- ❑ Use Meeting metrics

If you sit in a meeting more than 5 min and don't know why you are there, consider leaving

Lean Meeting Savings

One company we worked with cut both the frequency and, in some cases, the time in half for their production, finance, IT, forecasting, business development, and HR meetings, literally saving more than 4,500 hrs per year by seriously implementing and standardizing on effective meeting techniques.

Organizational Changes

If Lean is implemented properly, it impacts the entire organization (Figure 5.10). Organizational changes occur in three ways. They are manifested in structural changes, personnel changes, or a combination of both. Many concepts are discussed in the books, *Good to Great*, *Lean Thinking*, *Toyota Culture*, and *Inside the Mind of Toyota*.

When we start to discuss organizational changes, many middle managers become concerned with their jobs and start

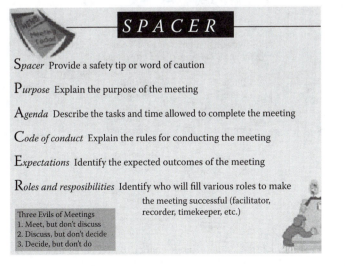

FIGURE 5.9 SPACER tool.

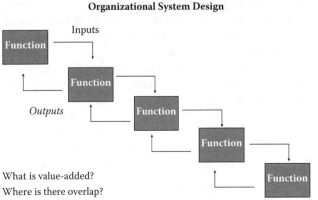

FIGURE 5.10 Organizational system design tool. Source: BIG archives - Original Source Unknown.

TABLE 5.3
Roles and Responsibilities Matrix

Decisions\Roles	Sales	Segment marketing	Insurance	Mutual funds	Marketing council	CEO	Finance	Human resources	Regional team
Product price C	R	C	C	C	C	A	I	X	X
Package design	C	R	X	X	A	I	I	X	I
Package price R	A	C	X	C	C	I	I	X	I
Forecast	A	R	C	C	C	I	I	X	X
Product design	A	R	C	X	A	A	X	I	I

Source: Adapted From Jay Gailbraith, *Designing Organizations*, Jossey-Bass Inc., 1995.
    R = Responsible; A = Approve; C = Consult; I = Inform; X = No Formal Role

to view Lean as a threat to their future. This concern needs to be recognized and addressed prior and throughout the Lean journey.

As structural changes occur, roles and responsibilities may change as well. As roles change throughout the organization, it is very important that we communicate these changes and how they will impact the individuals involved and the organization. We use a tool for this called a roles and responsibilities matrix. This tool is described in Jay Galbraith's book, *Designing Organizations*,[*] although there are other models out there (Table 5.3). When using this model, each person is assigned a level of ownership (role) to the responsibility. The level of ownership can be responsible, approve, consult, inform, or none. There should only be one person responsible for ownership/responsibility. Co-owners can cause confusion, redundancy, and excuses as to why a responsibility was not carried out. It is important to have clarity in roles and yet not have people become so myopic that things don't get done because they weren't assigned. For example, everyone should be able to clean up their areas and sweep the floor, as we all take pride in our workplace and jobs. We have and recommend using this model during a Lean initiative as well so there is a clear understanding of the key stakeholders and what each persons role is related to initiative decisions and participation, i.e., responsible, approval, consultive, inform, or no role.

Communication, Change and Lean

There is a well-known model study from UCLA[†] that discusses the components of communication (Figure 5.11). It states that communication is made up of 7% words, 35% tone of voice, and 55% body language. We have found this model extremely important with change and Lean. Since we always say one of the biggest problems with change is lack of communication and one cannot communicate enough, it is worth spending some time on this model. Since the introduction of e-mail, texting, and Twittering into society, think of the implications of the communication basis itself. Have you ever had someone misinterpret an e-mail or text message?

E-mails and text messages are only 7% of communication. Sometimes we can introduce a little more by adding a smiley face. What percent is telephone? The answer is 45% because we still can't see the body language.

Lesson Learned: *When you need to communicate with someone, consider the best way to communicate. Consider communicating in several different media (visual, verbal, e-mail, etc.) in order to effectively communicate the message. Sometimes there is no substitute for face-to-face communication. Consider having a trusted friend review your e-mails prior to sending (preferably someone with an opposite style to yours). The communication and mechanism should be multifaceted and outlined in a communication plan which should be monitored and tracked with the implementation. Right or wrong we have seen in many organizations communication is placed last on the priority list when in fact many obstacles or challenges could have been eliminated if communication had taken place prior to the event. Reflect back on changes or events that had occurred in past few years in your organizations, could you think of a few in which improved communication could have improve the outcome or acceptance?*

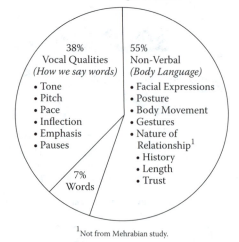

What's Missing in E-Mail?

[1]Not from Mehrabian study.

FIGURE 5.11 Communication model. Based on a study by Dr. Albert Mehrabian, UCLA. Referenced in Griffin, J. *How to Say It at Work*. Prentice Hall Press, Paramus, NJ, 1998.

[*] Jay Gailbraith, *Designing Organizations* (San Francisco, CA: Jossey-Bass) 1995.
[†] Based on a 1971 study by Dr. Albert Mehrabian, UCLA, referenced by J. Griffin, *How to Say it at Work* (Paramus: Prentice Hall Press) 1998.

COMPANY LOYALTY AND PROMOTION FROM WITHIN

There was a time, not so long ago, when company loyalty was a valued trait. When someone worked at many companies over a period of several years it was considered a negative, and they were thought of as "job hoppers" unable to hold a job. Today, most companies have moved away from this belief, and working at multiple companies is considered a positive; however, are you really in a job or company long enough to really understand the business or how to do the job? Some companies are actually referred to as "training grounds," where employees learn a job and then leave to go and work somewhere else that pays more money. What does the constant shuffling and low retention rate cost companies? If loyalty is no longer important, how do we know employees are putting their best foot forward to help the company?

Lean organizations embrace company loyalty, want to recruit, scrutinize, and hire the best people from the start, and pride themselves on how well they develop their employees.

LEAN SOLUTIONS: FREE LUNCH PROGRAM

At one company, we instituted the continuous improvement lunch program. Everyone is asked to implement a small improvement at their workplace. The rules are that it cannot be more than an hour and they can work on it with others. This is followed up in a week or two with a pizza or sandwich lunch where each person presents proof of their improvement in the form of a before and after picture or an explanation of the improvement. As each person concludes, they receive a warm round of applause. At the end of the presentations, each person is asked to make another improvement but, in addition, they are asked to have another person in the company work with them. These lunches are held every 2 to 3 weeks. Of course, there is no such thing as a free lunch: the price of admission is a small improvement.

SUMMARY

Change management, or the "people" component, can and will determine the overall success of any Lean initiative and, in turn, impact overall Lean transformation of an organization. There are many facets to a successful change management effort. It begins with a compelling need to change, a clear vision, communicating the next steps, and then leveraging change management tools to monitor and address resistance to change as it surfaces. Identifying pockets of resistance and managing with appropriate actions will require continual effort throughout the Lean initiative and will continue as Lean is disseminated throughout the organization. As you read through the rest of the book, we can't help but include pieces of change management. The most difficult part of Lean is establishing the culture of continuous improvement. The underpinnings of this lie in change management and leadership.

6 Lean Foundation

EXECUTIVE SUMMARY

This chapter sets the stage for the following chapters by using the "BASICS" model to look at Lean System Implementation. The BASICS model contains five phases:

Baseline
Assess/Analyze
Suggest Solutions
Implement
Check
Sustain

The BASICS system implementation model is provided as a simplistic roadmap or a guide to navigate through a Lean initiative or project. It can be used instead of, or in conjunction with, the traditional PDCA model or DMAIC problem-solving models. The Baseline phase begins with discussions surrounding:

- Voice of the customer
- Value stream mapping
- Supplier, Inputs, Process, Outputs, Customers (SIPOC)
- Consumer Quality Index (CQI)

The initial phase "B" which stands for baseline and its components are detailed within this chapter. The concept of ETDBW ("easy to do business with") is discussed as a customer orientation to your process and how easy it is for them to work with you.

The first phase basic includes "base-lining" key data elements of the process to understand the current state, including:

- Cycle time, Takt Time, first-pass yield (FPY), and current and future value stream states
- Takt Time = time available/customer demand
- Different levels of demand, including peak demand and average daily demand

Examples are provided to help understand calculations to assess the amount of staff needed for both of these entities. Inventory and concepts of work in progress are discussed.

Throughput time (also known as LOS, or Length of Stay) is calculated by adding the total processing, inspection, transport, and storage time, or the sum of all the components within a process. Staffing and inventory are integrated into this model.

KEY LEARNINGS

- Understanding of the BASICS model
- Listing of the ways to measure the "B" or baseline
- Voice of the Customer

- Understanding the concept of ETDBW ("easy to do business with")
- Being able to define cycle time, first pass yield and Takt Time
- Understanding LOS and its components

LEAN FOUNDATION
BASELINE IN THE BASICS MODEL

In God we trust. All others bring data.

—W. Edwards Deming

THINK—SEE—ACT LEAN

The Lean journey begins with becoming familiar with the Lean concepts, potential Lean results, and successes and lessons learned from other organizations. One must realize that, in order to become Lean, the organization will need to undergo a cultural transformation.

We discussed earlier that Lean is a new way of thinking, seeing, and acting. To THINK LEAN one must think about eliminating waste in every aspect of what is done every day. To SEE LEAN is to be able to see and learn what waste is and how to identify waste in all activities that we do, and then to ACT LEAN by taking action to remove the waste. We must enable and empower each employee so they can help in the daily process of eradicating waste.

Rolling out your Lean journey can begin in several ways. It can start with a Point Kaizen event, identifying a small subprocess or activity, a Five S event, or a Lean system pilot implementation, which is a larger transformation initiative. These topics will be discussed throughout the book.

SYSTEM LEAN IMPLEMENTATION APPROACH UTILIZING THE BASICS MODEL

For organizations serious about converting from their old batch-driven systems to Lean, which in healthcare could represent processes which would have significant throughput challenges due to batch type processing such as laboratory, surgical throughput etc. we recommend the larger transformation approach or what we call the Lean system implementation approach. This approach looks at the overall process from beginning to end, and has proved sustainable across many hospital systems all over the world.

To perform a larger transformational Lean initiative, we have outlined a model that can be used as a guide when applying Lean

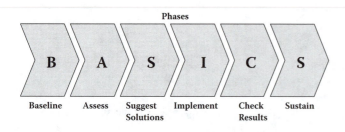

FIGURE 6.1 Executive summary BASICS graphic.

concepts and tools. There are six phases that follow the simple acronym "BASICS" (Figure 6.1). Each letter stands for the main theme for the activities that occur in its phase: *B*aseline, *A*ssess, *S*uggest solutions, *I*mprove, *C*heck results, and *S*ustain. In reality, the activities that occur in any Lean initiative can be mapped to most traditional methodologies, i.e., PDSA (plan, do, study, act), PDCA (plan, do, check, act), or DMAIC (define, measure, analyze, improve, control), etc.; however, we have found, as an example, that some of these models may not be intuitive for staff. The P in PDSA or PDCA, which stands for Plan, really doesn't provide the activities intuitively required, as one needs to do more than plan in the first phase of PDCA when initially converting from batch to Lean systems.

Many organizations that are deploying both Lean and Six Sigma have standardized their improvement roadmap to the acronym DMAIC. It works well for organizations implementing Six Sigma tools, and Lean activities have been and can be mapped to each phase. But it can be confusing because the Lean tools overlap and can be used in many of the DMAIC phases. We have found that remembering the acronym DMAIC and what each letter stands for can be challenging.

We have opted for a more simplistic model, hoping that it may be easier for staff to follow and remember as they go through the activities and steps. Within each of the six phases, we have highlighted, by category, what one may have to do, communicate, and deliver while moving from phase to phase.

The BASICS model contains Total Quality (TQ), Lean and Six Sigma tools (Figure 6.2). We will refer to this model throughout the book. The categories under each BASICS phase are:

Deliverables: provide an idea of what should be completed at the end of the phase

People tools/activities: activities and tasks related to facilitating change management and culture

Task tools: activities geared to the application of tools by phase

Implementation steps: outline critical tasks and activities that should be considered for implementation and moving to the next phase

Communication: activities related to communication throughout the initiative

Timeline: provides an estimated duration spent in each phase

The BASICS Lean system implementation approach is based 50% on the principles of scientific management, developed primarily by Frank Gilbreth and taught by Shigeo Shingo,

and 50% on change management discussed throughout the book. This approach is utilized to convert processes from batch to one-piece flow. Listed below is a summary of the BASICS steps to a Lean implementation.

Baseline
1. Charter the team and scope the project
2. Baseline metrics
3. Value stream map (VSM) the process
4. Determine the customer demand and Takt Time (TT)

Assess/analyze
5. Product Process Flow analysis—become the patient or product
6. Group tech analysis
7. Full work analysis of the operator/Job Breakdown Sheet
8. Changeover analysis

Suggest solutions
9. Make and approve recommendations
10. Create the optimal layout for the process
11. Design the work stations
12. Create standard work
13. Determine the capacity and labor requirements
14. Train staff in the new process

Implement
15. Implement the new process—use pilots
16. Implement Lean metrics
17. Incorporate Five S and visual controls
18. Mistake proof and TPM the process

Check
19. Lean Audits, Huddles, and Sustainability Boards

Sustain
20. Kaizen, Kaizen, Kaizen
21. Suggestions implemented from the floor are part of the culture
22. Plan do check act—over and over and over again

A Customer Service Story

The foundation of Lean starts with the customer. This sign was posted on the wall in a fast food restaurant in Madera, California (Figure 6.3). We actually witnessed an employee kick a customer out of the store who had complained about how his sandwich was made. The other customers were shocked and baffled as to what could have caused this behavior, knowing it could have just as easily been one of them booted out! What could possibly lead to these behaviors and a sign like this being posted for everyone to see?

We start with this story as it underpins many of the problems in many establishments today—the lack of customer service. We can all identify with the poor customer in the story above.

In the hospital, we often lose sight of our primary customer, which is generally the patient. We have internal customers as well, but we must never lose sight when we design our processes to ensure that they are focused primarily on our

Follow the BASICS to Implement Lean Sigma

	Baseline	Assess	Suggest Solutions	Implement	Check Results	Sustain
Deliverables	Baseline Metrics; Goals & Objectives; Assign Executive Sponsor; Communication Plan; Stakeholder's Analysis; Video Documentation; Customer Feedback (VOC); Customer Demand; Takt Time; Project Plan (timeline with milestones)	Value-Added Percents; Opportunity for Improvement; Quick Hits List; Group Tech Matrix - Identify Product / Process Families (by Procedure / Service Line / Diagnosis etc.); Stakeholder's analysis updated; Project Expected Results; Phase Gate Review	Capacity Planning; Bottleneck Identification; Layout / Master Layout; FMEA; Pilot Results; Quick Win Results and Celebration; Stakeholder's Analysis Updated; Phase Gate Review	Standard work Procedures; Standard work Station Design; Agreed ROI with Executive Leadership and Area management; Stakeholder's Analysis updated; Draft Control / Sustain Plan; Plan for Continuous Process Improvement phase Gate Review	Five S Adudit Sheet; TPM Checklists; Final Control Plans / Sustain Plans (includes Execrtive Monitoring of plan); Standard Work Plans (top to bottom); Phase Gate Review	Final Control Plans / Sustain Plans (includes Exececutive Monitoring of Plan); Cross training plan; Phase Gate Review
People Tasks and Tools (Not all these are tools??)	Phase Gate Review; Champion Training; MBTI; Team Skills; Communication; Change Equation; Hedgehog "Good to Great" Who "moved my cheese"; Capture Lessons Learned	Change Equation (Management); Team Dynamics (Forming, Storming, Norming, Performing); Don't Over React to Data or Team Dynamics Issues?? Not a Tool; Code of Conduct; Effective Meeting Techniques; Voice of the Customer Feedback; Lessons Learned	Change Equation (Management); Brainstorming; Share Pilot results and revisions; Capture Lessons Learned; MBTI	Change Equation (Management); Gemba Walks; Communication; Responsibility Matrix; Cross Training Matrix; Quick Response Team; Consider Lean Advisory Committee; Capture Lessons Learned	Change Equation (Management); Communication; Employee Satisfaction; Customer Satisfaction (Physician Satisfaction); Capture Lessons Learned	Right People on the Bus; Right People in the Right Seats; Succession planning; Change Management; Communication; Capture Lessons Learned
Task Tools	Voice of the Customer (survey's, interviews, SME, KANO etc.); Value Stream Mapping; Digital Video / Pictures; I.D. Customer Demand; Area Readiness Assessment; People Assessment; 60 sec Elevator Speech; Project Control Matrix; QFD House of Quality; Critical To Quality Matrix; SIPOC; Customer Value-Added Preposition; Process Capability; Equipment Condition (TPM); Develop Exit Strategy; Develop Resource Plan	Problem Solving model; Process Flow Mapping; Product Process Flow; Full Work Analysis; Current Work Procedures; Any Available Industrial Enineering data; SMED - Setup Reduction; Group Tech Matrix; Ten Cycle Analysis; Solicit feedback from process participants; Total Quality Tools -FMEA Workstation Analysis; DFMA????; Materials Strategy, Inventory Turns, and Supplier Data (# of, # certified etc.); Thru Put????	Part Production Capacity sheet; Standard Work Sheet (frontline, mid manager through executive); Standard Work Combination Sheet; Assess Roles and Responsibilities; Layouts - both area and master; Workstation Design improvements; Staffing Analysis and Plan; Kanbans; Updated ROI Analysis(does not have to be financial; Cost Benefit Analysis; Develop Exit Strategy; Ten Most Wanted List of Improvements for Pilot Area and Leadership; Production Smoothing; Level Loading (Heijunka)	Fit Up List (was this covered??); Five S; TPM; DOE (?? Do we want to include); Process moves from pilot to Adoption; Ongoing Data Collection Plan; Standard Work; SMED/ Setup Reduction	Audits; Control Plans / Sustain Plans; Lean Advisory Committee; Action Plans; Lean Accounting; Update ROI; Process Capability	Hoshin Planning; Balanced Scorecard; Consider Lean Advisory Committee; Five S Audit; TPM Audit; Ongoing Filming and Analysis; Ten Cycle Analysis; Collect Data; Six Sigma Tools
Implementation Steps	Develop Lean Vision - Shared Vision Model organizational and project; Select Leadership Steering Committee; Pick Pilot Area; Picl Pilot Team; Charter Team; Pick Champion; Develop Communication plan; Set overall goals / ROI; Budget for Pilot; Identify Potential Risks; Initial Walk Through With PI Consultant	Pilot Team: Assess the Product Flow; Assess the Operator; Assess the Setups; Solicit Feedback from process participants; Develop new work change management plan; Group Tech matrix; Build Ahead or Work Arounds in Place Prior to Implementation Phase	Layout Recommendations and Reviews and approvals; Project recommendations and approvals; Develop implementation plan; Develop new work procedures, guidelines or standard work procedures; Develop Kanban and Heijunka recommendation and materials strategies	Implement Layout Design Improvements including Five S and Visual Controls and Andon; Team Quick Wins that fit project plan; Implement new workstation Designs; Implement Standard Work pilot; Implement TPM pilot; Implement Kanbans and Materials Improvements; Gemba Walks; New Performance Metrics, Day by Hour and Month by Day Charts	Update Metrics; Review Metries vs Targets; I.D. Gaps; Gemba Walks; Develop Actions to address gaps	Transition to Area Supervisor or Dept. Head; Implement new Reward System; Implement Sustain and Follow up Plans; Gemba walks; Lean Projects Budgeted in Annual Operating Plan; Continuous Process Improvement plan; Create plan for Hospital Area Tours and Presentations
Communication	Leadership / Executive Briefings; PI Consultant Teleconference Prep Calls or Meetings; Contract for Change; Union Leadership Meetings where applicable; Rollout / Brief Pilot Area and Key Managers	Develop and Work communication plans; Develop Training plans; Weekly or BI monthly Leadership Updates; Bi-Monthly or monthly Exec Leadership Updates	Implementation Schedule; Suggested Milestone Posting	Visual Implementation Schedule; Miles Posting	Post Metrics; Visual Communication Postings	Visual Scorecard; Recognize Successes
Timeline	Up to 1 Month	2 to 4 weeks	Up to 1 Month	Up to 1 Month	Up to 1 Month	Up to 1 Month

FIGURE 6.2 Lean BASICS model.

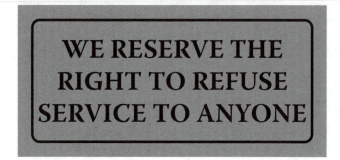

FIGURE 6.3 Fast food sandwich restaurant sign.

patients. There are instances in healthcare where, in order to design the most efficient patient process, we actually have to design the process around the surgeon or emergency department (ED) physician. This is a paradox with Lean. Why is this? In order to focus on the patients and get them seen as quickly as possible or, in the case of surgery, to make sure the surgery is performed on time, we need to focus on making our physician providers as efficient as possible. If the process is designed correctly, then the physician should pace the process or be the bottleneck. This is not a bad thing as we can only get patients through the process as quickly as our physicians can initially see or operate on them.

We have a variety of customer-focused tools in our Lean process improvement BASICS toolbox. The tools are not listed in any particular order and it should not be construed that every tool must be used during an implementation. We have worked in many hospital environments where they insisted we use every Six Sigma and Lean tool. We always challenge this type of thinking. If it is to train someone in a particular tool, that would make sense; but, otherwise, it is a waste of time to implement a tool just for the sake of implementing the tool! Only the necessary tools should be utilized to solve the existing problem. If we were working on repairing a bicycle tire tube, we wouldn't take off the pedals.

Lesson Learned: *BASICS tools should be used as needed to secure the necessary customer and stakeholder feedback, solve the particular problem at hand or to expose the waste necessary to identify the root cause to solve the problem that has been identified. In other words, use the tools that are needed to solve the problem—no more or no less.*

We have found many hospitals engaged in Six Sigma prior to learning about Lean. This can lead to difficulties when trying to implement Lean. In some organizations a "competition" between Green or Black Belts and so called Lean specialists or Masters develops, when, in fact, a synergy of the tools and concepts should be leveraged to gain a better result.

At Hospital X a Master Black Belt took over the Six Sigma and Lean efforts but, over the course of 2 years of restructuring, he was the recipient of a succession of leaders in an organization that had little or no Lean knowledge. They admonished the outside consultants for poor return on investments (ROIs) (which were the result of finance fighting

the new Lean systems) and implemented a rigorous project tracking *system designed to select only projects with the highest "finance-approved" ROIs.*

This true story, while in healthcare, is remarkably similar to that referenced in *Toyota Culture*[*] and is important to understand that Lean tools are a different toolset and should be considered complementary to Six Sigma tools. Both Lean and Six Sigma begin with the voice of the customer (VOC). Although both Lean and Six Sigma work toward quality improvement, through decreasing process variation, error, and defect reduction, frontline staff have a greater challenge with Six Sigma tools. Lean concepts and tools are better suited toward truly driving a cultural transformation. Lean encourages a different way of thinking, focusing on waste elimination, value-added activities, and process flow to achieve improvements.

In healthcare, because there are unstable processes with significant variation, most organizations find it more prudent to begin with Lean tools to identify and eliminate waste and streamline processes. As waste is taken out of a process and the process becomes more predictable and variation rises to the surface, we recommend following up with Six Sigma tools to refine and strive toward perfection. Otherwise, it can be a challenge to utilize some of the Six Sigma tools on widely variable processes; however, there are many Six Sigma tools and concepts related to measurement systems that augment the Lean tools in relation to data collection, interpretation, and change management. It is interesting to note Toyota does not have a Six Sigma program.[†] In an article by Mike Micklewright, he claims, "Six Sigma training is wasteful… It has watered down Lean efforts, it has watered down variation reduction efforts, it has created bureaucracies, it has isolated people," so he is putting his Black Belt up for sale![‡]

While this is extreme, we have seen this occur at some hospitals. We must keep in mind that all problem-solving models stem from Shewhart's plan-do-study-act. The Japanese changed it to plan do check act[§] (PDCA) and called it the Deming Wheel. It is also known in some companies as observe-orient-decide-act (OODA). The Department of Defense applies the cycle in its spiral development process of designing new battlefield technologies. BASICS fits the PDCA model with baseline, analyze, and suggest improvements aligning with the plan phase, implement is the do phase, C is the check phase, and the last S is the act phase. The Lean

---

[*] Jeffrey Liker, *Toyota Culture* (New York: McGraw-Hill) 2008, 29–30.
[†] Jeffrey Liker, *The Toyota Way* (New York: McGraw Hill) 2004. This book does not use complex statistical tools to explain the principles behind Toyota's success. On page 253, author Jeffrey K. Liker writes, "…Toyota does not have a Six Sigma program. Six Sigma is based on complex statistical analysis tools. People want to know how Toyota achieves such high levels of quality without the quality tools of Six Sigma. You can find an example of every Six Sigma tool somewhere in Toyota at some time. Yet most problems do not call for complex statistical analysis, but instead require painstaking, detailed problem solving. This requires a level of detailed thinking and analysis that is all too absent from most companies in day."
[‡] "Black Belt for Sale," *Quality Digest*, www.qualitydigest.com/print/4366, October 18, 2009.
[§] Matthew May, *The Elegant Solution* (New York: Free Press) 2007.

tools can be made to fit in just about any problem-solving model as long as common sense is applied.

BASICS fits the DMAIC model with Baseline aligning with Design and Measure, Assess aligning with Analyze, Suggest Solutions and Implement aligning with Improve and Check Results and Sustain aligning with Control. It should also be noted that Lean Six Sigma tools include all the Total Quality (TQ) tools. While we suggest the BASICS model as a way to convert batch to Lean flow, we still support use of the PDCA or PDSA model or the DMAIC model for ongoing improvement cycles once the initial Lean system implementation is completed, as long as the organization has a method it is comfortable deploying. The choice of model is not as critical as long as there is a consistent, logical, organized approach to ongoing problem solving in which every employee has been trained.

BASELINE METRICS

The first letter of our BASICS Lean foundation model stands for a baseline driven by customer value (Figure 6.4). If you don't know what your customer finds valuable or is willing to pay for, then you can't have a vision of what to improve. If you don't have process related metrics that show where you are, you can't possibly measure if you have improved.

This doesn't mean you can't improve, but how will you know if you did and by how much? During the baseline phase, the Lean roadmap is set up by determining the business problem(s) that needs to be solved as defined by the customer and capturing the "current state" of the process. Capturing the current state includes observing, mapping, and videotaping the process, understanding current metrics, potentially developing new or revising existing "process" metrics, and outlining the initial goals and objectives of the proposed initiative. During the baseline phase, a project charter should be created that outlines the Lean initiative, and both the executive sponsor and team should be selected.

Gathering baseline data is a key component in this phase and any subsequent recommendations for improvements must be driven by the notion of "managing by fact." We have found collecting data to be extremely challenging in hospitals and, when one does get data, one has to really question if they are reliable. This is where the Six Sigma measurement systems analysis tools can be leveraged. We find healthcare organizations collect data and accuracy is assumed. Often, as data is re-collected and scrutinized during Lean Six Sigma projects, data

inaccuracies surface, challenging the very data that everyone in the organization has been utilizing for years to make decisions.

DATA, REVENUE, AND HOSPITALS

Let's discuss what we normally find with the data at hospitals.

At Hospital X, we met with a Vice President of finance to work out our cost per case. Prior to the VP's arrival, we were provided with three different financial reports. After reviewing the reports, we found each report contained conflicting data. During our meeting, we confronted the Vice President with the problem. We thought we had stumbled on this great revelation only to learn she already knew of the problem. The reports came from three different hospital information systems that didn't talk to each other. We asked how she decided which report to use. She told us honestly that they just picked whichever report best fitted the need at the time!

We found that this is not an isolated case. Many hospitals have lots of data, but they are difficult to access, because they are spread across many disparate systems and databases, and the validity of much of the data is in question. Many hospitals do not have standard definitions for their "data touch points," such as 'surgery start', or 'patient in', and, if they exist, staff generally doesn't follow them because they either don't understand the definitions or they are too busy to capture the data in real time. Data collection becomes an estimate instead of a "true value."

Therefore, most hospitals have little valid and complete information when it comes to how long processes take, in many cases what their products or services really cost or what they should be charging for their delivery of care. Hospitals do not normally know how much revenue they are losing because of poorly constructed policies and processes. Another problem hospitals fight is the simple fact that staff generally only care about the patient and are not concerned with the financial health of the organization or "money." We hear them say, "We weren't trained about collecting charges or money in nursing school." They do not feel it is part of their job to know and when it is brought up we often hear "now you want us to only focus on finance and charge capture instead of taking care of our patients."

Lesson Learned: *First, we must recognize that the hospital is, in fact, a business and normally a large employer in the area and a benefit to the community. Without revenue and profit a business cannot survive, which puts every job in the organization along with the community benefit in jeopardy.*

If there is not enough revenue everyone will lose. Cost cutting and layoffs take place and new "cutting-edge" equipment cannot be purchased to advance healthcare.

While it is important that the first and foremost priority is taking quality care of the patient, there are two problems with the nursing attitude of "we are only concerned about the patient." In the current state of healthcare, it is imperative that healthcare workers understand how their actions impact the business. First, if charges are not accurately captured and

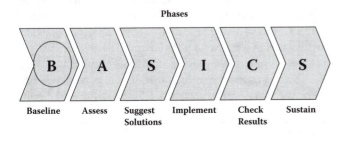

Phases

B) A) S) I) C) S

Baseline Assess Suggest   Implement Check   Sustain
                  Solutions   Results

FIGURE 6.4 BASICS model—baseline.

billed for services rendered, in the age of diminishing reimbursement, hospitals may be unable to survive. Nurses are more frequently required to assist in coding as part of their documentation "near real-time" in order to more accurately reflect services provided. In addition, if we choose to consistently use the most expensive supplies, then we will not be able to offer affordable healthcare.

Second, in the event that a staff member is ever called to court, medical legal questions could arise from having conflicting information in the medical record. Nursing staff have also received reprimands for consistently not charging for supplies.

Lesson Learned: *While we empathize with the clinical staff that the patient is the number one priority, we do ourselves and the patient, the ultimate customer, an injustice if we do not properly document and bill for services provided and all medical supplies used during the course of their treatment. We put the hospital and patients at risk from an employment, legal, community, and affordability perspective.*

Customer Satisfaction

Do You Know What Your Customer Really Wants? The Patient: "It's Really All About Me!"

First, it should be stated that all Lean Six Sigma and TQ tools should be implemented with the customer/patient in mind. Without the customer, we have no business. Our ultimate goal should be to provide the customer with the highest quality care, the right care, at the right time, in the shortest amount of time to do it safely, while giving the patient a great hospital experience. The tools we are going to cover are in the baseline phase of the model and are not necessarily in any type of prioritized order. The task and people tools are designed to extract the VOC; however, it is imperative that we begin each initiative by understanding what the customer values and desires. Too often when we go into hospitals we are told the customer expectations by the staff. When we probe a bit, we find that the expectations communicated were, in fact, not those of the customer but what the staff *thought* the customer wanted. We need to understand what makes a good customer/patient experience through *the customer's* lens, not the lens of the staff.

At Hospital X, during our process of improving their ED, we were told that patients (customers) did not want to move through the process. We were also told patients wanted to have one room and the same nurse throughout their stay. When we asked the patients what they thought, we were told that they did not mind moving as long as progress was being made and they did in fact, not need the same nurse throughout their visit as long as they received good consistent care. What was important to the customer was that they were seen quickly by the physician and that the nurse treated them nicely, professionally, and in a timely manner. They wanted the staff to continually communicate with them as they progressed through their visit.

It is surprising how many nurses and clinical staff forget or don't think it is important to communicate to their patients as they move through the process.

Lesson Learned: *Find out what is really important to your patients. Don't be afraid to ask them. Ongoing patient communication is the real key to increasing customer satisfaction. Lack of communication creates voids, and leads to anxiety as patients do not know what to expect and fear the unknown.*

Voice of the Customer Surveys

The only way to truly find out what the customer wants is to solicit feedback directly from the customer. There are many ways to obtain the VOC, such as holding focus groups, leveraging subject matter experts, and customer surveys. The customer survey can be done face-to-face, via e-mail, via Internet (i.e., Survey Monkey*), by phone, etc. The goal is to understand the "Big Y" or desired outcome of your customer and understand what is required (the 'x's' or little 'y's' necessary) to meet the Big Y. It is also important to feel the pain your customer feels and understand your customer's ultimate expectations or what they deem "valuable." There is nothing like experiencing the process yourself to feel what the customer goes through.

At many hospitals, we have witnessed the all-important phone call from the president or one of the senior leadership team, to notify the department director that one of their own is coming to the hospital. It may be for the ED or surgery, but this sets up "the all-important VIP visit" status for that patient. Everyone in the process scrambles to make sure everyone knows who the VIP is and when they are coming. It is not unusual for the referring leader to visit or accompany the VIP through the process. Often, this is the president's or senior leader's only exposure to how the processes really run. It is also the only time the staff may ever see them.

But, in actuality, the senior leader does not see how the normal process runs; they only see how the "VIP process" is run. So the leader gets a "warped," unrealistic view of the process.

Lesson Learned: *If you are the executive in a hospital organization and you have to call to set up a VIP visit, then your processes need much improvement. Otherwise, why would you call ahead to arrange the VIP visit? Shouldn't all patients get "the VIP" treatment?*

It is important when developing surveys to establish some type of objective, measurable criteria, and solicit open-ended feedback. The measurable feedback of customer satisfaction will allow us to see if we are improving. The answers we get to subjective questions provide significant value and insight into what customers are really thinking. It is important not to violate the survey rules, generally a 5- to 7-point scale[†] with

---

* http://www.surveymonkey.com/.
[†] http://www.surveygizmo.com/survey-blog/question-scale-length/ need a 5- to 7-point scale.

questions not written in such a way that they could lead to biased answers.

QUALITY FUNCTIONAL DEPLOYMENT

A sophisticated tool for customer feedback is called quality functional deployment (QFD). This tool is sometimes called the house of quality.

The QFD model facilitates the understanding of the VOC by determining the "true" customer's needs, features, and values. It then incorporates the customers desired level of performance that the process or product needs to deliver. This is accomplished by linking the needs of the customer to the design, development, production, and service required to deliver the desired results. QFD models can be time consuming to perform however they are an extremely valuable tool to utilize. There are new QFD models* being developed which may provide more wide-spread adoption as they may be more manageable to leverage in the health care setting.

It is important to develop ongoing customer feedback processes to make sure the changes we make as a result of continuous improvement are not negatively impacting our customers.

We were at Hospital X where one of our team members, who was also working with the ED, was told by the Vice President of the hospital that he had to increase patient satisfaction in the ED over the next 2 months. He knew his success or failure as an intern was riding on the results.

Does this type of directive sound familiar? What kind of problems can this type of open-ended instruction cause in an ED? Yet, it is typical of how we go about solving problems in hospitals today. Just go out and fix it. The intern tried various solutions only to find he did not significantly move the needle on patient satisfaction, but did end up introducing a significant amount of variation and stress into the ED process and staff as a result.

Lesson Learned: *Executives and managers should gain an understanding of "x" drivers for key metrics such as patient satisfaction to create reasonable expectations and time frames in order to drive success.*

EASY TO DO BUSINESS WITH[†]

The term ETDBW means that an organization is "easy to do business with." This discussion is inspired by the book, *The Agenda.*

Homework: *Call the company you work for, pretending you are a disgruntled customer or a patient with a problem or ask to speak with the CEO, then note how difficult it is to get hold of the person you are searching for and how long it takes. How many menus do you have to go through? How*

often did the computer not recognize your verbal response? How long are you put on hold? How many people do you have contact with? Did you get disconnected? Did you try to press 0 to speak to a person only to be sent back to the main menu?

Being ETDBW means that the business accepts orders or requests for service when and by whatever means it is most convenient for the customer. It means the orders or services are provided in the customer's terminology. It means the organization makes it painless for a customer to check the status of an order or result. Businesses need to eliminate the endless series of futile phone calls to uninterested and uninformed functionaries, who have been trained only to refer the caller to someone else equally uninformed or hang up because they exceeded their response time metrics.

It means the hospital or business sends a simple bill that is expressed in comprehensible terms—in other words, a bill that someone other than a cryptanalyst can decipher. In addition, hospitals have a greater responsibility that their customers understand, in terms of "simplistic language", what services are provided (tests) and instructions surrounding their care. Is your hospital or healthcare enterprise ETDBW?

Southwest Airlines is an example of ETDBW.

With Southwest Airlines, when I missed my flight, they still gave me credit. I can rearrange flights easily on line with no penalties vs. the hundred dollar or more change fees, seat fees, baggage fees, and miscellaneous charges from other airlines. I always try to fly Southwest Airlines but recently had to fly on another airline into one of their hubs to catch my flight home. This airline uses the hub model vs. Southwest's point-to-point model. Jim Womack refers to this hub model as "Huge Self Sorting People Movers"[‡] in his book "Lean Thinking." What is truly amazing is to see this "system" at work.

These "hubs" now have huge shopping malls and eateries for people with connecting flights who are stuck in the airport and really don't want to be there. Even if the other airlines wanted to change their business model, it would be much more difficult now that all this money has been invested in this hub system. Once the centralized model (hub system) is in place, things start growing in and around it, the stores, food plazas, massage therapists, etc., that are now well established in airports. The more entrenched the model becomes, the harder it is to change. Too many jobs now depend on it, which is similar to how government agencies seem to work.

Lesson Learned: *As soon as a wall is constructed, things get attached to it and run inside it, making it more difficult to take down. Another example is when companies invest a tremendous amount of money in batch and queue equipment, and then we are told they can't do Lean until they write off the equipment. This happens in all businesses.*

Having just boarded the plane, of a major (non Southwest airline) I noticed a gentleman who was last to arrive on the

---

* Information about both the New Kano Model and Blitz QFD® can be found at www.qfdi.org and free-to-download case studies at http://www.mazur.net/publishe.htm. The authors have not used and have no opinion on this model at this time but found it while doing research on the topic.

† Michael Hammer, *The Agenda* (New York: Crown Business) 2001.

‡ Jim Womack and Dan Jones, *Lean Thinking* (New York: Simon and Schuster) 1996.

plane. He shoved his briefcase into the overhead bin with a bit more force than normally required. Then, obviously upset, he went to his seat and asked a flight attendant for the name of the agent at the gate check-in. Not knowing the answer, the flight attendant turned to find one of the gate attendants on the plane and asked who was working with her at the desk. His first name was provided and the passenger was asked why he wanted it. He explained that this was his connecting flight on the same airline, and that his earlier flight had been delayed. After departing the tram and negotiating the huge escalator, he had run to the gate in order to catch this flight; only to find that the gate agent had given away his upgraded first class seat on an over-booked flight because he was late. The gate agent then told him, with a small smirk, "I did you a favor by even getting you a seat!"

How is that for customer service? The man, now sitting behind me in coach, asked for the agent's last name; they refused to give it to him and told him to go on the airline's web site to find the customer service number to register a complaint. Obviously, on this airline, only the Customer Service Department is responsible for any type of customer service. I was amazed that they never apologized to him!

Some systems come with inherent and predictable waste. The models used by non-Southwest carriers represent a "centralized," sometimes called "center of excellence," business model. Southwest uses a decentralized point-to-point model. Centralized models are characteristic of "batch" thinking.

By changing the paradigm and eliminating seat assignments, Southwest does away with all that waste. Boarding with no seat assignments seems to be as efficient, if not more efficient, for the business traveler than other carriers. It is also easier for the customer who now just grabs any seat and families with small children who now board after the "A" group, allowing them to sit together.

WHAT DOES ALL THIS HAVE TO DO WITH HOSPITALS?

Our experience with most hospitals is that their processes probably worked well at one time; however, over time, just about every hospital has added and built new rooms, operating rooms (ORs), towers, and in addition, may have added services and service lines. As they have grown and expanded, the old systems have been unable to keep up; new pieces of equipment in departments are placed wherever there is "room" rather than where they should have gone from a process flow perspective, thus creating numerous workarounds for the staff. The result is that, in many instances, nurse managers, directors, and other support staff have become very high paid "firefighters" and expediters, having to create work arounds in layouts and systems to get their day to day tasks accomplished. We then tend to promote those who are good with "get it done in any way possible (hero-like) behaviors."

Hospitals over the years have migrated more and more to centralization. Within most hospitals, transportation, registration, the laboratory, sterile processing, and scheduling are all centralized. What waste does this cause?

Standardization can help an organization become ETBW. What does standardizing on one type of plane do for Southwest? The number of seats is always the same, so the boarding process can be timed, maintenance is easy because only one set of parts has to be kept on hand, and planes can easily be swapped without having to adjust everyone's seat assignments.

What if all our surgical instrument equipment, supplies, and instrument sets were standardized like the planes at Southwest? What if all our processes were standardized as well? Standardizing can be applied almost everywhere in the hospital!

How often does the investment in existing systems get in the way of improvement? How often do we listen to our patients?

Homework: *Sit in any of your lobbies and listen to your patients. Ask them: How do they feel? How long have they been waiting? What do they need? What could have made their experience better?*

Lesson Learned: *Hospitals can learn a lot from manufacturing and other service business models. Yes, the Lean Production System is applicable to healthcare and, if given time and support from the top, can reap great rewards.*

CUSTOMER VALUE-ADDED PROPOSITION

As we have stated several times, we need to know our customers' expectations. Another tool for this is to develop a model of the customer's value-added proposition. This concept is covered in depth in a book entitled *The Agenda* (Figure 6.5). The organization needs to understand all the components that affect the customer's desired expectation and then decide how the organization wishes to position itself when compared to the competition. This proposition explores which attributes are considered key to the market being served and can graphically depict how the organization serves that market vs. the competition.[*] The example here is for a hotel. Based on our study of the VOC and the marketplace, we are offering a continental breakfast, decent room, and great business offerings at a low price. This tool can be leveraged to help understand what is critical to their customer's and/or physician's quality expectations and how they compare to local or regional competitors.

CUSTOMER QUALITY INDEX

As you begin to appreciate what the customer sees as value, the Customer Quality Index may be beneficial. The Customer Quality Index will help determine where one desires to be positioned in the marketplace by visually allowing one to plot services, products, etc., related to price vs. quality (Figure 6.6). While some manufacturers have a niche or differentiation strategy, our goal with Lean in hospitals is to be in the lower right-hand corner of the graph, providing the best care for the lowest price possible.

---

[*] Harvard Business Review; Michael Hammer, *The Agenda* (Crown Business Publishing) 2001.

Cutomer Value-Added Proposition			
Cutomer Value Criteria			
Eating Facilities			
Aesthetics			
Lounges			
Room Size			
Availability of Front Desk			
Furniture and amenities in room			
Best Quality			
Office Friendly - Internet, plugs			
Quietness of Room			
Price			
Scale	**Low**		**High**
		Level	
Note: Scales Are Ficticious - For Reference Only			

(Series in chart: Hotel Start Up, 3 star Hotel, Economy Hotel)

FIGURE 6.5 Customer value proposition. Source: Modified from Michael Hammer, *The Agenda*. (Crown Business Publishing) 2001.

We recommend that everyone becomes familiar with the Kano* model of customer satisfaction. As we go through our Lean initiatives and make improvements, we must not lose sight of the fact that, as customers of healthcare products and services, all patients and purchasers expect a "basic level" of customer satisfaction (basic vs. delighter as described by Dr. Noriaki Kano). They expect high quality and outcomes that meet the standard of care for services rendered, with zero defects or errors. Remember that waste, unnecessary steps, and lack of process standardization provide opportunities for errors and defects. This principle is also explained in the book, *Total Company Wide Quality Control*.[†]

As processes are designed, it is critical that basic customer needs are met and feedback loops designed so that further work can continue to move toward "delighting" the customers. Remember, if basic needs are not met, customers will look elsewhere, you will lose market share and may not understand why. In addition, as you add "improvements," make sure you understand these new improved activities and services that have increased customer satisfaction today will become tomorrow's expectations. Once the "delighter" is delivered and customers return, they will grow to "expect" the services that were used to delight and they will be disappointed if they

FIGURE 6.6 Customer quality index.

do not receive the same level of service or care. In healthcare, quality and customer satisfaction often get blurred in the patients' minds. They often assume quality, and relate poor customer satisfaction to poor quality care. These are just a few of the many tools that may help you better understand your customer and what you need to deliver.

BASELINE THE PROCESS

As we move through the B phase of the BASICS model, we need to gain an understanding of the current process. This includes understanding the process by going to the place where the process occurs and walking the process with the frontline staff, managers, and team. It is at this point that you need to "put your Lean glasses on," noting how the product and patient move from beginning to end, or for a service, what it takes from request to delivery. In addition, this allows you the opportunity to start asking why five times as you search for root causes and begin to identify waste and opportunities for improvement.

SIPOC—Process Mapping

A useful tool in understanding a process is called a SIPOC (process mapping) (Table 6.1). This tool is normally used in Six Sigma initiatives, but is essentially captured in Lean value stream maps. The acronym stands for suppliers, inputs, process, outputs, and customers. The SIPOC tool is particularly useful when the project or process is not clear. It is used to identify:

- The activities of the process
- The key elements of the process
- The suppliers to the process
- The inputs and the outputs of the process
- The customers and their requirements

There are several different versions of the tool, but the idea is to understand in detail each of these components as it relates to the process.

---

* http://en.wikipedia.org/wiki/Kano_model, Kano, Noriaki; Nobuhiku Seraku, Fumio Takahashi, Shinichi Tsuji (April 1984). "Attractive quality and must-be quality" (in Japanese). *Journal of the Japanese Society for Quality Control* 14 (2): 39–48. http://ci.nii.ac.jp/Detail/detail.do?LOCALID=ART0003570680&lang=en.

† Yoshio Kondo, *Company Wide Quality Control (Zenshateki Hinshitsu Kanri)* (translated by J. H. Loftus) (Japan: JUSE Press) 1993.

TABLE 6.1

SIPOC Example

Step	Supplier	Input	Process	Output	Customer
1	Surgeons offices	Patient referred to pre-testing	Registration—full and partial with copay request (hall patients only)	Patient registered and ready to complete pre-testing	Patient, surgeons, Pre-Op
2	Pre-testing nurses (retrieves patient)	Interview patient in person, vital signs, PICIC assessment, Med Rec, HOM entry	Nursing assessment	Patient determined to be ready for surgery, identify any ancillary testing needed	Patient, surgeons, Pre-Op
3	Pre-testing and ancillary staff	Complete blood draw, EKG, or x-rays	Ancillary testing (as indicated)	Laboratory, EKG, x-ray results	Patient, surgeons, Pre-Op
4	Pre-testing nurses (obtains patient name from phone list)	Interview patient over the phone, vital signs, PICIC assessment, Med Rec, HOM entry	Nursing assessment (phone patients only)	Patient determined to be ready for surgery, identify any ancillary testing needed	Patient, surgeons, Pre-Op
5	Pre-testing staff	Next-day surgery charts, consult notes, H&P, orders	Pre-testing chart completed	Chart has all required contents and patient is ready to go to Pre-Op	Patient, surgeons, Pre-Op

VALUE STREAM MAP (VSM) THE PROCESS

Value stream mapping is part of our baselining toolset. VSM techniques are explained in two books, *Learning to See** and *Seeing the Whole.*† Since the introduction of these books, many subsequent books utilize VSMs as part of their instruction. This book is no exception.

This tool has been used successfully in laboratories, pharmacy, radiology, ED, OR, catheterization laboratory, clinics, etc. (Figure 6.7). While a VSM is a good tool for virtually any type of process, it is one of the best tools for mapping administrative processes like scheduling, HR, revenue cycle, purchasing, sales, marketing, engineering, finance, and new business development. It can even be used to capture a physician or surgeon's office processes.

The VSM allows one to see the overall systems and subsystems and inter-related dependencies at work in healthcare inpatient and outpatient clinical or non-clinical areas as it follows the value stream that crosses departmental silos.

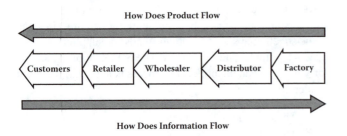

How Does Product Flow

Customers Retailer Wholesaler Distributor Factory

How Does Information Flow

FIGURE 6.7   VSM (value stream map) flow.

* Rother and Shook, *Learning to See* (Cambridge, MA: Lean Enterprise Institute) 1999.
† Jim Womack and Dan Jones, *Seeing the Whole* (Cambridge, MA : Lean Enterprise Institute) 2003.

VALUE STREAM DISCUSSION

The VSM is like a process map on steroids. It looks at how the product, or patient, physically flows through the process, as well as the flow and inter-relatedness of the information necessary to process the patient. It combines traditional process flow mapping, focusing on the longitudinal view of the process with data, to create a "roadmap" to help you identify opportunities for improvement. The VSM also has all the elements of the SIPOC tool built in. The VSM:

- Visualizes the flow
- Forces one to look at the big picture/system(s)
- Identifies the current state of the process
- Helps highlight the waste in the process
- Helps determine the sources (causes) of waste
- Provides a common language for discussing problems and improvements
- Makes necessary decisions about flow very apparent
- Enables innovation—brainstorm ideal and future states that leave out wasted steps while introducing smooth flow and leveled pull
- Provides a visual roadmap of prioritized opportunities to the strategic plan (i.e., projects and tasks) necessary for improvement (management tool to track progress)

VALUE STREAM MAPPING AND HEALTHCARE

There are hundreds of "processes" in the healthcare environment. There are high-level steps/activities, "process level" and "sub-process levels." A process box in a high-level VSM, if broken down, could end up being its own process, or sub-process VSM. The level and details depicted in VSM will depend on the business problem you are trying to solve. The VSM outlines the process and categorizes what is actually

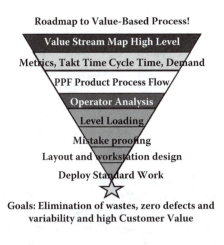

Roadmap to Value-Based Process!

Value Stream Map High Level

Metrics, Takt Time Cycle Time, Demand

PPF Product Process Flow

Operator Analysis

Level Loading

Mistake proofing

Layout and workstation design

Deploy Standard Work

Goals: Elimination of wastes, zero defects and variability and high Customer Value

FIGURE 6.8 Roadmap to perfection upside down pyramid.

process time and storage (waiting) time for the healthcare customer as they go through the process. It also shows the information flow, materials flow, and a timeline with a results box that shows the overall process vs. storage time. The value stream lends clarity to the process, helping to reveal process steps that impede throughput and highlight where waste and non-value activity are prevalent (Figure 6.8).

A flaw of most VSMs is when one assumes that just because a step is classified as a process step, it must be value-added; this is not the case. In actuality, VSMs typically mix up value-added and non-value-added activities in the process steps.

Lesson Learned: *We all want to think everything we do adds value, so some of us will play with the definitions of value-added to "make us feel better." This can do more harm than good. The goal of any process improvement tool is to highlight the waste in the process and expose variation. If we "end up deceiving ourselves" or work to make audit tool standards lower so that "we feel better," we are degrading the improvement process and lowering our standards.*

The value stream is the first layer of the process, which will help provide focus on areas that have opportunities for process improvement. The elimination of waste or non-value-added steps in a process will decrease the chance to make errors, decrease variability and streamline the process. This will be financially advantageous and yield an improvement in the quality of outcomes.

As stated earlier, process steps can include both value-added and non-value-added activities and, depending on the area being mapped, it may be impossible to provide intricate details. In healthcare, we can VSM both the patient and the information flow process independently. It is not unusual for the information flow, whether electronic or paper, to ultimately pace the progress of the patient. Value stream mapping an information flow process is very tricky because we are mapping information process flow boxes that interact with information flow system boxes at the top of the map.

VALUE STREAMS OBJECTIVES

- Visually identify process vs. storage steps
- Help to identify which steps can be eliminated, rearranged, combined, or simplified
- Facilitate opportunities to improve flow
- Enable opportunities to see where information systems should be able to talk to each other
- Identify where we can create pull systems
- Provide a vehicle to manage the area and feed employee "objective" evaluations
- Enable one to strive for perfection
- Creates a management roadmap to track the elimination of waste and improvements
- Updating your value stream maps is a great way to keep track of your progress over time

TRADITIONAL HOSPITAL SYSTEMS

When an organization is divided up by function (i.e., transport, laboratory, Pre-Op, PACU, registration, etc.) each department is only concerned with the processes in their area, Most traditional hospital organizations are set up in these functional silos. Due to organizational design, each department supervisor or manager is doing the best job they can within their span of control and within the department they manage.

In Hospital X we were developing a high-level VSM of surgical patients from the time they were scheduled for surgery to the time they reached the Post-Op recovery unit, only to discover we could not find one person within the surgery department who could describe the entire process. In addition, there were different managers for pre-testing, Pre-Op surgery and Post-Op recovery.

Lesson Learned: *Do not underestimate the silos in your organization. Even within the same service line there are silos that exist which need to be addressed so everyone is working toward the same goal.*

LEAN GOALS

When patients or customers are in contact with the organization or enter the facility they do not see silos. For example, their perception of the experience with the laboratory may begin with a phone call to a secretary or in the parking garage with cleanliness and signage.

Everyone in the organization should be aligned to the same goals with NO SILOS, where each patient is OUR patient, not THEIR patient. Some Lean ideas would be:

- Require that centralized departments become decentralized.
- Radiology (currently done with portable x-ray machines) and a mini laboratory co-located in the ED department, if possible.
- Each department responsible for its own transportation.
- Every department owns every patient and the patient's outcome.

- Put processes, materials and equipment in line and at point of use.
- Right size laboratory testing, i.e., implement tests at point of use like I-Stat®* Troponin point of care testing in the ED triage area, surgical pre-testing and Pre-Op areas.
- Level load and smoothly flow, with transparent handoffs, for patients across departments. View all departments as part of one overall system.
- Consider replacing functional department heads with one overall process owner or value stream manager who is responsible for the entire process flow including functional departments. This may involve reassigning persons within functional departments to report to the value stream manager.

In the hospital setting, value streams start with a supplier to the process (i.e., a doctor's office or vendor). We eliminate the functional view of the department and look to create product families (service lines) or value streams defined as a cross-functional value stream.

Parts of a Value Stream Map

VSMs have four major parts (Figure 6.9). In the middle of the map is the first, which is how the patient or information flows. At the top of the map is the second, or all the information system boxes required to make each process work or to status the process box. The third part is the timeline at the bottom of the information required for the map. The timeline is a saw tooth that has the storage time on top and cycle times on the bottom of the saw tooth which is totalled in a results box showing the overall storage vs. process time. The fourth part is the materials flow from supplier to customer.

Value Stream Map Icons

There are many references to VSM icons.† Figure 6.10 depicts some standard icons that we utilize, as well as lines to show manual information flows (i.e., someone hand-carrying information verbally or written and communication, such as fax, e-mail, snail mail, telephone, etc.).

We also utilize the balance of traditional Lean symbols (i.e., supermarkets, withdrawal, etc.); however, VSM could be as simple as hand-written sticky notes on a wall or as sophisticated as utilizing software packages to create VSM diagrams.

Value Stream Map Definitions

Our approach is to make the VSM as realistic as possible. The process box also includes a data box. So we try to get statistically accurate data to populate the boxes where we can as opposed to the entire map being a snapshot in time. While some maps can be done in a day, we find that when combined with teaching a value stream mapping team and collecting real data, it normally takes a week and sometimes 2 weeks for a large process (like an overall perioperative services VSM) in a large hospital. We normally create the map with paper and pencil and post it® notes. We send the team out to walk the process and interview the staff in order to begin the outline of process and storage boxes. The basic current state map can be drawn in less than a day sometimes less than an hour. We then send the team out to collect data for each process and storage box. The map undergoes constant changes as we invite stakeholders in to review the map. Getting accurate data for the process boxes can take from hours to several days depending on the VSM scope. The maps are reviewed by the major stakeholders along with the project prioritization schedule at the senior leadership debriefing. A normal schedule for a week long VSM event would be:

Day 1
- VSM training class
- Walk the process and interview staff
- Use yellow stickies and flip chart paper to outline the process and storage boxes

Day 2
- Collect data and fill in information flow system boxes.

Day 3
- Collect data, finish arrows to communication boxes, draw in materials
- Brainstorm ideal state
- Create ideals state map
- Brainstorm project list and separate task vs. project
- Note which projects could be done within the year

Day 4
- Create future state map
- Complete project prioritization
- Complete data collection
- Develop final report out and convert VSM to Visio®

Day 5
- Leadership presentation and team celebration

The VSM deliverables include three maps: current state, ideal state, and future state, in that order, and a prioritized project list. This provides the opportunity to fully walk through the current state or "reality" and then focus on what it will take to improve the clinical or administrative process. Many times we use Value Stream Maps in place of or as part of a hospital Lean assessment. It is a great way to figure out where to start a Lean project.

---

* http://www.abbottpointofcare.com/istat/www/products/Cartridge_ Brochure.pdf.

† Mike Rother and John Shook, *Learning to See,* Lean Enterprise Institute (LEI), 2003 www.lean.org; *Lean Lexicon,* by and published by the Lean Enterprise Institute (LEI), 2003 www.lean.org, Jim Womack and Dan Jones, *Seeing the Whole* (LEI) 2002.

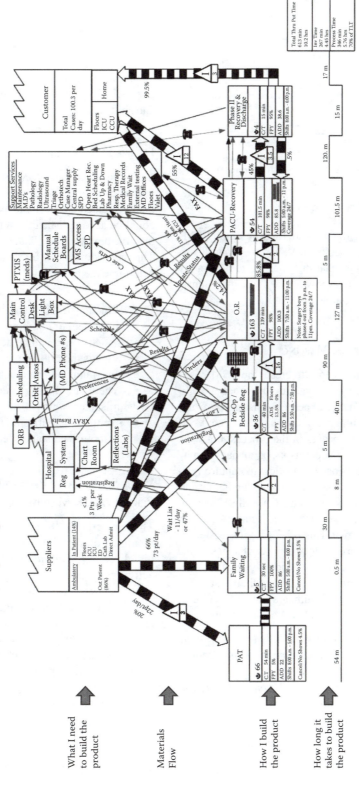

FIGURE 6.9 VSM (value stream map) parts.

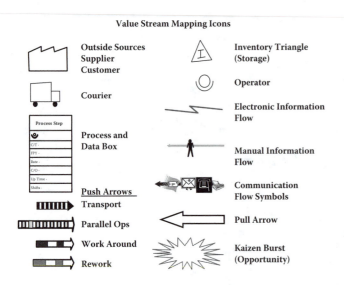

Value Stream Mapping Icons

Outside Sources
Supplier
Customer

Courier

Process and
Data Box

Push Arrows
Transport

Parallel Ops

Work Around

Rework

Inventory Triangle
(Storage)

Operator

Electronic Information
Flow

Manual Information
Flow

Communication
Flow Symbols

Pull Arrow

Kaizen Burst
(Opportunity)

FIGURE 6.10   VSM (value stream map) icons.

We are often asked what the rules are for developing VSMs in healthcare. Since all the books on VSMs are manufacturing based, we tell companies that the rules are to accurately depict your processes in whatever way makes the most sense. There are no hard, rigid guidelines.

CURRENT STATE VALUE STREAM MAPPING

As discussed above, the first step is to create the VSM based on the current state; this requires walking the process, gathering a team of subject matter experts consisting of front-line staff and those familiar with the process. The VSM must describe what actually occurs in the process, not what is written in policies or how supervisors or managers may believe the process is occurring. It is critical to capture reality in order to truly identify waste and non-value activity as described, as well as the supporting data. Once this is accomplished, the team moves on to define the ideal state. All of our VSMs are initially hand drawn. This is because it is easier for non-computer people to participate and make changes as the map is reviewed. For presentation purposes, we often convert these maps to Microsoft Visio® and print them out to flip chart size. This is because most healthcare executive cultures are not quite ready for hand-drawn VSM presentations.

Lesson Learned: *You have to pick the hills you want to die on. It is not worth trying to change executives' perceptions at a first-time meeting to consider A3 charts or hand-drawn maps. It is sometimes better to compromise on the Lean principles than lose a client or not have the opportunity to expose or implement lean in a department.*

An example of a hand drawn PACU value stream is shown in Figure 6.11.

IDEAL STATE VALUE STREAM MAPPING

Once the current state is constructed, a second VSM is performed, the ideal state map. It should be done as a brainstorming session in which the team determines what the process would be like if they were starting with a clean slate and all barriers were removed. Mapping the ideal process is looking at the process with:

- All the money in the world
- All the technology available
- What it could look like 5 or 10 years from now

Teams should not spend more than an hour on this step. The purpose is to get teams to brainstorm, get them out of the box, and shift paradigms to vision the possibilities.

FUTURE STATE VALUE STREAM MAPPING

Once the ideal state VSM is completed, the final step is to construct a future state map (Figure 6.12). The future state map is created by the same team and normally looks at what could be accomplished from the ideal state map realistically over the next year out, but can look out 2 years (Figure 6.13). This is accomplished by reviewing the current state map to determine the following:

- Which activities can be eliminated, rearranged, simplified, or combined?[*]
- Which events can be done in parallel?
- What is the critical path?
- How many people touch it?
- Where are there handoffs between participants? (mistakes, waits)
- Are there activities that are duplicated by the same or another person or department?

VALUE STREAM MAP PROJECT LISTS, PRIORITIZATION MATRIX, AND TRACKING

The team creates "Kaizen bursts" or potential projects, and identifies quick wins (changes that could be done immediately to improve the process, usually unnecessary waste activities) that can be implemented, to get the process from its current state to future state. As the team reviews and designs the "future state" process, the opportunities are placed in a list to improve process speed. Each opportunity is ranked based on impact to the strategic planning goals (Figure 6.14) (which may include service, people, finance, clinical, operations etc.), ease of deployment, and cost. In addition, ranking should occur to understand the risk and impact to other departments for each solution that is proposed. The list of potential opportunities provides a roadmap of continuous improvement activities that the clinical area can work on and track progress over the next year.

* Junichi Ishiwata, *Productivity Through Process Analysis* (New York: Productivity Press) 1997.

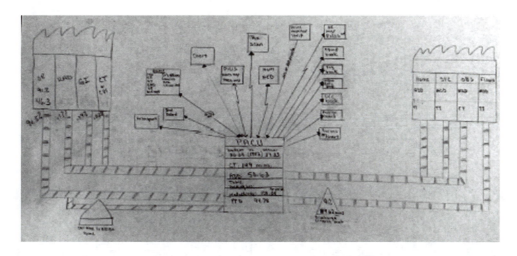

FIGURE 6.11   VSM (value stream map) hand-drawn PACU.

VALUE STREAM LAYOUT MAPS (SOMETIMES REFERRED TO AS SKITUMI MAPS)

During our VSM teachings, we always use the phrase that the process boxes "are a process, not a place." However, the information in VSMs can help guide layout revisions to help optimize flow. "Value stream layout maps" leverage the value stream mapping data by overlaying the process boxes (data) on top of the existing master layout. This is an excellent way for leaders to help visualize how their overall layouts create bottlenecks and waste. This is also a good way to look at your overall master layouts or block diagrams of the

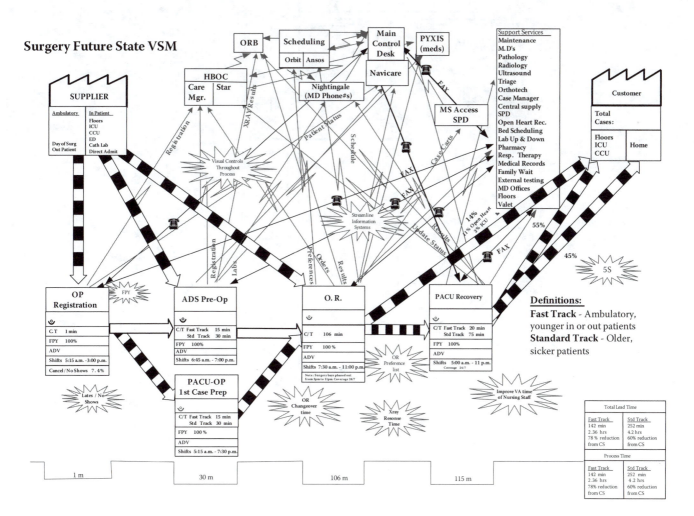

FIGURE 6.12   Future state value stream map example.

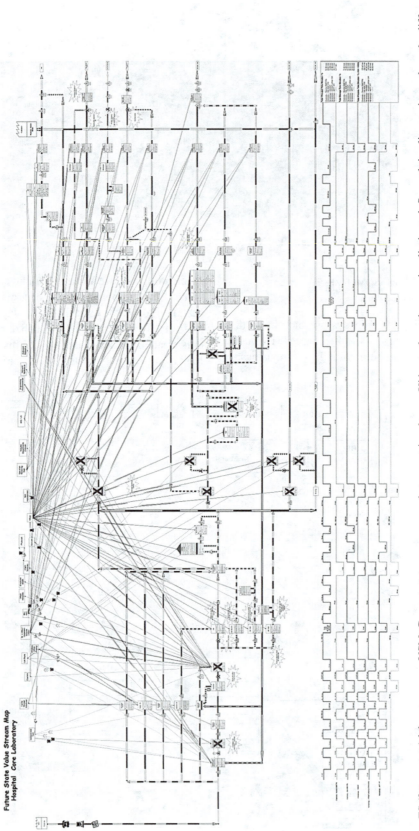

FIGURE 6.13 FS (future state) laboratory core VSM. Current state processes and storage triangles are X'd out where they can be eliminated. Several timelines exist to show the different paths lab specimens travel throughout the value stream.

Proposed Projects or Tasks Description	Ranking 1-low impact 3-med impact 5-high impact	Financial Impact (Cost/Benefit)	Ease of implementation	Improved Customer / Patient / Stakeholder Perspective	Cycle time impact	Future Perspective (Growth, Quality, Safety, etc...)	Total	
	Project or Task							Status
1	5 S OR equipment storage area	T						0	75% complete
2	5 S OR hallway	T						0	Open
3	Unclamp each instrument before sending to CS	T						0	100% complete
4	Eliminate instrument container washing process	T						0	100% complete
5	Improve Pre-Op patient information FPY	P	5	3	5	5	5	23	Open
6	Demand and supply matching for frequent used instrument sets	P	3	5	1	3	3	15	Open
7	OR scheduling process	P	3	1	3	3	3	13	Open
8	Improve 7:30 case start on-time	P	3	1	3	3	3	13	Open
9	Cross training for Pre-Op, PACU and Pre Testing staff	P	3	1	3	3	3	13	Open
10	Assess block time effectiveness	P	3	1	3	3	3	13	Open
11	Case cart assembly process standardization	P	1	5	1	3	3	13	90% complete
12	Level loading cases by: service line, instrument type, patient type	P	3	1	3	3	3	13	Open
13	Reassess Pre Testing demand and staffing need	P	1	5	1	1	3	11	Open
14	Visual control for processes (KPIs)	P	1	5	1	1	3	11	Open
15	OR room stock standardization	P	1	5	1	3	1	11	100% complete
16	CS demand and staffing need study	P	3	3	1	1	3	11	100% complete
17	Reduce unnecessary flashing	P	3	3	3	1	1	11	In Process (new equip purchase)
18	Align supply area to resource map (preference card)	P	1	5	1	1	1	9	80% complete (bin locations ID'd but needs to be uploaded by Surgery IS

FIGURE 6.14 Project prioritization matrix. When this matrix is prioritized to the strategic plan goals it provides the necessary linkage to align the department's projects and tasks with the company's goals. These tasks and projects become part of the process owners objective job goals for the year and are tied to their evaluation, bonuses (if they exist) and performance review.

hospital overall and develop high-level systemic approaches to improvement.

BASELINING THE PROCESS—DATA COLLECTION AND ANALYSIS—CURRENT STATE

Lean is about being able to "manage by fact" and understanding all the data related to the current process and what it can deliver. Next, we will go through the types of data needed to get a true picture of the best way to deliver customer value. The data captured in the baseline phase provides the foundation for the calculations and comparisons for the improvements as we methodically move through the phases. Although we will not be able to go through each and every item and tool mentioned in the baseline phase (B) of the BASICS model, we will introduce you to the key pieces of data and calculations in the baseline phase. We will begin to introduce demand, TT, cycle time, throughput time, staffing, peak demand, inventory, and work in process (WIP), and cover some key financial data points that we may want to consider. Many of these can be

collected in conjunction or while performing the VSM (as these can be data points contained within the process boxes).

CUSTOMER DEMAND

In Lean, everything starts with the customer, and the first piece of data we need is to determine true customer demand. Understanding customer demand is critical since it impacts what hours we need to be open and the number of staff required. It is an integral part of many of our other calculations. In a hospital or clinical setting, the best or most accurate demand numbers are based on current (actual) and future (or projected) forecasted demand. If we cannot get actual and forecasted numbers, we often have to rely on historical data. As we all know, sometimes history is not a good predictor of the future, as case mix, new services, and business development may alter demand.

We capture demand yearly, monthly, daily, by day of week, etc., and it is important to understand demand at the lowest possible level, especially if there are wide swings in demand cycles, such as in the laboratory "morning run." One of our rules with Lean is to always convert calculations to represent a day's worth or sometimes an hour's worth of demand. This is because it is easier for people to understand a day's or hour's worth of something vs. a week's, a month's or a year's worth. This will also make it easier to calculate the rest of the formulas as we work through the implementation.

As we begin to relate demand to activities performed, we must be able to analyze demand in terms of how or when it is needed. For example, we would be inaccurate at scheduling nurses in the emergency room if we based how many nurses we need on a daily (24 hrs) basis instead of understanding trends in demand by shifts, or preferably, in hours. If we scheduled staff equally throughout the day, we would find that we are overstaffed on nights and understaffed on days. Managers must recognize the importance of understanding and monitoring demand. If not, they may fall victim to "staffing to desire," where they will often find that they do not have the staff they need at the times they are needed, thus creating an artificial appearance that more staff is needed overall when, in fact, it is just not being scheduled properly to "match" the customer demand.

AVAILABLE TIME

Available time is equal to the total time per shift less uncovered breaks, meeting etc., where the workplace shuts down. In healthcare available time normally equals the total shift time as staff and managers cover breaks. However in some vet offices, general practitioner offices or commercial pharmacies it's not unusual for the office to shut down over lunch or planned break. If a normal shift was 10 hrs with an hour for lunch then the available time would be equal to 9 hrs. So the available time is actually the "work" time available for the department or unit.

TAKT TIME/PRODUCTION SMOOTHING

Most healthcare personnel are not familiar with the term Takt Time (TT) or production smoothing. TT allows us to look at a process or a group of activities and determine, based on customer demand and available time, how a process needs to run related to time. When we take yearly or monthly demand and divide it by working days, it aids in production smoothing or leveling the activities within the process; this will be discussed in detail throughout the book.

Takt* time (German root means metre, tempo, or beat) is equal to the available time to produce a product or service divided by the customer demand required during the available time.

PEAK DEMAND

Hospitals and clinics incur a phenomenon we have termed peak demand. In many areas, such as in the emergency room, OR, laboratory, radiology, and pharmacy, it can be difficult

---

* http://www.answers.com/topic/takt –Takt – Metre or time, as in *Dreivierteltakt* (3/4 time), *im Takt* (in strict tempo) etc., or bar (measure), as in *Taktstrich* (bar-line). http://www.websters-online-dictionary.org/definition/takt – German rhythm, clock time, stroke.

---

to level load the schedule. Even though the ED demand is predictable, patients do not necessarily arrive evenly spaced. It doesn't mean it can't be level loaded, but it is much more challenging and may require "non-conventional shifts" to optimize resources to meet customer demand.

Another area that has peak demand is surgery. The main driver is most surgeons want a 7:30 a.m. start or cut time and want to end their day by 4:00 p.m. or 5:00 p.m. This forces a large number of cases through first thing in the morning and drives when and how many resources (people, equipment, and facilities) are needed throughout the rest of the hospital to support it. Think about what impact this has on the entire organization and the staffing requirements for surgery. Thus, having all the cases start at the same time creates a domino effect of batching and drives when beds need to become available and when transport staff is needed. The number of Post-Op recovery staff and beds, as well as the need for critical care unit beds around the same time. Another driver is add-on or emergent cases. Imagine if we level loaded the demand each day. What differences would that make?

Peak demand can also occur during certain months of a year, such as seasonal (i.e., EDs in "snow bird" states during January to March). Peak demand can occur during weeks of a year, certain days (i.e., surgery Tuesday–Thursday) and during certain hours of the day (i.e., laboratory morning runs, ED after 5:00 p.m.). We have found that maybe with the exception of add-ons, surgery demand is as predictable as is ED demand (and even add-ons are somewhat predictable). We have modeled ED arrivals across several hospitals by hour and have predicted patients waiting to see the doctor at any time during the day or evening, to within 1–2 patients.

Peak demand drives a tremendous amount of waste. Supporting peak demand requires extra staffing, extra rooms, and extra equipment. Once peak demand is over what do we do with the extra staff, rooms, and equipment once the demand drops and rooms are left empty and staff turns idle? The goal is to level load demand, but until that can be done, we need to account for this peak demand or we will be unable to provide services.

Customer demand has to be analyzed in the same increment of time as available time to be compared with TT.

$$TT = \text{available time} \div \text{customer demand}.$$

CYCLE TIME

Cycle time is collected as part of the baseline phase so we can again understand the current state. It is calculated in different ways, but each should have the same result. They are:

1. The amount of *time* each person actually spends completing their part of the operation if the work is evenly distributed.
2. The daily or hourly available time divided by the daily or hourly demand of the process. (*Note: This is different from TT, which is based on the demand of the customer.*)

3. Dividing the total labor time (TLT) by the number of people in the process, again assuming it is evenly distributed.
4. Timed to the actual individual output of the process, i.e., the length of time between the discharges of each individual patient.

The collection of cycle time early in the Lean initiative provides a baseline of the activity or process. It is a very important data point since it can be used as an in-process metric. Once all or part of the waste is eliminated, it will be monitored in the "C" or check phase (BASIC). The current cycle time data will be compared to the future state cycle time of the proposed new process during the "S" or sustain phase of the BASICS model. The goal would be to match cycle times to TT, but they are generally not the same in healthcare owing to all the variation that exists in the processes.

CYCLE TIME AND TAKT TIME—WHAT'S THE DIFFERENCE?

To begin to "put the puzzle together," we differentiate between TT and cycle time. In order to optimize the process flow, we need a clear understanding of cycle time and TT. As we have previously discussed, cycle time is obtained through performing the product process and operator analysis. Cycle time is the actual working rhythm of the area or the amount of time each person must meet to complete their part of the operation.

Many use TT synonymously with cycle time, but we differentiate because we believe they are different. TT is a calculation that is based strictly on customer demand, where cycle time is based on the area's demand for that day or hour and/or the time it actually takes you to do a particular activity.

Our goal is to match cycle time to TT, but this may not always be possible. In a hospital, cycle time would be based on the demand at which we choose to "staff" or assign resources to perform activities in the area. Despite what is imagined, demand in hospitals is surprisingly predictable. In hospitals, due to scheduling limitations, based on hours one can work and jobs one can perform, it can be difficult to balance cycle times and TTs. Sometimes, we cannot always afford to staff to peak demand for all areas all the time, as this is not practical in all hospital settings.

Cycle time and TT can initially be confusing concepts. To illustrate, we will use the following example:

TT = available time ÷ customer demand.

In an OR we schedule 12 hrs shifts from 7:00 a.m. to 7:00 p.m. If the "demand" on a normal day for surgical cases is 45 cases, then our TT calculation is:

- Available time = 12 hrs or 720 min
- OR Room Time (Patient In to Patient Out) = 3 hrs (180 min)
- Total demand = 45 surgical cases per day

Takt Time = 720 ÷ 45 = 16 min.

The TT is based on AVERAGES and assumes everything is LEVEL LOADED (or evenly distributed). In order to complete the surgical schedule of 45 patients, the OR would need to process a patient in and out of the OR every 16 min. It is important to note that this has nothing to do with how long it takes to process someone or how many people work in the department. If the surgical case load for the day is more or less, then the TT would need to be adjusted.

Takt Time will also vary based on the number of shifts. Assuming the demand stays constant at 45/day the Takt Time would be:

- 16 min TT for 1 shift or
- 32 min TT if it is run for 2 shifts

This is because the available time increases and the demand remains the same.

The same effect can be achieved by running 2 parallel clinical processes* on 1 shift at a 32 min TT.

32 min TT ÷ 2 tracks = 16 min average cycle time overall i.e., 2 patients completed every 32 min.

We need to be able to balance the "line" or spread the work evenly across the area and flex resources to achieve maximum throughput. Sometimes, using these techniques helps to better balance work from shift to shift. Balancing the work has a corresponding effect on the number of people required in the OR. Based on the analysis, we need to be able to answer the following questions:

- What is the peak demand each OR should be able to meet?
- Are the ORs capable of performing each operation for each service line? In other words, are all OR room sizes and equipment standardized in hospitals?

See Chapter 15 which explores OR's in more detail.

DESIGNING CYCLE TIME TO TAKT TIME

Sometimes, we may choose to run at a faster or slower cycle time. This will cause us to over- or under-produce to Takt Time. To "design" a process leveraging cycle time information, we can alter the available time to run the process. We can do this by:

- Adding or taking away shifts (extending or decreasing the "work day")
- Adding or taking away rooms
- Running the rooms fewer days per week or fewer hours per day
- Combining or separating products/services in a work area or room

---

* "Cells" or "tracks" or in the case of the ORs it would be rooms

In the OR, for example, we may need to

- Open or close more ORs to meet the TT
- Add or balance the activities of the resources to a particular task to decrease the "rate limiting activity," thus reducing the "patient in" to "next patient in" cycle time
- Assess equipment cycle time such as the ability to clean/sterilize in a timely manner between cases
- Purchase additional or different equipment to facilitate flow
- Invoke work standards, standard work, and expectations
- Clarify roles and responsibilities among staff

Remember to assess everything that may impact the patient in and out of the OR. If we just looked at TT and cycle time and determined we had enough rooms to run a typical surgical day based on demand, we would be missing the opportunity to eliminate waste, optimize productivity, and grow our business within the current space. Each one of the Lean assessment tools product, operator, and setup provides a different piece to the Lean puzzle.

LENGTH OF STAY (LOS)

Since many organizations utilize Lean to tackle patient throughput issues, it is important that one gains an understanding of how LOS is calculated, as this is a key metric or key process indicator (KPI) in many businesses. Remember, it is important to calculate it consistently so that we can use it for comparison throughout the initiative as it is potentially an overall system-based metric.

THROUGHPUT TIME IS ALSO KNOWN AS LENGTH OF STAY

Throughput time is calculated by adding the total processing, inspection, transport, and storage time, or the sum of all the cycle times in a process. Once we have throughput time, we can divide it by the TT or necessary cycle time to determine the WIP (or work in progress) inventory required to meet the cycle time. Keep in mind that in hospitals, the products are patients and, hence, WIP in healthcare is synonymous with patients waiting for the next step.

The following is an example of the formula to determine the size of a waiting room.

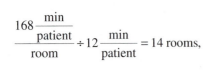

$$\frac{168\,\frac{\text{min}}{\frac{\text{patient}}{\text{room}}}}{} \div 12\,\frac{\text{min}}{\text{patient}} = 14 \text{ rooms},$$

If each patient spends 168 min of time waiting and a 12 min TT, then length of stay (LOS) divided by TT is equal to 14 rooms or 1 room that can house 14 patients to support the waiting area. Note: there is no cost accounting standard for this.

It is important to be aware that LOS includes value-added and non-value-added time. One of the primary goals every manager should have is to reduce the LOS without impacting another areas or department's LOS. Since LOS is such an important factor in all areas of the hospital and clinics, there may come a time when hospitals employ "value stream leaders" who would then oversee their overall LOS for a value stream or service line.

LENGTH OF STAY IS DIRECTLY CORRELATED TO INVENTORY

The longer the LOS, the more inventory or "patients" exist in the system. Inventory in manufacturing is totally different from healthcare in that the product can't talk to you while it is moving through the factory. Yet, the concept that hospitals can learn from factories is not that farfetched when you consider both have demand, time in which the demand has to be completed, and the need to reduce costs to be profitable and stay in business.

Inventory is divided into 3 basic types:

1. Raw material
2. Work in Process or Progress (WIP)
3. Finished goods

Raw material is material (or people) that have had no labor added to them. WIP is any raw material that has had labor added but is not finished. Finished goods are any material that has had all the labor added to them (with the exception of shipping to the customer).

A good WIP inventory analogy is a laundry example.

If we do our laundry every 2 weeks, how many days of clothes do we need? We need at least 14 days worth of clothes plus the time it takes to launder them. If it takes 3 days to launder them, then we need a total of 17 days. If we do our laundry once a week and it now takes a day to do the laundry, we can cut the inventory required from 17 days to 8 days. As we cut our throughput time and increase our first past yield (FPY, the total throughput yield of the system), our costs can't help but be reduced.

Tom Peters said, "In their book, Stalk and Hout say the consumption of time should become the primary business measurement performance variable,* i.e., ahead of the 'P' word profit. Sounds silly at first blush, sounds brilliant at second blush because if you get the 'T' word right then the 'P' word takes care of itself. There is no way in hell you can do a job in 4 hrs as expensively as you can do it in 9 months."[†] In addition, if we can reduce our throughput time we can now increase our capacity (assuming we have the demand).

LENGTH OF STAY—A KEY METRIC

We recommend LOS as a key Lean productivity metric along with other metrics on patient safety, quality and customer satisfaction. LOS can be used at the highest level to monitor patient-centered processes. Throughput time (LOS)

---

* George Stalk and Thomas Hout, *Competing Against Time* (New York: MacMillan) 1990.

† Tom Peters, "Speed is Life" video, Video Publishing House and KERA, 1991.

as a metric used for laboratory, pharmacy or nutritional service areas is very similar to manufacturing processes. Why is the metric LOS so important? This metric is important because most other metrics ('x's') are somehow related to or impact LOS, which would be our big "Y." The longer the LOS in a hospital:

- The greater the danger to the patient contracting a hospital or nosocomial* infection.
- The more it costs to house the patient.
- The more supplies required during their stay.
- The more labor required to take care of them.
- The fewer patients we can see, which drives the need for more space and rooms.
- The longer the throughput time, the longer the patients are tying up a bed, which means we see fewer patients our costs and opportunities for defects increase.

Every leader should understand that each extra minute of throughput time/LOS adds costs defined in a variety of ways, but most of that cost is hidden.

Understanding and managing LOS is critical to most hospitals as it impacts whether or not they can admit or treat that next patient in the ED or perform that next surgery or procedure. Managing LOS means the difference between whether or not we need to build that new hospital or doctor's office building, wing, add more surgical suites, add another MRI machine or build a larger facility. Managing LOS can impact the financial viability of the healthcare organization.

Homework: *Find out what every extra minute or hour of LOS costs you in your hospital or clinic.*

Safety, service, quality, delivery and cost all tie to the LOS metric. If we shorten LOS, our costs go down, our patient safety increases, our patient satisfaction increases, we deliver on time (meet the schedule), and we reduce our costs (and, in addition, we add capacity to potentially generate more revenue). The longer the LOS, the more complex our processes seem to become and the more frustrating it is for our staff members who are trying to move patients to keep the ED and ORs flowing. Longer throughput times drive holds in the OR and in the ED. In the OR, this results inpatient/surgeons' cases being delayed, which extends the workday and costs additional labor time or overtime; this does not include the "human life quality" costs. In the ED, extended LOS results in delays in access to seeing the physician; after 2–3 hrs patients start to leave. This is a safety risk for the patient and a potential loss of revenue for the hospital. Nurses and doctors get frustrated dealing with patients angry about having to wait so long to see them.

It is important to remember that LOS is related to patient mix and acuity, so LOS goals may be different at each facility. Comparing LOS over time at the same facility is best at the start, as long as patient mix does not change too much. While it is true that revenue will generally increase with shorter LOS, this assumes diagnosis-related group (DRG) payment (like Medicare) or case rate payments, there are still a few payers that pay on a per diem (daily rates), which pay more for longer LOS.

How do we reduce LOS? First, we have to understand what comprises LOS. LOS is made up of all the individual process cycle times that contribute to it. So we must look at total throughput time for a patient to get through our hospital, whether they enter through the OR, ED, catheterization laboratory, transfer, or direct admit until their exit by being discharged home.

Homework: *One action you can immediately take is to have all your managers and supervisors define throughput time in their areas, then calculate and understand what their cycle times and resulting throughput times are for the processes for which they are responsible. The more we reduce the cycle time for each process, the less inventory we need, the less rooms we need, etc. A format for that report is shown in Figure 6.15.*

We place a cautionary note, however, on metrics such as customer satisfaction and LOS, as there are a substantial number of contributing factors ('x's') to both of these metrics. One isolated Lean initiative may not—and we have found through experience that it will not—be able to impact all the contributing factors to significantly "move" the needle on these metrics, and a series of initiatives is required. For example, in the ED, if we did a survey and identified that customer satisfaction was important, we may need to measure and improve cycle time from door-to-doctor examination, along with nurse touch point communication and ancillary services to improve the overall LOS. If the ED had an internal Lean initiative, they could have a significant impact and control on all the factors except LOS. This is because ED LOS depends on the LOS or turnaround time of other departments, such as radiology, laboratory and, ultimately, the inpatient units. Therefore, Lean initiatives require understanding the "value stream" and how to integrate the silos.

NUMBER OF STAFF REQUIRED

LOS also impacts the number of staff or labor required to run the organization. The longer a patient stays within the system, whether it is in processing a registration, having a procedure, or being evaluating in the ED, it is necessary to understand the number or (headcount) of staff, the number of hours worked per week and skill level of each staff member. In a Lean initiative, capturing this data should be done at the beginning of the project. This will yield the amount of labor hours currently used by skill set.

---

* Louis M. Savary, *The Nun and the Bureaucrat* (Washington, DC: CC-M Productions) 2006.

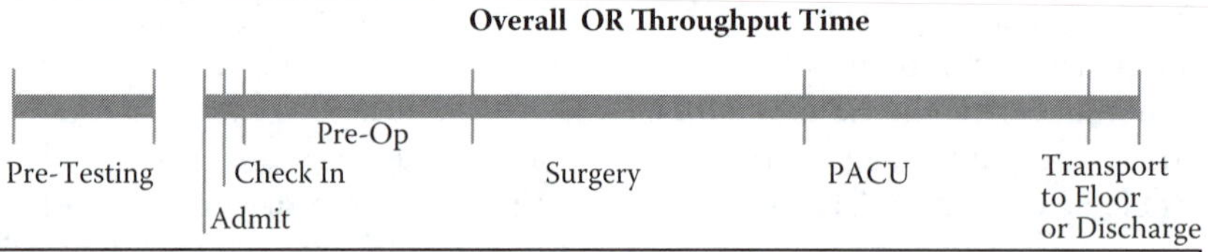

Overall OR Throughput Time

Sub Process	Cycle Time	Wait Times	Comments
Major Process: <u>Perioperative Services</u>			
List all you sub-processes and average cycle time for each process			
1. Pre-Testing	80 min	avg 10 min	Stand alone process
2. Admissions	5 min	avg 10 min	up to 30 min
3. Surgical Check In	5 min	avg 10 min	up to 20 min
4. Pre-Op	45 min	avg 60 min	up to 2 hrs or more
5. OR	110 min		
6. PACU	80 min		
7. Transport to Floor	10 min	up to 30 min	Nurse or tech moves
Totals for 2–8	**335 min**	**120 min**	**grand total 455 min 7.5 hrs**

FIGURE 6.15   OR overall throughput time.

So LOS or throughput time has a big impact on the number of rooms required in addition to the labor required in the healthcare environment. The longer the patient is in the process, the more resources they consume and the more expensive their visit or stay becomes.

Interestingly enough, the majority of hospitals do not have incentives built into their physician contracts or departments for LOS or for efficiency (i.e., door-to-doctor examination) times. In the ED, these two times are a dichotomy. Physicians in the ED, as a rule, don't handoff patients, so we end up trading LOS (i.e., disposition and discharge) with door-to-doctor examination time because there is only one physician and he can't examine 2 patients at the same time or examine and dispose/discharge 2 patients at the same time. If physicians ever determined that they could handoff the disposition of patients (which, in some cases, may not be desirable), this would alleviate the problem.

TOTAL LABOR TIME

The definition of TLT is the sum of value-added labor plus non-value-added labor. The TLT comes from the operator analysis section described later. Once we have the TLT we can divide it by TT or cycle time to determine the number of staff required, the total staffing hours and convert it to dollars. Later, this will help us to calculate any labor savings and improvement in productivity through the Lean initiative.

QUIZ

Problem1: *If it takes on average 5 days to get an inpatient through the hospital and the TT is 10 min, how many rooms do we need? If level loaded, how many patients would arrive and leave each day?*

Problem 1

$$5 \text{ days} \times 24 \text{ hrs} \times 60 \text{ min} = 7200 \text{ min.}$$

Number of rooms = LOS ÷ Takt Time = 720 rooms.

Number of paitents per hour = 60 min in an hour ÷ 10 min
Takt Time = 6 patients per hour.

Level loaded would equal 6 patients per hour every 24 hrs or 144 patients per day.

Problem 2: *If it takes 2 hrs to get results in an ED after the patient has been seen, and TT is 10 min, how big a waiting room do we need?*

Problem 2

120 min (waiting for results (LOS)) ÷ 10 min Takt Time = 12 patients in waiting room.

WEIGHTED AVERAGE

Often, we do not open or utilize "rooms" 24 hrs per day, whether it is in a procedural area, surgical suite, or even in a post-procedural recovery unit. We may "open" or make the rooms available for use based on demand. Sometimes, we have to calculate weighted averages in order to use some of the formulas.

Let's say surgery suites are utilized in the following manner (Table 6.2):

- 17 rooms from 7:00 a.m. to 3:00 p.m. (8 hrs)
- 10 rooms from 3:00 p.m. to 7:00 p.m. (4 hrs)
- 3 rooms from 7:00 p.m. to 11:00 p.m. (4 hrs)

What is the average number of rooms we use? We have to take 17 rooms + 10 rooms + 3 rooms = 30 rooms. The next step would be to take 17 rooms × 8 hrs = 136 hrs. We do this for each one and arrive at 188 for the total hours. We then divide the total hours for each room divided by the grand total of hours (188 hrs), see Table 6.2. This gives us the weighted average factor that we then multiply by the number of rooms, which gives us the weighted average number of rooms over the entire range of staffed hours from 7:00 a.m. to 11:00 p.m.

Remember, the goal is to manage by fact and understand your data. We need to discover what data are available in your

TABLE 6.2
Weighted Average Number of Rooms

Weighted Average Example					
1	2	3	4	5	6
			= col 1 * col 3	col 4/188	= col 5 * col 1
# of Rooms	Scheduled Hours	Hours	Total Hours	Weighted Avg Factor	Weighed Average Rooms
17	7 a.m. to 3 p.m.	8	136	72.3%	12.30
10	3 p.m. to 7 p.m.	4	40	21.3%	2.13
3	7 p.m. to 11 p.m.	4	12	6.4%	0.19
10	average		188	1	14.62

organization and what confidence level of accuracy can be placed on the data. The bottom line is that having data is great, but it is the human interpretation of this data that is critical. Sometimes, it helps to have a couple of people looking at the data to make sure the formulas are correct. The team, which includes the executive sponsor and Lean initiative owner, must understand the information and determine what is reasonable to accomplish in relation to the organizational goals. In addition, as situations change, the calculations must be redone to make sure that everyone continues to manage by fact or the system will break down.

FINANCIAL METRICS

Being able to articulate and quantify financial metrics can be important, especially early in Lean implementations when organizations are still trying to "prove the value" of adopting Lean. One challenge outlined below highlights some of the data points one might consider gathering during the initial phases of the initiative to begin to construct the financial component of the ROI.

MEASURING INVENTORY AND CASH FLOW

Most hospitals don't seem to formally track inventory consistently and, if they do, it is typically not very accurate. In fact, unlike manufacturers, cash flow is not even tracked as a key metric at many hospitals. Some hospitals have even said that if our cost of capital is only 4%–5%, why should we care about how much inventory we have? In fact, reducing inventory may negatively impact our profitability.

As a result, most hospitals have little or no idea of their inventory costs, whether in the surgical suite or emergency room or other departments, especially at the frontline management level. The cost of surgical supplies in storage, "lost" or excess and obsolete can be significant. The problem is that most healthcare organizations "think they know" what it is; however, we have found that in most hospitals the data are ripe with inaccuracies, which is scary because decisions are made on this data.

In healthcare, inventory can refer to many things: supplies, number of rooms, or even number of patients waiting (in different situations when it pertains to Lean). Related to financial metrics, we generally consider it as it pertains to supplies. Inventory can be expressed in dollars or number of turns or what we call days of supply (DOS).

Traditional inventory turns are expressed by[*]:

Sales or COGS ÷ last 3 months average inventory.

In Lean, we look at "forward looking" DOS, which is expressed by:

Sales or COGS ÷ next projected 3 months of average inventory.

We calculate DOS by taking:

Inventory dollars on hand ÷ a day's worth of average inventory.

In order to figure out a day's worth of inventory, we need to calculate the inventory used over a specified period and divide it by the number of days in that period. For example, if a surgical services department has $6 million in supply inventory and they use $1.2 million per month, we would take $1.2 million per month and divide by 30 calendar days per month:

$1,200,000 ÷ 30 days = $40,000 per calendar day.

If we take the $6,000,000 supply inventory on hand.

$6,000,000 ÷ $40,000/day = 150 calendar DOS.

Once we have DOS, we can calculate inventory turns:

Inventory turns = calendar or annual working days ÷ DOS.

For example:

365 days in the year ÷ 150 DOS = 2.43 turns per year.

[*] Erich Helfert, *Techniques of Financial Analysis* (Chicago, IL: Irwin Publishing) 1997, page 110; also www.inventoryturns.com.

TABLE 6.3

Short-Term Metrics—Results vs. Process Focused

Results Focused		Process Focused
Leading	**Lagging**	**Real Time**
On-time delivery	Inventory turns	Takt, cycle, and throughput time
Labor as a percentage of net sales	EBIDTA	Visual controls—delivery system by hour
Quality measures	Return on assets	Quality—immediate countermeasures and root cause
Cost of quality	Gross profit	Standard work audit
3 months forecasted DOS	Cash flow	Immediate patient feedback
Customer satisfaction	Contribution margin	Add on—unplanned stoppages number and hours
		Patient readiness

When figuring out par levels in surgery, however, the approach above would be misleading, as it averages the inventory over all 7 days of the week. When we figure par levels, we need to figure it out for each part individually (we call this a plan for every part (PFEP*)) and look at weekdays only and, in some cases, peak demand on weekdays (i.e., if we do most of our heart cases on 1 or 2 days), unless you are routinely doing cases on the weekends.

Note: *Most hospitals at the operational level prior to Lean initiatives do not look at inventory in this manner; however, the materials management area may track inventory turns.*

WORK IN PROCESS INVENTORY

Throughput time ÷ CT (Cycle Time) = amount of WIP inventory.

Consider the following inventory example related to equipment needed for surgical cases. If it takes 3 hrs to get equipment through the sterilization process and the CT is 60 min per surgical case, the number of equipment sets could be calculated. Knowing that it takes 3 hrs to perform the sterilization process (including transport and there are no other delays) or

$$180 \text{ min} \div 60 \text{ min (CT)} = 3 \text{ equipment sets,}$$

to run the system. It is important to be able to leverage the data and manage by fact to be able to know whether you have the right amount of equipment to do the work.

SALES OR REIMBURSEMENTS PER EMPLOYEES

Sales or revenue by itself is a misleading metric for hospitals and clinics, as the price charged does not typically represent what the hospital gets reimbursed nor does it often relate to what it costs to deliver the service. Also, hospitals in the United States are required to take patients whether the patient

can afford to pay or not.[†] This creates challenges for hospitals as they attempt to manage their costs without having control on what they can charge. For example, if the charge for "plasma" goes up, they cannot necessarily pass on the cost to their customers like many businesses can, as many of their payers' pay "fixed" reimbursements and some customers may not pay at all.

CONTRIBUTION MARGIN

Contribution margin, revenue, or reimbursements per employee are good overarching metrics for Lean. They are a high-level look at the contribution per employee and we should have a set percentage goal to increase this each year.

COST PER CASE

Cost per case can be another misleading metric; however, it can also be a key metric if used correctly; but we have to be careful how it is used and calculated. It can be a deceptive metric if one does not account for the weighted average of the case mix. For instance, orthopedic cases use very expensive implants. If the ratio of orthopedic cases increases, so will the overall average cost per case.

Our goal with Lean is not just to look at leading and lagging indicators but to focus on real-time process based metrics (Table 6.3).

DATA AND WHAT PEOPLE THINK

In the quest of gathering accurate data, over and over we ask people how long things take, with regard to performing activities within a given process. Most managers and staff provide an estimate; however when we videotape or conduct a time study, they are almost never correct. In fact, they are generally surprised once they are given the "real" data. As soon as someone says, "I think" or "it was" or "it should be," then one knows the person is not really sure. If our goal is to act on fact, then this becomes a problem. Why go into all this with Lean?

---

* Rick Harris, *Making Materials Flow* (Cambridge, MA: Lean Enterprise Institute (LEI) 2006.

[†] http://www.cms.hhs.gov/emtala/. In 1986, Congress enacted the emergency Medical Treatment & Labour Act (EMTALA) to ensure public access to emergency services regardless of ability to pay.

In order to improve, we need to know our starting point. If we can't baseline our metrics, we can't know how much we improved. Remember the old saying, "Minutes count but seconds rule."[*] It is very difficult, even with all the data and reports produced, to get good baseline data because the data are only as good as those entering the data. Having everyone working to the same data entry point definitions and capturing it in the same "reproducible and repeatable" manner in order to make sure it is accurate can be a difficult challenge.

For example, in one ED, we were told that the correct data was always entered and updated several times a day. Yet, when we dug deeper, we found it took at least 24 hours of reviewing every case from the prior day before the data was even 80% accurate. Think about it—these are legal documents! We found this not to be an isolated incident. Consider trying to meet a quality metric of door to EKG within 10 min and every staff member documents the time using unsynchronized clocks. Could this impact whether the metric was actually met? Other EDs take several days to calculate their actual arrivals and complete their charts. How can one manage the ED effectively without the critical information at the right time or in "real time or near real time" in order to make the adjustments needed to react to problems within a timely manner? After all, it is too late to fix the problem if the process has been completed, and the customer has left.

The baselining phase sets the stage for the Lean initiative. The scope is defined, the business problem they are trying to solve should be understood, and the executive sponsor should be on board. The executive sponsor and operational managers should understand their KPIs and identify the key metrics that will be impacted.

SUSTAINABILITY AND ACCOUNTABILITY

A culture of organizational accountability is critical in order to sustain Lean. Once we implement Lean in an area, there is a need for it not only to be sustained, but also continuously improved. When implemented, most processes may be 80% defined, the remaining 20% need to be further refined as staff works the process and identifies more opportunities to eliminate variation and waste. Without accountability in place, too often we see the areas or organizations backsliding.

Lesson Learned: *Once you implement Lean, any problem that shows up, even if you have had it for the last 30 years, will now get blamed on Lean.*

One fundamental and extremely challenging problem that we often encounter early in most healthcare organizations is a lack of accountability throughout the organization. Most organizations truly believe they have accountability

standards and measures in place; however, Lean initiatives will test the effectiveness of the organization's ability to impose top-to-bottom accountability.

As one engages in Lean, it will quickly become apparent that it is not all about the Lean tools. Lean consultants' roles within or outside our organizations are questioned repeatedly. What role do Lean consultants play?

We often respond that it is not unusual to spend more than 50% of our time in management consulting, teaching analytical skills, coaching, and acting as a catalyst and change agent; the other 50% of the time is spent teaching and applying the Lean tools. Often, we initially encounter basic "Management 101" type projects, i.e., determine how much inventory there is in surgery, baseline metrics, or develop basic reporting or productivity calculations for an area. There is nothing necessarily wrong with this; however, it shows the lack of resources or training programs in place to help the clinical talent that has been moved into management roles to get their basic analytical and managerial tasks completed. Managerial coaching is extremely important, as managing a Lean process is very different from that of a batch-type process. It is important to start this counseling and coaching immediately and help the manager build the infrastructure necessary to support the Lean culture.

PROCESS OWNERS DO NOT ALWAYS HAVE THE SKILL SETS NECESSARY TO MANAGE IN A LEAN ENVIRONMENT

Our experience in the United States is that:

- 40% of companies are either not exposed to it, dabble with Lean, or choose not to try it
- 40% will make ongoing attempts and struggle with it and may have pockets of excellence where several projects have improved and some have sustained
- 20% will try it with some level of success (5% of the 20% will go on to take it much further)

Many companies "talk Lean" but don't "walk Lean." If accountabilities are not in place and understood early in the initiative, then you will not change the culture and Lean will become a flavor of the month.

At Hospital X, we had an issue where, once the initial implementation was complete, the process excellence organization decided they were not responsible to ensure the brand new Lean implementations were sustained. Finance also stated that they did not have the responsibility to ensure the implementations were sustained. This really surprised us. We all agreed it was the process owner's job to sustain and improve, however the process owners were not far enough along in understanding the Lean management system or down the Lean maturity path to handle it. We brought up the issue with the Lean steering committee. In their opinion, it was the responsibility of the process owner to sustain. Of course, we agreed, but our concern was whose responsibility it is to follow up on the process owner until they are further down the path?

[*] Shawn L Noseworthy, RD, LD, MSA, Director of Food and Nutrition Services, Florida Hospital Memorial Medical System, 301 Memorial Medical Parkway, Daytona Beach, FL 32117 USA, shawn.noseworthy@fhmmc.org.

This is always an issue because, at most hospitals, there is little accountability throughout the management chain for metrics. As a result, if we leave "sustain and accountability" to only the process owners to continuously improve their metrics and adhere to their control plans it can be a recipe for disaster. A cultural change must occur and process improvement must become the way the organization does business. As the Lean journey begins, there needs to be a mechanism to track, monitor, and report on Lean deployments on an ongoing basis.

Since Lean is about the continual pursuit of eliminating waste, there needs to be a way to ensure that there are continuing cycles of improvement and that management and frontline staff members are actively engaged in operationalizing Lean concepts.

Lesson Learned: *It is critical to supply initial and ongoing training on how to manage in a Lean environment and provide opportunities to train new managers and employees in Lean thinking. Accountability and follow-up must be addressed if organizations are going to be successful. It should be part of the "High Level Lean Road Map." The senior leadership team must drive accountability to sustain Lean implementations through their line organization and continue to coach and develop the process owners.*

7 Basic Lean Concepts

EXECUTIVE SUMMARY

Chapter 7 continues using the BASICS system implementation model and looks at the "A," which stands for assess and analyze. It focuses on the different levels of waste that exist and how to assess the different levels including:

1. Obvious wastes
2. Five S type wastes
3. The eight wastes
4. Four or five wastes
5. Tribal waste
6. Hidden and unseen waste

It discusses that waste can easily become hidden or invisible over time. Sometimes we have to eliminate some waste in order to find other waste hiding below it. The large waste of overproduction and the importance of "just in time" process flow to help expose the waste.

The eight wastes are:

1. Waste of overproduction
2. Waste of time on hand
3. Waste of transportation
4. Waste of over-processing
5. Waste of stock on hand, i.e., inventory
6. Waste of worker movement
7. Waste of making defective products
8. Waste of people's talents

It is important to go to the actual hospital floor (*Gemba*) looking for waste. The 30-30-30 exercise is described where you stand and evaluate waste from that single spot.

Various problem-solving models are included such as DMAIC, PDSA, and PDCA. How to ask questions using the five Y's, the five W's, and the two H's is discussed—both tools that help us ask the pertinent questions and allow us to make sure we truly get down to the root cause including A3 strategy.

KEY LEARNINGS

- Understanding of the different levels and types of waste.
- Understanding the questions that must be asked, leveraging the five whys and the intense inspection that must occur to identify all waste.
- Understanding of the various models such as DMAIC and PDSA or PDCA that help evaluate the processes.

- Understanding that Lean still utilizes Total Quality (TQ) tools like fishbone diagrams, checklists and Pareto charts.
- Importance of *Gemba*—going to the actual location to inspect what is going on.

ASSESS/ANALYZE THE PROCESS

Time waste differs from material waste in that there can be no salvage. The easiest of all wastes and the hardest to correct is the waste of time, because wasted time does not litter the floor like wasted material...

—**Henry Ford, 1926**

The next letter in our BASICS model is *A*, which stands for *Assess/Analyze*. The main tools that make up this analysis are Product Process Flow analysis, full work/operator analysis, and changeover reduction. The goal of these tools is to uncover the obvious and, eventually, less obvious waste. This process of finding waste theoretically never ends.

So let's talk about waste. The heart of the Toyota system is eliminating waste. This is the main premise of the entire system. First, we need to expose waste and then get rid of it. Most of you are familiar with the seven wastes at Toyota, but these wastes are just a starting point, as there are many more types out there. We call these types the levels of waste.

LEVELS OF WASTE

1. The first level is obvious waste—low-hanging fruit (or walking on it).
2. The five S wastes—the easiest wastes to see.
3. The seven (eight) wastes—explained below.
4. Boiled frog waste—the waste that is hard to notice because it is old and we pass by it every day.
5. Tribal waste—sacred cows—waste in our culture and systems.
6. Hidden unseen waste—waste we don't typically see. You really have to hunt for it! The hardest waste to find, yet the most dangerous. Sometimes it is waste hiding behind other wastes.

LOW-HANGING FRUIT

This is the easiest waste because it is easy to see and very obvious to anyone looking at the area. It could be a long waiting line, things out of place, people walking to a printer, schedules not posted, charge nurse reviewing all the charts, etc.

FIVE S WASTES

We will discuss the five S wastes later in the book, but basically these wastes have to do with housekeeping. These wastes includes things not labeled, trash not picked up, or areas that need to be cleaned or swept.

THE SEVEN (EIGHT) WASTES

Listed in Table 7.1 are the seven wastes, including an eighth waste that we've added waste, which is the waste of talent, and examples of each.

HOW DO YOU FIND WASTE?

The most difficult waste to see is the waste that occurs in processes that we ourselves have created. When these wastes are pointed out to us, we tend to be defensive. This is normal behavior and justified in that it shows ownership over the process. We should take pride in everything we do. But because we take pride in our areas, we should be willing to expose the waste. Being defensive gets in the way because it discourages others from telling us when they see a problem or when they find waste in our area. In a Lean culture, we need to understand there is always a better way to do something. We may not always know how, so sometimes we just need to figure it out or solicit help to figure it out. The best way to figure it out is to constantly ask "why?"

Lesson Learned: *Never get too attached to your solutions and encourage anyone who tours your area to provide feedback—a list of good things and bad things they witnessed. Thank them when you receive it.*

To find waste, you have to go out and look for it, and then recognize it for what it is. Honda does this with an exercise they call the three A's,[*] which are to Go to the Actual Place and see the Actual Part in the Actual Situation (Figure 7.2).

In our Lean training classes, we ask our students to go out to the floor and write down waste wherever they see it. Many come back with 30–50 examples of waste. When we ask the supervisors what would have happened in the past if someone had come to them with a similar list, they tell us that they would have shut down, been defensive, and continued to do what they always did. When we ask them what they think now, once their eyes are opened, they say, "We see all this opportunity to improve!"

Examples, in addition to the eight wastes, include walking waste, watching waste, searching waste, large machine waste, conveyor waste, layout waste, meetings waste, and "picking up and setting down without using it" waste. Honda's three A's led to their Five P[†] program, which targets five strategic improvement areas:

1. best **P**osition—improve global competitiveness
2. best **P**roductivity—improve the process
3. best **P**roduct—improve quality and delivery
4. best **P**rice—decrease cost
5. best **P**artners—improve Honda/supplier relationship

Homework: *Can Honda's Five P's work for healthcare? Think about it and write down how it could work for you.*

30-30-30 EXERCISE

Taiichi Ohno was known for drawing a chalk circle around managers and making them stand in the circle until they had seen and documented all of the problems in a particular area (sometimes an entire shift) (Figure 7.3). Today the "stand in a circle" exercise is known as a 30-30-30 and is a great way to train someone's eyes to see waste and to provide structure for the team leader to carry out daily improvement or for the busy executive with limited time to go to the *Gemba* and see what is really happening. The exercise entails telling the person to stand in a circle for 30 min or more and just watch and look around to capture at least 30 wastes and then spend 30 min fixing one of them. When one spends time in the *Gemba* (the area where the work is being done) standing in the Ohno circle, you will see the gap between the target condition, if it even exists, and the actual condition.

Homework: *Go out and walk through your area or someone else's area. Answer the following questions.*

PEOPLE

- *What are people doing (or not doing)?*
- *Are we tapping their brains? Is there an idea board in the area?*

EQUIPMENT

- *What is the equipment doing or not doing?*
- *How smart is the equipment?*
- *Where is the high-volume equipment, like chemistry or hematology in a core laboratory, located?*
- *Is it batch or flow equipment?*

COMMUNICATION

- *How do we know if there is a problem?*
- *Is the area on plan or on schedule? The area should talk to you.*

VISUAL CONTROLS

- *Is the area Five S'd? Is the area neat and organized?*
- *Are there visual controls in place?*
- *Are there any metrics posted?*
- *Is standard work posted?*

---

[*] R. Dave Nelson, Patricia Moody, and Rick B. Mayo, *Powered by Honda* (Hoboken, NJ: John Wiley and Sons) 1998, 101.

[†] R. Dave Nelson, Patricia Moody, and Rick B. Mayo, *Powered by Honda* (Hoboken, NJ: John Wiley and Sons) 1998, 25.

TABLE 7.1
Symptoms of the Seven (Eight) Wastes

Over-Production	Waste of Idle and Wait Time	Waste of Transporting	Waste of Too Much Processing	Waste of Excess Inventory	Waste of Wasted Motions	Waste of Defects	Waste of Talent
Unbalanced staff scheduling	Idly watching equipment operate	Having multiple information systems	Asking the patient the same questions multiple times	Complex tracking systems	Inconsistent work methods	Mistakes made in-patient care	Staff not tapped for ideas
Unbalanced material flow	Idle people or machines	Inappropriate bed assignments on admission	Placing OR scheduling information in multiple systems	Multiple forms, multiple copies, multiple weeks' supplies	Long reach/walk distances	Patient returns (OR, readmit)	Staff not developed by their boss
Having more than we need of anything: supplies, beds etc.	Outpatient lab draw results take 1.5 hrs	Placing multiples calls to transport	Excessive duplication in OR, SPD, pharmacy, nursing units	No standardization of supplies	Centralized printers / copiers / fax locations	Frequent rescheduling of office appointments	Lack of discipline
Not notifying food service of diet changes and discharges	Surgeons waiting in between surgeries	Excess patient transfer/ movement	Multiple signature requirements	Long turnaround times on floor beds	Searching for anything, for example, equipment	Adverse drug events	Staff doesn't follow standard work flow
Extra floor space utilized	Unbalanced scheduling/ workload	PACU or OR backed up	Performing services patient doesn't need, for example, lab work	Unused appointment slots	Multiple patient handoffs	High infection rates and falls	Staff waits to be told what to do
Backups between departments, for example, ED to in-patient admit	Numerous and large waiting rooms	Temporary warehouses and multiple storage locations	Manual distribution of numerous report copies	Empty beds	Long lead-times	High incidence of bill rejects	Staff hired in from the outside
25% of surgical supplies picked and returned to the shelf	Reduced productivity (visible)	Walking intermittent samples to lab or going to get prescriptions multiple times	Sorting, testing, and inspection	Extra rework / hidden problems	Convoluted facility and workplace layouts	Utilization review, infection control, legal, and risk management inspections	Staff does same job over and over
Picking and opening OR instruments but not using them so they must be re-sterilized	Patients wait between multiple appointments	Staff copies patient chart for transfer between facilities	Duplicating physical assessment at triage and in treatment area	Duplication of supplies in temporary storage areas, patient rooms, closets, and so on	Prolonged Pre-Op testing times	Inappropriate communication of patient transfer mode with order entry	Poor morale
Scrap and wasted food	Techs move patients from PACU	Finished patient chart walked to financial counselor	Punching holes in paper to place in the patient chart	One surgical services cart alone had $250k of sutures	Poor workplace layout for patient services	Pharmacy refilling "multiple dose" medications	Staff not included in decision making or financials

Key Observation Work Sheet - Fill in each observation - 1 per page and summarize findings on Key Waste Summary Sheet								
Overview								
Waste Observation Number	Process Owner	Person Assigned Task		Standard Work Updated (If applicable)	All Employees Trained if Applicable	Persons Involved in Solution	Supervisor Sign off	

Detailed Findings	
Waste Discovered - Enter Text Here	Waste Discovered - Enter Before drawing or picture here
Enter Causes and Highlight Root Cause	What is a temporary fix you can implement
Enter Improvement Ideas (if applicable - fill in improvement idea cards and post on idea board)	What is the permanent fix you can implement

HC*/ LB	HC / HB
LC / LB	LC / HB

Enter Action(s) to be taken, responsibilities, Due Date and Follow Up Date						After Picture
Action To Be Taken	Responsibility	Due Date	Follow Up Date	Status	Reaudit Date	

FIGURE 7.1 Key waste observation sheet. * HC—high cost; LB—low benefit; HB—high benefit; LC—low cost.

LEADERSHIP

- *What behaviors does the leadership drive? Is it obvious in the area?*
- *Are there audits in place?*
- *Did you ask people what they are measured on?*
- *Are people afraid of their leaders?*

When we assess companies, we do this same exercise. We look to answer these questions and more. For example, do leaders role model the behaviors they desire? In a Lean environment, there is no place for egos and arrogance. Generally, when we do this exercise, we find that people are usually busy all the time. The next question we have to ask is, "What are they busy doing?"

Homework: *30-30-30 (a good time for this exercise is at the end of the day or right after lunch). Go spend 30–60 min (depending on time available) standing in one place (Ohno circle) in the hospital and see how*

FIGURE 7.2 Honda's three A's. Powered by Honda, Nelson, Mayo, Moody, John Wiley and Sons, 1998

FIGURE 7.3 Ohno circle.

many of the eight wastes you can identify. Shoot for 30 suggestions and then fix one that you find while you are there. It normally works best if you pick an area that is not your own.

Lessons Learned: *Now that you have completed your homework, what did you find? Did you find some waste? What level was it? If you were to tell the process owner about the waste you found, how do you think it would be received? If someone were to come into your area and tell you what they saw, how would you receive it now? How would you have reacted prior to this exercise? The key is not to be defensive; instead, recognize the waste that exists, and work to get rid of it. Generally, outsiders will see wastes that insiders do not see. Was it easier to identify wastes in an area that belonged to someone else? If that was your area to manage, supervise, or work, would you have found as many wasted activities? How would it have felt if you were the supervisor and the wastes were reported to you? How would you have reacted prior to this exercise? Are you a boiled frog?*

Sometimes, outsiders help to show us the waste that we don't see or we intentionally or unintentionally refuse to see. We all tend to be "boiled frogs." The key is not to be defensive. We should recognize the waste that exists, thank those who tell us, and work to eliminate it.

COST OF WASTE

Each time you have to search for something, consider who pays for that waste. Where does the cost of all this waste go? If you are idle, who pays for that idle time? The first answer is your company and the second answer is the customer (patient) or, actually, all of us as a nation in the form of higher healthcare costs. What is all this waste doing to your customer's experience? In factories, the products can't talk back; but, in hospitals and clinics they do, and often. Our customers can help us to identify waste we don't see. We need to listen to our patients, physicians, and co-staff members. Remember: Waste is like a virus; initially, it is hidden and incubates. If we don't treat it or get rid of it, it festers, mutates, and then grows and multiplies all around us. Waste creates workarounds to our processes. Waste creates poor staff and customer satisfaction because we are constantly searching for things and delaying patient care and treatment. Ultimately, waste decreases our ability to compete in the marketplace. Waste causes variation and imperfection in our processes. The big question is, do we have enough dissatisfaction with the waste to create a compelling need to change the system?

BASELINE ENTITLEMENT BENCHMARK

- Baseline—where we are today (measurement-wise).
- Entitlement—the best you can get with the current process or paradigm—normally 3X value-added time.

- Benchmark—implementing a totally new paradigm. The goal of the ideal state is to ask yourself what is not being done or can't be done today, but if it could be done, it would fundamentally change what we do.[*]

FIVE WHY'S

This familiar tool, which involves asking "why" up to five times, helps to get to the root cause of a problem.

PROBLEM STATEMENT

Urine analysis (UA) testing is taking too long (over an hour) to get results in the laboratory, and we just installed a new machine 2 months ago.

- *Why? The new UA machine is a problem.*
- *Why? The laboratory technicians don't believe the results.*
- *Why? They don't trust the new UA machine. They can't believe the machine is better than their old manual style of testing so they always run their manual tests to confirm it.*
- *Why? How often does it agree with the new machine? All the time. The new machine has never been wrong! In fact, the new machine has proven some of their manual tests were wrong.*
- *Why do they continue to conduct the manual tests?*
- *No one has investigated this before and forced them to stop the manual test.*

Lesson Learned: *It is not unusual for people to react to the symptoms of the problem without getting the facts. Sometimes, the problems are hidden. Sometimes, we believe we think we are experts only to find out we don't know what we don't know. For example, many times we only know how to do what we need to do on the machine and don't understand all its capabilities. As you reduce the waste in processes, you shrink the time it takes to get the patient or product through the process. If you get patients through the process faster, you then increase your capacity. We look at capacity as work plus waste.*

ANOTHER TOOL TO GET RID OF WASTE: THE FIVE W'S AND TWO H'S[†]

The goal of this tool is to work to find the root cause of a problem. How do you know when you have identified the root cause? The answer is: when you have fixed the problems so it never comes back. This is also called *Poka Yoke*.[‡]

---

[*] Joel Barker, *Business of Paradigms* video.
[†] Yuzo Yasuda, *40 Years, 20 Million Ideas* (New York: Productivity Press) 1991.
[‡] Shigeo Shingo, *Poka Yoke, Zero Quality Control* (New York: Productivity Press) 1986.

The five W's are composed of asking why for each of the five W's (*when?, where?, what?, who?,* and *why?*). The two H's are *how?* and *how much?*. This method is described in detail in Shingo's book, *Kaizen and the Art of Creative Thinking.*[*]

- **WHEN**—When is the best time to do it? Does it have to be done then?
- **WHERE**—Where is it being done? Does it have to be done here?
- **WHAT**—What is being done? Can this work be eliminated?
- **WHO**—Who is doing it? Would it be better to have someone else do it? Why am I doing it?
- **WHY**—Why is that work necessary? Clarify its purpose
- **HOW**—How is it being done? Is this the best way to do it? Are there any other ways of doing it?
- **HOW MUCH**—How much does it cost now? How much will it cost to improve?

The goal of asking the five W's and two H's is to get to the root cause and lay the groundwork for creative problem solving.

PROBLEM-SOLVING MODEL

Every company should standardize on a problem-solving model and teach it to every employee. Lean is continuous problem solving, so we need all our employees to have a common language when they get together to work in teams to fix problems.

Many companies/hospitals have standardized on the Six Sigma DMAIC model, Shewhart's Plan Do Study Act (PDSA), or the PDCA Deming model. The automotive companies standardized on the eight discipline (8D) problem-solving model (Table 7.2).[†] AlliedSignal (now Honeywell) had a nine-step problem-solving model (Figure 7.4). Regardless of the model used, it is important that everyone be trained in the model so they speak the same language. Most models are a spinoff of Shewhart's PDSA model. Most problem-solving models follow this format:

- What is the problem?
- Develop counter-measures.
- What is the baseline or point from which we are starting and developing the key measures around the process that will ultimately determine if you improved the process?
- What is the vision for where we want to be?
- What are the gaps between the baseline and the vision?
- What is the root cause? List all the gaps that exist. Filter the gaps into those you can control vs. those that have to be given to a higher level of management to solve.
- Brainstorm solutions to how we can overcome the gaps between the baseline and the vision.

[*] Shigeo Shingo, *Kaizen and the Art of Creative Thinking* (Hakuto-Shobo) 1959; English translation (Enna Products Corp. and PCS Inc.) 2007.
[†] Rambaud, *8D Problem Solving*, PHRED Solutions, 2007.

TABLE 7.2
8D Problem-Solving Model

The Global 8 Disciplines Are:	
1.	Form the Team
2.	Describe the Problem
3.	Contain the Problem
4.	I.D. the Root Cause
5.	Formulate and Verify Corrective Actions
6.	Correct the Problem and Confirm the Effects
7.	Prevent the Problem
8.	Congratulate the Team

Source: Rambaud, *8D Problem Solving*, PHRED Solutions, 2007. With permission.

- Implement the solutions one at a time.
- Check to see if they solved the problem.
- Start over again.

At Toyota, the word *problem* is not a bad word, contrary to most U.S. companies. If we don't admit we have a problem or develop systems to expose problems, then we will never reach world class. If we continue to bury problems, they just get worse. A good analogy for this is our patients themselves. If we have a problem, what do we do? We go to the doctor. What happens if we put off going to the doctor? In most cases, the problem will become acute. By the time we go to the doctor, the condition may be much more complex and difficult to treat. This is true for organizations as well.

Lesson Learned: *Make "problems" a good word. Find them, identify them, don't be afraid to call them what they are, and fix them so they don't come back.*

PROBLEM STATEMENTS

Go to the floor or department and discover first-hand what the real problem is. Test (ask why) to see if the answer is a symptom of the problem or a true root cause.

It is important to provide the necessary training to identify a good statement of the problem. A good problem statement should be an objective statement of the problem with any relevant data.

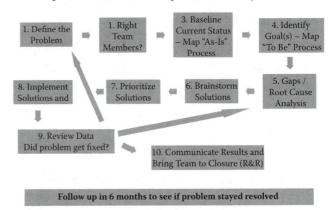

FIGURE 7.4   AlliedSignal solving model.

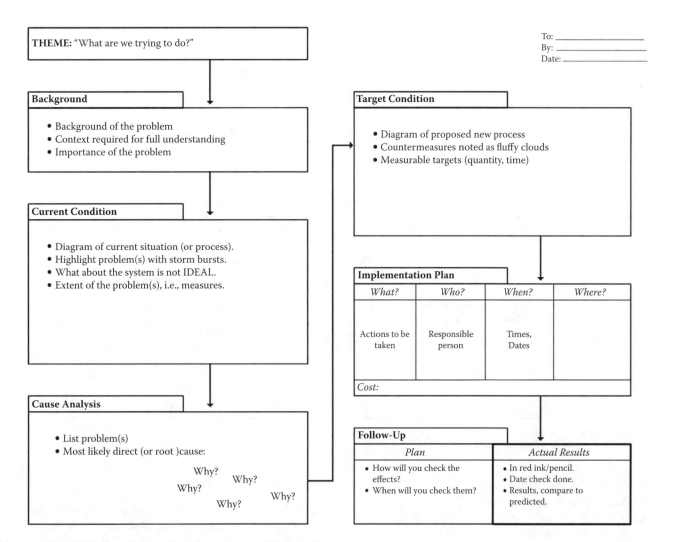

THEME: "What are we trying to do?"

To: _____
By: _____
Date: _____

Background

- Background of the problem
- Context required for full understanding
- Importance of the problem

Current Condition

- Diagram of current situation (or process).
- Highlight problem(s) with storm bursts.
- What about the system is not IDEAL.
- Extent of the problem(s), i.e., measures.

Cause Analysis

- List problem(s)
- Most likely direct (or root)cause:

Why? Why? Why? Why? Why?

Target Condition

- Diagram of proposed new process
- Countermeasures noted as fluffy clouds
- Measurable targets (quantity, time)

Implementation Plan

What?	Who?	When?	Where?
Actions to be taken	Responsible person	Times, Dates	

Cost:

Follow-Up

Plan	Actual Results
• How will you check the effects? • When will you check them?	• In red ink/pencil. • Date check done. • Results, compare to predicted.

FIGURE 7.5 A3 problem-solving model. Source: From Durward K., *The A3 Report*, "http://www.coe.montana.edu/ie/faculty/sobek/a3/report.htm" With permission.

It should not include a solution and should not be prescriptive (ties in with Baldridge criteria). It should be verifiable.

A bad problem statement would be

- 7:30 a.m. first case start times are 32% on time due to surgeons being late.

This is missing verifiable data and assumes the physician is the problem.

- 7:30 a.m. case start times are late, resulting in poor physician satisfaction.

This is missing verifiable data and assumes it results in poor physician satisfaction.

- 7:30 a.m. first case starts are 32% on time because we need to improve pretesting.

While the solution may be true, it might not be the root cause. Thus, it sets the problem solvers with a paradigm of what the solution should be.

An example of a good problem statement:

- 7:30 a.m. first case start times are 32% on time vs. our goal of 90% on time.

Clearly stating the scope and objectives of the project will help the team achieve the objectives.

FIGURE 7.6 Mr. and Mrs. Ishikawa October 1974. Source: Courtesy of Protzman Family Archives.

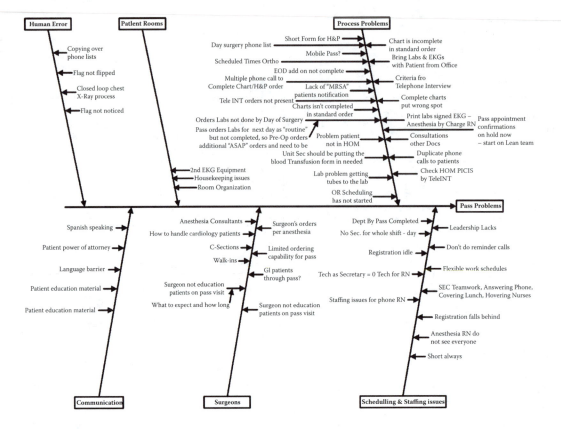

FIGURE 7.7   Fishbone example.

- Where does the process start?
- Where does the process end?
- What is the customer demand for the product?
- What is the peak demand the cell should be able to meet?
- What models/options are included or excluded?
- What sub-processes exist?
- How many shifts are used vs. how many should be used?
- Has new equipment been developed or bought that needs to be installed?
- What other objectives must be met (i.e., housekeeping, inventory, quality, space, others)?

ROOT CAUSE ANALYSIS—A3 STRATEGY

A great tool for root cause analysis is the tool Toyota uses called the A3 document (Figure 7.5). It is a way to get all your information in one place on one sheet of paper. A book that highlights this approach is *Understanding A3 Thinking: A Critical Component of Toyota's PDCA Management.*[*]

---

[*] Durward K. Sobek II and Art Smalley, *Understanding A3 Thinking: A Critical Component of Toyota's PDCA Management* (CRC Press) 2009, http://www.surveygizmo.com/survey-blog/question-scale-length/.

FISHBONES AND LEAN

Kaoru Ishikawa is credited with developing the fishbone tool (Figure 7.6). Today, this is known as one of the basic Total Quality (TQ) tools. These tools are very applicable in hospitals. The fishbone is a tool to help identify root cause. It works by putting the problem at the head of the fishbone, then brainstorming and categorizing all the reasons for the problems (Figure 7.7). The first layer of problems, which are placed on the main branches of the fish, is normally only the symptoms of the problems that we see. We then ask "why?" for each major branch, which creates sub-branches. We ask "why?" until we get to the bottom branch or root cause. This tool provides a way to see all the problems in an area at a glance. Fishbones are a great tool for collecting, categorizing, and root-causing feedback from staff.

It is important to leverage tools to gain an understanding of the root cause of the problem. Identifying root causes allows for the correction of defects and are essential in preventing problems from reoccurring which ultimately improves the overall process and quality of the result.

If you don't know where you are going, any path will take you there.

8 Basic Lean Tools

EXECUTIVE SUMMARY

This chapter continues with the assessment or analysis phase in the BASICS system implementation model. It defines a process as a series of actions and operations conducing to an end. Each action or process step is categorized as being value-added, non-value-added, or non-value-added but necessary (related to what the customer defines as valuable).

The criteria for value-added are:

1. The customer cares about the step and will pay for it.
2. It physically changes a thing.
3. It is done right the first time.

Shingo discovered, as he was studying production, that in the past it was always thought that process and operations were on the same axis; however, he recognized that there was the need to separate the two and study them independently and then merge them together. This is the Shingo methodology. The product process axis is analyzed first, and then we will analyze the operations (i.e., full work analysis of the operator) axis. We explore the differences between the product flow and the operator flow and why it is important to assess them separately. Product flow is performed by following a product (in this case, a patient) through the process, measuring the time increments and distance traveled, and identifying each step as value-added, non-value-added, or non-value-added but necessary.

The Product Process Flow uses a tool called TIPS. This stands for:

- Transport
- Inspect
- Process
- Store

One important example is explained by analyzing how physician rounding creates what are called "lot" delays.

The chapter discusses the concept of a group tech matrix. This is where the review of a process or products may be grouped into "like families," value streams or service lines. Point-to-point diagrams show the flow of a product or patient through an area and spaghetti diagrams are used to show staff/operator walk patterns, as this is an important Lean process which provides a very visual display of waste. Many times products or patients can literally travel a mile or more during a visit or stay.

The operator analysis is often based on videotaping and careful evaluation of the operators' activities. It can be broken into:

1. Required work
2. Unnecessary work
3. Idle time

Total labor time is discussed, as is workload balancing. This information can be used to obtain the right staffing levels.

We explore Frank Gilbreth's Therbligs, which are the 18 fundamental motions of a worker.

The processes of turnovers and changeovers are analyzed, which are, respectively, the procedures of turning over a room on a nursing unit floor or changing over a surgical suite from one patient to the next. It compares the changeover to the analysis of "a racing car pit stop" which is accomplished in seconds, exemplifying setup reduction techniques such as working on steps in parallel versus in series and further breaking work down into "internal "and "external" time. For example, steps can be carried out while the patient is out of the surgical suite time (internal, i.e., when the suite is down or unavailable for use by the surgeon) or things can be done only when the patient is still in the surgical suite (external). It discusses the concept of SMED, an industrial term that looks at reducing internal time to less than 10 min and stands for Single Minute Exchange of Dies on large stamping presses.

KEY LEARNINGS

1. Understanding the process of value-added and non value-added identification.
2. Understanding that product flow and operator flows contribute to different pieces of the Lean puzzle.
3. Understanding of, and discussing the concepts of, internal and external times and the value inherent in reducing setup or turnover times, which increase capacity and throughput velocity.
4. Analyzing the operator or staff to determine appropriate labor requirements.

ANALYZE/ASSESSMENT TOOLS

We have to grasp not only the Know-How but also 'Know-Why',

—Shingo

Phases

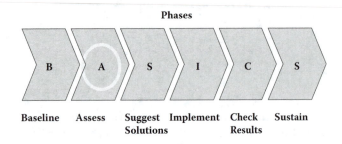

Baseline   Assess   Suggest   Implement   Check   Sustain
                       Solutions   Results

FIGURE 8.1   Basics model—Assess.

The tools in the assessment phase help break down the process layer by layer, as if you were peeling back an onion, to reveal the waste. The application of each tool enables us to drill deeper into what is really occurring in the process or "value stream" (Figure 8.1).

Utilizing Lean tools provides the opportunity to analyze a process from several facets. The first analysis tool is to follow the product. In healthcare, this can be a thing, like a drug, blood tube, x-ray, or chart, but more commonly, it is the patient going through the process. The second analysis tool is to follow the operator. The operator is the person performing the activities that transform the product or service into what is desired by the customer. This can be any person in the healthcare service delivery system, e.g., a physician, administrator, manager, unit secretary, nurse, or laboratory technician. The third analysis tool looks at turnovers/changeovers that may occur in the process. In healthcare, changeovers can be loading and unloading a patient from an magnetic resonance imaging (MRI) machine or turning over an operating room (OR) suite from one patient to another.

When we talk about the overall process flow, we are looking at the inter-relationship between process steps and the activities that staff perform. In Lean, the flow of the product/patient and the work of the operator/staff person are on two different planes (Figure 8.2). Applying the tools methodically will enable you to deconstruct a process into its individual sequence of steps, and then transform and reconstruct the process into one that improves customer value. The transformation within a process occurs through analyzing and eliminating waste, creating the right work flow, developing standard work, understanding working to customer demand, level loading the activity or demand, layout and design, and providing the right tools and quantity of supplies (inventory) at the right time and in the right place. The application of Lean tools results in a reduction of errors, decreased variability, improvement in throughput, increased productivity, and improvement in overall quality. Ultimately, these are financially rewarding to the supplier of the services or product.

We will continue to remind you that during each phase, change management must be top of mind. As you learn more about the tools and their applications, remember that when you initially expose people to the terms and tools, there is a language "conversion" that needs to occur from manufacturing to healthcare as the terminology and the manufacturing references can be foreign to healthcare workers. Examples include "operators" = staff or worker, "products" = patients or test tubes etc., "in storage" = waiting. This is extremely important in order to ease the transition and help in the adoption.

Lesson Learned: *Be mindful as you expose healthcare personnel to the Lean concepts and tools that manufacturing terminology can become a barrier to acceptance, as we often hear, "We do not work in a factory... we take care of patients."*

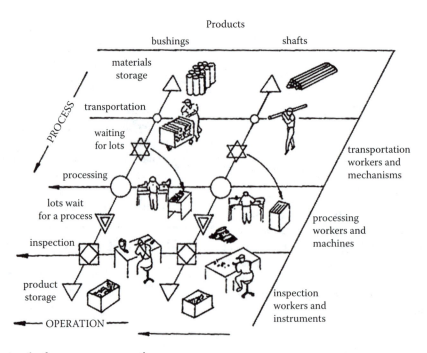

FIGURE 8.2   Shingo network of processes vs. operations.

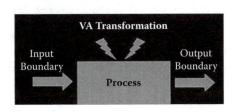

FIGURE 8.3 Process description.

BASICS—Assess the Process

Step One: Understand and Assess the Overall Process

A process is "a series of actions or operations conducing to an end; a continuous operation or treatment especially in manufacture."* Processes have an input and output boundary; a beginning and endpoint (Figure 8.3). A "process" takes place or is set in motion because "something" needs to be accomplished. The process provides some physical transformation to the product and/or emotional transformation to the patient going through the process. The goal within the Lean System is to expend resources only on activities that are "value-added to customer." Processes can also be broken down into sub-process steps. We categorize each sub-process/activity or step within a process into one of three categories of perceived customer value:

1. Value-added work
2. Non-value-added but "necessary" work
3. Unnecessary work or idle time

Value-Added

There are three criteria that must be met in order to determine if there is "value" within a process, with minor variations. Depending on the definition and source reference, the criteria for meeting customer value can be defined as:[†]

1. The customer cares about the step.
2. It physically changes the thing.
3. It is done right the first time.

A variation to the value-added definitions from above is any activity that meets the following three criteria:

1. The customer is willing to pay for it.
2. The activity physically changes the product: form, fit, shape, size, or function.
3. It is done right the first time.

Subjectivity comes into play when applying the above descriptions in "real life" healthcare scenarios as to the definition of what a customer "perceives as value." Based on our experience, we have chosen to alter the value-added criteria for healthcare:

1. Physically changes the product or physically or emotionally changes the patient for the better, as perceived by the patient.
2. The customer is willing to pay for the perceived value-added activity.
3. The activity is done right the first time.

When a step or activity meets all three criteria, we consider it value-added. We are often asked how to categorize when a patient asks a nurse a question or the nurse spends time with a patient because the patient is distraught or in need of emotional support. We consider any of these types of activities value-added because they are perceived by the patient as emotionally changing for the better.

Lesson Learned: *A "nurse's touch" is considered value-added.*

Non-Value-Added Activities/Work

If a process step/activity does not meet all of the above criteria, it will generally fall into the non-value-added category. Non-value-added activities generally rob us of time and/or resources, contribute to staff frustration and do not add value to the service or product from the customer's perspective. Non-value activities can be divided into three sub-categories:

1. Non-value-added but necessary work
2. Unnecessary work
3. Idle time

Needless to say, one can get into very heated arguments over what is value-added and what is not.

Non-Value-Added but Necessary Work

The largest cause of these arguments is process steps/sub-process activities that don't meet all three criteria, but meet one or two criteria. These steps we call not value-added but necessary. "Non-value-added but necessary" tasks provide an alternative if the evaluating person or group determines the majority of the criteria are met and/or the process cannot be eliminated and is needed to achieve the end result. Many times, these steps are regulatory requirements or hospital policy. In some cases, technology has not yet advanced to the point of eliminating the process step or task, but may in the future. Sometimes the process controls are not in place to do it right the first time. Examples could be filling out a medication reconciliation form, performing x-rays, or laboratory tests.

Unnecessary Work

Unnecessary work does not fit any of the three value-added criteria. They are simply tasks that shouldn't be done. Unnecessary tasks normally emanate from the following:

- Unclear or unwritten procedures.
- "Non-standard work."

---

* *Webster's Dictionary*, http://www.merriam-webster.com/dictionary/process.
† As defined in the AMA video *Time: The Next Dimension of Quality*, by the American Management Association; featuring John Guaspari and Edward Hay.

- "It's the way we've always done it."
- There was a good reason for it at one time but the reason for it no longer exists, i.e., technology changed or the original problem was corrected but we still do the activity as it was never removed from the process.

This is where many over-processing wastes originate.

IDLE TIME

We constantly see idle time when we watch videos of staff working their process. This can be due to employing a full time worker when in fact only "fractional labor" or a few hours of an employee was needed and, there is literally nothing for the person to do at that point (workloads are not balanced), the job was not designed well or the person is just plain lazy. It can also occur because of a misalignment between scheduled resources and customer demand. In any case, we don't normally view idle time as the person's fault; we view it as a fault of the system.

WARRANTED TIME EXCEPTION

In healthcare, we run into situations one would never run into in a factory, such as having to notify a family member their loved one is dying or a patient who has become a friend, passes away. Healthcare staff have difficult jobs that should be especially valued in our society. It takes not only a highly trained and skilled person, but also an exceptional kind of person to be a nurse. In these situations, we build this time into our analysis. Nurses, especially on oncology units or in high-stress areas such as the intensive care (ICU) or trauma units, need time to recover and recharge. The standard work should build this time in where it is warranted.

Lesson Learned: *Just because an activity "has to be done" does not necessarily make it value-added. We have to give the patient a nursing assessment, but the assessment, while it may be necessary, is still an inspection step. If you think about it with a very open mind, there is no physical change to the patient so it is considered non-value-added but necessary because it doesn't meet all three criteria. This does not mean the nurse is not value-added.*

One somewhat controversial example of value-added vs. non-value-added is the physical examination performed by a physician. Obviously, one would have to agree that the physician examination is necessary in order to identify physical changes which may aid in determining the course of treatment and/or patient care plan; however, it does not meet the strict value-added criteria. This is because the examination in and of itself does not physically change the person. We would argue that the examination is actually an inspection step by the physician to try to ascertain or identify the patient's presenting problem. Shigeo Shingo refers to the doctor examination this way when he states "judgment inspection… feeds information back to processing. It is like a medical examination… The sooner a symptom is identified,

the more quickly and efficiently the problem can be treated… In summary: Judgment inspection discovers defects, while informative inspections reduce them."[*] Deming said, "You cannot inspect quality into the product,"[†] and Henry Ford said, "There can be no quality without a standard."[‡]

A customer, however, may perceive value since the "physical inspection" or examination can reveal a problem or "no problem." Even though it may not meet the strict three criteria definition of value-added in which physical or emotional change occurs, it is perceived as necessary by the customer, so we would categorize the examination as non-value-added but necessary; however, this will continue to be controversial in many circles.

While the doctor examination is technically inspection, the words spoken by the doctor to reassure the patient ("you are going to be OK") are perceived as emotionally adding value by the patient. Therefore, we do agree that any communication regarding the diagnosis or plan of treatment anywhere during the process would be considered value-added. This is because we believe the dissemination of information to the patient at any stage is value-added, assuming it is emotionally changing the patient for the better. Future technological advances may someday eliminate the need for the physical examination by the physician.

ASSESS THE PROCESS—PRODUCT PROCESS FLOW (PPF)

This approach was developed by Shigeo Shingo, who first realized that "production constitutes a network of process and operations, phenomena that lie along intersecting axis. Improving production, process phenomena should be given top priority."[§] In the past, it was thought that process and operations were on the same axis.

That is why the heart and premise of this Lean improvement system is to separate the two and study them independently and then integrate them. We refer to this as the Shingo methodology. We will analyze the product process axis first, and then we will analyze the operations axis or what the operator does to the product. We do not have to do (PPF) analysis on any step that was eliminated in the value stream mapping process.

The PPF follows the product through the value stream. This tool cannot be done in a classroom or conference room. One has to go to the area (*Gemba*) and "become the thing, information, or patient" as it travels through the process and experience its path first-hand, asking questions as you go.

---

[*] Shigeo Shingo, *A Study of the Toyota Production System from an Industrial Engineering Point of View* (New York: Productivity Press) 1989.

[†] Mary Walton, *Deming Management Method* (New York: Putnam Publishing) 1986.

[‡] Henry Ford, *Today and Tomorrow*, Reprint edition (New York: Productivity Press) 1988.

[§] Shigeo Shingo, Japan Management Association *Non Stock Production: The Shingo System for Continous Improvement*, 1987 (New York: Productivity Press) 1988.

This process exposes the next layer under the value stream map of what is actually happening to the "product" throughout the process.

MAPPING THE PROCESS—IDENTIFYING PROCESS BOXES

In order to understand the PPF tool, one needs to understand "what defines a product." Lean publications refer to the "product" in various ways depending on what business problem you are trying to solve. The product can take many shapes or forms in the healthcare environment and is defined by what the customer desires.

When starting the process flow analysis we need to consider the business problem. What processes need to be analyzed in order to find what caused the business problem and what opportunities exist for elimination of waste or improvements? Sometimes, following the product as product transformations occur is not as easy as it may seem. It is important to remember that you must "become the product" at each step of the process to make sure that you accurately capture events from the product's perspective. This sounds easier than it is as just about everyone mixes up the product and operator when they are first exposed to this tool.

For example, a patient who presents to an Emergency Department (ED) is the "product" of the process flow of "delivery of care" in the ED.

In the ED setting, the "end product" from the customer perspective is the ED course of treatment. To determine the treatment, we need the results from the laboratory tests ordered by the physician. The test result starts as "a physician order," turns into a blood draw by the nurse, is then transformed into "test tubes" that are sent to the laboratory, placed in a blood analyzer, and finally transformed into "the result." The result is then reviewed by the physician to determine the proper course of treatment, which is what the customer desires.

In the pharmacy setting, the end product is the medication taken by the patient. The medication starts as a complaint by the patient, once verified, turns into an order by the physician moves to the pharmacy, is reviewed, then (filled) picked from the shelf, then sent to the floor, retrieved by the nurse, taken to the patient's room, and finally given to the patient by the nurse. The customer "value-added" is in taking the prescribed medication assuming it fixed the orginal patient complaint.

The concept of understanding "the product" in this context is sometimes difficult but extremely important as you begin to apply Lean tools to identify waste. In the beginning, we all tend to mix up the product piece and the operator piece.

PRODUCT PROCESS FLOW ANALYSIS TOOL

PPF is performed by following the product through the defined process. The PPF tool facilitates the identification of wastes through analyzing each process step required to get the product to the end of the defined process. We denote what happens at each step, where, and how far the product travels in each step. It is important to assess "customer value" at each step, assigning the appropriate designation as

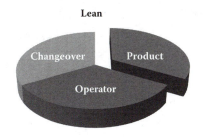

FIGURE 8.4 Pieces of Lean pie chart—product.

to whether it is a value-added process or a non-value-added but necessary process. This will help to determine which steps should be eliminated, simplified or combined with another step, also note any improvements that could help the process. Additionally, time increments and travel distance are measured for each step as applicable to determine the total throughput time and distance traveled by the patient or product (in other words the time it takes the product to complete the process), as well as any time a rework occurs. The combination of information flow and product flow provides a comprehensive analysis of the current state of the process from the "product" or "patient" perspective. (Figure 8.4)

A PPF can be performed by observation and documentation, or videotaping and analyzing each step. There are advantages to videotaping.[*] Shingo stated in his book, *The Toyota Production System from An Industrial Engineering Standpoint*, "We recently purchased a video camera and began filming operations on the shop floor. After each recording session, we'd invite the worker we had filmed, the improvement team concerned, and the worker's immediate supervisor and play the tape for them… We usually came up with lots of suggestions for improvement… and we'd implement the good ones immediately."

We follow the same process. As the product is tracked through the process, each step is analyzed individually. The tool uses an acronym we call TIPS,[†] which stands for transport, inspect, process, store. TIPS is utilized to analyze and categorize what is truly happening to the product at each step within the process.

Once we have baselined the existing process, we determine which steps in the process can be eliminated, rearranged, simplified, or combined. Once completed, we have a baseline and potential future time for total throughput.

The use of the PPF tools is described in Shigeo Shingo's, *Toyota Production System From an Industrial Engineering Viewpoint*, and also in his book, *Non Stock Production*. Process flow analysis is also described in the book, *IE for the Shop Floor: Productivity Through Process Analysis*.[‡]

---

[*] Shigeo Shingo, *A Study of the Toyota Production System from an Industrial Engineering Point of View* (New York: Productivity Press) 1989.

[†] Shigeo Shingo, *A Study of the Toyota Production System from an Industrial Engineering Point of View* (New York: Productivity Press) 1989.

[‡] Junichi Ishiwata, *IE for the Shop Floor: Productivity Through Process Analysis* (New York: Productivity Press) 1997.

TIPS ANALYSIS

There are four things a product/process can do:[*]

- Transport
- Inspect
- Process
- Store

Transport is the act of moving the "patient, product, or information" from one place to another. We look at both distance and time as the product or patient travels through the process.

Inspect is the act of checking or examining the "patient, product, or information" during the process. Inspection steps are highlighted to make problems in the process visible. As an example, if laboratory tests are ordered and the physician reviews the results, the testing itself is a process and the review of the results is considered inspection. Some inspection is needed at critical failure points of a process; however, if the process is optimally constructed, then no inspection should be needed. As stated in the book, *The Elegant Solution*,[†] in most companies today "getting it right has been replaced by getting it out." We must return to "getting it right" the first time. Processes should facilitate activities being done right the first time and should include mistake-proofing methods within the process whenever possible to eliminate errors and the need to inspect. In theory, inspection is really a non-value-added process step. We think Shingo separated out inspection (as it could be considered a non-value-added process) in order to highlight it because things were not being done right the first time.

Process or processing is the act that physically changes the product in form, fit, shape, size, or function. Changes to fix or correct the product—what we call rework—can typically be measured with amount, time, cost, yield, weight, etc.

Only process steps have operations that can be considered value-added. The other three criteria of TIPS (transport, inspect, and store) by definition are non-value-added. Our experience is that value-added processing is only a small fraction of the total time a product or patient spends in the process. It is not unusual for value-added to be less than 5%–10% of the total time the patient or product is going through the process.

Store stands for storage. In healthcare we use the word "store" to designate wait-time or idle time in a process. Our experience is that patients (and family members) spend most of their time in storage, normally alone, waiting for something to happen. We have found in all the analyses we have performed that it is not unusual to have storage (wait times) in the 50%–80% range or more (Figure 8.5). In their book, *Competing Against Time*, Stalk and Hout had a rule called the .05–5 rule.[‡] This rule "…highlights the

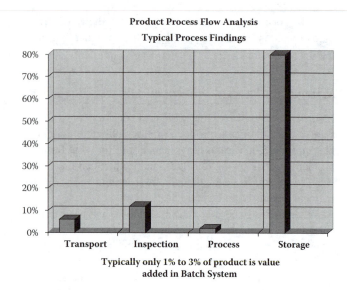

Product Process Flow Analysis

Typical Process Findings

Typically only 1% to 3% of product is value added in Batch System

FIGURE 8.5   PPF (Product Process Flow) analysis graph.

poor 'time productivity' of most organizations since most products and many services are actually receiving value for .05%–5% of the time they are in the value delivery systems of their companies." In other words, 95%–99.5% of the time nothing is actually happening to the product or, in our case, the patient.

They also go on to describe what they call the 3/3 rule. This rule states that during the 95%–99.5% of the time the products are waiting, they are waiting for one of three things:

1. Completion of the batch
2. Completion of physical or intellectual property
3. Management to make a decision as when to move the batch on to the next step in the process

In healthcare, we have found both of these rules to be true, even though they were originally constructed around manufacturing. With all this non-value-added activity, no wonder patients are frustrated as they go through the healthcare continuum of care.

We need to be careful as we identify and assign some activities or steps as storage. If a patient's body is recovering from an operation, we would argue this is not storage but value-added since the body is physically changing, or if a patient is receiving an IV medication, the waiting may be part of the treatment. The key is to be able to define at which point we move from when our body is recovering into storage or waiting. In some cases, we add an extra code to our spreadsheet to track recovery time. It is also worth noting that recovery time can be reduced, e.g., using non-invasive surgery techniques. This shows even value-added steps can be improved. Since storage in a process tends to be where the majority of waste occurs, storage can be defined with more granularity. This granularity helps us better understand what opportunities may be identified to improve the process.

[*] Shigeo Shingo, *A Study of the Toyota Production System from an Industrial Engineering Point of View* (New York: Productivity Press) 1989.

[†] Matthew May, *The Elegant Solution* (Free Press) 2007.

[‡] Stalk, George/Hout, Thomas, *Competing Against Time: How Time-Based Competition is Reshaping Global Markets* (Macmillan) 1990.

TYPES OF STORAGE

We said earlier that storage can be broken down into more minute detail. There are three types of storage:

1. RM—raw material
2. WIP—work in progress
3. FG—finished goods

RAW MATERIAL STORAGE

"Raw material" is a product or patient that has had no labor added to it. An example of raw material in healthcare would be the physician blood test order waiting to be assigned to a phlebotomist for collection. Another example is the patient's initial arrival into the waiting room prior to speaking to anyone or a box of blood test tubes waiting on the receiving dock for someone to open the package.

WORK IN PROCESS STORAGE

The definition of work in progress or process (WIP) is a product or patient that has had labor added to it.

An example of this would be a patient in the ED who was registered or triaged, or had some blood tests drawn and is now waiting for results. Another example is our package of blood test tubes that was moved to a desk waiting to be opened and received into the computer system.

FINISHED GOODS STORAGE

Finished goods is a product or patient where all labor has been added to it and the product or patient has completed the entire process. In a product's case, the only thing left would be to ship it to the customer or, in the patient's case, it may be where they are waiting for their ride to leave the hospital. Another example of finished goods might be a completed radiology test "dictation" waiting to be seen by the ED doctor. Finished goods for the package of blood test tubes would be when testing on the package was completed and the package was waiting in storage to be properly discarded (or go to the hazardous waste landfill).

FURTHER DELINEATING STORAGE— TYPES OF WORK IN PROCESS

WIP is a critical component within a process—especially in healthcare—because many services are time sensitive. Understanding WIP within a healthcare process is important as it contributes directly to customer service and expectations.

WIP translates to waiting or idle time for patients and families and delays in treatments. In essence, WIP is stored labor capacity or stored cash flow tied up in the delivery system that cannot be valued until it is completed and billed.

To better understand this conceptually, we need to understand the three categories of WIP. The first two were explained by Shingo[*] and the third we have added:

1. Lot delay: one piece or patient is waiting for the rest of the lot or the "linear batch to complete" prior to going to the next step.
2. Between process delay: the piece or entire lot is waiting for next step in the process.
3. Within process delay: we invented this delay more than 12 years ago as we found instances, especially in healthcare, where patients or things going through the process were interrupted, but it did not fit the criteria of a lot or between process delay. The definition of this delay is where a process is started and then interrupted or stopped before being completed.

Let's consider some examples of each delay.

LOT DELAY

Let's use the illustration of physician rounding again to describe the concept of a "lot delay." A physician arrives on a unit to perform morning rounds. The complete process of rounding encompasses the patient examination, documentation, and writing orders. The physician could have 10 patients on the unit and, because of the centralized location of the charting station, the practice is to examine 4–6 patients sequentially in a batch, one after another without stopping to document or write orders. When reaching the charting station, the physician proceeds to write their notes and orders for all 4–6 patients at once or in a "batch." Let's assume we are following and analyzing the first patient. The first patient is now waiting while the next 3–5 patients are seen. We consider the first patient in the process to be in a "lot delay" state, as their orders and notes are waiting until all the other patients are examined and orders written. We say the first patient or product is now waiting for the rest of their "buddies" to be completed prior to moving on to the next step.

POTENTIAL LEAN SOLUTION EXAMPLE #1

One improvement might be to implement computerized order entry (CPOE) by the physician to facilitate the elimination of "lot delays" through "real-time" computer documentation and time-order entry. The orders would be completed prior to leaving each patient room. This eliminates the batching of the patient's orders. When you multiply this times several hundred beds at each hospital, this can improve the process dramatically. Charts and nurses stationed outside the unit or at bedside (provided they are available there) help to eliminate the "batching" of documentation and orders.

---

[*] Shigeo Shingo, *A Study of the Toyota Production System from an Industrial Engineering Point of View* (New York: Productivity Press) 1989.

POTENTIAL LEAN SOLUTION EXAMPLE #2

Another batching issue we discussed earlier in the book is the fact that most physicians make rounds at about the same time each day. This creates a bottleneck of orders and nursing duties which need to be completed and batching of discharges. There is typically a large disconnect in coordinating discharge times. The batching process results in a large bolus of discharges late in the morning after orders get processed. This affects staff significantly by forcing them to try to get all their patients ready to go home at approximately the same time. Then housekeeping gets requests for a group of rooms to clean (turnover) at the same time.

This is a difficult Lean problem to manage, but it can be dealt with by trying to get physicians to round at different times or by changing some of the staffing ratios to coordinate with patient needs and physician preferences. If you think about it, the discharge process should start with the initial patient visit to their physician. The physician generally knows how long the patient is going to require in the hospital or it can be suggested by their insurance company. The expected discharge date and time should become part of the patient's chart right from the beginning. Some hospitals provide patients with schedule discharge times in an attempt to level load the discharge work. It can also be addressed by changing the discharge process as organizations move to proactive planning in the days prior to discharges and how physicians and nursing floors track and time their discharges. This would also help with patient and family expectations and improve customer satisfaction.

BETWEEN PROCESS DELAY

Between process storage delay is defined as any delay, waiting, or idle time that occurs while the entire lot of products, patients, or information is waiting for the next process to begin. Once again, in the manufacturing world, the use of the word storage is common. You will find that, in healthcare, there will be some resistance to the use of the word "storage" when referring to processes where the product is a "patient."

As an example: A patient presents to the laboratory for a routine blood draw. The process for the blood draw from the patient's perspective is

1. Sign in
2. Complete registration
3. Receive blood draw
4 Pay for visit or co-pay

If the patient has to sit idle in a wait or "storage" state in between any of these steps, it is an example of a "between process delay."

An example of information flow for a pharmacy or drug store is:

1. The order from the doctor's office waits on the fax machine
2. Then it waits to be entered into the system
3. Then it waits to be filled
4. Then it waits to be picked up

When the order waits (by itself, if one-piece flow, or in a group with all the other orders, i.e., batching), in between any of these steps it is considered a between process delay.

WITHIN PROCESS DELAY

We created the "within process delay" because, particularly in healthcare (sometimes manufacturing), it was found that many processes begin but then get interrupted at critical times. Interruptions in the middle of processes create unique challenges. Many times, errors occur when a standard process "flow" is disrupted. This can create rework (or the need to redo some of what was just done) or workarounds to make sure the process was in fact completed and performed correctly. Sometimes it's not till later when the nurse or physician discovers the problem do we realize the process was never finished, or worse, we discover it when the patient brings it up or reminds us.

We find this with medication administration where a nurse may have been interrupted, then got sidetracked and forgot to return to the original patient. Another example might be the patient/nurse discharge process. At the time of discharge, the nurse provides comprehensive discharge information, which includes going through each medication and having the patient read back the instructions to make sure the patient has full understanding of what was discussed. In the middle of the instruction about one of the medications, she receives a call about another patient, causing a delay in the discharge instruction process, creating idle or storage/wait time for the patient in the discharge process. Because of the delay, the nurse found she had to start over when she went to go back through the medication read-back, which we refer to as process "rework." Because of the nature of healthcare interruptions, "within process" delays generally cause some rework or redoing of part of the process to ensure it is completed properly. Within process delays need to be minimized as interruptions create opportunities for errors to occur, thus compromising quality and outcomes.

WHY BREAK DOWN TYPES OF STORAGE?

Since storage or waiting is non-value-added, being able to clearly identify what type of storage is occurring throughout the process is beneficial to determine the process improvement opportunity (Table 8.1). If one were to categorize all the steps as storage, one would miss the opportunities to improve on the throughput opportunities that exist in the process. For example, batching is only found where lot delays are present. Between process delays can normally be eliminated up front because they are normally hand offs where no value is added.

TABLE 8.1

PPF (Product Process Flow) Quick Reference Needs Work

Quick Reference Notes	Product Process Flows
When to use	Next Level of detail after VSM to determine opportunities to identify and eliminate "waste"
What it delivers	Follows the product through the process "value stream" used to identify: • Waste in the process • Determine value-added, non-value-added activity and non-value-added but necessary Baseline Metrics—throughput, critical path process metrics, value-added activities
How is it performed	Manually transcribed and/or videotaped • Walk through the process • Document product flow • Perform video or transcribed analysis

Analysis steps
Transport
Inspect
Process
 	
Store
	Product activities/process steps have four categories
	• Transport
	• Inspect
	• Process types
	  • Value-added
	  • Non-value-added
	  • Non-value-added but necessary
	  • Unnecessary or waste
	• Storage types—Raw Material, Work in Process, Finished Goods
	  • Lot delays
	  • Between process delays
	  • Within process delays

But once we implement one-piece flow, any remaining delay will be a between process delay. As we stated before, within process delays generally signify some type of interruption in the process and generally create rework. When we eliminate the interruption, we eliminate the delay. All these delays impact customer satisfaction and make the overall process more costly.

Total Throughput Time

A primary goal of the product analysis is to determine the total throughput time of the process. This will become important later, as it will tell us what the total amount of inventory or patients should be in the process. The total throughput time is the sum of all the time the product, patient, or information spends in the process.

Product Process Flow Worksheet

We use a worksheet to capture the PPF steps (Figure 8.6). We capture each step and note where it fits into our TIPS definition. We break down each step if it is a process as to whether it is value-added, non-value-added but necessary, or unnecessary, and we identify which type of storage the step fits. We accumulate the times the product or patient spends in each step and the distance traveled. Every step is questioned as we capture them as to why we do what we do and if we need to do it. We then look for opportunities to eliminate (omit), rearrange, simplify, or combine each step. We are left with a before and after analysis that gives us "as is"

vs. a "to be" number of process steps and times within each part of TIPS. The process analysis should yield a 20%–40% productivity improvement to the overall process vs. a batch environment.

Product Flow Point-to-Point Diagrams

Point-to-point diagrams are utilized to show the path of the product or patient through the layout of the area. This differs from the spaghetti diagram we use for operators. It is utilized to identify only product flow patterns. Because our layout will come from the PPF, this diagram is used to guarantee the product always moves forward in a point-to-point fashion. The product should never move backward in a process. If any stations are out of order, they will immediately show up as you draw the point-to-point flow of the product. Stations that are out of order or force the product to move backward should be corrected in future revisions to your layout.

Lesson Learned: *The product or patient should never move backward. It is OK for the person to move backward but never the product.*

From the product's perspective, the point-to-point diagram assists in creating a logical grouping of operations or machines based on the flow of the product. Anytime a renovation or new construction is being considered, the layout should be tested utilizing point-to-point diagramming for all products flowing through the process to ensure whatever is being conceptualized will result in a good flow through the area from the product and operator's perspective.

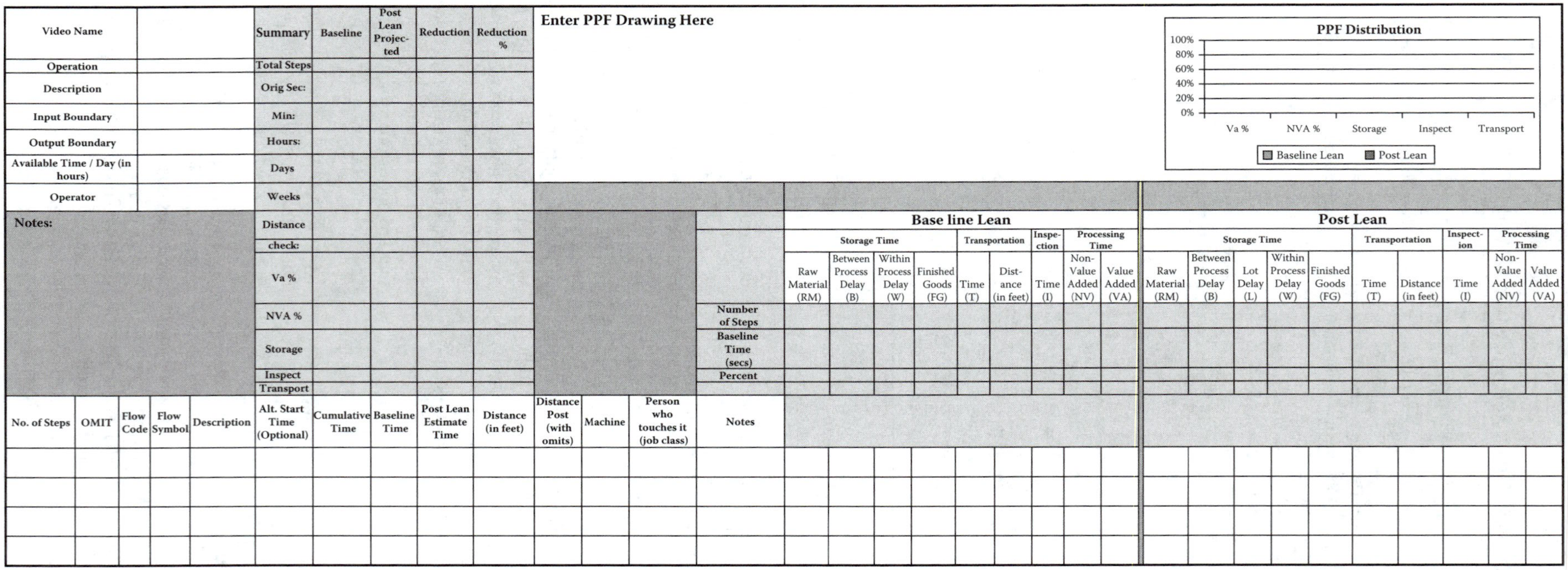

Enter PPF Drawing Here

PPF Distribution

100%	
80%	
60%	
40%	
20%	
0%	

Va %   NVA %   Storage   Inspect   Transport

■ Baseline Lean ■ Post Lean

Video Name		Summary	Baseline	Post Lean Projected	Reduction	Reduction %
Operation		Total Steps				
Description		Orig Sec:				
Input Boundary		Min:				
Output Boundary		Hours:				
Available Time / Day (in hours)		Days				
Operator		Weeks				

Notes:

check: | Distance | | | |
Va % | | | | |
NVA % | | | | |
Storage | | | | |
Inspect | | | | |
Transport | | | | |

Base line Lean

Number of Steps			
Baseline Time (secs)			
Percent			

Notes

			Storage Time				Transportation		Inspection	Processing Time	
		Raw Material (RM)	Between Process Delay (B)	Within Process Delay (W)	Finished Goods (FG)	Time (T)	Distance (in feet)	Time (I)	Non-Value Added (NV)	Value Added (VA)

Post Lean

			Storage Time				Transportation		Inspection	Processing Time	
		Raw Material (RM)	Between Process Delay (B)	Within Process Delay (W)	Finished Goods (FG)	Time (T)	Distance (in feet)	Time (I)	Non-Value Added (NV)	Value Added (VA)

No. of Steps	OMIT	Flow Code	Flow Symbol	Description	Alt. Start Time (Optional)	Cumulative Baseline Time	Baseline Time	Post Lean Estimate Time	Distance (in feet)	Distance Post (with omits)	Machine	Person who touches it (job class)

FIGURE 8.6 PPF (Product Process Flow) spreadsheet.

Pre-Testing – Point to Point - Cardiac Patient

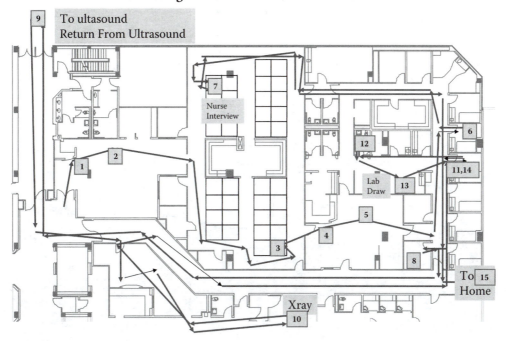

FIGURE 8.7 Point-to-point diagram surgical services pre-testing cardiac patient flow before Lean.

How to Do a Point-to-Point Diagram

The same teams who have participated in the PPF analysis should be involved in the point-to-point diagramming activity. The product point-to-point diagram is performed independently.

A team member is provided with a construction layout or sketches the layout on paper. As the product flows through the area, each movement is noted on the layout (Figures 8.7 and 8.8). Point-to-point diagrams should be created for both the base and revised "to be" layouts. We have also found that if the sequence is numbered in the point-to-point diagram, it helps in reviewing and utilizing the data to assist in sequencing equipment and supplies within a layout. We also recommend that the diagram is time- and date-stamped, as you may find varying product flows at different times, i.e., days vs. nights, weekdays vs. weekends.

Network of Process vs. Operations Defined

We have attempted to expand Shingo's separation between product, operator, and changeover and take it to the next level. To our knowledge, no one has broken down these processes into the pieces of Lean thinking each one provides. We studied this for literally years before it dawned on us that each analysis tool (product vs. operator's axis plus changeover) provides different answers for Lean improvement. We would like to propose that analyzing the product axis will provide the following pieces of the Lean implementation:

- Total throughput time
- Flow, flow, flow
- Layout and workstations

- Where rooms should be located in relation to the activity that is occurring
- Where the workstations should be located and the proper ordering of equipment and supplies
- The location of where standard WIP will be needed
- The standard WIP locations
- Machine times (running time of the process within a piece of equipment)
  - Examples: How long does it take to run a centrifuge in the laboratory, run a laboratory processor for a given test, send a fax or make a copy, wait for an elevator to open, ride an elevator, or send a specimen through a hospital tube system?
- Routings: which are the paths or sequence of steps the product or patients follow as they progress through the process?
- Travel distance for the product

Lesson Learned: *Using Lean tools enables you to understand and optimize what happens to the product or patient as they move through the process. Just analyzing and fixing the product axis piece of the network can yield as much as a 20%–40% productivity improvement.*

GROUP TECHNOLOGY MATRIX—STRATIFICATION ANALYSIS

There are books dedicated to group technology[*] in manufacturing. Our goal here is to familiarize the reader with this concept and provide an insight into how this can apply to sce-

[*] John L. Burbidge, *Group Technology* (London: Mechanical Engineering Publication) 1975.

PTEC –Point to Point Non - Cardiac Patient

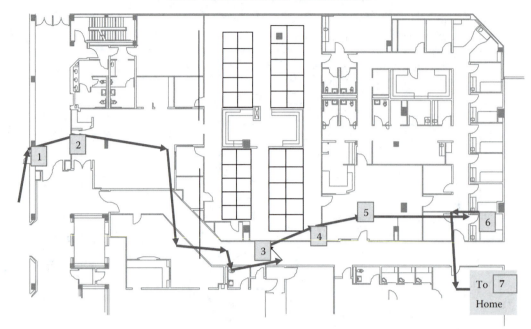

FIGURE 8.8 PPF (Product Process Flow) point-to-point surgical services pre-testing non cardiac patient flow after Lean.

narios within the healthcare domain. The group technology or group tech matrix allows one to view processes or products that may be similar, to be "grouped" into "like-families." We analyze volumes, product/process steps and equipment, skill sets utilized, service lines, or other criteria that may apply in order to try to find families of products.

The first step is to develop a product/process matrix and group the parts or activities into like-families based on the machines or processes utilized and in the order in which they use each machine or process.

An example would be to consider laboratory processing. In most cases, when comparing all the process flows for a specimen tube in the laboratory, we find that they break into families like chemistry, hematology, urine, and others. When getting a little more detailed, we find that many hematology specimens get centrifuged where a number of chemistry specimens get aliquoted. As we drill down on "categories," we can place specimens that are "processed" similarly or/and need the same analyzers together in the same "cell." Once we break down all the equipment that is utilized with each family, we determine if we have enough to support making a "cell." The centrifuges are now placed in front of each piece of equipment (this may mean smaller centrifuges) instead of being in a batched area.

Look at nursing unit rooms and determine what they may have in common and how they might be "grouped" in "like-families" with similar features to optimize flow, layout, and sequence. The goal is to move like products or things into the same "work area," potentially eliminating (or at least reducing) changeover (setup) times. These groupings can also occur based on geography and are sometimes referred by the term "unit based."

In another laboratory example, a new hematology test is being offered to the market. The test requires a new piece of equipment. This new piece of equipment can do the new test as well as several other tests that are currently done on another existing machine.

Typically, the machine would be purchased and placed wherever it would fit in the existing layout without consideration of the optimal placement of the machine. Optimal placement would consider the following:

- What specimen preparation might be required prior to processing
- The new tests that will be performed and the volume of tests able to be utilized by the equipment
- The machines before or after it
- Features of the existing tests performed on other machines should now be considered for the new machine
- The old machine may no longer be needed

The group tech matrix provides a mechanism for you to determine what the "product feature" similarities are and how to maximize these similarities to improve layout design, flow, and setup.

EXAMPLE: GROUP TECHNOLOGY APPLIED TO A SURGICAL SERVICES UNIT

Most hospitals have ORs dedicated to certain types of surgeries; however, we have found the number and locations of OR allocations that are dedicated to particular service lines are generally mismatched (Figure 8.9). The OR rooms have

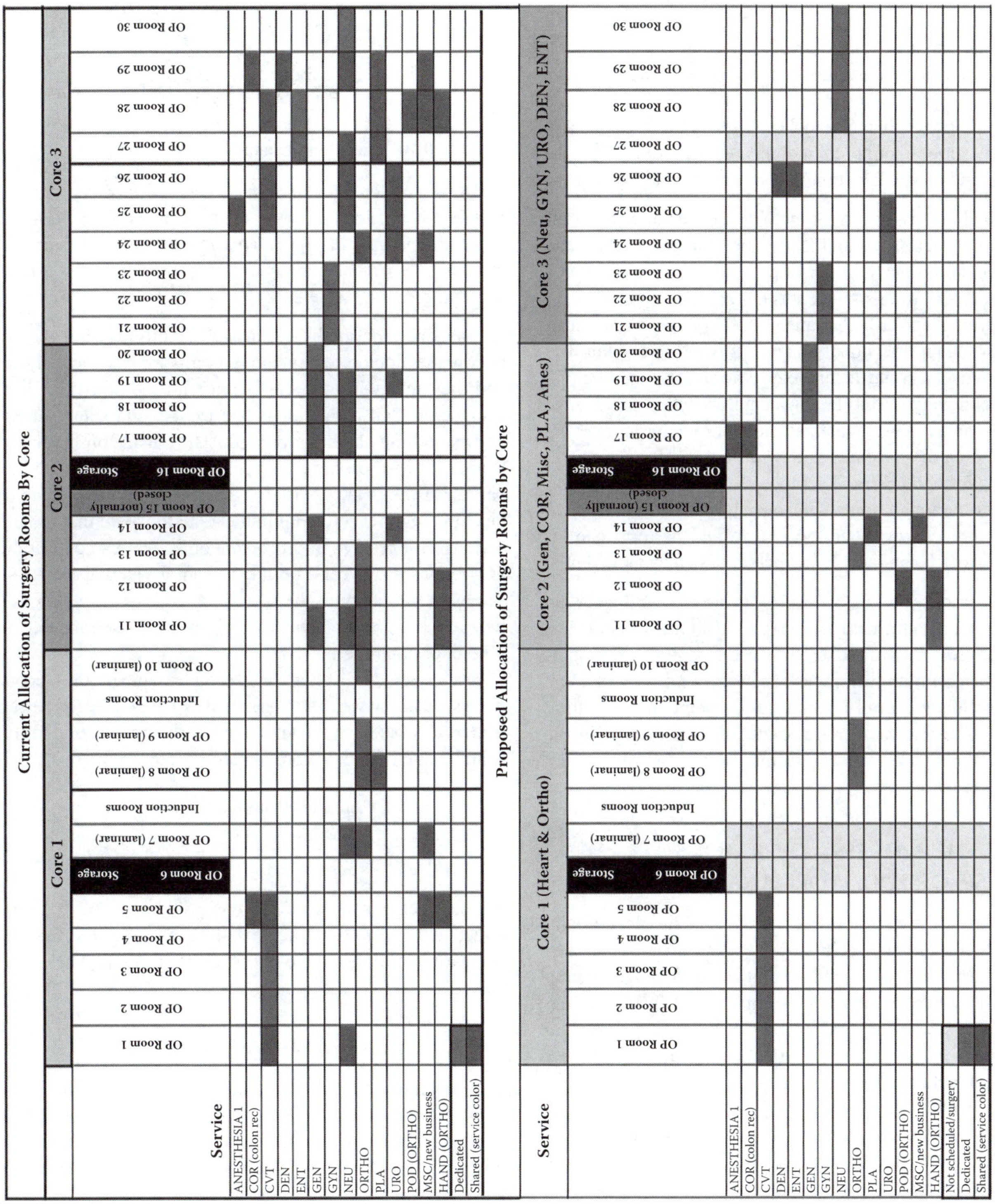

FIGURE 8.9 Group technology matrix— surgery rooms allocation.

normally not been analyzed based on similarities such as volumes, equipment supply use, turnover time, size of OR required to perform a given procedure, or the actual minutes of OR times used. These are all potential "features" that can be included in a group tech matrix to optimize the use of OR rooms. Once the appropriate number of rooms is determined to dedicate to a given service line, then the information in a group tech matrix can help you determine which surgical rooms to dedicate based on size and materials shared, again leveraging "features" or similarities and grouping to optimize layout and flow. A dynamic tool can be created so changes in case mix can be monitored and updated as surgical OR use changes, and room allocations can be adjusted accordingly.

Note: Technically, group technology is somewhat of a compromise between batch and Lean. For example, in the Lean world we would want universal patient rooms on the floors or universal OR rooms. Since it is not practical to have every room outfitted for an ICU patient or every OR room outfitted with laminar flow hoods and robots, we leverage families of rooms using group technology criteria. The idea behind group technology is to still implement flow but in "family-like grouped" areas. A surgical example would be grouping vascular with cardio-vascular as they utilize similar equipment and supplies, both types of procedures deal with vascular structures, although some surgeons specialize in peripheral vascular procedures others generalize and perform cardio-vascular (which can include peripheral vascular) procedures.

An example: The laboratory is, in essence, a big group technology or centralized area supplying all the hospital. The goal with Lean is to first streamline the centralized laboratory by using group technology; then the next level of Lean would be to have mini-laboratories or point of use testing solutions wherever they were needed, where they fit in the flow or, worst case, adjacent to the area and eliminate the centralized laboratory.

ASSESS THE PROCESS—OPERATOR ANALYSIS OR FULL WORK ANALYSIS[*]

In this section, we refer to the operator as any person who is part of the process (Figure 8.10). The operator term is unfamiliar to most in healthcare and we must caution you to clearly articulate the definition of operator. When speaking to frontline staff, you may need to interchangeably refer to the operator as a staff member to bridge the language barrier from manufacturing to healthcare.

Once again, we need to be reminded that we separate the product axis from the operator axis when doing analysis, and this is the secret for improving operations. Many times, focus is placed on what the person was doing, but not the product or patient going through the process. These must be looked at independently first, and then together after waste is eliminated from the process.

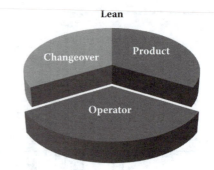

FIGURE 8.10 Pieces of Lean pie chart—operator.

Lesson Learned: *It should be noted that any step that was eliminated in the value stream mapping or PPF no longer requires operator analysis. This is why we do the analysis steps in the order of value stream map, product, operator, and changeover* (Table 8.2).

The operator analysis starts with filming the operator (i.e., nurse, doctor, technician, administrator, volunteer, etc.) and then reviewing the videotape with the operator, supervisor, industrial engineer (if one exists), and someone who knows nothing about the process. The outside observer's job is to ask "why" each step is performed since they don't have paradigms associated with the process. When reviewing the tape it is important to communicate to the team that the tape review is for process improvement only and that no disciplinary actions are ever to be taken from a videotape analysis. The goal of watching the tape is to analyze each step as to why it is done and what can be eliminated, rearranged, simplified, or combined.

We review each step on the videotape to the second, unless we know we can eliminate it. We then categorize each step as to whether it is value-added or non-value-added. If it is non-value-added, we break it down into:

1. Necessary but non-value-added work
2. Unnecessary work
3. Idle time

When the analysis is done, we basically have created a set of rather detailed job instructions. This becomes the basis for standard work later in the improvement process. The criteria for value-added is the same as for the product.

TIME IS A SHADOW OF MOTION[†]

With Lean, excess material and idle time always hide problems; however, not all problems result in extra inventory or idle time. When we watch videos, we look for safety and ergonomics first, but we also look at motions the operators take. The more motions a person uses to do their job, the longer it takes. Remember, Gilbreth said, "Time is a shadow of motion." If you can reduce the motions, the person is happier

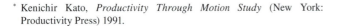

[*] Kenichir Kato, *Productivity Through Motion Study* (New York: Productivity Press) 1991.

[†] Shigeo Shingo, Japan Management Association *Non Stock Production: The shingo system for continous improvement*, 1987 (New York: Productivity Press) 1988.

TABLE 8.2

Full Work of the Operator Analysis

Step #	Omit	Description	Key Points	Reason For Key Points	Current TLT *seconds
1		Grab marker, fill in board, put marker back	Visual control	Charge nurse knows who is in each room	9
2		Walk to the outside of the counter			11
3	X	Sift through papers			6
4		Go get armband			5
5		Put stickers on armband	Patient must be identified correctly	So we prevent I.D. mistakes later in the process	17
6		Update check list with date, orders, blood consent, ID labs, and verify requisitions are same from what Dr. ordered			10
7		Sign signature sheet			10
8		Place check list, signature sheet, and orders in order			35
9		Finds consent and reviews procedure and updates the check list			27
10		Verify all lab work			24
11	X	Search for Blood Consent	Should not have to search needs improvement		30

*TLT - Total Labor Time in seconds

because the job is easier and management is happy because they are getting more done with the same person. It is a win-win solution.

Videotaping allows us to see waste we might not normally see and gives us a chance to see some of the hidden waste (waste behind the waste), which is the most difficult to see. It is important to never turn off the video camera once filming starts or you will lose chances to see and remove waste in the process.

One of the advantages to videotape is there is no disputing the information. What you see is what was done. Many times we hear, "Oh, I didn't realize I did that" or what we filmed was "unusual" and doesn't normally happen that way. Based on our experience, don't believe it. If it happened when you filmed it, you can bet it happens more than people think. We also spot other wastes in the video, such as over-processing, excess motion, searching, and transportation, to name a few.

Lesson Learned: *Management needs to support videotaping. You will get pushback on videotaping, as this is new to many in healthcare and can be intimidating. You can document a process through observation and written documentation; however, videotaping yields the best results as there is no dispute and other wastes can be identified* (Table 8.3). *If videotaping is allowed with staff review, in most cases the staff will gain an understanding of the value, through the review process and it is much easier to obtain "buy-in" to recommended changes.*

It is important to analyze each task to the second so it can be recorded correctly and split into the appropriate category. How we split the work varies depending on the area we are reviewing. In some areas, we may break down times for computer input or retrieving supplies into separate categories. It is important to break the steps up into what makes sense for the area in which you are studying. This task can be done by hand or on the computer.

WHY MAKE THE OPERATOR'S (STAFF PERSON'S) JOB EASIER?

Think about it, who really makes the money for us? The answer is the person on the frontline (floor) closest to the patient. Does it make sense to have the people who interact with the customers (patients) frustrated? In a time of nursing shortages, wouldn't it be easier to retain and recruit to an organization that strives to make the employee's job easier? Anyone in a management or support role doesn't directly make money for the organization; therefore, what is management's job? One of our favorite quotes is from Mike Walsh in the video *Speed is Life*, where he said, "Management's responsibility is to be worthy of its people."*

Why does management exist? The whole concept of middle management was started by the railroads back in the late nineteenth century. Frederick Taylor benchmarked the rail-

---

* Mike Walsh, at the time CEO of Northern Pacific railroad, "Speed is Life," Tom Peters, a co-production of Video Publishing House and KERA© 1991.

TABLE 8.3

Operator Quick Reference Guide

Quick Reference Notes:	Operator Analysis
When to use	Next level of detail after Product Process Flow which looks at each activity from the operator's or staff member's perspective to determine the "value" of each activity and to identify any steps which were not eliminated through the Product Process Flow or value stream map which was performed PRIOR to the operator analysis.
What it delivers	Identifies what activities that the operator performs that are of value througout the process step, and provides the total labor time needed for the process to occur
Used to identify	Waste in processes • Safety • Ergonomics • Excess Motions
Baseline Metrics	Value-Added activities as related to the product and operator Total Labor time needed to optimize the product Opportunities for improvement in productivity
How is it performed	Manually transcribed and/ or videotape

Analysis Steps	Walk through the process
	Document operator activities
	Perform Analysis
	• Analysis Types
	  • Value-Added
	  • Non Value-Added but Necessary
	  • Unnecessary
	  • Idle time
	Capture rework times
	Distance traveled baseline and improved (future state)

Final Report	Determine what steps can be eliminated, rearranged, simplified or combined within a process. Recalculate each of the above to determine potential opportunity for improvement in the future state. Can be used to determine preliminary ROI's

roads and brought middle management and cost accounting practices from the railroads to manufacturing and, eventually, service industries like hotels and healthcare. He took the supervisor's job and split it up into eight different positions: planning, production, route, inventory stores, instruction card and time study, order of work, recording and cost accounting, and disciplinarian.[*] This was the beginning of the functional organization we have today. At the time these jobs were created, they were designed to help the operators (staff) get more product out the door, and they were co-located in the production area with those that did the work. Yet, where are most overhead indirect staff and managers located today? The answer would be "in their offices," normally far away from the frontline. All one can do in an office is manage history, answer e-mails, and write reports. Does any of this make the operator's job easier? When you think about it, in a truly Lean organization staff positions need to be located on the floor wherever possible.

Lesson Learned: *Management's goal should be to work on making the frontline person's job easier by removing waste and making improvements. They should know, own, and constantly be working to streamline their processes.*

---

[*] Wrege, Charles D, *Frederick W. Taylor* (Irwin Publishing) ©1991; Copley, *Frederick W. Taylor* (Harper and Brothers) ©1923; Kanigel, *The One Best Way* (Penguin Books) ©1999.

TOTAL LABOR TIME

One of our major deliverables of operator analysis is total labor time. Total labor time is the amount of labor or work performed during the process by the operator to get to the end result. Machine time is not included in the labor time. The operator analysis should provide the baseline current "labor time," which is the total amount of both value-added and non-value-added labor time the operator performs throughout the task or process being analyzed.

After the operator analysis is performed, each step is reviewed to see if it can be eliminated, rearranged, simplified, or combined with another process. If so, those steps will be "omitted" or the estimated time for each step will be reduced, creating a future state total labor time.

SEPARATE WORKER FROM MACHINE

It is important, during analysis, when operators interact with machines to separate the work performed by the machine from the person. Machines should do hazardous, dangerous, boring, or repetitive work. People need to be "used wisely." We have run into several situations where people actually perform the work better than robots and others where the robots performed better than people. We have applied all the same Lean tools to analyze robots and machines as well.

People should have challenging work and be taught to constantly look for and identify improvements.

MACHINE TIME VS. LABOR TIME

We do not include machine time because the operator is not performing "the work" of the machine. An example of this would be centrifuging a specimen in the laboratory. The preparation of the specimen, placement of the specimen in the centrifuge, closing the lid, and turning on the machine are all part of the total labor time. The 8 min the machine is spinning, however, is not considered part of the labor time because the machine is doing the work and is captured in the PPF analysis. While the machine is working, the operator may be "waiting" for the spin cycle to complete or, hopefully, performing another task in parallel to the machine running. Examples where you might break down operator from machine time in healthcare would be hemodialysis, sterile processors, nebulizers, MRIs, and lab.

DELINEATING KEY DATA ELEMENTS

Calculating total labor time of a process will give you a picture of how much labor and, ultimately, how many staff members are needed to complete the one piece of whatever is being processed. The operator analysis should yield a 20%–40% productivity improvement to your overall process vs. a batch environment. In addition to capturing the labor time, the distance traveled is also captured as a baseline and future state. Leveraging the information to obtain the overall productivity improvement that is obtained by analyzing the PPF and operator analysis will be discussed in detail in Chapter 9.

WORKLOAD BALANCING

Some staff members may be perceived as inefficient, are not able, or do not have the desire to do work at the same level as others. In general, in order to minimize the resistance we may encounter, we subscribe to Deming's belief that most people want to do the right thing and want to keep busy.[*] When we are idle for periods of time, the day can really drag on, especially if there is a clock in front of you. We argue that, in most cases, it is the fault of management, not the staff that these perceptions occur. We normally find staff has not been provided with clear expectations nor have they been held accountable to any performance metrics or targets. In general, if there are clear expectations and good training for the job or task, the person will feel better and do what is required. In addition, if a person has not been empowered or trained in every operation, or does not have the right equipment or supplies it may not be possible for them to do the task at hand effectively or perform additional work. Occasionally, you may find the individual

that just doesn't want to work or do their fair share, but as Deming said, 95% of the time the "system" is the problem not the employee.[†] With Lean, we implement workload balancing, which means we try to distribute the same amount of work to each person. This helps promote a sense of fairness among staff and generally improves department morale. We often find stars among the workforce who never shined before, simply because they were never given the proper training or were just not given the opportunity to shine.

There are several components that we need to understand to achieve load balancing with a process or a given set of activities with a process:

- Available time
- Total labor time required
- Standard work
- Cycle time

To do this, we must understand how many operators are needed to do the work within a given cycle time.

$$\text{Number of Operators} = \text{total labor time required} \div \text{cycle time.}$$

HOW TO BALANCE THE WORK

If we have a process in which there are 30 min of total work and six people working, how much work should be done by each person? The answer is 5 min (or 30 min ÷ 6 people).

This requires each person to be given the same amount (5 min of work) and each person, in turn, must "do" his/her fair share of the 5 min worth of work. In order to accomplish this, we need to consider the skill set of the operators or staff performing the tasks or activities. This works well if everyone in a work area can all do the same level of work from a competency, licensure, and training perspective.

It is important to provide role clarity for each person and ensure each has the appropriate cross-training to enable flexibility across processes and between tasks, processes, and equipment. The process redesign and benefits must be outlined to staff so that clear expectations are set, and they have a clear understanding of their new roles and responsibilities related to the process. In addition, targets and expected results are explained and definition in role clarity is outlined. At this point, this should not be new to the staff, as frontline staff and supervisors should have been an integral part in redesigning the new process, identifying waste, and helping to create the "new work." This participation is critical to a successful implementation, as frontline staff has a clear understanding of the day-to-day value-added and wasted activities they perform. If we do not leverage their knowledge in the analysis and redesign, we will not obtain the expected results. Frontline staff and stakeholders must be a part of the redesign if the implementation is to succeed. Staff members

[*] Mary Walton, *Deming Management Method* (New York: Putnam Publishing) 1986.

[†] Mary Walton, *Deming Management Method* (New York: Putnam Publishing) 1986.

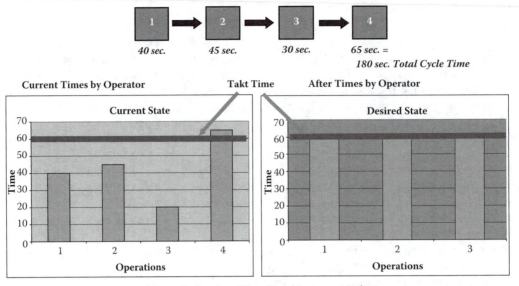

−work is evenly distributed for all workers to meet Takt time.

FIGURE 8.11   Operator line balancing.

need a full understanding of what is being done, why it is being done, what is in it for the company, and, above all, "what is in it for them" if they go along with the changes.

When we are line balancing, we must allow enough time for staff to perform each task. In Figure 8.11, the left hand graph shows the workloads for each person. Operator 1 has 40 sec, 2 has 45 sec, 3 has 30 sec, and 4 has 65 sec. Based on this simple load diagram, we can determine that work is accumulating between operator 1 and 2. Operator 3 immediately performs any work received and proceeds to really back up operator 4, who is the bottleneck.[*] We can predict that the cycle time, based on the theory of constraints,[†] is going to be 65 sec. This means operator 1, if forced to wait for operator 4, would have 25 sec of idle time, operator 2 would have 20 sec of idle time, and operator 3 would have 35 sec of idle time each cycle. But instead of being idle, they continue to work (batch) so the inventory will pile up. Remember, idle time is one of the things that can force us to batch. As before, we can predict how much work will pile up and where. Since operator 2 is the next slowest operator and they are 20 sec slower, then every four pieces we will back up a full piece prior to operator 4.

The line in each graph in Figure 8.1 shows the 60 sec Takt time. If we divide 180 sec of total work (40 + 45 + 30 + 65) or labor time by the Takt time of 60 sec, it shows we need 3 operators. We can then rebalance the work across the 3 operators to meet the Takt time and free up a person. What do we do with the person we free up? This is normally not a problem in healthcare, where well-trained, highly skilled resources are difficult to come by; however, it is very important that we

never lay anyone off due to continuous improvement activities, and there is a proactive plan in place to redeploy and retrain workers to other jobs or areas as this occurs.

Whenever we are training staff in the "new" or revised standard work, they often think we want them to rush. This is not the case. Staff should be coached not to rush, because if activities/tasks are rushed, mistakes and defects will occur. If we rush, quality will suffer, processes will need to be "reworked" and any time that you might have saved in elimination of waste will be lost in reworking defects. In addition, rework creates a financial burden that is not tracked and will lead to decreased customer satisfaction. The saying that we recommend posting in each new Lean system implementation is "Quality first; the speed will come." The other challenge we often face is while the work flow may be revised, the actual work is not and staff become so concerned with following the "new process" that they forget to do what is normally required as part of the job "that did not change." When this occurs, it can inadvertently lead to unjustified misgivings about Lean. As staff are cross-trained in new workflows, revised work, or new work, standard work and role clarity are extremely important to ensure that this does not occur (Figure 8.12).

Performing Lean implementations and applying Lean tools will enable us to become knowledgeable about how long tasks actually take to perform and enable reasonable targets to be established. An increase in productivity occurs when the process is redesigned with work in the proper sequence and balanced across the staff with the right tools, at the right time, in the right place to eliminate waste in the process.

Lean uses the terms "Mura" for uneven pace of production, and "Muri"—unreasonableness/excessive workload.[‡] It is important to remember that people are not robots. There

---

[*] Technically people can't be true bottlenecks because we can always add more people.

[†] The theory of constraints basically states that one can only go as fast as the slowest machine or person in a process. This is from a book by Eli Goldratt called *The Goal* (Great Barrington, MA: North River Press) 2004.

[‡] Taiichi Ohno, Setsuo Mito, *Just-In-Time For Today and Tomorrow* (New York: Productivity Press) 1988.

Job Type / Name	Sign In	Triage	Interventional	Discharge	Room RN	Charge Nurse
Joe Smith	1	2	1	2	1	1
Jane Doe	2	3	2	4	1	1
Mary Jones	5	5	4	3	2	2
ED Educational Training Grid (One Patient Flow)						
Not trained in clinical area				1		
Exposed to clinical area				2		
Limited training in clinical area				3		
Proficient in clinical Area				4		
Trained in the Clinical Area as Trainer				5		

FIGURE 8.12 Cross-training matrix.

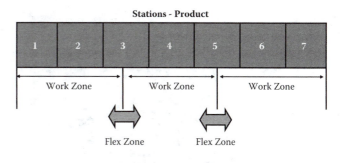

FIGURE 8.13 Baton flex zones.

are some situations that cause cycle-to-cycle imbalances, such as defective materials, slower patients, and unanticipated distractions. All these will impact the balance of work and flow of the process. The staff in each clinical area must be flexible and empowered to overcome these imbalances.

To facilitate work balancing, we utilize a concept Ohno referred to as "Baton Zones,"[*] or flex zones, which are areas where hand offs occur (Figure 8.13). The layout must be designed with short, easily shared steps around the zone. Long operations should be split into smaller steps. Avoid staff using their hands as fixtures because operator flexing will be constrained. When there is a significant mismatch between the planned balance points where service is being transitioned, the team should investigate to find a root cause and generate a corrective action.

Work imbalance occurs typically because a staff person did not follow the standard work, may not be flexing to assist a co-worker, or a "stop the line" strategy was not initiated so that the problem could be addressed. This can be a challenge in healthcare as we deal with patients and deliver services rather than build products. Patients, due to their disease processes, may take longer to perform a task such as a difficult blood draw, obtain a history, complete an examination, or a patient who just needs extra time for support or encouragement. People should understand that they still need to work as a team and flex as required even though they have an order in which tasks should be performed. We are still requiring them to "think" and "do" the appropriate activities to get the job done.

Standing/moving operation also promotes operator/staff flexibility and health. A staff member who sits is more likely to either build inventory or to wait (adding seconds or minutes to a process), as it takes more effort to get from a chair rather than rotate around when standing. You will find that staff members who are "used to" sitting for tasks may resist the suggestion of standing and vice versa. From an ergonomic

viewpoint, sitting is bad for you. It can lead to back problems and obesity, which can eventually lead to the possibility of early mortality.[†] You may need to transition from sitting to standing by adjusting counter heights that will allow the option to stand and perform activities. These will make the transition easier, as staff will find the task or activity they are performing easier to do if they stand. A general guideline for allowing "standup" chairs on the line is for operations or tasks where a person would have to stand in one place with no movement for 10–15 min at a time.

DIAGRAMS: SPAGHETTI DIAGRAMMING— OPERATOR WALK PATTERNS

When we map the walk patterns of operators throughout their work process, we call this spaghetti diagramming. Spaghetti maps highlight and aid in the identification of system waste in the areas of transport, location of supplies and equipment, rework, and poor flow that may not be readily apparent when performing operator analysis. Creating spaghetti diagrams helps drive future state: improvements to process flow, placement of equipment (adjacencies) and supplies. The goal is to have the right equipment and supplies at the right place, in the right order to optimize flow. From the operator perspective, we can create work zones. Work zones are based on the cycle time each operator must meet. So, in the example pictured in Figure 8.13, operator one may cover stations one, two, and part of three. If our demand increased, reducing our cycle time and requiring us to add an operator, then operator 1 may end up working at station one and part of station two before handing off to the next person. Operator 1 would wait for operator 2 to "pull" the part from them vs. working up to a point and setting the part down or waiting for operator 2. This shows work zones can change based on the number of operators and sequencing of units (equipment, adjacent processes, services, etc.). The goal is to create logical stations based on

---

[*] Taiichi Ohno, *Toyota Production System* (New York: Productivity Press) 1988.

[†] "Sitting Time and Mortality from all causes, cardiovascular disease, and cancer," Katzmarzyk PT, Church TS, Craig CL, Bouchard C. Pennington Biomedical Research Center, Baton Rouge, LA. http://conditioningresearch.blogspot.com/2009/04/too-much-sitting-down-is-bad-for-you.html. It's Dangerous, Charles Osgood on the CBS Radio Network. The Osgood File. June 10th, 2010; "Don't Just Sit There—It's Dangerous," Charles Osgood on the CBS Radio Network. The Osgood File. June 10th, 2010.

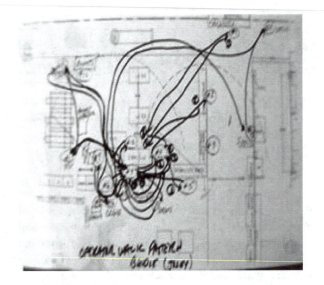

FIGURE 8.14   Operator spaghetti chart.

the PPF and then flex workers (flex zones) across the stations in order to balance the work.

How to Do a Spaghetti Diagram

The same teams who have participated in the operator analysis should be involved in the spaghetti diagramming activity. The spaghetti map for the operator is performed independently generally through observation or videotape. When performing the operator spaghetti diagram, it is helpful to number the steps as the operator goes through his/her tasks (Figure 8.14). We recommend that the date, time, operator, and operator skill level are documented. The team should determine the length of time to follow and map the operator's activity, which would be a true representative sample. For instance, you may follow a nurse for 1 or 2 hrs and when the nursing pattern begins to repeat, it means you have clearly reached a "representative sample of activity." For instance, you may note that the nurse may have already walked out of the area two or three times to get supplies, which clearly indicates that the location should be moved closer to where the actual work is occurring. Following the nurse for an entire shift may not be helpful or value-added.

You may choose to spaghetti diagram at different specific times of the day, i.e., shift change or on a surgery floor at the time when most patients are being prepped to leave the floor, in order to get the most benefit from the time the team is able to devote to the tools. You may consider providing a pedometer to the operator so that a baseline distance traveled can be calculated. "Travel" time is waste, inefficient and, more importantly, can be very tiring on staff. Proper planning of what you are trying to accomplish are key as you perform these tools.

The operator analysis helps focus on what to spaghetti diagram and highlight areas for future improvement. While the layout primarily comes from the product, bringing the

point-to-point and spaghetti diagrams together will help solve the overall layout.

Next, we will take the information and determine a new layout based on all the information gained from each of the tools utilized thus far. Once a new layout is proposed, a simulated PPF and spaghetti diagram of the operator should be performed. Numbering should be used for each step on the new layout to see how the "new" Product Process Flows.

The next step after this would be to take the layout and understand how the operator will work within the new layout, and where the supplies should be located.

Spaghetti diagramming can be very powerful in helping leaders, managers, and staff understand visual collision points, repetitive steps, travel time, and enable effective communicating of improvement opportunities at the "baseline level." Then post-diagramming reveals the results and additional improvements in the quest for elimination of waste.

Network of Process vs. Operations Defined

We have attempted to take Shingo's separation of product, operator, and changeover to the next level. To our knowledge, no one has broken down these processes into the pieces of Lean thinking each one provides. We studied this for literally years before it dawned on us that each analysis tool (product vs. operator's axis plus changeover) provides different answers for Lean improvement. We would like to propose the following "pieces" of Lean that will be determined by analyzing just the operator piece:

- Ergonomics/safety/fatigue
- Number of operators
- Line balancing
- Capacity planning
- Motion study
- Scheduling flexibility
- Standard WIP quantity
- Workstation design—tools and supplies sequenced in proper order of assembly
- Total labor time
- Operator walk patterns
- Ten cycle analysis
- Operator buy-in
- Baton zones
- Standard work
- Operator travel distance

As we move through the utilization of Lean tools to reach a Lean process to deliver the customer a quality end product, each tool discussed provides another piece of the puzzle required to achieve total process optimization (TPO).

Lesson Learned: *Using Lean tools enables one to understand and optimize what the staff (operators) does to the product or patient as they move through the process. Just looking and fixing the operator axis piece of the network can yield as much as an additional 20%–40% productivity improvement.*

MOTION STUDY—JUST WHEN YOU THOUGHT YOU WERE "THERE"

If you think you have improved all you can, let us provide you with a second thought.

Shingo has an example in one of his books where he takes a towel and soaks it in water. One by one, he asks his students to come up and wring out the towel. The first person squeezes out a lot of water, the next squeezes some water but not as much. But even the last student was able to squeeze out some additional drops. [*] *This exercise applies to waste as well.*

Once you are trained to see the waste for what it is, there is much to see. But sometimes waste is hidden by batching, excess material, and just because that is the way we have always done it ("boiled frog" syndrome). Once you "Lean out" the area, it becomes easy to see where there is variation and waste. But as you continuously improve the area, the waste becomes harder to find, yet it is definitely there. In some cases, it would be easy to say we have improved enough and we don't need to improve anymore; however, just like the towel example above, the waste is always there. You just have to keep squeezing the towel (Figures 8.15 and 8.16).

The tool for this is Frank Gilbreth's motion study.[†] Motion study involves analyzing what we do to the fraction of a second. As we discussed earlier, Gilbreth did his work with bricklayers. He owned a bricklaying company and was constantly searching for ways to improve the work processes and build buildings faster yet make it easier on those doing the work. Gilbreth filmed and studied the motions of his bricklayers and developed what he called "Therbligs," or the 18 fundamental motions of the worker. He found many of his bricklayers were wasting time getting their own cement or having to constantly mix the cement to the right consistency. He also noticed that they were doing a lot of walking, searching, and bending over. He analyzed their work down to the right and wrong way to pick up a brick. He totally standardized how the wall should be built, brick by brick. He hired people to make sure that the cement was always the right consistency. He invented and patented adjustable scaffolding to adjust the height of the bricklayers to the wall so that they did not have to bend over. He had a rule that his bricklayers should always be laying brick and should never have to take more than one step in any direction. This was all part of the scientific management movement of the Industrial Revolution in the early twentieth century. Gilbreths's Therbligs are listed below (Figures 8.17 and 8.18):

Class 1: The essence of an operation (highest value)

- Assemble
- Disassemble
- Use

FIGURE 8.15 Gilbreth bricklayers materials (before). Source: Frank Gilbreth, *Motion Study.* Boston (USA: Stanbope Press) 1911.

Class 2: Preparatory or follow-up motions

- Transport empty
- Grasp
- Transport loaded
- Release load

Class 3: Incidental motions

- Search
- Find
- Select
- Inspect
- Pre-position or re-position
- Hold
- Prepare

Class 4: These should be eliminated, if possible

- Think or plan
- Rest for overcoming fatigue
- Unavoidable delay
- Avoidable delay

The only Therbligs that can be value-added are assemble, disassemble, and use. Gilbreth's original work was done with bricklayers and is documented in a book called *Motion Study*, circa 1911. Gilbreth also used the techniques we are describing in a hospital setting. He created a hospital OR in his home, which was depicted in the original film "Cheaper by the Dozen."[‡] Gilbreth videotaped the tonsillectomy operations on his children and himself so that he could study the motions that the doctors were utilizing and work to streamline

---

[*] Shigeo Shingo, Japan Management Association *Non Stock Production: The Shingo System for Continous Improvement,* 1987 (New York: Productivity Press) 1988.

[†] Frank Gilbreth, *Motion Study.* Boston (USA: Stanbope Press) 1911.

[‡] "Cheaper By The Dozen," 20th Century Fox, 1950.

FIGURE 8.16 Gilbreth bricklayers materials (after). Gilbreth added "material handlers" or "water spiders" as we call them in Lean whose main job was to make sure the brick and concrete was always available and that the concrete was always mixed to the proper consistency. This way the brick layers could concentrate on just laying brick. He could build buildings much faster than his competition so he won most of the bids. Source: Frank Gilbreth, *Motion Study*. Boston (USA: Stanbope Press) 1911.

them. Our approach is to typically analyze operations to the second and, when we have exhausted improvement opportunities at that level, move to motion study. We have come across operations in healthcare where each person only has a few seconds worth of work in their process. We have successfully used motion study techniques to reduce these times by more than 50% per operator, effectively doubling their capacity. The concept of eliminating waste in motions and transforming them into work is known as labor density. The formula for this is work divided by motion with a goal of 100%.[*] One thing to keep in mind is that not all motion is work. Only work that is value-added or necessary should be considered true work.

100% Efficiency with Humans

Looking at from a very analytical lean or motion study purest point of view an operator who uses both hands and feet at the same time is 100% efficient (a drummer is a good example). How close can we get to this in healthcare? Normally, we look at use of both hands simultaneously as 100% efficient, but technically it is only 50% efficient since we are not using our feet. People who use one hand as a fixture to hold something while the other hand is working on it are only 25% efficient and are also a common reason that operations cannot be split between two persons. Watch the work being performed. Can a fixture be made to hold the part for the person and free up the other hand? In healthcare, think of the daVinci robot®, where the surgeon sits at a console and simultaneously uses both hands and feet to manipulate the robot. It has robotic

arms that, in fact, free up assistant surgeons' hands; they no longer have to be exposed to ergonomic challenges associated with laparoscopic instrumentation.

Operator Resistance

In healthcare, clinical personnel are trained to "get the job done" despite any obstacles and are encouraged and rewarded to perform workarounds. Since they have become accustomed to workarounds in their day-to-day life, we encounter resistance in redesigning processes and re-allocating work activities. Proactively sequencing "work" in the order it needs to occur, providing the right tools at the right place at

FIGURE 8.17 Gilbreth bricklayers' wrong way to pick up a brick. Source: Frank Gilbreth, *Motion Study*. Boston (USA: Stanbope Press) 1911.

---

[*] Japanese Management Association, *Kanban Just-in-Time* (New York: Productivity Press) 1986.

FIGURE 8.18 Gilbreth bricklayers' right way to pick up a brick. Source: Frank Gilbreth, *Motion Study*. Boston (USA: Stanbope Press) 1911.

the right time, and standard work may be very challenging concepts, and personnel may find it difficult to believe that it will actually occur. We often find that because they are trained to deal with emergencies and "rewarded for saving the day," it is often challenging for them to change from a reactive work model to a proactive model in which "work-arounds and saving the day" are essentially eliminated.

ASSESS THE PROCESS—CHANGEOVER ANALYSIS

Changeover analysis is the third assessment tool and it is performed in that order (Figure 8.19). The analogy we use for turnover is that of a pit stop. How long does a NASCAR pit stop take? The fastest pit stop on record is around 12 sec.* On the Winner's Circle[†] tape it takes about 14.7 sec. It is important to note that 14.7 sec is the clock time. In Lean changeovers, we make a distinction between clock time and labor time. While the clock time is 14.7 sec, we look to see how many operators there are to determine the labor time. If there are seven persons doing the changeover, we calculate

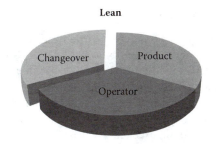

FIGURE 8.19 Pieces of Lean pie chart—changeover.

the labor time by multiplying seven times 14.7 sec, which equals 109.3 sec. Could the pit stop have been done with one person? The answer is yes, but how long would it take? At least the 109.3 sec, but probably longer owing to travel distance and extra movements which would be required. Since races are typically won by fractions of a second, we would probably lose the race. What characteristics make the pit stop concept successful? Doing things in parallel, standard work for each person, and lots of practice all contribute to the Lean formula.

Another concept we use is to break the work down into internal time vs. external time. In the pit stop example, anything done while in the pit is considered "internal time." Examples would be changing the tires or refueling. Anything we can do while the car is going around the track is considered "external" time. For example, we could get the tires ready and located in the pit area ahead of time. So, if you think about it, the 14.7 sec is only a measure of the internal time, not the external time. Why do we focus on internal time? Because this is the amount of time the asset is not available for use, i.e., the car is not racing around the track.

The next step we use in setup analysis is to break down each step into its component parts or categories. Shingo describes these in his book, *A Revolution in Manufacturing: The SMED System*.[‡] The four components of setup reduction are: preparation (P) and organization, mounting (M) and removing, calibration (C) measurement and testing (positioning), and trial (T) runs and adjustments. These terms are challenging for healthcare workers, so being able to convert the language and thought process to healthcare is essential to adoption.

The process we use for changeover reduction then is to videotape the changeover. This means we need a video camera to follow every person involved in the changeover. Examples in healthcare are the ED (changeover of rooms), housekeeping, or surgical rooms. Once we have the videotape, we break down each step from the video, preferably with the person we filmed, a supervisor, and someone who knows nothing about the process present. We initially break it into what we call the "As Is" condition. Each step is divided into either internal or external and one of the four categories we outlined earlier (PMCT). We also note distances traveled where appropriate.

* http://en.allexperts.com/q/NASCAR-Racing-2068/Pit-Stop.htm. Copyright ©2008 About, Inc. AllExperts, AllExperts.com, and About.com are registered trademarks of About, Inc. All rights reserved. There is no official record. It is estimated to be around 12 sec.

† "Winners Circle" was produced originally for Cosma International, an automotive components manufacturer, to help its workforce understand the power and simplicity of quick changeover techniques. However, it was so well done that it was subsequently released for the general marketplace. The film brilliantly blends clips of racecar pit crews with a Cosma work team attempting to reduce the changeover time of its 800-ton press from 2 hrs to 10 min.

‡ Shigeo Shingo, Andrew Dillon (translator), *A Revolution in Manufacturing: The Smed System* (New York: Productivity Press) 1985.

HEALTHCARE SETUP TRANSLATION

We normally refer to setups in healthcare as turnover or changeover. Single minute exchange of dies (SMED) was originally developed for changing over dies in large presses used in automotive stamping applications, like a fender on a car. This means the changeover is accomplished in 9 min 59 sec or less. Anything 10 min or more would be considered double minute (digit) exchange of dies.

When analyzing room turnover, each person that has a role or need within changeover will need to be analyzed and have his/her work deconstructed. We divide up tasks in the video into the following categories:

Preparation (P) and organization, which is gathering and preparing tools, information, or anything needed ahead of time for the "changeover." For example:

- Is the bed available with an IV pole and a "roller" to move the patient (technicians, assistants)?
- Does the patient need blood for potential transfusions on standby (nursing personnel)?
- Is the next patient prepared to enter the room (by the surgeon, OR staff, and anesthesiologist)?
- Is the anesthesia equipment prepared?
- Are the clean supplies ready (support staff/assistants)?
- Checking to see if the correct case cart is pulled, any additional instrumentation is needed, especially if there are implants involved.

Mounting (M) and removing includes removing or taking down the previous setup and preparation for the next activity, which could include removing the patient, changing beds, and cleaning up, which can only be done while the patient is out of the room. For example:

- Removing the patient from the room
- Cleaning the room
- Making the bed (unless the patient is prepared in an induction room)
- Moving the next patient into the room

Calibration (C) measurement and testing (positioning) includes making sure things are accurate and ready for setup and that machines are ready for use. Normally these occur after the patient is in the room. For example:

- Calibrating equipment or pre-testing required for anesthesia monitoring or surgical equipment to make sure it is functional and functioning properly.
- Positioning the patient for surgery (ortho cases) Getting the bed to the correct height.

Trial (T) runs and adjustments. Normally these occur after the patient is in the room. For example:

- Actions needed to be taken as a result of "pause for the cause." This is where the surgeon stops to make sure everything is correct and in order prior to beginning the operation.

- An instrument set is not ready so another one has to be retrieved to use in it's place.
- Multiple screws and fittings required for knee replacement.

The next step is to invoke the SMED process, which Shingo developed from 1950 to 1969.[*] This can be thought of in healthcare as SMER (single minute exchange of rooms). There are three steps to the SMED process.

1. The first is to identify internal vs. external work. We do this in our video analysis.
2. The next step is to convert internal to external work wherever possible. So we question every step as to whether it can be converted from internal to external work. This enables us to shorten the clock time on the changeover.
3. The third step is to eliminate, rearrange, simplify, or combine all remaining work.

To complete our analysis, we go back over each step to determine what the "to be" state will look like if we can make improvements to the changeover. We also look for whatever we can omit or how we can shorten the time it takes for each step by making improvements. Initially, it is not unusual to find that most of the internal time is spent on preparation and organization; however, preparation and organization should be almost totally external time and completed before the patient enters the room. Our goal with the other two steps, calibration and trial runs, is to eliminate the need for them. This means the 14.7 sec in our pit stop should only be for internal steps that are related to mounting and moving the patient or product.

In healthcare, SMED can get confusing. The concepts, however, are very applicable to many settings, such as laboratory changeover of equipment/reagent changes, turning over patients such as bed or room cleaning, or radiology, catheterization laboratory and surgery room "turnovers." In addition, the non-clinical areas of laundry, nutritional service areas and even engineering services may have equipment setups.

WHY REDUCE SETUPS? BENEFITS OF SMED/SMER

Reducing setup time immediately increases capacity. The goal is to reduce the time it takes to do a changeover so that the fixed asset can be freed up and utilized as quickly as possible. In surgery it may be an OR that we need to turnover quickly so we can maximize the surgeon's time and get patients in and out faster. In ORs, we have been able to get surgeons one or two more operations a day in the same amount or less time with less waiting between cases. On the floors and in the ED and radiology, it is turning over the room between patients. In the office, it can simply be reloading paper or toner in the copying machine.

---

[*] Shigeo Shingo, Andrew Dillon (translator), *A Revolution in Manufacturing: The Smed System* (New York: Productivity Press) 1985.

We propose that analyzing just the changeover will provide the following pieces of Lean:

- Enabler for one piece or one patient flow or smaller batch sizes
- Immediately increases capacity
- Enabler for mixed model and ability to supply in sets
- Provides quick response to demand changes
- Enabler for more reliable delivery of care
- Capital asset utilization rates increases (if demand is there)
- Reduces material handling
- Results in standardization
- Improved operator safety
- Improved patient/product quality and integrates five S and mistake proofing

ANALYSIS SECTION REVIEW

To review, we started with surveying our customers and finding out what was important to them and what challenges they experienced with the current process. We also interviewed the staff and constructed fishbone diagrams to help categorize and determine the root cause of the problems they faced. Problem is not a bad word; in fact, identifying and bringing attention to problems needs to be encouraged. We need to surface problems by lowering the inventory, eliminating storage or waits, and rework to uncover hidden wastes, remembering that waste hides more waste.

We then determined our customer demand and peak demand (in some cases to the hour) and calculated our Takt time. The demand is the number of patients, products, or services that need to be "processed." Demand could be the number of customers who present to the Emergency Room for treatment in a particular hour, day, month, or year. From the pharmacy's perspective, they would be more interested in the number of medications they need to "fill" in 15 min, 60 min, or daily, so the demand from the pharmacy's perspective might be medication fills per hour or average number of medication filled per patient. Takt time is equal to the available time divided by customer demand or the beat to which we need to construct our new system.

Next came the value stream map, which provided a high-level systemic view of the overall process, identifying process vs. non-process-based activities and a baseline view of throughput for the overall process. Part of our calculations included determining value-added vs. non-value-added time, cycle time, and throughput (LOS) time. The findings and opportunities identified through the value stream map helped us to gain insight into what areas needed improvement and where to focus the next level of tools. Our assessment tools included the PPF, operator analysis, and changeover analysis. It is optional at this point to go back and update the value stream map with the analysis-based data.

Utilizing the PPF tool, we looked at how the product or services "flowed" within and throughout the process. Information was gathered on the time and distance it takes to go through the process or service. We used the eight wastes to identify the value-added percentage along with the process steps that could be eliminated, rearranged, simplified, or combined. We now look at the remaining steps to see which ones can be done in parallel. The product also gives us total throughput time, which we can use to calculate how much inventory (product or patients) needs to be in the system to meet the Takt time. In healthcare, the ability to measure and track throughput as a metric is key to improving processes. There are many processes for which throughput is uniquely defined; one example could be "a stat medication order," where the throughput metric could be defined from the time the medication was ordered by the physician to the time the patient actually received the medication from the nurse. In radiology, an example of throughput would be the arrival of a patient in radiology at the registration desk to the completion of the examination or, better yet, the patient receiving the examination result. Throughput is a key metric in Lean and should be a key metric for every department in every organization. We also pointed out that just because we have to perform a step does not make it value-added. Determining the new flow and new layout begins with the knowledge gained from the PPF analysis.

The next step was performing the operator analysis, which looked at the process from the operator's or staff's point of view and provided a baseline for "labor time." We were then able to eliminate, rearrange, simplify, or combine the steps as they relate to the staff member doing the work. This helped streamline the work of staff persons to make sure that the activities being performed were value-added based on what is "really" needed to achieve the results. Observations during this process provided opportunities to make sure that the staff person had been provided with the "right tools or parts" at the "right place" to get the job done with the least amount of effort, thus the least amount of wasted motions and activity, again using "the eight wastes" as a guide. This provides the basis for standard work and balancing our operation steps. The operator analysis gave us total labor time, which we can now use to calculate how many staff we will need in our newly designed process and area layout.

Then we performed the changeover analysis, which looked at the turnover of the room between patients and the opportunities that existed to convert internal steps to external. Reducing turnover time frees up capacity (beds) throughout the system. It also makes our surgeons much happier as they can get more cases done in the same amount of time, which can be financially rewarding as well.

The overall goal is to achieve a new process flow, free of waste and non-value-added activities. In healthcare this often equates to improving both patient and information flow. Improving flow is fundamental to achieving customer value and delivery of expected results.

Remember, it is essential to ensure that we have clear definitions of each metric. These include precise starting and ending points for the process, how, when, where, and who is collecting it, and over what time frame. It is important that consistency in the metric collection process is obtained. The definitions need to be discussed and clearly understood by all stakeholders to avoid downstream confusion of what exactly is being reported.

To summarize, we have the following key process metrics coming out of the analysis phase: available time, Takt time, throughput time, total labor time, and changeover time.

Lesson Learned: *The real key with Lean is figuring out the product axis vs. the operator axis and changeover axis separately and developing the solution for all of them together.*

9 Putting It All Together

EXECUTIVE SUMMARY

This chapter covers the first S in the BASICS system implementation model, Suggest Solutions. In this chapter we explore:

- Using our future state or "To Be" models for each of our assessment tools
- Designing cycle time to Takt time
- Understanding bottlenecks
- How to balance the workload among staff so that labor distribution is fair
- The value of cross-training
- The principle of *Heijunka* or level-loaded scheduling
- Standard work and leader standard work
- Layout and workstation design
- Lean materials, *Kanban*, plan for every part and supply chain management

One must understand the current and future demands in order to account for both peak and ongoing demand, and leave 50% of current demand for growth potential. It is important to understand cycle time and demand volumes, Takt time and calculating the total labor time from the full work analysis.

Standard work and work in progress are critical underpinnings, as are inventory and supply chain management.

This chapter reviews work in progress, that is, patients who are awaiting treatment and why bottlenecks are created. It defines the term "Herbies," now referred to as "pacemaker," which is the bottleneck point in the process. It is important to understand that people should never be a bottleneck, since we can always add more people. Only machines should be bottlenecks but in hospitals this is sometimes not the case. This chapter emphasizes the importance of prioritizing quality of treatment over speed.

We discuss the principle of *Heijunka*. Which is the sequence of leveling, balancing and smoothing out the schedule or workload. This should result in a steady, constant, error-free workflow and is one of the defining points of Lean. It is a challenge in hospitals since level-loading can become exceptionally difficult, particularly during such processes as Pre-Op evaluation, Pre-Op scheduling, and lab collection.

Standard work is a critical piece of Lean. This is defined as:

1. Cycle time
2. Work sequence
3. Standard inventory

The chapter also includes a discussion on automation and semi-automation, in which semi-automation can provide 80% of the improvement at only 20% of the cost, while full automation takes 80% of the cost to get the additional 20% increase in productivity.

An extensive overview of layouts and spaghetti diagrams. Different types of layouts (U-shaped, the straight line and other diagrams) is included, as is the disutility of islands in the middle of a workspace and emphasis on flexibility. The guidelines for proper layout are:

1. No isolated islands
2. Consider safety and ergonomics first
3. Reduce motions of staff
4. Eliminate or limit doors, drawers and walls
5. Flexibility should be general, from utility grids in ceilings to multi-process-capable, cross-trained staff
6. Use of modular furniture on wheels
7. Create visual controls
8. Co-locate executives near the hospital floor areas
9. Do not rework inside the cell
10. Develop a master layout
11. Get layout approval and establish a "Lean Layout Review Board."

There is also an abbreviated discussion of inventory and supply chain management. This includes the use of a *Kanban* system utilizing different methods to manage materials both internally and with suppliers.

KEY LEARNINGS

- Understanding of how to leverage and integrate the different analysis tools, including value stream mapping, product process flows, operator flows and changeover, to implement a future state Lean environment.
- Understanding the criticality of standard work.
- Importance of balancing the schedule and workload for *Heijunka*.
- Understanding the importance of layouts and inventory management in Lean flow.

Focusing on the first S in our BASICS model (which stands for suggest solutions), the goal of this chapter is to introduce the balance of the tools and how to proceed once the analysis is completed. There are many pieces to a Lean implementation and they are all interconnected. The material in this chapter will walk through the relationships and how the data collected up to this point can be leveraged to prepare you for your implementation. It will discuss suggesting solutions for improvements and making

Phases

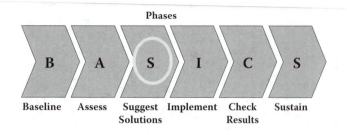

Baseline   Assess   Suggest   Implement   Check   Sustain
                    Solutions   Results

FIGURE 9.1 BASICS model—Suggest Solutions.

recommendations to management to secure their buy-in and approval (Figure 9.1).

The information obtained from the staff during the value stream map, product process flow, operator analysis, and changeover analysis help us develop the key data elements: cycle time, Takt time, demand, available time, and TLT. We then use the analysis to develop standard work, calculate SWIP, design the new layout, and create the new work station/area design. Materials/inventory management supports the new flow of delivering the service or product to the customer. It is important to note that this is a ready… aim… fire… approach, but it is not analysis paralysis. With enough practice, the tools can be applied quickly (in the span of hours, depending on scope).

USING THE FUTURE STATE "TO BE" AND FUTURE STATE ANALYSIS TO DESIGN THE NEW PROCESS AND IMPLEMENTATION

The key elements that need to be considered in your optimal flow design are all derived from the analysis tools we described earlier.

- *The future state value stream map helps provide a road map for areas and projects to focus process improvement, identify wastes and throughput opportunities, and our current state metrics.*
- *Knowing the current and forecasted customer demand and "peak" demand is critical.* We should design our new processes and layouts to 50% of the current demand or to the demand forecasted in the hospital strategic plan in order to encompass future growth.
- *Determine the available time, which is the amount of time available to do work or perform an activity.* An example might be the pre-admission testing area, which operates from 6:00 a.m. to 5:00 p.m. for an available time of 11 hrs or 660 min of operation, while an area such as an emergency room, which is open 24 hrs, has an available time of 1440 min.
- *Understand the Takt time (customer demand divided by available time).* This helps determine the "beat" or "pace" of the activity that needs to performed as well as assists in balancing the workload.
- *The future state or what we call the "To Be" product process flow and point-to-point diagram showed us how the flow should look.* This is where we begin to

design the new layout for the area. This can be done with a computer-aided drawing (CAD) system, but it is usually best to get a "to-scale" diagram of the area and use "paper dolls" or "cutouts" to see how everything fits. It is not unusual to go through many versions of the layout before getting it right. Each time we develop or change the layout, we need to draw a new point-to-point diagram of how things are going to flow using the layout guidelines that we will discuss in more detail later. We need to optimize the layout and work station design to create a "Lean" layout that places the sequence of steps/activities in the correct and/or parallel order.

- *The "To Be" full work of the operator analysis and spaghetti diagram showed us how to optimize operator walk patterns, locations for point-of-use storage, and work station design.* The work station must have the "right tools at the right place" to perform the activities in the proper sequence within the process.
- *The "To Be" changeover analysis showed us what our additional capacity can be.* The key now is to determine if we have the resources necessary and determine the time frame to implement the changeover ideas. We need to calculate the capacity for the areas before and, then after, to determine if they can support the input to and from the area implementing the turnover project. For example, if we can do one or two more surgeries per day per surgeon, can Pre-Op and post-anesthesia care unit (PACU) support the new demand numbers?
- *Calculate the total labor time (TLT) from the full work analysis.* The TLT is equal to the sum of the total value-added and non-value-added labor time. It is the amount of time staff members spend on activities within a process. The demand, available time, and TLT will drive the number of staff or operators needed to run your process, and impact your work area design.
- *Understand the desired cycle time and new staffing model.* The cycle time comes from the operator analysis, the demand and the takt time. We need to figure out how many operators are needed to support the current peak demand and forecasted demand. We then need to make sure we can balance the workload for the staff. After balancing the workload, we will have the cycle time (the amount of time each person must meet to complete their part of the operation or activity within the process). It is calculated by dividing the available time by the volume demand of the new process. It also equals the TLT divided by the number of operators/staff members (if work is balanced evenly). The new layout needs to be reviewed to ensure we have room for the number of persons required to support current, peak, and future demand.
- *Determine if standard work can be applied.* Have the employees in the area help develop the standard work and train to the defined standard work. Make sure to plan for demand fluctuations related to

staff and resource (supply) requirements. This often requires a new staffing model for the area. The plan should include how to run the area with one or two less in case the demand drops or one or two more persons in the event the demand increases.

- *Determine the standard work in process (SWIP).* This calculation determines the minimum amount of inventory that is necessary to perform the task safely and meet the required cycle time. Be aware that batch operations normally require at least double the inventory. The quantity of SWIP may change with revisions to the throughput time, cycle time, and number of operators or staff in the cell or changes in customer demand. In healthcare, often the SWIP is actually patients going through or waiting during the process. We can design the waiting areas based on the projected waiting times divided by the cycle time we plan to run. Keep in mind that we want to design these areas to incorporate present as well as future demand. Consider any innovations or changes from current state such as deploying "pagers for family members" which may decrease space needed in waiting areas (as long as you are actually going to implement).

- *Adjust inventory and understand materials and supply chain management.* Make sure the layout has enough room for the "right amount" of supplies available at the "right time" at point of use, in other words available when needed and room to grow if necessary.

- *Create a plan for every part with a focus on how and where each item will be replenished.* Some options for replenishment include fixed time or fixed quantity *Kanbans*.

- *The layout needs to be flexible.* Put work stations on wheels, don't hard pipe machines, and install flexible utilities wherever possible so that if we have to move equipment or work stations in the future it is not a barrier.

One can now see why we spend time analyzing the process. The analysis of the data will lead you to the optimal solution.

UNDERSTANDING DEMAND AND RESOURCE NEEDS

When converting a process from batch to one-piece flow, there may be some substantial time savings just from running one piece or one patient at a time. Customer demand, cycle time, TLT, and standard work are directly related to one another. In earlier chapters, we discussed calculations relating to staffing to demand. Now it is time to put the calculations into practical use.

Example 9.1

If on average, 120 patients per day come to the Emergency Department (ED) and need to be signed-in, triaged, and seen by the physician, then the average daily demand (ADD)

would be 120 patients per day. The hourly demand would be $120 \div 8$ hrs (for an 8-hrs shift) or 15 patients per hour. This can be extremely important to understand, as this will impact how and when one might want to schedule staff in a clinical area. Since it is difficult to adjust staff to smaller than hourly increments, we normally use hourly demand when looking at staffing resources and balancing labor. Resources can be optimized by scheduling staff to the actual customer demand or arrivals by hour. In healthcare, we have found that managers fall into the routine of scheduling staff in routine shifts—7:00 a.m. to 3:00 p.m., 3:00 p.m. to 11:00 p.m., 7:00 a.m. to 7:00 p.m.—without really understanding when patients arrive or when peak patient services are required.

In the emergency department example, the waiting room is normally filled with patients waiting for care because demand by hour and cycle times of activities have not been analyzed. Often, the physician and staff scheduled hours do not align with the patient arrivals by hour. Therefore, the correct number of staff, scheduled at the right time, performing the right activities is not available, and bottlenecks occur. Working in the healthcare environment, we have found that demand in most areas, even the emergency room, is very predictable. There will always be times when emergencies occur, such as the "bus accident" however, if the manager or supervisor reviews hourly, daily, and seasonal demand, the right resource scheduling is possible.

Using the same demand in the emergency example above, let's examine the initial two process steps in the emergency room arrival: patient sign-in and triage.

Patient sign-in and triage cycle times are determined by performing an operator analysis on each process and understanding the specific tasks involved and the cycle time necessary to perform these activities. An example of sample data is outlined in Table 9.1.

The next step is to review the information in the chart to determine the number of staff needed per shift and the ability to schedule them to fit the hourly demand. We calculated the available time for performing activities for the 7:00 a.m. to 3:00 p.m. shift at 480 min. Understanding the available time, we can now calculate the number of staff needed.

To meet current average shift demand:

Method 1: Total shift labor time ÷ available time = # of staff or operators to meet current demand

Sign-in 600 min ÷ 480 min = 1.25 staff

Triage 720 min ÷ 480 min = 1.50 staff.

In the example above, the TLT to perform the task, contains both value-added and non-value-added activities. When determining final staffing for a given process, be careful that you take into account all the activities or tasks the individual is performing. Another way to calculate number of staff is to take the TLT divided by the cycle time or Takt times (see method 2).

Method 2: Takt time = 60 min/hrs ÷ 15 patients/hrs = 4 min/patient
TLT for 1 patient ÷ Takt time = # of staff

Sign-in 5 min ÷ 4 min = 1.25 staff

Triage 6 min ÷ 4 min = 1.50 staff.

TABLE 9.1

Sample Data Sign-In and Triage

Patient sign-in	Available Time (min)	Total Labor Time For 1 Patient (min)	ADD (Average Daily Demand: 7:00 a.m. to 3:00 p.m.)	Hourly Patient Demand: 7:00 a.m. to 3:00 p.m.)	Takt Time (min)	Required Labor for all patients (min)	# of Staff Required Method 1 = RequiredShift Labor/ Available Time	# of Staff Required Method 2 = TLT/TT
Patient sign-in	480	5	120	15	4.00	600	1.25	1.25
Triage	480	6	120	15	4.00	720	1.5	1.5

Takt time will give you the theoretical, whereas cycle time will give you the actual, unless Takt time = cycle time.

Since we have a person and a fraction of a person (we call this fractional labor), we can't necessarily utilize a fraction of a person, which means that for sign-in the person will be idle 75% of the time. If we only had one staff member assigned to each of the tasks, we would fall behind the pace and the beat of the process would be disrupted, creating bottlenecks or "wait states." So, the solution would be to cross-train the staff to flex from work area/activity to work area/activity, if possible, and capitalize on minimizing fractional labor.

In hospital environments, this is difficult, as only certain people can do certain jobs. When we divide out the numbers, anything above 0.9 people can be rounded up to a full person. The challenge is to eliminate enough work from the area to get the fractional person somewhere between plus and minus 0.1. The key is to divide the work as evenly as possible and have the people in the areas flex to cover minor variations in cycle times. Sometimes, some of the steps can be offloaded to other areas when appropriate to facilitate the balance. Imbalances that are less than about 10% of cycle time will usually not be a problem and are handled by flexing staff or operators. Flexing operators can take two different forms. Ohno uses the analogy between swimming relay handoffs and baton relay handoffs* to describe the differences in flexing. Swimming relay handoffs require the next worker to wait until the person prior to them completes their work, whereas a baton relay handoff allows work to be handed off before it is completed but requires the operator to be able to perform that work.

In order to do this, we need layouts that support flexing, and each person has to have the necessary skills to carry out each of the tasks involved. At many hospitals, this creates an initial barrier; for example registration may be centralized, located in partitioned cubes (isolated), or doesn't want to cross-train non-registration personnel. Sometimes, to flex labor we may decide to staff a level up or even create a new higher-grade position. For example, staffing with a nurse vs. a technician as the nurse could carry out additional duties where the technician could not. This involves a cost-benefit decision. Is it worth paying a higher skilled salary vs. having a technician idle 50%–75% of

the time? Often we find this analysis doesn't take place, and many times finance discourages this line of thinking.

In the example listed above, an option would be to add a second triage nurse as a backup for times when there are more patients waiting than 1 nurse can handle or if triage takes longer than the average 5 min, as there are variations in the time it takes. Another option would be to add up the TLT of 600 min for sign-in plus 720 min for triage and then divide by 480 min of available time to determine the combined labor needs, which would equate to 2.75 operators or staff. This again assumes that staff are interchangeable and again assumes that the layout is flexible and the work can be balanced.

Every time there is a change in demand, a change in products or services offered, a change in process, or new machinery introduced (i.e., robots or new diagnostic equipment), it necessitates recalculating all the numbers in order to re-balance the work flow. World-class companies see these changes as opportunities to improve and eliminate even more waste in the process. Be careful with elements of a job that may have been categorized as a group of operations with a large chunk of time. Sometimes these can be split up to get the work to balance. As a normal rule of thumb, we analyze operations down to the second to avoid this problem. Bottlenecks may also be caused by machines that require extended machine cycle times or that have larger capacity to run multiple tests or processes. Ask yourself, what can be done to separate the machine work from the human work or to divide up the machine tasks across different machines?

Now consider the following ED example, which will pull together the concepts of a target metric, cycle time, Takt time, demand, and available time.

APPROPRIATE RESOURCING CAN DRIVE METRICS

Example 9.2

Patients present to the emergency room for critical care, urgent care, and for non-urgent treatment care. Urgent and non-urgent patients (patients who leave the same day) expect to see the physician within 20 min of arrival, which is defined as the time the patient sign in to the time the physician examination is started. So, we need to ensure delivery of value to our customer by making improvements to achieve a door-to-physician time less than or equal to

---

* Taiichi Ohno, *Toyota Production System* (New York: Productivity Press) 1988.

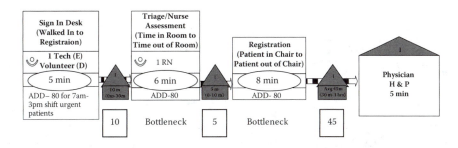

FIGURE 9.2   VSM (value stream map) ED boxes before—needs work.

20 min. A value stream map was created and the data revealed the demand through the ED was 15 patients per hour (average) for the 7:00 a.m. to 3:00 p.m. shift. Ten of the 15 patients per hour were non-urgent. The average baseline cycle time from door to physician was 79 min (5 + 10 + 5 + 6 + 8 + 45) (Figure 9.2).

- Sign-in: 5 min (with a range of 1–15 min)
- Triage: 6 min (with a range of 0–25 min)
- Registration collection of demographic information: 8 min (with a range of 2–20 min)

To calculate demand for non-critical patients:

- Available time = time per shift 7:00 a.m. to 3:00 p.m. = 8 hrs × 60 min = 480 min (note: lunches are covered by staff or charge nurse)
- Hourly non critical demand = 10 patients per hour (note: demand by hour does not always equal the average)
- Daily shift non critical demand (8 hrs shift 7:00 a.m. to 3:00 p.m.) = 80 patients per day
- Total process time from the process boxes = 19 min (5 + 6 + 8)
- Total storage times in the triangle boxes = 60 min (10 + 5 + 45)
- Total throughput time door-to-MD = 19 min process time + 60 min of storage (patient wait) time = 79 min on average (ranging from 33 to 234 min)

Since the Takt time is:

$$60 \text{ min} \div 10 \text{ patients} = 6 \text{ min}$$

So, we need to design a process where Every 6 min, a patient sees the physician to be able to achieve the Takt time or "pace" of how patients arrive to the emergency room.

If each process step is not completed at or below the 6 min Takt time, then a "bottleneck" or wait state will occur creating excess WIP, i.e., patients waiting.

Remember, any excess WIP or idle time is the sign of a problem within a Lean system. A bottleneck is the constraint, (where the capacity of the machine cannot meet the demand) in any series of operations in a process. Per the theory of constraints, which is explained in detail in a book entitled *The Goal*,[*] the cycle time will always be equal to the slowest machine or slowest person in the process. We refer to these constraints as "Herbies." In theory, a person (Herbie) should never be a constraint as we can

always add people but we cannot always add or speed up machines. In essence, only machines should be bottlenecks in a process. This is a good and bad news story. The bad news is we have a backup or bottleneck. The good news is we not only know we have a backup, but we also can now predict when the backup will start, how long it will last, and how many patients will queue up.

Bottlenecks occur in the process if each of these tasks is sequential and we have only one work area for each process staffed with one person. The sign-in process is 5 min and the subsequent processes are 6 and 8 min, respectively. So the slowest process is 8 min, which means we can't go faster than 8 min cycle times unless we add people to or speed up the registration process.

We cannot meet the 6 min Takt time as the process is currently configured. So the backup starts at registration (8 min CT) Sign-in has an average of 1 min of idle time compared to the takt time but is 3 min slower than registration. Every cycle, we get 2 min behind per person (6 min per arrival vs. 8 min for registration). So, for every 4 patients, one will back-up after triage and before registration. Assuming no variation, we would never have a back up at sign-in. Hence, we can predict the queue (Figure 9.3).

Let's say our demand changes to 12 patients per hour. Now patients arrive every 5 min (new Takt time), which would create a backup starting at the triage nurse (6 min CT). Now there is no idle time at sign in. Now for each patient, we lose 1 min at triage and 3 min at registration. We can predict that every 6 patients we will back-up a patient before triage because the triage nurse is losing 1 min for every patient that arrives. Registration is losing

[*] Goldratt, Eliyahu & Cox, Jeff. *The Goal* (North River Press) 2004.

Queuing Example			Queuing Example		
# of Patients	6 minTakt Time Arrivals	Registration Cycle Time Queue	# of Patients	5 minTakt Time Arrivals	Registration Cycle Time Queue
1	6	8	1	5	8
2	12	16	2	10	16
3	18	24	3	15	24
4	24	32	4	20	32
5	30	40	5	25	40
6	36	48	6	30	48
7	42	56	7	35	56
8	48	64	8	40	64
9	54	72	9	45	72
10	60	80	10	50	80
11	66	88	11	55	88

FIGURE 9.3   VSM (value stream map) operator load chart.

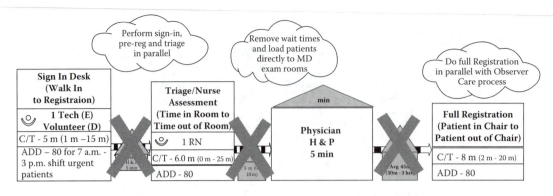

FIGURE 9.4   Future state ED VSM (value stream map) process boxes.

3 min per patient arrival (8 min–5 min). So for every 8 patients, Registration gets 3 patients behind.

In the above example, the cycle time for a history and physical examination by the physician is 5 min, so we are not going to meet customer expectations or the 20 min target metric owing to the bottlenecks in the process (Figure 9.4).

In real life, because we experience these bottlenecks and the added complexity of acuities in the ED, the triage nurse will start to shuffle the order of patients sent through the process in order to treat "sicker" patients first (i.e., the essence of the word triage). This then changes the first-in, first-out sequence of the patients to "see the physician," which further impacts the ability to meet the customer-defined 20 min target and contributes to even more bottlenecks within the process. Understanding Takt time and process cycle and wait times will help assess the resources and staffing required to balance the workload.

Sometimes, we may be in a situation where we cannot "run to customer demand." An example of this might be if we had an employee out sick. If we could not find a replacement, we would run to a slower cycle time than Takt time and we would fall behind, and patients would wait. If later in the day additional staff came in, then we might be able to run at a faster cycle time than our Takt time and whittle down the queue.

The next step would be to perform either an analysis of cycle time through observation with a stopwatch or perform a formal product process flow and operator full work analysis with a video camera to determine if any of the activities that occur in each of the sub-processes of door-to-physician could be eliminated, simplified or combined, or rearranged to be done in parallel.

In the example below, it was determined the "wait states" between processes could be nearly eliminated once we analyzed the Takt time, cycle times, and resource needs. In addition, the staff felt, since the value proposition was in

seeing the physician, "full" registration could be done in parallel later in the process. Operator full work analysis was used to determine standard work and provide cycle time information that will be used to calculate the amount of staff needed to meet the customer expectations (Figure 9.5).

TRUE BOTTLENECKS

A true bottleneck is defined as a machine that runs 24 hrs a day and can not meet Takt time. In healthcare, the ED room can be a true bottleneck, as witnessed when the ED goes into inpatient "hold" status, where patients are unable to be moved to units and therefore remain in a "wait-state" in the ED resulting in lengthy delays or diversions. How we handle a true bottleneck is different from other constraints. Other constraints can be made up with overtime or speeding up the machine, etc. But true bottlenecks must be managed intensely to mitigate any lost time. It is important during the analysis phase to look at the processes as an overall system and determine whether there are any true bottlenecks lurking.

CROSS-TRAINING

Staff need appropriate cross-training to perform the tasks and have a clear understanding of the benefits to the customer, and the organization and to address "what is in it for me" as it relates to each person. Cross-training is normally the first thing needed in order to achieve the desired workload balancing. Staff members must be multi-process capable to fine tune the work distribution. This necessitates that they learn more tasks or operations within a cell or work area. One way to facilitate this training is to use a cross-training matrix and post it on the team communication board to keep track of which staff members are trained up to what level in each task.

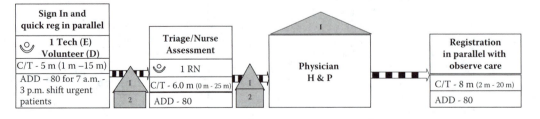

FIGURE 9.5   ED VSM (value stream map) process boxes after Lean. With the improvements in parallel processing we now have 11 min process and 4 min storage = 15 min total cycle time.

TABLE 9.2

Cross-Training Matrix Sample

Name	Task 1	Task 2	Task 3
Jane	3	3	4
Karl	4	1	0
Loretta	0	4	2

Legend: 0 = untrained, 1 = in training, 2 = produces quality tasks, 3 = meets cycle time, 4 = can train others

How to Construct a Cross-Training Matrix

Each staff member that works in the area is rated based on a set of objective measures (0–4). These ratings should be continually monitored and revised. If a staff member has not worked in a particular area or performed the task for a given period of time (i.e., 6 months), they should either be re-certified or lose their status for that operation (Table 9.2).

In an environment where continuous improvement is practiced, the tasks or operations will be continually improving and changing. This requires the staff to be trained on the latest developments and standard work in the area. The goal for the area should be to have all staff at a status "3" or above on all operations/tasks. This is just one example of cross-training matrices that can range from simple to complex.

HEIJUNKA—SEQUENCING ACTIVITIES, LOAD BALANCING

Production leveling, also known as *production smoothing* or—by its Japanese original term—*heijunka* (平準化[*]), 平 means "a plain, flat, level," 準 means "standard, level," and 化 means "change."

Level loading is a technique for reducing the *mura* waste and is vital to the development of production efficiency in the Toyota Production System and Lean manufacturing. The general idea is to produce intermediate goods at a constant rate, to allow further processing to be carried out at a constant and predictable rate.[†]

In manufacturing, this concept is utilized to level out production of various or "mixed" models. This concept allows Toyota to run multiple car types down the same line one model after another. This can only be accomplished with flexibility built into the layout, equipment, utilities, and people. The idea behind this concept is to schedule your patients evenly so as not to create batches of patients coming in at one time. In some areas of hospitals this is easy to do, and in some areas it may be near impossible to do.

In a hospital setting, this mixed model concept could be interpreted as running multiple types of surgery at the same time or running various levels of acuity down a Lean care track in an ED. In order to properly sequence activities within an operation, one must understand the order of the activities and in most cases, the information flow. Often, the information flow will actually pace the progress of the patient through the process. The product process flow analysis gives us this data and then we combine it with the "amount of demand" and type of demand in products or services to determine the sequence.

Once the proper sequence is determined, the flow of the patients must be balanced and evenly distributed to the extent possible. In Lean, we call this demand smoothing, level loading, or *Heijunka*. We then need to match the product process flow (understanding the "critical value-added and non-value-added but necessary activities") to what is "required" by the operator or staff person within the amount of time (cycle time) it takes to perform those activities that come from the full work analysis. We need to be able to optimize the delivery of products or services within the time frame the customer desires or that which is demanded by the process Takt time.

When all the patients arrive at the same time, it creates a domino effect across the system, pulling on all system resources at the same time, disrupting first-in, first-out and the ability to concentrate and effectively prioritize the work. A simple example might be pre-admission testing. 40 patients were scheduled by the physicians' offices to come to the clinic as outlined in Table 9.3.

The majority of the patients arrived for pre-admission testing between 6:00 a.m. and 9:00 a.m. If the total cycle time (and labor time) for the visit was 60 min, to meet the early morning demand we needed 10 staff members; this resulted in more staff and more labor costs than needed throughout the day, as the majority of work was performed in the initial 3 hrs. If the area was staffed to handle only the average workload, then a bottleneck would occur and some patients would wait for over 5 hrs ultimately resulting in dissatisfied customers. The process owner of the area surveyed the customers and found that patients didn't mind coming in throughout the day. By still providing the desired morning appointments and revising the open slots, they were able to level out the rest of the day (Table 9.4). Staffing was improved, morale was better, and they were able to make their targeted times and output to meet demand.

Another example of level loading would be to set up the clinic schedules at an even rate each hour and then staff to that rate. Figure 9.6 shows the patient is in and the chart is ready.

Another example is the *Heijunka* box we used in the pre-testing department (Figure 9.7). Each slot represents half-hour increments. The night before, it is loaded with each patient by schedule time. In the back is a no-show and cancelled slot. We immediately know by hour who is late and how many are scheduled for that hour. Each slip contains spots to fill in process times so we can track the cycle time of each step and the overall throughput time. The times were manually entered into an Excel spreadsheet and goals were set for the overall time the patient spent going through the process. The goals were based on obtaining a complete and thorough assessment of the patient along with collecting all required labs and x-rays.

The fact that hospitals, in general, do not level load their schedules creates a tremendous amount of waste in their systems in extra labor and overtime costs.

---

[*] Translation provided by Professor William Tsutsui, Associate Dean for International Studies, Professor of History, College of Liberal Arts & Sciences, The University of Kansas.

[†] Taiichi Ohno, *Toyota Production System* (New York: Productivity Press) 1988.

TABLE 9.3
Before Pre-Testing Schedule

Hours	Available Time per hour (min)	Patients Scheduled	Cumulative patients	Percent of Total Daily Patients	Takt Time	TLT Per Patient (min)	Appointment Total Labor Time (min)	# of Staff Needed Method 1	# of Staff Needed Method 2
6:00 a.m. to 7 a.m.	60	10	10	25.0%	6.0	60.0	600	10.0	10.0
7:00 a.m. to 8 a.m.	60	8	18	45.0%	7.5	60.0	480	8.0	8.0
8:00 a.m. to 9 a.m.	60	6	24	60.0%	10.0	60.0	360	6.0	6.0
9:00 a.m. to 10 a.m.	60	3	27	67.5%	20.0	60.0	180	3.0	3.0
10:00 a.m. to 11 a.m.	60	3	30	75.0%	20.0	60.0	180	3.0	3.0
11:00 to noon	60	4	34	85.0%	15.0	60.0	240	4.0	4.0
Noon to 1:00 p.m.	60	2	36	90.0%	30.0	60.0	120	2.0	2.0
1:00 to 2:00 p.m.	60	2	38	95.0%	30.0	60.0	120	2.0	2.0
2:00 to 3:00 p.m.	60	2	40	100.0%	30.0	60.0	120	2.0	2.0
Daily	540	40			13.5		2400	40	40

In many cases, all their resources are needed at the exact same time. Examples of this are getting patients ready in Pre-Op for 7:30 a.m. starts, and the morning collection run for the phlebotomists. In most hospitals, the a.m. phlebotomist collection or "morning run" requires that blood draws are performed over a short interval of time for a large number of hospital inpatients as the results need to be available for physicians morning rounds. This causes an extreme burden for laboratory services and resources from 2:00 a.m. to 7:00 a.m. every morning. It is very difficult for a hospital to hire phlebotomists to work 4 to 5 hrs per day from 2:00 a.m. to 7:00 a.m. to meet this peak demand. This is one of the cases where demand and staffing is difficult to modify. One might consider cross-training to flex phlebotomist staff during off-peak times to other laboratory tasks such as receiving, or review by floor the time that the laboratory results are truly needed for the "internal customers" (physicians) by reviewing the physician rounding schedules to see if there is any potential to level the workload.

Level loading surgical cases throughput the week and throughput the day has been shown to be very beneficial in

TABLE 9.4
Heijunka (Level Loading) After Pre-testing Schedule

Hours	Available Time per hour (min)	Patients Scheduled	Cumulative patients	Percent of Total Daily Patients	Percent of Total Daily Patients Per Hour	Takt Time	TLT Per Patient (min)	Appointment Total Labor Time (min)	# of Staff Needed Method 1	# of Staff Needed Method 2
6:00 a.m. to 7 a.m.	60	5	5	12.5%	12.5%	12.0	60.0	300	5.0	5.0
7:00 a.m. to 8 a.m.	60	5	10	25.0%	12.5%	12.0	60.0	300	5.0	5.0
8:00 a.m. to 9 a.m.	60	5	15	37.5%	12.5%	12.0	60.0	300	5.0	5.0
9:00 a.m. to 10 a.m.	60	5	20	50.0%	12.5%	12.0	60.0	300	5.0	5.0
10:00 a.m. to 11 a.m.	60	4	24	60.0%	10.0%	15.0	60.0	240	4.0	4.0
11:00 to noon	60	5	29	72.5%	12.5%	12.0	60.0	300	5.0	5.0
Noon to 1:00 p.m.	60	4	33	82.5%	10.0%	15.0	60.0	240	4.0	4.0
1:00 to 2:00 p.m.	60	4	37	92.5%	10.0%	15.0	60.0	240	4.0	4.0
2:00 to 3:00 p.m.	60	3	40	100.0%	7.5%	20.0	60.0	180	3.0	3.0
Daily	540	40				13.5		2400	40	40

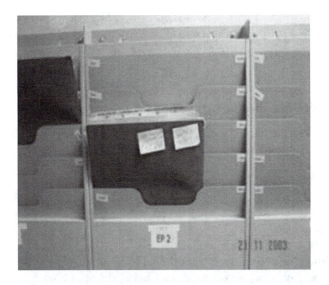

FIGURE 9.6 Heijunka appointment scheduling box EP laboratory.

some hospitals, improving the ability to free up bed capacity and improve ED flow. Level loading the cases directly impacted the number of beds needed on the same days of the week, spreading the need throughput the week. Remember, hospital services and resources are inter-mingled and adjustments in one clinical area can directly impact other clinical areas. This concept, while simple, is very important to making our Lean processes run smoothly. The goal in Lean is to staff the process based on data thus managing by fact. Then work to improve the process and layouts to take out costs. If you focus on the process, instead of cutting costs, you will get the results.

STANDARD WORK

We traveled recently to Scotland and somehow got the courage up to rent a car. I handed the agent my license and credit

FIGURE 9.7 Heijunka scheduling box unsed in surgical services pre-testing department.

card but when he placed my credit card into the machine it wouldn't work. Apparently, in the U.K. the credit cards have a chip so the card is no longer swiped as in the U.S. Fortunately he had a way to swipe the card as well. He then explained a couple of differences about the car, a VW Passat. For example, the key is no longer turned in the ignition. It is instead completely depressed into the ignition and with one foot on the brake and one foot on the clutch it starts up. We took our luggage to the vehicle and I went to the driver's side only to find the passenger seat. Of course, we are in the U.K. now, so I went over to the other driver's side and sat down. It was a beautiful car. I figured out the ignition and the parking brake and slowly ventured out with the mirror on my left side and left handed stick shift to drive on the left side of the road. Having made it through two traffic circles and a right hand turn in front of traffic to the hotel two miles away I figured I could manage driving anywhere. We then ventured out to the highlands to visit "whiskey" country. We were moving along and I was following the speed of traffic when I saw the first speed limit sign with a 30 on it with a red circle around it. I looked down at the speedometer and noticed it was in miles per hour and in addition there was a digital speedometer in the middle that was Kilometers per Hour. I wasn't sure which one the sign was for but since everyone seemed to be going 30 miles per hour (much faster than 30 km per hour) I figured we must be in miles per hour. As we got out into the country there was a strange absence of speed limit signs. Just signs that had a black circle with a slash on a white background. Since I was the lead car I wasn't sure what this meant. Several cars started passing me so I figured I must be going too slow. Then we saw signs that showed a picture of a camera and said speed cameras in use. I was panicked as I didn't know the speed limit and the car rental agent made it very clear we were responsible for any tickets. We eventually were able to ask some of the locals questions we had concerning their standards. Between the innocuous road signs, chip credit cards, clutch and driving on the left hand side it was quite an adventure and somewhat stressful. Scotland is a beautiful country and has one foot in the metric system and one in the English system. This reminds me of the space vehicle designed by NASA that had problems because some engineers designed using the metrics system where others used the English system of measure.

Lesson Learned: *The message here is that when things are not standardized it is easy to make mistakes.*

Story

Excerpt from The Five Patients by Michael Crichton[*]
Surgeon: *"Give me the smallest Fogarty you have."*
Circulating Nurse: *"Here is a number four"*
Surgeon: *Let's have a look at it, opens it up, "it looks too large, are you sure you don't have something smaller?"*

---

* Michael Crichton, *The 5 Patients* (Books) 1970.

Scrub Nurse to Circulating Nurse:" I know we have a six at least"

Circulating Nurse: But a six is larger than a number four" (she said it hesitantly because numbers do not always run the same way. For instance, urinary catheters nasogastric tubes run in proportion to size—a number 14 is larger than a 12. But needles and sutures run in the opposite direction, an eighteen is much larger than a 21.

Circulating Nurse: "Well see if there is something smaller." There wasn't. The Surgeon made a small cut in the artery wall, and found he could slip in the number four Fogarty without difficulty.

This story illustrates problems have existed with standardization for years within healthcare. When increasing numbers could mean larger or smaller products there is more chance for error and confusion among staff.

The "Holy Grail of Lean" is standard work. Without standard work there can be no improvement in the process, no flexibility, and no guarantee of quality from the process. If we are going to create a continuous improvement environment, standard work must be the foundation of every process. Each operator must be trained and must execute the steps in order for each operation the same way, every time. Taiichi Ohno said, "The first step toward improvement is standardization; where there is no standard, there can be no improvement."[*]

This does not mean that operators are robots. As the operators get into a rhythm doing standard work, we want them to constantly think about how to improve the processes. It is the supervisor's job to spend at least 50% of their time encouraging and implementing process improvement ideas. All improvements should be documented by updating the standard work and then training all the operators. Then every operator must use the new method until it is improved again.

Policy and procedures are not the same as standard work. A policy and procedure dictates what we do and, sometimes, what is expected and who is responsible. How does this compare to standard work?

Standard work is defined by Ohno[†] as three items:

1. Cycle time
2. Work sequence
3. Standard inventory

JOB BREAKDOWN/FULL WORK ANALYSIS

Behind or underneath standard work are job breakdown instructions with detailed steps and times so anyone can perform the work (assuming proper training and certification dexterity, etc.). In the BASICS approach we breakdown the job to the second

as part of the full work analysis. Included in the analysis are key points for each step (how you do the work) and reasons for key points (which is why you do the work). The premise for all standard work is Training Within Industry (TWI).[‡]

DEVELOPING STANDARD WORK

When planning standard work, it is important not to overburden or overwork employees. Once the waste is eliminated, the goal is for employees to work at a normal pace and create an environment where employees are able to take on additional tasks and become multi-skilled and multi-process-capable. Productivity increases and employees become more valuable and more marketable without working harder.

A good analogy for standard work is a pass play in football. Each time, the operator (receiver) must run the pattern (sequence of operations) in the same amount of time. (cycle time) in order to complete the pass. If an operator does not follow the play or is too slow or too fast, they will not catch the ball. As a result, football teams videotape plays, review the tape to look for improvements, and practice, practice, practice. The same is required to implement and sustain Lean.

Another good analogy is an orchestra. Have you ever heard a fifth grade orchestra play? How do they sound compared to a symphony orchestra? Let's look at our three components of standard work. What is the sequence of operations or steps? If you answered the music or each note, that is correct. Think about it. Every note must be played in the exact order and the right note needs to be played. What if everyone in the symphony orchestra did what a lot of our employees do and decided to play the notes in the order they want to play them? After all, forcing them to play the music as it is written would make them robots, wouldn't it? What if each person in the orchestra believed that they had a better way to play the music? What if they paid no attention to the conductor (supervisor)? What if they never practiced?

The next component of standard work is cycle time. What represents cycle time in our example? Cycle time is represented by the length of each note and the need to play the note for exactly the correct amount of time. It is important to differentiate cycle time from Takt time. Standard work must be based on cycle time because to run to Takt time may not always be feasible. For example, Takt time may dictate that the line or area is run with 1.5 people, but we can't run with half of a person. Therefore, we must run with two people. This means we have to recalculate the time using two people, which is going to give us a cycle time that will run faster than Takt time. This means we will over produce unless we stop the line when we meet the required output or we find something else for the half a person to do each cycle. In the hospital environment, this is further driven by the difference in skill sets and the need to have additional people (not just fractional) to run the area. In addition, since there is so much

---

[*] Japan Management Association, *Kanban Just-in-Time at Toyota.* (New York: Productivity Press) 1989.

[†] Taiichi Ohno, *Toyota Production System* (New York: Productivity Press) 1988.

[‡] Donald Dinero, *Training Within Industry and Training Within Industry Manual* (New York: Productivity Press) 2005.

variation in some cases with how certain patient care must be delivered, we may have to have a range of cycle times in the standard work.

The SWIP inventory can be viewed as the instrument the musician is playing. In some cases, a musician may have more than one instrument in the inventory due to the demands of the musical score.

The difference with the fifth grade orchestra is that they don't always hit the right notes, they don't always get the timing right, and they may not have exactly the right instruments. Like a symphony, standard work first has to be created (i.e., the musical score or the football play). Then it takes training and education and lots of practice to make sure we hit the notes correctly and follow the beat. The beat in our musical example is like the Takt time, which is comparable to the time signature of the score (i.e., 4/4 or 3/4 time). Standard work is actively being deployed in healthcare to improve quality; examples include: the process in administering blood products, SBAR, and handoff communication.

Most good operators will intuitively see the need for standard operations once you start to try to balance the line. The line cannot be balanced without standard work. Standard work cannot be implemented until all the parts and tools are available in the correct order (product process flow) for the operators to do their job.

Standard work is the foundation for continuous line improvement, line flexibility, and quality improvements. Each staff member must be trained and must execute the steps in each operation the same way every time. Does that mean we can never improve the process? No! We can improve the processes and, in fact, encourage process improvements by suggesting that line staff come up with improvements, try the improvements (to ensure results), document the improvements, train the staff on the improvements, and make sure each person uses the new method until it is improved again.

Lesson Learned: *The only way this system can work is if we give the supervisors time to carry out the improvements.*

TRUE STANDARDIZED WORK

Some make a distinction between true standardized work and standard work. True standardized work is obtained in the results and found by standard work audits, which means we follow the steps in an exact repeatable sequence and hit the times with the right standard work in process (SWIP) for each step every time. Another term for standardized work might be one-piece, balanced, synchronized flow. Standard work means we follow the steps, but because of variation in the process, we don't always hit our times. Machines, for example, do true standardized work. In some cases, if the line is set up properly, an assembly or semi-automated line can achieve true standardized work. True standardized work can be very difficult to obtain in some hospital processes owing to the variation that exists between patients and acuities.

STANDARD WORK FORM

Standard work is derived from the full work analysis we did earlier. After documenting the operator steps, key points and reasons for key points, we go back and look for items to omit or items where we can save time through the improvements brainstormed during the analysis process, i.e., eliminate, rearrange, simplify, or combine. The steps that are not omitted are then rearranged into the proper sequence and become the basis for how to do the job. This becomes the basis for standard work.

Table 9.5 shows a standard work form. The standard work form is primarily designed for the supervisor. It is constructed at a higher level than the full work analysis (job breakdown). We have added columns for key points and reasons for key points, which were derived from the TWI.[*] We have also merged what is called a standard job sheet, which depicts a layout of the area. The standard job sheet is used to show the operator walk patterns, denote safety items, WIP storage, number of operators, quality checks, and pipe locations. This form can be adapted to any area. We normally create standard job sheets for plus or minus one or two operators so the supervisor can run the process short or with additional staff.

WORK STANDARDS

Work standards are different than standard work and are designed around jobs that do not repeat or only repeat every so often. In some cases, the work standard may have times for each step or a range of times for each step. Remember, we can only implement true standardized work where we have constant repeatable operations with little or no variation. This means all tools, materials, supplies, and equipment, are ready in their proper locations and in the right amounts necessary and on hand exactly where they will be needed.

In healthcare settings, this is not always possible. No 2 patients are exactly the same, and since we are generally in the repair business, we can encounter substantial variation between patients and what is required to treat each patient may be different. For example, in the emergency room, some patients may simply need a prescription for an antibiotic while others need a full workup of diagnostic tests and x-rays. In the clinic setting, elderly or immobile patients take longer to process. So, in many cases we have to implement work standards in addition to or as part of standard work. Sequence of operations, SWIP, and/or cycle time may vary. In some areas, we have struggled to even get to a work standard because every patient is so unique, i.e., coming out of surgery. In PACU, we ended up with three categories of work and standardized the sequence of operations to the extent it made sense within each of the three categories:

1. *Patient arrives in PACU*
   Every patient presents differently so these tasks are listed but do not necessarily follow the same

---

[*] Donald Dinero, *Training Within Industry and Training Within Industry Manual* (New York: Productivity Press) 2005.

TABLE 9.5

Standard Work Form

Nurse Job Standard Work														
Area	Total Labor Time	Available Time Minutes	Daily Demand	Takt Time Minutes			HEAD COUNT:		1	3	4	5	6	
							CYCLE TIME:							
							HOURLY OUTPUT:							
							DAILY OUTPUT:							
Standard Work Area:							Layout Area and Walk Patterns							
Job Step #	Nurse Description (what they do)	Key Points and Quality Notes (how they do it)	Reasons for Key Points	Min Time (secs)	Max Time (secs)	Avg Time (secs)	Cumulative Avg Time Minutes							
1														
2														
3														

sequence. We adjusted the steps to fit 60%–80% of the patients. Here we had to include a work standard.

2. *Nurse is cycling patient*
   These steps are repeated: monitoring and assessing the patient. The only issue here is if a patient changes acuity levels, then the steps would obviously change. In this case, we could include sequence of steps and cycle time.

3. *Patient has met criteria and is ready to be discharged*
   These steps were the most repeatable and could have cycle times attached.

Lesson Learned: *The Lean tools are a guide and cannot be "cookie-cuttered" into every healthcare application, even from site to site. You have to do what makes sense for the area in which you are working and use the tools appropriate to that area.*

Eventually Standard Work Can Lead to Semi- or Complete Automation[*]

As we standardize work and activities, we can now see opportunities to semi-automate or completely automate tasks. This concept, especially in the United States, is met with resistance. Yet, this is the nature of technological change. People should not have to do mundane, repetitive, boring jobs all day long. If a machine can do it, we should let a machine do it. We cannot let the fact that a person's job may be eliminated get in our way of improving a task.

We need to make sure we don't lay anyone off due to continuous improvement and that we invest in re-training those displaced for new or revised jobs. Our experience is jobs can be semi-automated (i.e., using a power screwdriver vs. a manual screwdriver) and realize 80% of the improvement for about 20% of the cost. It normally takes the other 80% of the cost to get 20% more improvement by fully automating tasks. The Shingo chart shows this path from manual to semi-automation to full automation (Figure 9.8).[†]

Lesson Learned: *It is not until machines are doing tasks that we can start truly mistake-proofing operations.*

Leader Standard Work

The concept of leader standard work supports the overall system. This means every employee up to the CEO has standard work as a basis for their jobs. The work is less standardized the higher one is in the organization. David Mann, in his book *Creating a Lean Culture*,[‡] describes "leader standard work" in detail.

Whether you are a supervisor or CEO you may wonder why you need Leader Standard Work. One reason is it truly helps manage your day, and the other is to set an example and role model the behaviors desired from the rest of your organization. It doesn't mean everything is done to the second, but starts to allow the groundwork for *Gemba* walks or "rounding," which used to be called "managing by walking around," and blocks out your calendar so it is done each day. When a leader rounds several times each day they are:

[*] Shigeo Shingo, *A Study of the TPS From an Industrial Engineering Viewpoint* (Productivity Press) 1989.

[†] Shigeo Shingo, *The Shingo Non Stock Production: The Shingo System for Continuous Improvement* (New York: Productivity Press) 1988.

[‡] Mann, *Creating a Lean Culture.*

Type	Hand Functions				Mental Functions			
	Principal Operations				Marginal Allowances			
	Main Operations		Incidental Operations		(Usual Method)		(Toyota Method)	
Stage	Cutting	Feeding	Installation Removal	Switch Operation	Detecting Abnormalities	Disposition of Abnormalities	Detecting Abnormalities	Disposition of Abnormalities
1 Manual operation	worker	worker	worker	worker	worker	worker	worker	worker
2 Manual feed, automation cutting	machine	worker	worker	worker	worker	worker	worker	worker
3 Automatic feed, automation cutting	machine		worker	worker	worker	worker	Machine that stops automatically (worker oversees more than one machine)	worker
4 Semiautomation	machine		machine	machine	worker	worker	Machine (worker oversees more than one machine)	worker
5 Preautomation (automation with a human touch)	machine		machine	machine	machine	worker	Machine (automation with a human touch)	worker
6 True automation	machine		machine		machine	machine	machine	machine

FIGURE 9.8 Shingo transition to automation. Reprinted from Table 3 on page 71 of *A Study of the Toyota Production System* by Shigeo Shingo,© 1989 Productivity Inc, PO Box 13390 Portland, OR 97213, 800-394-6868. www.productivityinc.com. With permission.

- Checking visual controls
- Attending huddles
- Encouraging improvement suggestions
- Sitting in on a quality circle
- Performing a Five S, standard work, or *Heijunka* audit
- Answers a question from a supervisor with "what do they think they should do"
- Suggests an A3 root cause analysis

It shows the staff that these things are important and reinforces the desired behaviors and helps develop their ability to think.

CAPACITY ANALYSIS—PART PRODUCTION CAPACITY SHEET

Ohno said capacity is equal to work + waste.[*] Throughput time is how long it takes for a patient or product to get through the entire process. It is composed of process time, transport time, and wait times.

Lean has a tool called the part production capacity sheet (Table 9.6). Once we have analyzed the area, this sheet is the vehicle to pull all the data together. This sheet is described in many books but is well-documented in the book, *Toyota Production System.*[†]

LAYOUT DESIGN

The PPF and operator analysis help to determine the proposed changes to the product flow and how the operator activities will be improved within the new flow. The point-to-point and spaghetti diagrams help to show how the product flows through the current layout and the challenges the product and operator experience in the current state. The next analysis peels down one more level to workstation design. It is critical to look at the layout and work station design as part of the process improvement. Most base layouts are generally full of the waste of transportation, which leads to the waste of over production (batching), waste of inventory, and waste of idle time. If the layout is not fixed or the work station design corrected, it may be virtually impossible to achieve the targeted results.

MASTER LAYOUTS

Typically, we recommend companies begin our implementation approach with a pilot area. Once the BASICS tools are implemented, the companies now have an idea of the time and dedication required to pursue this implementation strategy. When the first project is completed, we suggest they put an overall implementation plan together. Part of that plan should be to develop a master layout early on in the process. The advantage of creating this master layout is, as we implement ongoing improvement we can work to begin to move or place the new lines, machines or work stations where they fit in the overall new Lean master layout. We have seen companies save a tremendous amount of time and expense getting their layout right the first time as opposed to moving entire areas multiple times per year. In manufacturing, we utilized this strategy when we purchased companies and moved their manufacturing to our plants. We would use the BASICS tools to figure out how to move and transition their batch processes to Lean

---

[*] Taiichi Ohno, *Toyota Production System, Beyond Large Scale Production* (New York: Productivity Press) 1978.

[†] Yahsiro Monden, *Toyota Production System* (Institute of Industrial Engineering) 2002.

TABLE 9.6
PPCS (Part Production Capacity Sheet) Histology

Part Production Capacity Sheet (PPCS)	Available Time (hrs/day)	Available Time (min/day)	Available Time (sec/day)	Customer Demand (units/day)	Takt Time (sec)	Factory Demand (units/day + scrap)	Required Cycle Time	Total Labor Time	Number of People Required
Description — Histology	24.0	1,440.0	86400	990.0	87.3	990.0	87.3	245.0	2.8

Basic Time   ***Capacity***

Specimen	Manual operation time	Machine processing time	Completion time	Loads per day based on completion time	Max container batch size	Machine container capacity per hour	Max machine capacity per day	SWIP	Number of machines required
Description of process	(sec)	(sec)	(sec)						
Cumulative times	245	33302	33547						
Percentage manual op. and VA time	0.7%	99.3%							
Work sequence									
1 Tissue prep	60.0	30,501.0	30,561.0	2.0	150.0	2.0	600.0	350.2	1.7
2 Embed	10.0	21.0	31.0	2,787.0	1.0	1.0	2,787.0	0.4	0.4
3 Cutting	60.00	80.0	140.0	617.0	1.0	1.0	617.0	1.6	1.6
4 Staining	10.0	2,700.0	2,710.0	31.0	30.0	6.0	5,580.0	31.1	0.2
5 Signout	105.0		105.0	822.0	1.0	1.0	822.0	1.2	1.2

processes. This forced us to run the new area Lean. Many hospitals will move the batch processes "as is" and then try to Lean them out; however, this requires more space initially and loss of productivity until or if the area is converted over to Lean.

In hospitals, moving areas is very expensive and difficult because of the need for containment and patient safety. The biggest opportunity for Lean master layout development is during a re-design of an area or a totally new hospital or clinic construction.

Lesson Learned: *There is an inherent danger in initially value stream mapping a sub process. This danger presents itself in the fundamental concept of the value stream itself. If we only look at one value stream, we are not necessarily seeing the "big picture." This is why it is important to do a high-level value stream map for the overall organization, which depicts how all the individual value streams work together. There should be an executive position in the organization that is always looking at how all the value streams (processes) function and work together and assess improvement opportunities to streamline the overall organization. The master layout should be considered at this level. If individual value streams are working on improvements but are isolated, then, essentially, we are still supporting silos even though they have been "Leaned". Too often we see layouts implemented by well-meaning managers or teams but because there is no "knowledgeable Lean review" they are not really Lean but still implemented.*

CREATIVITY BEFORE CAPITAL

When we begin a process improvement project, we always recommend the concept of "creativity before capital." Money doesn't solve every problem. We can generally make many improvements for no investment or minor expense dollars; however, it has been our experience that most hospital layouts are in need of some type of major construction as part of a Lean project.

The best time to design a new layout is when a new building is designed, but most hospitals miss this opportunity because either the hospital or the architect are not aware of Lean layout and work station design principles. This oversight can cost hospitals millions a year in hidden costs.

It is recommended a budget or dedicated "funds" for potential layout or equipment improvements be established and set aside, in the event they are required. If this is not done prior to the start of a project, the approval process may delay the project timeline and, if the funds for the improvement are not approved, it may impact the ability to achieve the outlined results.

The optimization of the layout and work station should be performed in conjunction with the frontline staff for the new process. Leveraging the knowledge of the frontline staff will provide an overall better design and, in addition, help facilitate the adoption of the new process and layout. Remember the change equation, which includes both the "change" and

FIGURE 9.9   Isolated islands.

the "acceptance." One can develop a great process change or re-design, but if we do not continually work on the change side of the equation, the result may be zero.

Do not underestimate the potential resistance to change when implementing a new process. The goals of effective work station design and layout optimization is to facilitate the flow of the product through the process and minimize travel distance. The following can impact flow related to layout and work station design.

LEAN LAYOUT DESIGN—CONFIGURATIONS— DETERMINING THE NEW FLOW FOR THE AREA

Most healthcare managers have not been exposed to the concepts widely deployed in manufacturing related to layout design. Understanding these basic design concepts and their benefits and then applying them to healthcare design will provide significant opportunities in process improvement. When reading material related to Lean, particularly in the manufacturing domain, there are references to "cell" or "work cell." This is a foreign term to most healthcare managers. The definition[*] of work cell is the physical or logical arrangement of all resources (people, machines, and materials) associated with the performance of an activity or task. As we discuss layout, we may refer to this cell-related definition. An example of a cell could be the work area that performs all chemistry tests in a large laboratory or the area where all hematology tests are performed, i.e., the "hematology cell." The patient unit on the floor could be referred to on a large scale as a work cell as well.

The main goal in layout design is to design areas that flow and do not contain isolated islands. Figure 9.9 shows three people who cannot flex or help each other out. We see these designs all the time in hospitals. Each of these workstation is an isolated island which prohibits flexing and leads to fractional labor.

From a workflow perspective, particular "cell" shapes have been identified that facilitate work or process flows. Generally, the shape of a cell is mostly determined by the requirements of the process. Functional layouts may require that the product is moved within the department many times to get processed. For example, the blood sample or test tube

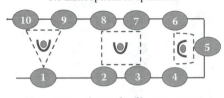

Materials replenished from outside the line.
No interruptions to operators.

Operators on the inside of layouts ensure
maximum flexibility and teamwork.

FIGURE 9.10   U-shaped layout.

is delivered to one spot, dictated by the tube system location in the department, and then "received' adjacent to the tube system, and then transported to another room where it is centrifuged and then another room where the test on the blood sample is performed and resulted. In this example, the operations are isolated by functions, and functions occur in silos. If there are errors in the processing, it is normally difficult to locate where the error occurred. In addition, if there are questions about the sample, communication is hindered by the functions occurring in different areas in isolation.

The staff at the beginning of the laboratory process (receiving end) does not really understand how long it takes from the time the specimen is received until the result is sent because the total process is divided functionally in different rooms or areas of the laboratory. When the processes are located in cells or workspaces that are in sequence and adjacent to each other, the team members understand their part in the total process. We normally find that the most utilized areas are, for some reason, located farthest from the beginning of the process.

THE "U-SHAPED" LAYOUT

Layouts can be in an L shape, S shape, C shape, etc. Shapes such as A, T, F, E, or R layouts, for example, would contain isolated islands. The U-shaped layout has some advantages over other shapes (Figure 9.10). The main benefit is the ability to share resources. The staff is better able to help each other should the need arise. Communication among the staff is easier, especially between the beginning and end of the process or part of the process that you are trying to improve. Walking distances are shorter and the person can work while they are standing and moving. Staff will be more productive yet potentially feel less fatigued. This layout maximizes the ability to flex the staff across operations. It can be run with one person or multiple persons. If, for example, it is run with three persons, one person could do stations 1, 9 and 10, or 1, 2 and 3. If one person runs 1, 9 and 10 then that person controls the input and output of the area, so we can never start more than we finish.

Materials and supplies are replenished from the outside so there is no interruption to those working inside the area. When building new layouts or work areas, effort should be made to have most of the operations take place in the same area with one team. This facilitates communication, as errors

Materials replenished from outside the line.
No interruptions to operators.

Walk   Walk   Walk

Operators on the inside of layouts ensure
maximum flexibility and teamwork.

FIGURE 9.11   Straight line layout.

are found and communicated among team members. This motivates team members to problem solve to avoid mistakes. U-shaped layouts do not have to run counter-clockwise. The advantage to counter-clockwise is to those of us who are right-handed. It is important to note that accommodations need to be made for left-handed people, as applicable, especially in work station design.

STRAIGHT LINE LAYOUTS

Straight lines or linear layouts allow resources to move down the line sequentially for the process (Figure 9.11). Staff can still flex in a straight line, but the flexing is limited to the operator immediately before or after. The drawback to this layout is that, with one staff member, the travel distance is longer from operation one to operation six, however, the process generally dictates the layout.

PARALLEL LAYOUTS

Parallel layouts are designed with the staff on the inside to facilitate resource sharing as staff can move across to the other parallel line or down the same line (Figure 9.12). Materials and supplies are replenished from outside the work area or cell to minimize interruptions. This layout works well in a high-mix, low-volume environment.

OTHER LAYOUT CONSIDERATIONS

Layout and work station considerations should include baton zones or flex spaces in between work process zones. These areas are located before or after standard work zones in which operators/staff can flex to absorb minor variations in time. From a healthcare perspective, consider the pre-admission testing visit

Materials replenished from outside the line.
No interruptions to operators.

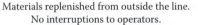
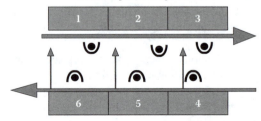

FIGURE 9.12   Parallel line layout.

that we will discuss in further detail later. Some patients may require an electrocardiogram (EKG) while others may not, so there can be variation in how one might move a patient through activities that occur during a pre-admission testing visit.

Since all patients are not created equal, one must consider areas where the layout can handle a "back-up." Back-ups are normally patients, and since they represent excess inventory, then the goal should be able to eliminate the backups in the process. Again, consider the pre-admission testing department. If the blood draw/EKG area is short a person, patients may back-up and require chairs in which they have to wait. If the nurses draw blood in the same room where they interview the patients then patients will normally back-up in the pre-admission waiting area.

Lean layouts should promote flexible workspace and design. Layout re-designs should result in a decrease in overall space and travel distance needed to perform a task and minimize fractional labor. If the re-design does not save space, then we need to understand the variables that caused the space to increase. In most cases, space increase would be due to changing technologies for new equipment or dramatic increases in projections volume.

Guidelines to Layout Re-design—Non-Negotiable

Guideline #1: No isolated islands

Rationale: The golden rule is not to build isolated islands into your layout. Isolated islands are areas where we isolate workers and prohibit flexing. We see this in hospital settings all the time. Isolated islands create the need for fractional labor, which means that a person may only have 50% of their time assigned to a task. They may not be able to be assigned any more duties because they either aren't capable, may not want to do another job, or cannot flex to help someone else out because they are too far away (distance). They may have a barrier that precludes them from flexing; an example of this is the nutritional tray line (Figure 9.13). Notice that the operators are boxed in by equipment and carts of dishes or food, and the layout prevents them from performing other tasks.

Guideline #2: No or limited use of doors, drawers, and walls

Rationale: Walls are bad! Drawers hide clutter and provide a space for "just in case" supplies, which increase inventory and impact the organization financially by having hidden excess cash in "un-needed" inventory. If cabinets need to be installed, remove the doors. If doors or drawers have to be installed, make them "see through," so when looking for items, they are clearly visible. This will also assist with Five S to de-clutter and keep the area clean.

There will be much resistance to this guideline. Staff and especially supervisors and managers will come up with many reasons for why we need walls, doors, and drawers. They have become accustomed to what they have today and are challenged to make the paradigm shift to an open "shared" environment. The hospital will have to define what a "customer" area is and what it needs. We have designed many

FIGURE 9.13 Tray line isolated islands.

"customer" areas without doors and drawers and we tape out items and areas, where allowed.

We have found that there is seldom a true need for walls, doors, and drawers.

Lesson Learned: *Have the courage to challenge conventional guidelines and regulations, as many are antiquated and can be overturned. Some are misinterpretations of regulatory requirements or The American Institute of Architects (AIA) guidelines. There are times when we have had to go to accreditation agencies to get clarifications, additions, or changes to existing guidelines to facilitate Lean designs.*

Guideline #3: Flexibility

Rationale: What you are building today may change tomorrow. Build "grids" for water, electric facilitates flexibility and extended use (Figure 9.14). Providing utilities in a grid enables flexibility in future space use. Grid-type layouts allow for "plug and play" air, water, and gas connections. In addition, should you need to move a piece of equipment to another location to improve the flow, or take on a new line of business, it makes sense to change the sequence. Flexible utilities can make the change cost effective. Maintenance should move each piece of equipment with the paradigm "that it can be moved twice as fast the next time." There will be resistance in general to grid utility construction, which can cost more up front but will

FIGURE 9.14   Flexible utilities.

provide huge savings in future re-designs. Many organizations start projects with limited budgets and have difficulty justifying future cost avoidance measures when they have limited funds available for a basic project.

Guideline #4: OBA Gauge

Rationale: The rule is that racks and partitions should be no higher than four foot, where possible. This is called the "Oba Gauge." A four-foot-tall Japanese Lean sensei named Mr. Oba was notorious for insisting that nothing in the factory be taller than his eye-level. This resulted in the "Oba Gauge" for a visual workplace. The idea is to avoid creating view-blockers in your workplace whenever possible. It is also called the "four-foot rule" or "1.3 meter rule." Five and six foot high cubicle walls and doors create "isolated" islands or silos in work environments. Cubical walls should be no more than three or four foot high offices to encourage line of sight management (Figure 9.15). Use modular furniture to facilitate ease of movement, cell or work area re-design

FIGURE 9.15   Lean office layout.

and configuration. We are seeing more organizations adapt to the use of modular furniture. Use clear glass for offices to encourage open door policies.

Guideline #5: Review layout and work station design for travel distance and "ergonomics," limit reaching, and have staff stand, if possible

Rationale: Travel and motion are non-value-added activities identified as "wastes." They also cause fatigue and impact your workforce, so whenever possible, they need to be eliminated or minimized. Sitting may cause staff to reach unnecessarily and the up and down activity may be more detrimental ergonomically than standing. There will be resistance to "stand and move rather than sit." When staff is provided with the appropriate mechanism, such as padded mats and high counters along with health safety and environmental reviews, we can overcome most, if not all, objections. We have even found when areas are set up for one-piece or one-patient flow and staff members are allowed to sit, they find themselves preferring to stand and walk. This depends solely on what activity they are required to perform and how long they may be standing in one place. If the activity requires a constant up and down movement or someone has to stand in one place for a long period of time (10 or 15 min), then they should sit because standing and not moving is bad for you. Each situation needs to be assessed on an individual basis. Overall, our analysis shows standing and moving in properly designed layouts to be up to 30% more efficient than sitting at one station.

Guideline #6: Staff should be located on the inside of the "work cell" and replenishment should be from the outside

Rationale: Locating staff on the inside facilitates movement of staff as they are able to flex across process steps, promotes resource sharing, and provides shorter travel distances. Replenishing supplies from outside the work cell or area limits interruptions of "cell activity" when supplies are needed.

Guideline #7: The layout should be designed with flow and visual controls in mind

Rationale: Point-to-point diagrams must be constructed for all proposed layouts. These diagrams should include both the flow all products and inbound and outbound materials. Cell layouts should remain constant regardless of the amount of operators (within reason).

Guideline #8: Co-locate executives and office staff on or near the floor or areas with their products/patients

Rationale: How can an executive manage a hospital from a separate building or floor? We need to be co-located on or near the *Gemba*. This aids in assisting any interruption of flow on the line and ensures a quick response to any staff problems.

Guideline #9: Don't plan rework inside a cell

Rationale: If you absolutely must have a rework area, make sure it is painfully visible and that someone is accountable.

Statistics on WIP and cash flow, and cost of poor quality (COPQ) for the area should be posted and visible.

Guideline #10: Develop a master layout early on in the project

Rationale: The master layout can be constructed in less than a day but sometimes can take a week or more to get it right. It does not have to be perfect, but will serve as a guide to the core team and a vision to the rest of the organization of how things may look in the future. We typically get it 80%–90% correct the first time.

Guideline #11: Layout approval

Rationale: Establish a Lean layout review board. There should be a Lean layout expert developed at your site with the power to say "no." This person should be thoroughly trained in the Lean principles and be able to offer an explanation and suggestions for layouts that are not acceptable. The layouts should be explained in a meeting to the staff, facilities or engineering department, supervisors, and process owners prior to submittal for approval. Reasonable suggestions, which do not violate the principles, should be incorporated. Be careful with new installations not to add additional workspace if data does not support it. Every time we have added additional workspace that people just had to have, it has resulted in the additional workspace collecting junk. An analogy for this would be the exercise bike which becomes a clothes hanger.

Guideline #12: Housekeeping

Rationale: A place for everything and everything in its place! Each place should be labeled with the equipment name, supply or part name, and location. Consider appointing someone or a team to implement Five S Kaizens frequently and sponsor shredder days or housekeeping days several times a year. Take before and after pictures of each project area. Videotape a baseline of your entire plant prior to starting Lean improvements.

How Do We Know when the Layout is Right?

This is a difficult question to answer, but we find it to be somewhat intuitive. You just know when you get it right when all point-to-point diagrams work and the metrics support it. Some metrics we use are total space, travel distance, number of operators, inventory, percentage of fractional labor, etc. When the product flows, the operator travel is minimized, changeover can be performed quickly, and there is room for expansion, we know the layout is close to being correct. Keep in mind that, as we continue to implement improvements or expand capacity, the layout may need to change. This is why walls are never in the right place and it is important to have work stations and equipment on wheels with quick disconnects, etc., to facilitate easy and ongoing layout changes. As improvements are implemented, most layouts continue to shrink over time. In developing the layout it is important to separate human work from machine work. Once the layout is in place, we need to immediately implement and audit standard work methods where possible, balance work across all

operators, and train and cross-train operators as soon as possible to minimize the number of staff required to support the operation. The layout should provide for standing/walking, moving operations, and have room for SWIP.

There are instances where several days or even weeks are spent trying to get the layout right. Sometimes, we have found one has to step away from it for a while and then come back to it. Something else that normally works is when we suggest rotating all or parts of the layout 90 degrees to see what that does. It is important to make sure, where applicable, that machines with the highest volume are located nearest the work entry point(s). Keep in mind that many people design the layout in the right order within a work "cell" in sequence to create flow; however, this is only part of the equation. Yes, it is true that you will get improvement by having the activities in the right sequence and moving activities closer together; however, if you have not looked at smoothing or load balancing the work, in essence, you have only completed part of the task and have not level loaded the work to facilitate flow and, thereby, not eliminated potential bottlenecks.

Work station Design

We always get frontline staff involved in the work station design. When we watch the videos, we find the staff actually show us how to set up their work. The goal is to set up standing moving operations where possible. Any good ergonomics and safety person will confirm that moving and walking is better for you than sitting all day. Standing in one place is bad for you. When we set up work stations, we design them for standing up and, if sitting is necessary, we put in "standing height sit down chairs." We want work stations to be as flexible as possible. This means wheels with no hard piping, conduit, or tubing. Work stations need to be safe and ergonomically designed with standing mats. Lean, ergonomics, and safety all work very well together and is part of our "Respect for Humanity" principle. We should always make provisions in our work stations for workers with disabilities.

We have already discussed the importance of engaging frontline staff, frontline supervisors, and managers in the process of layout and work station design. Often, we find work stations are changed on the fly at every shift change based on how the next employee performs their work. It is critical that the frontline staff is fully engaged in the re-designing of their work stations, as it reinforces acceptance. Once the base layout is determined by re-designing the process flow, each work station or area within the new layout needs to be designed to ensure the following:

- What supplies are needed?
- What is the placement, order, or sequence of the supplies for each work area or station? and that each is labeled by location.
- What equipment is required? Larger pieces of equipment may tend to drive the overall layout. We call these monuments. One has to take into consideration mechanical and electrical "fit up" requirements like

high voltage electrical connections, water lines, air lines, gas lines or venting/ducting requirements. Some equipment when initially considered doesn't take into account other pieces of equipment which may be necessary to support it like manifolds, cooling addons or hydraulic modules.

- What should be near each work station (fax, phones, copiers, etc.)? (Again, the larger layout will drive adjacencies, but remember what may be needed related to support these in the adjacent work areas).
- What size and amount of supplies are needed?
- How many work stations are needed?

We recommend team members consisting of frontline staff and supervisor plan out the work station and locate all supplies and needs on the drawing. Work stations should be designed to the product flow (not the operator time). The team needs to decide on quantity and location for inventory and "buffer" or back-up supplies, and discuss the replenishment or restocking of supplies to determine the impact to work station design. If during the process a "collection area" needs to be considered, such as in a laboratory re-design where there may be multiple collection points for specimens within a larger "work cell," discussions should take place to make sure that appropriate locations are built into the work station design. It is recommended that, if multi-shifts and staff are sharing work areas, each person on each shift has the opportunity to review the work station re-design and process and that there are standards and audits put in place to ensure compliance.

The list of tools and supplies was documented when we did the full work operator analysis. When setting up work station designs, we will normally run a pilot with the staff person. We literally go step-by-step, where applicable, lining up their materials and supplies in the proper sequence in order to minimize reaching and excess motions. We then draw an outline around it or tape it out and label it. This is a very time-consuming process that requires much patience by the staff person and the Lean team. Once we get everything in place, we have the operator run the work station and then make adjustments, since operators will normally forget something or something will not be in the right place. When we are comfortable that everything is set up correctly and they have practiced, we will videotape them and then sit down and review the videotape. After reviewing the videotape, we will make other improvements or adjustments as necessary. Once we are satisfied that things are running well, we will look at formally re-designing all the work stations.

There may be cases where we duplicate equipment or supplies on the work stations so that the product keeps moving forward and allows the opportunity for other operators to flex. If we were to set everything up on one work station with the supplies not in the exact order, i.e., we put a fixture in the middle of the work station, this would force the operator to stay in one place, probably sitting, and would not allow anyone else to flex in and help.

STAND UP VS. SIT DOWN STATIONS WITH CHART FLOW

In a pre-testing clinic at Hospital X, we designed a new flow and work station for assembling patients' surgical charts. This involved essentially setting up a line where all the forms were placed on a counter in the order they were assembled. The clerks simply grabbed a hard chart and then picked up and placed each form from the form bins into its proper position in the hard chart. In the current layout, due to the configuration of the nurse work station counter, we could not set up the forms properly so the clerks had to slide their chairs back and forth, and they hated it. Of the three clerks, one had some physical issues that made it difficult to stand up, so she resisted the stand-up operation. We brought in a health, safety, and ergonomics expert who agreed the operation should be "stand up." We ended up suggesting a compromise solution, which was to install a new standup height counter, but provided a "standup–sit down" chair for the other operator. We have designed lines in the past to accommodate staff with wheelchairs.

Lesson Learned: *Standing and walking is normally up to 30% more efficient than sit-down operations. We also need to be able to develop solutions that work just as well for our physically challenged individuals.*

WORK STATION DESIGN SUMMARY

- Work stations do not have to be designed to meet the Takt time as long as operators can flex across the stations. The problem with designing stations to Takt time is that the Takt time may change and then we are faced with changing the work stations every time the Takt time changes.
- Do we have the right amount of inventory? We need a minimum amount of WIP to meet the Takt time and do it safely. The SWIP at the line or in the area is based on Takt time and the throughput time.
- Stations are initially designed based on what logically makes sense to build the product or process the patient.
- Work zones need to be designed for plus or minus two operators based on the number of operators required to meet the current cycle time or Takt time.
- Stations should be designed to support peak demand with maximum options.
- The layout should not change based on changing the number of staff.
- The layout may change based on ongoing improvements.
- Supplies and tools should be in the exact order of use and should be within reach, even if duplicate supplies are required.
- Determine appropriate inventory amount.
- As you design your workspace, ask yourself the following questions:
  - Do you have doors and drawers as hiding places?

- Is the furniture bolted or is it readily movable?
- What is the state of the infrastructure? If a new piece of equipment had to change location, how difficult or costly would it be to partially re-design the work area?
- Have you calculated the distances that the product and staff need to travel between processes and to get the supplies they need to do their jobs? Where are the staff members located in relation to the flow of the work that needs to be performed? Are there collisions which may occur between staff members or opportunities for products to get mixed up?
- Are there walls or doors impeding flow?
- Can you visually identify bottlenecks with the process?
- Are tasks or processes that occur sequentially located near each other to enable flexing of resources?

MASTER LAYOUTS AND LEAN DESIGN

LEAN AND ARCHITECTS

There is a real need for architects to learn Lean because just about every hospital design today is not Lean. Many hospitals ask us to review a new design that is so far along in design stage 4 or 6, (see Table 9.7), that any changes would be impossible owing to the high cost of the changes.

Lessons Learned: *Now we ask at what stage the design is in and, if it is in the final stages, we politely refuse to comment. Why? Because at this stage all we will do is frustrate and upset anyone involved in the process unless they are really willing to spend the money on the changes. Lean should enter at stage 1 and latest at stage 2.*

When designing buildings with multiple clinics, don't design a central registration area. Registration should be located within each clinic. Central registration areas create bottlenecks and delay patients and ultimately the physicians.

In new buildings or construction, there may have been thought given to layout adjacencies and equipment placement. We have found that, in many instances working with architectural firms in healthcare over the years, the architects believe they have given consideration to equipment placement

TABLE 9.7

Stages of Design

1.	Conceptual development
2.	Block Diagram
3.	Rough Layout
4.	Area Design
5.	Initial Schematics
6.	Detailed Schematics

and process when designing workspace. More often than not, the architects increase space based on volume projections and then apply square foot multipliers to determine the amount of space needed to support the project. Recently, there has been an increase in the number of architectural firms now utilizing Lean principles to help guide their design process, still they may be reluctant to push back when managers and staff ask for "non-Lean" designs. When analyzing the architect's layout, do point-to-point diagrams for every product/patient in the process. Again, the overarching goal is to provide a flexible work area and work station designs to be able to adapt to future needs and provide an environment conducive to continuous improvement.

DO WE REALLY NEED TO ADD MORE ROOMS OR SPACE?

Most hospitals underestimate the need for Lean design. The first question asked should be if we really need to add rooms or space. In the pre-Lean environment, the need for additional rooms, which appear to be required, may, in fact, not be needed once the Lean project is completed.

At Hospital X, we were working on Leaning a laboratory, both core and non-core (Figure 9.16). The architects were told the laboratory expected to double its output over the next 3 years. So what did the architects do? They doubled the floor space for both laboratories. Once they doubled the floor space, there was no longer room for both laboratories on the same floor. As a result, the decision was made to move the non-core laboratory offsite to a two-story building. By the end of our Lean laboratory project, we were able to reduce the architect's footprint for the core laboratory by close to 30% and the non-core laboratory by the same margin. In addition, both laboratories could have remained on the same floor. But since the new building was so far along, they continued down that path. By moving the non-core laboratory to another building, a whole set of additional waste was created.

Lessons Learned: *When we do need more space or rooms then it is important to Lean out the processes first and then, and only then, make changes to the layout. It is important to remember that each layout needs to be as flexible as possible. Hard piping, hard walls, and immovable equipment, are bad, as are centralized nursing stations, materials, and supplies. To the extent possible, we need grid work in the ceiling so utilities can plug and play. This may be more expensive up front but saves significant dollars in the future.*

LAYOUTS DRIVE LABOR COSTS—CONSIDER ADJACENCIES

It is amazing to see how much waste can be built into a layout. How does this happen? While some architects may consider the flow, most don't. They tend to put things where the customer wants them and then work to make everything else fit, which doesn't always mean it flows. We have never seen an architect do a point-to-point diagram. This does not

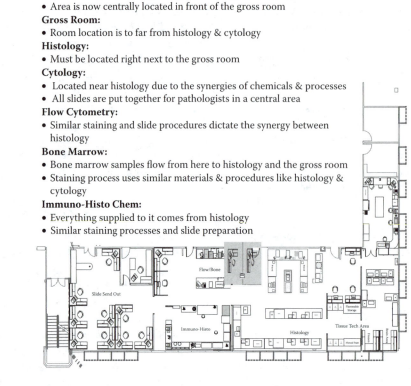

Non-Core Adjacencies:
Accessioning Area for Cytology & Histology:
- Area is now centrally located in front of the gross room

Gross Room:
- Room location is to far from histology & cytology

Histology:
- Must be located right next to the gross room

Cytology:
- Located near histology due to the synergies of chemicals & processes
- All slides are put together for pathologists in a central area

Flow Cytometry:
- Similar staining and slide procedures dictate the synergy between histology

Bone Marrow:
- Bone marrow samples flow from here to histology and the gross room
- Staining process uses similar materials & procedures like histology & cytology

Immuno-Histo Chem:
- Everything supplied to it comes from histology
- Similar staining processes and slide preparation

FIGURE 9.16 Lean laboratory master layout.

necessarily mean it's never done; we have just never witnessed it.

When isolated islands are designed, we end up paying for the fractional labor of that person who then ends up being idle. There is not a cost for this in the architect's proposal. A significant amount of thought is provided from the implementing department; however, many times there is not much thought given to how the new design may impact other departments.

Layouts should be designed to support the overall flow of the support area, clinic, or hospital. Overall flow is just as important—if not more important—than the flow within a department. Hospitals need to be thought of as a system with many departments and information flows interacting all the time.

Hospital X asked us to design a new hospital ED with Lean tracks but then decided not to Lean out the ED in the existing hospital. We advised them that if they did not implement Lean in the existing ED, there is no way they would be able to run it when they moved to the new Lean ED design. The new Lean area would run much worse with the old processes, if at all.

Lesson Learned: *The hospital must be prepared to run Lean if they are going to design Lean. One cannot design a Lean hospital and run it with the old batch-driven systems!*

For example, when designing an ED, we need to consider the location of radiology and laboratory in the master layout. Ideally, we would build these areas into our ED layout. If

this is not possible, they should be considered when viewing adjacencies.

Layouts should:

- Minimize travel distance and excess walking
- Avoid isolated islands and support flexing
- Include point of use storage
- Incorporate IT systems at point of use

EDs are one of the two main front doors of your hospital. The other front door is the routine entrance for surgery patients and visitors. It may also be the door to your outpatient facilities and services (i.e., pharmacy). The ED should have a front door for patients and a separate door for ambulances. One may want to consider separate entrances for outpatient radiology or laboratory testing.

Lesson Learned: *If you are going to compete with stand-alone outpatient facilities, you have to offer similar parking and easy access as the outpatient facility.*

SOME PRACTICAL EXAMPLES OF LEAN DESIGNS

- Surgery should have admitting (registration) as part of the waiting area or be able to provide the functions of registration at the surgery area to eliminate the step of going to registration.
- The waiting area should be on the same floor as surgery or preferably adjacent to the surgical area.

- Sterile processing and materials should be located on the same floor as surgery, Pre-Op, and PACU.
- Surgery should form a U-shaped. Unless designing encapsulated surgery flows, i.e., individual surgery tracks, then Pre-Op and PACU should be adjacent so resources can be shared.

Surgery U-Shaped Layout

conceptual –not to scale

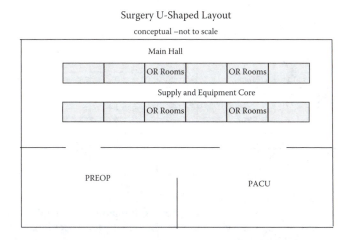

- The ideal surgical layout would have all rooms the same (universal). For cost and practicality reasons this is not always possible. Otherwise, assign rooms geographically by family-based demand.
- Surgical suites should have cores in between where materials and equipment can be stored based on the families of rooms located within the core.
- There should be pass-through access to enable restocking of materials without having to enter the rooms.
- There should be a clean and a dirty side, with an entrance for patients and an entrance for staff.
- Each room should have point-of-use materials and equipment (based on the group tech matrix).
- Consider adding induction rooms so anesthesia can prepare the patient prior to surgery. One room can be shared between two ORs.

Surgery Cell

conceptual –not to scale

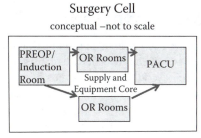

NURSING FLOORS

When designing nursing floors, one should consider adding point-of-use material storage in the room or, worst case, immediately outside the room. Many hospitals are already doing this. Remember centralized storage areas; whether they are for materials, nursing station, medications, etc., bring the "centralized" waste along with them.

Large centralized nursing stations, in general, are "waste attractors." We have to travel to them and we socialize at them. Many hospitals are moving to smaller point-of-use nursing stations or getting rid of them altogether in favor of in-room or room-side charting. These are often called "pods."

ICU floors should be close to surgery. Patient floors can be grouped by service line, where possible.

OTHER DESIGN CONSIDERATIONS

- Surgery should be near the ED in case an emergent surgery is required, especially in level 1 or 2 trauma hospitals.
- Laboratories should be near both the ED and pre-testing areas.
- Radiology may be divided between inpatient and outpatient. If there is a high outpatient volume, it should have an outside entrance. It should also be located near the surgery pre-testing unit. Demand should drive location of the radiology areas. All layouts should allow for the process owner and staff to be located in or near the area.

LEAN AND REGULATORY ENVIRONMENT

In Lean designs, you must be willing to challenge the convention. We have had instances where we had to go back to regulatory bodies, like the Joint Commission on the Accreditation of Healthcare Organizations (JCAHO)[*] or the State Agency for Health Care Administration (AHCA),[†] and have them approve our designs. We occasionally come up with rooms that don't necessarily fit existing criteria. For example, EDs had provisions for examination rooms and waiting rooms (non-patient care area), but did not have a classification for the "observe care" area we created. This was where patients who were waiting for test results or, in essence, didn't need a formal bed or room, could wait and have limited care as needed until all the tests and results were complete. Patients were monitored but they were not in an actual room. If care was given, it was provided in a room attached to the area. There was no criteria for this in the AIA, AHCA or JCAHO guidelines.

LINE DESIGN CRITERIA

There are key criteria elements that must be considered when designing your new process layout or "line." Once again, the

---

[*] What is JCAHO? The Joint Commission on the Accreditation of Healthcare Organizations sets standards for healthcare organizations and issues accreditation to organizations that meet those standards. JCAHO conducts periodic on-site surveys to verify that "an accredited organization substantially complies with Joint Commission standards and continuously makes efforts to improve the care and services it provides."

[†] About the Agency for Health Care Administration (AHCA): "This Agency was statutorily created by Chapter 20, Florida Statutes as the chief health policy and planning entity for the state. We are primarily responsible for the state's $16 billion Medicaid program that serves over 2.2 million Floridians, the licensure of the state's 36,000 health care facilities and the sharing of health care data through the Florida Center for Health Information and Policy Analysis. Our mission is Better Health Care for All Floridians."

term line is manufacturing-based but can be easily transferred to the healthcare domain as healthcare has "lines" as well. We do supply customers with services, and we have processes that act in many aspects like assembly lines. Examples of these would be a "pre-admission testing visit" where there is an expected "result" that consists of a series of tasks or activities that have to occur in order to achieve that result.

Example: Pre-Testing Visit

Scenario #1

Let's examine the process of the pre-admission testing visit, which would include the following components: having blood work drawn (laboratory testing), EKG, x-ray, consent signed, and medical history taken. The goal would be to have all this completed with preliminary results from the laboratory tests back within 85 min, before the patient leaves, in case additional laboratory tests are needed. This ensures that the patient does not have to make a return visit.

In this example, an appropriate layout or design can significantly impact the clinic's ability to achieve this result (Table 9.8). These are the average times for the steps at a high level. If the current process was done in this order, without reference to how long each of the activities needed to be performed, they would never be able to achieve their goal of 85 min. This excludes looking at the seven wastes and the activity and time between each process step, like the travel between clinical areas or laboratory specimens, which have to get transported to another location for processing.

Scenario #2

If we just reorder the "line" of work, we can get closer to our overall goal. The example in Table 9.9 illustrates that, conceptually, a healthcare process can be the same as an assembly line's activities linked together to achieve a customer result. This example did not go into the detail of the transport or co-location of services and adjacencies of departments in order to achieve maximum throughput and minimum cycle time. It did provide a very simple view of how looking at one process can be performed linearly while the steps in two different sequences can

TABLE 9.8
Clinic Steps Before

Steps	Time (min)	Cumulative Time
Enters the clinic, signs in	1	1
Patient Registration (demographic and financial)	8	9
Medical History Taken	25	34
Consent Signed	5	39
EKG Taken	10	49
X-Ray Taken	30	79
Laboratory Draw (results take 70 min)	6	85
Lab Results Received	70	155
Total Goal < 85 min		155

TABLE 9.9
Clinic Steps After

Steps	Time (min)	Cumulative Time	
Enters the clinic, signs in	1	1	
Patient Registration (demographic and financial)	8	9	
Laboratory Draw (results take 70 min)	6	15	Lab Results Time Starts Here
Medical History Taken	25	40	25
Consent Signed	5	45	30
EKG Taken	10	55	40
X-Ray Taken	30	85	70
Lab Results Received		85	
Goal < 85 min			

provide different end results. By moving the laboratory draw up to step #3 in the process, it enabled "parallel" processing of the remaining activities that had to occur to meet the goal of 85 min.

This would be very easy to do if this were the only component that impacted a customer going through a process; however, there are many variables that influence a process, such as hourly demand and the number of patients or services being provided.

Using the example above, what if the specimens were not taken immediately to the process area or the laboratory test ran in "batches" and the specimen had to "wait" for the next batch cycle to run. These may be items the clinic process may have not considered when setting the original goal. In using average cycle times, you may end up with significant variability from average process time (yielding a large standard deviation) in results when you do not fully understand what is going on in "interdepartmental or between process work cells." There may be downstream opportunities to improve as you go beyond the area over which you have control. In order to optimize the process flow, the following are criteria required as you look at your process re-design.

LEAN MATERIALS AND SUPPLIES

Many books have been written on inventory and supply chain management in Lean deployments. Lean inventory or materials projects are beyond the scope of this book. We feel that we would be remiss if we did not include highlights of some of the basic concepts related to supply replenishment, inventory, and materials management that need to be considered in any Lean implementation.

INVENTORY

When re-designing your value stream, we need to understand what and how many supplies are needed to perform the activities/operations within the process. For example, where Lean has not been fully implemented within your organization, we can probably go into any clinical area and open drawers only to find the same supplies in multiple places throughput the clinical area. In re-designing the work area and process, one of the key concepts is that the right supplies and equipment or tools are needed at the right place at the right time to perform the activity. Too many supplies take up valuable space and cause waste. If departments are spending money on redundant overstock supplies that are not tracked and are found stashed in drawers waiting to expire, then they do not have the funds available to spend on other activities. Excess inventory is always the sign of a problem. Richard Schonberger's book, *World Class Manufacturing: The Next Decade*, has suggested inventory turns be utilized as one of the prime measures to rate companies on the ability to sustain continuous improvement.[*]

SUPPLIES NEEDED AND PLACEMENT

The supplies needed to perform a task and placement of the supplies is determined by videotaping and observing staff members performing their task. As mentioned earlier a good operator will actually show us how to design their work station. During the video analysis, we hold discussions about who uses the supply, why each supply is used, what it is, how it is used, and where within the work station should it be placed for best access. The quantity needed may impact the location and/or timing of the replenishment of the supplies. Supplies and equipment should be placed in the order that they are being used during the care of the patient. There should be agreement across all parties that share the workspace about the locations and quantity required. All shifts should have input into the work station layout and design. This sounds simple; however, there can be a significant amount of "change management" with the people component involved. In addition, there are techniques utilized in Lean to help sustain work station design, such as labeling and outlining, where supplies and equipment should be located to provide visual cues when equipment is misplaced. Supplies that are needed all the time should be at point of use. Supplies needed once a day can be further away and supplies used once a week or month further away still.

PLAN FOR EVERY PART—AMOUNT OF SUPPLIES/INVENTORY NEEDED

The plan for every part (PFEP) provides a mechanism to track and determine the supplies needed, current demand, and the current state inventory information. We need to know where they are located, how many will be replenished, and a buffer plan to ensure that supplies will be available to meet peak demand. While many of us have created Lean materials spreadsheets in the past, they didn't seem to have an official name until the book, *Making Materials Flow*, was published.[†] The PFEP can be created manually, but is easier to manipulate in

an Excel spreadsheet. The PFEP involves literally listing every single part used in the process or area. Then we look at each part to determine the lead time, daily quantity required, days of supply on hand, safety stock, and appropriate Kanban sizes. This rather large spreadsheet is dynamic and needs to be maintained at some frequency in most areas because volume or mix of cases can change, thereby impacting the minimum, maximum, and reorder quantity levels. The charge nurses or service team leader should have the final say on the minimum, maximum, and reorder quantities.

How many "quantity" at the work station "at the right place" is generally based on the demand for the supply, how long it takes to replenish it, supplier minimum ordering size, supplier quality issues, and demand variation, which create a beta or risk factor associated with re-supplying the part. We generally add a small buffer of supplies called safety stock to cover this risk.

Each clinical area should understand what it is that they have in the way of inventory of supplies, and how much they use based on their demand (daily). In addition, for each supply, they should understand the replenishment process from the supplier, including how it is supplied to them (i.e., by box and the number in the box or the unit) and the lead time to obtain additional supplies, which will impact the minimum, maximum, and reorder point of each type of supply required.

The amount of supplies and bins or containers and the size of the equipment or supply bins will determine the size and number of shelves which impact the layout. We need to "right size" the bins or containers which supplies are utilized to the actual demand. If the containers or bins are too large, the tendency will be to overstock the bins. This can lead to organizational cash flow issues, due to money being tied up in excess inventory. In addition, over-ordering and overstocking raises the potential to purchase supplies that will only become expired.

LABELING

Labeling of supplies and where they are placed, such as shelves and bins, is important (Figure 9.17). The front of the bins should have the bin location and the quantity and description of the supplies in the bin. The back of the bin tells how or where the bin is re-supplied. Labeling is an important part of visual controls and is a critical component when implementing Lean initiatives, to help eliminate the waste for searching. Labeling shelves should include a designation for the particular rack, shelf row, and position on the shelf row. In Figure 9.17, in the example to the right, the location for the top left box is A1A, referring to Rack A Shelf #1 Position A on the shelf.

KANBAN

Kanban (看 watch over 板 a board), where kan, 看/カン (literal—watch over a board for a period until one) is a concept related to Lean and Just-In-Time (JIT) production. Kanbans facilitate inventory supply replenishment. The Japanese word Kanban is a common term meaning "signboard" or "billboard." According

[*] Richard Schonberger, *World Class Manufacturing: The Next Decade* (New York: The Free Press) 1996.
[†] Rick Harris, *Making Materials Flow* (Cambridge, MA: Lean Enterprise Institute) 2006.

Rack A

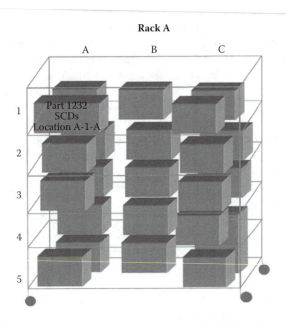

FIGURE 9.17 Example of how to label a specific location on a shelf on a rack.

to Taiichi Ohno, the man credited with developing JIT, Kanban is a means through which JIT is achieved.[*]

The purpose of a Kanban system is to control the flow of material by providing inventory as a buffer in order to synchronize two disconnected processes. Because Kanbans are inventory, we need to constantly work to minimize the amount of materials. A Kanban trigger or signal can be an empty space, an empty bin, a piece of paper, an electronic signal (lights, electronic data interchange), or an icon (e.g., rolling golf balls down a tube).

A Kanban is a signal designed to trigger an event. The term Kanban is used not only to describe the system, but also the individual bins or cards in the system. A Kanban card or empty bin can signal the need for the material to be replenished or it can serve as an order for production to begin in order to replenish the parts. Kanbans are described in detail in many books so we will only briefly describe them here. The simplest type of Kanban is called a two-bin system (Figure 9.18 and 9.19). A two-bin system is composed of two separate bins containing the same parts, with one bin placed behind the other. When the first bin empties, the bin is removed and the second bin, full of parts, slides down into its place. The empty bin is now the Kanban, or signal to replenish it. In all our years of implementation, we have found that when using this simple system, we never run out of parts. When you depend on a computer report to tell you when to reorder, you typically end up with a bunch of parts you don't need and you run out of the parts you do need. With Kanban, we virtually never run out of any supplies. Kanban is similar to the re-supply of milk when the milkman would take your empties and replace them with full bottles.

The Kanban system can be a one-bin system as well, if the parts are replenished every day (Figure 9.20). Normally in a one-bin system, the bins are refilled to the top, as one might refill bread in a store. This is called a "breadman" system. In some areas, the nurses scan into a terminal the quantity of supplies taken. This information is immediately passed to the stockroom or supplier as data for replenishment. This is called a point of sale system. Another way to trigger replenishment would be a water level line drawn or painted in the bin. When the parts go below the line, then it needs to be replenished.

Kanbans can also utilize card systems. In this system, the card is taken from the empty bin and placed in a holder. This is called a Kanban post. At certain frequencies during the day, the material handler or "water spider" collects the cards in the post. The cards are then taken to the storage location for the replenishment material or the card is taken from the replenishment material and put into another post to be reordered from the supplier. The card from the original bin is then placed on the new bin of materials. The new bin of materials is then returned to the original location in the area. This is called a withdrawal Kanban system. There are many types of Kanban systems, which have been documented by Ohno, Shingo, and Monden.[†]

Kanban systems regulate the inventory in a production system as the volume or rate of the process changes. But Kanban systems have two major failure modes. First, the Kanban system was originally designed in the PFEP to support a certain maximum volume. If this volume is exceeded, there will be parts shortages. Second, if Kanban cards are lost, inventory will not be replaced. If there are too many cards in the system to begin with, it will create excess inventory. Ongoing audits of the cards in a Kanban system are required to ensure that all the cards are present. Some people will complain this takes extra time to find all the cards. If cycle counting of parts were done prior to Kanban, use this time to audit Kanban cards instead. Training of the entire area and vigilance is necessary especially for the first installed Kanban systems.

$$\text{Kanban formula} = \frac{\begin{array}{c}(\text{total lead time to replenish}) + \\ \text{safety stock} + \text{buffer stock}\end{array}}{\text{container size}}.$$

KANBAN REPLENISHMENT

WHAT PARTS DO WE KANBAN?

Kanban systems are sometimes referred to as supermarkets since they were the premise for the idea. The simplest

[*] http://dict.regex.info Japanese to English dictionary, http://www.saiga-jp.com Kanji to English.

[†] Japan Management Association, *Kanban Just In Time at Toyota* (New York: Productivity Press) 1989. Yahsiro Monden, *The Toyota Production System* (Institute of Industrial Engineering) 2002; Shigeo Shingo, *The Shingo Non Stock Production: The Shingo System for Continuous Improvement* (New York: Productivity Press) 1988.

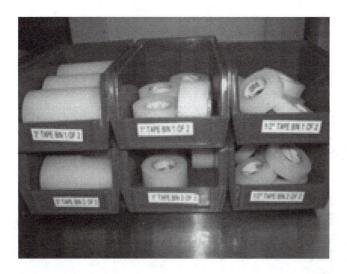

FIGURE 9.18   Two-bin Kanban system example. Operators take from top bin first. Empty bin is signal to replenish. Drawback to this setup is operators can draw from both bins and could have FIFO issues when second bin is returned.

way is to consider any part for Kanban that has a consistent demand over a user-defined period. This may be daily, weekly, monthly, or sometimes even quarterly. Parts that are specially ordered or ordered once a year are normally not good candidates. Some utilize the coefficient of variation[*] (CV) to determine which parts to Kanban or to set safety stock levels.

CONSTANT TIME OR CONSTANT QUANTITY

Kanbans can be replenished in two ways. Constant time means they are replenished the same time each day or several times a day. This is referred to as a "breadman" type replenishment, which is similar to grocery store shelves being restocked each night (Figure 9.21). Constant quantity is like the two-bin system above. It may empty out at any time, but we refill it with the same quantity every time.

TYPES OF KANBAN

There are several types of Kanban. These are explained in the first six chapters of a book entitled *The Toyota Production System*.[†] The main types are withdrawal and production Kanban. Remember, Kanbans are triggers to make something happen. Withdrawal means I go to a shelf with my empty bin, grab a full bin, and leave the empty. The empty may be replaced by an area, stockroom, or a supplier. If there is a card system, then I take the card from the new bin and put it on the empty bin. A production ordering Kanban uses the empty bin to trigger the need for production

FIGURE 9.19   Two-bin system operator draws from first bin then 2nd bin slides down. First bin is signal to replenish. Operators could still draw from second bin but this bin setup is more clear.

(vs. a work order or request) by the area to replace the parts in the bin.

KANBAN SYSTEM RULES

Kanbans should only be used when we can't link processes directly connected. Kanban cards should only be used when we can't use more simplistic systems, like an empty bin or space. The later process always goes to the earlier process to pick up material. The earlier process produces or is replenished according to the Kanban quantity and sequence. If you are using cards, all parts must have Kanban cards attached. Parts must be supplied 100% defect free. Since Kanbans are excess inventory, the goal is to reduce the number of Kanban cards over time through smoothing demand and shortening the cycle time.

WATER SPIDER FOR REPLENISHMENT

Sometimes we call the material handlers "water spiders," like the "water beetle" that frequently scurries around. The material handlers or water spiders replenish the parts in the empty bins or when triggered by a Kanban card. The water spider concept can be deployed outside the materials supply system as well, such as transporting specimens around a laboratory from one area to another. The goal is to enable our operators or staff members who are working with the product or patient to stay with the patient and not be interrupted or inconvenienced by having to search for supplies. This increases productivity and efficiency in the area.

TOTAL COST MATERIALS MANAGEMENT

Strategic buyers look at the total cost of material throughout the value stream, not just price variance or history. Total cost includes the cost of the raw material, supplier inventory on hand, replenishment frequency, overhead elimination, cost of receiving and inspection, defects and scrap in manufacturing, response time to engineering, quote and problems, setup and tooling, shelf life, warranty and the requirements imposed on the supplier's vendor, etc.

---

[*] CV is computed by dividing the standard deviation of the usage by the usage mean. One can also look at the standard deviation of lead times to the mean. Other more complicated factors that can be considered are throughput velocity, machine utilization, and autocorrelation processing time.

[†] Yahsiro Monden, *Toyota Production System* (Institute of Industrial Engineering) 2002.

FIGURE 9.20   One bin system with terminal. Supplies are replaced nightly based on the POS system.

TRUE PARTNERING WITH SUPPLIERS

The goal is to move suppliers from the typical antagonistic environment to one where the supplier becomes a true partner or an extension of your facility. True partnering involves getting your suppliers involved early in the design phase to suggest cost-saving ideas for materials used, labor required, setup time reduction, and standardized tooling requirements. Suppliers can suggest, for instance, off-the-shelf materials that they currently stock or material substitutes that may be cheaper. Suppliers should be given target costs for delivery, schedule, and quality with a pre-determined sharing formula when they can beat those targets. True partnered suppliers do not cut margins; they reduce their costs. The goal is to keep your partners as viable sources by maintaining reasonable profit margins. Partnered suppliers will respond immediately to production problems.

I was working with Hospital X on their materials process. One of the steps in the process is to double check the count of the inventory (spot check) prior to releasing the order to the distributor. This is in addition to the cycle counting they are already doing. We asked if this was a value-added step. Everyone said yes because we have to do it. I asked why they have to do it. They said they can't always be sure the count in the perpetual inventory system is correct. I asked why this was. They said it was because people were too lazy to scan out the material they needed or didn't have time to scan in the

materials. So we asked again, "Is this really value-added?" The answer was that yes, everyone who has this perpetual inventory system has to do it.

The point is no one looks at or sees this as waste. But in reality, we have "spot checks" in our process because we can't trust the system to be correct with regard to what inventory is really in the bin. So we inspect the bin to see how much is there. Inspection is waste. Just because we need to do a process doesn't make it value-added. We have to be able to see and recognize waste that is and has been in our processes for years and years and have the discipline and fortitude to call it what it is… waste or Muda.

INSOURCING VS. OUTSOURCING

There is a move in industry to outsource as much as possible. With Lean thinking, we tend to go the opposite way. In manufacturing, many times we pull production back into the United States from China and Mexico where it is going to be used in the United States. In general, when one outsources they give up control of the item or service and are at the mercy of the supplier. If you have true partnering with suppliers this can work, but where you don't, it can be a disaster waiting to happen.

EARLY SUPPLIER INVOLVEMENT

Engaging suppliers early in any of your Lean initiatives, where the goal would be to decrease inventory, can save significant dollars and should be a part of overall materials cost-reduction strategies. Once suppliers are engaged and partnering with your facility, they should receive report cards on their progress for quality cost service and delivery (QCDS).

ENFORCING QUALITY WITH SUPPLIERS

Long-term agreements (LTAs) should have built-in quality requirements with the ultimate goal of zero defects. Suppliers should have ongoing requirements/challenges to reduce the cost of the product whether it be through design

FIGURE 9.21   Supermarket.

or taking waste out of their processes. Suppliers should have stipulations that require they implement Lean Sigma programs. Delivery should be on time to the customer's requirements, not to the supplier's ability to deliver. Service should be rated based on some agreed-on criteria up front in the contract. Supplier financials are an important part of any LTA. Most suppliers have ratings that can be obtained through Dunn and Bradstreet or other credit rating agencies. It is important to make sure your suppliers are financially viable.

Electronic Data Interchange

Electronic data interchange (EDI) refers to the ability of supplier and customer computer systems to talk to each other. It eliminates the need for paper purchase orders or other paper-based transactions. Many times these systems will allow the supplier to see the customers' part's usage, etc. There are also electronic and Internet-based Kanban systems available in the market today.

FORECASTS

Forecasts are a necessary component of any materials system; however, we always say an "accurate forecast" is an oxymoron. The problem with forecasts is the longer the forecast horizon, the less accurate it tends to be. The goal of JIT is to reduce the cycle time so we can forecast out days or weeks vs. months.

FLEX FENCES

Flex fences is a concept that provides flexibility to an LTA. Flex fences look at the overall horizon of the agreement and build in risk mitigation plans in the event that the projected volume was to increase by 10%–30% or reduce by 10%–30%. For example, we may pay the supplier to keep some extra raw material on hand so we can increase our volume by 10% over a specified period of time. We may arrange with our supplier to have 30% of the material just about completed all the time in case our volume increases rapidly.

10 Implementing Lean in a Healthcare Environment

EXECUTIVE SUMMARY

This chapter deals with the implementation phase (I) of the BASICS model and the integration of new layouts, workstations and materials. It also includes discussions on Five S, Visual Controls, Mistake-Proofing, along with the Checking (C) and sustaining (S) phases of the BASICS model.

The Lean team and the supervisor must prove that the newly-implemented process can perform as expected, and they must document and train in the new process. It is the leadership's job to continually check the process in order to make sure it is running properly.

It is up to the team assigned to the area or work area (including the supervisor, planner, engineer, etc.) to sustain the gains and continuously improve the operation of the targeted area. The team should debrief the staff and other stakeholders on the improvements that have been made.

Lean is a minimum 5 year commitment which, if implemented correctly, should continue indefinitely. It needs to have top management buy-in, passion, drive, unwavering commitment and the relentless pursuit of perfection to ultimately succeed. The chapter discusses Kakushin, a serious blossoming improvement plan that is defined as a revolutionary change.

The significance of the team charter is also emphasized. It should not just provide a road map for the team but should also create a "pull" for the team, provide a structured approach for leadership interventions and create a vehicle for leadership.

Point Kaizen training is different than a Lean system kaizen implementation. Point Kaizen is typically a 5 days class 1 day of training; 3 days of work on the hospital floor; and a Friday morning PowerPoint report of the activity completed. This approach sometimes makes the process difficult to sustain once the event is over; however, Point Kaizen events are great sustaining tools. "Ready-Fire-Aim" is a good way to get management to do something and to start changing but the Point Kaizen approach has a poor chance for true success as a stand-alone strategy.

Often embedding Lean in an area and training can take months of working with experts and much susequent work long after the experts have gone. It is truly a continuous improvement process. Different implementation models are discussed and compared with the BASICS model.

LEAN IMPLEMENTATION TIPS

- Work hard to keep it simple.
- Manage by exception wherever possible.
- If you cannot do it all at once, phase it in.
- Pareto rule (80%.... 20%....).
- Skeptics are good, cynics are bad.
- Naysayers are not always against you.
- Dedicate as many resources as possible.
- Always start closest to the customer.
- Demand, Takt, flow, balance (flex), standardize, improve.
- It is not unusual to find that what you believe to be the bottleneck is not the bottleneck.
- Involve all of the employees.
- No one should lose their job as a direct consequence of continuous improvement.
- Do not try to do everything at once.
- Do not waste too much time on concrete heads (batchards).

Different types of teams are also explored:

1. Problem-Solving Teams: Implementation Teams (Kaizen or *Kaikaku*, Lean or Six Sigma)
2. Information-Gathering Teams
3. Leadership-Chartered Teams

Visual Management System Components are a way of visually indentifying when something is working or is abnormal without having the actual observer having to look at a computer or ask someone. It should be instantly noticeable to anyone looking at it.

There are four components of a visual management system. These are:

1. Five S's
2. Visual Displays
3. Visual Controls
4. Visual Management

Chapter 10 covers the Five S's or

- Seiri—sort and arrange
- Seiton—store and organize in its proper place
- Seiso—sweeping, shine and clean
- Seiketsu—standardized within and on the new system
- Shitshuke—sustained discipline and changing the old habits to new habits for good

The concept and importance of *Poka yoke*, which means fail-safing or mistake-proofing a process is reviewed.

TPM (total productivity maintenance) and overall equipment effectiveness (OEE) are discussed. Goals focus on eliminating machine down time and keeping machines running efficiently.

- Create the leadership road map
- Create a Lean steering committee – but make it the senior leadership team
- Lean consultants should report to the CEO
- Create a Lean organizational infrastructure
- Obtain leadership and physician buy-in up-front
- Have a communication plan
- Leadership must actively engage and participate with Lean
- Leadership must lead and drive Lean changes, not just support them
- Do not permit Lean to become a finance-driven FTE witch hunt
- Work to establish the Lean culture, not just the tools
- Insist on updating standard work
- Do not reward workarounds
- Do not encourage the victim syndrome
- Meetings are good but conducting too many can be counter-productive
- Get everyone involved in the analysis phase
- Dedicate resources up-front; never short-change resources
- Include a strategy for accountability and sustainability as part of the continuous improvement (CI) roadmap
- Adopt and integrate standard work and create a suggestion and reward system
- Continue videotaping after the consultant has left
- Do not make people redundant after Lean implementation
- Do not shortcut the tools
- Training is key
- Identify the process owner and the team leader up-front
- Consider changing the reward system over time
- Do not attempt to reduce the Lean implementation timeline by 50%

Key Learnings

- Lean is a long-term commitment that never ends, resulting in a major cultural change.
- Understanding the Five S's.
- Understanding visual controls and other Lean tools.
- Understanding what role Kaizen should play.
- Lean is not easy; it takes commitment, perseverance and planning.

HOW TO IMPLEMENT LEAN METHODOLOGY

You can do it to them or with them. We would rather do it WITH them than to them.

We are now into the implementing phase of the BASICS model (Figure 10.1). To recap, we have baselined the project,

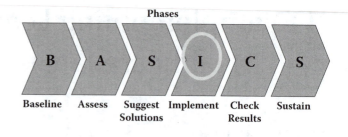

FIGURE 10.1 BASICS model—implementation.

assessed the project, and developed and suggested solutions. We typically report out to the senior leadership team. The report outs can be held after each phase (letter in the BASICS model) or based on agreed up-front milestones in the team charter. Some hospitals call these report outs "tollgate or phase gate reviews."

This chapter deals with the implementation of the new layout, workstations, and materials piece explained in earlier chapters. We are also going to discuss Five S, visual controls, and mistake proofing, along with the checking and sustaining phases of the BASICS model. Part of sustaining is ongoing Kaizen and we will discuss the differences between Kaizen and Point Kaizen events in detail later in the chapter.

THE LEAN SYSTEM IMPLEMENTATION— ARE YOU READY FOR IT?

Do you have a compelling need to change your organization? Do you have a burning platform? Do you have a fundamental dissatisfaction with how things are done today and the waste that is prevalent in all your processes? Are you willing to get the entire organization involved, including your board of directors? If so, then you are ready. If not, in the long run, you will not be successful. Remember: 40% to 80% of companies do not sustain the Lean journey or fail.

What Type of Commitment is Required?

We tell companies that Lean is a minimum 5 year commitment that never ends! It is a journey, not a "quick fix" solution. It requires resources, a plan, and an unwavering commitment. We recommend budgeting up-front for Lean and paying for it with savings from the projects.

The term "project" is somewhat of a misnomer with Lean, in that the word "project" has an ending connotation to it. Technically, once we end a Lean project, we are really just beginning the improvement that is necessary for the area, process, or changes to the overall system being implemented.

Implementing Lean changes is not always easy. Not everyone is going to buy in to the changes. Sometimes, in the early phases, there are some casualties that are too tied to the old way of doing things. While it is important to coach and motivate to help these people buy in, it is not worth spending all your time on the 10% or so who will refuse to change. Taiichi Ohno ran into the same problem when he first started implementing his new system. In his book, *The Toyota Production*

System, Ohno states that one has to "Use your authority to encourage them."[*] "When he (Ohno) introduced Kanbans to the Toyota production process, he was forced to resort to holding his position against many complaints from his foremen to his boss. He had to rather forcefully urge his foreman to go along with the system resulting in a number of complaints that he was doing something ridiculous and should be stopped. Fortunately the top manager trusted him and told him not to stop."[†]

By sticking with his new system, he eventually introduced it company-wide, even though it was not a smooth transition. Had top management not backed Ohno, the system we know as Kanban today probably would not exist. This passage from Ohno's book, *The Toyota Production System, Beyond Large Scale Production*, who consider Ohno as the "Father of the Toyota Production System," supports the notion that top management must change its way of thinking, make a commitment, and show strong support for Lean if it is to be successful. This also means that the traditional system on which top management relied on for so long has to change.

Ohno goes on to say,

> Organizational leaders must comprehend factors such as inner and outer environmental changes and the demands and directions of the times. Based on these factors, the corporation must indicate what must be done from the top-down. In the production plant, from the bottom up, employees must propose ways to improve human relations, increase productivity and ultimately reduce costs through improvements to their own workplaces. I believe it is this harmony and discord, the magnified effect between the top-down and bottom-up styles that cause insanity in the minds of people working there. Based on my experiences in the production plant, I know that in the beginning, people tended to resist change, whether large or small, making the atmosphere not conducive to implementing change. However, if the employees were frantic, we were crazy! In the end, we forced our way through and persuaded the others. The whole process of developing the TPS took place this way. From the late 1940s to the early 1960s, with everyone in opposition, it was called the abominable Ohno Production System. People refused to call it the Toyota Production System. When I confirmed the validity of the system and tried to implement it, everyone objected vehemently. To overcome this resistance, I had to quarrel and fight. And since the numbers were against me, I had no choice – I went crazy. This differs from an 'ambitious spirit.'[‡]

We think it is important for the reader to realize that, whether it is manufacturing or healthcare, Ohno's quote applies. Lean is not always easy to implement and it is not always nirvana where people get together to sing the praises of the Lean implementation. This is especially true since many people, owing to companies that only use Lean to cut manpower, now equate Lean with loss of jobs, which is really the antithesis of Lean. In reality, if implemented properly, Lean saves and creates jobs!

Lesson Learned: *Whenever implementing Lean, people are going to resist changes. As leaders you have to hang in there and support the changes, and maybe even for a period of time, "brute force" the changes, for several years until the new culture "sticks."*

What is *Kaikaku*?

Kaikaku, 改革, reform or reorganization.[§] It is a term noted in Jim Womack's book, *Lean Thinking*,[¶] and is the subject of a book of the same name. In the book, *Kaikaku*,[**] it is described as "A great transformation in awareness and in actual business. It is a large fundamental change of policy, practice or awareness." [††]

Kakushin[‡‡]

Kakushin, 革新, is a serious blossoming improvement plan, defined as revolutionary change driven by the leadership including at board level. An example would be in 2006, Toyota was even questioning its basic Kaizen approach. The result was the initiative by then CEO Mr. Watanabe to cut the number of components in their car by half. This was on top of the 2004 initiative to improve 173 system components and to cut procurement costs by 30%.[§§]

The BASICS approach we use to transform cultures from batch to Lean described in this book is a different implementation approach than the Point Kaizen event type approach. It is more along the lines of the *Kakushin* and *Kaikaku* approach, utilizing Lean system implementations or what some call System Kaizen. These are typically 4 to 14 week implementations based on applying the tools of scientific management of both time and motion study.

When converting processes from batch to flow, we use the BASICS tools described in the earlier chapters in order to assess and improve the entire system. Then we use the Kaizen (ideas from the floor) and Point Kaizen events to sustain and drive continuous improvement. The goal is to create a culture within the hospital where most of the improvement suggestions emanate from the staff on the floor doing the job every day and giving supervisors and managers time to implement the improvements.

---

[*] Taiichi Ohno, *Toyota Production System* (New York: Productivity Press) 1988.

[†] Taiichi Ohno, *Toyota Production System* (New York: Productivity Press) 1988.

[‡] Taiichi Ohno, Setsuo Mito, *Just in Time For Today and Tomorrow*. (New York: Productivity Press) 1988.

[§] http://dict.regex.info Japanese to English dictionary, http://www.saiga-jp.com Kanji to En.

[¶] James Womack and Dan Jones, *Lean Thinking* (Simon and Schuster), 1996. www.lean.org.

[**] Norman Bodek, *Kaikaku* (PCS Press) 2004.

[††] Norman Bodek, *Kaikaku* (PCS Press) 2004.

[‡‡] http://dict.regex.info Japanese to English dictionary, http://www.saiga-jp.com Kanji to En.

[§§] "Evolving Excellence," December 2006, http://www.evolvingexcellence.com/blog/2006/12/toyota question.html.

When we do Point Kaizen events, we do them a little differently than traditional Kaizen blitzes, in that we continue to use the "ready-aim-fire" approach vs. the typical Kaizen approach of "ready-fire-aim." We pick an area to improve, assemble a team, videotape and analyze it, and then make improvements. We get more proficient in the tools the more we utilize them. In some cases, on smaller scope projects, we can get through all the necessary BASICS tools in a day or less.

IMPORTANCE OF LEAN PILOTS

We recommend using Lean pilots. We start off with small pieces within the project, apply the Lean tools and work out the "kinks" prior to converting the entire area. A phased approach gives everyone time to voice their opinions and secure the necessary staff buy-in from the area. We also suggest involving the engineering/maintenance and health safety and environmental departments on the team full time or part time.

KEEP THE OWNERSHIP WITH THE LINE ORGANIZATION

The real key to implementing and sustaining Lean is to create a "PULL" for Lean from the top. The CEO needs to set goals and expectations for the line organization, which can only be met by implementing Lean and Six Sigma. It is important to keep the ownership with the process owner and not let it fall to the Lean team. The Lean team can unknowingly take the ownership by simply doing the charter or doing the scheduled report outs. These tasks must stay with the line owners in order to be successful long term.

LEAN IMPLEMENTATION OBJECTIONS AND RETAIL SALES TECHNIQUES

OBJECTIONS ARE GOOD!

Many feel that if they object or want to discuss proposed Lean ideas, they will be perceived as negative. This couldn't be more off target, because we need people to ask the difficult questions. Just because people ask difficult questions does not mean they are negative. But once the questions are answered, are they on board with the changes?

To start the discussion, one needs to understand the true nature of an "objection." There are three answers that one encounters when trying to sell an idea: yes, no, or the objections, i.e., what about this or that?

Remember, if someone objects to an idea, they have not said "no." Objections come from our paradigms that we discussed earlier. Objections are actually a way for the person to try to buy in to the change. If one can satisfactorily answer all the objections, they get the sale. Therefore, we look forward to objections. When someone does say "no," one normally responds with "why?" The question "why" is designed to solicit the objection. Once we have the objection, we must work to overcome it. Sometimes it can be overcome quickly, while other times it may take training, a series of

long discussions, or showing the person an example of where their objection was overcome, i.e., benchmarking. Some of us just need to see it to believe it. Once we see it, there is no stopping us from going after it. Once we overcome all the objections, we need to go for the "close."

Lesson Learned: *It is key that each objection is individually addressed or you will not be able to gain complete buy-in or closure.*

TYPES OF CLOSING QUESTIONS

There are several closing processes taught in retail sales. Some of them are:

- The direct close
- The indirect close
- The positive negative close
- The assumed close

These techniques work with change management as well because we are trying to "sell the change," or in this case, "Lean," to the organization. Let's explore the different types of closes.

The *direct close* is simply asking the person if they are willing to go along with the change. Then be silent until they answer.

I used to work in sales for a retail tile, paint, and wallpaper chain store. One evening I spent more than an hour and a half working with a husband and wife planning their bathroom. They had much difficulty agreeing on what they wanted. We laid out many tiles and wallpaper samples. When they finished the difficult process of picking out the tile and paint, they finally came to agreement on their wallpaper. I asked them if they would like to "go ahead and write it all up." At that moment, one of my salesmen interrupted and asked me a question. The husband and wife started discussing what they picked out and weren't sure they were happy and started looking at more wallpaper. In that instant, I had lost them. We worked together for another half hour before they once again agreed on what they wanted to purchase, which was exactly where we ended up the first time. I asked them if they were ready to go ahead with the purchase. This was the moment of truth. The husband silently walked around the rows of colorful tiles and then down the wallpaper row and back to where I was standing. The whole time I was silent. Then he said, "Yes, let's write it up."

With Lean, this could be asking someone if they would like to be on the Lean team or if they would like to start Lean in their department.

The *indirect close* is accomplished by answering an objection. It goes something like this... The customer found a tile they liked. I asked if they liked the tile. They said they did but wanted it to be "no wax." The response was, "So if I were to tell you it was 'no wax' you would take it with you tonight?" They said yes, I said yes, and we closed the sale.

The *positive negative* close is taking into consideration what a customer initially states is a key characteristic they are seeking. For example, I had a customer that stated as soon as I met them that they wanted a tile that had to be glued to the floor. We looked at several tiles and they found one they liked. My closing question was, "Well, it's a great tile and will work perfectly for you based on all the criteria you need. The only problem is you have to glue it!" Well, the customer looked at me like I was an idiot and said. "But that's what I want. I want one that needs gluing." I said, "Oh, alright then" and wrote up the sale.

I used this in healthcare. I was told by a manager that they wanted to implement Lean in the emergency department (ED) so they could increase their volume. When we were done touring the area and talking with the staff in the area, I said my assessment is that Lean would work very well in their area but he needed to understand that if they implemented Lean, he needed to be careful because word of their improvements would get out and spread. I showed him data to prove we had seen an initial 10% bump in initial volume each time we improved the ED processes. He said, "That's not a problem for us; that's what we want!" I said OK and we implemented Lean in their ED; they saw a 10% bump in volume with an empty waiting room after 2 a.m.

The *assumed close* is accomplished by just starting to write up the sale. While writing up the order, it is not uncommon to hear the husband and wife saying, "Are you happy with it? Are you sure you want it?" They agree they want it and sign on the bottom line.

These same closing techniques, which are legitimate and ethical, can be utilized in selling the change you desire and help overcome the resistance to change. The most important thing to remember is that most of us are only good at selling something we really believe in. If you really believe in Lean principles and have seen it work over and over again, it becomes an easy sell.

When someone does object to implementing Lean in their area, the first thing we try to ascertain is the objection. If the objection is that it is "going to make my job more difficult," our response might be, "so what you are saying is, if we could show you how it would make your job easier, you would buy in to the change? OK, let's show you how it will make it easier to do your job in the long run." Once the discussion is complete, we are ready for the closing question: "so now that we have shown how much easier your job will be to manage in the new Lean environment, are you willing to work with us on the change?" Then be silent because he who speaks first loses.

Badgering and the Closing

Why is it important to be silent after asking the closing question? Have you ever been to a store where the person asks the closing question "Would you like to buy the carpet tonight?" While you are thinking it over they say, "Well, you know it is very good carpet and it will last a long time and we have free installation, and it is the best carpet in its class." Before you know it, all you want to do is get away from this person.

By him/her continuing to speak, he/she now gives you more cause for objections and reasons to walk out.

This behavior translates into "begging" you to buy the carpet and the person appears "desperate" to get the sale. We see this same behavior with ideas and change.

Lesson Learned: *Don't badger. Sell your case based on data and facts, not what other people think. Be confident, believe and be passionate in your responses, back them up with data and past results, answer the objections, and close the sale!*

GENERAL OVERARCHING LEAN IMPLEMENTATION TIPS

- Work really hard to keep it simple.
- Manage by exception wherever possible.
- If you can't do it all at once… phase it in.
- Pareto rule (80%…. 20%….). The Pareto* principle normally applies to Lean implementations. Focus on the 80% you can impact and save the 20% to work on later.
- Skeptics are good, cynics are bad. We encourage skeptics. After all, they keep us honest. Cynics are convinced it will never work, thus anything you do will be wrong. If you can turn a cynic, they become zealots, but it takes a tremendous investment in time but they can become your best salespeople.
- Leverage your informal leaders as they can significantly influence your ability to achieve buy-in and acceptance.
- Naysayers are not always against you. Many times, they just honestly believe it won't work. It is OK to be negative as long as they are not cynical. We can normally bring them along once the new process is up and running and they physically see it working.
- Dedicate as many resources as possible. We find that each person you can dedicate to improvement pays for themselves ten times over. In the long run, we need to free up 50% of our supervisor and managers' time to implement improvements.
- Always start closest to the customer. This rule has never failed us, but it is somewhat counterintuitive. People say that if the sub-process isn't working, then

* http://en.wikipedia.org/wiki/Pareto_principle. The Pareto principle (also known as the 80–20 rule, the law of the vital few, and the Principle of Factor Sparsity) states that, for many events, roughly 80% of the effects come from 20% of the causes. Business management thinker, Joseph M. Juran, suggested the principle and named it after Italian economist Vilfredo Pareto, who observed in 1906 that 80% of the land in Italy was owned by 20% of the population. It is a common rule of thumb in business, e.g., "80% of your sales come from 20% of your clients." Mathematically, where something is shared among a sufficiently large set of participants, there must be a number k between 50 and 100 such that $k\%$ is taken by $(100 - k)\%$ of the participants. k may vary from 50 (in the case of equal distribution) to nearly 100 (when a tiny number of participants account for almost all of the resource). There is nothing special about the number 80% mathematically, but many real systems have k somewhere around this region of intermediate imbalance in distribution.

the final process closest to the customer won't work. While this might be true, by acting on the later process we create the true pull requirements for the earlier process. If you attack the earlier process first, then all you do is bottleneck the process prior to the later process.

- Demand, Takt, flow, balance (flex), standardize, improve.
- It's not unusual to find that what you think is the bottleneck, is not the bottleneck. People only think they know where the problem is until they study and analyze the root cause of it.
- Get all the employees involved. Treat people like people—we can't emphasize this rule enough!
- No one should lose their job directly due to continuous improvement.
- Don't try to do everything at once. Prioritize and stay focused. This does not mean you can't multitask, but too many projects at once can be a recipe for disaster.
- Don't waste too much time on concrete heads (batchards). Give them some time and coach them to buy in, but in the end, you may have to find a new home for them—in or out of the company.

TEAM CHARTERS

Team charters are a necessary tool prior to starting any project. Team charters include entry and exit strategies, budgets, and detailed scopes. They are contracts with the teams, implementing department, and the leadership or steering committee.

At Hospital X, Bill, the Lean specialist, was working with his second clinic. The first had been very successful and was even toured by other hospitals. As the second clinic kicked off, Bill met with the leadership to review the charter his team had prepared. The leadership took the position that they had already done one clinic and there was no need for a formal charter for the second team. How wrong they were! About 3 to 4 weeks into the project, the team champion/sponsor was on vacation for several weeks. During this time, certain members of the team took over, alienated Bill and ostracized him from the management meetings. Meanwhile, the clinic leadership team decided that they wanted no part in the changes and the effort stalled. Because there was no charter (the result of an uncommitted leadership team), there was no escalation plan. As problems surfaced, the team started "infighting." It was further complicated by a new hire whose job was to project manage (micro-manage) the team. The project manager was not familiar with Lean or Six Sigma. Instead of meeting with Bill and learning the Lean implementation process, the project manager met with the team and laid down his rules and how his project was going to run.

Lessons Learned: *The significance of the team charter is not just to provide a road map for the team, but also to create a "pull" for the team, provide a structured approach for leadership interventions, and create a vehicle for*

leadership to follow-up and sustain during and after the initial implementation.

The charter is a symbol of management commitment and provides an escalation process and ultimate ownership for the team and its results in the event that they run into any resistance to change.

DIFFERENT TYPES OF TEAMS

Many books have been written on all aspects of teams. Our purpose here is to differentiate between different types of teams utilized in or with Lean. When we do a value stream mapping (VSM), we develop a list of opportunities. Some of these opportunities are simply tasks that can be assigned to an individual (and should have only one owner). An item is deemed a project because, after much discussion, it is determined to be more complex than one individual can or should fix, and a team is required. We break teams into three categories:

1. Problem-solving teams: implementation teams (Kaizen or *Kaikaku*, Lean or Six Sigma)
2. Information-gathering teams
3. Leadership-chartered teams

PROBLEM-SOLVING TEAMS

These would include senior leadership and management teams, in other words, everyone's job in the organization is problem solving and continuous improvements, i.e., developing new paradigms.[*] The ideas of paradigms[†] are critical to Lean thinking. We must be able to recognize when we are in a paradigm; this is very difficult.

INFORMATION-GATHERING TEAMS

Information teams only gather and research information and report back to the chartering body. In the book, *40 Years, 20 Million Ideas*,[‡] Toyota talks about how they utilize information teams outside work and how it is an honor to be selected for one of these teams.

LEADERSHIP-CHARTERED TEAMS

Implementation teams are chartered by the board of directors, CEO, a senior level executive or CEO led Process Improvement Committee, given a budget and empowerment level.

TEAMS

As Lean is implemented throughout a facility, people must learn to work together as a team to accomplish their tasks. If the people assigned to an area are not taught how to work together, performance can suffer and stress levels can increase.

---

[*] Joel Barker, The New Business of Paradigms (C) 2001.
[†] Joel Barker — Original Business of Paradigms, 1989.
[‡] Yuzo Yasuda, *40 Years, 20 Million Ideas: Toyota Suggestion System* (Productivity Press) 1990.

Teams go through four stages of development: forming, storming, norming, performing.* During the forming stage, the team is going through an exploration period. Team members are cautious and guarded. Sometimes, confusion and anxiety are experienced as individual differences surface within the team. The team facilitator can help by sharing relevant information, encouraging open dialogue, providing structure, and developing a climate of trust and respect.

During the storming stage, the team feels defensive. Conflict cannot be avoided during this stage. The team must deal with the issues of power, leadership, and decision making. They will challenge the wisdom of the leader. The team facilitator should engage the team in group problem solving, establish norms for looking at different points of view, discuss decision-making procedures, and encourage two communications (Figure 10.2).

At the norming stage, the team feels as though they have made it through the storm. Team members become committed to working with one another. Trust, the most essential ingredient in team dynamics, begins to evolve. The team facilitator guides the team to talk openly about issues and concerns. Positive feedback and support for a consensus decision-making process will help the team grow.

The performing stage brings a sense of team identity and commitment to the team and its goals. The team has learned to work together. Communication is open and information is shared. The team facilitator should observe the team and offer feedback when requested. Encourage ongoing self-assessment and mentor the team to develop to its fullest potential.

GUIDELINES FOR THE SUPERVISOR

- Be a leader and lead the work area.
- Create an atmosphere that encourages adherence to standard work.
- Run the daily team meeting/huddle.
- Make timely and effective decisions.
- Be able to prioritize and delegate.
- Be the role model for the work area (i.e., attitude, breaks, etc.).
- Make the numbers and meet the schedule.
- Understand how the area should run and run it properly. Make sure people have tools and materials to do their jobs. Know each job thoroughly and be able to train others in standard work and hitting the times. Manage the standard work in progress (WIP) in the area. Manage breaks, lunch, and start times.
- Ensure the day-by-the-hour chart and the month-by-the-day chart is filled out.
- Deploy people properly, make sure people stay in their areas, and flex as required. If you have extra people in the work area, make sure to move them to another area.

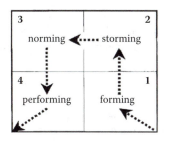

FIGURE 10.2 Four stages of teams. Psychologist, B.W Tuckman in the 1970s, developed this model and Tuckman suggests that there are four team development stages that teams have to go through in order to be productive. The four stages are: Forming when the team meets and starts to work together for the first time. Storming, when the members within the team start to "jockey" for position and when control struggles take place. Norming when rules are finalised and accepted and when team rules start being adhered to. Performing when the team starts to produce through effective and efficient working practices.

- Discipline people as required.
- Clearly display the standardized work sheet in the area.
- Keep the area clean. Make sure tools are put back after each shift.
- Cross-train everyone in the area and rotate jobs at some frequency—daily, weekly, or monthly.
- Create a top ten problem action item list for both the team and upper management.
- Take swift and effective action on ideas generated by the team.
- Update the standard work as suggestions are implemented.
- Attend production meetings and update management, escalate as appropriate.
- Float into the line as needed or ensure someone is available to float.
- Be responsible to immediately respond to problems in the area with appropriate action and then document on the day-by-the-hour chart.

TRAIN THE STAFF IN THE NEW PROCESS

The next step is to train the staff in the new process. This is done by taking the standard work developed by the team based on the video analysis and communicating it to the rest of the staff. We typically do this in small groups and ask for their input as we go. Sometimes, it is necessary to pull the whole staff together in order to get everyone to agree on what the steps for the standard work are going to be. Most of the time, the person's job doesn't change, just the order or when they do the steps in the job.

TYPES OF TRAINING

It is important to train your organization with an overview of batch systems vs. Lean systems, Lean principles, Six Sigma, Total Quality (TQ) tools, and change management. Training

---

* With permission of Bruce Tuckman 1965, original "Forming-storming-norming-performing" concept, http://www.businessballs.com/tuckman-formingstormingnormingperforming.html.

should focus on tools 50% and people 50%. For those of you who have implemented changes, you already know that the tools are easy to learn compared to getting people to change.

OVERVIEW TRAINING

Lean overview training can run anywhere from 1 hr to 5 day sessions. We recommend basic overview training for the entire organization. It should be part of the training and communication plans. While it is true that Lean cannot be totally learned in a classroom, if the classroom training is done properly, many tools can be implemented on leaving the class. There are also advanced Lean training classes and a variety of Lean certification options available. The participants are exposed to Lean principles in several ways.

In the 5 day overview training, participants learn through lectures, interactive exercises, and a small Kaizen event. They experience teamwork and team building and typically meet new people inside or outside the organization. Participants include those who are going to be working on their first Lean project, key stakeholders, suppliers, and customers of the pilot project. We have run the classes with everyone from the president to floor personnel. Prior to the class, we normally videotape the processes from the pilot project and analyze them in the class. Participants are tasked to implement at least one improvement when they leave the class. This results in an opportunity to get the class back together to follow up on the improvements. When we get them back together, we encourage them to make another improvement and to get someone else to make an improvement as well. We serve a free lunch with the price of admission being an improvement. When everyone in the class is exposed to Lean, it makes it much easier to implement each project. This training becomes part of a larger, more comprehensive training plan. Interestingly enough, we have many people who have repeated our 5 day training a year or two later. The advantage is that once a person has implemented and learned Lean principles and tools, they continue to get something new out of it. We have had all levels of healthcare personnel attend our manufacturing 5 day classes (normally a year or so after they started their Lean journey). Other training options include a 3 day, 2 day, 1 day, and various hourly training sessions.

Lesson Learned: *Where an overview training session is not utilized, it is much more difficult to implement and sustain the project.*

ON THE JOB LEAN TRAINING

On the job training is provided during an event or implementation. It is important to review the Lean principles and whatever specific tools are going to be involved prior to implementation. Essentially, Lean system Kaizen implementations are ongoing training in each of the Lean tools that are necessary for the project. This training is invaluable, as it is totally based on real-life implementation as opposed to the classroom. The overview classroom training should be a pre-requisite for an implementation. It saves a lot of time covering the principles and reasons for implementing Lean as opposed to trying to do it as you go.

EXECUTIVE TRAINING

Executive training should be the same as for implementers; however, this is difficult to accomplish. The best way to learn Lean is by doing it. Most executives don't feel they have time to learn, so we prepare overview training for them. This training is generally 1 to 2 1/2 days. We have had many executives get much more involved and attend 5 day overview training, drop in during implementation training, and lead training and Point Kaizen events.

THE LEAN IMPLEMENTATION MODEL

The implementation methods model describes the different approaches to Lean and compares them to Toyota (Figure 10.3). This whole discussion is confusing as the word Kaizen appears in all four methods. In order to clarify, let's examine each method.

- Method 1 is the implementation model we have been promoting in this book based on the BASICS model and followed up with PDSA (plan, do, study, act).
- Method 2 is made up of Point Kaizen events. This process will be discussed in detail in this chapter.
- Method 3 is the goal of a Lean culture. This is where 80% or more of the ideas are generated from the floor every day and implemented by the team leader or supervisor.
- Method 4 is composed of high-level chartered teams that are looking at benchmarking the rest of the world and constantly assessing the overall continuous improvement system of the company.

GENERAL DISCUSSION OF THE FOUR METHODS

Once the area has been converted to flow with the BASICS model, we utilize method 2, Point Kaizens, as one method of sustaining. We also use Point Kaizens occasionally as a way to introduce a new company to the power of what a dedicated team can accomplish in 1 week. Most companies and 95% of consultants have been using method 2 to try to convert from batch to Lean. Most of their training material and certifications are developed around this Point Kaizen approach. We will discuss the pros and cons of this as an approach to convert batch to flow. What took seven Kaizen events and 2 years at one company to implement flow on one line was surpassed at the same company using the BASICS approach during one 8 week system Kaizen implementation in another area that looked at the entire product line from beginning to end. It is a very powerful system. However, the Point Kaizen approach seldom leads to method 3, which is the overall goal of a Lean culture. Method 4 uses the Good Ideas club to sustain and continuously improve the other three methods.

Method 4 Good Idea (GI) Club Board / Executive Level Chartered Strategic Kaizen Teams Continuous Learning CI System Responsibility Toyota uses 10%	Method 3 True Kaizen Ideas Flow From Floor & Implemented by Team Leader Sustain Toyota uses 80%	Method 2 Point Kaizen Events Initial Sell Sustain U.S. uses 80% to 100% Toyota uses 10%	Method 1 System Kaizen Implementation Should be used for Batch to Flow Conversions
This is the Goal!		95% consultants	5% consultants
CEO & Board should own	CEO & HR should own		

FIGURE 10.3   Lean implementation methodology.

KAIZEN (METHOD 3) VS. THE TRADITIONAL POINT KAIZEN (METHOD 2) EVENT APPROACH

What is Kaizen? Kaizen 改良する* (this is kairyō suru, which means to improve). Kaizen is 改善 a Japanese word, Kai 改 meaning change and zen 漸 meaning gradual. Kaizen is interpreted in English to mean continuous small or incremental improvements. The term Kaizen and Point Kaizen often get confused or used interchangeably. Point Kaizen events and Kaizen are *different* concepts. Toyota's Kaizen approach is based on the Toyota House with the 2 pillars of JIT and Jidoka supporting the roof (respect for humanity) with the foundation being standard work, Heijunka, visual controls, TCWQC and TPM (Figure 10.4).

Kaizen

Kaizen is the idea that every employee is contributing ideas and small improvements every day. Supervisors and managers are given time, at least 50% of their day, to implement these changes. These small ideas each day turn into thousands of suggestions and significant bottom-line profitability on an annual basis.

Point Kaizen Events

A traditional Point Kaizen event requires a team of 6–8 people who are dedicated for a week to an improvement effort. Point Kaizen event training is typically a 5 day event, with the first day being training, the next 3 days on the floor or in the office making changes with a report out, and "celebration" on the fifth day. In reality, we have found Kaizen events can range from a 1 hour event to 2 to 3 week events, although this is rare. The events require a full-time dedicated team during this time.

Point Kaizen events require very specific, focused, realistic goals that can be accomplished within the event's time frame. These are typically sold by consultants as "ready-fire-aim" events and contain the same day of training for each Point Kaizen event forever. Each event ends with the team going back to their regular jobs and a 30 day list of actions to complete. Ready-fire-aim means you just go do it without any planning.

POTENTIAL PITFALLS OF THE TRADITIONAL POINT KAIZEN APPROACH

Many consultants today use Point Kaizen events to implement Lean. There can be problems with this approach when doing large conversions from batch to flow. It is important to understand that Point Kaizen events are an easy sell to company management because they only tie up 6–8 people for a week, and they get management on board with Lean. Management doesn't have to do anything but give up a person here or there for a week and attend the report out. They are initially amazed at what a dedicated cross-functional team

---

* Translation provided by Professor William Tsutsui, Associate Dean for International Studies, Professor of History, College of Liberal Arts & Sciences, The University of Kansas.

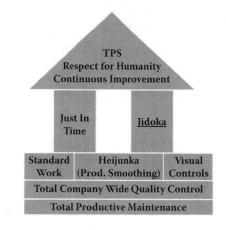

FIGURE 10.4   Toyota house.

can accomplish in a week. The team appears, based on the PowerPoint presentation, to get great initial results. Note: Point Kaizens can be leveraged to achieve "quick wins", but should be used with caution as discussed below. In many cases, the results are great, but after several months management finds out that they are difficult to sustain and can't understand why.

The next pitfall is that most Point Kaizen event report outs contain a 30 day list. Unfortunately, the dedicated teams are only put together for a week so there is no one left to follow up the 30 day list. Then the company assigns the list to the area supervisor, but this doesn't work either because the supervisor is too busy fighting day-to-day problems or can't get the list done. As a result, many Point Kaizen events don't sustain the improvement. The other problem using Point Kaizen events as an implementation strategy is there is only so much one can accomplish in a 1 week event. Point Kaizen events are designed to make small and large improvements within the week and rarely lead to organizational cultural transformations.

On large healthcare service lines, like inpatient, laboratory, ED, or operating room (OR), only a small part of a line can be attacked in a Point Kaizen event. For instance, changeover of one surgery room might be targeted for an event. If you don't hit a process that is on the critical path, roll it out area- or system-wide and sustain it, then the results don't get to the bottom line. In addition, the old processes still exist. In many cases, you are still batching into and out of the improved area. This also makes it difficult to sustain.

Our results are not getting to the bottom line... We are having trouble sustaining the improvements... We are not able to complete our Kaizen newspapers and 30 day lists... I can't put that many people in the Kaizen Promotion Office or run all the events required based on 1 event per 100 persons in the company. These comments were common at all of Company X's sites. While weekly events were very successful in the short term, they were typically difficult to sustain in the long term or even the week after the event. The consultants told us that this was normal. We were also told that we may end up changing the layout up to 10 times a year and that was normal because each event is looking at a different piece of the process. The important thing was to just go out and change something; don't study it, just try it.

If you are a hospital administrator in the middle of a typical week in the OR, imagine I come to you and say we are going to do a Point Kaizen event in your area this week. We are going to change your whole process design around, and it may work or it may not but that's normal. We want to just ready-fire-aim and "go do." Or imagine you are in construction and I say, "Let's just change that steel to plastic; it's cheaper and we can get it quicker." Or "Let's just change this layout. After all, if we don't get it right the first time, we will just re-do it ten or twelve times this year until we get it right." Or I am a doctor and I say let's not do the operation the standard way; let's improve it by just trying something new. We don't need to study or plan for it; after all, it might work. Consultants told us it's not unusual to take 3 steps forward and 2 steps back. After all, you can't expect to get it right the first time every time. Doesn't this type of logic sound absurd? Yet, we are letting ourselves be reeled into this type of approach with traditional Kaizen events.

Sound management techniques and training typically would reject and, at most, discourage this type of thought and approach. In fact, when we explain this approach during our Point Kaizen event training sessions, it is often met, at first, with disbelief and amazement; however, owing to the reputation of Kaizen consultants and films showing great results, we are often misled to believe that this panacea exists and that our sound judgment should be replaced with a "just do it" philosophy. The films do not show where these efforts fail and the potential costs of failure.

We believe, as a stand-alone improvement philosophy, the Point Kaizen approach to Leaning out entire companies is dangerous not only to American but also global manufacturing, healthcare, and service industries. If the Point Kaizen event approach is not completely understood, it can result in the opposite of the desired effect. It then becomes a failed effort or a very expensive (the consultants time is not cheap) yet failed proposition. We believe many companies have failed, leading to scrapped Lean initiatives owing to their experiences with the traditional Point Kaizen event approach. We have often heard, "Oh, yeah, we tried that Lean stuff before and it won't work here!"

DISADVANTAGES OF POINT KAIZEN EVENTS USED FOR FIRST TIME IMPLEMENTATION

1. The term "event" in and of itself does not signify continuous improvement and the typical Point Kaizen event approach is "ready-fire-aim, not ready-aim-fire." The Point Kaizen event has to be scoped to something that can be accomplished in a week (really three or three and one-half working days), but, typically, companies try to tackle too much at once. They tend to sub-optimize processes because only so much can be accomplished in a week. Sometimes this is not enough time to make it work or for staff to understand or learn the new way. Staff are typically not trained well in new procedures and many times the new procedures are poorly documented, if at all. So, if they do get it up and running but someone is out sick, the supervisor doesn't know what to do. The process introduces variation and some areas have been shut down for days, weeks, or even months after a poorly planned event. Area staff are left with the results of a Kaizen event (and in some cases all the mess), but no support to clean it up. Many times, in people's haste "to do" or make changes, safety, ergonomic, and local and state regulations are violated.

2. They are difficult to rollout as an overall system strategy. They are a slow approach and don't work well for initial batch to one-piece flow conversions. Changes to a system are not normally planned well

and opportunities exist for many unintended consequences after the team leaves. During an event, there is only time to work on a piece of the process; we don't have time to take a step back to look at the whole process, i.e., to look at the big picture. We found with Point Kaizen events, TQ teams, or Grass Roots Teams, sometimes we spent a week trying to improve a process that, when we looked at it from a system view, could have been eliminated. Instead, we wasted valuable time trying to improve it.

3. Most Point Kaizen events are based on what management thinks are the problems, but have not collected data to know for sure. It is difficult to sustain improvements if an event is done in the middle of a process and supporting systems are not improved. We still have push systems before and after the new Lean part of the process; therefore, it is very tough to maintain. 30 day lists are typically not followed up or require extensive resources to complete. On average, 50% or less of Point Kaizen events sustain over time. There are normally no audit systems to follow up.

4. Teams get in line for "events," delaying improvements. *At one company, a supervisor came to me and said, "I bought all the quick-change tooling we need for this one machine but I can't get on the Kaizen event calendar to get it installed!"* There is normally not enough time to get standard work in place and sustain it and the supervisor doesn't know how to run it.

Many companies form Kaizen promotion offices. These contain the trainers for Kaizens and people freed up as part of the Kaizen events. While, in concept, Kaizen promotion offices make sense, they are seldom successful and become easy targets for layoffs. In addition, since the Kaizen trainers are dedicated, they end up spending a lot of time in the office instead of on the floor making improvements or training line management how to lead events.

5. Kaizen events feed the CEO's desire for quick returns for little investment. They tend to turn into Friday "shows" for management, free lunch for the team, and a checkmark off the list that the kaizen event has been completed for corporate. Some companies are measured on the number of Kaizen events instead of the continuous improvement measures they should be monitoring.

6. Some companies have "Initiativitis." They try to implement different pieces of the Toyota process system (TPS) separately. Over several years, a Fortune 100 company had launched separate initiatives with Five S, Focused Factories, Kanbans, Process Flows (TQ Speed), Process & Wall Mapping, not to mention 4 days of TQ tools training, facilitator training, and Point Kaizen events, etc. But they never put all the tools together and integrate them with the Lean culture. As a result, the improvements

became difficult to sustain and most people figured they could just "wait it out."

7. Reward systems are not changed to support continuous improvement.

8. In many cases, the Kaizen event approach typically makes one more dependent on consultants. Once management sees the first report out and the enthusiasm of the team, they are hooked. They immediately want to roll out more events. This is reinforced by the notion that we only need to dedicate a team for a week to get great results. The consultants provide 1 day of the same training for every event, which is not enough to learn Lean or understand the philosophy behind it. Therefore, the teams become dependent on the consultants' knowledge. Since the consultants encourage creation of a Kaizen promotion office to coordinate the events and the company does not have enough trained personnel, the consultant can typically expect 1 to 2 years worth of engagement. Many companies use the number of events as a measure vs. process-based continuous improvement measures.

WHY IS THE POINT KAIZEN APPROACH SO PREVALENT?

To be honest, Point Kaizen events are great marketing tools for consultants and easy to sell to management and companies. They are quick and easy and only need 4–6 people dedicated for 1 week. It is amazing what a group of dedicated, smart, talented, and knowledgeable people can accomplish in a 3 to 5 day time frame. Kaizen consultants encourage the team to stay up very late Thursday night to put the presentation together. Then the team reports their successes to senior leadership: reductions in cycle time, distance traveled, WIP, space, etc. Management then salivates over these ready-fire-aim improvements and schedules more events. The Point Kaizen events or blitzes become a very easy sell. It is also easy to quickly train new consultants in this approach.

In 1996, I was invited to attend a Point Kaizen event in Japan. We were also told we would see several world-class companies, including Toyota. The Japanese senseis provided their day of training, which was translated to us. The trainer was great, although 90% was what we already received in every other day one of 5 day Kaizen event training.

We spent 3 days working in a Japanese electronics plant. To a novice, this Japan trip is phenomenal and can provide much needed paradigm shifts for traditional managers. Our Japanese senseis said "Go find improvements, bring them back to us and we will implement them." When we asked if we could videotape, we were told "no time for videotape... go do..."

Please keep in mind that we had several years of Lean experience by this time. As usual, Tuesday to Thursday, we found many opportunities for improvements. Then they wanted us to stay up until midnight Thursday when we had our presentation done by 8:00 p.m. I think this was just so we could say we stayed up late Thursday night. The next surprise was our sponsor wanted us to put results in our report we did not achieve. We refused and said if they did, they could deliver the report.

What we learned was that this trip was all about the big show and selling more Point Kaizen events. After talking with our sponsor consultant guides, we determined that any idea we thought of that they had already thought of would be implemented fairly quickly. If a tool or fixture was needed, it would magically appear overnight; however, when one of my colleagues came up with a modification to a machine that they had not thought of, we were told "they had to study it first." On Wednesday morning, I came up with a new layout for their surface mount line. Once again, we were told that they would have to study it first. This cemented for me that ready-fire-aim was primarily designed to get Americans, Europeans, and other countries to just start making improvements. If this was the strategy, it worked, and they are still very successful with the Point Kaizen approach.

During my 2 years on an organization's Champions Club, the subject of Kaizen blitzes came up during one of our meetings. Everyone at the table had just presented improvements that they had done at their plants. They all had similar experiences with Point Kaizen events as we had at my old company and acknowledged they were not the right tool to convert an entire factory from batch to Lean. But, Kaizen blitzes sell and get companies involved, get initial results, and motivate them to start up Lean programs. There was no simple alternative, so everyone agreed to stay with Kaizen blitzes because something was better than nothing.

Lesson Learned: *The first lesson learned was that we need to study new improvement ideas vs. just doing them. Ready-fire-aim is a good way to get management to do something and to start changing, but the Point Kaizen approach has a poor chance for true success as a stand-alone strategy. A new approach is needed other than Point Kaizen events if the United States or any other country is going to be truly successful at sustaining Lean. Once the consultants leave, most companies revise their Point Kaizen event approach and Kaizen Promotion Office because of the sustaining issue and lack of getting to the bottom line. I still hear the same complaints today from manufacturing companies and hospitals. The BASICS system Lean approach is the answer, but it takes time and resolve to implement because it is a ready-aim-fire approach and requires a significant commitment up-front of project and training resources.*

With all these negative comments, one might think we are against Kaizen events. But we are not! Kaizen events have their place and should be a part of your improvement strategy, but not your entire improvement strategy. We believe Point Kaizen events should be utilized as a management introduction to continuous improvement, to get people on board with Lean, and can be extremely beneficial as one of the tools for sustaining Lean to augment the continuous improvement program to foster the Lean cultural transformation.

ADVANTAGES/RESULTS OF KAIZEN EVENTS

- If properly scoped and chartered with the right expectations, Kaizen events can provide great results, and a lot of change can be accomplished in a very short time frame. We have completely changed entire layouts overnight.
- Significant productivity and space improvements can be made within the specific area being targeted.
- They promote organizational team building with visibility to the senior leadership team. They showcase the power of dedicated cross-functional teams to make quick changes, which help break down functional barriers.
- They can be a good training and sustaining tool to help develop a continuous learning organization.

We find that there are many projects that lend themselves to the Kaizen event approach. Some of these are:

- Setup/changeover reductions
- Five S
- *Poka yoke*, etc.
- TPM pilot
- Visual displays or controls
- Smaller area layout improvements
- Processes that can be improved within the week time frame, employees trained and the supervisor left with a complete standard work package

In order to utilize Point Kaizen events as an overall implementation approach, there has to be a cohesive strategy with multiple sequential events in one area and a ready-aim-fire approach. Toyota did not get Lean doing Point Kaizen events. Point Kaizen events came much later, after the company was converted to flow.

Lesson Learned: *Based on all the reading we have done it seems that at Toyota about 10% of improvement comes from Point Kaizen events, 10% from leadership-chartered improvement teams, and 80% from employees and supervisors (team leaders) on the line every day.*

We have developed a new, revised Kaizen approach in order to convert the Point Kaizen event to more of a ready-aim-fire style event with training tailored to the event. We recommend against generating a 30 day list, as it has been our experience that these are seldom followed up unless the proper resources are dedicated and management has the discipline to bring the outstanding items to closure.

Our revised Kaizen approach is composed of the following:

- Senior leaders should lead the event and the training.
- Charter the team properly.
- State the target improvement and expectations up-front.
- Focus the team and provide the right team members and resources.
- The Kaizen team must be dedicated during the event.

- Give the team priority over resources, especially maintenance.
- Act on fact, use the BASICS tools, videotape, and utilize a ready-aim-fire approach.
- Provide overview training to all participants.
- Follow up each day with the team or team leader.
- Make sure all changes are documented prior to the end of the event.
- Make sure changes are communicated to the product team ahead of time and secure their buy-in.
- Implement changes.
- Report out to the senior leadership team at the end of the week's event.
- Make sure that any remaining action items are turned over as recommendations to the area or functions responsible.
- Have a follow-up meeting with management to ensure all actions are closed out.
- Have a follow-up audit or review in 1 week or at 1 month intervals (as needed) to ensure the improvements in the area are sustaining.

VISUAL MANAGEMENT SYSTEM COMPONENTS

There are four components of a visual management system. These are:

1. Five S
2. Visual displays
3. Visual controls
4. Visual management

FIVE S

Whether or not Five S (5S) is implemented as a separate initiative, it becomes a part of every implementation. As we make changes to the layout and workstations, we implement Five S as we go. Some organizations add an S for safety and call this 6S. Five S is the beginning step and part of a larger whole, called visual management systems. The goal of visual management is to make problems jump out and be visible.

When a work area is neat, clean, and orderly, it is a more efficient and safer work area. The Five S's are a method for creating and maintaining this type of work environment. Listed below are the Five S's with original Japanese words and different American definitions, depending on the source:[*]

Seiri—整理[†]—proper arrangement, sort, clean up, clearing up, organization: The first step is to separate and consolidate those items that are necessary for the proper functioning of the work area (tools, fixtures, work instructions, parts, etc.)

from the unnecessary items. Get rid of those items that are unnecessary.

Seiton—整頓—arrange, put in order and store, set in order, order, orderliness, organize logical order, neatness: Arrange items so they can be retrieved immediately in the order required. Make a place for all the necessary items and put them in their place. Identify their appropriate place by outlining the area (shadow boarding) or labeling the space.

Seiso—清楚—neat, tidy, shine, cleanliness, cleaning, pick up: Operators clean the work area daily. Sweep the floors, wipe off the machines, and keep a sanitary work area. Make sure everything is neatly in its place.

Seiketsu—清潔—cleanliness, standardize, neatness, maintaining a spotless workplace: Find ways to keep the overall environment neat and clean. Are there ways to reduce dust, dirt, and debris that make the cleanup easier? How are old documents purged from the area? Can we eliminate safety hazards?

Shitsuke—躾—discipline, sustain, conduct, changing work habits, training: Discipline and training. The most important step of all is to maintain the area once it has been created. Everyone must follow the standardized procedures for cleaning and organizing. Continue to look at the whole area, not just your workspace.

Many areas audit regularly to track their improvement. The area team uses the audit results to focus their improvement efforts and increase their score on the next audit. The area team should review the audit results, brainstorm suggestions for improvement, and take the necessary actions.

The observation form can be tailored to the plant. A plant that does chemical processes will have some different items than a plant that only does assembly. Remember to include safety as part of your Five S audits.

Five S is about two major items—housekeeping and discipline. Housekeeping is about the old saying "a place for everything and everything in its place," but it is also about discipline. Putting things back in their place is the most difficult part of Five S. The leader of the area sets the standard for Five S and Lean overall. If someone does not put something away where they should and the leader says nothing, then effectively the leader has just rewarded that behavior. We all need to be part of setting the standard at the highest levels if we are to be considered world class.

VISUAL DISPLAYS

Visual displays are signs and bulletin boards that communicate information. They do not enforce any action, only communicate the name of an area, machine, or some other type of information.

VISUAL CONTROLS

The analogy for visual controls is the human body.[‡] When the body has a problem, it lets you know. It may be in the form of a fever, pain, bleeding, blister, etc. Once your body

---

[*] Nelson, Mayo and Moody, *Productivity Five S Series, Powered by Honda*; Shimbun, *The Five S's, Visual Control Systems*; Hirano, *Putting Five S to Work*; and Ohno, *Workplace Management*.

[†] Translation provided by Professor William Tsutsui, Associate Dean for International Studies, Professor of History, College of Liberal Arts & Sciences, The University of Kansas.

[‡] Taiichi Ohno, *Toyota Production System* (New York: Productivity Press) 1988.

signals a problem, it needs to be taken care of right away or it tends to get worse. This is true in the hospital or clinic as well. The goal is to make problems visible so they can be fixed right away and then fix them so they don't come back. The work area should "talk to you" and communicate its condition as you walk around it.

Visual controls are different than visual displays as they help remind us but usually don't force certain actions. For example, a stoplight tells a driver to stop, but it doesn't force the driver to stop. The driver stops because they know if they continue there may be some negative consequence, like an accident or a ticket. They are communication tools to help the systems within an area respond to customer demand and changes within the environment. These controls come in many forms, but the common denominator among them is that they cause an appropriate action when a visual signal occurs. The following is a list of examples.

- When a Kanban card is placed in the post office box, it triggers the right number of parts to be made or replenished.
- In a laboratory, when an andon light is turned on, it may signal to a technician that the processing line needs attention or to a supervisor that a machine is down.
- Electronic whiteboards or tracking boards in an ED may signal when a new order has been written that needs action or an abnormal lab has been resulted.
- In surgery, electronic tracking boards may signal where the patient is in the process, signaling what actions need to be taken.
- In pharmacies, empty bins or water level marks prompt a visual cue that supplies need to be replenished.

Measurements of the process in the area are visual controls that are updated by team members and are used to drive improvements. Day-by-the-hour charts are a simple form of area metric. When the area is performing to the Takt time, it is meeting its target metrics. When the area misses its Takt time, comments are noted on the chart to help the teams follow up with countermeasures and root cause corrective actions. The charts are used to facilitate team meetings and become the primary communication tool.

The goal is to create visuals so anyone can walk around the area and know what's going on and how we are doing without asking anyone.

Story

Ironically, when we create our Lean environment in factories, we use the emergency room as an example. We ask 5 day training class participants the following questions regarding creating a Lean environment:

1. Does every second count?
2. Do I need all my tools and supplies at point of use (POU)?

3. Do I need standing walking operations?
4. Does everyone need to know their jobs and have standard work?

The answers are a resounding "yes" to each question. Then I go on to explain and ask what the difference is between a factory and an emergency trauma room:

1. Does every second count? Yes.
2. Do I need all my supplies at POU (Point of Use)? Imagine the doctor says, "Scalpel," and the nurse says, "Wait a minute doc, it's in the cabinet over there!" After searching, she can't find it and says, "It must have been moved out of the room to the "core" supply area!"
3. Do I need standing and walking operations? Imagine they wheel you in to the emergency department and all the doctors and nurses are sitting on chairs.
4. Do we need standard work? Imagine if all procedures were not standardized.

We were able to observe a trauma case in action. There were actually two trauma bays in one big room. As we waited for the patient arrival, the number of staff in the room increased, filled with excitement and anticipation.

While watching, it was obvious that:

1. Every second counted.
2. The trauma doctor asked for an instrument, and the nurse proceeded to search through all the case carts and couldn't find it (seconds lost). The nurse asked the doctor if there was something else she could use. The doctor indicated there was and told her what to get. The nurse found it and handed it to the nurse assisting the doctor.
3. Everyone was standing and walking and seemed to work well as a team.
4. Everyone seemed to know their jobs and tried to anticipate the doctor. But they were all over the place. Several times, the doctor ask for something and either it wasn't there or a nurse had to run out to the hall supply closet to get it (again seconds and minutes lost).

After the trauma was over and the room was cleaned, we took a look at the layout and the nurse walk patterns that I had drawn during the case. Some questions immediately popped into my mind:

1. Why couldn't the nurse find the instrument or supply requested?
2. Why did another nurse have to go outside the room several times for supplies? We talked with the nurse, who said they frequently run out of materials due to empty bins. We asked what happens if materials are not in the closet. She said she has to run downstairs

to central supply. This is with a critical patient on the table!

3. *What would happen if there were two traumas going on at the same time in that room.*

We reviewed the materials bins, and noticed several were empty. At that point, the materials person showed up to inventory the bins.

We asked him why the bins were empty. He said they only refilled the bins once a day. We asked what happens when there is a patient on the trauma table and the bin is empty. He said, "Oh, they just run down the hall to the supply closet and get what they need." We said, "But the patient could be dying!" He said, "Well, that's how we've always done it since there was a cut back on FTEs 5 years ago!"

We then asked who set the PAR levels on the bins. He didn't know but guessed it was someone in materials. So now, we hesitate to use the trauma room as an example with factories.

VISUAL MANAGEMENT SYSTEM

The goal of a visual management is to make *abnormal* conditions immediately visible using Five S, visual displays and visual controls, and taking the premise one step further by incorporating root cause, countermeasures, andon, risk mitigation, TPM, and mistake proofing. The goal of the system is to prevent or mitigate the defect. An example of each component can be found in automobiles.

Let's say you leave the headlights on in the car. What happens? The car has a light that shows your headlights are on (visual display). If you take the key out of the ignition it makes a noise (andon) to make you aware that your lights are still on. The next level is where it mistake proofs it by turning off your lights for you after a pre-programmed length of time. The lights going out is the final signal of the visual management system. The car now prevents the defect by mitigating the error and preventing the defect (dead battery). We discuss visual management from a supervisor's perspective later in the chapter.

SIX SIGMA AND LEAN

Many hospitals that have started their Lean journeys with Six Sigma have found similar problems to those occurring with Point Kaizen events. Like Point Kaizen events, Six Sigma is a tool. Six Sigma tools are designed to attack variation. The Six Sigma tools and TQ tools are basically the Deming and Juran tools repackaged and remarketed. Like Point Kaizen events, if we try to implement Six Sigma tools in an area that has not been "Leaned out," i.e., established flow, pull, standard work, Five S, POU materials, etc., then the only way one can get an improvement that hits the bottom line is to hit the critical path and sustain it. Also, how can one show improvement in a hospital area that is a mess and has no data? Six Sigma tools are designed to eliminate variation and help to work toward the Lean target of zero defects. But Six Sigma encounters challenges when trying

to achieve a transformational culture change in the sense of the culture change that comes with Lean thinking. True Lean culture changes transform the *"thinking and actions"* of the entire organization.

In our experience, 95% of the time it makes more sense to implement Lean first, clean up the area, organize it, put standard work in place, and let all the problems come to the surface. As the problems arise, use Six Sigma tools where appropriate to fix them.

SIX SIGMA TOOLS

Six Sigma is a statistical measure of quality. It means 3.4 defects per million opportunities with a one Sigma shift. Six Sigma is a collection of tools (FMEA, MSE, DOE, process mapping, and control plans). Six Sigma differs from Lean in that Lean requires companies to make major system changes. Implementing Lean pulls for changes in your organization and reward systems. Our experience is that 60%–80% of improvements come from Lean. If you implement Six Sigma first, it is difficult to see and sustain improvements because nothing is standardized. We have a saying in Lean circles that "Variation is the enemy of Lean." Six Sigma is about reducing variation. Lean and Six Sigma should be integrated initiatives.

LEAN GOAL IS ZERO DEFECTS—DIFFERENCE BETWEEN AN ERROR AND A DEFECT

Six Sigma tools are designed to measure, highlight and eliminate defects, the only way to get to zero defects is to eliminate the error before it occurs. Therefore, it is important to understand the difference between an error and a defect. An error is a mistake that is made; a defect is a problem that occurs as a result of the error that was made. Shingo often referred to this in his books as the importance of separating cause from effect. An example would be as follows: the error was leaving the lights on in the car, while the defect is that the battery died. Mistake-proofing is a critical component of Lean and provides a mechanism to eliminate the errors so defects won't occur.

Many organizations use statistical process control (SPC). SPC is a good program that can help on a Six Sigma journey, but SPC will not ensure zero defects since the defects are detected after they are made. The goal of Lean is 100% defect prevention at the source. Lean processes require defect-free patients and processes to support a JIT system. JIT is getting the right "good quality" part or the "properly prepared" patient. If this is not the case, then the system breaks down and delays occur.

Six Sigma has various strategies for quality control and creating control plans. Lean has strategies as well. Shingo conveys these in his book, called *Poka yoke.*[*] Ultimately, the

---

[*] Nikkan Kogyo Shimbun, *Poka yoke* (New York: Productivity Press) 1988; Singo, *Zero Quality Control* (New York: Productivity Press) 1986; Hinckley, *Make No Mistakes* (New York: Productivity Press) 2002.

need for control plans in a truly Lean environment should disappear as any abnormalities should be clearly and immediately visible in the workplace in real time. However realistically control strategies are needed as it is difficult to "mistake proof" 100% of the opportunities where errors can occur even though that is the goal.

POKA YOKE (FIGURE 10.5)[*]

- 1 in 2000 surgical patients suffer from a retained foreign object
- Two-thirds of these retained foreign objects are surgical pads, essentially large pieces of fabric that promote tissue visualization and prevent tissue trauma during surgery
- Retained foreign objects add 4 days to the average hospital stay, result in 57 deaths, and cost more than $1.5 billion annually.

Poka yoke—ポカヨケ—distraction proof, is a Japanese term that means "fail safing" or "mistake proofing." A *Poka yoke* is any mechanism in a Lean process that helps staff avoid (*yokeru*) mistakes (*poka*). Its purpose is to eliminate product defects by preventing, correcting, or drawing attention to human errors as they occur. The concept was formalized, and the term adopted by Shigeo Shingo as part of the Toyota Production System. It was originally described as *Baka yoke*, but as this means "fool proofing" (or "idiot proofing"), the name was changed to the milder *Poka yoke*.[†]

The idea of mistake proofing started with Toyoda in the spinning loom factory.[‡] Since then, the Toyota Motor Corporation has spent the last 60 years improving on the concept and always striving for perfection. The first step to *Poka*

yoke is self-inspection. This is where each operator inspects his/her own work. The next level is called successive check inspection. This is where each operator inspects the work of the previous operators in addition to his/her own work. The next level is 100% inspection at the source. This inspection is done by a machine, not a person. The only way to get to zero defects is to have 100% automated inspection at the source and catch the mistake, not the defect. This is the basic idea behind *Jidoka*. Here is an example of mistake proofing (Poka yoke) at home.

Our house had an attached garage. The door from the garage to the house was right next to my office. When one of my children would come into the garage during the winter, they, like most kids, left the door open. The realization of the door being open was delivered by a cold blast and then a steady stream of air into my office. Over the course of the next couple of months, I tried everything I could think of to get the kids to shut the door when they came in. We talked to them nicely. We explained why we needed the door closed when they came in and then moved to the frustration mode accompanied by shouting at them to close the door, every time they came in. The next step was looking at some type of punishment or negative consequences to get them to pay attention and listen to us. We made them come back each time to close the door. Even this didn't work. Then, one day as I was strolling through the local hardware store, I noticed an item called a "self-closing hinge." I purchased the hinge and installed it immediately on my arrival home. Once installed, everyone's life in the house returned to peace and calm. When the kids came in, the door closed itself—no rush of air, no punishments, and life was good! Installing the hinge was such a simple fix; yet, the first thought is normally to blame those in the system whom we perceive are creating the problems.

Lesson Learned: *You cannot inspect quality into a product[§] or process.*

TYPES OF CONTROL AND WARNING DEVICES[¶]

- Contact device: contact is established between the device and the product.
- Fixed value method: part must be a certain weight or it won't work.
- Motion step method: product must pass inspection before proceeding to the next step.
- Design-out defect: the ultimate goal is to eliminate errors by designing your products or processes Lean.

Once you clean up the areas and standardize the work, then the variation sticks out. Six Sigma tools are designed to fix the variation. The Lean tools and Six Sigma tools integrate nicely.

[*] Figures and information supplied by Soterios Reppas, Technologies Solutions Group. M. J. Zinner, T. A. Brennan, E. J. Orav, D. M. Studdart, and A. A. Gawande (2003) Risk factors for retained instruments and sponges after surgery, *The New England Journal of Medicine* 348, 229–35; S. Morris, D. Morris, and A. Macario (2006) Initial clinical evaluation of a handheld device for detecting retained surgical gauze sponges using radiofrequency identification technology, *Archives of Surgery* 141, 659–62.

[†] www.Wikipedia.com. Harry Robinson (1997) "Using Poka yoke Techniques for Early Defect Detection," http://facultyweb.berry.edu/jgrout/pokasoft.html. Retrieved May 4, 2009. Shigeo Shingo and Andrew P. Dillon, *A Study of the Toyota Production System from an Industrial Engineering Viewpoint* (Portland, OR: Productivity Press) 1989, p.21–22. John R. Grout and Brian T. Downs. "A Brief Tutorial on Mistake-proofing, Poka yoke, and ZQC," MistakeProofing.com. http://www.mistakeproofing.com/tutorial.html. Retrieved May 4, 2009. "Poka yoke or Mistake Proofing: Overview. The Quality Portal," http://thequalityportal.com/pokayoke.htm. Retrieved May 5, 2009. Nikkan Kogyo Shimbun, *Poka yoke: Improving Product Quality by Preventing Defects* (Portland, OR: Productivity Press) 1988, p.111, 209. "'Pokayoke.' The Manufacturing Advisory Service in the South West (MAS-SW)," http://www.swmas.co.uk/info/index.php/Pokayoke. Retrieved May 2, 2009. 8. http://dict.regex.info Japanese to English dictionary, http://www.saiga-jp.com, http://thequalityportal.com/pokayoke.htm.

[‡] Taiichi Ohno, *Toyota Production System* (New York: Productivity Press) 1988.

[§] *CCS Training Manual*, Charles Protzman Sr. and Homer Sarasohn, 1948–1949 (prepared by Nick Fisher and Suzanne Lavery of ValueMetrics, Australia), p. 138.

[¶] Shingo, *Zero Quality Control* (Productivity Press) 1986.

Mistake Proofing Example - RFID Hardware
(Patent Pending – Technologies Solutions Group)

Sponge and RFID tag

RFID wand and
wireless link

An RFID antenna tuned to 13.56 mhz is positioned in a kickbucket where sponges are commonly disposed of. The antenna is suspended from an apron forcing all RFID sponges through an opening while reading the unique ID. This data is decoded and sent via bluetooth (2.4 Ghz) to a tablet unit where specialized software records all sponges transactions from beginning to the end of the procedure. If it is deemed a sponge is left in the body a tethered wand antenna is passed over the body to detect the missing sponge. It is then reconciled in the system. All reconciled data is sent via WIFI (802.11 b/g) to a middleware piece sitting on a central server. Derived from this data are various file formats which can be used for applications across the enterprise.

FIGURE 10.5 RFID example. Courtesy of Technologies solutions group RFID Operations@t-sgrp.com.

EXAMPLES OF CAUSE AND EFFECT

- Process: car crosses over railroad track
- Defect: train collides with car at railroad crossing
- Warning device: use a sign and/or sound to warn the operator
- Control device: put up gates to prevent the car from crossing
- Design-out defect: design a bridge over or under to the railroad track, which prevents the error and the defect

Lesson Learned: *Goal is defect prevention at the source.*

TOTAL PRODUCTIVITY MAINTENANCE

Total productivity maintenance (TPM) involves everyone in the organization, from top management to the staff person on the floor. With TPM, the staff members now share in the maintenance and upkeep of the equipment. They take care of day-to-day checklists (adding oil to a machine, changing over reagents) and maintenance takes care of difficult problems. The analogy for this is like taking care of your car. You wash it, check the fluids, put gas in it, but when there is a big problem, you take it to a mechanic.

TPM has all sorts of application in hospitals. There are machines everywhere, but we don't always think about them. Sterile processing has washers and sterilizers, radiology has x-ray equipment, surgery has "C" arms and anesthesia equipment, and the floor nurses use medication storage machines and have machines at the bedside that monitor vitals. All of this equipment has to be maintained.

With Lean, the nurses become the front line for maintenance when reporting problems or making minor fixes to machines.

TOTAL PRODUCTIVITY MAINTENANCE GOALS

- Eliminate unplanned machine downtime
- Increase machine capacity
- Have fewer defects
- Reduce overall operating costs
- Allow for minimum inventory
- Increase operator safety
- Create a better working environment

OVERALL EQUIPMENT EFFECTIVENESS

The goal of overall equipment effectiveness (OEE) is to take metrics that individually might look good and look at them together. The metrics are:

1. Scheduled available time (any unplanned downtime or changeover time counts against this)
2. Operating rate—rate or speed at which the machine is scheduled to run
3. Defect rate—percentage of good parts

Let's say we were running a piece of laboratory equipment. Ninety percent of the time, we had planned for the machine to be down for normal maintenances. We had to slow the machine down due to a service issue so it was operating at 90% of what it was rated and we had 95% good results, i.e., 5% had to be retested.

These numbers by themselves look pretty good, but they hide the true utilization of the machine. OEE multiplies these percentages together ($0.9 \times 0.9 \times 0.95$) to determine the true capacity (77%) of the machine.

New Maintenance Paradigm

In the Productivity Series entitled TPM,[*] there is an interesting quote: "Maintenance should be looked at as Capacity Generators." Consider the following quote, when it is time to cut heads, where do we normally start? We normally start with "indirect labor." The first indirect labor target is normally maintenance. After all, what do they really do? We can outsource them if we have to, right?

Sometimes this perception is unwarranted, but other times it is due to poor management of maintenance resources or lack of discipline and accountability. Laying off maintenance first is easy to do because it is quick money on paper, but what does it cost us in the long run? When we let maintenance go, all the little day-to-day problems don't get fixed or, sometimes, even worse, well-intentioned people try to fix them. Over time, our equipment shuts down or stops running all together.

Lesson Learned: *Look at maintenance not as a cost center but as a profit center. After all, they are capacity generators.*

Lean and Maintenance in Hospitals

Lean creates job security for the engineering and maintenance of hospital facilities. We are constantly asking maintenance to remove doors on cabinets, install flexible workstations, remove walls, change nursing stations, make us POU locations, and do mock-ups for pilots. So maintenance really wears two Lean hats. One is helping us with Lean changes. The other is considering that maintenance, itself, can be Leaned out!

At Hospital X, we needed some major layout changes to support Lean. We found out that major changes were needed to overhaul the venting and filtration systems. These changes were not necessary for our project but were overdue to the hospital's ongoing maintenance. Instead of budgeting for maintenance needs, the hospital waited for major projects to tack on these large dollar tasks. The ventilation added about $2 million in cost to our ROI. Fortunately, management chose to look at these improvements as ongoing maintenance of their system vs. tying it to our project. The capital improvements weren't required by Lean but that was the only way maintenance could get money to fund the changes.

Lesson Learned: *We need to budget for predictive and preventative maintenance. Maintenance should not be looked at as a cost center but as a capacity generator.[†] It is easy when cutting costs to cut maintenance budgets and FTEs first. This*

may save money in the short run but can cost exponentially more in the long run.

Here is an example of maintenance involved with Lean. We needed to move a large piece of equipment to the third floor of the building. The machine was too big to fit in the elevator, but it would fit in the shaft if they cut the machine in half. Maintenance did just that. They cut the machine in half, moved it up the elevator shaft, and welded it back together. The head of maintenance told me that they had a new maintenance paradigm: "If you are going to move something, move it in such a way that next time you have to move it you can move it twice as fast!"

Construction Challenges

When implementing Lean there will be construction challenges; regulatory agencies, permitting bodies, joint commission requirements[‡], and AIA guidelines[§] all impacting construction projects. It helps to get maintenance involved early on the team and to train them in Lean principles and make sure they are always in the communication loop and planning. TPM should not be just a maintenance initiative; it should be a company-wide initiative. The best way to start TPM is by creating simple checklists for each piece of equipment.

HOSPITAL AND IT SYSTEMS

Whenever we value stream map hospitals, it becomes apparent how many different and unconnected information systems typically exist. Contrast this with most factories, which have typically one material requirements planning (MRP) system or enterprise planning (ERP) system. Hospitals tend to have laboratory information systems, registration systems, insurance verification, surgery system, ED system, bed management, pharmacy and stat system, scheduling, overall hospital information system, electronic record software, instrument tracking systems, billing systems, materials management systems, marketing or forecasting systems, desktop software and bar coding and other scanner support. This is not a complete list and does not include all the manual information that is charted.

IT also provides services: data backup and retention, risk management, help desk, software loading, computer maintenance and upgrades, software control, network installation and support, and shared drives.

IT has potentially three hats with Lean:

1. Streamlining the internal IT processes
2. Connecting and streamlining the overall information flow
3. Supporting Lean system implementation and Kaizen teams

[*] TPM, Productivity Video Series©.
[†] TPM Video Tapes—Productivity Series.
[‡] Joint Commission on Accreditation of Healthcare Organizations.
[§] http://info.aia.org/nwsltr_aah.cfm?pagename=aah_gd_hospcons.

Streamlining internal IT processes utilize the same BASICS tools we have discussed throughout this book. The first step is to value stream map the processes and then apply the product and operator tools. Streamlining overall communication involves building interfaces so all the different IT systems can talk to each other. This is not an easy task. There are ERP systems available now for hospitals.

Lean teams require varying levels of IT support throughout their improvement journey. The initial need is data that can be ported to Access or Excel. Other support needs involve POU printers and supplying software needs to the team.

The real key when improving processes is not to purchase software to fix problems or streamline a process until after the process has been "Leaned" out. In addition, the software needs to be flexible. It needs to support Kanban applications and frequent changes or modifications to support ongoing improvements to standard work. It is important to remember that software does not solve everything. In many cases, we have suggested holding off on purchasing additional systems or scrapping them altogether. A major Lean tenet is don't tie operators to machines; use check blocks or boxes or touch screens, etc. There are several books on Lean and IT now, including *Easier, Simpler, Faster*[*] and *Lean Software Strategies*.[†]

Phases

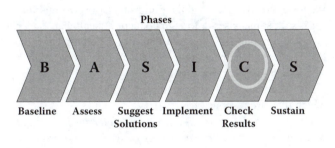

FIGURE 10.6   BASICS model—check.

BASICS—CHECKING THE NEW PROCESS

The Lean team and the supervisor must prove that the new process implemented in the area performs as expected and document the new process (Figure 10.6). It is the leadership's job to continually check the process in order to make sure it is running properly. In order to check the process, we need metrics, standard work, and visual controls in place. After the area has been run for a short time, some ongoing "fine tuning" will be necessary, followed by continuous improvement. Make sure the area has appropriate metrics in place (e.g., a day-by-the-hour chart) visible for all to see, accompanied by daily huddles to monitor progress and solicit employee suggestions. When we experience a problem, we need to address it in real time by working through the problem-solving process.

Phases

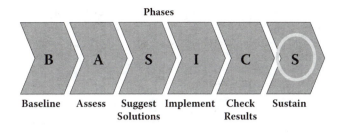

FIGURE 10.7   BASICS model—sustain.

BASICS—SUSTAINING THE PROCESS

It is up to the team assigned to the work area (including the supervisor, planner, engineer, etc.) to sustain the gains and continuously improve the operation of the targeted area. The team should debrief the staff and other stakeholders on the improvements that have been made. Any follow-up items should be small and easy actions.

SUSTAINING TOOLS

SUSTAIN PLANS/CONTROL PLANS

While we have created sustain plans, control plans, and combinations of the two, one needs to realize that the term sustain plan is somewhat of a misnomer and not sufficient for a Lean implementation (Figure 10.7). When a Lean system implementation is completed, there is generally an exit strategy for the dedicated Lean resources. This is the point where the consultant, internal or external, leaves the project. The exit strategy should contain the conditions and deliverables that must be in place prior to that exit.

A control plan generally has a list of metrics that the area must continue to meet. When one of the metrics falls out of control, then some predetermined action that is noted in the control plan is followed until the metric is back "under or in control."

The sustain plan is a little different in that it contains the control plan and includes actions necessary to sustain the implementation. But the idea behind Lean is that we do not just sustain, but continuously improve. Therefore, the sustain plan should be renamed "the continuous improvement plan."

In his book *Creating a Lean Culture*,[‡] David Mann describes four necessary criteria to sustain Lean:

1. Leader standard work
2. Visual controls
3. Accountability
4. Discipline

These criteria are combined with the notion that the role of the team leader or supervisor must change from 100% running the business to a combination of running the business and improving the business. Toyota actually builds in 50%

[*] Jean Cunningham, *Easier, Simpler, Faster* (New York: Productivity Press) 2007.
[†] Peter Middleton, *Lean Software Strategies* (New York: Productivity Press) 2005.

[‡] David Mann, *Creating a Lean Culture* (Productivity Press) 2005.

time for the supervisor[*] to continually improve the business. In the United States, if two supervisors had 50% of their time available, we would probably work to lay one of them off.

LEADER STANDARD WORK

We have expanded on this concept to include all standard work. Standard work is the vehicle that has helped Toyota capture and sustain all their improvements. It also provides the vehicle to transfer areas from an old manager to a new one without skipping a beat.

VISUAL MANAGEMENT

We discussed this concept briefly earlier. In the context of creating and sustaining a Lean environment, we expand visual controls to visual management. At first this is a tough concept for hospital administrations and doctors to comprehend. Most hospital administrations utilize reports to manage their areas. What's wrong with reports?[†] Reports are history, and usually so much time has transpired that one cannot get to the root causes of any problems. In addition, based on our experience, the data in many reports is so suspect that it is scary to think that anyone uses it to manage or make financial decisions.

The goal with Lean is to manage in a REAL TIME ENVIRONMENT. This has many implications for hospital administrators. We need go to the floor, get our information first hand, manage by fact, and encourage and challenge our people to think through and solve problems.

Imagine you are a director who is told by your boss to go to the floor and do a Gemba Walk. On your first trip, you will find your people are busy all the time. In fact, when you first go out to the floor, you will probably be in their way. Most of your managers are probably spending 80%–90% fighting fires and 10%–20% running the area. You look around to see what is going on, but all you see are whiteboards or maybe an electronic screen.

You go over to the charge nurse and ask what is going on. The charge nurse says, "Why are you here? Is something wrong?" In any case, she tells you to wait until she is free to talk to you. During that time, a surgeon tells you his case was delayed because his instruments weren't ready. An anesthesiologist grabs you and complains that the Pre-Op nurse did not have his/her patient ready. A nurse tells you that she was yelled at by the surgeon because the preference card was not right, and she had to run to three different supply areas/ closets to find what was needed. That was after she called Materials who said they had no one who could run it up to her.

I knew of one charge nurse who was suddenly reporting to a new director. The new director held daily status meetings in her office, which the charge nurse was told to attend. Because she was attending so many meetings, her area started slipping and the status meetings got longer and longer. As a result, her area continued to slip more and more and she was eventually terminated for mismanagement of her area.

Lesson Learned: *When "overhead" office staff people aren't busy, they create work to justify their jobs. This creates more work for the people on the floor who are already busy. We need to evaluate the value-added from the office environment and review every report to see if it is value-added.*

Does any of this sound familiar?

This example represents typical surgical areas in most hospitals. Everyone works in a reactive atmosphere and crisis management dominates. Our managers are congratulated and rewarded for working around the system to fix problems.

So how do we set up a visual management system? First we have to "Lean out" our processes so they flow. We need to get all supplies and materials at POU where they are needed. We need to Five S the area and organize our equipment. We need to reduce any unnecessary equipment and supplies. Once we establish flow and clean up and organize the area, we need to start putting process focus metrics in place and make them visible.

ACCOUNTABILITY

We have already discussed the importance of accountability. This is, in some cases, a foreign concept to healthcare supervisors and managers. Many will require coaching and training to beef up their analytical skills and business acumen. Accountability is a big problem in most hospitals. People are typically not held accountable and don't have metrics for which they are responsible.

At Hospital X, I interviewed every leader in the surgical services area. One of the questions I asked each person was "how are you measured?" Most said they are told during their annual reviews if they are doing a good job. I couldn't believe that virtually no one had any metrics. They were not held responsible for anything. If they did have a metric, they could not tell me how they were currently performing against the metric. No one knew any of their cycle times or quality metrics. One person told me that they had a budget to meet and was grilled on it each month, but there were never any positive or negative consequences if they did not meet their target.

If we are going to follow a clinical management model, we need to train our clinical staff in business processes, analytical skills, supervisory and leadership training, and financial management. We also need a probationary period where clinicians can see if they like management or would prefer to stay in a caregiver role.

Many hospitals have lost their chain of command and respect from the staff for their leaders. After all, the leadership doesn't really know what goes on every day. As a result, they react and dictate edicts in order to change things. The HR movements of the 1960s and 1970s[‡] have left us with

---

[*] Jeffrey Liker, *Toyota Culture* (McGraw Hill) 2008.
[†] Brian Maskell, *Making the Numbers Count* (New York: Productivity Press) 1996.

[‡] Henry Ford and Samuel Crowther, *My Life and Work* (Garden City, NY: Garden City) 1922.

little or no discipline in our work areas. People think discipline is a "bad" word and processes are not documented. In many cases, they are not properly trained or developed to manage others. As a result, we continue to promote leaders who have no clinical knowledge or clinicians who have no business savvy. This results in an organization where the leadership is unable or literally does not know how to hold people accountable.

We need to return to the days of promoting from within. We need supervisors who have done the job, know the job, and can train in the job. This tribal knowledge is the basis for standard work. Most hospital procedures are poorly documented. This trend must change if Lean is to survive.

When hospitals, or any company for that matter, have leadership running the company who don't know the business or service line, then the organization is in jeopardy. When a consultant has to be called in to help with restructuring the organization or provide (vs. facilitate) strategic planning, then there is, potentially, a weakness at the top.

Titles Tend to Get in the Way

We have been in hospitals where there are as many job classifications as one would find in a union. Job classifications create waste. In some cases, they are necessary because of the training required, but in others they inhibit flexibility.

Titles denote, to some, the excuse not to be flexible. If I am a tech, for instance, why should I sweep the floors; that is housekeeping's job. If I am a surgeon, why should I help with the changeover? While many of you reading this may be exceptions to these rules, there are many who are not. Henry Ford said,

> Because there are no titles and no limits of authority, there is no question of red tape or going over a man's head. Any workman can go to anybody, and so established has this become a custom, that a foreman does not get sore if a workman goes over him and directly to the head of the factory. The workman rarely ever does so, because a foreman knows as well as he knows his own name that if he has been unjust it will be very quickly found out, and he shall no longer be a foreman. One of the things we will not tolerate is injustice of any kind. The moment a man starts to swell with authority he is discovered and he goes out or goes back to a machine. A large amount of labor unrest comes from the unjust exercise of authority by those in subordinate positions and I am afraid that in far too many manufacturing institutions it is really not possible for a workman to get a square deal. The work and the work alone control us. That is one of the reasons why we have no titles.*

Ford also said, "We expect the men to do what they are told. The organization is so highly specialized and one party is so dependent upon another that we could not, for a moment, consider allowing men to have their own way. Without the most rigid discipline we would have the utmost confusion."[†]

This quote should not be interpreted as there should not be a hierarchy or chain of command. If anyone went to Ford about a problem with one of his senior leaders, he would suggest the person take up the problem with them first. Today, the organization Ford created is referred to as a molecular organization.

Discipline

Discipline is a key in Lean environments. Without discipline, there is chaos. We need people to have the discipline to follow standard work, put things back where they belong, follow through on audits, conduct root cause analysis, and create the continuous improvement environment.

Staff Involvement

The importance of including staff in the Lean analysis and journey cannot be overemphasized, as most organizations don't fail in analysis, waste identification, and process redesign; they fail in sustaining the "change." The ability to sustain the process is related to communication, staff participation, training, role clarity, reward programs, and clear expectations of expected results and the importance placed on sustaining and improving from every level of leadership.

YOU GET WHAT YOU EXPECT; YOU DESERVE WHAT YOU TOLERATE[‡]

Additional Sustaining Tools

Once the Lean system Kaizen implementation is completed, there are several sustaining tools:

- Training within industry
- QC circles
- Point Kaizen events
- Ongoing Kaizen (ideas generated from employees on the floor)
- Company-chartered continuous improvement groups

The ultimate vehicle for sustaining, regardless of the approach, is the constant updating of the standard work to capture all improvements.

Lesson Learned: *Implement Lean first, then Six Sigma. As you Lean out the process and establish flow, clean it up and begin to get work standards in place or standard work; the variation now stands out and is immediately obvious. That is when we bring in Six Sigma tools.*

Repeat the Cycle!

Remember that "continuous improvement" must become a way of life. After a line has been converted from batch to

---

[*] Henry Ford, *My Life and Work* (Garden City, NY: Garden City) 1922.
[†] Henry Ford, *My Life and Work* (Garden City, NY: Garden City) 1922.
[‡] Unknown, *Reader's Digest.*

one-piece flow, use Kaizen events as a way to sustain the cycle. Kaizen events can be hours or days, but have a cross-functional dedicated team working on improvement.

LEAN SPECIALIST AND LEAN MASTER

Many companies, hospitals, and manufacturers believe one can train up a Lean specialist rather quickly. A Lean specialist would be defined as someone competent in the Lean tools with an understanding of the culture. In our experience, this is not the case. Whether or not this is possible without working in the Toyota environment is debatable; however, there are a number of books and articles, e.g., by former Toyota insiders, which give us a deeper insight into the culture.

To become what we would consider a Lean specialist takes an average of 6 to 9 months working with a sensei who is well-grounded in the tools of scientific management, Lean principles, and change management. At Toyota, the Japanese senseis remained on site with NUMMI (the former GM/Toyota joint venture in California) leaders for an average of 3 years and longer to train them in the Toyota system. This is a difficult concept for the United States' "want it right away" and "impatient" culture. We define a Lean specialist as one who has read certain Lean books, can lead and conduct a Lean system implementation in addition to Point Kaizen events on their own, and has been exposed to office, assembly, machining, and setup environments.

We have another categorization called a Lean Master. This is somewhat of a misnomer in that we don't believe anyone ever truly masters Lean, but the title seems to be used in many companies. This title designates someone who is well read in Lean and has implemented system and Point Kaizens and established a track record of sustained improvement for 3 to 5 years. There are two categories of Lean Master. One is technically proficient in the tools, while the other is proficient at training and "train the trainer" activities. We separate this, as not everyone is good at conducting training classes.

LEAN HOSPITAL IMPLEMENTATION (SYSTEM KAIZEN AND POINT KAIZEN) LESSONS LEARNED

CREATE THE LEADERSHIP ROAD MAP

It is important to have a leadership Lean/Six Sigma implementation road map. Lean should be part of the strategic goals and, as such, should be tracked and measured the same. Failure to have a map is like driving with no compass or shooting arrows without a target. It leads to pockets of success and fractured results.

MAKE SURE YOUR ORGANIZATION IS READY

Some organizations are just not ready and shouldn't implement Lean. If there is no compelling need to change or fundamental dissatisfaction in how things are done today, it will not be successful.

CREATE A LEAN STEERING COMMITTEE—BUT MAKE IT THE SENIOR LEADERSHIP TEAM

Part of the leadership road map should be the creation of a Lean steering committee. I can hear you say that the last thing we need is another committee. Yet this committee can and should be made up of the senior leadership team or some subset of the team. Since Lean should be a goal in the strategic plan, it should be no different than reviewing any other strategic plan goal to see if the company is on target.

The Lean steering committee should review the team charters to make sure the projects align with the overall vision and that the teams are on schedule. Each senior leader should be a champion and participate in the implementation with the team. The goal of the steering committee is to break down the most difficult organizational barriers, the sacred cows, and assist in any way possible to make the teams successful and work to develop the Lean culture.

LEAN CONSULTANTS SHOULD REPORT TO THE CEO

In many companies, we have reported to someone other than the CEO. We normally end up reporting to the process excellence leader or the director of operations. We find this is a short-sighted approach. If Lean is a strategic goal, and the goal is truly cultural transformation then the consultants should report to the CEO. Only the CEO is empowered to break down all the barriers in the organization. Consultants can only be effective and successful to the level of leadership to which they report. If they report to the director of operations, then much can be accomplished in operations, but none of the other functional silos will participate directly. They might have someone on a team, but that will be the extent. And of course, everything is fine as long as they are not implementing in your area (my backyard, so to speak). Whenever we work with the CEO or owners of companies, our progress and level of penetration in the organization is almost double that as opposed to when we don't. It becomes the consultant's job to "work their way up to the CEO."

Another problem that consultants run into is that, in many instances, the designated person they report to is not necessarily keeping their superiors informed. When the person the consultant reports to leaves or is asked to leave, which happens more than one might think, the person who takes over (the superior) has no idea what the consultants have been doing. This is also indicative of not having a Lean steering committee and a road map.

At Hospital X, we conducted a very successful Lean Six Sigma implementation on a clinic. The plan was to take our lessons learned and expand the approach to the balance of clinics within the organization. The implementation at the second clinic was a struggle. As successful as the first clinic went, the second one went poorly. The main reasons were lack of leadership and physician buy-in to the changes and standard work. We recommended to the senior leadership that the problems be worked through at the second clinic prior to moving on to the next. Owing to budget reasons and

*the need to meet an already agreed to implementation sched-
ule, our advice was ignored and they proceeded on to the
next clinic. As feared, the third clinic leadership and physicians resisted the changes and asked why they should have to
implement physician standard work if clinic 2 did not have
to. Eventually, the whole clinic multisite implementation was
halted and, of course, all the problems were blamed on Lean.*

Lesson Learned: *Don't move on to the next one until you
have solved the problems and paradigms of the current
implementation.*

CREATE A LEAN ORGANIZATIONAL INFRASTRUCTURE

There needs to be a basic infrastructure in place for implementing Lean and it should be part of the leadership road
map. The process excellence team should eventually fold
back into the organization in staff jobs. A key failure mode is
when finance identifies the process excellence group as "easy
pickins" to be laid off to increase profits in the short term.

OBTAIN LEADERSHIP AND PHYSICIAN BUY-IN UP FRONT

Part of the leadership road map should be a communication
plan, a training plan, and a contract for change. Have everyone sign the contract for change. The contract for change is
designed to put everyone on notice of the go forward plan and
expectations, and secure the buy-in up-front. Failure to do
this can lead to failed implementations.

COMMUNICATION PLAN (FIGURE 10.8)

There is a saying that "you cannot communicate enough" during any type of organizational change. Our experience is that
this could not be a truer statement. A communication plan
should be established up-front detailing the tools, frequency,
method of delivery, and responsibility for the item. For example, we are going to publish a Lean newsletter, twice a month,
via email and hand out at the cafeteria and the process owner
is responsible. The importance of ongoing communication
cannot be emphasized enough! Communication can determine whether a project will be successful and sustain. It can
impact how Lean cultural transformation will be viewed.

TRAINING PLAN

To be successful, development of a training plan is crucial. The training plan should include short- and long-term
plans as well as some type of auditing or assessment process. It should also include development of an infrastructure
to support the ongoing training required with a continuous
improvement, learning organization.

LEADERSHIP CANNOT STAY IN THEIR IVORY TOWER

The CEO cannot manage a Lean transformation from their
office in an "ivory tower." The CEO must get involved and

go to the *Gemba*. CEOs who truly "get" Lean participate in
the training and are involved as teams implement throughout
their organizations. They talk with the staff and join them
in the lunchroom. In some cases, they move their offices
to become more accessible. They don't listen to hearsay or
accept excuses; they hear issues first hand, and they eliminate leadership "perks." They talk to their patients in addition
to their physicians. They see laying people off as a failure
on management's part. They are the first to take a pay cut,
if necessary. Leaders must role model the culture they are
trying to create.

LEADERSHIP MUST LEAD AND DRIVE LEAN CHANGES, NOT JUST SUPPORT THEM

If the CEO is not trained properly or does not support Lean,
it will ultimately fail. An untrained CEO, even in a support
mode, can be dangerous because the culture change starts at
the top and the decisions made at the top are still based on
the old batch environment. So, even if the CEO believes they
are supporting it, they may be doing irreparable harm and
not realize it. This is because a Lean management system
requires different reactions and behaviors than the old batch-
driven systems.

LEADERS MUST PARTICIPATE IN LEAN. YOU CANNOT "GET IT" IN A TWO HOUR OR FOUR HOUR POWERPOINT PITCH

It takes time to understand all the implications of Lean thinking to develop and sustain a Lean culture. It takes benchmarking, reading, and understanding what a Lean culture is
in order to be successful in creating one. It takes leading a
Point Kaizen event or participating in an implementation and
attending training to even begin to understand the Lean tools
and concepts.

DON'T LET LEAN TURN INTO FINANCE-DRIVEN FTE WITCH HUNTS

Lean can easily turn into finance-driven FTE witch hunts.
Finance is normally the first major barrier we run into in
Lean implementations. This is again because the old ways
of measuring and cost accounting normally make the Lean
initiatives initially look poorly. If all the organization desires
is a way for the financial department to eliminate FTEs, the
word will get around and people will resist participation in
Lean initiatives, any videotaping or making improvements
for fear their jobs will be eliminated.

WORK TO ESTABLISH THE LEAN CULTURE, NOT JUST THE TOOLS

Some organizations just focus on the Lean tools. The tools
are easy compared to the people piece. If we just focus on the
tools, you may realize "pockets of excellence," but it will ultimately not sustain because the Lean culture was not created.

Meeting	Purpose	Owner	Key Tasks	Frequency	Duration	Delivery Via	Date	Location	Attendees/Distribution
Surgery PI Project Proposed Communication Plan									
Kick-Off Meetings									
Data Support	To discuss the data needs of four OR projects and how to support: 1. Material/supply. 2. OR Metrics green bell project. 3. OR Scheduling VSM/baseline performance 4. PASS Phase 2		Meet to allocate data support resources		1 hr	meeting	Week of 9/18	OR admin	
VSM participation	To seek black bell and green bells who may be available to support data collection for the creation of VSM in OR scheduling		Communication requesting available resources to assist with documentation of VSM of OR scheduling		Once	email	9/18	Main – OR	13B
OR Scheduling VSM and Baseline Performance	To inform of plan for VSM and baseline performance assessment in Or Scheduling. Secure team members and time commitments		Inform of role as process owner and secure team members, inform of timeline		1 hr	meeting	Week of 9/18	OR admin offices	
PASS Phase 2	To discuss with the PASS project, his role as process owner and time commitment. Also, identify team members and time commitments		Meet to discuss PASS Phase 2 project		1 hr	meeting	Week of 9/18	OR admin offices	
PASS Phase 2	To discuss scope, charter document, and overview of process. Specifically discuss team members and time allocation to project		Set Dale and Create Agenda For Meeting		1 hr	meeting	Week of 9/22	PASS breakroom	
VSM validation/PASS Phase 2	To interview for OR information (VSM) and inform of failure Or project plans		Interview for VSM information (VOC) and inform of failure PASS projects, order sets		30 min	meeting	09/22/08		
All Employee PEP (Lean) Kick off Meetings	Formal Kickoff of Project with all employees in Surgery, SPD, Materials. Other areas impacted		Need Script to answer change questions		Utilize 1/2 hour of weekly staff meeting (scripted)	meeting	Week of 9/22		Surgery Staff including SPD and Materials
Physician Kick Off Meetings- TBD	Formal Kickoff with Surgeons and Anesthesiologists		Need Script to answer change questions. Select Physicians and Choose Venue		Utilize existing Board or Staff meetings	meeting	TBD		All Physicians

FIGURE 10.8 Communication plan example.

Insist On Updating Standard Work

Without standard work, Lean will fail. Standard work is the glue that holds the entire system together. Without standard work, there can be no ongoing improvement nor can one capture the improvements made. Improvements become person dependent and disappear with that person when they leave.

Do Not Reward Work Arounds

If the old "hero of the day" and "work around" culture prevails, Lean will fail. When we work around a problem, we don't solve it, so it ultimately comes back! Lean only sustains in cultures that learn to address root cause and fix problems so they never come back.

The Paranoid syndrome

At Hospital X there was a medical director who had outlasted several administrations. He chaired the surgeons committee and was the "go-to" guy for all the surgeons and anesthesiologists in the hospital. He basked in the glory of being the person all the surgeons confided in and loved to complain to management about all the problems.

He had participated in numerous process improvement projects in the past, none of which were successful, to the point that only one or two action items might have been accomplished on each. This shielded him from any changes and kept him as the "go-to" person for his peers.

As we implemented Lean with the approach outlined in this book, we started making changes fairly quickly. He could not believe things were actually changing this time and the changes were sustaining. On the surface, at our weekly steering committee meetings, he told us what a great job we were doing; however, he became very concerned and paranoid that his role would change and he would no longer be needed. He viewed the changes as a threat vs. an opportunity. This became very unsettling to him and he started to resist the changes. Eventually, he stalled our project, made life very difficult for the Lean team with management, and refused to approve many of our changes. Because the team was successful, despite his efforts, management finally saw him for what he was, a "concrete head." Senior management tried to coach him through it, but he felt he didn't need to change with 1 year left before retirement. We ended up having to work with him until he retired.

Don't Encourage the Victim Syndrome

This person, the victim, like Eeyore,[*] tends to have that "cloud over their head" all the time. They cannot accept the changes nor take responsibility for them in their area. Although they were involved in the changes, they felt threatened and turned everything we did together into something that was "done to them" even though they agreed with all the changes.

Physician Resistance to Lean

In manufacturing, we have found machinists tend to fight Lean the most. They are very independent and typically start out not wanting any part of standard work. In the hospital world, the machinist seems, in some cases, to be replaced by the physician.

At hospital X, we were piloting our new ED system approach. The physicians involved with our team were part of and embraced the changes. The medical director, however, would not get involved and totally disagreed with our changes. He refused to speak directly with the team and purposely distorted our very positive results from their ED medical group during a budget presentation to the hospital CEO. This set the team and the ED rollouts back several months. After much coaching from his own physicians and finally witnessing first hand the changes, he reversed his position with the CEO, but by then the damage was done.

While some physicians truly embrace Lean and some actually drive the changes, most tend to initially resist or downright fight the changes. When they see the positive impact of Lean, they eventually come around. This brings up a point. Most Lean consulting is sold through the administrative side of hospitals. There is a real need to sell Lean through the physician/clinician side. Dr. Nelson, a physician trained in Lean, states, "The likelihood of a successful implementation in a hospital or clinic setting is directly proportional to the time spent engaging the physicians prior to initiating change. It is critical to understand their needs, to demystify Lean and to get their commitment for involvement in making tests of change. Sustaining a successful implementation may be as dependent on physician recognition of the improvement in their professional work lives as continued senior leader commitment. Value for physicians from more efficient and safer patient care processes can be a powerful force for sustainment."[†]

Meetings are Good but Too Many are Bad

Meetings serve a useful purpose. They help us communicate and share information or problem solve. But are they all truly necessary? In too many hospitals in which we have worked, the leader's "Office Outlook®"[‡] calendars are literally crammed full of meetings every day, with many double- or triple-booked! We can't possibly run our organizations if we are meeting all the time!

Homework: *Pick a day and examine your meeting request(s). Ask yourself—Is the meeting really necessary? If so, is it necessary for you to be there? Is there an agenda? If not, how can people come prepared? Is the meeting really value-added and focused on the patient? Does it have to be an hour or in 15 min increments?*

---

[*] A.A. Milne, *Winnie the Pooh* (London: Methuen) 1926.

[†] Dr. Michael Nelson, Blue Corn Professional Services, Personal Communication. *From Introduction To Sustaining Lean In Healthcare: Developing And Engaging Physician Leadership.* To be published by Productivity Press in Summer 2010.

[‡] Microsoft Office Outlook 2007 & 2006.

Try setting the meeting to your actual agenda time, such as for 37 min instead of the usual hour. If we schedule it for an hour, we tend to find ways to fill the time. If it is a problem-solving meeting, try meeting on the floor or in an office, wherever the source of the problem lies, to discuss ways to fix the problem.

Get Everyone Involved in the Analysis Phase

Get as many people as possible in the targeted area involved in any Lean implementation from the beginning. The analysis tools are designed for that purpose. Many times we are told that people cannot be pulled to watch the videotapes. Without the people in the room during analysis, we can only guess at what they are doing. Even if we have someone else there that does that job, they still don't necessarily know what the person we filmed is doing. This is especially true in environments where everyone does it differently.

The other point here is that people will try to cut the analysis time by having the team do the analysis first and then bringing the person in to discuss the video. While it can be done this way, it is a poor process. The person who was filmed does not get to participate in the enlightenment process that occurs watching what they do on the tape nor do they participate in any of the discussions leading up to the idea. They will also fight the results when they are told that they should be able to do that job in one-third to one-half the time they do it now. When they participate in the analysis process, they are part of omitting steps and the subsequent suggestions and are then part of the reduction in time and can go back and trial the new process.

Give Lean System Implementation Time to Work Before Trying to Change the Underpinnings

With any new process, it takes time to work. Everyone tends to resist the new process because it is different. We also fall victim to the systems thinking law of "unintended consequences." This law states that whenever we implement changes, no matter how much planning, there will always be something we forgot. Don't worry though, because the people in the area will be more than happy to point the mistakes out to you. As a result, we need time to work out the "bugs" and get the new processes working before scrapping it to go back and do it the way we have always done it before. It is very important not to over-react to comments or feelings people initially have prior to giving the new system a chance to work.

Dedicate Resources Up Front

When starting the first Lean projects, we recommend a 100% dedicated cross-functional team of people to go through the BASICS process. We have tried the "part time" approach, and it NEVER works. The reason is that the day-to-day problems always win out over the needs of the improvement team. While we know it is very difficult, it is critical to backfill these people so that they can participate 100% of the time learning the tools and implementing the new Lean process.

Include a Strategy for Accountability and Sustaining as Part of the Continuous Improvement Road Map

In the overall implementation plan there has to be consideration given to how the project will be followed up and sustained. Keep in mind, sustained means ongoing improvement. We typically implement control plans and sustain plans with every project. Since the Lean management system is new to the organization, we have learned that the process owners do not have the discipline, Lean knowledge, resources, or accountability to hold the gains and continually improve.

At Hospital X, this became a big problem. Once the project was done and the Lean team moved on, the organization believed it was the process owner's job to sustain and continue to drive improvements. We agreed! However, if the process owner, from a Lean maturity standpoint, doesn't know what needs to be done and there is no one to coach them on their standard work, it will ultimately fail. Finance said it was not their job to sustain it or make sure they met the ROI, which finance drove up-front. The process excellence staff organization said it was not their job to make sure it sustained because they were moving on to the next project. In addition, there was a major reorganization in the works within the hospital. This created quite a quandary, which by the time we departed, was never resolved.

Don't let this happen to you. Include this action plan in your Lean leadership road map. Encourage HR to play a role by "beefing up" people development and assisting leadership in creating the culture of accountability and discipline. This is a new set of skills that needs to be taught along with the vision and expectations of the new culture we are trying to create.

Listen to Your Lean Consultants/Experts

Many companies get to a point after 3 to 6 months where they think they know enough to do it all themselves. Every company seems to go through this phase. People get to a point where they know enough to be dangerous and dangerous they become. Why do companies hire Lean consultants? Many times we have asked ourselves the same question. They refuse to put the Lean steering committee together; they stop listening to the Lean consultants and do what they want to do. Then, they come back to the Lean consultants and ask why Lean isn't working and blame it on the consultants.

So what are we to do? As Lean consultants we have to occasionally let them falter. It is the only way they will learn. Any good Lean consultant will admit there is still much that they do not know. We are always learning. When you think you know it all, it is time to quit!

Adopt and Integrate Standard Work and Create a Suggestion and Reward Systems

Toyota first learned about suggestions systems from Henry Ford. Toyota's suggestion system is described in the book,

40 Years, 20 Million Ideas. It is a fascinating read. Their model is not based around a suggestion box, but by having suggestions encouraged every day by the team leaders (supervisors) and implemented in real time. If it doesn't work, then they continue to try until it works or they go back to the way it was before and then try another improvement idea the next day. Once suggestions are implemented, the team leader updates the standard work in order to permanently capture the idea.

Continue Videotaping After the Consultant Leaves

We worked with Hospital X for more than 2 years. They would invite us back quarterly for "maintenance," which meant sitting down with their teams, reviewing their projects and events in the works, and offering suggestions. In addition, we would always pick out an area to work on improving while we were there. This was normally over a 1 week period.

The first thing we would always do is baseline metrics and videotape following the BASICS model. We would walk through the tools and make great improvements. Eventually, one of their process excellence people said to me, "I guess we should be videotaping and following the model while you're gone." (i.e. not try to shortcut activities).

We are not sure why this phenomenon exists, but it seems once we leave, the day-to-day activities take over, and there seems to be no time to follow the BASICS model. They tend to go back to "shooting from the hip."

We have always been successful using the BASICS and PDSA models. It has never failed us, yet if you are not careful, people tend to go back to the way it was always done before.

Don't Leave Managers in Place Who Aren't Going to Get It

One of the biggest obstacles we face is the manager or supervisor who is just never going to "get it." They don't buy in to Lean. They are normally from the "my way or the highway" philosophy of managing or they just plain look at this whole Lean thing as a threat to their job and the way they have always done it before. Our policy is to coach and mentor, coach and mentor, but eventually it becomes pretty obvious the person is not going to "buy in." Many times they go into a "stall" mode where they are always talking how great Lean is and outwardly agreeing with the team, but behind the scenes, they are stalling and doing everything they can to thwart the team.

Our experience is that 40%–70% of frontline supervisors and managers can't make the switch from cop to coach. If you keep them, they will kill the project and blame it on Lean or Six Sigma. It is important to move them to another area where they can be an individual contributor or moved out of

the organization. It is difficult to do and most organizations wait way too long to address the problem and then wonder why they don't get the results.

This ties in with the ongoing review to see if we have the right people on the bus and if they are in the right seats to take us to the next level. With Lean, the need for the hero has gone away. It is also difficult when this person, who has so often been the "hero of the month," has to let go and focus on the process.

Don't Lay People Off after Lean Implementation

As stated before, our goal is to never lay off anyone as a result of continuous improvement. This does not mean there cannot be layoffs due to a recession. Toyota and other companies have found a way to deal with recessions by hiring temporary part-time people. When you work for Toyota, it is a lifetime commitment. When you leave Toyota, they don't invite you back.

Don't Shortcut the Tools

If we shortcut the tools, then we shortcut the results. It is really that simple.

Encourage Lean Architectural Designs

Traditional architect designs are not Lean. If a Lean consultant is brought in, it is best to bring them in during the conceptual phase of the project prior to drawings.

Include a "Go Forward" Person on the Team

When implementing multiple sites or campuses, it works best if the prior campus team contains a person from the next campus to be implemented. We call this a "go forward" person. This is a great way to load the next campus team for success.

Train, Train, Train

One cannot train enough with Lean. There is so much to learn. There are more than 300 books on Lean as we speak, many of the best now out of print. Creating a training plan up-front and following it is critical to success. The training is no substitute for the experience of implementing on the floor, but good interactive classroom training does have a role with Lean. Initial training can be as short as an hour or up to as long as 3 months or more at different intervals.

Ultimately, the training and ongoing continuous improvement culture becomes the role of the team or group leader with the assistance of HR and management. *You don't really learn the material until you have to train the materials!*

Create an Escalation Process

It is critical to have an escalation process in place to help the improvement teams or supervisors remove barriers to

* Yuzo Yasuda, *40 Years, 20 Million Ideas* (Cambridge, MA: Productivity Press) 1991.

improvement. Many times, people are afraid to complain to their bosses or their bosses may be the problem. Failure to have this process in place will force these issues to be hidden and not surface. The escalation process should go to the CEO. Several times, we have had to go to the CEO during Lean implementations to make the final call.

IDENTIFY THE PROCESS OWNER AND THE TEAM LEADER UP FRONT

Document and communicate roles and responsibilities for everyone in the organization.

At Hospital X, we were speaking with a manager and asked to whom he reported. He said he reported to two different directors in the department. I asked each director who the manager ultimately reported to, and neither was sure. I asked the administrator over the area who the manger reported to. He said he reported to Director 1 and why was I asking. I told him that no one I asked was sure. Then he said, "Well, he also sort of reports to Director 2 as well." One director was administrative and one was clinical. This caused a lot of confusion and resulted in little accountability.

Lesson Learned: *When all else fails, ask, "Who owns it?" If there is even a moment of hesitation in the response there is a problem.*

CHANGE REWARD SYSTEM

If we implement the new Lean system but leave the old reward system in place, what will be the outcome? The new system will never sustain. We must change the reward system to align with the new desired Lean behaviors. This should be part of the Lean road map.

LEAN MATURITY PATH

People and companies go through phases. These phases follow traditional change models. One can tell where a person or organization is in the Lean maturity path simply by the questions they ask. For example, if someone asks, "Will Lean work here or will Lean work for us?" we know they have not started Lean. When someone says, "We really aren't changing fast enough," we know they have moved into a new phase of their understanding of Lean.

IT'S JUST A BUMP IN THE ROAD

Many times, especially during suggesting solutions, or implementation, the team will run into problems and setbacks. A legal or compliance person will tell you something can't be done, or somehow the team has inadvertently upset someone. We have come to refer to these as "bumps in the road." At the time, they may seem like major issues or problems, but once we work through them, they become minor. This is a time to consider the communication model. Sometimes face-to-face communication is best during these "bumps."

MULTIPLE SITE ROLLOUT STRATEGIES

SITE/AREA SELECTION

We generally suggest putting a cross-functional team of individuals together to form the team. We pick a pilot site and pilot line based on the following criteria[*]:

- Most important, it must be successful.
- We must have open-minded leadership willing to participate on the team, take ownership, drive and sustain the change.
- We need the process owner to spend 80%–90% of the time on the team.
- The pilot should prove that the BASICS tools work.
- Where it makes sense, we should be able to transfer results to other campuses and standardize the processes.

TRYING TO IMPLEMENT SEVERAL PROJECTS AT ONCE WITHOUT SUFFICIENT RESOURCES

Resources become a critical ingredient when implementing Point Kaizen events or Lean implementations. If you can't resource it, don't launch it! We have seen and been part of many efforts that failed because the implementing area, while really wanting to make the changes, couldn't free up the necessary or the right staff to make the changes successful.

BEWARE OF CONFLICTING IMPROVEMENT APPROACHES, MULTIPLE CONSULTANTS

There are pros and cons associated with multiple consultants working on the same area. If the consultants have clearly defined expectations that complement each other or implement with exactly the same methodology, this is not a problem. But problems are created when each consultant is working on the same area with different implementation models, skill sets, or approaches. It is important when implementing to standardize the approach and problem-solving model. The pros are organizations will learn something different from each consultant. The cons are it can get very confusing to those implementing as to what process they are supposed to follow and which consultant is right when there is a difference of opinion. It is also difficult for the consultants because most consultants don't like to share their approaches, methodologies, and software or training materials.

DON'T TRY TO CUT THE LEAN IMPLEMENTATION TIME LINE BY 50%

Beware of always wanting to cut the implementation time on the next project by 50%. This seems to occur in every hospital and with every multisite implementation. While

---

[*] Influenced by Mark Jamrog, principal, The SMC Group.

implementations can be sped up, it doesn't necessarily mean that it is a good thing nor does it mean they can be cut in half. We need to take the time to get people involved, teach them the tools, and figure out those items that are unique to the next area in which we are implementing. Remember the "people piece", change can be difficult and takes time. It seems this lesson always has to be learned the hard way.

COOKIE CUTTER APPROACHES

While many areas across different hospitals and clinics are similar, we have found none that are exactly the same. For this reason, we highly discourage "cookie cutter" type approaches. It is important to go through the analysis steps (BASICS) in each implementation in order to get the buy-in from the existing staff. This does not mean that once the formula is created it can't be implemented quicker, but it is important not to try to implement it too quickly or it will not sustain. Remember Lean requires people to think differently than they are used to. If they don't go through the process of actually seeing their "wastes" in the process for themselves they will have difficulty in accepting any new process proposed.

SCRIPTING AND CUSTOMER SATISFACTION

Our experience is that there is a high correlation between those hospitals that embrace "scripting" and employee-centered initiatives and their patient satisfaction numbers. These hospitals also have leadership support from the top down to do whatever it takes to make the customer happy.[*] Some hospitals have had success in the ED setting by hiring a non-clinical "hospitality" person whose sole job is to talk and primarily listen to patients and help them in any way possible.[†]

Listed below are some best practices we have witnessed in hospitals that were in the top 90th percentile Press Ganey[‡] for patient satisfaction. Here are some of the things they implemented:

1. Physician award system: There are four areas of recognition in their physician reward system: (1) humanitarian award, (2) outstanding service to patients, (3) outstanding service to the health system, and (4) outstanding service to fellow colleagues. The doctors love it and it holds the administration accountable.
2. The five pillars of excellence is a form of performance management. It recognizes the following: (1)

best service, (2) best people, (3) best quality, (4) best growth, and (5) best cost.

3. Team/peer interview for hiring and implementing a 90 day probationary period for new employees, with the team leader able to terminate the orientee resulted in a huge increase in the retention rate of the employees.
4. Scripting guidelines: acknowledge, introduce, time, expectation of procedure, and thank.
5. Team leader is dependent on his/her staff's productivity. The team leader receives a monetary reward for the department's accomplishments. The team leader rarely quits or leaves the position. The team leader takes total ownership.
6. Service hallway with white grease board: The purpose of this board is to allow interdepartmental communication. Basically, a large communication board allows for any staff member to convey a message. We have also seen this at a large national hotel chain.
7. Champions of the month: Every month a 30 min recognition program is in place for those employees who volunteer in community service. Their names are put on display in the hallway.
8. Physician satisfaction board: Hospitals receive a monthly score from physicians. More than 160 physicians participated. Of the physicians interviewed, a percentage ranks each department, i.e., of the 82% of physicians interviewed, 95% gave a particular department a good score.
9. Bright ideas board: This is the heavy hitter of awards for suggestions. If the hospital saves $5000 or more from an employee's suggestion, the employee will receive a percentage of the savings.
10. The hospital focuses on the Press Ganey Priority Index, which are the top 10 questions in the report. If these questions are addressed and mastered, the chances of the rest of the Press Ganey report being stellar is significant.
11. Uniforms: Each department has a standard unique uniform so that each area is easily identified by patients, families, and other employees. Arrangements for discounts and sales are made with uniform companies who come to the hospital to supply employees.
12. Real-time communication mechanism/phone system: Each nurse carries a floor phone or a Vocera®.[§] The nurse's patients have the nurse's number so that they can call the nurse for any need, such as pain medication.

[*] Al Stubblefield, *The Baptist Health Care Journey to Excellence: Creating A Culture that Wows* (Hoboken, NJ: John Wiley) 2005.
[†] Louis M. Savary and Clare Crawford-Mason, *The Nun and The Bureaucrat* (CC-M Productions) 2006.
[‡] http://www.pressganey.com.
[§] www.vocera.com.

11 Executives and Lean

EXECUTIVE SUMMARY

Senior leaders have been through many quality initiatives and need to have a deep understanding of Lean's worth for it to be successful. This is a cultural change for their organization, and they must understand how it leads to a competitive advantage.

They need to be responsible for resources and accountability as well as creating a measurement system to make sure Lean is successful. Executives must set up a communication plan and commit to training at all levels of the organization including the board. Communication is a critical success factor. They must ensure resources are committed and jobs are backfilled so staff can commit to the Lean project.

Senior leaders must lead by example and must go to *Gemba*, meaning they must actually see how things are done on the floor. Barriers must be removed: Leaders need to help set the control process so once the Lean initiative is underway they are sure it continues to be successful. It is important they create a fair and just culture as a background for this cultural change. Physician engagement is critical to this process.

The chapter also discusses various organizational structures of a corporation, noting that American corporations tend to have many organizational levels, which can make it very difficult for communication and harder to implement Lean. It also discusses how to pick a consultant and the expertise required to be successful.

KEY LEARNINGS

- Executives are responsible for driving the cultural change within the organization.
- Understanding the critical role leaders play in supporting Lean, evaluating Lean metrics, removing barriers, setting goals and allocating resources.
- Importance of showing commitment and support leading Lean by example (i.e., *Gemba*, etc.).
- Communication is vital.

"We have successfully leveraged Lean concepts and tools to avoid the cost of a multi-million dollar expansion of our Food Production Center, saved approximately $3.5 million in building a non-core laboratory, and used the savings to re-design the in-house laboratory and implemented Lean tracks in our Emergency Departments which significantly reduced the number of patients that left without seeing the doctor on all our campuses."

—**Lars Houmann, FACHE**

President and Chief Executive Officer, Florida Hospital, Florida Division, Adventist Health System

INTRODUCTION

Lean and other quality initiatives often do not find their way into a company through senior leadership. These projects normally start at the middle-management level and trickle up and down. Senior managers usually believe they have a good understanding of quality initiatives while often their understanding is not as deep as they believe.

You do not need to go to Japan to see Lean at work. There are many companies to tour in the United States, including Toyota. Most associations offer tours of companies working on Lean, including the Association of Manufacturing Excellence, the Society of Manufacturing Engineers, the Institute of Industrial Engineers, the Society for Health Systems, and the Institute for Healthcare Improvement.

There are many good books for executives to read. They are listed in Appendix 3 in the suggested reading section.

BEEN THERE, DONE THAT

It is important to understand that senior leaders have been through many quality initiatives over the years. Many can still remember the days when total quality management (TQM), continuous quality improvement (CQI), and the other alphabet soup initiatives were the quality programs *du jour*. While many senior executives may have only fleeting memories of most of these initiatives, they seemed to come and go on the whim of executive consultants and experts. It is understandable why many senior executives are skeptical and perhaps even cynical of new quality initiatives that come in the vernacular of a group of initials or new "sound bites." In addition, many of the results derived from other quality initiatives are not culturally transformational nor do they mirror results we have seen achieved through Lean initiatives.

Along with this superficial understanding of quality initiatives, it is not surprising to find that many senior leaders and executives believe they have a better understanding of these programs than they do, and most think they have a good understanding of how to deliver high-quality patient care. It is not until they get personally involved with Six Sigma and Lean that they begin to understand what they do and do not know. In these difficult financial times, the cost of implementation is also a significant barrier.

Learning Lean can be difficult for most executives since many are busy with operational and leadership functions. Even the thought of taking the time to sit down and understand Lean and other quality initiatives is quite daunting with everything else piled up on their plates. One of the most difficult tasks of getting Lean into an organization is the "coaching up" that executive high-level staff must do to their most senior leadership to get them to understand the level of value, level of commitment, and the investment in time and energy to realize a Lean organization. If executives somehow find the time to truly understand Lean and its impact, they will discover it is not just another quality improvement initiative. Lean provides concepts and tools that will fundamentally change the way organizations do business and ultimately make their jobs as leaders much easier in the long run.

COMPETITIVE ADVANTAGE

Our current healthcare spending model in this country is unsustainable. The ability to provide increasing quality of care at decreasing cost through organizational efficiencies is paramount. As healthcare gets more competitive and unit cost reimbursements decrease, it will become more imperative for organizations to become more efficient. Not only will executives need to understand the potential financial impact from a bottom line perspective, but they will also need to be able to lead the organization in understanding that eliminating waste will reduce the number of steps, thereby reducing the opportunities for defects or errors to occur. This will ultimately lead toward improving the overall quality of the service and care delivered to the customer (both internal and external) and the end result, over time, will positively impact the organization.

With the creation of the Hospital Consumer Assessment of Healthcare Providers and Systems* (HCAHPS) survey, hospitals are becoming increasingly aware that their reputation for quality and patient satisfaction can drive consumer choice. They are now recognizing that it is necessary to view patients as customers because they are held accountable for their customer service track record in a very public forum. Executives need to place emphasis on the importance of obtaining the voice of the customer (VOC) to fully understand what is value-added from the patients' point of view, which may be different from how they have viewed their organizations in the past. Gaining an understanding of Lean concepts and principles and deploying Lean tools to optimize operations will become a competitive model that enables corporate sustainability in the long run. Over time, Lean will move from being utilized to achieve a competitive advantage to a way that companies operate in order to survive.

Lesson Learned: *Lean is the competitive advantage today and a way of survival tomorrow.*

BOARD OF DIRECTORS TRAINING

Every Lean system implementation or journey should be supported by the guiding principles and values of the organization.

The board of directors is playing a more active role in organizations, both strategically and operationally. As boards become more accountable, not just for the financial health of an organization but also for the quality and outcomes of that particular institution, it becomes imperative that the board understand the quality and improvement initiatives taking place in the company. The board of directors is responsible for setting the strategic direction of the organization; therefore, they must receive training in Lean in order to understand the value of Lean and drive the Lean transformation from the top. Top-down leadership is critical to rolling out and sustaining Lean and a commitment of significant resources to achieve organizational improvement. One needs to recognize the executives on the board have many of the same challenges as other executives in terms of time commitment, prior quality improvement experience, etc.; however, it is imperative they understand the potential impact Lean can bring to an organization in order to fully support the initiatives. It is interesting to note many hospital boards have members from industries other than healthcare which are practicing Lean such as manufacturing or service based companies and are now enlightening fellow hospital board members as to the benefits of introducing Lean programs. In addition, the process excellence organization should report directly to the CEO and the board. This will place attention to the importance of the transformation, while providing the most senior executives direct access to what is occurring in the deployment.

DIFFERENCES BETWEEN LEAN AND SIX SIGMA

Executives often find themselves in a position where they have to explain why they are advocating Lean and/or Six Sigma and the differences between Lean and Six Sigma. While both tool sets start with the Voice of the Customer (VOC), Lean is focused on improvements to flow and throughput velocity through standardization of tasks and improving efficiency by reducing non-value-added activities and removing waste. In a Lean culture, small incremental improvements are made every day by everyone in the organization.

Six Sigma is a more methodical model aimed at improving processes by reducing variation. Healthcare organizations often find it difficult to begin with applying Six Sigma tools, as the processes are ridden with waste and a significant amount of variability. In order to achieve the greatest impact toward improving the process, we apply Lean concepts and tools first, in order to eliminate waste and streamline processes, and then apply Six Sigma tools to reduce variation.

Most projects or initiatives use a combination of both Lean and Six Sigma tools, since they both work well together.

DEFINE REALITY FOR THE LEAN INITIATIVE

Executives can become familiar with Lean concepts, tools, and benefits by attending healthcare forums, reading literature, or formal training. They begin by identifying areas within the organization in which there is a compelling need to change. In most circumstances, these are areas in which there

---

* http://www.hcahpsonline.org/home.aspx.

is poor performance based on either patient complaints, poor satisfaction scores from patients, physicians or staff, falling volumes, or an area's inability to move its metrics.

Occasionally, Lean projects are initiated prior to potential capital investments to validate, consolidate, or redesign an expansion. Senior executives must select Lean projects that carefully align with corporate goals and strategy to allow buy-in from the entire healthcare team. It is the executive's responsibility to engage in the process of "project or initiative selection" to make sure the area and the potential initiative being considered has a proper scope with clarity in the project definition, with expectations that are realistic, and aligned to the strategic plan of the organization.

We have had many executive-level conversations on where in the organization to begin Lean initiatives, as in many cases the areas with the most opportunity for improvement have experienced ongoing organizational challenges. There may have been weak management or they may not have had the appropriate support to make the necessary changes to be successful. It is critical for the executives to assess and understand potential challenges a Lean initiative may encounter and be willing to remove barriers and provide the support needed to enable success.

A key component of any initiative or project selection is setting in place accountability along with roles and responsibilities for the initiative. The executive must make sure that all the stakeholders understand the initiative, timeline, expectations, and deliverables. They need to be realistic and clearly communicated with area leadership and staff prior to the implementation rollout. It is important that the executive demonstrates an ongoing strong and active level of support to show that the Lean or Six Sigma effort has the highest priority.

Communication is critical! Everyone, including frontline staff, supervisors, managers, and team members should understand the goals and objectives to be achieved, how the Lean initiative will help the clinical area achieve the goals, how they (staff and managers) will be impacted by them, and what is in it for them if they meet the deliverables. These are basic change management questions that need to be addressed and re-addressed throughout the initiative. The staff needs to clearly understand what the organization is trying to accomplish and what role they play in helping the organization reach that goal. This can be done by attending departmental meetings with the area management, personally kicking off the project, holding weekly update meetings, making department rounds, and continually interacting with the staff in the area in which the initiative is occurring.

Review the objectives, goals, and timeline during status update meetings, allowing time for key designated team members to discuss challenges, successes, and lessons learned.

RESOURCES AND ACCOUNTABILITY

It is up to the leadership to work with the area managers, supervisors, and even the finance department to make the necessary resources available. Often, staff feel overwhelmed with the amount of work they have to do and it is a very

difficult transition to take time out of one's daily work to be 100% dedicated to a Lean team. The senior leadership is responsible to select the teams and encourage multi-disciplinary cooperation to bring the right people to the table. They must dedicate the resources and time needed to change processes, to carefully set the stage, and identify appropriate roles and responsibilities for these teams.

Lesson Learned: *Leadership must be prepared to "backfill" those on the team, as these projects don't work with "part-time" resources. The day-to-day tasks will always win out.*

It is the responsibility of the executive and critical to the success of the Lean initiative to allow the time needed to change their culture. Executives need to be aware that the teams engaged in these initiatives spend 20%–30% of their time in training concepts and tools and 70%–80% of the time in change management responding to the cultural component. Some organizations create a separate "budget" so that the time for employees who are engaged in the initiative are not "charged" to the department budget.

Lesson Learned: *Culture changes normally take 3–5 years with a passionate and dedicated CEO and senior leadership team communicating the vision, consistent message and adhering to a strong value system centered on adding customer value along with respect and appreciation for their employees. Eventually, everyone is on the Lean team, as Lean becomes the way we do business.*

In healthcare settings, managers are often promoted from within and may have little experience in these areas. Frontline nurses who have been excellent in that role may be placed in management positions but may have limited management experience or training. This is somewhat unique to the healthcare profession. Thus, the selection of projects and the setting of appropriate expectations and goals become even more critical. In addition, leadership must be willing for staff, managers, and team members to take chances, and make and learn from their mistakes.

LEAN SHOULD BE WHERE THE ACTION IS

It is important that the Lean team, process excellence organization, and the area leadership are co-located where the action is. Many companies have put their process excellence or quality departments off-site in other buildings and sometimes even at other hospitals or clinic locations. It is critical the Lean group is on-site and any Lean activity be visual to the frontline staff. This is a very important piece of the cultural change. The Lean change program must be in front of everyone, every day, and successes published throughout the organization.

REMOVING BARRIERS

It is the responsibility of the executive to listen attentively, ask questions, and be prepared to help to remove barriers as appropriate to keep the Lean initiative on track. Barriers often encountered are cultural, territorial, accountability challenges, team resource availability, and financially driven such as budgetary constraints or capital needs. There may be times when new equipment or funding for layout reconstruction are identified, and executives can play a pivotal role in championing resource needs within the organization.

Lean is a different way of thinking and managing. Some areas may have performance issues with managers or staff who may be competent but may not have the necessary skills needed or may not be receptive to adopting Lean as a new way to do business.

Executives are constantly faced with determining if they have the "right people on the right seat on the bus." Our experience has been that every Lean initiative has staff "changing seats" or "leaving the bus." In most cases, managers or staff members recognize that they do not want to engage in the cultural transformation and opt to move to other areas or leave the organization. As these challenges present themselves, the executive leader will play a key role to make sure the right leaders are in the right place to drive the initiative to the next level. The area leadership must be held accountable to sustain any improvement and drive continuous improvement activities forward.

Executives must be willing to work through personnel changes and engage human resource managers to help resolve staffing barriers. If the area executive believes that the outcome of the Lean initiative may be staff reductions, there must be a plan to move staff to other areas. Normally, attrition will provide open spots for those freed up. We do not recommend layoffs during or surrounding a Lean initiative. This will prove counterproductive and rumors will travel like the plague relating Lean to layoffs. It will then be extremely difficult to engage other areas within the organization in Lean initiatives.

If Human Resources is engaged early on, they can provide advice on opportunities for employees as reductions occur and provide counsel on options for staff or managers who may resist the cultural transformation necessary for the Lean initiative's success. Often, we put people we free up on existing or future process improvement teams until we can find a home for them.

MEASUREMENTS TO DRIVE OUTCOMES

The next major issue for leadership is to set up the processes for measurements. This is particularly critical in healthcare, where, often, quality measurements can be difficult to evaluate. In healthcare, accountabilities and measures are critical to a Lean initiative; without this, Lean will not be sustainable. "Floor" management and daily huddles are necessary to facilitate communication with frontline staff to "debrief" daily operations and receive feedback for continuous opportunities of improvement.

Outcomes measurement is the gold standard in healthcare; however, in healthcare we must often measure process or care instead. There can be many process steps in the care of a patient. By improving these process steps we assume or

in many cases, the literature supports improved outcomes. An example might be a patient with a heart attack (a code STEMI) that is seen in the emergency room and because the clinical literature supports better outcomes an aspirin is prescribed. The morbidity and survival of the patient become the outcome measure. The literature supports many of these processes. They lead to positive outcomes and it is under this assumption we look at these "process" of care metrics. It is critical that leadership set up a dashboard where these measurements are tracked on a regular basis to actually prove that our pre- and post-results are what we expect. In many cases the numbers are not large enough at a single institution or the time frames long enough to look at outcomes, this is where benchmarking can be helpful.

It is also very important to set up a measurement system that looks at measurements in real time so that effective changes can be made immediately. Patient care and quality outcomes are time-sensitive factors. There is little value in looking at measurements at the end of the month only to find out "after the fact" that we have a problem. Additionally, we have to look at individual measures, not just averages or extremes, to know whether we have improved the process. It is not helpful to look at only extremes of measurement, since variation can be an issue. One of our sayings is "variation is the enemy of Lean,"* and we have to focus on keeping the standard deviation variants to a minimum.

The challenge, initially, is that very few processes within healthcare follow a normal distribution. There is extreme variability as standard work has not been deployed and staff may perform tasks differently on different shifts. We must stabilize the process through a Lean initiative and gain an understanding of what is important to the customer. This is accomplished through eliminating non-value-added steps, which will result in decreasing variability and "clean up" the process, which then highlights the remaining true variation.

WHO IS TO BLAME?

The measurement piece must be focused on improving the process. It is sometimes very tempting and easy to find someone or something to blame when there is a problem. We have to recognize that at least 90% of the time, the process or "system" is at fault, and focusing on people misleads us. An example often used in healthcare is when something goes wrong; we default to doing "more education" and focus on individual learning. This is often not the correct approach. Often, when we look back at the process, we find out that it has been broken for some time and that simply re-training will not solve the problem. We have to go back and analyze the process to determine the true systemic root cause.

We need to discover what in our system allowed the "error" by the staff person to be made. How do we "people proof" or mistake proof critical processes to prevent the error and resulting defect from ever occurring again? We have to get beyond depending on the individual's personal

---

* Influenced by Six Sigma saying.

knowledge, training, experience, skill, and memory. No one intentionally decides that they are going to come in to work today and purposefully make mistakes. Many industries have deployed mistake proofing to eradicate unwanted behaviors, fully understanding that people don't want to make errors and feel terrible when they make them, especially when people's lives are at risk.

YOU ARE WHAT YOU MEASURE

Executives need to set the standards! They need to choose the metrics or measures that they want to achieve, that are aligned to the organizations goals, and provide clarity to management about what is being measured, who is responsible, how (baseline, targets, and stretch goals) results are going to be evaluated, and how often the results should be reported (timeline, daily, monthly, quarterly). It is important that these results are posted real time in the department, not just on a cluttered bulletin board or mixed in with other paperwork.

In healthcare, we often suffer from information overload. We are so busy trying to get so much information out to the line level staff that we are naïve to the fact that very little is grasped. We need to whittle the data down to information and train our staff in the vital few metrics that are important. This information should be shared at standing "huddle" at the department meetings every morning in a very visible graph-like fashion so it can be looked at and evaluated quickly. The ability to select representative data points to measure core processes, with clear definitions, with real-time reporting on an executive dashboard to monitor performance is critical to continuous process improvement and to achieve organizational excellence.

CONTROL OR SUSTAIN PROCESS

Executives must supervise the creation of a "control or sustain" process for all improvements. If the executive does not follow up on Lean changes, managers and supervisors will assume that it is not a priority. This means that once a change is put in place, a real-time measurement process must be put in place to keep track of the process. The most difficult part of Lean and Six Sigma is to make sure the process stays in "control" and continues to improve. The process should be measured before and after on a continued basis, or one cannot determine if the improvements to the process are sustained. It is the responsibility of the executive to review the measures and make the area managers and staff understand the expectations and set accountabilities in place. This may mean the initiation of both positive and negative consequences for the staff in order to create accountability and discipline for the measures.

The target measures must be established at the beginning of a Lean initiative ("baselined"), and once the improvement is established, constantly improved, otherwise things have a tendency to backslide to the old less efficient "way we have always done it" (Figure 11.1).

If the expectations are not met, then the executive must work with the process owner (i.e., department leader) to identify the root cause and put a corrective action plan in place.

Any process deployed should have key metrics and/or measures that are reported through the chain of command starting at the frontline, to supervisor/manager to director to senior executive, so the senior executive can gauge how well the process is performing and be able to identify challenges. These metrics and/or measures should be incorporated into the leader standard work. The senior executive should work with their leaders to help them grow and develop by holding them accountable to sustain and improve the process measures.

Lesson Learned: *When the executive's bonus rides on the measure, the measure normally improves. The question is: "Is it the right improvement?" The answer is: The right improvement is driven by giving the process owner the right tools to determine how to improve the process. The wrong improvement is driven by the senior leaders providing all the answers and focusing only on results.*

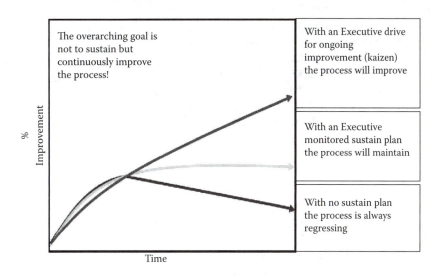

FIGURE 11.1 Improvement curve.

LEAN AND AUDITS

Looking at the Toyota model, there are a number of key areas emphasized in the development of their Lean process. The first one was auditing. Auditing can be utilized in a variety of ways and it can play a key role in identifying opportunities for improvement on a day-to-day basis. It can be leveraged to monitor a recently implemented improvement in order to understand the level of control or adoption.

In healthcare, auditing can take the form of a written audit assessment or can be a form of "rounding," where the executive's focus is on mentoring the area leadership to think through ongoing and visual process improvement. The premise is that key process metrics are reviewed on a day-to-day basis by management and leadership in "real time." This allows for immediate corrective action and achieves the best results.

Executives can set a clear line-of-sight accountability from the frontline staff to the executive, by incorporating audits, measurement reporting, action plan updates to resolve challenges, monitoring the results of audits, feedback mechanisms from staff, suggestion implementation, and incorporating continuous improvement into leader standard work, where the executive "leads by example" to drive ongoing performance and improvement.

CULTURAL CHANGE

In healthcare, patients or patient families are often not thought of as "customers". Leaders must drive staff to think about what the customer desires and what the customer perceives as value-added. This is the heart of Lean. They must start to understand the Lean processes at the ground level and have a better understanding of what happens in the work place. They must move into a listening mode and encourage communications up and down the hierarchy. It is essential that managers and employees see executives engaging in and leading Lean initiatives. One example would be conducting "*Gemba*" walks or rounding to see problems firsthand and to know what is going on in the workplace.

Senior leaders and executives need to move the organization into thinking more about delivering what the customer wants. They must develop their staff and encourage root cause problem solving by learning the art of "asking why five times." If leaders don't change their behaviors and the reward systems, the culture will revert to the way it always was. The only people who can change the culture are the CEO and the senior leadership team.

"PROJECT-ITIS"

One of the challenges in many corporations is to get out of what is called a "project mentality." Companies launch project after project, hoping something will "stick." Even if these are Lean oriented, sooner or later, they run out of staff to continue these projects or the same staff members may be assigned to every project. We have been at several companies where they have many projects going at the same time. The oldest project seems to fall out of control once the staff readjusts their sights on the newer projects. This is why a change in culture is so critical. We must move out of the "project-itis" mentality and move toward creating an environment of change based on process-focused improvements.

HUMAN ERROR FACTOR

Current hospital culture and training combined with years of tradition, paradigms, and poor hospital information systems have all contributed to the broken hospital systems we see today. Physicians have had to react and deal with these systems, getting reimbursed less and less for their services, while malpractice insurance skyrockets. A number of states have capped their insurance judgments.[*][†][‡] Since 1986, 38 states have reformed joint-and-several liability rules; 23 states have enacted statutes limiting non-economic damages, and currently 18 states have such statutes in place; and 34 states have restricted punitive damages. Yet doctors are human, hospital staff are human, and all doctors and staff, even the best, make mistakes. Why? Because humans are, based on a poll of several Master Black Belts, at best from less than 1–3 Sigma. This means doctors average 66,800 mistakes per million or more. While most are probably minor, every once in a while a major one is going to occur, even to the best.

The temptation not to report a medical error should never be underestimated. One published study disclosed that only 50% of house staff physicians who admitted making serious clinical errors disclosed their errors to medical colleagues, and only 25% disclosed them to the patients or their families. In another published survey of laypersons, only 1–3 of respondents who had experienced medical errors said that the physicians involved in the error had informed them about it. Still another survey, asking European physicians whether they would disclose a medical error to patients, found that although 70% responded that physicians should provide details of such an event, only 32% would actually disclose the details of what happened. A similar percentage of American physicians (77%) echoed the same opinion.

A British researcher explains this reluctance to disclose by pointing out that physicians who commit medical errors frequently question their own competence and fear being discovered; they know they should confess but "dread the prospect of potential punishment." These reactions are "reinforced during medical training; the culture of medical school and residency implies that mistakes are unacceptable and point to a failure of effort or character."

Nurses, hospitals, and anyone who works within a hospital are subjected to malpractice risk. Hospitals are struggling with how to create a "just" culture of honesty with patients, while trying not to increase malpractice claims. How do you push a "just" culture when society is always looking for blame

---

[*] Liker, Toyota Culture.
[†] http://www.webmm.ahrq.gov/perspective.aspx?perspectiveID=50.
[‡] Source: http://uspolitics.about.com/od/healthcare/a/01_tort_reform.htm.

(especially within the U.S. legal system)? Doctors have years of habits—both good and bad—influenced by society and our legal system, as well as ethical dilemmas created constantly by new technology. When we implement Lean, we start to bump up against these old habits. It is interesting to note how much medicine and medical technology has changed over the years, yet, in most cases, our processes have not!

Lessons Learned: *The ability to deploy Lean is directly related to the culture within your organization. Culture change is the biggest obstacle to implementing Lean and lack of systems thinking is the biggest obstacle to implementing the right tools and improvements.*

Fair and Just Culture*

The Lean cultural change needs to include what used to be called a "blame-free" culture. This is probably not practical since a blame-free culture is not ideal or practical. The new terminology is more accurately called a "just" culture. This is a culture where, when things do not go right, they are looked at critically from an operational standpoint. If it is a hospital systemic process issue, it is dealt with at that level. If it is truly an individual person's accountability, such as the person refuses to follow the standard work or abide by the new system, then appropriate action should be taken. Thus, it is not really a blame-free culture, but a fair, just, and accountable culture that focuses on dealing with problems at an accurate level and in an efficient manner, keeping the patient at the forefront of everyone's concerns. If a process has been broken and not followed for years, it does not seem right to punish an individual for not following it when something goes wrong.

In the Lean model, the culture is based on "Respect for Humanity." Whether we call it "just" or "blameless," this new culture is critical in order for Lean to work.[†] A Lean environment should encourage employees to feel free to uncover and share problems. The goal is to have every problem exposed, identify the root cause, then act on and fix the problem so it never comes back. If the employee is too afraid to admit to a mistake, we will never know a problem existed or, worst case scenario, the problem manifests itself and eventually results in something serious, such as a hospital-acquired infection or the death of a patient. If employees do not feel comfortable identifying wastes within their processes and exposing problems, Lean will not permeate the organization.

A good model for making sure that all aspects of a project are clearly evaluated is to focus on evaluating the critical areas of safety, quality, delivery, cost, inventory and morale.

A new worker on the Toyota line had accidentally scratched the underside of a front fender of the car as he carried out his operation.[‡] He debated whether to tell the team leader because, after all, no one would probably see

it. He pulled the andon cord and the supervisor came over. The worker told the supervisor the problem. The supervisor asked him how it was caused. The worker told him. Together they came up with both a short-term (counter-measure) and longer-term solution to fix the problem so it would never come back. At lunchtime, the team leader pulled everyone together and congratulated the worker for pulling the cord and telling him about the problem. Everyone clapped for him.

Lesson Learned: *Does everyone on your healthcare staff feel free to admit to problems immediately as they occur? If we don't surface the problem, we can't fix it. If your culture is based on fear and retribution, employees will not surface problems and everyone loses.*

As we can see from the story above, there are two ways to approach problems—one is positive and the other is negative. Some hospitals have been very successful at creating this "just" culture.[§] Other hospitals may just be beginning the journey; however, this may truly be one of the most difficult programs to implement, as it may require an organizational culture change.

Communication, Communication, and more Communication

An important piece of a Lean environment is that leadership should set up a two-way communication process where line level staff can use their experience to safely identify existing problems and comfortably contribute ideas that they feel are valued and should be acted on. These ideas should be acknowledged by management. One way to do this is by putting up a bulletin board that tracks, open and honestly, any employee suggestions and creates a dialogue to get more information about particular suggestions (Figure 11.2). This dialogue must then be acted on, putting a process in place to take the suggestion and operationalizing it. All this should be in a public forum and be both posted and discussed, so that people feel that their ideas are taken seriously and have value. Providing staff with a mechanism to make recommendations and publicly displaying the impact of their suggestions will drive cycles of continuous improvement, foster employee engagement, and help sustain Lean.

Communication is a critical enabler and can be facilitated by holding regular meetings every morning. This should be a brisk meeting, 5–10 min, also called "standup meetings or huddles." These meetings should deal with issues of the day, talk about difficult problems, and talk about changes in patient's status. They also need to address efficiencies of care, which is not necessarily a standard topic in today's environment. These meetings can also be where new information is shared from a process change and where results can be shared with the group.

In addition, in order to achieve a transformational change, executives must create ongoing lines of communication

---

* Joint Commission on Accreditation of Health Care Organization 10/07 vol 33 #10.
† Mann, *Creating a Lean Culture*. (Productivity Press) 2005.
‡ Liker, *Toyota Culture* (McGraw Hill) 2005.

§ http://www.webmm.ahrq.gov/perspective.aspx?perspectiveID=50.

FIGURE 11.2   Ideas board.

with managers and staff to share the organization's strategic goals and to reinforce the organization's priorities. They must ensure that each employee understands how each can contribute to help the organization to achieve its goals. If reinforcement is not continued, attention and priorities will fade, and the progress to achieving the strategic goals will diminish.

GEMBA[*] – WHERE THE TRUTH CAN BE FOUND

"*Gemba* 現場 translated to "on the spot," the actual place," or "the real place" where value is created." One of the most important aspects of Lean is the "walk around" or going to the *Gemba*. The *Gemba* should be a visual workplace and it "should talk to you" by making problems immediately visible (Figure 11.3). Going to the *Gemba* provides the opportunity for executives, managers, and supervisors to develop their employees by reinforcing organizational priorities and encouraging them to think through the problem-solving process. This is done by the executive going to the area and seeing what is actually occurring on the frontline. The executives can engage employees in active communication related to topics important to the organization and obtain direct feedback from the staff.

The executive or manager may choose topics for each *Gemba* to drill down on potential issues that have been identified and then encourage the area leaders to take the opportunity to ask why five times to get to the root cause of the problem. An environment of transparency and trust must be created. Clear, concise, open, and honest dialog must be continued. Suggestions and feedback must be accepted and evaluated without an initial reaction. No ideas are "stupid."

In a healthcare situation, walking around the hospital or a medical office, talking to patients, vendors, and line level staff helps to create critical communication both upward and downward. *Gemba* walks allow staff to see the commitment of the executive team and vice versa. The staff can communicate issues that are affecting them on a very real day-to-day basis.

When was the last time you had lunch with the frontline staff in the cafeteria? This is routinely done by Japan Airways President and CEO Haruka Nishimatsu. In both a CNN and CBS Sunday Morning[†] interview, he stated he likes to eat lunch with the employees "in order to share and to raise morale and motivation." His philosophy is "there is no one at the top or bottom. A boss is in the same boat as their people. You either share the work and sacrifice together or the company will sink." He goes on to say, "If you have a problem, don't blame the person you are dealing with, blame the person in charge." In the same segment, Southwest CEO Gary Kelly says, "It won't work if leaders treat themselves one way and employees another."

It is also important that the executive be among the patients, as they are the ultimate customers of the system. They can give feedback on the things that are working and not working in a very direct and meaningful way.

WHAT QUESTIONS SHOULD YOU ASK WHEN DOING A GEMBA WALK?

- What are your challenges, problems, issues?
- What have you improved today?

---

[*] www.saiga-jp.com, kanji to English dictionary, http://dict.regex.info Japanese to English dictionary.

[†] CBS Sunday Morning, aired February 2009, entitled "Economy Class," produced by Marsha Cooke and edited by Randy Schmidt, CNN interview on You Tube, http://www.youtube.com/watch?v=858t44psmww&feature=rec-LGOUT-exp_fresh+div-1r-2-HM.

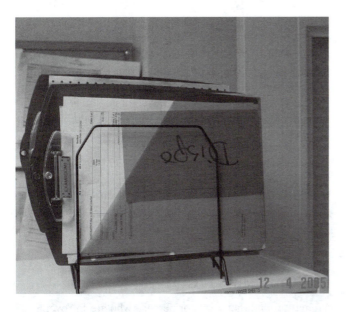

FIGURE 11.3 Visual control ED disposition rack in first in first out order (FIFO).

- Audits - Are they up to date? What problems are they having?
- How can I help you?

Lesson Learned: *An executive must be open and accessible. Get out of the ivory tower and find out what is going on in your hospital first-hand at the Gemba.*

MEETINGS

Meetings are often the bane of existence in a corporation. Meetings take up a tremendous amount of time and often take up most of many executives' day. Meetings in and of themselves are not necessarily bad; however, in many companies, both the number of meetings and the meeting inefficiency create a tremendous waste of time. In looking at this from a Lean perspective, if the time is not actually spent adding value to the customer, then one must question the value of the meeting(s). Meetings should be carefully orchestrated in terms of what their purpose is and what their outcomes will be, making sure that this will all add to a better product (patient care). Many organizations undergoing a Lean transformation actually "Lean" the meeting process by eliminating redundant or ineffective meetings that are not value-added to the internal or external customers, deploying structure and rigor in meeting design. Companies are moving to designated "no meeting days" to allow managers to dedicate more time to managing frontline operations and staff.

PAYING FOR SUGGESTIONS

One complicated issue is when to compensate for suggestions. There is no easy answer. Some people feel that paying for suggestions is paying people for work that they should already be doing. Other companies feel that the value of suggestions and savings should be transferred back to the

individual employee. Many companies introduce some type of gain-sharing or bonus system in which all employees receive an equal amount vs. a percentage of their pay. This is an individual company decision, and there are pros and cons to all approaches. The goal of many Lean organizations is to eliminate all wasted activities, redundancies, and create error- or defect-free processes; doing this will eliminate steps and improve cycle times and rework, thereby increasing the productivity of each worker. By increasing productivity, we need less staff to do the same work so companies will become more profitable. These profits should be shared with employees. The goal should be to pay 20%–30% more than your competitors, thereby attracting and retaining the best employees and facilitating recruitment and retention of highly talented staff. Toyota's suggestion system is described in the book, *40 Years, 20 Million Ideas.*[*] Employees are generally paid small amounts for their ideas, but when they receive a payment, they share it with their co-workers. After all, without their co-workers they could not have implemented the idea.

PHYSICIAN ENGAGEMENT

One of the most difficult challenges for executives in the hospital and healthcare setting is engaging physicians. Increasingly, physicians feel pressures from the outside world, both financial and administrative. Rising administrative issues around healthcare coverage, patient financial engagements, and ongoing malpractice issues have clearly increased the stress and anxiety that weigh on physicians on a day-to-day basis. Physicians are also feeling less focused and engaged in the hospital setting as we move toward a more "hospitalist" model. Many physicians are moving out of this environment, with hospitalists taking over these roles. Hospitalists can be contracted, employed, or independent. Depending on which role they take, other physicians will have more or less engagement in the hospital. It is challenging to engage a physician in something they believe is oriented toward the hospital's needs. Most hospital processes are seen as hospital issues and not physician issues. Often, it is difficult for physicians to focus on these things and to understand that fixing these processes will make their lives easier. Some organizations get the physicians involved up front with a "contract for change" where the expectations of the Lean initiative and the physician involvement are clearly stated. The Lean tools apply to physicians' processes the same as any other process in the hospital. Some physicians have improved their independent office operations and are seeing the benefits. Videotaping is a great way to surface improvements that Emergency Department (ED) physicians, surgeons, and hospitalists can make to improve their bottom line or be able to make the same revenue in less time. It is critical to bring physicians on the Lean journey and have them participate in Lean projects that directly impact their daily activities, as

---

* Yuzo Yasuda, *40 Years, 20 Million Ideas* (Cambridge, MA: Productivity Press) 1991.

their feedback provides the physicians perspective of the process. It also serves to facilitate the acceptance of the new process and can be beneficial as the physicians can see that the hospital administration is working toward improving activities that directly impact their workflow. We have had staff who are resistant to the change go to their physician "allies" in an attempt to de-rail the proposed changes. However if the area physicians are knowledgeable about what is occurring they can assist in the change management and help to defuse potential situations.

THE COG IN THE CHAIN OF COMMAND

We have learned over the years that every once in a while a middle management person can become a "cog" in the wheels of the organization. This person could be anywhere in between the CEO and the person on the floor, but normally they are director level or above. They are typically out to make a name for themselves. They are not team players (but they talk like they are) and they are not interested in developing their people. Information from the top is filtered through this person to their reports based on what they desire to pass on and filtered up to their manager so that no information that makes this cog look bad goes any further.

At one company, an employee had information that there was no way they were going to meet a particular customer schedule. Even though they told their boss, their boss refused to let them tell his boss, the general manager. At another company, a room full of "old boy network" directors outright lied to a new general manager about the production schedules. They confidently conveyed everything was on schedule when it was not. Why? In the past, the old general manager never left his office, so the directors could tell him whatever they wanted. If the new general manager had not gone to the floor himself, he would never have known the true production status. You would not want to have been in the next production meeting!

What does this say about our organizations? One can see why Toyota develops a leadership culture focused on going to the floor to witness what problems exist first-hand.

THE EXECUTIVE AND THE ORGANIZATIONAL STRUCTURE: THE PROBLEM WITH TOO MANY LAYERS

The problem with layers in an organization is that each layer feels it has to make a name for itself and put its stamp on the processes, and each layer has to be involved in the decision process. Every person in the chain of command adds at least one more step to the process. Each level makes decision making longer, less precise, and more convoluted. Each level creates opportunities for defects and translation errors. So, by the time your message gets to the recipient(s), it may be unrecognizable.

In the Tom Peters' video "Speed is Life," Mike Walsh, CEO of Northern Pacific Railroad, explains the problems he ran into with layers in his company. He talks about how he chopped six layers of management over a 120-day period because he could not get his decisions through the organization. Walsh stated, "This is a big problem in American business today. You have, by and large, a set of frustrated CEOs because they can't make the organization respond to what they decide to do because the combination of layers and bureaucracy simply defeats them. As I have said before, the organization wears you out or waits you out, or both!"*

Lessons Learned: *The more levels in an organization, the longer it takes to make decisions and react to changes in the marketplace. The more levels, the less responsive the organization is. The more removed the "C" level—CEO, CNO, CMO, CFO—is from the frontline, the more "results oriented" and reactive the organization tends to be.*

"OVERHEAD" STAFF LAYERS

We have found that layers or persons who are in "overhead" (staff) positions and don't have enough work tend to create more work for those of us who already have too much work to do. In order to justify their "overhead" position, they tie us and our frontline staff up in meetings to the point we have difficulty supervising. This creates a "Catch 22" for those who report to them. They generate seemingly endless e-mail request for reports, information, and status, and call countless meetings, meetings, meetings. Their mantra is "We are corporate staff and we are here to *help* you!"

Lessons Learned: *Those in overhead positions without enough work create non-value-added work for the rest of us. Convert staff or overhead positions to line positions wherever possible.*

THE EXECUTIVE REQUEST

Often, the executive makes what seems like a simple request, but it sometimes turns the organization upside down. For example, a senior vice president asks the vice president for some information. It may not be something he really needs or wants, but the vice president then gets the assistant vice president in a meeting to review the senior vice president's request and determine how to answer the request (in a way that makes them look good and seem intelligent). The assistant vice president calls in the administrator and tells them what they want. The administrator goes to the directors and requests another meeting to decide how to get the data and information to answer the request. The directors call a meeting with the nurse managers to get the information. The nurse managers call a meeting with the nurses to get the information. Then nurse managers meet to firm their response to the director so they look good. Then the director and administrator meet again to go over the data/information and also massage it. They create a wonderful PowerPoint© presentation. Then the administration reviews it with the assistant

---

vice president, who calls a meeting to review it with the vice president, who massages it again to present to the senior vice president.

With some requests, the loop is cycled through several times at various levels until the information is thought to be good enough to be passed on. We can all think of examples where this has happened. Think back to your last budgeting process.

THE GOAL WITH LEAN IS FLATTER ORGANIZATIONS

With Lean, our goal is to flatten the organization. The goal is five levels or less!

TOYOTA'S FIVE LEVELS—TOYOTA HIERARCHY LOOKS LIKE THIS[*]

1. Group leaders
2. Managers
3. General managers
4. Vice president
5. President

The president at Toyota makes no more than 11 times the lowest paid person in the company. Toyota still follows the lifetime employment model; if you leave Toyota, you can never go back to Toyota, but you can still work at a subsidiary. Toyota organizations are similar to a living and breathing organism. In fact, in recent years, U.S. CEOs have made vastly more than their counterparts in other nations. In the United States, the average CEO pulled down a staggering 475 times what the typical American worker earned.[†]

How is decision making impacted in flatter organizations? Let's start with a one-person company. How long does it take to make decisions? As the company grows, it takes on more complexity. At first, all small companies' managers (3–10 people) wear many hats, and roles and responsibilities are shared. Our experience is that when companies hit the point where their leaders start to specialize or are assigned to one area or department (such as a director vice president over materials, one over nursing, one over laboratory, one over finance, etc.) that is when problems and the silos begin, turf wars start and competition really sets in for the top position. This is the beginning of what was termed "big company disease."

We have actually witnessed first-hand where registration (which was centralized) refused to decrease their cycle times because they were not part of that department and their director required that they meet 25 min cycle times. So they would only see patients every 25 min, even though this made patients wait in the lobby. After all, it wasn't their problem or even the problem of the patients who waited; it was the problem of the department for which they were doing registration. Why should they see a patient faster than the standard on what their pay is based?

We see nursing floors that won't take a new patient (when rooms are available) because they are ED patients, not theirs. We see ED dedicated or urgent critical areas with open beds that will make a patient wait for 3 hrs for fast track to open. We see upset materials people who refuse to fill stockouts because they are "mad" at a person or persons in an area. We see transport people who won't help out because "it is not their job." The more layers, silos, and centralization that exist, the worse it gets, and it is our patients, who are supposed to be our primary customers, who ultimately suffer.

What does this mean for the executive? First, one must have an awareness that these types of situations may be occurring in your organization. Second, there is the realization that we must reduce the layers and convert as many staff positions to line positions as possible. As you implement Lean processes, you should be able to cut or transition 30%–50% of your overhead staff! What kind of savings lay here?

VALUE STREAM MANAGERS IN THE LEAN ORGANIZATION

The goal in Lean is to create value stream managers who own and are accountable for the overall process. Functional managers are still required but should matrix to the value stream managers. In some hospitals, these are called service lines; however, the concept of service lines is different at different hospitals. In manufacturing, a value stream is equivalent to what used to be called a small business unit, where the value stream manager would have an entirely cross-functional organization reporting to him/her, but were responsible "soup to nuts" for the entire operations—from sales and marketing to delivering the product. In hospitals, the value stream is more difficult to determine. Some would argue that the operating room and ED are value streams, but they don't encompass the entire flow of the patient. So should they really be value streams? In our view, a value stream would be a service line or combination of similar service lines that own the patient from their arrival until the bill is paid.

As we transition to Lean, old traditional jobs change. We no longer need five or six supervisors in nutrition. Why? Because now the Lean line is contained in a much smaller area, visual controls exist, and visual signals like Kanban drive replenishment. Our demand becomes more predictable and waste decreases, which makes it easier to trigger orders from suppliers. We may now see the need to start combining roles, i.e., technician and secretary, etc., driving the need for more flexibility and cross-training.

The hospital executive, in conjunction with the physician and nursing executive, needs to rethink the entire organization to align it to best customer value and quality care.

---

[*] Gary Convis speech to annual MWCMC meeting, 2008.
[†] "Gannett Co. Lays Off Thousands As CEO Pockets Millions," By Marc McDonald Wednesday, July 1, 2009, posted by Marc McDonald @ 4:50 p.m.

ROLE OF THE EXTERNAL CONSULTANT

When first starting out, it can save a lot of time and money to hire an external resource to help lead you down the path. The consultant should base their business on transfer of knowledge and helping you develop your own internal resources. The consultant should be a change agent and a catalyst for change.

At some point, the consultant should transition from a sensei to a Lean resource. Consultants come in varying price ranges. It is best to seek and check out the consultant's references prior to signing a contract. You should build in a clause that, if you are ever not satisfied with the consultant for any reason, you can immediately terminate them and only be liable for expenses incurred to that point.

Most consultants will pay for themselves within a year; however, this is difficult to measure when you are using traditional accounting measures. You should agree with your consultant up front what will be considered Lean savings, if this is a requirement of launching the effort. Over time (2–3 years), most hospitals realize that determining return on investment (ROI) for every project is not a value-added process and that it results in much wasted time to assemble and justify, with most never being followed up. CEOs and executives learn to implement Lean because it is the right thing to do. You may not see real bottom line results until several years into the process, as it takes time to implement the changes across the system.

SUMMARY

Lean transformations are cultural movements that need to be led by senior level executives. In order for this to occur, executives at all levels must be knowledgeable and achieve a full understanding of the impact Lean will have on the organization. Beginning with the customer, Lean can provide a strategic competitive advantage through improvements in quality and safety by reducing the opportunities for errors and defects and by eliminating wasted activities. The elimination in defects and waste will yield financial returns in patient safety and adverse events, and improvement in productivity, reduction in throughput, and enhanced capacity. Executives must communicate organizational priorities by "walking the walk," by going to the *Gemba* and setting first-hand, clear, line-of-sight accountabilities both vertically and horizontally throughout the organization. This will require patience, coaching, mentoring of supervisors and managers, and fortitude and perseverance when challenged by skeptics. If one looks to Toyota, however, one will find that the journey, the lessons learned, and the results will be rewarding.

PUNCH LIST OF CONSIDERATIONS/ IDEAS FOR THE EXECUTIVE LEADER

- *Lead by example.* Visit your project teams. Five S *your* office. Move your office or add an office to the floor. Drive problem-solving mentality by example. Participate in or lead a Point Kaizen event. Eliminate PowerPoint© presentations and switch to A3s. Don't waste time reviewing good things done by your reports—focus on problems, highlighting and telling managers to think and solve for themselves. Go to the *Gemba*—talk to your surgeons, talk to your surgeon's offices, talk to your surgeon's staff on the floor. Help overcome the "not invented here," "not our way," and "can't be done—regulations, legal, policies" syndromes. Understand that 40%–60% of frontline supervisors have difficulty making the change from "the old way to coach." Conduct a, Five S *Heijunka*, or standard work audit on the floor.
- *Train* your board members, staff, and your employees in Lean. Consider creating a training center. Create leadership development programs.
- *Create a Lean culture* that is action oriented and focused on execution. Make continuous improvement part of the strategic plan. Implement Hoshin planning. Create a Lean system implementation plan with an oversight Lean steering committee. Don't put expectations on the Lean team… put them on the line owners. Create a "pull for Lean" throughout the organization.
- *Encourage problem sharing.* Create feedback loops so you can hear what you need to know vs. what you want to hear. Conduct skip-level meetings with your employees or, better yet, have lunch with them. Have Town Hall meetings on Lean and Six Sigma. Create (with pay) a surgeon/anesthesia feedback committee.
- *Organize realignment.* Move staff jobs to line jobs. Conduct succession planning to lowest levels. Consider a move to value stream leaders. Eliminate layers in your organization. Don't put leadership in separate off-site buildings. Eliminate "employee of the month" and executive perks. Consider salary caps and bonus systems. Consider lifetime employment. Train and establish Lean accounting and convert cost accountants to Lean project leaders.
- Develop process-oriented metrics vs. results.
- Use Hoshin Planning to align strategic goal deployment with the staff in the workplace.

12 Roles and Responsibilities of Managers and Supervisors

EXECUTIVE SUMMARY

Supervisors and managers need to be actively engaged, helping to develop the team charter, clarify and define the scope of the Lean project, establish metrics and provide support and guidance throughout the Lean initiative. This chapter examines how Lean is perceived by middle management which is defined by how their leaders frame it. The critical issues are:

1. The clarity of the initiative
2. Expectations
3. Management Visibility
4. Role of the executive leadership
5. Role of the Lean consultant
6. Timeline
7. Resources
8. Bonuses/rewards
9. Lean training

The manager must be actively engaged in the process. Forty to fifty percent of mid-level managers initially resist Lean initiatives, since they are perceived as being potentially threatening to their jobs. Lean is often initially viewed as a separate task, but ultimately it becomes how they do "the work."

It is important that managers select key staff to be involved in Lean initiatives rather than "expendable" staff. They must pick the best staff for these critical projects who can be viable future leaders for the organization. The concept of firefighting/problem-solving versus fixing the root cause is discussed using visual systems and other Lean tools. The concept of standard work and auditing is discussed in relation to management and the importance of critical thinking. The issue of ongoing audits is part of a Lean change in culture.

In Lean organizations, the staff is often much more satisfied with their jobs, leading to higher job retention.

Delegation of responsibility is discussed and the importance of the different levels of empowerment, such as:

1. Being given instruction on what to do
2. Asked what to do
3. Recommending and taking action
4. Take action and notify
5. Take action and notify periodically

The issue of empowerment and speed to empowerment are important along with the levels of authority needed for that empowerment.

KEY LEARNINGS

- Understanding of the critical roles in creating expectations and the role that managers and supervisors play in Lean.
- Understanding the importance of selecting the right staff and creating the right work environment.
- Understanding the appropriate staff delegations and the hierarchies of those delegations.

If you're any good at all, you just know you can be better...

—Lindsay Buckingham
Fleetwood Mac

SETTING THE STAGE: ROLE OF MANAGERS AND SUPERVISORS

Supervisors and managers (hereinafter referred to as management team) need to be actively engaged in helping to develop the team charter, define and clarify the scope of the Lean project, establish metrics, and provide support and guidance throughout the Lean initiative.

The question that needs to be understood by mid-level management from the executive leaders as they engage in the Lean initiative are:

- How visible is the initiative within the organization? Is this the first Lean initiative? The perception of being "targeted" for a Lean project may be perceived negatively by a clinical area management team.
- What is the problem, what needs to be improved, and what would success look like? What are the expectations of the results of the Lean project?
- What is the scope of the project?
- What is the timeline of the project?
- What is the role of the executive in the Lean initiative?
- What is the executive's perception/expectation of managers' and supervisors' roles and responsibilities for the success of the initiative, especially if they have not been exposed to previous Lean initiatives?
- Are they receiving Lean consultant support and training?
- What resources will need to be provided to the clinical area managers and supervisors?

- Will the manager and supervisor be able to backfill staff or other resources to be engaged in the Lean initiatives?
- How will the cost of backfilling for the resources be accounted for? Many healthcare organizations are labor constrained and they do not, culturally, proactively accommodate for Lean initiative resources.
- Will the Lean initiative impact any bonuses?
- What is the communication expectation between the managers, supervisors, and executive related to the Lean initiative?
- What is in it for them? The fear of the unknown may cause reluctance to participate.
- How will the progress and results of the initiative be communicated throughout the organization?

The level of support displayed by the management team throughout the Lean initiative makes a significant impact on the overall project success. It has been our experience that 40%–60% of mid-level managers initially resist Lean initiatives. In many cases, they opt to alter their roles either during or after the implementation and, in some cases, will sabotage the implementation in subtle ways.

Some managers and supervisors may fear they do not have the ability to do what they are being asked, and the Lean initiative will normally take them way out of their comfort zone. If you add the fact that the goal of Lean initiatives is to expose all the wastes in their area of responsibility, this can be paralyzing to many individuals and, as with any change, they can view this as potentially threatening to their job or how they are perceived as a manager.

Managers and supervisors should view the Lean initiative as an opportunity to showcase their talents. They need to become proficient in Lean concepts and tools with the expectation that they will drive Lean continuous improvement initiatives within their clinical areas. Every supervisor and manager we know who has embraced Lean has actually improved their careers and moved up in the organization. A significant number have become internal Lean consultants and/or green belts. It can be a great career pathway, merging one's expertise in clinical care with process improvement.

DO YOU REALLY WANT TO KNOW WHAT I SEE? DO YOU REALLY WANT TO KNOW WHAT I THINK?

Charlie Chan used to say, "Your eyes see but they do not observe." We think this statement characterizes the waste that is inherent in all our processes. One has to train oneself to observe the waste that exists before one can start eliminating it.

When you hire or assign an internal or external Lean consultant and they tour your healthcare department, clinic, or administrative area, they see waste everywhere; in places you don't see or may not be able or willing to recognize as waste. There are different philosophies or strategies on how

to communicate what the consultant sees to those whose area is being toured or, in the external consultant's role, to those who are prospective employers.

One Japanese sensei was not bashful about rubbing our noses in the *muda* (Japanese word for waste). He would tell us how stupid we were as managers to allow this waste to go on.

We had one manager ask what we saw after we toured his area. We told him we thought it was a complete and utter mess! He actually agreed and thanked us for being so honest.

We have found however the brutally honest approach doesn't always work. At another company where this approach was used, the managers were so put off with the response we were never invited back!

So now we always start out by asking, "Do you really want to know what we see?" If so, we will be happy to point out some of the waste we see and honestly tell them. If they say yes and become very defensive (normal behavior), we stop because we know they thought they could handle it, but really can't. The management team must learn to be able to put their Lean glasses on and take an objective look at the waste which is actually occurring in their work areas.

KEY RESPONSIBILITIES AND TOOLS FOR MANAGERS AND SUPERVISORS

The following subsections outline the key responsibilities of managers and/or supervisors.

COMMUNICATION

It is equally important that the cultural change starts at the top and is communicated throughout the organization down to the line level staff. The management team can never communicate enough when going through any type of Lean change. This is where the action needs to begin.

Line level staff must start looking at things differently and must be attuned to the fact that just because they have always done it this way does not mean it is the right way. They must start looking for waste and inefficiencies, and have the confidence and be in an environment where they communicate freely and openly with their superiors.

This is a cultural change in a hospital environment where things tend to be extremely task oriented. The nurses must change their thinking from simply looking at the task of giving a patient a drug or moving a patient from A to B, to looking at the process from either a patient and/or hospital perspective. This is sometimes an extremely difficult change for any line level staff who may feel totally overwhelmed with the day-to-day functionality of their current role. Newer computer systems make this even harder by creating "task" lists as part of the patient routines.

The management team plays a critical role in communicating to the staff all the information related to the Lean initiative. The importance of communication cannot be overemphasized. We have a saying: "When they are tired of hearing the message about the Lean initiative, they are probably just beginning to get it." Multiple means of communication should be used, such as meetings, communication boards, newsletters, Intranet, e-mails, etc.

It is important to communicate with your staff so they understand what it is you are trying to improve and why it is important to the organization and patient. The line level staff should not see this as a new project or initiative, but as part of an ongoing effort to improve and nurture the new Lean environment.

In a healthcare environment, most line level staff members are very caring and patient-centric individuals and it is important that they view their role as improving patient care. They need to understand that better care is not just about doing that particular function that day, but looking at the whole process outside their standard scope. They need to look at things from a multi-disciplinary perspective, which is a major cultural shift. How would you want your family to be treated?

If Lean is viewed simply as a new project, it will not be very effective. It is important that leaders are seen on the floors helping to create this cultural change, but also that the change really must be a "bottom-up" approach in terms of the staff looking for improvement opportunities and sharing this with their leadership.

Most staff view Lean as an additional task to their job. In the beginning, this is true. Time is spent learning and implementing Lean tools, but day-to-day work still has to be completed. But over time, the transformation should occur and Lean becomes "how we do our jobs." This sounds easy, but it's not. If you are a manager or supervisor going through the initial Lean system implementation and culture change, it is very difficult.

The challenges that a nursing manager will have to face include following standard work, auditing standard work, holding staff accountable, and maintaining discipline. Some staff will embrace the changes while others will fight them. Nursing managers will encounter ongoing negativity and resistance to change from that portion of the staff fighting the change. Be prepared, as some staff may try to sabotage the change; some may even call the Joint Commission on Accreditation of Healthcare Organizations (JCAHO) and state agencies, while others will go covert and fight you behind your back. It is not unusual to have to remove those who are never going to buy or for others to request ask to be moved.

In the book, *Baptist Healthcare Journey to Excellence*, CEO Al Stubblefield gives the following example:

In October 1995, I walked into our board meeting and promised that we would raise our patient satisfaction scores from the eighteenth percentile in patient satisfaction to the seventy-fifth percentile in 9 months. This was a radical but (I hoped!) achievable goal, and I believed that creating some quick wins was crucial to our success. When I walked out of the room after making that announcement, one of my senior officers took me aside and said, 'Do you realize what you just did in there? You set us up for failure!' Part of my reason for sharing this is that 9 months later, when we had not only reached the seventy-fifth percentile but surpassed it, that officer was no longer with the organization. He and a

handful of others who were unwilling to embrace our new culture had to be replaced.[*]

So, why all the negativity? Implementing Lean is very unsettling to those who are comfortable in their jobs. Anyone who has gone through change will admit that change can be very difficult. Despite all the talk about current problems, people tend to be generally happy with their jobs, and with the *status quo*. They may frequently complain about certain things or conditions, but deep down they either really like things the way they are or they are good at managing the informal workarounds developed over the years. This brings us back to the change equation,[†]

$$C \times V \times N \times S > R_{change},$$

Do people really have the *C*... a compelling need to change? If not, they simply will not change. The senior leadership and management team must create the "burning platform to create the compelling need to change for their employees."

As a leader, you can't always be everyone's friend and be a great supervisor. Someone has to do the scheduling, discipline, documentation, etc.

You must remember that each person may be impacted differently and the answer to what is in it for them will change based on their perspective. For example let's say the Lean initiative reduces throughput in the Operating Room and we now get done in 9 hrs what used to take 10 hrs. The surgeon will be happy as their day will end earlier. But the staff will see it in different ways. Some will see this as a positive, a chance to leave on time, while others will see this as negative because they lose an hour of overtime which impacts their income. It is important to understand the changes from their point of view and work with them to frame these changes in a positive light.

IDENTIFY AND PROVIDE RESOURCES

The manager or supervisor of the area may be asked to identify individuals to participate directly with the Lean consultant on the process excellence "core team." This is the group who become the subject matter experts (SMEs) for the team and will be driving the activities of the Lean initiative. The team members selected should be the informal leaders of the staff to help facilitate input from co-workers and help to communicate the changes that will need to be implemented. Many times, we find that managers or supervisors select staff to engage in Lean initiatives because they are available, expendable, or maybe on light duty. A manager who has not been exposed to Lean may not realize that selecting key employees who are viable as future leaders can be advantageous.

---

[*] Al Stubblefield, *The Baptist Health Care Journey to Excellence: Creating a Culture that Wows* (Hoboken, NJ: John Wiley) 2005.

[†] This equation was modified from the $D \times F \times N > Rc$ from Gleicher, Beckhard, and Harris.

Lesson Learned: *Ultimately, the team is only as good as its members. If the best people are selected for the team, the best results will be achieved.*

Many times, managers and supervisors view having to "give up" staff to be on teams as an imposition, as they may not be given additional budgetary dollars to backfill staff. Others may feel burdened if they take on the workload of their co-workers who are given what may be perceived as a work hiatus to be on the Lean team. These issues are all challenging but the quicker we fix our processes, the easier our jobs will become.

It is important that the managers and supervisors communicate to co-workers why they selected who they selected along with the timeline. Being a Lean team member can be challenging. It is not uncommon for staff on the initial team to be ostracized by their peers. It is the role of the managers and supervisors to provide support to the team members throughout the initiative and work to communicate effectively and provide a positive work environment. The management team needs to provide continuous process improvement activities, driving quick wins, Kaizen, and other area Lean improvements once the initial Lean initiative has been implemented.

TIME MANAGEMENT AND THE "FIRES"

As part of the management team, you may personally experience or have to deal with an employee who pushes back before, during, or after the Lean initiative in response to the changes being made. The normal response from the nurse to our requests for changing the process is "we don't have time to do this!" But why don't they have the time? Normally, it is because they are too busy doing their normal job or just fighting the everyday normal "fires." Why do they have to fight fires every day? Where do the fires come from? The fires or inefficiencies are everywhere.

Most people have a love/hate relationship with these "fires." Staff say they hate to fight them and will complain about firefighting, but yet, deep inside, they get great satisfaction from conquering and extinguishing (at least for the time being) these fires. In addition, most staff are rewarded or recognized for saving the day for coming through with the impossible. Over time, this can be very wearing. Firefighting is an inherent skill set in healthcare workers. Most staff, managers, and supervisors are all very good at fighting and working around the internal, formal systems.

There is a saying: "Today's problems come from yesterday's solutions."[*] For example, the boss decides he or she knows how to fix a particular problem and tells the employee to implement the fix. Meanwhile, a patient complains, an auditor shows up and finds the nurses aren't following a procedure; someone calls in sick or has to leave early. Then, the directors want a report or analysis on a patient service issue, and on top of this, reports are due tomorrow, and you're late for a meeting. So where do all these fires come from? They come from behavior and variation inherent in the organization's or clinical area's current culture and processes… in essence, the system! Firefighting is a sign of a reactive culture.

Lesson Learned: *Firefighting doesn't solve problems; only root cause analysis solves problems. As long as we firefight, we may extinguish the fire, but it is guaranteed to come back. With Lean, we replace firefighting skills with Lean management system skills.*

So think of the "fires" as problems with the processes, problems with time management, or problems with behaviors of people, ultimately problems with our "systems." These problems cannot all be solved by writing people up or blaming individuals. These are systemic problems and need systemic solutions. Managers and supervisors need to gain a solid understanding of Lean concepts, principles, and tools so that when changes are made in Lean initiatives and staff pose questions and concerns, they can address them with confidence.

Lesson Learned: *To implement Lean, we need to change the systems. Fires eventually go away and managing becomes easier. Blaming people interferes with exposing the inherent problems in the system. Also remember, excess materials, wait times, and idle times are all signs of a problem in the system.*

STANDARD WORK AND HEALTHCARE

One of the critical components of a Lean initiative is developing standard work for processes that are routinely performed, to eliminate errors, provide role and task clarity, and decrease variation within an activity, task, or process. It is not uncommon when rolling out standard work to hear, "Oh, you want us to be robots." We confront the perceptions of standard work directly. All employees from the executive level to the frontline staff must understand that the goal of standard work is not to make employees robots, but to improve the quality of our work and allow for the implementation of continuous improvement.

Nursing schools train us to be critical thinkers and the U.S. culture is very individualistic.[†] Therefore, standard work meets resistance in the United States, no matter what the setting. Yet, when we do not standardize, everyone does the job differently and quality suffers. We also lose our chance to improve the process. Let's say we have a process with steps one, two, three and four; we all do the steps in a different order and we find a way to eliminate step two. What will happen when we tell everyone to eliminate their second step? Everyone will eliminate a different step. Let's say we have a laboratory specimen in the process and we leave to go to lunch. How can someone pick up where we have left off if everyone does it differently? The person taking over will have to spend time assessing what's been done in order to move forward. What is the chance that a step could be missed?

A new laboratory technician started in a clinic. The standard work was to draw blood and immediately label

[*] Peter M Senge, *The Fifth Discipline*, Doubleday, 2006, p. 57.

[†] Liker, *Toyota Culture* (McGraw Hill) 2008; Mann, *Creating a Lean Culture* (Productivity Press) 2005.

the specimen with the patient's name. Instead of following the standard work, the technician put the blood tubes in his pocket (batching) and called in the next patient. Over the course of just 1 week, he mixed up patients' blood samples three times. We all know how dangerous this is! The technician refused to follow standard work and was replaced.

Lesson Learned: *When hiring people, it is important, once Lean is in place, to communicate our new Lean expectations during the interview process that we expect all employees to follow standard work and that everyone is expected to contribute improvement ideas daily.*

We must spend time convincing healthcare workers they can still "critically think" while doing standard work. Clinical judgment and critical thinking will always be part of healthcare. This issue is synonymous with convincing physicians that standard orders are not cookbook medicine. We may want our physicians to use checklists, but we need their expertise for the unplanned or unusual. The movement toward evidence-based medical care is aiding in the adoption of standard order sets. We still need physicians to deal with the undefined, the exceptions, and the large part of medicine that is still "art."

Remember, standard work has been readily practiced in healthcare; physicians are taught and have always applied standard work in how they perform and document history and physical examinations. In addition, subjective, objective, assessment, and plan (SOAP) notes, situation, background, assessment, recommendation (SBAR), universal protocols, documenting times of patient orders and blood transfusion processes are also examples of standard work practices that have been readily adopted. Proper standard work methods help ensure quality and protect us legally. When encountering resistance to standard work, it is helpful to provide examples of how standard work has been applied in healthcare to improve quality, safety, and communication. The computerized physician order entry (CPOE) is helping to create standard work and mistake-proofing medication ordering and drug interactions.

Once developed and implemented, it is important to audit standard work. This is the supervisor's and manager's job. The frequency is negotiable, but auditing standard work is important for several reasons:

1. It is important to maintain quality and control over the process. Note: one can only sustain the quality if it is built into the standard work.
2. Standard work is key to sustaining and maintaining a disciplined Lean environment.
3. The auditor should not only be reviewing to make sure the person is following the standard work, but also constantly looking for improvements or asking employees for ideas to change the process in order to make the person's job easier.
4. We need to make sure we are adhering to any new changes to the standard work.

At Hospital X, we implemented standard work in their pretesting area. The charge nurse over the area stated she stopped auditing the standard work. When asked why, she said it didn't matter to her in what order people did things as long as they did them, and she saw no point to the audit. She also said she was told that since everyone was hitting their cycle times (and performance metrics), she no longer needed to do the audits. Consider what your response would be as her manager?

Our response: She was asked if she considered patient safety important. She was then reminded of all the problems that had been encountered with quality prior to implementing standard work. It was explained that auditing should not be looked on as another task added to her workload, but as an opportunity to ensure the quality and safety of the patient as well as a mechanism to look for additional improvements. When the audit is done, the results should be immediately fed back to the individual being audited. If problems are found, we need to get the staff together and identify root cause and brainstorm countermeasures and implement solutions. Auditing can be performed by any individual, assuming they are trained in the process of how to do the audit and document the results. By fixing the problems so they don't come back, it makes our jobs easier as charge nurses or managers. If we can find a way to mistake proof the problems, then the need to audit diminishes.

When supervising and auditing, we need to make sure that the standard work steps are being followed in the proper order in the right amount of time.

Auditing standard work is like balancing your checkbook. You never know if the bank is going to make a mistake.[*]

Just because people are meeting or exceeding the cycle times or metrics doesn't mean they are necessarily following the standard work. The only way one can know for sure in this environment is to conduct the audit. There will always be some variation, especially when the tasks involve interviewing patients, as each may require a different level of interaction. When we find huge variations in time, it normally means people are not following the standard work. It should be noted that we are using the term standard work in some healthcare areas somewhat loosely when compared to manufacturing. Some areas in healthcare are really using work standards vs. standard work owing to the lack of repeatability and variation inherent in patients; however, this should not be used as an excuse not to continue the pursuit of true standard work by using Six Sigma tools to reduce variation.

Lesson Learned: *We can eliminate audits only when we eliminate the need for the audit. Auditing is not necessarily Lean but a counter measure. The goal should be to create visual controls with real time feedback so we can fix the problems as they occur. When the process is under control and feedback mechanisms installed we should no longer need the audit.*

---

[*] Willie Grace, Manager, Presbyterian Hospital, Albuquerque, NM.

IMPLEMENTATION

Once the pilots are complete and the new Lean process is initiated in an area, enough time must be given for the implementation to work. When the new process is fully implemented by the process owner and the team, it is normally 80%–90% "complete." During the early phases, we sometimes end up maintaining two separate systems: the old way of doing it in parallel with the new way of doing it. This is a confusing and difficult time during implementation. It is basically organized chaos; however, once the area is converted to Lean, the rewards will come. Managing the Lean way is easier and more fun than the old way; however, the way we manage in Lean must change from the old way we manage.

Changes or adjustments to the new Lean process need to be based on fact, not on what people think. For some reason, when implementing changes to a process or creating a new process, some of the staff will immediately want to change the new process without giving it a chance to work or getting sufficient data to show a problem exists. If we allow this to happen, we end up making changes with no data, based on gut feel or opinion. In many cases, the changes they want to make, oddly enough, will tend to resemble the old process. What should we do in this case? If we give in to the changes, we will go back to the way it was before. Is that an option? How was the process before? Inevitably, we will have all the same problems we had before!

Lesson Learned: *As the manager or charge nurse, it is important that the staff is guided and coached to make the changes based on data, facts, and sound Lean principles and to resist resorting to shortcutting the process and making process changes "on the fly."*

The new process that has just been implemented is very fragile and needs to be given the support, nurturing, and time to stabilize as it moves into the "control" or check results and sustain phases. Now is the time to get ideas from the staff and do ongoing Kaizen or Kaizen events to continue to drive improvement.

PROBLEMS WITH BEHAVIORS

There is a common phrase that one often hears when discussing behaviors: "You get what you expect." This saying reigns true throughout many of life's situations, including the workplace. Ultimately, as a manager or supervisor, one gets the behaviors the organization or culture rewards. These behaviors can be "desired" or "undesired."

Homework: *Identify the most desired and least desired behaviors in the organization, area, or process. If desired, identify how those behaviors are being rewarded and keep those systems in place. Identify any rewards behind the undesired behaviors and develop plans to eliminate them. Replace them with preferred behaviors and change the reward system to encourage the new desired behaviors.*

A book called *Bringing Out the Best in People* by Aubrey Daniels,[*] can help with this homework assignment. In this book, Mr. Daniels discusses "fact-based" performance measures and the necessary role of consequences, both positive and negative. This is a gross simplification of the book, but we have found this to be extremely useful in dealing with organizations.

UNDERSTANDING EMPLOYEE SATISFACTION

Homework: *List on a piece of paper ten things that would make one satisfied as an employee, then as a manager, then as the CEO. Do you see any common items in these lists?*

No matter what our role is in the organization, most of us want to understand what is expected of us and be empowered to achieve it. In order to be successful, we must be provided with clear direction, organizational priorities, and the ability to create processes to do our jobs safely and efficiently. We need to be able to obtain the right tools and supplies to do our jobs and leave feeling like we accomplished something and we are part of a winning team. This is impossible to achieve if processes, areas, or people are out of control and not standardized.

The combination of Lean and change management tools can help make us successful. Lean initiatives take place on the frontline, requiring managers, supervisors, and frontline staff to engage together to develop a problem-solving culture. In order to make the appropriate improvements, staff must learn to identify waste and be able to make suggestions and/ or take action to eliminate waste and defects.

An additional benefit of a Lean culture and Lean environment is the employee satisfaction and commitment that comes with it. Employees like being involved in improving the organization, and ultimately, better patient care and outcomes. This employee satisfaction can translate to less nursing turnover, as well as a healthier and more productive work environment. Increasing cultural change in this direction can increase efficiency, which increases satisfaction, thereby creating a positive directional change that may save jobs in the future. There can be significant savings in employee retention.

MANAGEMENT AND SUPERVISOR PERFORMANCE

One of our Lean principles is not to be idle. We call idle time "pure waste." A good manager or supervisor can keep several balls afloat at once. For many, this is a learned behavior. One of our Lean goals as managers is to spend at least 50% of our time on continuous improvement and 50% running the business.[†]

Continuing with our firefighting analogy, firefighters don't have any time left at the end of the day for continuous improvement and eventually "burn out." The only way we can survive and improve is to get our fires under control

---

[*] Aubrey Daniels, *Bringing Out the Best in People* (New York: McGraw-Hill) 1994.
[†] Liker, *Toyota Culture* (McGraw Hill) 2008

and start putting them out permanently so the embers can't restart. Only then will there be time left to start improving our processes. The more we improve, the more we contain and eventually extinguish the fires. Managers may resist this and initially find it hard to believe, but putting out these fires permanently will ultimately make their job easier.

Imagine if everyone had what they needed when they needed it, if everyone did things the same way and staff was empowered to identify waste and come up with ways to eliminate it. How much easier would it be to manage the area?

The problem we encounter here is outright fear. Some managers are concerned if they will be needed anymore. In the past, they have held key information about the process "close to the vest" to make it harder for anyone to replace them. Now they are being asked to share this information.

Their processes are videotaped and we expose their "dirty laundry" for everyone to see! Is it any wonder some resistance builds up! This is why it is so important to manage the "people" piece and change management piece of Lean, and teach managers to embrace the change as an opportunity.

But in the end, who would you rather hold on to? Would you rather promote the employee who is the micro-manager, constant firefighter, and hero of the day? Or would you rather promote the employee who admits he/she is no longer needed in that role and worked themselves out of a job by following the Lean principles? If you are the employee, do you want to do the same boring job forever or continue to grow, develop, rotate positions, increase your skill sets, and become more marketable?

Delegation

Lean initiatives require a level of comfort with delegation. Engaging frontline staff in problem solving and supporting them in the initiatives requires that managers must be able to empower and delegate activities they may not have in the past for a variety of reasons. Managers or supervisors may choose not to delegate because they do not think anyone else is as qualified to do the task, or the right person wasn't hired and didn't have the right job description or appropriate role clarity. Some managers just like to do everything themselves. There is a comfort level knowing every detail and making every decision, in "micro-managing," as it were.

The manager may not be proficient in coaching or mentoring. Part of the job of a leader is to develop those who work for us. How do we overcome delegation challenges? It is done through empowerment. Managers need to have confidence that their employees have the ability and skills to perform tasks independently. Confidence is achieved through the development of the staff. To do this, we use a tool called the empowerment or freedom scale.[*] The scale is composed of the following five levels:

1. Told what to do
2. Ask what to do
3. Recommend, then take action

4. Take action, notify at once
5. Take action, notify periodically

These levels represent the comfort levels between a manager/supervisor and direct reports or team. They can be utilized for individual tasks, job descriptions, and team projects, etc., Let's discuss each of these levels.

Level 1

An example of Level 1 begins on the first day of work or when the staff member is presented with a new task. The staff member is so new that they may not even know where the bathroom is yet. At which level will he/she be working? The Level 1 employee does specifically what they are told, normally nothing more or less. In this mode, one may find the employee standing around with nothing to do because he/she is done. If asked why they did not tell someone they were idle, they will respond, "I wasn't told to do that!" In some cases, this phase and Level 2 are good opportunities to ask the employee if they see any waste or "stupid" things we seem to be doing that could be improved.

Level 2

As employees progress at the task or job, and managers gain a better understanding, their comfort level with the employee or team increases. Additionally the employee in turn feels more comfortable in the task. The managers will then tell the employee to start asking what to do next.

Level 3

At this level, managers are much more comfortable with the employee and the employee is much more confident and competent with the task. Now the employee is told to recommend what they think should be done next. If they present a problem, they should be asked to think about what the answer might be prior to giving them the answer. The problem and solutions are discussed and decisions are made jointly on a course of action. This forces the employee to start to *think* on their own and is the first step to moving the employee out of the "micro-managing" mode. This will also increase the morale of the employee because they are now contributing to the organization with their ideas and recommendations.

During a visit to a manager's office, the conversation kept getting interrupted by phone calls. During each phone call, he listened to the problem and gave the caller the answer. When this was brought to his attention, he was totally unaware of what he was doing. He had always done it this way.

Lesson Learned: *This is a sure sign of a micro-manager. Every decision has to go through them! We all get a certain satisfaction of being the boss, the person who does it best and can make all the decisions. But every decision we make is stifling our employees and endangering the organization. Why? Because we are not developing our people and the "bench strength" needed for the succession plan. In some organizations, we have forced managers to tie their hands together for a day in order to force them to delegate. At the end of the day, they can't believe how hard it was and how their old behaviors were ingrained.*

---

[*] Coopers and Lybrand. Allied Signal TQ Training Course - 1994.

Every employee in a Lean environment should be moved to Level 3 as quickly as possible. This requires ongoing training and mentoring to be successful. Managers who have trouble with this level stick out once you know the "tell" signs. When an employee comes to a manager with a problem and does not come prepared with a *solution* or *recommendation* and the manager simply answers the question or provides the solution, employees are forced to stay at Level 2. Most of the time, this is done unconsciously. But when the answer to the question or the solution is provided to the employee, what will happen the next time they encounter a problem? Managers will be asked for the answer. Some employees enjoy this, as it keeps them from ever taking any accountability or responsibility for their actions. They actually see this as job security because they can never make (or learn from) a bad decision.

As a manager, you find yourself not being able to get everything done because you are constantly answering everyone's question or solving problems. The manager becomes the fire chief and is awarded the firefighter's hat. While there is a certain joy or satisfaction some of us may experience with this, it is not supportive to the growth of employees. We are denying them their ability to develop and prosper. We are rewarding them for not thinking and are encouraging a non-learning organization. In some cases, these managers see this as job security because there is, typically no one to replace them. On the other hand, they may have difficulty moving up in the organization because there is no one to take their place.

Homework: *The next time an employee comes to you with a problem or question, the most important rule is to ask them, "What do you think we should do? What recommendations do you have for me?" Force them to think! And move them to empowerment Level 3.*

Level 4

At this level, managers are very comfortable with the employee, and the employee or team is totally competent with the task(s). Employees are told, "From this point on, I am going to trust you to take the appropriate action and implement the correct solution to solve the problem or complete the particular job or task at hand." The manager, however, also tells the employee or staff to notify them immediately of the actions taken. This is just in case they missed a step or did not totally think things through, to mitigate risk. Employees are trusted, but managers may want to make sure things were done properly or provide "damage control" if necessary. Managers must make sure that employees at this level are on a professional growth plan to move up within the organization, so employees can develop to their full potential.

Level 5

At this level, the manager and the employee are very comfortable with each other and the process; the employee is competent and can be trusted implicitly. Employees are told to make whatever decisions are necessary and report back via a weekly, monthly, or quarterly report.

LESSONS LEARNED WITH EMPOWERMENT

- Don't empower too fast. If people are empowered too quickly, you may think they are ready, and they may not have had the time needed.
- Make sure the empowerment levels are clear. We have seen many teams created to solve problems. The teams meet, develop ideas, and then implement them. Ideas may be implemented without working through the ramifications on another department. Level clarity is critical so expectations of managers and staff are understood. This is important at the individual and team level.
- A person or team can have different levels of empowerment for different tasks. For example, tasks at which an individual has excelled might be at Level 5. The manager is totally comfortable with the individual's level of performance at a given task. On a new task, the same individual is at Level 3 until proficiency is attained. Different problems also may require different levels of empowerment. A high risk or high expense problem may push the level back.
- One must have the authority and resources to operate at the level assigned. Individuals or teams need to perform the functions or tasks to the extent required in order to be at the level assigned. This is a two-way scale for both the manager and the employee.
- Levels of empowerment can be a great tool for personnel evaluations. The employee identifies what tasks are associated with their job and creates a list. Each rates the levels of empowerment they feel the employee is at for each of their key tasks or job overall. Where there are discrepancies, a good framework for ongoing discussion and employee development is provided.

THE JOURNEY OF A LEAN SENSEI WITH A STAR WARS® ANALOGY

At some point, Lean Thinking clicks, the light bulb goes on, and the young Lean Padawan starts to "Truly see." They begin to see the levels of waste and see how the Lean tools and principles really work to reduce the waste. They may not totally believe it will work yet, but they are on their way down the right path.

Anyone who has experienced this Lean journey can probably think back to some experience, training, exercise, video, seminar, or conversation that opened their eyes. Once their eyes are opened, they continue down the path utilizing the tools, until they get enough training and experience to really believe it works.

The analogy of "The Force" in Star Wars* *is not too far-fetched. It can take from several months to several years for people to get "it" and really believe that Lean principles and*

---

* *Star Wars.*

philosophies work. The Star Wars sayings fit well with Lean: "Try do not, There is no try, only do, Jedi Knight you think you are? You must unlearn what you have learned, Mind what you have learned, save you it can, Feel the force; beware of the dark (batch) side."

We have found all these phrases apply to those going down the Lean sensei path. *There is no try.* When we implement Lean, we need to mistake proof the implementation so that there is no turning back. To go back to the way it was before …*leads to the dark side it will!*

Many times, especially if we have higher levels of education, *we must unlearn some of what we have learned.* I had to unlearn my entire cost accounting for operations class. Traditional cost accounting gets in the way of Lean. Almost all of us are born with the "batch is better" paradigm. This is the "dark side" to Lean and is always fighting us.

Jedi Knight you think you are? For the next phase of Lean, the young Padawan must choose the Darth Vader or the Yoda path. The Darth Vader path consists of "we know it all now, we are confident we are right, we no longer need a sensei!" They think they are Jedi Knights way before they are even close. Toyota didn't leave its protégés with NUMMI, the California joint venture between GM and Toyota, alone for several years.[*] Yet, at most companies, they get one Lean project under their belt and management thinks they are done and can go it alone. After 6–9 months they want to change the training and implementation processes, cut the implementation times in half, shortcut the Lean processes and then wonder why they have trouble sustaining it.

---

[*] Jeffrey Liker, *Toyota Culture* (New York: McGraw Hill) 2005.

ON-LINE LEAN TRAINING

There is never a good time for training. You must make the time for training, however don't think you can do all the training on-line.

At Hospital X, we were told to put all Lean training on the back burner. There was no time or money for training. We highly recommended against this approach but were told to implement anyway. So we trained the persons on our team as we went, which worked fine. When rolling out to the rest of the area we, of course, met a lot of resistance as people did not realize or understand what we were trying to accomplish. The training-on-line program they were developing was still not completed after a year. We told them on-line training will allow people to learn the terminology, but one cannot learn everything about Lean through on-line training. Eventually they agreed with us and we taught their management the Lean training course.

Lesson Learned: *It is a powerful tool when the leadership team can conduct the Lean training course with an expectation for their staff to be able to train as well. Lean training was accomplished for each employee within the area, which allowed the implementations to proceed much more quickly and more smoothly with great buy-in and suggestions from the staff.*

Lesson Learned: *The Lean journey is a constant journey of learning. Only by doing do we learn and, by sometimes failing, truly learn. Implementing Lean can save you, your job, and the organization by improving profitability through reducing waste and variation in healthcare processes. "Mind what you have learned" may the force be with you on your Lean journey!*

13 Finance, Marketing, and Our Hospitals

EXECUTIVE SUMMARY

Hospitals tend to focus on cost in relation to either FTEs or supplies but often do not look at the real costs, nor do they see the hidden costs of running a hospital. Often financiers are in charge of budgeting and only look at the cost side of the equation. They often do not consider:

1. Hidden costs
2. Traditional accounting and Lean
3. Inaccurate or incomplete data

Hidden costs can significantly contribute to financial performance. More money is lost in hospitals from things that are not tracked than from things that are tracked. Hospitals track FTEs, supplies, but do not always track inventory dollars, inventory turns, excess and obsolete inventory, supplies opened but not used, restocking supply labor, retention/training costs, staff impact by IT issues, centralized printers, centralized departments, poor area designs/layouts, time spent on workarounds, or time spent searching for equipment and supplies.

Other hidden costs can include:

- Cost of management meetings and firefighting
- Cost of holding a surgery or procedural room waiting for the anesthesiologist or surgeon to arrive
- Cost of uneaten and consequently discarded meals
- Cost of idle time and unnecessary searching by staff and physicians
- Cost of people who leave the ED without being seen
- Cost of a surgery or procedural cancellation or delay
- Cost of rework when things are not done right the first time
- Cost of medical errors and hospital-acquired infections
- Cost of layoffs—fractional labor

It is important to change the focus from cutting FTEs to a process improvement culture.

There are often complaints of lack of space in hospitals. It is often more the way the space and the processes are managed. Cutting FTEs is often a short-sighted approach and is a practice of "lazy" management.

Invoking budgetary reductions without a plan to identify and eliminate forms of waste and identify and understand hidden costs can impact quality, service and patient safety.

Expected Lean results are:

- A 20–80% increase in productivity
- A 75–99% throughput time reductions

CMS continues to work on a "Roadmap for Implementing Value Driven Healthcare in the Traditional Medicare Fee-for-Service Program" with the VISION FOR AMERICA: Patient-centered, high-quality care delivered, and will play a role in the years to come.

The budgeting process can go on for up to 6 months or more at some hospitals, and organizations spend a tremendous amount of hidden, non-tracked costs preparing and negotiating the budget.

In many healthcare facilities we have found problems with "charge capture." The nurse may feel the patient is the only important issue and may not understand why it is necessary to capture all their charges.

Inventory inaccuracy and poor inventory control are discussed in some detail, with the cost of poor inventory management being significant. Capital equipment with poor processes and physical layouts leads to an increasing need for expensive capital equipment. Standardization of equipment and materials has huge opportunity in cost savings.

Information Systems (IS) costs and hidden IS costs are reviewed. Organizations need to recognize the impact to computer systems within the organization. Computer systems can negatively impact an organization through poor or slow performance or if they do not integrate or "talk to each other," thus breeding inefficiency; additionally, some systems are expensive to maintain.

There is a discussion about point of use (POU) supplies and the critical role materials management, inventory control and supply planning plays in a hospital setting. The inaccuracy of inventory counts in a hospital is an unfortunate standard, and can be very costly. Many hospitals focus on centralization of supplies and storage, which is just another form of batching.

Staffing: Census managing is the practice of scheduling nurses for a full shift and then, if the census changes, staff are sent home early without pay or are forced to use vacation time in order to receive full-time salary. This is a poor practice, is reactive scheduling, and can lead to moral challenges as staff that need their full-time salaries may be unable to meet their monthly payments. In the hospital, we are told to focus on FTEs, but it is important to focus on what type of FTEs and the skill-sets required.

Contribution margins and earned value analysis (EVA) are important financial metrics, as are return on capital and return on net assets. It is important to focus on growth and revenue management, not always on cost-cutting and FTE-cutting. The concept of critical mass or the certain minimum number of people to run an ER/OR is a critical concept.

Lean accounting is different in that we put standards (i.e., standard work) in place based on data-based targets utilizing real-time metrics. The goal is to continually reduce the standard time with no negative impact to quality, safety or patient satisfaction. There is no longer a need for variance reporting if Lean is implemented properly, since this is addressed in standardized work and visual controls. Lean accounting uses no traditional cost accounting standards at all. With Lean accounting, we collect the costs by value stream. We do not differentiate if it is direct, indirect or overhead. Cost-accounting personnel are moved back into the line organization to work on process improvements and support the value stream (or Service Line) managers with information and analysis.

KEY LEARNINGS

- Understanding the importance and value of locating hidden costs in the healthcare system.
- Looking beyond FTEs and evaluating a process and profitability.
- Understanding the different type of accounting we must have in a Lean environment.

Costs do not exist to be calculated. Costs exist to be reduced.

—Taiichi Ohno

We have never considered any costs as fixed. Therefore, we reduce the price to a point we where we believe more sales will result. Then we go ahead and try to make the price. We do not bother about the costs. The new price forces the costs down.

—Henry Ford[*]

The CEO of a company, Hospital and Clinic Chain, Inc. (HCC), was sitting at his desk after his 9:00 a.m. arrival thinking how good life was. He was #1 in a growing market; his surgeons had some complaints, but overall they were generally satisfied. His hospital metrics were about average compared to other hospitals in the benchmark database, most of the quality measures were being met, and his costs were under control because his finance people really ran and controlled the hospital. In fact, they had just gotten through the budget and cut 10% of their full-time equivalents (FTEs) over the past year. The surgery marketing forecast looked good (10%–15% growth); however, the emergency department (ED) had 4- to 6-hrs waits and patients were required to come in 3–5 hrs early for surgery. Fifteen percent of their patients left the ED without seeing the doctor, but it had been this way for years. In fact, the diversion rate only increased by 1% last year. They had a new feedback and suggestion system that they felt was working very well, and everyone in the organization was telling the CEO exactly what he wanted

to hear. The board would be happy at the meeting tonight and life would be good.

A couple of months went by when the CEO heard that a nearby but smaller hospital was working on initiating a Lean program based on the Toyota Production System. The CEO was convinced making cars had nothing to do with how hospitals run. The CEO sat back and thought that program would soon become a flavor of the month. He thought to himself, "We are not manufacturers; we are clinicians and working on cars is different from working on people."

As the busy season progressed, HCC lost a large surgeon group to the nearby hospital, but this was not a big surprise, as he knew they were targeting that Service Line, and there was no cause for alarm. By summer, he heard the other hospital had dropped its ED waiting times to less than 1 hr on average, with patients seeing doctors in 30 min or less. And their LWBS (left without being seen) was less than 2%.

As budgeting season approached, finance told the CEO that they would have to cut another 10% of FTEs. The CEO asked why. Finance said marketing did not hit its forecast in surgeries, and ED volume was decreasing. The CEO responded, "But we are in a growth market." Finance said, "Yes, but that nearby hospital is taking our surgeons and our market share, so, we have to cut FTEs to make the budget." The CEO countered, "But if we continue to cut FTEs, our service levels will drop." The finance officers said, "No, because our volumes are decreasing, service levels will remain the same." So they cut 10% more FTEs.

Over the next year, the CEO found they were losing more of their top surgeons to the nearby hospital. Surgery volumes decreased and the hospital started losing money. Finance told the CEO that they needed to cut even more staff since they were losing money. The CEO asked his surgeons why they were leaving. The surgeons said that they could get more cases done in the same amount of time at the nearby hospital. The CEO thought to himself," I wonder what our surgery turnaround times are?" but dismissed the thought and put his PowerPoint® together for tonight's board meeting. After what the CEO thought was truly a great PowerPoint® presentation, the board asked him to resign.[†]

INTRODUCTION

The Centers for Medicare and Medicaid Services cites, "Expenditures in the United States on health care surpassed $2.2 trillion in 2007, more than three times the $714 billion spent in 1990, and over eight times the $253 billion spent in 1980. Stemming this growth has become a major policy priority, as the government, employers, and consumers increasingly struggle to keep up with health care costs."[‡] As healthcare costs continue to rise, placing a greater burden on

---

[*] Charles Allen, *My Life and My Work Henry Ford* (Lippincoft) 1919, p. 166.

[†] Story inspired by the book Lean Transformation, Henders, Larco, The Oakley Press, 1999.

[‡] Centers for Medicare and Medicaid Services, Office of the Actuary, National Health Statistics Group, "2007 National Health Care Expenditures Data," March 2009.

the country, it will become even more important to understand the contributing factors of the rising costs (hidden wastes yielding hidden costs) and how to eliminate them in order to restrain the current trajectory of healthcare spending. Simply cutting cost will not be effective. It will be all about doing more with less… Lean.

This chapter is divided up into three parts. The first part deals with Lean savings, the second part deals with hidden costs, and the last is about the impact traditional finance and Lean solutions have on an organization. We included many stories of the pitfalls of traditional accounting on the healthcare organization in the hopes it may be useful to those reading the book. We also include lessons learned that show the need for a new way of thinking and the need for new systems. The third part is composed of Lean and Lean accounting solutions, which are a different way of thinking and reporting financials.*

PAYING THE PRICE—UNDERSTANDING WHAT IT COSTS TO RUN YOUR BUSINESS

We contend that more money is lost in hospitals from things that are not tracked than from things that are tracked. What do we track? FTEs and supplies, but we don't always track inventory dollars, inventory turns, excess and obsolete inventory, supplies opened but not used, restocking supply labor, retention/training costs, staff impact by IT issues, centralized printers, centralized departments, poor area designs/layouts, time spent on workarounds, or time searching for equipment and supplies. All these play a role in productivity as well as costs to operations and capital.

During a project at Hospital X, we followed a nurse for 25 min looking for a positioning item the physician needed in the operating room (OR). She finally found it and took it from another room. What do you think the next nurse will have to do when she finds the item that she needs is now missing? How much time do we lose in surgery when the patient is not brought back until the room setup is completed? What is your cost per minute or second of surgery? Again, none of these costs are normally tracked. If one doesn't fully understand and track the costs of doing business, then opportunities to improve may go undetected and are lost.

Occasionally, we are asked to review new layout designs for departments or hospitals. At Hospital X, the architects created several isolated spaces because this is what they thought the department wanted. Eventually, every architect seems to get into the mode of "we can't put it there, so let's put it over here," with no regard to process flow. Supplies are normally centralized, creating lots of walking for the staff. Layouts can double or triple your labor costs. But finance never looks

at layouts from a cost-of-use perspective. There has been a trend with some architectural firms to begin leveraging Lean principles in the design process, but this is not the norm.

"RESULTS-DRIVEN MANAGEMENT"

The CEO and CFO are typically behind results-driven management. Our goal with this chapter is not to "bash" or undermine the accounting or finance profession. The people in these roles are highly skilled and talented. There are rules and laws that must be followed. Yet, the philosophy that changed the role of finance from a reporting body to one of finance driving "results" in the organization is now engrained in our organizations from the teachings of our leading business schools. Over the last several years, we have found that this philosophy can lead to destructive behaviors (consider Enron, sub-prime mortgages and subsequent bank bailouts, General Motors, Bernard L. Madoff Investment Securities, LLC Ponzi scheme, etc.). Our goal here is to highlight the systemic problems inherent in the traditional accounting approach and show some of the pitfalls that exist. We hope the following will provoke thought and will be taken in the spirit of the need for continuous improvement.

HOW WILL YOUR ORGANIZATION DEFINE LEAN SAVINGS?

When an organization is in the early stages of Lean adoption and the cultural transformation has not yet occurred, management finds itself in a position to financially justify the "Lean initiatives." After all, at this stage, Lean is not embedded in the way they do business. The expected results will depend on how Lean is "brought" into the organization. In most cases, we have found that the early expectations are always in the form of "bottom-line" results in the form of FTE reductions.

To illustrate, let's review the expected Lean results we discussed earlier in the book. Each result is qualified in Table 13.1 as to whether one could easily translate the results into hard savings, defined as "bottom-line to budget" FTE savings; soft benefits, which contribute to but may not yield a direct quantifiable "bottom-line" budget reduction; and cost avoidance (a real savings but again is not an operational "bottom-line" reduction; however, it is a capital savings).

Most finance leaders repeatedly ask us how the Lean initiative will impact the bottom-line and what can they remove from the budget at the end of the project. This is due, in part, to the fact that Lean is normally brought in at a time when the organization has a compelling need to change and is most likely in need of bottom-line savings.

One cannot argue that all the savings listed in Table 13.1 are beneficial and will result in clinical, service, and operational process improvements and will ultimately contribute to the financial success of the organization. In our experience, however, most financial leaders especially in the initial Lean implementations only want to know the bottom-line FTE reductions they will receive and when (since this will directly impact this year's budget).

* Brian Maskell and Bruce Baggaley, *Practical Lean Accounting*, Productivity Press, 2004. Brian Maskell and the BMA Team, *Making the Numbers Count*, Productivity Press, 1996. Brian Maskel, *The Lean Business Management System*. Brian H. Maskell, Bruce Baggaley, Nick Katko, David Paino, BMA Press, 2007. These books are available from the BMA website (www.maskell.com), from Amazon.com, and other business book websites.

TABLE 13.1

Expected Results Breakdown

Expected Results	Hard	Soft	Cost Avoidance
20%–80% increases in productivity	√		
50%–90% reductions in patients waiting		√	
Resulting in increased patient satisfaction		√	
75%–99% through put time reductions		√	
Resulting in significant decrease in LOS—days are decreased to hours per patient		√	
20%–50% reductions in space			√
75%–95% reductions in distance traveled		√	
10% or more reduction in process imperfections		√	

Hospital X was considering a large expansion of its food production center, which was part of its nutritional services department. After learning about Lean, they embarked on an initiative to determine if they could streamline processes, eliminate waste, and decrease (avoid) costs during this capital project. A key executive in the organization who had a financial background initiated the Lean program but left the company mid-way through the program. The area management fully supported the endeavor and the Lean initiative continued, ultimately proving that the new expansion was not needed, and the organization saved millions of dollars in capital outlays. In addition, the metric improvements outlined in the beginning of the initiative were met, and several hundred thousand dollars in labor savings were identified (which was significant as this represented several FTEs of savings, as the employees were not highly paid workers).

Near the end of the initiative, the Lean team gathered to present its final results. Several of the executives in attendance had not been on the journey, since the key executive who left suddenly had not briefed his superiors or peers on the Lean initiative's deliverables or progress.

The area management, team members, consultants, and those who had been on the journey clearly understood the progress made. The key deliverable originally assigned to the team was to determine if this sizable expansion and millions of dollars were needed. The team was very excited about presenting the results. The cultural transformation began as area management, who once believed the expansion was needed, were convinced they could do the same amount of work in less space by eliminating waste and streamlining processes.

As the team reported out, many executives nodded in approval of the area management and teams' accomplishments; however, during the report out a new "finance manager" whose primary focus was "FTE/labor savings today" shunned the cost-avoidance results. Since he was so focused on bottom-line results, millions of dollars in cost avoidance for

a new or facility expansion, in his eyes, did not yield hard savings. Not understanding that cost savings was the objective of the initiative and being somewhat short-sighted, he continued to inquire and badger the team and Lean consultants as to why there were not more labor savings. In his words, "Any Lean consultant worth his salt saves 10 times what they are paid in labor savings," leaving the team feeling that the millions the team avoided in construction spending counted for little.

His focus on immediate "labor savings" clouded his ability to see the true benefits of the project. Had the expansion project moved forward as planned, much additional labor would have been needed in the years to come to run the expanded nutritional services area. This is not including the additional "hidden costs" like transportation and excess motion waste we often don't think of when we are only focused on "cutting labor" to drive down costs.

Lessons Learned:

1. *Continually monitor and update new participants and key stakeholders on the progress of the initiative and have action plans to address engagement and "buy-in" to align goals and objectives. Clearly outline the line of sight "wastes" and how they will impact organization of soft and hard dollars, and tangible and intangible benefits that will aid in the Lean cultural transformation.*

2. *Decide up front how Lean savings the type of savings the organization deems valuable and how and by whom they will be calculated. Will cost avoidance even be considered? How will material savings be defined? Make sure these savings assumptions are included in the team charter up front.*

3. *Viewing only FTE savings as bottom-line is a very dangerous and misleading approach to process improvement and Lean. There are many hidden costs that don't show up in traditional finance reports.*

HIDDEN COSTS—THE SIXTH LEVEL OF WASTE

This section is dedicated to the sixth level of waste. This level is the waste that hides behind the obvious wastes and are difficult to see. It doesn't show up in financial reports. Shigeo Shingo was quoted as saying, "*The real problem is when people do not recognize waste when they see it... the most dangerous kind of waste is the waste we do not recognize.*"[*] Better known as hidden costs. Examples of hidden costs are:

- Cost of management meetings and firefighting
- Cost of holding a surgery or procedural room waiting for the anesthesiologist or surgeon to arrive
- Cost of meals not eaten and discarded because the patient is not in the room (meals batched)
- Cost of idle time and unnecessary searching by staff and physicians

---

[*] Shigeo Shingo, *Non Stock Production: The Shingo System for Continuous Improvement* (Productivity Press). 1988.

- Cost of nurse constantly having to follow up on other departments
- Cost of people who leave the ED without being seen by a physician (LWSD) or leave against medical advice (AMA)
- Cost of a surgery or procedural cancellations or delayed surgery cases because the patient wasn't ready, arrived late, wasn't cleared medically, or equipment failure
- Cost of rework (FPY) everywhere
- Cost of medical errors and hospital-acquired infections
- Lack of patient throughput. What does an extra unpaid day of stay cost? On the other side of the equation, what does an open room cost? What does a minute of patient throughput time cost?
- Cost of layoffs—fractional labor
- Cost of 7:30 a.m. OR cases not starting on time
- Cost of census managing

These are just a few examples of hidden costs. We could sight hundreds if not thousands of hidden costs that occur each and every day that contribute to the cost of providing affordable, high-quality healthcare. If seriously pursued, eliminating the hidden wastes can impact the ability to reform healthcare today and in the future. But why are these costs hidden? The answer is because we don't track them and have no system in place to expose them.

Most organizations are accustomed to the day-to-day workarounds and do not view this activity as costly, when, in fact, if many of these wastes were eliminated, the result would be a better product or service with less rework, fewer defects, and higher quality with less associated costs. In most cases, however, when any financial challenges occur, the first cost-cutting measure that most organizations take is in the form of labor or FTE reductions.

The "wastes" that contribute to hidden costs are like leeches sucking the life blood out of the organization. Like leeches, we don't always notice them right away, and they are difficult to remove.

Why don't we track them? Because in many cases we don't have accurate data, the information may be difficulty to quantify, or there are no resources available for manual collection or we just don't consider them that important. What data do we track? Budget and FTEs! Why? Because they are easy to track and visible! Historically, it is what has "always been" tracked and it is acceptable within the industry. So our focus is on what we call "results management" with the results defined by finance. How many finance people have worked as a nurse or technician on the floor? How many finance people have run an ED or surgery department?

Because organizations need revenue and need to meet a budget to remain viable, it is the finance department's responsibility to monitor and report on the organization's financial health. Thus, it seems that finance plays an integral role in running most of our hospitals and corporations around the world, but in many cases, they have little

or no domain knowledge.[*] This is a key ingredient of "Big Company Disease." In the end, we don't fix our processes and we are forced to cut FTEs to meet finance's targets. Who is to blame? The blame can only go to our system, our culture, and our business management programs. If we blame people, we won't solve the problems. Who ultimately creates the culture? The leadership team does, which, in turn, creates our systems. Only the CEO and senior leadership team can change the focus from cutting FTEs to a "Process Improvement Driven Culture." If you fix the processes, the results will come.[†]

Finance plays a pivotal role in most healthcare organizations as they attempt to control costs through trying to improve productivity by forcing labor reductions each year as they go through the budget cycle. Administrators are under constant pressure to cut labor and supply costs each month; we are not discounting there is some merit to managing labor and supplies, but it is not the only way to control costs.

What behaviors does this type of focus drive? In most cases, managers are told they need to reduce labor and expense costs by "x" percent, which requires the elimination of staff and a scrutinizing each month of any budget variance in overtime or supplies. We have found that, when this occurs, managers tend to eliminate or not fill any open or "vacant" positions. Since they have not altered the way they do business, managers must then go through a process where they identify services they can reduce or eliminate, or transfer those services they once performed to another area to achieve the expected results. Although this method can result in "labor reductions" and reaching budget, it does not normally result in a true "improvement" of productivity and can potentially impact the quality and safety of activities and services that should be provided. Normally, these problems go undetected until the "blow up" and it is determined that something fell through the cracks when the position was eliminated.

In Hospital X, the nursing department was asked to decrease overtime on their units. In reviewing the activities, they found that the nurses on the units often accompany critical patients to Pre-Op, and this can take between 2 and 3 hrs of time, waiting for them to go from the floor unit to Pre-Op to surgery. This task/service had been provided by nursing for many years. In the pursuit to meet their budget, they unilaterally determined they would eliminate this service. Surgical services then had to scramble to try to determine how they were going to care for the critical patients waiting for surgery.

Lesson Learned: *Invoking budgetary reductions without a plan to identify and eliminate wastes and identify and understand hidden costs can impact quality, service, and patient safety. It can overburden employees who are now required to perform the same tasks in the same*

[*] Kenneth Hopper and William Hopper, *The Puritan Gift: Reclaiming the American Dream amidst Global Financial Chaos* (New York: I.B. Tauris) 2009.
[†] David Mann, *Creating a Lean Culture* (Productivity Press) 2005.

environment "ridden with wastes" with less staff, or perform fewer services that may impact patient satisfaction or safety.

Centers for Medicare and Medicaid Services (CMS) is continuing to work on a "Roadmap for Implementing Value Driven Healthcare in the Traditional Medicare Fee-for-Service Program" with the "VISION FOR AMERICA: of Patient-centered, high-quality care delivered."[*] The paper published in 2008 laid out value base purchasing (VBP) goals.

GOALS FOR VALUE-BASE PURCHASING:

- Financial viability: where the financial viability of the traditional.
- Medicare fee-for-service program is protected for beneficiaries and taxpayers.
- Payment incentives: where Medicare payments are linked to the value, quality, and efficiency of care provided.
- Joint accountability: where physicians and providers have joint clinical and financial accountability for healthcare in their communities.
- Effectiveness: where care is evidence based and outcomes driven to better manage diseases and prevent complications from them.
- Ensuring access: where a restructured Medicare fee-for-service payment system provides equal access to high-quality, affordable care.
- Safety and transparency: where a value-based payment system gives beneficiaries information on the quality, cost, and safety of their healthcare.
- Smooth transitions: where payment systems support well-coordinated care across different providers and settings.
- Electronic health records: where value-driven healthcare supports the use of information technology to give providers the ability to deliver high-quality, efficient, and well-coordinated care.[†]

Even though many of the goals are "payment system based," the premise is providing value to the customer (the patient), the payer (CMS) and, ultimately, the taxpayer, who helps fund the healthcare system, to ensure value for the services purchased. Understanding the value stream across the continuum of care and being able to identify and eliminate hidden wastes will impact the ability to deliver high-quality, cost-effective care and will enable organizations to begin to work within the VBP models that are being proposed under CMS.

---

[*] "Roadmap for Implementing Value Driven Healthcare in the Traditional Medicare Fee-for-Service Program," CMS, December 2008 paper. http://www.cms.hhs.gov/QualityInitiativesGenInfo/downloads/VBPRoadmap_OEA_1-16_508.pdf.
[†] ibid

HIDDEN COST OF CENSUS MANAGING

"Census managing" was touted as the next best thing since sliced bread in healthcare. Census managing is scheduling nurses for a full shift and then, if the schedule changes, sending them home early without pay or forcing them to use vacation pay. This is a terrible practice and equates to lazy management scheduling. It follows the thinking behind pushing accounts payable out to 45, 60 or, in some cases, 90 days or more. When did this become acceptable in the business world? Is this respect for humanity? Isn't this really poor management? What does this do to employee morale? In some hospitals, they cut the percentage of the full FTE to meet budget. So a 40 hrs week becomes a 36 hrs week (0.9 FTE) with 4 hrs less pay. This is similar to the food industry cutting the size of the container but charging the same price. In order to impact the process of how organizations invoke "reductions," it is important to understand the cost of doing business.

Lesson Learned: *This is a waste of talent. We should learn to properly plan our schedules. If we have excess people, couldn't we use them to work on further improving our processes? Consider developing a list of all the things that we never have time to do or work on and divide it up by the hourly requirement for each task. Next time we have nurses available, have them work on the list. Consider creating quality circles in which the nurses and/or technicians could participate.*

HIDDEN COSTS OF MISMATCHED STAFFING

Departments tend to be staffed based on what we call demonstrated capacity. This term is also applicable in manufacturing. An example of this is staffing our department based on what one sees everyday on the surface, thus not managing based on facts or data. Another example is when the area experiences unanticipated surges or wide variability in demand. Sometimes the need for the additional staff is only 3 or 4 hrs but they are scheduled for a full 8 hrs shift. Since they are only utilized for the peak demand and may not be cross trained to do other tasks, they may sit around or find busy work to fill the remainder of their shift.

Demand cycles that are not managed properly can result in supervisors going to their management and saying they need more staff. The area staff complains about a variety of things, such as being too busy or having too much work, having staff on sick leave and even complaining of safety issues. Many times, these complaints are directly tied to the surges in demand or date back to years ago when something extraordinary happened, but they always refer to it as happening in the present.

Most of these things are the result of inherent wastes that have built up in the process over many years. It is difficult to see the situation clearly because we become "boiled frogs" and forget the way it used to be. Managers ask supervisors and staff to put a case together to fight for more people or more space.

Each year as the waste increases, if they can convince management, they temporarily "fix it" by adding more staff, rooms, equipment, etc. Over time, there is a migration from the old way that actually used to work with the existing staff. Over time the experienced staff members get fed up and leave and the remaining people forget how the work used to be accomplished without the problems they are currently experiencing.

Often what is found is that the addition of more people actually creates more waste. Often we find managers staff to desire and not demand. This can result from a variety of reasons from personnel requests from employees for a particular shift or work schedule to the manager not tracking and monitoring demand in their clinical area. Shifts in customer demand may occur without a corresponding adjustment to scheduled times for staff. Often managers adhere to traditional set "shift times" without analyzing whether they should be staggering staff schedules to meet demand cycles. These all can contribute to mis-matched staff to demand and result in waste, often contributing to agency and overtime costs.

If there is no standard work or training programs, the problems are exacerbated. Because everyone is trained by someone different and, eventually, the same tasks and the same jobs are done in different ways, it leads to quality and safety concerns. Making decisions regarding space or labor based on demonstrated capacity is dangerous and can be extremely costly. Lean offers an escape from this trap by analyzing the process and collecting data on which to make sound "data-driven" budgeting and staffing decisions, thus managing by fact. These situations are found both in manufacturing and in hospitals.

When the Lean team first arrives and visits the clinical areas, we generally hear from staff things like, "We don't have enough space, we don't have enough rooms/beds and we need more people or we don't have the supplies or equipment we need."

When asked what managers use to construct or adjust their budgets, in many cases they say, "Well, I ask my people in the area." Therefore, budgets are based on perceptions, past experiences, and assumptions. In most cases, there is little or no data, and so the requests for more people and rooms continue on. It is no wonder that finance is always focused on cutting labor through FTEs.

But does adding rooms or people really fix the problems? We would argue that it works for a while, but it really just hides the underlying problems. "Waste hides waste" for a time, but then the problems come back worse than before because the root causes of the problems were never identified and fixed. The organization (including finance) has no process to keep track of these hidden costs and normally has weak standards or standards based on purchased benchmarked databases. Finance does what they do best during the budgeting process. In an attempt to keep the organization financially viable, they spend their time pushing back and insisting on cuts in FTEs and supplies, hoping that managers and directors will cave in and meet these seemingly impossible goals. Many of the perceived impossible goals could be achieved or even surpassed if managers were taught how to identify and eliminate wastes and streamline their processes.

Once educated, managers need to work together with finance to develop the goals and outline the improvement plan (which may need to be a multi-year journey) to achieve the goals.

Since Hospital X needed to reduce costs, each department was required to contribute by reducing labor or FTEs. The radiology department decided to let one of its technicians go, and everyone was happy because they saved one FTE. But what did it cost? In the long run, they could no longer support the number of outpatient CT scans, so they cut the schedule back by 40%. Outpatient CT scans generated significant revenue, but no one ever looked or recognized the revenue they were losing.

Lesson Learned: *Cutting FTEs to meet budget without understanding the impact is a short-sighted approach to any type of improvement. FTEs are an easy target, but this practice can be a symptom of uninformed management. Millions of dollars are lost in a hospital due to these hidden wastes. Financial reduction targets should require a "process improvement" or waste elimination plan outlining how the goals will be achieved.*

Hidden Cost of Minimal Staffing and the Concept of Critical Mass

Most hospitals processes (due to layouts and skill sets) have a "critical mass" of personnel to operate. This critical mass is defined as the number of people required to support the area if only one person were to walk in at any time. When organizations staff at or below critical mass, they may meet our FTE goal, but may compromise patient quality, satisfaction, and throughput. Remember, one bad patient experience will most probably be communicated to at least ten people. For example, if we staff to minimal labor requirements (or FTEs) in ED and patient waits are too long, where do they go next time? How will it impact the LWSD (left without seeing doctor) percentage? Do we measure it? If patients wait for outpatient services in a hospital, where do they go next time? Patients are consumers and consumers are becoming savvier, even in healthcare. Ultimately, they will go to places that are "easy to do business with" (ETDBW) unless they only have one choice in the area. If they have a bad service experience in one area, will they come back to the same facility to have another service? These FTE cuts are, in, and of themselves, short-sighted, but this goes back to our business schools and overall financial system, which is quarterly (short-term) focused. So, in the words of a Lean sensei, Mark Jamrog, "We make the numbers, but at what cost?"* If we have the ability to take market share from our competitors, why not staff accordingly and grow the business? Departments need to be allowed to start staffing for growth *as long as* they are continuously pursuing opportunities to eliminate waste. We have found that this is a difficult concept and practice for healthcare organizations to adopt.

---

* Mark Jamrog, principal, The SMC Group.

HIDDEN COSTS IN OUR BUDGETING PROCESSES

As we have discussed, we have watched several budgeting processes at various hospitals with some amazement. The financial arm of the organization determines the global reduction required, pads it, then breaks it down by department, and sends it out to each department as their budgets for the upcoming year. The budgets include the expected "reductions" that are needed for the organization to remain fiscally sound. Managers and directors spend at least a month and, in many cases, months in preparation determining what their needs are for the upcoming year and what they are going to cut (in most cases in labor (FTEs) and supplies) to meet the budget that they were provided by the finance department. Jockeying occurs between departments to offload people and services in order to meet the reductions, as the negotiation process begins.

We have witnessed the budgeting process go on for literally 6 months or more at some hospitals. Organizations spend a tremendous amount of hidden, non-tracked costs preparing and negotiating during the budget season while everything else literally gets put on hold. Managers and directors cannot be accessed because they are too busy either getting ready for a budget meeting or attending one. In many cases, any preparations to justify increases are wasted as they are told, "It's not enough money; we need you to come up with more cost cuts." In the end, finance dictates to all the managers the final budget. It begs the question, "Why don't we just cut the months of work out of the process and tell the departments what you are going to mandate to them in the end anyway?" Often, the budget numbers are pushed down so low that there must be a give-back at the end. It almost feels like the budgeting process isn't complete until a certain pain threshold is reached.

At Hospital X, surgery was told by finance that they had to add 1000 cases to their surgery budget. Adding cases was the only way that they could justify the budget put in place, since surgery volume drove their labor and supply budget. No one validated that obtaining an additional 1000 cases was possible in the current market. There was no market share analysis performed or marketing plan in place to work on getting the cases. Despite the surgery manager's protest, the 1000 cases were added to the budget for the upcoming year. In addition, current processes in surgery could not even handle 1000 more cases, so they spent the next year explaining each month why they weren't making their budgeted 1000 cases. Then a strategic shift occurred; as Lean was implemented, they started finding millions in revenue they were not capturing. After many meetings, they were allowed by finance to convert the 1000 cases over to additional revenue capture and meet their finance target that way.

Once the budget is in place, to what extent are people measured against it? How realistic are the assumptions that are made? How good is the data behind the assumptions? How much padding and positioning goes on throughout the year tying up and wasting time that could be used on making improvements and cutting waste? We are not saying that finance should not ask the tough questions and expect good financial performance; however, there are other methods that can be leveraged that need to be considered to achieve the same or better goals.

HIDDEN COST OF CHARGES NOT CAPTURED

In many healthcare facilities, we have found problems with "charge capture" in numerous operations. Perhaps the nurse feels the patient is the only important issue and may not understand why it is necessary to capture all their charges, or may not feel that it is part of their job, thus charge capture becomes a minor concern or an afterthought. We have found these "deeply hidden" wastes turn into losses that can run into millions of dollars per year at larger hospitals. While there may be attempts to track the more obvious areas, such as registration capture in an ED, we find it is seldom a "key" metric that is tracked and shared with management and staff.

HIDDEN COSTS IN MATERIALS REPLENISHMENT

Hidden costs in materials can be found throughout most hospitals. How often are materials not stored where they are needed? What is the impact and how does finance reflect the cost of material stock outs?

The materials department at Hospital X only replenishes surgery materials in trauma rooms once a day. We asked the materials person what the nurses do when they run out of stock in one of the bins. They responded that the nurse has to go down the hall to the supply closet or call down to central supply to get the needed supplies. What if there are none available? The reply was that then they have to call a nearby hospital. "No big deal." They do it all the time!

How much does excess stock cost us in cash flow and space, shelving, restocking, etc.? What additional labor does this add to the organization and how does this balance against the cost of having the stock in the right place at the right time when it is needed? But these costs are not captured anywhere in financial systems or scorecards. It is not unusual on inventory projects to find tens of thousands of dollars in obsolete or expired inventory.

Hospital X didn't utilize a formal materials list. Many of their materials were subcontracted to a distributor who was supposed to manage the inventory. The roles of the hospital and its partnering distributor were not well defined, which caused blame and waste in all the handoffs inherent in the process. We found the physical inventory counted was only 10%–15% of the actual total sum of supplies purchased each year. Finance had a "calculated" number it inserted each year to make sure the hospital hit its profitability number.

HIDDEN COST OF SOFTWARE THAT WILL SOLVE ALL OUR PROBLEMS

At Hospital X, a Lean initiative was planned in the Sterile Processing Department (SPD); however, it was delayed due to the instrument tracking system being installed. We suggested they abandon the tracking system until we worked with them to create Lean processes. We also stated that a tracking system may not be necessary once we were done. Since they already had the $250K approved, they didn't want to take a chance on losing the capital at year's end, and they couldn't carry the money over to the next year or they would lose it. So they purchased the system anyway. Because they went ahead with the tracking system, the Lean initiative was not started until more than a year later. When we asked how the tracking system was going, we were told that they took it out because they didn't have the manpower to keep it running, and the SPD supervisor who oversaw the implementation was transferred to another department.

Hidden Costs Associated with Centralizing Sterile Processing

What does it cost to centralize the Sterile Processing Department (SPD) in a remote location such as a basement or on a floor other than where the OR or other heavy users who need access are located?

At Hospital X, we were told to develop suggestions for Sterile Processing and the OR materials supply room. We suggested moving it back up from the basement to the surgery floor, where it belongs. This started a very politically charged response, to put it mildly. After all, they just spent a lot of money to buy new large washers. The return on investment (ROI) stated that it made sense to move it downstairs because they could now have more space to centralize the area. The fact that it was two floors down didn't seem to matter, except to the OR nurses who fought the move and lost.

When we analyzed the move, we found it actually cost them more money in hidden costs than it saved despite the ROI, which showed less than one-year payback. In the past, the instruments were taken down the hall to the SPD. Smaller washers were quicker, and a larger percentage of items were washed by hand. Washing by hand was actually better and faster, in many cases, because the bone chips and other assorted fragments can get caught in instrument trays in the washer. Since they processed the cases one cart at a time, the turnaround time for instruments was about 1.5–2 hrs. Since the new SPD area downstairs required an elevator ride, the dirty case carts would sit upstairs until someone decided to put them in the elevator and send them down. An unintended consequence of the move was that instruments would fall off carts and end up in the bottom of the elevator shaft. The washing process now took about 20 min per case cart, but the washers ran for 45 min. The sets would be taken out of the washer and put on a shelf to cool. Since the case carts were "batched" downstairs, they got mixed up, and when the SPD put the sets back together, they were often missing instruments that had gotten separated, so the instruments sets piled up on a table waiting for the balance of the set to arrive. If a set was only missing one or two instruments, they would replace it with a new one or "rob" it from a similar set. The sterilization took another hour, with additional time for cooling, so the overall process now took 3–5 hrs to turn around one set. This doubled the time of the

old process. This contributed to the hidden costs that were not accounted for in moving the operations downstairs. So why did it cost more to move it downstairs? In addition to all the capital costs to set up the area, they now had to buy more instrument sets since the turnaround time was so long. Instrument sets are very expensive and, obviously, were not included in the ROI, and no one bothered to recalculate the ROI after the move.

Lesson Learned: *It is extremely difficult, at times, to conceptualize all the "x's" that will be impacted by a large-scale change; however, stepping back and trying to gain a full understanding is critical. Layouts in hospitals are important. The further the distance, the more batching, the longer the turnaround times, and the more equipment needed to compensate. Also, sometimes a manual process is better than the machine (automated) that replaced it.*

Hidden Cost of Inventory Management

When we visited Hospital X, we inquired about their inventory accuracy. They weren't sure but estimated it at around 95%. When we watched the case pickers on video, we noticed the first step was to pull up the pick list and manually go through the list of parts. Prior to picking the parts, they counted all the major parts on the list, which they knew typically had problematic counts. Sometimes this could be several hundred parts per day. Once the parts were counted, they went into the system and adjusted the inventory numbers based on their hand counts. While observing the operator or staff member adjust the counts, we saw that several of the counts were entered incorrectly and had to be readjusted. We determined the accuracy rate was about 40% at this stage. Once all the counts were adjusted in the system, they reprinted the pick ticket and proceeded to pick the supplies for the case. At the end of the day, they did a "cycle" counting process. This is where a random set of parts is manually counted and then adjusted. The cycle counting turned out to be about 80% accurate and that was after all the daily adjustments.

This was supposed to be a perpetual inventory system, but there were several problems inherent in the system. How much labor time do you think was "lost" to rework and adjustments because of the poor system and process? The first problem was that anyone and everyone had access to the supplies and minimal effort was in place to ensure that supplies removed were documented, especially on evening and night shifts. The next problem was the human error factor related to all the adjustments. This was because not every part existed in the system, and the supplier constantly changed parts from Just In Time (JIT) inventory to non-JIT inventory, and there was not a good process in place to inform the material handlers. This resulted in orders not showing up the next day as planned. Complete orders were being cancelled if one of the items had the wrong information entered into the system. The affected department supervisors would not find out about the cancelled order until the next day when the orders arrived or didn't arrive.

Lesson Learned: *It's amazing what is identified by observing or videotaping a process. How much money was lost in the expensive rework procedures being done by the material handlers, by the materials not being there when needed, or all the phone calls made to notify affected departments? Every hospital has these types of problems. They may not be exactly the same, but they are out there, ever-lurking and hidden from view.*

Hidden Costs and Lack of Standardization at a System Level Throughout the Hospital

At Hospital X, the surgery pre-testing department spends 7 min entering data into the first system and then spends an additional 7 min re-entering the same data into a second system. Why? Because there is no integration or interface feeding information from one system to the next. When we inquired, we discovered that the interface required was not purchased originally because they had to reduce the capital cost of the system so they could meet the ROI.

Lesson Learned: *The costs of not standardizing throughout the hospital is staggering. Yet, these costs are not accounted for thus hidden from the typical financial reporting systems.*

Hidden Costs in the Software Solution

Many times, we have seen software solutions requiring major dollars touted as the answer to all of the hospital's problems. Often, a good job is performed investigating the system costs, but no one investigates what it is going to cost to keep the system fed (operational), including the number of staff required to input the data required to maintain the integrity of the system. In addition, once the system is purchased, in many cases the implementation is targeted for cost reduction. Often, the organization allocates funds for the initial training and implementation. In some cases, instead of sending their best people to training, they send the "available" people. Most often, this results in poor rollouts and many times the system is setup incorrectly.

Most IT vendors sell the ROI based on using all the features and functions of the system. The organization expects that ROI, and ultimately falls short of achieving it as the appropriate resources are not allocated due to budget cuts, and is not able to fully leverage all the features and functions as intended. In many cases, even though enough resources might be allocated to perform the initial implementation, they fail to recognize the end-users learning curve and what resources are needed to guarantee current and future users are trained appropriately to ensure continued data integrity. In many cases, refresher courses are needed to reinforce learning that may or may not have been achieved on the initial implementation. The type of system being rolled out can significantly impact areas such as charge capture and revenue recognition for many years.

At Hospital X, the IT department purchased a new software program but didn't have the end-users (nurses)

participate in the software selection process. On investigation, we couldn't determine what criteria were utilized to justify the purchase, but it certainly wasn't cycle time. When we performed a comparative time study of both systems, the data revealed that it took end-users three times longer to enter the information in the new system because of the need to navigate through the addition of several more screens to achieve the previous result. In addition, system performance and response time had degraded as well.

The next problem the nurses encountered was that, during installation of the new software, the computers were reprogrammed and their documentation was sent to a new centralized printer in a nursing station 50 yards away (the organization wanted the information to flow to a "secure" printer). As it turned out, the printer was no more secure than the printer next to the nurses' workstation. The CEO happened to stop in when we were analyzing this video and was so embarrassed he immediately called IT and fixed both problems.

At Hospital X, IT installed a new computer system. When we videotaped and time-studied the new process, it was so slow it was delaying patient care. By showing the video to the director, we were able to get "temporary" permission to make the process of documenting within the system more efficient and effective by doing the paperwork manually while the system was upgraded, since manually was three to four times faster than the new computer system.

Lessons Learned: *When implementing new IT systems, it is important to understand current state vs. future state impacts of deployment. Do not assume that implementing a new system will improve productivity, efficiency, quality, and safety. Videotaping and/or simulating activities that are being impacted can be very useful to identify enhancements that need to be made to streamline the process, help obtain approvals from leadership to change the process or, in some cases, go back to the old manual processes, when appropriate and don't put the new software system in place until AFTER you have 'Leaned out" the process.*

LEAN SOLUTIONS AND LEAN ACCOUNTING

Lean is about managing by fact, deploying concepts that will drive elimination of waste and leveraging tools and formulas that are data driven. Once we implement Lean in an area, understanding what tasks are value-added to the customer and what it takes (the work effort based on time) to get the process done becomes clearer. The data is based on hard evidence and backed up by videotape analysis.

It's amazing how many times we go into an area and find out that they are planning on adding more staff, beds, or rooms, but when we study the process and do the calculations, we tell them they are not going to need them.

Once Lean is implemented, if management requests a labor reduction, the supervisor now has a standard package of data that will show the impact to the department or value stream. In fact, management should require the Lean tools be applied to any requests for additional staff or resources.

As Lean is adopted in more areas, the budgeting process becomes easier and the role of finance in the organization should change. In fact, financial analysts may find it easier to identify areas where productivity can be improved and labor reduced. The budget becomes straightforward as Lean calculations determine exactly how much capacity and labor is required for each area. Some Lean organizations go "beyond budgeting" and provide financial forecasts each month and loosen themselves from the snares of the annual budget process.

Lean finds other operational savings by eliminating wastes and streamlining processes. When the overall revenue stream for improvement is targeted, we normally find an increase in collections. In accounting, we find many opportunities to improve accounts payable, receivable, and the capital allocation and budgeting process. In pharmacy, we revise processes to eliminate waste in mixing drugs and reducing expired drugs, etc.

It is sometimes difficult in the early stages of the Lean journey to get complete "buy-in" by finance leaders who may not see the Lean day-to-day operational and cultural changes as truly significant. If we can't get them involved on teams up front, we tend to find it takes a series of Lean initiatives over a year or two until the transformation of Lean thinking takes hold in order for finance to begin to buy in. Unfortunately, it may be difficult to see a direct financial performance link to some Lean healthcare initiatives in the short term.

Lesson Learned: *Have finance leaders read up on Lean accounting, send them to a Lean accounting seminar or get with a Lean accounting expert consultant up front. Make sure finance is involved supporting the teams and has members on your teams up front.*

Lean is not a short-term solution or "quick fix." It is not unusual to take 2–3 years to see truly sustained results really start to impact the bottom-line, even though one may see the results immediately in the areas you are improving. Remember, it took Toyota more than 50 years of applying Lean principles for continuous improvement to become the world's number one auto manufacturer.

LEAN—IT'S ALL ABOUT THE PROCESS, NOT LABOR OR FULL-TIME EMPLOYEE REDUCTIONS

We are firm advocates of improvements in productivity. Productivity improvements in general are a byproduct of Lean, but what we strive for is to improve the process, create flow, and make the customer experience the best it can be. We not only obtain productivity increases, but we generally achieve improvements in quality (reductions in defects), safety (error reductions), space requirements, morale, etc. It is extremely important not to be focused solely on FTE reductions but to be able to embrace the full impact that applying Lean concepts and tools can bring to the organization with the Lean Cultural Transformation.

When we initially create a Lean process in an area, it normally impacts a small part of a department's overall process and budget so we are only going to initially impact a small

portion of the overall costs and ROI. Eventually, the organization achieves results, eliminating the need to prove the ROI and Lean is viewed as a tool to perform as continuous improvement and is "just the right thing to do."

COST ACCOUNTING STANDARDS— TRADITIONAL ACCOUNTING VS. LEAN ACCOUNTING

The following discussion is purposefully somewhat lengthy. The reason for this section is that this is the one of the major areas that creates conflict with Lean. Our initial discussions with CFOs tend to be around cost accounting standards and how Lean deals with them. It should be pointed out that, if hospitals do not utilize labor standards, the labor tends to be set on experience and day-to-day demands.

LEAN ACCOUNTING APPROACH

With Lean accounting, we eliminate cost accounting standards and the concept of earned hours in the traditional sense, and cost accounting staff are moved back into the line organization to work on process improvements and support the value stream (or Service Line) managers with information and analysis. Early on with Lean implementations, this is way too far over on the perceived weirdness indicator (PWI) scale for the financially focused individuals. We find it generally takes about 2–3 years to get financial areas on board with the notion of standards and Lean accounting. So, we will spend the next several pages trying to point out the problems with the traditional cost accounting systems.

Lesson Learned: *The best use of cost accountants I ever saw was several years ago when a well-known Fortune 500 company converted its cost accountants to Lean project leaders or team members.*

EARNED HOURS

This system is so engrained that there are several companies whose sole existence is based on operational analysis (i.e., labor management reporting). In the healthcare environment, the labor budget is normally set based on labor standards that are assigned for variable staffing, which is normally "earned" and directly tied to patient or product volumes. The formulas include a variety of drivers, including patient days, adjusted patient days, laboratory tests performed, acuity-based adjustments or other methods that had been created in order for an area to "earn hours for work performed." All the formulas try to achieve the same goal: to determine labor hours needed so that earned labor or allocated labor dollars fluctuate with volume. As the volume increases, more labor hours are earned. If volume falls, then managers must adjust the staffing accordingly (such as proactively sending staff home based on "census" and managing to the labor standard), so as not to go over or beat the budget.

In addition, there is also a fixed staffing component for labor that will not be directly related to changes in volume. This can be both a blessing and a curse. If labor standards are generous and volume increases, then the clinical area will have, in some cases, a budgetary allowance that exceeds what is truly needed. This can cause managers to manage more loosely because they know they will meet their budget. If the labor standard is inaccurate to the downside, however, the clinical area will forever find itself justifying to management why it is over budget. The decrease in flex labor causes the clinical area to feel they are continually fighting a battle to obtain adequate resources to provide the required service.

Standards in most hospitals are generally set by utilizing benchmark data. There is always a concern with benchmark data as with all benchmark data, definitions can be interpreted and there may not be full transparency as to how the labor standard was created and if benchmark is exactly the same at the entity that it is being compared to, thus the labor standard may not reflect that organizations reality.

To determine how the surgery standards were set, we sat with the sales representative from a major healthcare operations analysis company that provides productivity and standards data. The standards were set on a combination of observations and employee interviews that were then compared with "similar" hospitals; but some of the standards were set incorrectly. For example, the standard for a clinical area included costs for the department that were not included by other hospitals providing "similar data." So the comparison data was misleading.

STANDARDS AND VARIANCE REPORTING

The typical variance report is generally distributed late and contains historical and unactionable information. Yet, we spend hours or even days researching and trying to explain the variances to management. To what benefit?

Since this information is generally not available in "real-time," operational managers must learn how their budget relates to actual staffing. When managers or supervisors get a report showing they are over budget, they work harder at sending staff home, and if they are on budget, they tend to be more lax with staffing. This can have little relation to what is actually occurring on their unit or department. In most instances, they do not, on an hourly or daily basis, manage staff to what is going on in the process. Instead, they manage to the budget. No more, no less. There is no push to improve; if they are meeting their budgeted labor allocation, they are satisfied and complacency sets in.

LEAN ACCOUNTING APPROACH

Lean accounting is different in that we put standards (i.e., standard work) in place based on data-based targets utilizing real-time metrics. The goal is to continually reduce the standard time with no negative impact to quality, safety, or patient satisfaction. There is no longer a need for variance reporting

if Lean is implemented properly, since this is addressed in standardized work and visual controls. Lean accounting uses no standards at all. Goals are set based on our future state map plans for improvement, which derive from our demand, operations, and financial planning, which is derived from our strategy deployment, which is derived from our strategic plan and flowed throughout the organization via Hoshin planning.

THE PROBLEM WITH COST ACCOUNTING STANDARDS

If the organization has determined that they are using benchmarking data and implementing labor standards to drive budget and labor management, one needs to understand that once labor standards are introduced and adopted, they tend to remain fixed and can take an extreme amount of work to adjust. When managers or employees perform better than the standard, then they may want more money. If they have a generous labor standard, we have found that they do not readily volunteer to adjust the labor standard to reflect a tighter standard. How does any of this drive improvement?

When the clinical area beats the standard, they may adjust it (raise it). This is probably rational and reasonable if one buys into the whole "standards" thing, but the mere act of raising it is a disincentive to the department. Why should anyone work to improve the standard when they figure out the standard is just going to be raised? What is in it for them? This is what drives "soldiering". Soldiering is where an employee or employees as a group agree on how much work they are going to perform. Anyone who "works harder" gets harassed or gets their car "keyed" by fellow employees.[*]

Lesson Learned: *Traditional cost accounting standards, contrary to popular belief, seldom drive improvement. Brian Maskell of BMA Associates, said, "Think about it – if they did, every hospital would be world class."*[†]

TRADITIONAL COST ACCOUNTING QUESTION

Cost accounting standards typically are calculated by the following equation:

$$\text{Worked hours} \div \text{units of service.}$$

As stated earlier, however, cost accounting standards can be very misleading and, when utilized as metrics, can drive some crazy behaviors. There are several problems with these types of standards:

Who set the standards? How are they set? How often are they updated and who is responsible to update them? What exactly are we trying to measure? When we only use direct labor in a standard it can be misleading. How much indirect labor is necessary and is it counted? How do you define output

---

[*] Principles of Scientific Management, Frederick Taylor, 1911.

[†] Correspondence dated December 31, 2009, from Brian Maskell of BMA Associates, BMA website (www.maskell.com), was highly influential in this section.

on a nursing floor? Should it really be determined solely by the number of patients per nurse per hour? Or earned hours per patient day? What if the acuity of the patients is different? Is the standard then recalculated?

Benchmarking companies utilize activities to help drive the assigned labor standard and other variables and, in many cases, managers are not even taught how the standards are calculated or how to manage to them. Once that transfer of knowledge occurs, in most cases, if a manager is promoted or leaves, the subsequent manager is not trained and now manages to a number in a report without understanding the variables that contributed to its creation.

In addition, we have repeatedly uncovered that even good managers who have responsibility across multiple areas do not understand whether the area is under a fixed labor model in which there is no adjustment for volumes changes, or flexible labor. We have repeatedly discovered areas where they were under fixed labor models that, in fact, needed flexible labor standards. The challenge has been that as this is uncovered, in most cases, the financial department allow the manager no incremental increase and requires the standard assigned "fit into the current budget." In many cases, this is not a true comparison to what it takes to perform actual tasks to the labor standard assigned. So the dilemma continues. Even though there are significant challenges with labor standards, we have never found a standard we could not meet or significantly beat with Lean improvements.

Lesson Learned: *The main caution and danger is that people measured on labor standards only work to meet the standard, but they do not consistently work to improve on it.*

"THE LABOR STANDARD REPORT SAID WE SHOULD HIRE THREE PEOPLE—LEAN ACCOUNTING SAID NO!"

Hospital X is using a well-known standards reporting company. After we Leaned out one of the pre-testing departments, the set labor standard remained the same. Owing to our productivity improvements, we had days where we were performing at a rate that was 175% of the current standard. Based on the strict definition of the standard and actions dictated by the standard, we were considered by everyone who saw the report to be way understaffed and, in fact, for several weeks the manager was asked to add three people to the department.

PRE-TESTING LEAN ACCOUNTING APPROACH EXAMPLE

At Hospital X, part of our Lean improvement was to revise the appointment scheduling and build a Microsoft Office Excel©-based staffing model based on the new standard work and cycle times in the department. We also implemented a day-end visual computerized report that kept track of productivity and daily demand. We installed a Heijunka system that, in addition to level loading, kept track of all the individual cycle times in the department.

With these real-time metrics in place, we knew we didn't need to add anyone and, in fact, once additional changes were put in place, could have handled additional volume with the same staff. The models were manual but took no more than 15–30 min per day to update. The need for the labor report was eliminated, yet we had to follow it because that was part of the finance labor management system. It is interesting to note that each monthly "labor standard" finance report we received for each of the OR manager's departments had errors in worked hours. The only way we were able to resolve the errors was with the manual data collection we implemented with Lean. It begs the question: How many other department "labor standard" reports had errors?

Lesson Learned: *Just because the labor standard report says additional people are needed, once the area has been "Leaned," it is not necessarily true.*

SKILL SETS VS. THE NUMBER AND COST OF FULL-TIME EMPLOYEES

Healthcare is a complicated labor environment. It is somewhat inflexible in that many processes can only be performed by certain skill sets. The concept of full-time equivalents (FTEs) is used in the healthcare environment vs. manufacturing. An FTE is normally 2080 hrs/year.

Lesson Learned: *Finance tends to focus on FTEs but not necessarily on the costs and skill sets of the FTEs. An example of the challenges which are encountered when too much emphasis is placed on FTE variance reports and the unintentional consequences having managers accountable to reporting the numbers versus being able to the address the bigger picture.*

Consider the following example at Hospital X

The serviceline coordinator in the operating room was responsible for turnover. When she analyzed the turnover process, she recognized that she could decrease her turnaround time if she had two surgical assistants help with room cleaning in parallel, instead of one nurse doing the same tasks in series. She brought this to her director's attention. They discussed the benefits which revealed that no additional dollars would be added to the overall budget for two assistants versus one nurse and in fact the day would probably end sooner or they would be able to add another case thus generate more revenue. Even though he agreed with her assessment he would not comply with her request because at the monthly budget review meeting he was accountable not only for budget but for the variances in earned FTEs. The addition of the surgical assistant hours would not be earned in the current model and would raise a red flag in additional FTEs the variance report. He felt he would be subject to additional scrutiny as the current financial leadership focused heavily on FTEs even though they would remain budget neutral. Her request for the improvement was denied.

LEAN ACCOUNTING APPROACH

On several projects, we have been able to replace nurses in certain processes with a technician, which realized lower FTE costs, and we have needed to replace technicians with nurses, secretaries with technicians, or a technician 1 with a technician 3, which results in increased costs, even though the number of FTEs remained the same.

Lesson Learned: *We need to get the right skill sets in the right job in order to maintain flexibility and reduce fractional labor time. Budget numbers need to include not just FTE but budget dollars as well.*

LEAN ACCOUNTING APPROACH

Not all standards are bad. Lean has standards based on hard data and we use this data to guide our decisions. Setting standards is different from standardization. As we move from functional departments to value streams, what do we do? What are the implications for organizational structure? One can argue that Lean does have standards, which we would agree—but not in the sense of traditional cost accounting systems. It is a different type of system.

In Lean, we don't need a published finance "labor standard" report a month later. Once we implement Lean, we know the total labor time and Takt time or required cycle time, and we can determine the proper staffing level. We then put visual controls in place to make it immediately obvious.

Lesson Learned: *Lean is about reducing waste and exposing hidden costs. Lean tools make waste obvious and easy to quantify, but only to the extent to which the Lean project will impact the area.*

CONTROLLING THE COST OF DOING BUSINESS—IS IT POSSIBLE?

Many organizations—including healthcare—are faced with determining who ultimately is responsible for the patient value stream as it relates to cost control. In an environment where one might be paid a "case rate" (DRGs) for all services rendered for the patient admission, which would include radiology, surgery, supplies, etc., who should be responsible for cost containment? How can one manage to eliminate waste across the continuum when the costs for the services delivered within that admission are managed by a group of functional departments (in silos). This organizational structure creates a challenge for hospitals as they try to control costs in order to meet a fixed reimbursement. For instance, for drug-related group (DRG) 105 (heart valve replacement), a director may be responsible for the cardiac floors, the intensive care unit, the progressive care unit, and the catheterization laboratory, but may or may not be responsible for surgery, admitting, transportation, radiology, or the laboratory departments. Yet each of these may contribute to the length of stay and the resources used for the patient assigned to that DRG. The physician also contributes intimately to the length of stay

and the resources used, but is not a direct part of the value stream.

ALLOCATING OVERHEAD

If finance is spreading overhead by square foot (or some other method), we would postulate that we will never know the true costs. For example, what if radiology has the same square footage as Pre-Op? Which one has higher overhead costs? Obviously, the answer is radiology, with the cost of its magnetic resonance imaging (MRI) machines and electricity required to run the area. If we spread these costs evenly, it has the effect of raising the costs of Pre-Op and lowering the overall cost of radiology. This mistake has been made at many manufacturing companies over the years. At one of our manufacturing plants, we used this cost accounting methodology and ended up eliminating our most profitable line while keeping our least profitable line.

LEAN ACCOUNTING APPROACH

With Lean accounting, we collect the costs by value stream. We don't differentiate if it is direct, indirect, or overhead. We eliminate the need for earned hours and the need for absorption accounting.

Prior to implementing Lean accounting, we utilized contribution margin when possible to understand what can be gained from improvements. We consider labor cost to be fixed, and when we use contribution margin, we only take truly variable costs. In addition, we recommend that one understands the true overhead of each area. We also like to modify the contribution margin approach to look at all FTEs vs. separating out direct and indirect employees. This includes centralized and supervisory personnel. This way, one gets a look at the total costs vs. slices of direct or indirect costs. When making decisions, we look at the true impact on the value stream costs and profitability. This includes everybody and everything that is in the value stream; however, monuments—like radiology, i.e., MRI, computed tomography (CT), etc.—create a problem, and we have to allocate them in a more simple way.

Another good measure is earned value analysis (EVA).[*] This metric focuses on return on capital or return on net assets (RONA).

WHY DO WE? WHY CAN'T WE?

Why do we need to track every supply on a case? What is the labor cost to accomplish that? What is the value-added? In manufacturing, we expense the cost for category C and B items, and we manage and account for category A items. Why can't we do the same in hospitals?

---

[*] David Young and Stephen O'Byrne, *EVA and Value-Based Management* (New York: McGraw Hill) 2001. EVA is equal to return on net assets–weighted average cost of capital × invested capital [(RONA − WACC) × invested capital].

Departments vs. Value Streams (Aka Service Line Management)

Traditional hospitals are organized by departments that have become more numerous with the ongoing effort to centralize. Centralization and specialization have created territorial and department silos encouraged by the DRG accounting and budgeting by department. While the costs for the DRG are rolled up to the director level that may be held accountable for cost containment, each department is managed in a silo.

Lean Accounting Approach

Some hospitals have started moving toward the Service Lines concept. I wouldn't be surprised if that is how hospitals were structured many years ago before all the specialization that has occurred. If set up properly, these Service Lines would equate to value streams in Lean. This is a relatively new concept for hospitals. As CMS is working toward establishing global payments under the acute care episode (ACE) demonstration testing, the use of the bundled hospital and physician payment for cardiac and/or orthopedics,* the ability to look at the patient value stream will become increasingly important.

We don't always agree with the Service Lines hospitals create, but we do agree it is the right way to proceed. Some hospitals set up ED and OR as Service Lines. We think this warrants further thought and analysis. It is certainly easy to pick these, as the emergency room and surgery are feeders to the hospital. Surgery tends to be a primary source of revenue for most institutions. Generally, as they try to increase market share, they strategically select Service Lines such as cardiac, neurosurgery, or orthopedics. These, in essence, are value streams.

An example of a true value stream would be the cardiac value stream. The value stream would start with the patient's visit to his/her physician or cardiologist, followed by admission to the hospital either through the ED, direct admit or surgery, to the cardiac nursing unit floor(s), and end with their payment and follow-up call from the hospital. We would create a value stream manager whose responsibility would be to "own" the entire process, from process improvement to marketing and growing the business. There may even be segments of value streams within the cardiac surgical value stream, such as interventional or even medical patient value stream, depending on how one determines the best way to view the services rendered.

Some departments are pretty straightforward. A stand-alone urgent care or urgent care co-located within an ED should be its own value stream. Support services like transport, registration, pharmacy, medical records, etc., that generally cross all Service Lines should become decentralized and "point of use" to each value stream. The centralized areas like radiology, laboratories, etc., might consider decentralization and have more point of use testing in the future. For example, each ED should have a real-time, portable x-ray machine or potentially locate a portion of radiological procedural testing in the adjacent vicinity and additionally have access to rapid, real-time, point of use laboratory results. The analogy is similar to testing bays in manufacturing or shipping, which is initially centralized, but eventually decentralized and put on the end of the assembly lines.

Where it gets complicated is the EDs and surgery. These would need to be deconstructed to determine potential value streams. For example, emergency patients who are admitted could be the front end to several value streams such, as cardiac, vascular, or general surgery.

Brian Maskell, an acknowledged Lean accounting expert from BMA Associates, states:

> All financial reporting is done at the value stream level with little or no allocation. Having said that we allocate facility costs square foot (but we do not fully absorb them) and we allocate monuments (MRI, etc.). Facility cost allocation is done solely to provide an incentive to the Service Line managers to reduce the amount of space they use. We want to grow the business without needing to acquire more buildings. Typical monuments are the Radiology/Imaging, Lab, Pharmacy, etc. Over the longer term we will dismantle these monuments and have them within the Service Lines organizationally. Financial reporting tends to be weekly by value stream and Service Line. The Service Line manager has responsibility for the P&L. We create Box Scores showing the operational Service Line/value stream measurements. These include the weekly operational measurements, the financial results, and capacity utilization. Capacity shows how much of our people's time is spent doing Productive Things vs. Non-Productive, and the remaining available capacity. These (Box Scores) are used for reporting, decision making, to understand the impact of Lean improvement, and any time you need to understand a value stream's performance.[†]

SHOULD YOU ALWAYS BENCHMARK OTHER HOSPITALS?

Benchmarking is a process where we compare our institution to similar institutions. True benchmarking, however, involves selecting a process and benchmarking it against not only similar companies but also non-similar companies that have similar processes and then implementing those improvements. For instance, if you wanted to benchmark how to process orders, you may go to an Internet company that is good at that process. The problem with just looking at benchmark data is that, many times, what is reported to the benchmarking firm is not necessarily aligned with how it may be measured at your company. Organizations need to fully understand the reference to which they are benchmarking themselves to ensure validity.

---

* "Roadmap for Implementing Value Driven Healthcare in the Traditional Medicare Fee-for-Service Program," CMS, December 2008 paper, 21. http://www.cms.hhs.gov/QualityInitiativesGenInfo/downloads/VBPRoadmap_OEA_1-16_508.pdf.

† Personal correspondence with Brian Maskell of BMA Associates (www.maskell.com).

Hospital X has scheduled a Kaizen to improve its approach to meals in the long-term-stay nursing home. The purpose is to increase customer satisfaction. This Kaizen will include a manager from a local hotel and a manager from the McDonald's across the street.[*]

For some processes, like nutritional services, it may be better to benchmark a fast food restaurant or a hotel's "room service." For billing and collections, we may benchmark an insurance company or credit card company.

Other considerations with benchmarking data are: How good is the data? Is there clarity in the definitions? Does everyone measure cycle time for turnovers the same way? For instance, the benchmarking data definition may have been patient in to patient out. But, some hospitals have different measures based on what their system can collect. Organizations may have different definitions for patient in. For the nurse, it may be when the stretcher crosses the room threshold, or for the anesthesiologist, it might be when the patient is placed on the OR. There may not be clarity in each facility as to what variability is built into the metric; e.g., when does the 7:30 a.m. case start? Is it "cut" time or "patient in the room" time. If it is patient in the room time, is it based on when the patient leaves Pre-Op (where the metric is 7:30 a.m. + 6 min) or when the patient crosses the OR threshold.

PHYSICIANS AND COST STRUCTURE

Why do surgeons feel they are always being told what to do, administration is constantly changing the rules, and no one listens to them? We don't seem to show outwardly that we cherish our surgeons and appreciate their importance and what they bring to the table. This normally doesn't become evident until they take their problem to the CEO.

Why don't physicians play a larger role in reducing our hospital's cost structure? A hospital is only as good as the sum of its highly skilled, trained, and talented physicians. Without the physicians we have nothing. Tools and materials are very important to surgeons, since life and death can hang in the balance. Do physicians play a role in our hospital cost structures? The answer is a resounding "yes." Often organizations do not directly share with the physicians or surgeons the impact of their behaviors, thus passing up an opportunity to collaborate to reduce waste. We have seen that once physicians are provided the opportunity to review and understand their impact that they more readily engage in working toward improving the hospitals processes and financial profitability. This can be very powerful when presented comparatively against their peers, however we can not emphasize enough the importance of ensuring data accuracy when working with physicians.

Lessons Learned: *Capital equipment, surgical instrument sets, and cost of necessary supplies are all impacted by the*

physicians. We need the physicians to be our partners in reducing overall value stream costs.

STANDARDIZING ON EQUIPMENT

In Lean, our goal would be to standardize preference cards, to the extent it makes sense, across all surgeons by case type. Many surgery directors would find value in doing this; however, most would find accomplishing this in their current environments is another story. There is a significant amount of money to be saved by standardizing equipment and supplies across the board; there is probably a safety component as well, as staff would not have to be trained on multiple types of equipment that does the same function. How do we accomplish this? We need the physicians involved up front to help align the incentives to drive the behaviors we desire. Departments (in the future, Value Streams) need access to accurate data on a timely basis. We have found in many cases physicians are not aware of what is available or the cost comparison of supplies they utilize. This may be easier to achieve if global (bundled) hospital rates are established in the future. We need to modify physician contracts and relationships to encourage level loading schedules, standardizing order sets, equipment and supplies and safely reducing patient length of stay.

LEAN AND MARKETING

While reducing costs, it is important to begin to increase "marketing," or grow the business. In many instances, the impact of Lean initiatives will not be realized if marketing is not engaged. As waste is eliminated, the organization may find that throughput time is reduced and they are able to provide more services with the same or less staff and in the same amount of time. Marketing needs to proactively develop plans to generate more business to fill available new capacity. Most hospitals we have encountered do not have strong marketing departments. While some may have qualified marketing personnel, they tend to lack clarity in the alignment between organizational strategy, operational infrastructure, and marketing. Some marketing departments have plans and great ideas but, in many cases, they do not have good data to support their projections.

One hospital had targeted growth for surgery and created a new business plan and strategy that seemed sound, yet it was lacking hard data projections. The forecasts provided were "soft," in other words, what people hoped would happen. They determined there was market share to gain, but there was no clear plan to align the operational infrastructure to the growth plans.

At Hospital X, marketing had determined that the hospital needed to grow the neurosurgical business. They targeted neurosurgeons who had the potential to increase case volume to the hospital. The plan was successful and neurosurgical case volume increased; however, a problem was created downstream when there were not enough instruments sets,

---

[*] Story furnished by Brian Maskell of BMA Associates. BMA website (www.maskell.com).

supplies, Post-Op recovery, or unit beds to accommodate their patients.

There was no one responsible for the overall neurosurgical Service Line. In addition, in the pursuit of increased market share, the marketing team made operational promises for 7:30 a.m. start times, block times, and dedicated teams. There was no clear plan to execute these promises with the operational team, so when the surgeons arrived they were unable to deliver. Marketing saw its job as increasing business, and executed its plan, but the lack of engagement across the continuum yielded unintended negative consequences.

With the value stream model, this story would no longer apply. Since value streams would be in place, marketing would fall under the value stream manager. The value stream manager would need to consider coordinating marketing within the Service Line(s) and integrating the marketing plans with operations to ensure successful integration to support ongoing growth.

Marketing would provide the initial voice of the customer, both internal (physicians) and external (patients), across the organization to help identify the customer requirements related to service expectations. Now it can proactively put plans in place to deliver on the customers' needs. For instance, if the organization determined that it was going to rollout a marketing campaign to grow the ED, not only will the organization need to make sure there are enough rooms or treatment space within the ED to meet customer demand in a timely manner, but it would also have to have the ability to move patients out of the ED to inpatient rooms available to support the anticipated "mix" of patients.

The value stream manager should provide an expectation of the demand by hour (projected/anticipated) to make sure there is a plan in place to appropriately staff both ED physicians and nursing staff to support the anticipated growth. The same would be true for anticipated surgical growth, so the surgery department can provide the correct number of instrument sets, materials, and scheduling options to accommodate the new growth.

We have seen organizations develop plans to grow surgical volume and not communicate the plans to the anesthesia groups, which creates a challenge to anesthesia when they are expected to support the increasing demand, yet are not aware they needed to recruit staff to execute the surgical plan, causing strain in physician and hospital relationships. As volume grows, support services such as radiology, laboratory, pharmacy, case management, and even hospitalists, etc., may be impacted by an increase in demand. It is critical that growth plans are communicated across the value stream of the patient care continuum and that plans are in place to ensure they can meet the demand.

Hospitals may need to consider revising how they view particular departments related to cost vs. revenue-generating entities. For instance, surgery generates significant revenue for most hospitals and needs to be viewed within the organization as a revenue center instead of a cost center. Once organizations consider surgery as a revenue center, it becomes easier to apply the appropriate resources in terms of people and capital to support growth.

While all this seems to be common sense, it is often difficult for organizations to understand clearly the financial benefits of Lean in the current cost accounting environment. Results may take 6 months to a couple of years to be fully recognized because the value stream of the patient crosses the entire continuum of care, and several initiatives may have to be performed sequentially, extending over a period of years, to make a significant impact. It is important to engage the financial management team in the process so that they can understand the value and help assist the Lean teams and managers in quantifying the results in order to achieve "buy-in" and adoption of a Lean culture and conversion to a Lean accounting-based structure.

When pricing services in the Lean value stream, we employ something called target costing. Once aligned in value streams, we use the voice of the customer to understand the value created by each value stream. This takes us back to the equation "selling price − cost = profit." The customer sets the selling price. We work out how much can be charged for each service, and then work out the cost level in the value stream by subtracting required profit from the target price.

We then target Lean implementations or events to drive reductions in cost (by eliminating waste) and reposition the Service Line into the right place financially. In healthcare, this is made (in some ways) easier by the fact that prices are largely set by insurance companies and the government. But it is a mistake to just take these numbers and ignore the value created for the patients. If we can calculate the customer value into real numbers, then we have the customer value driving Lean change. This is a difficult concept for most hospitals.

Lesson Learned: *Lean and Lean accounting principles drastically change the way we view traditional financial methodologies. Once Lean is organized around value streams, it enables a totally new paradigm to emerge, but will result in major changes to the overall organization.*

14 What It Means to Have a Lean Culture

EXECUTIVE SUMMARY

It is important that each organization:

1. Understands what a Lean culture looks like or what we call "The People Piece"
2. Carries out a Lean culture assessment
3. Set up a roadmap to a Lean culture
4. Identifies the barriers to continuous improvement
5. Works to sustain and improve

In a culture change, 50% is people and 50% is scientific management.

Lean culture is only attained when you are tapping into and implementing the ideas of everyone in the organization on a daily basis. It is a culture where we offer what the customer desires with the highest quality, in time, and at the lowest cost. There needs to be a long-term focus with the bottoms-up view looking at root causes, people contributing new ideas every month, keeping inventory to a minimum, level-loading, moving away from batching, and visible metrics.

Pearls of advice:

- Be patient with the process but insist on results.
- Don't confuse effort with results.
- Create a "no excuses" environment.
- Pause briefly to reflect on your successes then move on to the next one.

High Level Steps to Implementing a Lean Culture are detailed:

1. Utilize skip levels to see what your employees are thinking.
2. Education and training.
3. Create a pull for Lean.
4. Create a Lean implementation plan.
5. Create or utilize the existing senior leadership team as a Lean steering committee.
6. Baseline metrics.
7. Implement a pilot—utilize the BASICS implementation model.
8. Take daily *Gemba* walks.
9. Sustain with tools like Hoshin planning/policy deployment.
10. Create a continuous improvement environment where suggestions are encouraged and implemented throughout the organization everyday.

With Lean, we try to repeatedly improve performance by 30% or 50%. Often there are:

- Technical barriers
- Technological barriers
- Cultural barriers

The first barrier is almost always top management and finance which must be brought into the educational process. Companies that are truly Lean do not worry about ROI because they know it is the right thing to do. This can be a learning and cultural adjustment for the leaders in the organization and particularly within the finance areas as they are traditionally focused on "bottom-line" results. HR needs to facilitate, support and help drive the Lean culture starting with the hiring process. Most healthcare organizations still utilize the old-style subjective employee evaluation systems. This should be replaced with objective and subjective criteria supported by 360 feedback.

Key Learnings

- Realizing that cultural transformations take time and are necessary for enterprise-wide Lean adoption.
- Understanding that leaders must create a pull for the Lean culture and drive and facilitate the cultural transformation.
- Understanding the steps to create a Lean culture.
- Understanding the resistance-to-change and the technical, technological and cultural hurdles to Lean.
- Understanding the barriers in leadership that must be overcome to evaluate and implement Lean.

The leadership has to get involved; you can't do this from the front office. You have to be there in jeans and work boots, moving the machines yourself.

—Joe McNamara
VP, Global Operations, ITT Control Technologies

ORGANIZATIONAL DISSEMINATION OF LEAN

By now you have probably gained a better understanding of what it means to be Lean and the concepts, philosophies, and benefits an organization can achieve if Lean was adopted and deployed throughout the organization. In order to disseminate Lean across an organization, a cultural transformation must occur. In order to create a Lean culture, one must understand what makes up a Lean culture.

The customer should be the main focus of the Lean culture. This means the organization must have a way to tap the voice of the customer for each process and communicate it to the employees. The organization must develop and adopt process-focused metrics geared to improving the patient experience.

This topic is covered extensively in several recent publications. *Toyota Culture*, written by Jeffrey Liker, explores Toyota's Lean culture in much detail. David Mann's *Creating a Lean Culture* outlines the important components in a Lean culture. Dwane Baumgardner and Russ Scaffede's *Leadership Road Map*[*] lays out a guide for the CEO and board members of a company to implement a Lean culture. In the book, *The Baptist Health Care Journey to Excellence: Creating a Culture That Wows*,[†] Al Stubblefield describes his journey to change the traditional hospital-based culture. These are excellent references and, when taken together, provide a comprehensive road map on what and how to change the culture. The premise of each book explains that culture is a direct reflection of the beliefs and value systems embodied by the CEO and senior leadership team. Ultimately, others can influence the culture, but changes to the culture start with executive team.

We will briefly cover the following topics associated with implementing a Lean culture:

1. Understand what a Lean culture looks like—"the people piece"
2. Lean culture assessment
3. High-level steps to implementing a Lean culture
4. Barriers to continuous improvement
5. Work to sustain and improve it

UNDERSTANDING WHAT A LEAN CULTURE LOOKS LIKE—"THE PEOPLE PIECE"

While you can read up on all these topics, there is no "one-size-fits-all" solution. Every organization is unique; however, there are several common principles, approaches, and barriers encountered, as well as lots of *lessons learned* that can be garnered from organizations going through a Lean cultural transformation.

As we have stated many times, the Lean culture is only attained when you are tapping into and implementing the ideas of everyone in the organization, every day. Everyone in the organization is continuously and relentlessly working to eliminate waste which we offer what the customer desires with the highest quality, just in time, with the lowest cost and great patient experience. It is a culture where people enjoy

coming to work, they are not afraid of layoffs or census managing, and get paid more than the competition. The culture is role-modeled by the leadership, which is open and accessible to all their employees.

Standard work, to the extent it makes sense, is developed by the employees who are disciplined and take pride in everything they do. Standard work is prevalent in all layers of the organization and employees have what they need, when and where they need it; if they don't, they are empowered to work toward achieving it. Staff and physicians are encouraged to surface root cause problems with visual controls that provide a direct line of sight to their patients/customers and their expectations and quality.

The business incorporates real-time visual management systems with accountability and discipline where the frontline workers understand the chain of command and how they contribute to the specific goals in the strategic plan. Supervisors are promoted from within and are knowledgeable, accountable, and train their employees in their standard work. Employees work as a team, with an understanding that each and every patient is "their" patient. Staff members are cross-trained with the idea that no job is beneath them (i.e., anyone can mop the floor or pick up trash). PowerPoint presentations are replaced by A3 reports or another one-page standard form to provide a common way to communicate across the organization. The leadership is guided by a set of values and social responsibility to their communities. They respect and develop their employees, foster company loyalty, and encourage employees to think. The Lean organization is aligned by value streams (which breaks down the silos) with a focus on improving the overall process every day. While this is not an all-encompassing list, it embodies the highlights.

IMPORTANCE OF THE 50% PEOPLE PIECE

While some shrug off the need to bring everyone along on the journey, "the people piece," as we call it, cannot be underestimated and must be appreciated and constantly worked on in order to be successful. Implementing the Lean Six Sigma tools, while not always easy, are child's play when compared to implementing "the people piece" of these culture changes.

Understanding that people will make or break an organization's ability to fully deploy Lean is even more critical if you are a service organization. This is because, in most cases, the elimination of waste in service organizations occurs through process changes and deploying standard work and cannot be achieved or assisted by sequencing equipment and "layout" changes.

This requires that people "buy-in" to the process changes and standard work being implemented. If there is partial or no buy-in, then sustaining will be difficult. While it is easy to talk about the people piece and values by which the company will live or principles that will guide it, it is a very difficult environment to create, takes an incredible amount of work and perseverance, and must be driven from the top to be ultimately successful. The amount of time that this will take should not be underestimated.

---

[*] Russ Scaffede, owner, Lean Manufacturing Systems Group, LLC and management consulting consultant, vice president of manufacturing at Toyota Boshoku America. Past general manager/vice president of Toyota Motor Manufacturing Power Train, past senior vice president, senior vice president of global manufacturing at Donnelly Corporation, co-author of *The Leadership Roadmap: People, Lean & Innovation*, with Dwane Baumgardner and Russ Scaffede (Great Barrington, MA: North River Press) 2008.

[†] Al Stubblefield, *The Baptist Health Care Journey To Excellence: Creating A Culture That Wows* (Hoboken, New Jersey: John Wiley & Sons) 2005.

PEOPLE VS. TASK—WE NEED A BALANCE

If the goal is to truly have a cultural transformation, each employee should perform activities as defined by the customer with the least amount of waste. The desired behaviors need to be embedded within the organization by communicating, training, and reinforcing from the highest level of the organization. Most companies are still unable or unwilling or simply uneducated in how to create this "people piece" of the Lean culture. Too often, we treat people as replaceable or expendable, and we don't work to develop their talents. We call this the eighth waste: the "waste of talent."

If one gets too focused on "the people side," however, we lose discipline at the frontline and people will tend to do as they please. We can lose productivity and will hear comments like "How can you expect that person to work all day?"

Once during a Lean system implementation, we had an employee express that he was emotionally distraught because he never had to work all day. Sixty to eighty percent of his day was doing nothing as he watched the person across from him work non-stop, shouldering the burden of the operation. This employee complained to us that we couldn't expect him to work all day; in order to do so, he would need significant time, i.e., months, to work up to getting used to working all day. He then went to HR to complain. This is a true story.

You also see this phenomenon when managers have to just about "bribe" their employees to do a task that management cannot perform. At Toyota, everyone starts on the frontline. Even engineers start on the line so that they understand the systems, how the car is made and what their employees go through to make the car. What is interesting is that many of these principles were developed in the United States and were taught to the Japanese post-World War II. Unfortunately, the U.S. did not continue to leverage them.

In healthcare, we find managers often do not understand what employees have to do to perform their tasks. This is, in part, because licensure or specialized training is required to perform many activities. It is not always common practice for managers or other support staff to start on the frontline. When they join the company, they are placed at the level their licensure or degree dictates. In addition, it is not always common practice to have employees shadow each other to understand what they do. While they may shadow the person doing their job, they do not take time to understand the entire process from the patient's perspective. For example, we have found that staff in the operating room do not understand what happens in pre-testing, the Pre-Op area, or in the recovery area. On the opposite end, many clinical staff members are promoted because they are "good clinicians" and are not adequately trained or prepared to manage employees. This may cause an imbalance between the people component and the "data" or scientific management component.

VISION

In order to have a cultural transformation, the organizational leader must be able to define and articulate where the company is headed and what the "next level" of improvement will look like. Joel Barker says, *"A leader is someone you choose to follow to a place you wouldn't go by yourself."*[*] Successful Lean companies articulate and spread their Lean vision across the organization. Toyota combines this vision with its ongoing worries to create what some call "healthy or cultural paranoia" or a never-ending "compelling need to change". They create this healthy paranoia throughout the company regardless of their position in the industry. They do not celebrate when they hit a major milestone[†] because it is expected. Yet, they always worry about the competition and are concerned that they are not changing fast enough or are growing too fast and use this "worry" to constantly drive improvement.[‡]

ORGANIZATIONAL VALUE SYSTEMS

Does your organization have a set of values it truly lives by? Typical values are integrity, trust, etc. Successful Lean companies have a set of guiding principles and values that the companies truly live by. For example, As of this writing Toyota has not laid off any permanent employees since the 1950's even during the 2008 and 2009 recession.[§¶] Most companies have values, but they seem to be in name only. They say they believe in the values; however, the decisions that are made are not necessarily based on their values, nor do they live by them. Organizational leaders must role model their values by example. If they don't, then employees start to lose trust and not live by them either. Companies that live by their value systems include their values in their employee evaluations as subjective criteria.

In the book, *The Leadership Road Map,*[**] the authors dedicate the first half of the book to principles and values creation systems. When we hand this book out to executive leaders, they tend to skim through the first half of the book. When we ask them what they thought of the first half, they almost always respond, "Well, I already knew all that and it was somewhat a waste of my time."

We feel the key to these chapters is that one will find that it is easy to say "I know every organization has values" and CEOs know it is important to have company values but, in the end, do organizations really put their value systems into practice?

We then ask the leaders if their employees can state their company values. What would your employees say if we asked them the following: "Does your leadership live by those

---

[*] Joel Barker video, "Leadershift™ Five Lessons for Leaders in the 21st Century," American Media Inc, Distributed by Star Thrower.

[†] "CBS Sunday Morning, Under the Hood," Steve Glauber Producer, David Bhagat, editor, June, 2007 based on comments by Norm Buffano, senior vice president of Toyota.

[‡] "Toyotas All Out Drive To Stay Toyota," *Business Week* Vol., December 3, 2007.

[§] Employees were let go as a result of the joint venture NUMMI plant closure. Temporary employees have seen layoffs however that is why they are temporary. Toyota has considered voluntary job cuts with early retirement options and has offerred buyouts

[¶] Big Three U.S. automakers (Reuters) - Even though Toyota Motorpickup as "the truck that's changing it aAntonio are not immune from the threat

[**] Dwane Baumgardner and Russ Scaffede, *The Leadership Roadmap: People, Lean & Innovation* (Great Barrington, MA: North River Press) 2008.

TABLE 14.1

What we Believe

We believe that business enterprise has the opportunity to become the most positive influence on our society by providing a cultural environment in which people can realize their gifts, apply and develop their talents, and feel a genuine sense of fulfillment for their contributions in pursuit of a common inspirational vision.
Barry-Wehmiller: "What We Believe"
At Barry-Wehmiller, our **Guiding Principles of Leadership** define our vision of a dynamic corporate culture based on trust, respect and a genuine commitment to the personal and professional development of our team members. By striving to live these principles each and every day, we put our organizational values into action and advance our goal of measuring success by the way we touch the lives of people.
We believe that creating a truly successful environment—one that brings out the best in people and translates into strong business results over time—is our leadership challenge.
We believe that in every interaction, our customers are entitled to proactive and insightful communication with competent individuals who care about our customers' needs and the quality of their experience with our products, with our services, and with us.
We believe it is our responsibility to help our team members learn not only the fundamentals of our business, our products and our services but also realize the leadership skills needed to create an empowering and fulfilling environment.
We believe that embracing the leadership tools of **Lean (L3)** will allow our team members to fully engage their heads, hearts and hands to create products and services that are competitive and responsive to our customers' needs.
We believe that the convergence of **Lean** and our **Guiding Principles of Leadership** is critical to securing a rewarding and sustainable future for our associates by allowing us to compete effectively.
We believe that the decisions we make when filling leadership positions are critical as these people are stewards of our unique culture.
We believe that the fusion of our unique culture with the clarity of our vision is a powerful combination critical for long-term growth.
We build GREAT people who do EXTRAORDINARY things.
PACKAGING • ENGINEERING & IT CONSULTING • CORRUGATING • PAPER CONVERTING

Source: Courtesy of Robert Chapman, CEO, Barry Wehmiller, January 10, 2009.

values? Do your leaders make decisions based on those values? Does the leadership put the values into action?"

In most cases the answer is "no!" This is such an important point. We all know values are important, but most companies don't "walk the talk." One company that does "walk the talk" is Barry-Wehmiller. *Target Magazine* profiled CEO, Bob Chapman, and the "unique management system that truly embodies the people-centric, sustainability-focused principles of the Toyota Production System."[*] In the article, Mr. Chapman proposes the equation: "People + Process = Performance." We feel this embodies how important the people piece is to Lean (Table 14.1).

Mr. Chapman expounds on this equation by saying,

We realized about 8 years ago that we didn't have any 'stated values'. We 'thought' we had a 'good culture', but if you asked someone what that was, it differed by individual. But, about 8 years ago, we gathered a few people together to understand some of the leadership initiatives we were trying and we decided to 'study' articles on leadership in preparation for this meeting. In the course of the meeting, we started talking about what 'good' leadership should look like and we articulated the guiding principles of leadership. We had a general vision of growth, value and liquidity, all financial before this time and due to this articulation of our guiding principles of leadership, we refined our 'vision' to people, purpose and performance. It is fundamentally about how we touch lives of people, but to do so we need an inspiring purpose and then we need to execute/live this purpose by performing! It has totally transformed our sense

of purpose. We have recently taken it to another level and now state what we believe! It is our sense that all of these statements are in harmony and have evolved over time. We call it L3, Living Legacy of Leadership, as we are striving to develop and live leadership principles that are so profound that they will become deeply imbedded in our organization and serve as a sustaining leadership practice for generations to come. We believe that business enterprise has the opportunity to become the most positive influence on our society by providing a cultural environment in which people can realize their gifts, apply and develop their talents, and feel a genuine sense of fulfillment for their contributions in pursuit of a common inspirational vision. We found the Toyota system, and most all Lean leadership practices to be all about numbers, waste reduction, inventory turns, quality, improved financial performance and we 'realized' that the employee engagement aspect of Lean was a powerful leadership practice that could allow us to engage the heads and hearts of our teams, not just their hands, and create a more fulfilling environment for them daily. That is the problem with Lean. We do it for the wrong reasons. It is clearly a way to cure the decades old practice of paying people for their hands, when they would have given us their heads and hearts for free 'if' we just knew how to ask. Lean is a wonderful way to ask![†]

Homework: *Does your organization live its values in its day-to-day operations? Is it obvious to your ultimate customer, your patient? Does the organization use its principles to truly measure and guide the decision making?*

[*] "Capturing the Competitive Advantage of Employee Fulfillment," *Target Magazine* Vol. 25, No. 3, 2009.

[†] Correspondence from Robert Chapman, CEO, Barry Wehmiller, January 10, 2009.

Pearls of Advice

- Be patient with the process but insist on results
- Don't confuse effort with results.[*]
- Create a "no excuses" environment (toward improvement).
- Pause briefly to reflect on your successes, and then move on to the next one.

Managing Resistance to a Lean Culture Change

Every organization has a resistance to change. This resistance to change is embodied in the trials, tribulations, and outcomes of past change efforts. If the organization has demonstrated historically that other initiatives deployed were unsuccessful, then there will be more resistance to change. If the change is not supported or driven by top management, it will not last because employees will not view Lean as a priority. Successful Lean companies overcome the resistance by creating a compelling need to change and providing a positive vision of where and what they aspire to as the future state or next level, and then display activities and resources to support the vision.

Lean Culture Assessment

Homework: *Table 14.2 is a self-assessment that can determine where your organization is on its Lean journey. We have selected attributes that align with each type of culture. This can be used to help assess your organization. Place an X where you think it best fits your organization.*[†]

This assessment includes just a few of the attributes of a Lean culture. On which side does your organization seem to land?

Assessment Issues and Discussion

Are your people motivated to do a good job? Do they take pride in their work or just do enough to get by? Would they want to put in the extra effort because the organization makes them feel valuable? Is company loyalty encouraged? Company loyalty used to be coveted; today it is discouraged. It is no wonder we have the Enron's of the world. We seem to have lost our way!

Motivation and Continuous Improvement

That's the one nice thing about winning is you never second-guess yourself afterwards.[‡] The way to truly motivate people is to give them a vision to which to aspire and lead them there. Make them feel part of a winning team, part of your successful organization. If you expect your people to put in extra time, do you put in extra time as well? Does the executive team role model the behaviors you desire from your staff? Would your people say they work for a world-class organization with world-class processes?

By all current standards, you may think your organization is successful, but remember—success breeds complacency. Do you *really* demand continuous process improvement, or do you drive strictly financial-based improvements that middle management accomplishes through census managing or ongoing service and staff cuts? When was the last time you improved your processes? When was your last innovation? In the words of Sir John Harvey Jones, "*If you are not progressing, then you are regressing.*"[§] The more complacent your organization gets, the more vulnerable you are to the competition.

There was a time when layoffs or census managing were considered a failure on management's part. Today they are commonplace. After all, in the traditional model, people are considered expendable. It doesn't matter how much we have invested in training them. How do we treat our customers? Some companies actually refer to their customers as "units" as opposed to patients. Which side currently best fits your organization? If the answer is traditional and you find you embody more of the traditional organization, don't despair!

A goal of the Lean culture is to have 20%–30% less labor than your competition but have a 15%–30% increase in market wages over your competition.[¶] People should be rewarded for being more productive. What would be the advantages of this outcome? Employee retention would be at an all-time high. We all know how expensive it is to train people in their jobs and the culture. What is your employee turnover rate today? Job-hopping used to mean you weren't employable; now, if you don't change jobs people perceive something is wrong with you!

Another key element of companies in the past was the notion of "promote from within." Toyota still follows this today. Yet, in the United States, it seems it is more often "promote from without," and employees' opinions are not as valued as those of external consultants.

---

[*] Vic Chance, vice president of worldwide operations, Cordis Corporation, a Johnson and Johnson Company.

[†] Includes input from Jim Dauw, president, ITT Control Technologies.

[‡] Quote from Erik Seidel ESPN World Series of Poker 9-14-10.

[§] Video: "Trouble Shooter Series," BBC Television.

[¶] *From Detroit Free Press*

The UAW is losing its edge in pay compared with non-unionized U.S. assembly plant workers for foreign companies, even as Detroit automakers aim for deeper benefit cuts to trim their losses.

In at least one case last year, workers for a foreign automaker for the first time averaged more in base pay and bonuses than UAW members working for domestic automakers, according to an economist for the Center for Automotive Research and figures supplied to the *Free Press* by auto companies.

In that instance, Toyota Motor Corp. gave workers at its largest U.S. plant bonuses of $6,000 to $8,000, boosting the average pay at the Georgetown, KY, plant to the equivalent of $30 an hour. That compares with a $27 hourly average for UAW workers, most of whom did not receive profit-sharing checks last year. Toyota would not provide a U.S. average, but said its 7,000-worker Georgetown plant is representative of its U.S. operations.

Honda Motor Co. and Nissan Motor Co. are not far behind Toyota and UAW pay levels. Comparable wages have long been one way foreign companies fight off UAW organizing efforts.

February 1, 2007.

TABLE 14.2

Traditional vs. Lean

Traditional Healthcare Culture	Mark "X"	Lean Six Sigma Healthcare Culture	Mark "X"	Traditional Healthcare Culture	Mark "X"	Lean Six Sigma Healthcare Culture	Mark "X"
Short-term focused		Long-term focused		Lots of searching for everything		Five S'd organized areas	
Results-oriented metrics		Process-focused metrics		Lots of PowerPoint© presentations		One page A3 presentations	
Metrics located on computers		Metrics visible for everyone to see		Employees good at one job		Cross-trained and cross-functional "flexible" teams	
Management owns the numbers		Everyone owns the numbers		No time for training, too expensive		Mandatory training minimum 40 hrs per year	
Finance drives improvements		Quality and voice of customer-driven improvements		First day—on the job training		First 2 weeks learning culture prior to training	
Finance-driven decisions		Analysis and value-added data-driven decisions		Hire anyone that breathes		Strict selective criteria—teamwork and discipline	
Many management levels		Few management levels		HR backs employees that don't perform		HR backs managers and employees coached to "get them on the right seat in the bus"	
Autocratic		Participative and "bottom up"		Subjective evaluations		Objective and subjective evaluations with development and succession planning incorporated	
Management heavy		Empowered at the lowest levels		Special executive perks		No executive perks	
Management tells what to do		Management asks, challenges staff and offers help		Executives considered "suits"		Executives considered coaches and mentors	
Manage by "gut" and experience		Manage by fact		Ivory executive tower		Executives and managers co-located with employees	
Shoot from the hip fixes (not "data-driven")		Analysis data-driven fixes based on A3 root causes		Executive dining lounge		Executives eat with employees in cafeteria	
Band-aid type fixes		Permanent "root cause" fixes		Layoffs		Executives take pay cuts first, no one laid off	
Mistakes punished		Mistakes rewarded		People considered expendable		We invest in our people and cherish them	
People not paid to think		People expected to contribute new ideas daily		Organization silos		Value stream organization	
People don't have goals		Hoshin planning—line of sight to strategic plan		Normal maintenance		Total productivity maintenance	
"It is the ED's patient, not mine"		Every patient is "OUR" patient		Receiving		Point of use (delegate quality)	
Batching predominant		Flow driven		Inventory stores		Point of use materials storage (POU)	
Overproduction		Produce what's needed when it's needed		Cost of quality as a percentage of sales		Poka Yoke	
Erratic demand and staffing		Level loading and staffing to demand		Fake Lean		Lean seriously	
Reactive environment		Proactive environment		Finance		Lean accounting	

(continued)

TABLE 14.2 (CONTINUED)
Traditional vs. Lean

Traditional Healthcare Culture	Mark "X"	Lean Six Sigma Healthcare Culture	Mark "X"	Traditional Healthcare Culture	Mark "X"	Lean Six Sigma Healthcare Culture	Mark "X"
Firefighting rewarded		Firefighting eliminated		Managers expedite		Managers spend 50% on improvements	
Lots of inventory (nurse stash)		Minimal inventory, no stash		Buyers are order placers		Buyer/planner/scheduler	
Muda or waste everywhere		Improvements visible everywhere		Physician preference cards		Generic preference cards	
Employees frustrated end of day		Employees feel sense of accomplishment each day		Kaizen events		True continuous improvement	
People talk behind others backs		Daily huddles surface employee concerns and ideas		HR		Lean culture	
Little or no standard work		Standard work documented (and people follow it)		Minimal accountability		Hierarchical chain of command with all defined roles and responsibilites	
Few or no audits		Many audits		Managers 100% run business (firefight)		50% manager time budgeted for improvements	
People have repetitive dull work		People have meaningful and rewarding jobs		Meeting goals		Never satisfied with goals	

Source: Includes input from Jim Dauw, President, ITT Control Technologies. With permission.

In some companies, we have people constantly bidding and competing for their jobs. What type of environment does this create? Deming preached management must migrate away from managing by fear, yet at many companies this fear is embraced. In hospitals, we don't generally see management by fear but typically the opposite; there is little or no management accountability at all.

Back to the assessment. Did you rate yourself honestly? Would your employees agree with your ratings? Why not have some of them fill it out and see? An example is embedded in Hospital Consumer Assessment of Healthcare Providers and Systems (HCAPS) a "willingness to recommend." Not only does management need to be concerned about whether patients would be willing to recommend, but a gauge could be would your employees willingly recommend your hospital to customers in the community? Would your employees want to have services performed at their place of employment?

The first step to improvement is recognizing the need for improvement. But is it enough? Is there a compelling need to change? Remember the change equation: $C \times V \times N \times S > Rc$? If you *do not* have a compelling need to change after completing the checklist, then you may as well put the book down now and file it for future reference until you are ready. If the answer is yes, then, by all means, please read on!

Homework: *Review your check marks and make a list of where the gaps exist between the Lean culture and the traditional culture characteristics and behaviors.*

HIGH-LEVEL STEPS TO IMPLEMENTING A LEAN CULTURE

STEP 1: UTILIZE SKIP LEVELS TO SEE WHAT YOUR EMPLOYEES ARE THINKING

Use skip level meetings to meet with two levels below you without their manager or supervisor. Ask the manager or supervisor what you will hear from their employees and see how close it is. Then meet with the manager or supervisor to discuss what was heard and implement improvements based on same. There must be no retribution by the manager or supervisor for this process to work.

STEP 2: EDUCATION AND TRAINING

Educate yourself first on the Lean culture. Read Lean books, find a Lean sensei (knowledge and tools practitioner), find a Lean hospital or Lean manufacturing company to benchmark, attend Lean business seminars, join SME, AME, IIE, LEI, or other Lean organizations, take Lean training seminars, attend Lean executive roundtables, etc. Learn as much as you can about Lean Six Sigma. Learn the difference between Lean approaches, i.e., Point Kaizen events vs. Lean system implementation projects. Remember: Lean culture starts at the top.

Train your board of directors in Lean and get their support. Consider assigning a group to monitor your Lean activities. Consider creating a benchmarking group. Toyota has various committees at the board level to facilitate and support its continuous improvement efforts.

Train your senior leaders. Set expectations related to improvements and have each area create its plan to improve, monitor these plans and help to remove barriers. Create an executive team of Lean Six Sigma role models. Consider having "lunch and learns" to discuss Lean books or implement other teach-back techniques. Train everyone in the organization in Total Quality, Lean, and Six Sigma tools. Lead through example, make the training mandatory and make executives attend the training without their BlackBerrys®. If you are the CEO, once you have learned Lean Six Sigma, lead some of the training or participate on an implementation team.

STEP 3: CREATE A PULL FOR LEAN

If you are the CEO, put together your vision and values and Lean implementation plan. Then have every leader develop and report their process cycle times and overall throughput times.

Create a pull for Lean by telling your senior team they have to cut cycle times by 50% over the next year. Make sure your strategic plan contains a continuous improvement strategy. Make sure at every meeting that you emphasize Lean and A3 problem solving. The only way to truly sustain a Lean organization, especially if you have dedicated Lean Six Sigma resources, is to drive Lean goals, i.e., goals that can only be met by Leaning out the process. These goals have to be driven from the CEO level to create the pull for Lean initiatives. Without this pull, your dedicated continuous improvement folks have to "push" Lean. The more you "push" Lean, the more resistance you will meet. One can get good results initially by putting the ownership on the Lean resources, but they alone cannot sustain it because they don't have authority over the people in the department.

STEP 4: CREATE A LEAN IMPLEMENTATION PLAN

Create an organization-wide implementation plan, including your Lean vision, values, training, and communication plans with deliverable milestones. Make sure all functional area and value stream managers have a say in the plan. Communicate your vision, values, and guiding principles. Put it on wallet-sized cards and distribute them to everyone in the organization. Communicate, Communicate, Communicate! Remove the "blanks" and make sure everyone is communicating a similar message. If their are voids in communication employees will fill them in and in many cases it will be with messages that you have not intended to deliver. Utilize a variety of techniques to get the message out as not everyone responds to the same communication methods. Know that not everyone is going to be able to make the journey and be prepared to deal with them quickly.

Seek and receive approval from the board and the physicians on the Lean system implementation plan. Consider having each person sign a "contract for change or physician compact,"* outlining the vision and approach to be utilized.

Don't be afraid to amend the contract as you incorporate improvements to your strategy; however, every signer must agree to live by the contract or seek employment elsewhere.

Review your organizational chart. Drive accountability and discipline throughout the organization. Do you have the right people on the bus and in the right seats to get you to the next level of your plan? Every 6 months to a year, review your plan, your metrics, and your organization.

STEP 5: CREATE A LEAN STEERING COMMITTEE

Convert your senior leadership team into your Lean steering committee. Remember, Lean becomes the culture, the way you do business from now on.

Homework: *Determine the big Y (i.e., your most desired output or goal for your hospital or department delivery system). Then list all the inputs (Xs) that are required to meet the big Y. Then check to see if you have metrics in place that support each of the Xs. You will be surprised how often you don't!*

STEP 6: BASELINE METRICS

Baseline your current performance metrics. Establish "process-focused" cycle time and throughput time metrics and goals for every process in every department. This means your leadership team will have to become familiar with every process and sub-process in each department. Create process-centered metrics to support the results-oriented metrics you currently have and understand the linkage between them. Have each department conduct the Big Y exercise.† Map the line of site from the frontline worker through the executive leaders making sure that each employee has a clear understanding how their job directly impacts the strategic goals of the organization, and how they can contribute to the organizations success.

Take baseline videos and pictures everywhere. You will be surprised to see how fast things change. It really pays to take pictures so you can create before and after examples for staff.

STEP 7: IMPLEMENT A PILOT—UTILIZE THE BASICS MODEL

Pick a pilot area and implement a Lean project. If you need help, hire a consultant to guide you. It is not unusual to take 6 months to a year to learn the Lean tools. Toyota had its Lean senseis spend 3 years with each U.S. manager at NUMMI to teach and coach them in the system.‡

Kick off your implementation with a Lean training class. Lean training classes work best for teams that are implementing Lean or to provide an overview of Lean to your organization. Lean cannot be learned in the classroom or from online training. One has to learn the principles and then go practice/implement them. We have found 1 and 5-day or more

---

* Harvard Business Review, Virginia Mason, 9-606-044, Richard Bomer, Erika Ferlins, January 11, 2006.

† ValuMetrix® Tool, ValuMetrix® Services of Ortho Clinical Diagnostics.
‡ Gary Convis talk to MWCMC, April 16, 2008.

sessions very helpful as a supporting tool for creating a Lean culture and have many testimonials to back it up.

You can implement Five S with your Lean projects and Point Kaizen events or launch Five S cleanups, i.e., some organizations have "dumpster days." Five S can be a lot of fun. But it is important to plan Five S ahead of time. We are not fans of "if in doubt, throw it out." We have seen millions of dollars of equipment thrown out this way. Create a disposition and discard process.

Again, once Lean training is conducted, the CEO and his/her staff should become the trainers. Continue to implement improvements and continue to hit projects/areas already implemented to continuously drive them toward world class.

STEP 8: GEMBA WALKS

Get out of your office! Walk around! Conduct audits, talk to employees. Get out of your ivory tower, encourage suggestions, and ask employees how you can help. Eliminate all the reports and create visual metric boards in each area. Remember, if you improve your in-process metrics, the results will follow. This is a big leap of faith but necessary to succeed in creating a Lean culture. Eat lunch with your employees. Encourage them to think; don't give them the answers. Ask them what their metrics are. Quiz them on Lean concepts.

STEP 9: SUSTAIN—HOSHIN AND SUGGESTION SYSTEM

Implement and formalize *Hoshin* planning bottom-up goal deployment. Then establish a formal, Lean-type, suggestion process—not a suggestion box! Toyota's suggestion system is described in the book, *20 Million Ideas in 40 Years.* Recognize, reward, and publicize successes. Remember, rewards do not have to be monetary. Consider having yearly events to recognize best improvements.

STEP 10: CONTINUOUS IMPROVEMENT

Take your Lean culture quiz every 6 months and report the findings to the board-level Lean committee. Update your roadmap or "plan" of continuous improvement to continue to narrow the gaps.

Our every day employee goals for a Lean culture can best be embodied by the words of Joel Barker, *"When you combine the paradigm pioneering concept with Kaizen or continuous improvement, the speed of your paradigm curve is increased. Now when the settlers ask is it safe out there? The Pioneer says sure it's safe, but there's nothing left for you."*

But to do this we all have to improve our jobs every day. As Joel Barker goes on to say, *"1/10th of 1 percent is just fine but you have to do it every day".*

Initially, it doesn't sound like much, but imagine the power of one-tenth of 1% every day by every employee:

One-tenth of 1% × 10 days = 1% improvement × 100 days = 10% × 1000 days = 100%.

Company X, which had been around for approximately 125 years, was complaining about the problems it continued to experience. We wanted company X to really think about serious improvement, so we took a chance and honestly inquired, "You've been in business for more than 100 years; shouldn't you have it just about right by now?" Fortunately, despite our candid questioning, we were invited back and worked with them to make huge improvements. Sometimes you have to provoke companies to get that "compelling need to change."

BARRIERS TO CONTINUOUS IMPROVEMENT

There are three main types of barriers: technical, technological, and cultural.

1. Technical barriers examples
   - Lack of communication
   - Lack of data
   - Process changes

These can be overcome by team empowerment, clear project charters, change management, and communication plans.

2. Technological barrier examples
   - Information systems
   - Equipment/infrastructure costs
   - New technology, i.e., RFID systems, etc.
   - Centralized vs. decentralized equipment decisions

These may be more difficult to overcome; however, understanding upfront that there may be challenges is important. If the organization's infrastructure is composed of many IT systems which don't communicate with each other, then engaging technology teams or identifying IT personnel to be part time or full time on the Lean implementation teams may be an answer.

In some cases, there may need to be an openness to revert temporarily to a manual process while changes are being made to the IT software or systems. It may be necessary to implement a temporary freeze on rolling out new technologies until the areas can be "Leaned," i.e., waste is eliminated and the process is streamlined.

Capital and operation funds should be set aside pre-project to address challenges that may already be known by the area or IT department so, as recommendations surface, the funds are available for enhancements.

3. Cultural barriers examples
   - Sacred cows—paradigms—not invented here, "We've always done it this way"
   - Organizational barriers—department/silo-focused, lack of HR support
   - Lack of leadership buy-in, resulting in management stall tactics

---

* Video: "Paradigm Pioneers," Joel Barker, president, Infinity Limited, distributed by Chart House International© 1993.

- Financially, results-oriented, driven, short-term thinking resulting in sliding back to results-focused and shoot-from-the-hip behaviors
- Putting everything on a computer
- No time for training or training costs too much
- Laying off your black belt or dedicated Lean resources
- Expecting the Lean dedicated resources to own the changes

These barriers are the most difficult and typically can only be overcome by the CEO creating:

- An open-minded culture where any sacred cow is open to questioning
- A clear implementation road map
- A "manage by fact" culture
- Having everyone sign contracts for change
- Real-time visual controls
- Leading by example, clear communication

If Lean is "brought in" at the middle management level, they will tell you their biggest barrier is almost always top management. We hear it over and over. Middle managers will state "they (top management) don't understand Lean or what we are trying to do." The next barrier we hear is finance. They tell us, "Finance still wants ROI results-driven metrics." It is difficult for financial analysts and managers to understand the impact of results-focused metrics and that it may take 6 months to a year to achieve bottom-line results. Finance often tells middle managers, "We don't care about Lean accounting because we still have to answer to auditors and regulators," since this is the way the organization does business.

The next department barrier is human resources. For example, during a Lean initiative there is a charge nurse who doesn't want to engage in Lean. Human resources' solution is to place the nurse on a 6-month development plan and, thus, the Lean program in that department grinds to a halt and stalls for 6 months or more.

EFFORT TO OVERCOME EACH BARRIER TYPES

The rule of thumb is technical barriers take 1X effort to overcome, technological take 10X effort to overcome, and cultural take 100X to overcome. Only the CEO and their leadership team can truly overcome the cultural barriers. Why? Because the CEO is the only one who has the authority over everyone and every department in the organization.

WORK TO SUSTAIN AND IMPROVE WITH LEAN

As we have discussed, in order for Lean to be truly embraced and strategically entrenched within an organization, a cultural transformation needs to occur. We have seen Lean sustained in "pockets" in many organizations by management and staff who believe in Lean and have seen the results; however, if Lean has not been embedded as the way the organization

does business, ultimately the improvements will turn into what we call "Lean light," or a watered-down version. The organization will not attain what they could nor will it be able to sustain once the area staff or "believers" move on, and more than likely the area will go back to doing things the way they did before. Therefore, it is important that an organization begins to gain an understanding of how it operates from a leadership and cultural perspective to recognize what challenges it may face in adopting Lean philosophies. This is why the overall success rate with Lean is so small.

HOW DO YOU GET THE CEO ON BOARD?

In order to sustain Lean, the CEO must be on board. This doesn't mean they have to be on board in the beginning, although this is the ideal. Getting them on board will depend on the CEO's exposure to Lean. Encourage them to read, benchmark, and attend executive Lean seminars.

It can be difficult if you are trying to create a Lean culture within a traditional organization. In traditional organizations, the CEOs and financial officers are looking for short-term, quick, and large ROIs. If the organization is traditional, they will respond best if they are shown quick results on one or a series project(s). Many times, Lean goes on for a couple of years, and the CEOs still have not totally bought in. This is mainly due to pressure from the CFO. We normally end up having very candid discussions with the CEO and CFO over their investment in the effort and whether or not they are serious about implementing Lean and embedding it into their culture. This conversation has worked at more than one hospital.

Story...Lean in County Government

*Erie County Executive, Chris Collins, who came to politics from business, has made Six Sigma a focal point of his administration. Through his high profile position, he has brought attention to the system… His Six Sigma director, Bill Carey, said the first wave of projects have generated $4.9 million in savings. Additional projects are under way or being planned.**

COMMITTING THE RIGHT RESOURCES TO SUSTAIN

When rolling out Lean, many organizations bring in an outside resource or consultant to act as a sensei helping to lead and train management staff in Lean concepts and tools. Leaders of organizations need to make sure there is clarity of the consultant role. The consultant's job should be to make sure the organization eventually becomes self-sufficient in being able to propagate Lean internally.

It is the consultant's job to do the improvement *with* management and the team, not *to them*. To be successful, the ownership must stay with the frontline staff process owners or Lean will not sustain. The operational process owners need to be told up front that they own the projects,

* "Six Sigma backers say commitment is key," *The Buffalo News: Business Today,* December 22, 2009, by Matt Glyn, update October 11, 2009.

timeline, control, and sustain the plan as well as the overall success of the projects. The consultant, internal or external, is there to help and support them. There must be an exit strategy for the internal or external consultants to transition the area back to the process owner. The process owner needs to continue ongoing cycles of improvement once the team has disassembled.

Dedicated Lean organizational resources are necessary to get the changes started. It is important to have dedicated process improvement resources or Lean specialists within clinical areas dedicated to drive continuous cycles of improvement. Over time, these resources must be folded back into the organization in management and frontline roles. Because most healthcare organizations don't have staff in roles that are initially equipped to handle this accountability, discipline, and responsibility, this skill set will need to be developed.

Care must be taken to protect these dedicated Lean positions, as these tend to be viewed as "easy to cut" positions, since they are not perceived to be dedicated to frontline patient care. The organization should place future potential leaders in the Lean specialist roles to develop them for future roles and incorporate them into their succession planning. When Lean specialists transition back into the line organization, they will reinforce Lean concepts and help drive cultural change across the organization as future leaders. We have witnessed time after time, if there are not good development plans in place or leadership does not buy in, the Lean specialists will leave the organization.

Lesson Learned #1: *We need to put development plans in place for all our middle managers and supervisors, which provide adequate training to successfully manage in a Lean culture environment.*

Lesson Learned #2: *If you are going to invest in highly skilled training and Lean-dedicated resources, you must provide and structure challenging development plans for them along with a vision for their futures. Anyone who is dedicated to improvement activities initially worries about their job future, since they are not tied to a department or value stream.*

HUMAN RESOURCES AND LEAN

Human resources should help facilitate, support, and drive the Lean culture. Most healthcare organizations are still utilizing the old style, very subjective employee evaluation systems. It is not unusual for the subjectivity to be based on personalities. In the new evaluation system, employees should have a subjective and objective component with a 3- to 5-year development plan. The subjective component should be based on how they are living each of the company values. The objective component should be based on their overall performance to the goals mutually developed with employee and supervisor to meet the strategic plan.

Toyota uses a system for this, called *Hoshin* planning. *Hoshin* planning provides a mechanism so that every employee can understand how his/her personal goals directly relate and impact the strategic planning goals of the organization. Organizations must constantly focus on and understand the gaps to obtain the next level of the vision. This is not a management by objectives (MBO) approach!

In order to drive the correct behaviors, employees need to be evaluated on how they are living the new company values and guiding principles. If employees don't live and role model the company values, even if they have exceeded their objective goals, there needs to be a process to correct the behavior. The values (people piece) must carry equal weight with the tools (objective) piece. Failure to do this will result in a non-Lean culture.

Every leader should be evaluated on how well they develop their people. The evaluation should include a professional growth plan outlining the employee's aspirations and what position he/she might be seeking in the next 1–5 years. The manager and employee should each fill out a copy of the evaluation, meet to assess where they agree and disagree, and then together explore the gaps. Once the gaps are discussed and agreed on, the employee should jot down actions they plan on implementing over the next year to overcome the gaps. This becomes their development plan.

The development plan should include an ongoing training plan that leverages books, formal school classes, webinars, seminars, movies, benchmarking, etc. The 360-degree evaluation technique between employee, supervisor, and peers can become a very powerful tool for objective feedback.

SUSTAINING THE CONTINUOUS IMPROVEMENT CULTURE

As we stated earlier, the goal is to sustain the continuous improvement culture. It is truly a wonder that Toyota has somehow managed to sustain this culture for so long. Sustaining is the most difficult part of any Lean journey. One can lose the culture very easily and quickly. The new system is fragile and vulnerable until both the tools and "people piece" are cemented into the organization at the top.

We have seen companies lose the culture they worked so hard to build with the change of a president/CEO or CFO. We have seen companies lose it because the CEO and CFO never totally understood the new system. We have seen companies lose it because they lost the "tools piece" and stopped videotaping, stopped acting on fact, and reverted back to the "shoot-from-the-hip" culture. It gets even more difficult in challenging financial times with declining reimbursements. Of course, this is when it is most critical and important. So what do we do? Probably the best example is to figure out how Toyota did it.

Toyota has continually worked at the model. They have created a learning organization. They constantly focus on building "cars that sell." They don't lose sight of the customer. They constantly retrain management in the fundamentals of the system. They have totally changed their systems and organization to support the Lean philosophy. Their CEOs don't monitor the stock price daily and don't make millions of dollars a year. They value their employees, but there is still a rigid command and control discipline in place.* The glue that seems to hold it all together is the "standard work paradox." The paradox is standard work is rigid in that everyone must follow it, yet flexible in that everyone is constantly trying to improve every operation every day and then updating the standard work. If you were to ask Toyota, however, I bet they would tell you that they are still working on the system and know that they have not discovered all of its secrets.† If they feel they have a long way to go, what does that say for the rest of us? However, it takes a continual pursuit toward excellence and even great companies stray, look at what challenges Toyota has experienced in the past with previously unheard of recalls. Will investigative research reveal that there was a fundamental change in the way they were doing business that caused their quality to be questioned? One can only speculate at this junction and understand that this journey requires diligence and perseverance to stay course from the executive leaders.

---

* E-mail from Russ Scaffede, owner, Lean Manufacturing Systems Group, LLC and management consulting consultant, vice president of manufacturing at Toyota Boshoku America, past senior vice president of global manufacturing at Donnelly Corporation, past vice president of Toyota Motor Manufacturing Power Train, co-author of *The Leadership Roadmap: People, Lean & Innovation*, with Dwane Baumgardner and Russ Scaffede (Great Barrington, MA: North River Press) 2008.

---

† Many of their secrets are in Jidoka, which is mistake proofing and safety built into all their machines that cannot be seen.

Section III

Selected Lean Implementation Case Studies

15 Surgical Services

Now we begin Section III, the Lean implementation case studies.

The primary goal behind these chapters is to eliminate the excuses that often surround implementing Lean such as "we are unique", "it won't work in my department" or "clinical practice is unpredictable". Lean can and has worked in virtually every area of the hospital. The case studies in section III are limited representative examples of implementations we experienced over the past several years. There are many more examples not only in hospitals and clinics but in Veterinary Medicine, Healthcare Architectural Design, and Private Practice etc. We hope the case studies can give the reader an idea of how Lean can be applied to gain an understanding of the "possibilities" and provide a starting point for your Lean journey. Our hope is that you see value and expand the scope into areas that are yet to be explored and that the solutions we share are surpassed in the future. One thing we have learned over the many years of Lean implementation is "there is always a better way, we just have to continue to work to discover it." We hope hospitals continue to share their continuous improvement successes which will accelerate the transfer of knowledge and create Continuous Learning Organizations.

The case studies are designed to show how the tools have been successfully implemented at various hospitals. This does not necessarily mean these are the best/ or only ways to apply Lean, but shows how others have implemented in their pursuit to eliminate waste and shares their lessons learned. The case studies vary in length with surgery and ED being the most lengthy as they are some of the most complex processes within the hospital vs. GI Lab which we were able to walk through and apply all of the tools within 1.5 hrs! Please note these case studies represent implementations, not the traditional Five Day Point Kaizen Event approach. The chapters are formatted similarly to the extent that each one looks at the traditional processes, problems with the process, and "what" and "how" Lean tools were applied. The book is written so most chapters can stand alone, therefore you will find some repetition.

Many chapters were co-written by a person who implemented Lean in their own department. For instance, Nutritional Services includes select insights and Lessons Learned from a "Director Level" Leader who went through our Lean implementation process. For those would like to see the breakdown in the math, some chapters provide detailed calculations.

Lean and Six Sigma have a very comprehensive tool chest, and when integrated with a Lean Culture, create a very powerful system which we hope we have managed to convey in the next several chapters.

SURGICAL SERVICES: OVERVIEW

Since surgical services is such a large value stream we have dedicated a significant number of pages to its coverage. In order to organize it for the reader we have broken the chapter into an overview section with lessons learned and Lean solutions and then a detailed section which drills down to a level of 'how to implement' and calculations. It should be noted the Lean solutions discussed were successfully implemented and sustained but may not necessarily be the best solution for every hospital since each hospital is unique. They are shared here to give the reader an idea of how Lean was successfully applied.

Traditionally What We Find in Most Operating Rooms

Lean initiatives are generally recommended by hospital administrators for several reasons. Surgery has always been a main driver of hospital revenue, but now it is under pressure. Surgical reimbursements are dropping, surgeon malpractice insurance is increasing, and there is increasing pressure to provide value based healthcare. Profitable heart surgeries have been replaced by minimally invasive technological breakthroughs (i.e., stents) and advancements in medical treatments.

The implementation of HCAHPS (Hospital Consumer Assessment of Healthcare Providers and Systems) survey by CMS implemented in October 2006, with the first public reporting in March 2008 has caused hospitals to look more closely at the drivers of patient satisfaction. Patients now have a venue to view comparative information on hospitals which could be utilized to help them determine where to seek elective and non-emergent care.

Global Impact of Operating Room Flow— Organizational Conflicts—Competition for Beds

It is no surprise that surgery and emergency departments (EDs) compete for the same hospital beds. As a result, when surgery demand is higher on Tuesday, Wednesday and Thursday, floors back up, inpatient holds increase in the ED (sometimes forcing diversions), patients back up in the post-anesthesia care unit (PACU) which sometimes leads to holding patients in the OR suites. Management typically responds with reactive-type counter measures, which can be costly. Normally, they want to add rooms (patient, ED, Pre-Op, ORs, etc.) to fix the problems. But adding rooms is typically a "shoot from the hip" short-term and sometimes short-sighted solution. Adding capacity may alleviate the challenges for six months or a year, if that, but once we fill those rooms up, what happens? We experience the same problems as before, but now on a larger scale because the root causes of the original processes were never identified and never fixed. In addition, the rooms are typically added under the stress of meeting a deadline or budget, and architects attempting to please their customers and budgetary constraints may cause rooms and support services to be placed wherever they fit. Typically, architects do not analyze process data and, if they do, they use a multiplier of square footage, i.e., today's square footage multiplied by 50% projected growth. This yields a 50% larger footprint that tends to be more costly than needed. Architects sometimes look at process flows, but most often default to what the staff want, which is to base the new layout on their current batch-based processes. Architectural firms almost never challenge managers when it is related to administrative space desired. Designs are produced based on past experiences or what other hospitals designed vs. the Lean concepts. Generally, one ends up with adhoc layouts without any type of overall flow or capacity analysis. More often than not, even when flow is considered, rooms and equipment get "squeezed in" to areas that are "available," thus disrupting any type of product flow or minimizing travel distance. In the layout example shown, storage, equipment, and a pharmacy were placed between PACU, Pre-Op, and the ORs. In reality, the best Lean layout is often not feasible owing to constraints within an aging building or it is cost prohibitive to remodel (Figure 15.1).

Lesson Learned: *Adding rooms is a very costly solution. It is essentially creating excess inventory that hides the root cause of the hospital's problems. It is an easy way out. If we improve our processes and reduce throughput time, we won't need the additional rooms (unless there is a significant growth plan to add volume). In the event we need to add rooms, we need to consider an ideal Lean layout first (no constraints) and then adjust it to meet the constraints inherent in the existing building.*

Hospitals need to ensure revenue streams are maintained amid the changing healthcare environment. They need to retain and attract physicians by creating an efficient environment where surgeons want to bring their cases. Often, we hear complaints from our physicians "customers" because they are "unhappy" or dissatisfied. Our first step is to survey the surgeons, anesthesiologists and hospital staff to identify the issues. For a sample VOC Survey see Table 15.1. At most hospitals we categorize the issues by patient flow, however, we have chosen to view the issues from the Customer Point of View. While ultimately the patient is the "end" customer in the hospital business model, the surgeon can also be viewed as an external customer. The staff and administrators represent internal customers to each other as they are linked to one another throughout the process i.e., Pre-Op is a customer of Admitting, OR is a customer of Pre-Op, PACU is a customer of the OR and the floors are customers of PACU. To elucidate, in most hospital models, the surgeons bring the customer, "the patients", "with them" to the hospital. Without the surgeons, with the exception of the ED or medical admissions who may require surgery, the hospital would have few surgery patients. Surgeons generate billings for the hospital in addition to surgery revenue as patients need ancillary services such as radiology and lab, rehab, consults and inpatient unit hospital stays. The surgeon and hospital revenue streams may vary depending on whether the surgeon or hospitalist becomes the admitting physician. Some surgeons prefer to only perform surgeries and let the hospitalists take care of the admitting and attending or the "follow up" portion of care. So this is somewhat of a unique case in Lean where we have two main customers, surgeon and patient. We must be able to satisfy the surgeon and take care of our ultimate end customer "the patient" as they progress through our hospital processes the before, during, and after surgery. The basic assumption is if we can satisfy the surgeons, anesthesiologists, staff and administrative issues, the patient will have a good experience. The exception to this issue would be where the patient is undergoing a procedure they really don't need or is being over processed in some fashion. We have categorized the major issues we find in our surgery assessments below:

I. Physician (surgeon and anesthesiologist) Satisfaction Issues
   a. Poor surgeon utilization – (i.e., surgeons have to wait between cases)
   b. Patient Readiness
   c. Pre-Testing Clinic bottlenecks and flow
   d. Lack of Standard Orders
   e. Late Starts
   f. Turnover Time
   g. Lack of Bed Availability
   h. Staffing
   i. OR Scheduling
   j. Lack of standardization

II. OR Surgical Team (Staff and Administrative) Issues
   a. Organizational Silos - centralized departments i.e., Transport, Bed Management
   b. Reactive Management
   c. Non Standardized, Incomplete, or Undocumented Processes
   d. Lack of Measurement Accountability
   e. Poor Data Availability
   f. Non-Integrated Data Systems
   g. Data Validity

Let's briefly explore each of these issues.

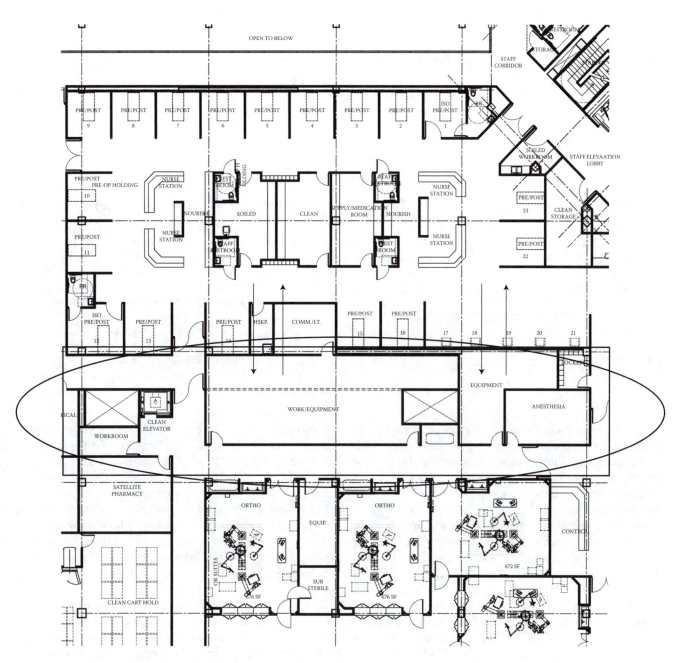

FIGURE 15.1 OR design drawing Note: Flow from Pre-Op to OR is blocked by work equipment, storage rooms and mechanical equipment.

I. Physician (surgeon and anesthesiologist) Satisfaction Issues

When we implement in surgical services we start with a physician and staff satisfaction survey. A sample of survey results can be found in Table 15.1. In many instances, the physicians' complaints are well founded. We find significant waste and workarounds every day by each staff member in order to get the patient through the system. In addition, when analyzing the "value stream of the surgical patient" as defined from pre-admission to post-operative

(Post-Op) bed placement (in actuality, one might start the value stream at recommendation for surgery and end at payment received). It is difficult to find many staff who have a full understanding of the activity that takes place across the entire value stream. One has to engage participants from every area to gain a true picture of what the "patient customer" encounters as they navigate the surgical value stream.

Ia. Poor surgeon utilization – i.e., Surgeons have to wait before and between cases. We define surgeon utilization as

TABLE 15.1

VOC (Voice of the Customer) Survey Results

Voice of the Customer – VOC Feedback From Survey Only Items With Multiple Responses "What Is Your Main Frustration" Key Common Concerns point to Efficiency, Staff Resources		
Surgeon Team **Issues** Prioritized	**Anesthesiology Team** **Issues** Prioritized	**OR Surgical Team** **Issues** **Not Prioritized**
38 Responses	38 Responses	66 Responses
1. *Turnover* 2. *Lack of Staff* 3. *On Time Starts* 4. Training of Current Staff 5. Block Time 6. Loss of Information 7. No Designated OR for Emergent Cases 8. Equipment 9. Scheduling 10. Labs 11. # Of OR Rooms 12. *OR Throughput*	1. *Lack of Staff* 2. *Turnover Time* 3. *Waiting in OR for PACU Bed* 4. Incomplete Pre-Op Preparedness 5. *Delays* 6. *Inefficiency* 7. *PACU Holds* 8. Equipment	• *Lack of Staff* • Education of Staff • Incomplete and Poor access to Supplies • HIS Time Consuming and not Real Time • Poor Evaluation Process and Reward System • Poor Scheduling Process • Accountability, Cooperation, *late Arrival* and Treatment by Physicians • Communication & Team building • Management Enforcement of Key Operational and Safety Policies

"surgeon in to surgeon out" divided by the "patient in to next patient in" or total surgery case time. We find surgeon efficiency according to this definition is generally 40% to 50% (and the surgeon's perception is less if for example, a first assistant closes, and there is not a second team standing by to start the next case).

At most hospitals, it is the anesthesiologist group's availability and many times availability of the surgical team that drives the schedule. This impacts the ability to provide physician block time, or flexibility in adding cases, and impacts potential revenue and surgeon satisfaction. Yet, much of this is hidden to the surgeons unless they are actively involved with management in improving the process. Surgeon utilization also impacts the hospital's global budget related to staffing, supplies/instruments, and capital equipment. Most of the issues we discuss throughout the chapter impact surgeon utilization at some level. In reality what leads to surgeon satisfaction is providing solutions which alleviate surgeon idle time. Many hospitals attempt to use flip rooms to decrease surgeon idle time, however this can be problematic as this only works if there is an additional (new) team which would include staff and anesthesiologist to start the next room at the "right" time to begin the case for the surgeon. This tends to work best if the surgeon has a physician partner, resident or mid-level provider who can get the "next" case going until the surgeon can complete the prior case (surgeon out) to minimize idle time of the anesthesiologist, team and room. Flip rooms can create a challenge for the hospital if too much anesthesia or room and staff idle time is created, as it may have to hold OR suites "vacant" for a period of time (which now impacts room utilization) until the surgeon completes his prior case in order to "flip" to the next room. This can impact the satisfaction of anesthesiologists who want

to optimize their day (by generating revenue) performing back to back cases so they do not sit idle waiting for the surgeon to finish the prior case. In addition, this may require additional surgical teams who if the timing is off will wait along with anesthesia for the surgeon to complete the prior case, burning FTE dollars which are not generating revenue for the hospital. In essence there are opposing views of what determines physician satisfaction, between the surgeons, anesthesiologists, hospital administration, and surgical services staff which need to be balanced.

Ib. Patient readiness really comes down to two major components: Does the patient have medical clearance for the procedure and is the patient properly prepared for surgery which would include consenting, marking and preparation? We have found after implementing Lean in several surgery departments, the tests for medical clearance are generally ordered by the surgeon. However, it is not the surgeon who really decides if the patient goes ahead with the procedure. This decision is ultimately that of the anesthesiologist. Therefore the patient needs to be prepared based on a combination of surgeon and anesthesiologist orders. We have found this is normally a "weak link" in the chain on the day of surgery. The patient will arrive in surgery with all the surgeon's orders carried out only to find the anesthesiologist needs another test or piece of information to approve the move to the OR. The surgeon ends up being delayed but normally is unaware of the newly imposed requirements and assumes the Pre-Op/pre-testing process is flawed. In summary we need to concentrate in parallel on improving both the pre-testing process and surgical order sets.

Lean Solutions

Standard Orders

We recommend meeting with the surgery Operations Oversight committee (which should include physician representatives from each subspecialty along with anesthesia and administrative representatives) or a cross specialty adhoc committee which includes the lead anesthesiologist (if there is not an existing committee structure) to work together to develop or revise an existing "standard" order set which clearly defines the expectations for overall surgery clearance. The order set is generally in the form of a grid (with checkboxes of orders) to guide surgeons through best practice recommended orders. The format and content may vary for each hospital depending on the case mix and acuity level of the patients treated.

Pre-Testing Clinic

We work on streamlining the Hospital's Surgical Pre-testing (or Pre-Admission Testing) Unit. We create standard work and level load the schedule. We develop process focused metrics around cycle times and real time customer satisfaction. We give control of their schedule to the unit vs. having the OR or central scheduling handle the appointments. We develop quality metrics (see Figure 15.2) and Pre-Op (internal customer) feedback to make sure all the orders are carried out properly. We engage physician offices to educate them on the new order-set, pre-testing processes, facilitate communication and emphasize the importance and impact of following "standard work" related to surgical orders and accessing pre-testing.

Ic. Late starts frustrate both physicians and staff. These can be measured and root causes (or defects in the process) should be defined and addressed.

Lean Solutions: *Late starts have generally two root causes. The first is the patients aren't ready for surgery and the second is the surgeon is late. Generally the surgeon is late because the patients are never ready so this becomes a "catch 22" type problem. With Lean we pareto the reasons for late starts (defects) and set the surgeon lateness issue on the back burner. This is because if the patients are always ready to go on schedule the surgeon will have the confidence in the staff and schedule to show up on time. We generally find the most common root causes for lateness tie back to patient readiness issues and lack of a clear definition of what a "patient ready for surgery" looks like. We create a standard checklists and a standard physician order set to create a ready patient and then create visual controls to sustain our results.*

Id. Turnover time drives capacity and surgeon "wait times" and is generally a surgeon and anesthesiologist dissatisfier at every hospital and many surgical outpatient centers. Organizations may not have agreed to what the right metric is for turnover and more importantly, the definition of turnover being utilized may not have been clearly communicated, so physicians and staff reviewing it may be interpreting it differently. For example, when reviewing the metrics surrounding turnover, hospitals may report 'patient out to patient in,' 'surgeon out to surgeon in,' or 'surgeon close to cut'. To really understand what is occurring operationally, however, one may have to break down the process to a more granular level.

Figure 15.3 represents the surgery turnover sequence of activities. One could potentially collect and measure any of these data points related to processes within the operative time frame. For example, one could measure the following cycle times:

- 'Patient out' to 'ready for patient' or 'room ready'
- 'Ready for patient' or 'room ready' to 'patient in room' or 'wheels in'
- 'Patient out' or 'wheels out' until 'surgeon cut'
- 'Patient in room' or 'wheels in' to 'patient out of room' or 'wheels out'

It is important that each process data point is clearly defined and communicated so the data is accurately understood and captured. It is important to note that each measure encompasses benefits and drawbacks and therefore may drive different levels and types of improvement suggestions.

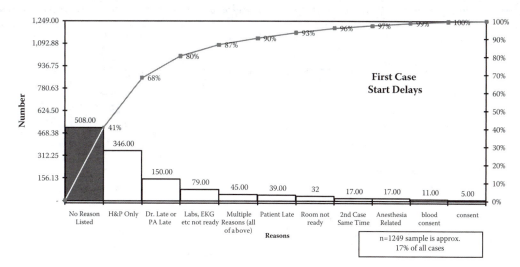

FIGURE 15.2   First case delays. Note: The number one reason is "no reason listed". We find this lack of data to be normal at most hospitals.

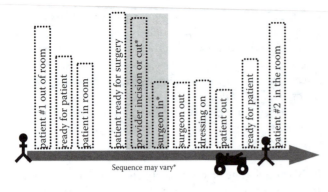

Sequence may vary*

FIGURE 15.3 Turnover time.

Many organizations only utilize 'patient out to patient in' to gauge turnover efficiency; however, there are conflicting goals in efficiency between surgeons, administration, staff, and anesthesiology related to OR utilization and efficiency. One may not want to routinely measure and report each data point on each sub-process; however, being able to identify waste and opportunities that need to be improved at the sub-processes level can be extremely valuable in getting to the root cause of any problems at hand. Surgeons want to minimize their "idle time" and, if asked, their definition of turnover is really related to their perceived turnover time 'surgeon out to surgeon in,' which would equate to the time they exit the OR room to the time they make the surgical incision or in some cases begin the next procedure (if they have resident or midlevel provider who started the procedure) on the next case.

The appropriate metric should be determined by where you would most likely identify the wastes. The turnover metric could be "close" (of the first patient) to "cut" (on the next patient), which is more of an operational metric vs. the surgeon efficiency metric. 'Patient out' to 'patient in' is routinely measured and reported by most ORs, which gauge only the physical room cleaning, and maybe some patient preparation activity but does not include all the anesthesia- or surgery-related activity. If you look at 'surgeon out to surgeon in,' it will capture inefficiencies within the overall system related to turnover, setting up

the room, availability of anesthesia, and even timeliness of surgeon. It will even capture inefficiencies related to whoever is left to close the patient (resident, assistant) and steps required prior to moving the patient out of the room, which is not captured in the metric 'patient out to patient in'. It will not capture downtime of the room and the inefficiencies the OR faces or anesthesia encounters while they are waiting for the surgeon to move from room to room (Figure 15.4). Thus, surgeons are most efficient if they have 2 ORs, and 2 teams (which would include 2 anesthesiologists), so they could complete one case and go directly into the next case to minimize their "idle time." From the room and resource utilization perspective, the hospital or anesthesiologists would rather have cases booked sequentially to prevent "gaps" within the surgical schedule, which are created while a room, team, and anesthesiologist remain available in a "wait state" for the surgeon to complete the preceding case. This creates conflicting measures, makes the OR potentially underutilized, and drives additional staffing resources and more surgical suites.

Lean Solutions: *We videotape the process and standardize the room turnover to work much like that of a "pit crew" in a NASCAR race. We can generally reduce turnover times by 50% or more during the first pilot. We identify other defects that contribute to turnover time such as pick sheet accuracy, case picking, supply availability, and standard work related to understanding room ready for the next patient.*

Ie. Bed Availability - We find bed availability is a function of the overall process flow, centralized transport, how physicians round and discharge patients, and the efficiency of support services like lab and Radiology.

Lean Solution: *Start by fixing the inpatient and overall hospital patient flow prior to working on surgery or the emergency department, as cycle times for ancillary support services can derail process improvements that are made in surgery and emergency department. For example, if patients are ready for surgery but transport is late in moving them to*

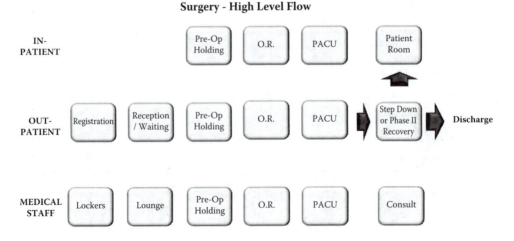

Surgery - High Level Flow

FIGURE 15.4 Surgery high level flow.

surgery it delays the case start and will negatively impact the process flow in the operating room.

If. Staffing generally has three components. The first is surgeons prefer to have the same staff for every operation. This represents an ongoing struggle between the surgery directors who need to keep their staff skills up and cross training so they can staff their surgery schedule during the week and on weekends. The second component is having enough 'competent' (from the physicians perspective) staff available. Travelers and agency staff add a level of uncertainty and sometimes complexity to the mix. Some travelers are very good and some are not as good but all of them have to get used to the new environment, culture and policies within the OR to which they are assigned. The third component of staffing is cost. There is always pressure on the surgery director to meet budget so there is a constant struggle to maintain the "work-life balance" of the staff with a surgery schedule which is typically not "nailed down" until the morning of surgery and requires constant reshuffling of rooms and staff by the charge nurses to meet the schedule, handle emergent cases and while trying to adhere to the budget.

Lean Solutions: *In conjunction with level loading the surgery schedules we develop a skills training matrix which outlines staff trained by service, technology and level to help in guiding appropriate staff skill mix for a case. A "Group Tech" matrix is developed which helps to further refine geographically which rooms each service line is assigned and then adjust the instruments and supplies accordingly. We videotape the staff and physicians and create standard work which leads to a new staffing model. One can start to see Lean solutions begin to overlap across each area as all of surgery in an integrated system dependent on the overall hospital flow.*

Ig. Scheduling: The last item is level loading of surgical schedules. There are three components to level loading the schedule. The first component is the leveling of the surgeries by day of week and the second is leveling the schedule during the day and the third is leveling by specialty. The first component, batching patients on days of the week, normally Tuesday through Thursday can lead to holding patients in the ORs because there is no room in PACU. Some floor units backup as all the patients are competing for beds leaving other days with a low census in these units.

Starting a large number of surgical cases at the exact same time in the morning (i.e., 7:30 starts) drives crazy behaviors throughout the rest of the hospital as all the transporters are needed at the same time for an hour period to bring patients to the OR. All the OR staff are needed at the same time to prepare for the 7:30 cases creating a tremendous amount of pull for resources at the same time. This creates problems which are generally concealed within the overall system. This lack of level loading creates peaks and valleys in demand drive excess staffing costs and ultimately result in delays of patients and services throughout the hospital.

The third component is level loading by specialty. One wouldn't want all their neurosurgeons to operate on Mondays and Tuesdays as this would create a demand for all Neuro ICU beds on Monday and Tuesdays as well as creating a competition for services needed by those patients because the need is now batched as the majority of patients are "pulling for the same case affiliated resources" around the same times throughout their hospital stay. This leads to shortages in Neuro equipment sets, Neuro OR rooms, and "Neuro trained" staff and materials. The "issues" created by these three components are again generally hidden but directly drive a significant amount of patient, physician and staff dissatisfaction.

Lean Solutions: *We work with surgeons, anesthesiologists and administrators to assess each service line to level load both the weekly and daily schedules and show them the benefits which can be gained. It involves some sacrificing on everyone's part but in the long run we can get the surgeons more cases in the same amount of time each day. The surgeons need to be willing to be open minded and flexible to adjust their office hours, and the administrators and surgeons have to be willing to change the overall approach to scheduling and staffing. The goal is to achieve a work-life balance for everyone involved while maintaining quality, achieving lower costs and increasing patient satisfaction.*

Ih. Lack of standardization—drives excess costs for equipment sets, shortages of equipment sets, increases in flash sterilization, increased maintenance costs, significant hidden waste in terms of wasted time spent hunting and gathering, and surprisingly results in surgeon dissatisfaction. We find physicians generally do not like to compromise when selecting instrumentation or agree on a "standard" at the service line level. When this is attempted, organizations are often faced with surgeons pushing back on administration and the non-standardization continues. This practice is very costly as hospitals are unable to control their equipment and capital budgets with the continued "one-off" purchases.

At Hospital X, a perceived "profitable" surgeon desires new or additional instruments just for his or her own use. The instruments are non-standard and costly. The surgery director explains there is no money in the budget this year, which sets off a chain of events. The surgeon goes directly to the COO or CEO and complains. The CEO/COO typically overrides the surgery director, who is then told to purchase the instruments and is now over budget. At budget time, the surgery director is then chastised by the COO or CEO for being over budget.

Lean Solutions: *As part of Lean implementations we strive to standardize anywhere and everywhere possible. We work with physicians to standardize instrument sets and supplies, we work to standardize staff supplies and stock them at "point of use" and with physicians and administrators on capital equipment purchases. We create standard work to the extent possible not just for staff jobs but for administrators (such as creating Leader standard work) and for how off line tasks are performed like developing the weekly schedule and updating the group tech matrix or staffing models. Engaging physicians and making them part of the improvement process (contract for change) will help to standardize where it makes sense and reduce costs throughout the system.*

Lesson Learned: *Get your house in order first i.e., your processes under control, before you address the physician arrival issues. The problems mentioned above are just a few of an overall list that could be mentioned here. I'm sure you can think of many others. Why do we have these problems? It is important to understand these problems are symptoms and cannot be fixed or sustained by attacking them individually. They come with and are part of the **overall system**. While some hospitals are better than others, most have similar problems and there is always room for improvement. The only way to fix these problems is to **change the system**.*

II. OR Surgical Team (Staff and Administrative) Issues

IIa. OR Surgical Team (Staff and Administrative) Issues—Centralized departments drive batching and delays throughout the hospital. They are created with good intentions, to develop economies of scale and to fully utilize staff but in reality they are many times the root cause for bottlenecks and delays throughout the hospital.

Hospital X decided to centralize Sterile Processing (SPD) and move it from the surgery floor to the basement. They purchased new big "batch" washers and added transportation which created a new SPD process that now takes three to four times longer than the old process. They even took on sterile processing needs from other hosptials in their system. While on the surface this may seem to make a lot of sense, due to economies of scale, the increased cycle time to turn around instruments drove significant unplanned costs and delays (for example the need for three to four times more instrument sets) which were obviously not part of the initial ROI for the project. It also created much staff and physician dissatsifaction but since so much money was spent it on the new centralized basement system could not be reversed. In some cases this is done to create space for new ORs on the surgery floor, but if we had "Leaned out the process", decreased turnover times, and level loaded the schedules would we have needed the new ORs? It is important to use the 5 Why tools whenever making these types of centralizing decisions. Do we really need to centralize?

Lean Solution: *Decentralize staff functions wherever possible. This means the value stream department will have to educate and cross train their staff to ensure efficiency and staff utilization. For example, consider decentralizing transport and lab or work to eliminate the need or necessity for some departments like bed management. In some cases we decentralize most of a department while keeping a small centralized portion where it makes sense. We also will install "point of use" testing, for example "mini-labs" where it makes sense that can meet the 80% of the diagnostic needs for the area or department.*

Lesson Learned: *We understand the ongoing arguments and discussions which exist around centralization. However, keep in mind centralization is ultimately "batching" and one should approach the pro-centralization "economies of scale" arguments very skeptically as the waste encountered by having to schedule and manage the new "centralized"*

department generally outweigh the benefits resulting in patient and staff dissatisfaction.

IIb. Reactive Management—is a lack of managing by fact – this issue was difficult to categorize as it generally affects the subsequent decision making for all of the hospital. Our hospital systems are generally difficult to "data mine" and the validity of the resulting data is normally questionable. Most of the data we need for Lean does not exist. i.e., the cycle times for each step in a process. Each of the department silos has their own perceptions of challenges the "patient/customer encounters" upon which "reactive" or "shoot from the hip" type decisions are made. For example, when interviewed, one may find that surgeons normally complain about turnover, start times, and the fact that the patients aren't ready for surgery. In Pre-Op, anesthesiologists often complain of inefficiencies related to patients not having the right tests ordered and that the necessary paperwork is incomplete or unavailable. Surgeons are mostly insulated from this directly, but experience it through case cancellations, increases in turnover time and "surgeon wait time" resulting in a decrease of their overall utilization. Most of this blame is placed on the nurses in pre-testing, Pre-Op or the ORs yet many times the root causes for the delays can be traced back to the physicians themselves i.e., illegible orders, new anesthesia requirements, or patients not informed or confused by the physician's office pre-testing clinic as to whether or not they should take their medicines or how many hours to fast prior to surgery.

Lean Solution: *Identify service line value streams to develop a continuous improvement roadmap to facilitate throughput, and identify drivers of defects in order to improve service, quality and cost across the system.*

IIc. Non standardized, Incomplete, or Undocumented Processes—represents a lack of standard work. We find this inherent in many hospital processes and is a main failure mode of state and other regulatory audits which can also surface as issues in quality. Lack of standardized processes become obvious as we film different staff or physician members doing the same jobs. Root causes go back to the lack of documentation and the fact everyone is then trained differently depending on who they learned the job from and "how they have always done it before".

Lean solution: *Develop, implement and educate in standard work where applicable from frontline staff to executive leaders throughout the hospital or clinic environment.*

IId. Measurement Accountability—Employees tend not to have hard measures to which they are held accountable; if they do exist, employees are not readily aware of the metrics or how the metrics align to that of the overall organization. When we asked employees what they are measured on, they respond:

- They are not sure how they are measured.
- It is based on whatever their boss communicates at evaluation time.
- They think they are measured on customer satisfaction, number of complaints, or physician satisfaction.

Even if they can come up with a measure, we find they cannot normally tell us how they are performing against the metric or explain to us exactly what the measures are, their goals for the year, or how the measures are calculated. In most cases they do not have a full understanding of how their day to day tasks impact the departmental metrics or how their day to day activities align to the overall organizational goals.

Lean solution: *The goal with Lean is to adopt and manage using "process focused" metrics which are directly tied to the overall organization goals for the year and are supported and attained in conjunction with complying with and living the organization's value system. In Lean this system is called Hoshin Planning. Examples of process focused metrics are takt time, cycle time, throughput time, first pass yield (FPY) at every step, rolled throughput yield, customer demand by hour, planned vs. unplanned downtime, and OR turnover times. Process-driven metrics require an immediate explanation and countermeasures when an abnormality occurs, followed by a root cause determination of how to fix it so that it never comes back.*

IIe. Poor Data Availability and Non-Integrated Data Systems—We have found obtaining accurate data, "data mining" or trying to drill down into data extremely challenging at every hospital, some worse than others. At some hospitals, IT system disconnects drive the need for surgical services to invest in its own IT personnel to write reports which can be exported to Microsoft Excel or Microsoft Access and distributed to management. Accurate operational or process based data is not available or difficult to obtain and normally requires manual collection. It is surprising how much data we have obtained from nurses who keep their own manual logs. Many times since chart data has to be input after the fact we don't have access to simple things like number of admitted Pre-Op patients by hour or by day until 2–3 days later after the charts have been coded and completed.

IT systems which don't talk to each other create rework by imposing redundant duplication of data entry in different systems or keying in missing data due to "one way" interfaces (communication) from one system to another. An example is where we found pre-testing software which did not talk to the lab information system so the same data was entered into both systems. There is still much manual paperwork, faxes and phone calls which are very prone to legibility issues and human error.

We have found in many cases the surgeons' offices have the wrong patient names, and other critical information like DOB, so the wrong charts get pulled or can't be found due to the limited "search capabilities" of the existing software or lack of training of user personnel. Other examples are "screens" which do not update each other causing the same information to be typed over and over again. We witness "system timing out" messages while the nurses are still entering data causing them frustration as they have to re-log in and start the data entry over again. We find IT likes to centralize printers, faxes (and sometimes even computers) because it is easier "for them" rather than giving each nurse a fax/printer or their own computer. So the nurses have to stop during their patient interviews to go get the print out from the IT designated secure centralized printer (normally not the closest to them) and bring it back in order to review it with the patient.

IIF. Data Validity—Most of the time there is little or no documentation surrounding the definitions of the data and where there are they are not followed. Additionally there is little data integrity with respect to the data collection methods to ensure data reproducibility and repeatability. Data entry is a very low priority for surgical nurses whose main focus is always on the patient. Many times we get into in-depth discussions over what a "to-follow-on" case means and in virtually no circumstances is detailed data kept on cycle times within each department i.e., registration time, registration to check in, check in time, check in to Pre-Op entry, Pre-Op time, Pre-Op to surgery, etc. Sometimes it is tracked on electronic boards but they are on a different system than the surgical system and not everyone enters their times in a timely manner or using the same definition. Real-time data are almost non-existent unless there is an electronic tracking board in place. Financial data are abundant but may require manipulation to understand, and are generally not timely. When data are available, the definitions must be confirmed, as well as the validity and formulas. For example, at one hospital their inpatient data was suspect. They would classify a patient as an "observation" patient (<24 hrs stay) but the patient would end up being admitted. We found they never went back and changed the status of the patient. At another hospital they recovered millions of dollars in charges for patients which were not categorized properly in the surgical system and found more money in supplies where Pre-Op didn't realize they had to charge the patients for certain supplies. They thought they were bundled charges. And the list goes on and on.

Lean Solutions: *Here are some limited examples of what we find when we implement Lean. First we call everyone together so we can standardize all the definitions throughout the area. We identify opportunities where redundancies in data collection and input occur and work with IT on implementing software solutions that interface between systems. We create manual time collection systems until we can implement bar coded or other more automated collection systems. We create Microsoft Excel® based spreadsheets and pivot tables until the surgical IT personnel can generate the reports. We train the supervisors, managers and charge nurses in their existing standards and reporting mechanisms and teach them how to do Lean Staffing Models. We look at RIFD or other tracking systems for materials where needed. We add simple things like pick locations to surgical pick lists used for case picking.*

Lesson Learned: *Question all data received prior to utilizing for analysis and decision making. When data doesn't exist put in a manual collection system until it can be automated. This will be met with much resistance but we can't improve the processes if we have no data on which to base our decisions or to be able to ascertain if the solutions implemented fixed the problems and is sustaining.*

Conclusion – Do you consider the Operating Room a Cost Center or a Profit Center?

Many operating rooms (ORs) are treated and function as cost centers instead of revenue or profit centers. Managers are primarily measured on cost accounting standards and variances to determine how well they met their budget. This puts the main focus on reducing full-time employees (FTEs), not servicing the customer or growth in volume. Many managers do not understand how their accounting standards were developed. We often uncover mistakes in the labor standards and how fixed and variable resources are assigned.

Lean solution: *The OR should be treated as a profit center with a focus on growing the business; however, one needs to be able to develop the data to understand which service lines are profitable.*

SURGICAL SERVICES: DETAIL

INTRODUCTION—WHAT WE FIND

Surgery is a system that is intertwined and integrated within the hospital. Our findings include (Figure 15.5):

- Unbalanced surgical schedules.
- Multiple delays throughout the day.
- Poor data.
- Unclear definitions related to turnover time, lack of understanding of "what is really" causing delays—root cause of the issues.

- Workarounds are accepted and rewarded when staff "saves the day".
- Staffing is to desire, not demand.
- No standard work or role clarity (and normally no written procedures or work instructions) exist.
- OR utilization and true OR capacity based on existing data is initially difficult to quantify.
- Low surgeon utilization efficiency (does not mean surgeons are not efficient but that surgeons spend 50% or more of their time waiting).
- Lack of standardization of supplies and instrumentation.
- Metrics and targets do not measure what is important to the customer and are not communicated to the frontline staff.

TYPICAL SURGERY PROJECTS

Each one of the activities in Table 15.2 could be Lean initiatives an organization may choose to undertake in its quest to improve surgical services.

HOW CAN LEAN IMPROVE OPERATING ROOMS?

Most Lean initiatives start with a value stream map (VSM). This enables the clinical area to begin to understand what occurs across the entire surgical process, from the time the recommendation for surgery is made to the time the patient exits the Post-Op recovery unit (Figure 15.6). The VSM can even be taken further downstream to the time the patient is discharged from the hospital. The beginning and endpoint of the VSM depends

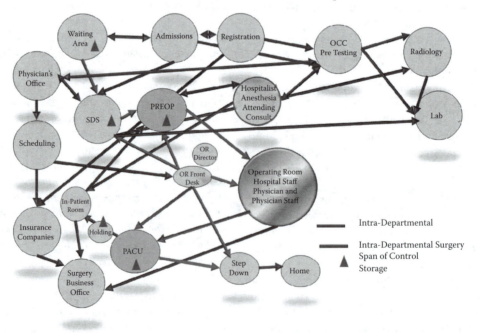

Architectural Point Of View – Inter-Relationships

How Much Control Does The OR Director Have Over The System?
How Do We Compete With Stand Alone Surgical Centers?

FIGURE 15.5 Inter-relationship diagram OR.

TABLE 15.2

OR Potential Projects

Assessment (Overall Throughput)	Pre-Op Flow	OR Turnover	Block time rules and utilization
Group Tech Matrix (capacity)	Pre-testing on floors	Billing / Revenue Capture	Sterile Processing
Physician Standard Orders	OR Flow	Forecasting/Marketing	Physician's offices
Pre-testing Flow	PACU Flow	Standardization of instruments	Patient tracking system
Scheduling	Case picking & Materials	IS System related projects	OR Layout

on the level of detail desired and the goal the organization is trying to achieve. Once the VSM is done, it is followed by a product process flow (PPF) (Table 15.3) (following the patient), point-to-point diagram, full work operator analysis (following the staff, which would include nurses, surgeons, and others), and spaghetti diagrams (Figure 15.7). It is surprising how much time a patient can spend waiting and how far a patient is required to walk during the pre-testing process. One organization found that a patient scheduled for *cardiovascular* surgery was required to walk almost one mile in order to complete all their tests.

These tools can help you understand what surgeons desire as well. From the surgeon's point of view, it is often, "I need what I need when I need it!" This ties in with Lean's principle of Just in Time (JIT). Most truly efficient surgeons take the comment "you and your team work as a well-oiled machine" as a compliment. Standard work plays a significant role in applying Lean in the surgical clinical areas. Many surgeons already practice Lean, which is exactly how highly skilled surgical teams work. One can go into many ORs and find teams that work together know the standard routine; the surgical technician anticipates each step of the surgeon (through applying standard work for that procedure) and hands the surgeon the right tool that is needed at the right time it is needed. The goal is to become so standardized that operations go smoothly and safely with high quality. What better tool is there than videotaping a resident or young surgeon and reviewing the tape together to look for improvement opportunities? When we have filmed surgeons, they identify many opportunities where they could improve. Occasionally new ideas for instrumentation or supplies emerge.

Even though there is a "feel" component which can only be gained through experience with many operations, if the best surgeons are filmed, training films can be created and standardized work can be used as a teaching tool for residents and medical schools. Flexibility, flow, mistake proofing, JIT, standardized work, etc., integrate perfectly with surgeons in the OR. These tools can also be applied not only in perioperative services, but also extended beyond to physicians/surgeons' offices to improve their infrastructure and patient experience.

We have divided the surgical services Detail into ten sections as outlined below:

I. Everything Starts With Demand
II. Pre-Testing—the Path to Patient Readiness
III. Pre-Op
IV. Group Tech Matrix
V. OR Layout/Capacity
VI. OR Room Turnover
VII. Surgical Services Materials Readiness
VIII. Post-Anesthesia Care Unit (PACU)
IX. Lean Leadership and Staff Readiness in the OR
X. Overarching Results.

SECTION I EVERYTHING STARTS WITH DEMAND

At Hospital X, surgical case demand was 60 surgeries per day. Pre-Op had 10 beds and PACU had 14 beds. The first "batch" of 17 patients was told to arrive in the Pre-Op area between 5:30 a.m. and 6:00 a.m. for 7:30 a.m. starts. Therefore, peak demand was 17 patients over 2 hrs, Takt time was calculated at

$$2 \text{ hrs or } 120 \text{ min} \div 17 \text{ cases} = 7.05 \text{ min.}$$

Each morning, the 10 Pre-Op beds were filled, and overflow went to some of the 14 Post-Op care unit beds.

Pre-Op had a staff of 5 nurses. How can we determine if that is adequate staff? Through video analysis, it was determined the total labor time (TLT) for Pre-Op nurses averaged 40 min. Therefore,

$$\text{Number of nurses required} = 40 \text{ min} \div 7.05 \text{ TT} = 5.67$$
$$\text{Pre-Op staff,}$$

or, in actuality, 6 nurses are needed each day at peak demand to perform the clinical tasks (Table 15.4).

What happens when one is sick? In general, the other nurses or the supervisor may pick up the tasks, but if not, we can predict (since 5 nurses can only see 15 patients in 2 hrs) that 2 patients will not be ready for surgery in time and case delays will occur.

The average length of stay (LOS) for surgery is 108 min. PACU is 145 min and Pre-Op is, by default, paced by surgery. Once the patients are moved to the OR, the 10 Pre-Op and 7 of the Post-Op care unit rooms free up as patients move through the process and the next "batch" of 10 patients arrives to begin the process again. The Takt time is now 10.8 min (108 min ÷ 10 patients).

Number of operators required is 40 min ÷ 10.8 = 3.7 nurses.

We now have an extra nurse. With 5 nurses, the patients are ready in 80 min and all the patients wait for an average of 28 min. What happens if a surgeon finishes early and needs a patient who is not in Pre-Op? There is no more room in Pre-Op and the surgeon will have to wait.

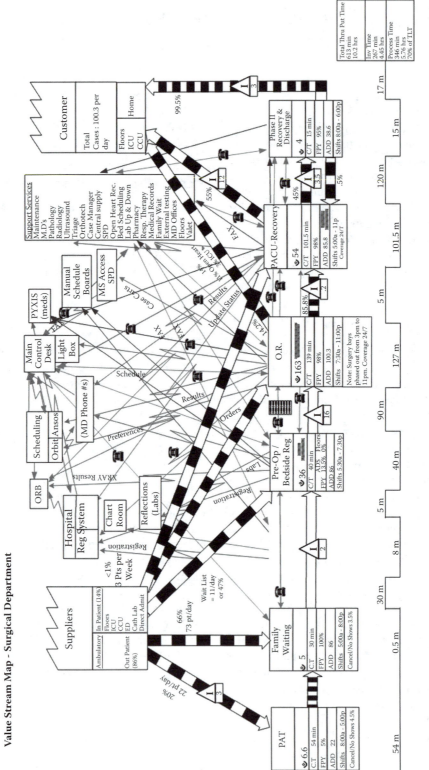

FIGURE 15.6   Surgical VSM (value stream map).

TABLE 15.3
PPF (Product Process Flow) Cardiac Patient

Summary	Baseline	Post Lean Projected	Reduction	Reduction %
Total Steps	82.0	36.0	46.00	56%
Orig Sec:	13,266.0	10,387.0	2,879.00	22%
Min:	221.1	173.1	47.98	22%
Hours:	3.7	2.9	0.80	22%
Days	0.5	0.4	0.10	22%
Distance	4,326.0	1,239.0	3,087.00	71%
check:	13,266.0	10,387.0	2,79.00	22%
Va %	31.61%	40.37%	−8.76%	−28%
NVA %	32.75%	33.52%	−0.77%	−2%
Storage	26.38%	19.14%	7.24%	27%
Inspect	0.00%	0.00%	0.00%	#DIV/0!
Transport	9.26%	6.97%	2.29%	25%

Note: Patient travels almost a mile.

Lesson Learned: *When you're working on something (someone) you don't need, you can't be working on something (someone) you do need.*

Since PACU averages 145 min LOS (patient in to patient ready for discharge), what is going to happen when the second round of surgeries come out? We can't answer the question, as we are missing an element of the total time. We have 'patient in to patient out' for surgery given as 108 min. We don't have 'patient out to patient in', or room turnover time. If room turnover is 40 min we can predict PACU will have the time (145 min vs. total OR time of 148 min), but we can assume there may be delays as the times are so close. If transport from PACU averages more than 3 min we will have delays because PACU technicians will be busy transporting to the floor.

What happens if our Post-Op care unit is holding six inpatients at 5:30 a.m. in the morning and no floor beds are available until 10:00 a.m.? The Post-Op care unit now has to care for the 6 inpatients (which is probably not in their budget) in addition to getting the seven Pre-Op patients ready for the OR or to go back into Pre-Op. But once the seven Pre-Op patients go to surgery; we still only have eight beds

Pre-Testing – Point to Point - Cardiac Patient

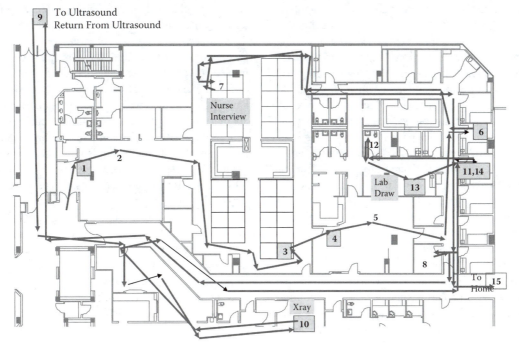

FIGURE 15.7   Point-to-point diagram cardiac.

TABLE 15.4

Nurse Cycle Time Example

# Nurses	Avg TLT/PT Minutes	PTs/Hr	Total Per Hr
1	40	1.5	1.5
2	40	1.5	3.0
3	40	1.5	4.5
4	40	1.5	6.0
5	40	1.5	7.5
6	40	1.5	9.0
7	40	1.5	10.5

available in PACU because six are still filled with inpatients. 14 patients will be arriving from the OR in the 8:00 a.m. to 9:30 a.m. range. The Post-Op care unit now has to plead with bed management to find unit or ICU beds for 6 patients as soon as possible or the OR will go into a hold mode.

With the OR time average of 108 min plus turnover of 40 min, our 'patient in to patient in' time is 148 min. What if PACU averages 165 min, what's going to happen next?

$$165 \text{ min} - 148 \text{ min} = 17 \text{ min}.$$

Surgical procedures are being completed at a faster rate than the patients can exit the Post-Op care unit; therefore, a bottleneck is created and the result is holding patients in the ORs.

Our options to address the bottleneck are:

1. Add more Post-Op care unit rooms
2. Add more Post-Op care unit nurses
3. Eliminate inpatient boarders (who are waiting for beds within the hospital)
4. Reduce LOS in Post-Op care unit

One must be aware that Lean is an ongoing problem-solving methodology and approach. This is the linkage Lean shares with Joel Barker's "paradigm concepts". The first three solutions are all normal reactive solutions to a problem when one doesn't follow a problem-solving methodology. Solutions 1, 2, and 3 are based on the symptoms or current paradigms; however, what needs to be asked is "what is the root cause of the problem?" The root cause is "the system's" batching the arrival and surgeries of our patients. Imagine the stress placed on the overall system by 17 patients arriving at one time. They all hit admitting at once! So at 5:15 a.m. the admitting area is backed up, but doesn't open until 5:30 a.m. Now a large admitting area and several registration personnel are required to meet peak demand. Next, the 17 patients descend on the surgical waiting room and Pre-Op area. Now it appears more Pre-Op beds and staffing are needed because everyone's rushing each morning to Pre-Op these patients who are prioritized based on their surgeon (if they are a high producer or very vocal) or anesthesia (if a "block" is required) or in some cases no priority system is in place. Patients arrive in varying states of "readiness" for their surgical procedure depending on the pre-testing already completed and resulted, so every morning the following problems occur:

- Incomplete charts.
- Inaccurate or incomplete consents.
- Surgeon orders are either not done or are incomplete.
- History and physical examinations (H&Ps) were not provided by the office, or were provided the night before to pre-testing (which does not open until 7:00 a.m.) but needed in Pre-Op or the faxes were lost somewhere along the way.
- Surgeons are late.
- Blood work is not complete, i.e., type and cross, etc. or additional testing is required based on patient and chart examination by anesthesia.
- Inpatients co-morbid medical conditions have not been addressed medically clearing them for the surgical procedure.

Nurses scamper to get the ORs ready and backfill missing personnel. Nurses then try to find missing supplies and equipment either because they were missing, cases were not "picked" (process of gathering routine supplies and equipment for a case) accurately, they were used on a previous case and have to be cleaned, or the preference card was wrong inaccurate or incomplete. Now 17 patients are rolled in procession into the OR, and once surgery is completed, 17 patients are moved into the PACU/Post-Op care unit. Then the second "batch" rush starts.

SURGERY IS LIKE A REPAIR SHOP

Surgery in its simplest form is like an auto repair shop. Clinicians may have difficulty with this analogy, but there are some similarities. Obviously, surgeons and clinicians are highly trained and skilled, and people are not cars, but parallels exist. As consumers, we take our car to the auto shop (which could be the surgeon's or physician's office or hospital), because there is a problem that needs to be "diagnosed", determine what needs to be done and repair the issue. Patients go to surgeons so they can diagnose the situation, and determine a course of action (repairs needed or medical treatment or recommend surgical intervention). Auto shops (hospitals) have highly trained and skilled technicians (physicians and ancillary personal) that carry out the repairs (surgical intervention). Sometimes, certain parts are back ordered (such as a specialized instrument, implant or screw) which delays the repair. Each repair (surgical case) is different and requires different equipment and supplies. If you were the owner of the repair shop (hospital), what processes would you set up to deliver your service in a low cost, high quality, and efficient manner in order to generate revenue?

1. Scheduling—If this was your shop (surgery dept), how would you setup the schedule? In reality, in most car shops, some people may call ahead while others drop off their cars without warning (thus add-ons). Most people drop off their cars in the morning on their way to work, therefore the majority of cars or peak demand occurs first thing in the morning. In addition, Mondays and Fridays tend to be the busiest with pent up demand for service on Monday

and the desire on Friday for service prior to the weekend. Operating rooms have the same challenges with unleveled work load. Cases are not level loaded throughout the week and peak demand occurs in the morning as physicians ask all their patients to show up at the same time in the morning for fear if the first patient doesn't show or has an issue they will sit idle waiting for the next case or even be bumped. What is the impact when all cars come in for service at the same time? What would be the added costs of heavier schedules on certain days? Would the shop need more bays, more tools and supplies, and more labor on those days? Does it have enough bays (OR suites) or will cars get behind schedule? Does the shop know how long an oil change will take, as well as any other repair? Again, if you owned the shop, would you standardize your equipment, tools, and supplies or would you buy different equipment, tools, and supplies for each mechanic?

In many cases, hospital surgical services management teams may recognize the challenges they face internally when cases are not level loaded throughout the week. When they have 20 cases to staff 1 day and 10 the next day, there are challenges in anesthesia coverage and extra instrument sets needed to meet the peak demand. They may not have enough speciality OR rooms, and Post-Op beds creating delays. Most managers do not recognize the impact they have on the entire hospital when assigning block time (scheduling cases).

Illustration: *There is one six-surgeon, neurosurgical group practicing at Hospital X, scheduling all their cases on Mondays, Wednesdays, and Thursdays. This causes peaks and troughs in staffing and rooms/beds in both the OR and in the neurosurgical intensive care units, transportation, and other ancillary services such as pharmacy, radiology, and laboratory. The system becomes stressed on Mondays, Wednesdays, and Thursdays owing to the non-leveling of cases. Cases need to be scheduled so there are no equipment conflicts that can negatively impact the same surgeons which then creates a need for more equipment sets and the resulting work to clean, sterilize, pick, and maintain them which stresses the sterile processing department and then the floor units that receive the patients.*

Lean Solution: *Work with the neurosurgical group to see if some of the surgeons in that group could adjust their office hours and perform cases on Tuesdays and Fridays. This would level capacity in OR, demand for instrument sets, ICU and medical surgical beds, etc. This simple example illustrates the organizational and cost reduction impact that leveling in the OR can have.*

2. What if each mechanic wanted his/her own tools? This is not uncommon practice, but who pays for them? The mechanic does. The problem with having employee-owned tools is that they can interfere or aid with standard work, especially when the mechanics customize them and no one else has the tool. When the mechanic leaves no one can figure out how the mechanic performed the job.

Surgeons and physicians typically do not see standardizing supplies and instruments as important. Why? One reason is

because they are not paying for them. In addition, they may find it intrusive to their practice, as in general, they want to use the tools/instruments with which they have become trained and comfortable, and therefore any change is met with resistance. How does this impact staff that have to stay proficient with the varying pieces of equipment. Do physicians standardize equipment and supplies in their offices? Do they level load their office schedules? Do they maximize their time in their offices?

The auto repair shop and surgery have synonymous goals:

- Level loading
- Standardize parts and supplies
- Flexible (cross trained) labor
- Optimizing throughput in and out as quickly as possible, providing high quality with zero defects

What do we do if we only have one oil change person or one front-end alignment person? How would that impact the overall operations or goals? What if they were out sick or have a doctor's appointment?

What would happen in the hospital environment with only one specially trained surgeon, surgical technician, housekeeper, transporter, etc.?

There has been a slow migration of physicians leaving private practice to become hospital-employed, and we are beginning to see a shift in willingness by some physician groups to break down barriers and work more toward common goals.

Lesson Learned: *Level loading, standardizing on supplies and equipment, flexible labor, and optimizing throughput are important to creating and sustaining a Lean environment.*

SECTION II PRE-TESTING—THE PATH TO PATIENT READINESS

The surgical processes, in its most simplistic form, can be divided into several steps: Pre-Op testing, which could take place anytime from the day of surgery to several days prior; registration Pre-Op; surgery (OR); and Post-Op (PACU) period. These areas in combination form the overall OR process flow. In order to flow, four key process focused areas must be addressed:

- Patient readiness
- Materials and equipment readiness
- OR turnover
- Staff readiness (includes surgeon and anesthesia)

We met with the surgery director and asked her to explain the problems they were having, and then proceeded to walk through their process. The main problem was they couldn't get patients through the surgery process efficiently, and everyone in the system was blaming everyone else. The surgeons were blaming the nurses. The nurses were blaming anesthesia and transport. Everyone was blaming management, and it was a very unhappy and unprofessional environment. We asked to see if they had any data related to their processes. They had limited data from their system and what they were able to produce for us wasn't accurate. (We have experience this problem at many other hospitals.) We explained that with Lean they may be looking at making some significant "out of the box" changes to their overall system. They said they knew that and that they were ready to "break plates" and never look back. The next 6 weeks was spent collecting and sifting through the data, value stream mapping and assessing where the problems were. What we learned was that no one person or group was to blame. Blame only hides problems. We ultimately found the problem was the overall perioperative services system.

While cycle times are important, it turns out that the first pass yield (FPY– or percent of "right the first time" units of work) in the VSM held the key to the problems. *Their biggest problem was that patients were not ready when it was time for surgery.* As a result, cases were not started on time, schedules backed up, patients waited, and surgeons lost faith in the system and experienced lots of idle or wasted time. Surgeons decided it didn't make sense to arrive on time for a 7:30 a.m. case since patients were never ready to go until 8:00 a.m. Additionally, when patients are consistently not ready on time, surgeons tend to tell all their patients to come in even earlier for surgery, all at the same time in the morning around 5 a.m., so that they can adjust their schedule to accommodate whichever of their patients are ready first. This just adds even more of a peak workload on registration, surgery waiting and Pre-Op and adds to the confusion and frustration of nurses, case picking, sterile processing, anesthesiologists and surgeons. Many surgeons thought the problem was long turnovers and blamed the nurses, when the problem was actually that their patients weren't ready to go into the room for their surgical procedure. The next step was to root cause the problem. The FPY in Pre-Op was less than 30%, which was caused by patients not being sent by the surgeons to pre-testing, thus arriving to the Pre-Op area the day of surgery without everything they needed to go through with surgery. It is also a problem with Pre-Op in that they do not have the resources or support services available to totally process (work up) the patient the same day of surgery within the required cycle time, hence the need for a separate pre-testing visit prior to the day of surgery. (There are some other benefits to pre-testing early with the ability to collect additional revenue and prevent certain cancellations day of surgery for complex patients. We found if the patient arrives totally prepared for surgery, the surgery process starts out efficiently. However if the patient arrives the day of surgery and needs re-evaluation or is delayed because the preparations are not complete, perhaps the patient ate, needs additional testing or x-rays, or took prohibited medications, the process starts behind and will seldom catch up. So the real area we first needed to focus on was getting patients ready for surgery.

We focused on the surgical information flow processes first and then the pre-testing department. When we first walked into pre-testing, we noticed a crowded lobby. Only about 20% of patients were being pre-tested. The pre-testing office was like walking into a chaotic town center. Papers were everywhere. The copy machine and fax machines were all centralized in another room and the manual schedule was difficult to read. Six to eight nurses were doing nothing but clerical work; receiving faxes, filing, and calling offices instead of seeing patients. What a waste of talent! During our analysis of pre-testing we discovered several of the problems had root causes that originated in surgeon's offices and related to anesthesiology requirements for medical clearance.

Patient readiness (quality) should be one of the number one Lean measures in surgical services, followed by turnover time which includes cleaning, setup, materials, case picking, preference cards which all impact throughput time.

If patients are ready, surgeries are quick and smooth. But why aren't patients ready? Patients may not be required by their surgeon to go to pre-testing prior to the day of surgery, or if they do go, the pre-testing process may be inadequate to provide the intended result. If the pre-testing process was good, i.e., FPY reached 100%, it would indicate that everything performed was accurate and right the first time and the intended results were achieved. What would the impact be of having a patient show up on the day of surgery with all the testing and documentation complete? How long would it take to get the patient ready? Would the patient still have to come in as early? Just consider how positively this could impact the patients, physicians and hospital staff, i.e., fewer Pre-Op beds needed and labor savings as patients will not need to be prepped or monitored for as long while "waiting" for surgery.

When analyzing patient readiness, we have identified several key tasks directly related to pre-testing which will ensure patient readiness:

1. Create a Standard Order Set for Surgical Clearance: A standard set of physician orders needs to be jointly developed by the surgeons and anesthesiologists, which guarantee not only medical clearance by the physician/surgeon, but also anesthesia clearance as anesthesia ultimately makes the decision if the surgery goes ahead or not

2. Adoption of Standard Orders and Need for Pre-testing: The physicians and their offices need to adopt a standardized pre-testing process that would include supplying standard orders prior to the patient's arrival at the pre-testing facility. The other option is for the physician's office to perform the required pre-testing.

3. Mandate Pre-testing (at a minimum for first case starts and for key patient populations): Develop a mandate that pre-testing is important and required as it plays a major role in patient readiness and impacts first case on-time starts. The pre-testing area needs the ability to have any abnormal results reviewed by the surgeon and the anesthesiologist and immediately acted on.

4. Efficient Pre-testing Clinic: The pre-testing clinic needs to have a formalized review process, streamlined, standardized work flow, and level loading of patients.

TYPICAL PRE-TESTING "PATIENT READINESS FOR SURGERY" PROJECTS

1. Patient readiness project assessment (overall)
2. Define and standardize what it means to be "ready for surgery" on the day of surgery (outpatients or same day admits)

3. Define inpatient "ready for surgery"
4. Develop surgery Pre-Op standard order form driven by surgeons and anesthesia which outlines the necessary tests for medical clearance
5. Surgeon office education and communication of the new process
6. Patient flow—pre-testing to OR
7. Information flow—pre-testing to OR
8. Pre-testing infrastructure
9. Pre-Op area assessment
10. Standardize Pre-Op checklist
11. Standardize inpatient Pre-Op checklist
12. Standardize timing of completion of inpatient readiness
13. Communicate definition of "ready for surgery"

THE PRE-TESTING MODEL

Each hospital we visit seems to have different models for pre-testing. These will be discussed later in this chapter. Which one is best? From a Lean and systems view, pre-testing is an "inspection" process. The ideal would be not to have to do it at all. The next best solution would be to do it on the day of surgery, and there are a few hospitals doing this. But most hospitals cannot do it on the day of surgery because their processes are not robust enough to support the "testing results" turnaround times (TAT) necessary. Waiting until the day of surgery to perform "readiness checks on all patients" could result in an increased number of last-minute cancellations and impact patient and family satisfaction.

TRADITIONAL PRE-TESTING PROCESS

The ultimate goal is to create a "robust" pre-testing process by surfacing any problems that may cause the surgery to be cancelled or delayed. When the patient arrives on the day of surgery, we want them to be "defect" free with all the forms and tests that can be completed prior to that day documented, and reviewed for necessary actions to medically clear the patient. The only activities left the day of surgery are those that must be completed within the perioperative time frame, i.e., diabetics or patients on blood thinners may need repeat blood tests.

Let's look at where the opportunities are to streamline the process. We have to start with the initial patient visit to the surgeon. What is the surgeon's job? The surgeon determines if the patient may benefit from surgical intervention, discusses the options with their patient, the benefits and risks of surgery, and the right to a second opinion. They see their job initially as explaining the surgery to the patient and answering any questions. They may or may not decide what orders are required, but the orders written for surgical preparation are from their (the surgeon's) perspective and may not meet the same needs of the anesthesiologists or hospital to "clear" the patient for surgery. The patient is then handed over to the office staff. The office staff pulls the order

sheet (protocols) for the designated surgery and then calls the hospital to schedule the pre-testing visit along with their assigned OR scheduled time or refers the patient to a physician to do the pre-testing work.

There are several ways a patient may be "prepared or receive medical clearance" to become "ready for surgery." From the hospital perspective, this process results in "paper" (laboratory and x-ray results, various consents, orders, H&Ps all arriving by fax or e-mail) from multiple sources for next-day surgeries to surgeries several months out. Gathering and sorting this in the pre-testing clinic requires a vast number of personnel and most hospitals utilize nurses to handle all this paperwork. We have found that this incoming "paperwork" is often received in multiple places within or outside the pre-testing department, making coordination and consolidation virtually impossible. Test results, consents, and other paper-work can be lost, causing frustration and rework for the surgeons and their offices, and for the pre-testing clinic. The surgeons and their staff then have to chase down, secure, and resubmit to pre-testing or Pre-Op on the day of surgery, the appropriate documents for medical clearance. In addition, in many organizations there has not been an agreed upon "standard for medical clearance" between all the anesthesiologists and surgeons requiring more testing and rework for nurses and patients, creating more confusion and delays. In many cases, even obtaining agreement from one anesthesiologist to another is extremely difficult.

Most hospitals have a screening or interview process referred to as "medical clearance" and have "forms" such as consents which need to be completed by the patient prior to surgery. Who evaluates the patient varies across the organization. It may be a hospitalist, nurse anesthetist, or a pre-testing nurse in the "pre-testing process." On the day of surgery, the final review is carried out by a nurse anesthetist and/or anesthesiologist.

NEED FOR STANDARD ORDERS

The need for standard orders arose as we reviewed the faxed orders received into the pre-testing department. Typical problems we encountered are the following:

- The orders are illegible.
- Patient names are spelled wrong (birth dates are normally correct, but the computer system doesn't search by birth dates).
- Every office order form is different and some are different from within each office.
- Many times, patients arrive with no orders, forcing expedited calls to offices.
- Variability from surgeon to surgeon on their pre-testing orders and procedures.

These manual processes and paperwork deciphering create a ripe environment for errors and ongoing work for both the pre-testing department and the surgeon's offices. It is no wonder this all-important relationship is sometimes so strained. Some pre-testing departments actually have a "do not call list" where surgeons have refused to allow them to call their offices. As a result, we have found that surgeons can unintentionally be their own worst enemies. Whose responsibility should it be to make sure the patient is ready? One would assume it has to start with the surgeon. But we find that this is not the case. Ultimately, the anesthesiologist decides what is required and determines if the surgery "goes according to schedule if at all."

In many cases, pre-orders written by the surgeon do not agree or do not contain everything the anesthesiologist requires to assure that the patient is medically ready and cleared for safe surgeries, i.e., sleep apnea, etc. The surgeon and anesthesiologist each are coming from different patient care perspectives. The anesthesiologist must ensure the patient is healthy enough to administer anesthesia, can make it through the operations, and then be able to wake up.

One of the challenges we have encountered is the lack of clarity in definition of medical clearance, i.e., an agreement across all parties (surgeons and anesthesia) of what medical surgery clearance ultimately entails. Some anesthesiologists have told us that surgeons simply don't have the knowledge necessary to screen their patients according to the criteria required by anesthesia. While surgeons and anesthesiologists believe they are in agreement, we have found when you dive into the details, there is not an "agreed" on standard tests, results, and reports needed to "clear a patient" for surgical intervention. Thus, depending on the anesthesiologist reviewing the case on the day of surgery, the expectations of what needs to be done vs. what has been done may not match what needs to be done in their opinion and so the delay begins.

We also have found that even among anesthesiologists and/or nurse anesthetists there are disagreements as to what criteria or expectations are required and what constitutes "medical clearance" for surgery. We witness this in every hospital when one anesthesiologist takes over another's patient.

STANDARD PRE-TESTING AND PRE-OP ORDER SETS

Lean Solution: *In order to eliminate the patient readiness problem, it is necessary to create a standard order set for pre-testing and Pre-Op. This order set (see Figure 15.8) contains both the surgeon criteria and an agreed-on anesthesia clearance criteria in the form of a grid based on patient condition and what anesthesia tests are required. We have found it typically takes a year or more, once a serious effort is expended to undertake the initiative. The end result is an astounding increase in patient readiness, reduction or elimination of early morning surgeon calls, improved office/pre-testing and Pre-Op relationship, reduced cancellations, and happier patients.*

The first step to creating standard orders is to get all the anesthesiologists to agree on what is necessary by patient demographics and surgery type and develop medical clearance criteria. The next step is to develop the standard order set, which incorporates the "anesthesia" medical clearance

criteria. The next step is to have the organization, including surgeons, trained in and adopt the standard orders as part of their processes. The surgeon then completes, signs, and dates the orders for each patient. The surgeon's offices have to complete the forms and schedule the patient's surgery and pre-testing visit before they leave.

HOW TO: THE PROCEDURE TO CREATE STANDARD ORDERS FOR "MEDICAL CLEARANCE FOR SURGERY"

1. Meet with chief of anesthesia/designated leader of the anesthesia practice and surgical medical directors. Meet with any other policy or procedure committee necessary that will be involved in the approval process for the forms. Include the legal department, if necessary.
2. Propose standard orders and answer the "change" questions:
   a. What is the change?
   b. Why is it necessary?
   c. What is in it for all parties involved (this will be different for different stakeholders)?
3. Solicit thoughts and/or objections. We view objections as good. Once the objections are overcome, we can move forward.
4. Have chief of anesthesia/designated leader of anesthesia practice and appointees create standard anesthesia requirements.
5. Have the chief of anesthesia/designated leader of anesthesia practice get consensus for all anesthesiologists to agree.
6. Approve final draft and standard orders for piloting and put on Internet.
7. Pick first and second round pilot surgeons.
8. Meet with pilot surgeons and explain the new system, expectations, and what will be shared with their offices.
9. Meet with their offices and educate them on the new form and process.
10. Implement first round pilot for 2 weeks, and monitor system. Call offices 2 or 3 times a week to see how it is going, and if they have any improvement ideas. Check with anesthesia medical director 2 or 3 times per week to see if any patient was not ready due to missing anesthesia requirements and change form as required.
11. Roll out second round of pilots (same as first).
12. Roll out the rest of the system. This must be done individually; it does not work with "lunch and learns."

The surgeon should be provided with an area on the form to add any additional orders as necessary to the standard order form (see standard order form). Since many surgeon specialties already have Pre-Op standard orders by surgery type, an alternative would be allowing them to use their standard forms in conjunction with the new "standard order form

Print Form

PASS ORDER SET

Instructions: Fax completed for to   . Any questions call   . Email address:

Surgery Date [ ] Patient Last Name [ ] First Name [ ] MI [ ] ○ Male ○ Female

Procedure [ ]

Anesthesia Preference: ☐ Local ☐ MAC ☐ General ☐ Acute Pain Block: (type) [ ] ☐ **Choice**

Patient Type: ☐ In patient ☐ Observation Patient (<24 hours) Out Patient Center [ ]

☐ MRSA Precautions Required ☐ Latex Allergy ☐ Special Requirements [ ]

Note: One of the pre-admission testing options below is mandatory prior to surgery

PASS

○ Pass Phone Call - This option for patients requiring no labs or testing   Preferred time to call? [ ]

○ Pass Visit   Pass Scheduled Date [ ]   Time of Visit [ ]

RECOMMENDED LABS

Medical Condition / **Test required by PASS Protocol**	CBC w/o Dif	EKG	BMP	PT/ PTT INR	K+AM DOS	CMP	U-HCG AM DOS	C-Gluc
Cardiovascular		X						
HTN		X						
Smoking > 20 packs year								
Pulmonary disease		X						
Renal Disease	X	X				X		
Dialysis	X	X			X	X DOS		
Diabetes	X	X						X DOS
Bleeding problems	X			X				
Liver Disease				X		X		
Obesity (BMI OF 40 OR >)		X						
Possible Pregnancy							X	
Current Malignancy under treatment	X	X						
Diuretics			X					
Digoxin						X		
Anticoagulants (Coumadin)	X			X DOS				
Steroids								
Other		☐	☐	☐	☐	☐	☐	☐

Additional Orders/Labs:

☐ Type & Screen
☐ Packed Cells
☐ Platelets
☐ FFP
Auto Blood Available
☐ PFT Screening
Carotid Ultrasound
☐ Pull Films
☐ Clip &Prep Location
☐ Type and Cross

Units [ ]
Units [ ]
Units [ ]
Units [ ]

☐ PFT
☐ Pull Old Chart
☐ MRI/CT DOS
Only (10 am starts or later)

Enter any additional orders necessary here [ ]

ANTIBIOTIC PROPHYLAXIS (all antibiotics will be given within one hour prior to skin incision unless otherwise ordered)

☐ SCIP Protocol for Pre-Op antibiotics   Cefazolin ☐ 1 gm ☐ 2 gm ☐ Vancomycin 1 gm IVPB

Other [ ]

Please list any allergies [ ]

DVT PROPHYLAXIS

☐ SCIP Protocol for placement of compression devices ☐ SCD/Plexpulses ☐ Ted hose knee high ☐ Ted hose thigh high

☐ **Do not** use DVT prophylaxis compression devices

MEDICAL CONSULTS

☐ Admit to Doctor: [ ]

☐ Cardiac Clearance Consult: Scheduled for: [ ]

☐ Other Consult: Doctor's Name: [ ]

Physician Signature [ ]

Printed Name [ ]

Current Date [ ]   Time Signed [ ]

Patient Label

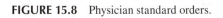

FIGURE 15.8 Physician standard orders.

for medical clearance." The standard order forms need to be readily accessible to all surgeons and their offices, along with other forms outlined by the organization (such as surgical consent, blood consent, etc.) that need to be completed before the patient enters the OR. We normally provide this form on the Internet so any updates are real time to the surgeon's offices.

Each surgeon's office may need to be educated on the new forms and the necessary process steps to streamline readiness. Education should include standards related to how to:

1. Call to schedule patients for surgery
2. During the same call to schedule the surgery, transfer to pre-testing to schedule the pre-testing appointment
3. Streamline where the documentation needs to be sent. Options for sending: scan, fax, or e-mail order form or consent to one pre-testing location

Take caution: Before mandatory pre-testing is fully implemented, one may want, in parallel, to streamline operations in the pre-testing area. Consider a Lean initiative looking at the pre-testing operations and infrastructure to make sure that it is easy to do business with (ETDBW). Pre-testing must be able to provide a high quality service level to their patients. If not, patients will complain to the surgeon's office, and then the surgeons will no longer want to participate in the new pre-testing process as outlined.

KEY CONSIDERATIONS

If there is not adequate space or staff to meet the projected demand within the pre-testing department, the manager may determine that they "pace" the physician office training of the new process and "rollout," to meet the ability of the clinic to meet the demand of their customers (physician offices). The team should work closely with ancillary support services that are needed during clinic operating times to ensure that laboratory and radiology etc., can meet the new customer demand.

STANDARD ORDERS ROLLOUT— GENERAL LEAN PROJECT SYSTEM IMPLEMENTATION CONSIDERATIONS

PHYSICIAN ACCEPTANCE AND ADOPTION

In general, if one is considering a Lean initiative in surgical services, it is important to engage physician leaders to steer the initiative. This group could be a committee that already exists within the organization or a new one developed to oversee operations within surgical services. It is recommended that whether considering an existing committee or developing a new one, the members include representatives from each large surgical subspecialty, administration, anesthesia, and surgeon leaders. The committee should determine what projects should be engaged, assess the progress, remove barriers

and make "surgeon" decisions related to the projects. As an example, the committee should review the new standard orders that incorporate medical clearance. We have found this helps in physician change management and to remove physician-related barriers to facilitate compliance. In addition, it provides a mechanism for the Lean team to get feedback on what is important from the customer's viewpoint.

HOW TO IMPLEMENT THE PHYSICIAN OFFICE COMPONENT

Physician Office Education

Key activities

- Selecting pilot surgeon offices
- Training and coaching offices on the process
- Results and full implementation

Selection of Pilot Offices

When implementing standard orders, it is best to identify 2—maybe 3—surgeons to pilot the implementation. The requirement for the first pilot is simply finding a surgeon(s) who is willing to try the new process and activities, be open-minded, provide feedback, and make it successful. In addition, it is helpful to identify an informal leader within the surgical arena, a surgeon who is respected and will be able to drive the adoption of others once the pilot phase is complete.

Once the surgeon(s) agrees to the pilot, it is necessary to meet with the involved physicians, the director of surgery, and director or group leader of anesthesia (and other stakeholders, as identified) to explain the new process and desired behaviors and outcomes.

We create an education packet which explains to the offices the new process with a practical run-through of the new standard order form, where it is located, how to download it or complete it on the Internet, and the procedure for furnishing it to pre-testing.

Necessity for Pre-Testing

It is necessary to explain to the office staff the challenges and current statistics relating to patient readiness for their surgeon. In addition, it is important to explain why patient readiness is so critical to starting surgery on time and what is in it for them (patient and surgeon satisfaction, and, in addition, they may receive fewer phone calls and rework in trying to obtain last-minute results that may have been lost).

Necessity to Schedule Pre-Testing at least 3–10 days (whenever possible) Prior to the Surgery Date

Other obstacles to same-day testing is the timeliness or TATs for laboratory results and x-rays; in addition, some organizations have expressed challenges related to reimbursement for tests performed the same day of surgery. The argument for three plus days prior is that it provides a buffer that allows time for processing tests (laboratory and radiology), review of the results, and implementation of corrective actions, or additional testing that may be required. Having pre-testing performed prior to the day of surgery provides a relaxed atmosphere to interview the patient and ascertain if any other complications could arise prior to the day of surgery. It is not unusual to find patients who aren't sure of their surgeons' names or don't even fully understand the surgery they are contemplating.

Pre-testing can alleviate potential problems that, if not identified and addressed, may cause cancellations on the day of surgery. Cancellations the same day of surgery can be very disruptive to both the patients and their families who have emotionally and logistically prepared for surgery. In addition, same-day cancellations also disrupt the surgical schedule and impact, staffing, anesthesiologists, and other patients.

General Considerations in Working with surgeon's Offices:

- Consents need to be signed in surgeon's office
- Provide contact numbers for faxing and feedback
- Agreement that the offices send their patients to pre-testing and pre-testing will take care of everything for them
- If the offices send them to an outside provider, i.e., internist or family practitioner, separate laboratory, or radiology center, etc., then the doctor's office is responsible to convey all the reports and furnish them "as a package" to pre-testing
- Explain the process for how "any abnormals" will be handled

LEAN PRE-TESTING MODEL

The pre-testing Lean initiative should utilize the following tools: VSM, base-line metrics and photos, five why's, PPF (TIPS) analysis, operator full work analysis (FWA), layout review, capacity and staffing analysis and scheduling. In most cases, we have found that a new layout is required, deploying standard work and a staffing plan ("staff to demand"), which would include forecasting and level loading demand. We have found that once standard orders are implemented, demand for pre-testing grows. It should be noted that pre-testing is, in fact, inspection and, therefore, a non-value-adding activity. Eventually, the goal should be to eliminate the need for or minimize the amount of pre-testing criteria and time necessary.

PRE-TESTING INFRASTRUCTURE

When we work with pre-testing, our goal is to work two parallel projects. One is to implement the standard orders initiative, including the development of the form, physician education, and pilots, and the other is to improve the flow and efficiency of the pre-testing clinic.

Pre-testing infrastructure must be streamlined before one considers mandated pre-testing. Takt time will tell us how many rooms will be needed to see patients. PPFs and point-to-point diagramming are beneficial in determining the layout and new work flow through the unit. PPFs will help identify where and when phlebotomy and electrocardiograms (EKGs) are performed. full work analysis will aid in determining value-added steps, workstation design, where to place printers, faxes, and other equipment. FWA will reveal TLT; that, when divided by Takt time, will help in determining how many staff will be required. One must remember that today, volume may be low, but on adoption of standard orders and mandated pre-testing, demand will grow. Forecasting growth related to rooms required and staff is extremely critical to meet customer needs and must be considered in the new layout. Customer surveys may be needed to determine the optimal times (hours and days) to operate the clinic to maximize patient satisfaction.

We have discovered many models for pre-testing. Each has pros and cons and can be influenced by many variables. We have identified the following different pre-testing models to date:

1. Surgeon performs some pre-testing in office (patient and sometimes results not sent to pre-testing area).
2. Family physician or internist performs pre-testing (referred by surgeon not sent to hospital pre-testing clinic).
3. Patient drives the process (patient provided orders by surgeon and patient determines where to go).
4. Pre-testing performed by pre-testing clinic nurse phone call only (no visit) to determine which patients should come in to be seen by an anesthesiologist and schedules appointments for others.
5. All patients are sent by surgeons' offices to the hospital pre-testing clinic where the process is:
6. Nurse in pre-testing performs pre-testing interview, carries out standard orders, follows up on results, and communicates with surgeons or physicians, as needed.
7. Phone call by pre-testing nurse, followed by a visit to pre-testing clinic (nurses).
8. Combination of nurse interview and anesthetist nurse screening.
9. Anesthesia (physician) screens patient in pre-testing (or their office) and nurse in pre-testing does interview.
10. Hospitalist screens patient in pre-testing clinic and nurse does interview. Hospitals using this model swear by it. They will tell you a nurse is not a doctor. In addition, the hospitalist can complete the H&P and consents needed for surgery.
11. Physician's assistant (PA) or advanced registered nurse practitioner (ARNP) in pre-testing area screens patient and nurse does interview.
12. Some hybrid combination of all the above.

We have found that pre-testing clinics with standardized processes are the most successful. In addition, depending on the contracts with the anesthesia groups and hospitalists, models that include physicians in pre-testing may be cost prohibitive for many organizations. There can also be complications where hospitals have more than one hospitalist group. Pre-testing models are influenced by the ability to charge for services rendered by physicians in the clinics (anesthesia, hospitalist, etc.). Depending on the surgeon's relationships with the local family practitioners, and internists, there may be some reluctance to refer patients to physician hospitalist groups in the pre-testing clinic. Other concerns result as to who is the "attending" or admitting physician. In some cases, the hospitalist model is very effective if the hospitalist becomes the "attending" physician. They are then responsible and reimbursed for the care of the patient, which frees up the surgeon to do more surgeries. As discussed, the ultimate goal with standard orders and pre-testing is to make sure that the patient is ready the day of surgery and the case does not get cancelled or rescheduled.

TRADITIONAL PROCESS FLOW AND ISSUES OF THE "READINESS FOR SURGERY PROCESS"

The process starts with the patient consenting to surgery. The surgeon begins by writing orders and then, in most cases, the office staff will normally provide the patient with a packet of information that includes what the patient can expect. The office may tell the patient at that time or inform the patient that they will be notified of the surgery date and time. They may tell the patient to call for a pre-testing appointment, or schedule it for the patient, or have pre-testing done that day (depending on the timing of surgery and pre-testing models and process in place).

PRE-TESTING PHONE CALL PROCESS

Some pre-testing models only make phone calls first, but most combine with visits. Once the pre-testing nurse is able to contact the patient, she/he will go through the routine assessment and enter the patient information into a computer. This facilitates patient time spent in the clinic, and provides insight into medical history. If it is determined that the patient has complicated medical risks and the case could be delayed or cancelled, the patient is instructed to come in for the pre-testing process and medical clearance. Most pre-testing managers want all their patients to visit to ensure they are properly prepared. Most can be quoted as saying "A phone call is not the same as "hands on.""

PRE-TESTING PATIENT INTERVIEW

During the interview, the nurse enters the patient's information into the surgical information system. Some hospitals simply collect the information to have on hand and use for decision making. Other hospitals utilize this tool to trigger consults during Post-Op care. This is both good for the patient and good for the hospital.

THE PRE-TESTING MODEL—PATIENT VISIT

When patients go to pre-testing, they are normally checked in by a person who will ask the patient to sign in and, complete any forms that may be missing (Figure 15.9).

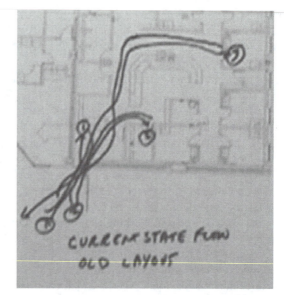

FIGURE 15.9   Patient flow diagram.

At some point, the patient is called to registration to verify insurance information and co-payment collection. The patient is then directed back to the waiting room to wait for the nurse. The nurse takes the patient's vitals, fills out a nursing assessment (if they have them), completes orders for any other test results and x-rays (as needed), and provides instructions for the day of surgery. At some point, a phlebotomist comes into the room to draw blood and/or do an EKG. The nurse then completes the process and makes sure the consents are proper and signed. After this, depending on the model, the patient may see a nurse anesthetist, physician, or whoever is responsible for reviewing the patient's information. They may examine the patient and determine if they meet all the criteria. If rendered necessary, he or she may then order an additional laboratory test (blood draw or EKG) or contact the surgeon.

PROBLEMS TYPICALLY ENCOUNTERED

- Nurse productivity is low.
- Management thinks they need more rooms.
- Forms are everywhere.
- Chart making is batched in sections.
- Wait times for patients are long.
- There is a long LOS for the process.
- Matching up paperwork from different sources is often difficult. I have seen processes where 6 to 8 nurses were needed to match up paperwork which was coming from doctor's offices, independent laboratories, physician offices, etc., for surgeries days to months out.
- Chart completion percentage at Pre-Op is low.
- Orders may or may not be in the chart when patient arrives.
- FPY at Pre-Op is low.
- There are no standard orders to follow (across all surgeons).

Hospital X Lean Results in Pre-Testing are Proven

A financial-based decision was made to close a small pre-testing department at a day surgery site adjacent to the main hospital campus. The department had 3 nurses with an average of 13–17 patients per day. The main campus pre-testing clinic was able to absorb the additional volume with no increase in staff. The 3 nurses were re-deployed elsewhere in the hospital. In addition, the clinic has increased volume by 38%, increased patients per nurse by 19.4%, and improved on-time chart completion from 36% to 70% using more stringent criteria. When this was conveyed to the unit secretaries, their faces lit up and they said, "We are going to keep raising it!" The clinic has been able to eliminate virtually all overtime. In addition, by changing the information flow and how charts were assembled, they were able to work on completing charts up to 2 weeks or more in advance, when just getting the next day's charts used to be a struggle. Everyone prefers the new system.

Level Loading the Schedule

Hospital X was having difficulty staffing the unit and patients were experiencing long wait times. When analyzed, *it was determined that staffing did not match the demand nor the wide variation in the times that patients arrived. The schedule was controlled by the OR, not the pre-testing unit. We transferred control of the schedule to the pre-testing unit, thereby giving them control over their own destiny. The first thing we did was to level load the appointments. This is called Heijunka (Figure 15.10). The software had to be "fooled" to accomplish this, as the software scheduled by room, not by the hour. Once we implemented the Heijunka system, the demand averaged out per hour and the nurses could easily manage the demand. The nurses were much happier and less frustrated. We then implemented visual controls for registration (Figure 15.11) so they always knew who was at which registration desk, next door. We*

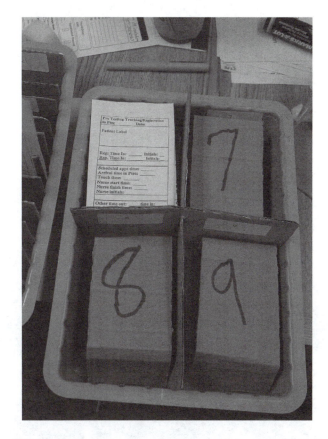

FIGURE 15.11   Registration visual queue.

then implemented Heijunka cards (Table 15.5) where we captured the cycle times for each part of the process and logged them into a spreadsheet each day real time. A day-by-the-hour sheet was created and each room had an in and out envelope in which the Heijunka card would go (Figure 15.12). Now we knew who was in what room all the time.

FIGURE 15.10   Heijunka box.

TABLE 15.5
Heijunka Cycle Time (CT) Card

Pre Testing Stats					
Patient Label					
Appt. Time:			Date:		
Circle Type: K	M	DS	RR	GI	OB
Lab EKG CXR UA					
Check In:					
Reg In:			Out:		
Ord. Start:			End:		
Room In:					
Nurse start:			End:		
Anes In:			Out:		
BD/EKG In:			Out:		
Nurse Name:					
Comments:					

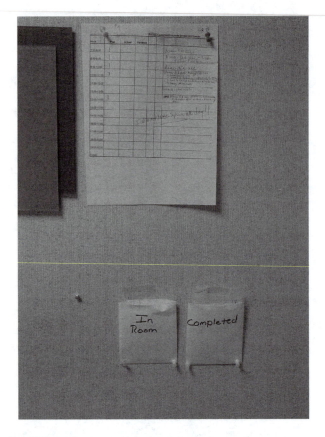

FIGURE 15.12   Pre-testing visual day by hour.

The charge nurse now had tools to manage and improve the system (Table 15.6).

HOSPITAL B—STANDARD WORK—THOUGHTS AND DISCUSSIONS SURROUNDING THE INTRODUCTION OF STANDARD WORK TO STAFF IN A PRE-TESTING CLINIC

As part of a Lean initiative, the nurses were filmed as they performed their daily activities within the pre-testing area. Each step the nurses performed was documented and a FWA sheet was created. Two acting charge nurses (who were on the Lean team) met in private to review each of their steps from their film on the FWA and came to agreement on how they would set up new standard work and sequence of operations. A job breakdown sheet (JBS) was created. When asked what they thought of the process, they were surprised how differently they each performed the patient interview. They did things in different order, asked different questions and, in some cases, certain questions were not asked at all. The standard work concept was introduced to the entire department during an afternoon huddle meeting where we reviewed the "idea board." The meeting was held each week as part of our Lean initiative with a goal to get it to a 10-min "standup" meeting. We explained the advantages of standard work along with how it would help ensure the quality of patient care. As one might imagine, we were met with some resistance and comments such as:

- "We were trained to do nursing independently and now you want to tell us what to do!"
- "Our licenses are at stake and, since you are not a nurse, you don't understand that."
- "If you make us do everything the same, we will forget and quality will be compromised!"
- "You don't care about the patients; you just want us to be robots."
- "Nursing is an art form learned over years of experience. It is not a science."

After the staff vented their concerns, it was explained that many processes in the hospital are broken, which is why hospitals continually fail audits. At risk is the safety and welfare of our patients, which should be put first in our decision making. When everyone does a process differently, what are the chances that each patient is getting the same high-level quality of care? How would you measure it? You couldn't because everyone does it differently. You can't implement an improvement across the board when everyone does it differently. In many cases, most procedures were not written down. Everyone is trained by a different nurse with different tribal knowledge and opinions on how things should be done. How can quality be better in this environment?

We explained when everyone does tasks differently it is actually dangerous and is supported by a recent example where a nurse bypassed protocol (bed management) and a patient was literally lost in the system.

The goal is not to change what the nurses do, but to structure it so every patient gets the same necessary standard and high quality of care. We must document the process and improvements to the process (no longer person-dependent) in order to:

- Train new hires
- Have the ability to audit the process
- Pass audits and incorporate changes as a result of audits
- Create a video for new hires (on standard processes)
- Obtain consistent times and expectations for the process across all nurses
- Know how far a patient is through the process with any nurse at any time
- Make their job easier
- Highlight variation in the process to encourage ongoing continuous improvement

We told them we had done this many times before. We then passed out the "straw man" of the job breakdown sheets (Figure 15.13) of their daily tasks that the 2 charge nurses created. All the nurses were given the opportunity to review it for a week and to see what changes, if any, they wanted to make. The department grumbling and rumor mill continued throughout the week, and we were told that morale was way down. This is typical of what will occur through a Lean initiative, as there is normal resistance to change. We walked the nurses through the change

TABLE 15.6
Heijunka Cycle Times

	Data												
Date	Average of Reg CT	Average of Reg Wait Time	Average of orders CT	Average of Order Entry Delay Time	Average of Exam Room Wait Time	Average of Patient Exam Room CT	Average of Nurse CT	Average of anesthesia CT	Average of anesthesia Wait Time	Average of BD/EKG Wait Time	Average of BD/EKG CT	Average of LOS/Throughput Time
19 March	0:04	0:03	0:02	0:06	0:16	0:28	0:32	0:05	0:03	0:04	0:09	1:10
20 March	0:04	0:09	0:01	0:04	0:17	0:28	0:32	0:05	0:04	0:04	0:10	1:18
24 March	0:04	0:06	0:01	0:02	0:15	0:31	0:33	0:04	0:03	0:04	0:09	1:17
25 March	0:04	0:03	0:03	0:04	0:15	0:32	0:35	0:05	0:04	0:06	0:07	1:17
26 March	0:03	0:04	0:03	0:05	0:21	0:31	0:33	0:05	0:01	0:20	0:08	1:13
27 March	0:03	0:08	0:02	0:03	0:18	0:32	0:35	0:05	0:06	0:33	0:09	1:23
30 March	0:05	0:05	0:03	0:04	0:22	0:36	0:41	0:05	0:04	0:05	0:08	1:29
Grand total	0:04	0:05	0:02	0:04	0:18	0:31	0:34	0:05	0:04	0:12	0:09	1:19

Nurse Standard Work

Area	Total Labor Time	Available Time Minutes	Daily Demand	Takt Time (Mins)
Pre Testing	2,842	700	42	17

HEAD COUNT:	1	3	4	5	6
CYCLE TIME:	2842	947	710	568	474
HOURLY OUTPUT:	1	4	5	6	8
DAILY OUTPUT:	15	44	59	74	89

Layout Area and Walk Patterns

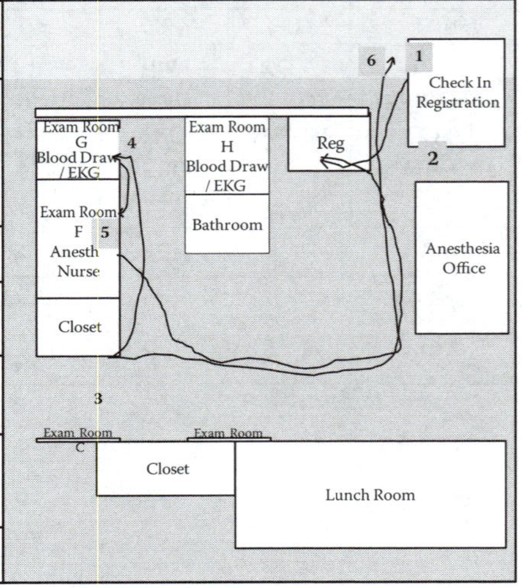

(Layout diagram showing: Check In Registration; Reg; Anesthesia Office; Exam Room H Blood Draw / EKG; Bathroom; Exam Room G Blood Draw / EKG; Exam Room F; Anesth Nurse; Closet; Lunch Room; Exam Room; Closet; Exam Room C; with walk pattern numbers 1–6)

Standard Work Area: Surgery Pre Testing Clinic

Job Step #	Nurse Description (what they do)	Key Points and Quality Notes (how they do it)	Reasons for Key Points	Min Time (secs)	Max Time (secs)	Avg Time Secs	Cumulative Avg Time Mins
1	Pick up chart, and go to room or get patient from lobby	If there is no patient, you should make a phone call. If there is a patient, Reg will put the patient in your room if you do not have one in there. If all the rooms are full, Reg will put the chart in the file (labeled on the counter) and put the patient in the lobby	Our priority is visiting patients first and then phone calls. However phone calls are very important and have to get done as well.	120	160	140	140
2	Prep the chart outside	checklist, signature sheet, consents, check orders and labs, stickers if needed	We don't watching us prep the chart and they think we are ignoring them	60	120	90	141.5
3	Get the patient if necessary. Flip flags as required. Then Introduce yourself to the patient and explain the process.	See script	It is important we follow the script especially in the case of dealing with more difficult patients	60	80	70	142.7
4	Log into PICIS and HOM. Locate the patient in the computer but go to HOM first	see procedure for logging into PICIS and HOM	Let Patient Know We are going to repeat some of the information Reg just asked you.	60	60	60	143.7
5	Begin Charting	Verify correct DOB and DOS and review orders. Have patients sign consents, Check bib? sheets and armbands if applicable and review spelling of sticker		300	300	300	148.7
6	Look for med list in chart, then chart meds, in HOM, Allergies, height, weight, advance directives and print			300	300	300	153.7

FIGURE 15.13 Nurse job breakdown sheet / standard work.

that was recommended, discussed why it was being made, how it would affect them, and if they changed what was in it for them. We also explained that standard work would not be set in stone, and the expectation would be to continually improve it. A week later, the "big" night came. We met with the staff after clinic was closed. We showed the nurses a movie about taking time out of processes. After the movie, the manager of the area debriefed the movie and told everyone that Lean was about giving our patients the best care and making sure the patient chart and patients were ready for surgery.

We handed the meeting over to the 2 charge nurses who reviewed the activities step by step, in the standard work. Listed below is how the review started. The charge nurse said:

Step 1—Grab the charts

"Does everyone agree?" asked the charge nurse, who was dreading this exercise. All eleven present agreed! Ok, Only 39 more to go.

Step 2—Introduce yourself to the patient

Does everyone agree? Rules were set prior to the meeting that one person would talk at a time. Well, it didn't last long. One nurse asked about preparing the chart. "We have to sign the signature sheet, fill out consents…" Another nurse said, "I just tell the patient what I'm doing and it is not a problem." The first nurse said, "When I do it, the patients think I am ignoring them and make comments."

I then asked what other nurses thought and they all started sharing their thoughts and feelings, some more passionately than others. When we were done, we added a new Step 2, prepare the chart prior to entering the room with the patient.

Step 3—Take vitals

One nurse stated she takes vitals right away while the computer is loading the programs. Another nurse does it about ten steps down, another does it toward the end, and yet another does it at the end. As facilitator, I had each nurse give the reason they did vitals when they did them. One said she did it toward the end because she found when she did it right away, some patients were so nervous she had to retake the blood pressure later. So by doing it later in the process, the patient was more relaxed and they got a good reading. After much discussion, we decided to move it toward the end of the process.

Note: *And so it went on and on, with everyone discovering how differently they each did the same job, how everyone had a different approach, and how many left important questions out and others asked questions that weren't necessary. In one case, 1 nurse felt her job and license were on the line if she didn't mention every single drop-down box regardless of how the patient answered the questions. The system is designed so that if a patient answers "no"*

to a question, one moves on to the next question vs. continuing to ask the patient if they have any of the ten items in the drop-down box that they already answered "no" to. It instantly became clear why this nurse had the longest interview times, sometimes taking more than an hour and a half for a process that should average 25–30 min. This nurse felt we were lowering our standards and not being thorough. The rest of the nurses very nicely explained to her how the system was designed to work and that, as long as they properly documented the patient's responses, we still maintain the same high level of quality and it would never jeopardize her license. Over an hour later, we were halfway through the document and adjourned for the evening. We would schedule another "movie" night to conclude the exercise.

Lessons Learned and Ideas Implemented from Various Lean Pre-Testing Initiatives

- Deployed standard work which was agreed on by consensus
- Standard work must incorporate the motto "quality first, the speed will come"
- Created visual cues to track patient visits outside each room
- Nurses do not have to continually log in and out of different computers
- Created a new chart flow so the nurses could follow up and complete their patient

Before, moving from room to room between every patient, nurses had to give the charts to the charge nurse to keep them centralized and not lost. So, the "system" created a process where the charge nurse had to follow-up and complete every chart. There was no time to supervise or watch the flow. The new process freed up the supervisor to work on ongoing improvements.

- Assigned a nurse to a specific room each day—benefits:
  - Had a place for personal items.
  - By creating separate rooms for lab, EKG, and vitals, we were able to replace six "unfriendly" examination beds in each room with recliners. We also eliminated the interview rooms as a bottleneck and saw more patients. This freed up several computers and eliminated a lot of gathering (and socializing) at the nurse's station.
- Standardized the rooms—designate a leader for this effort and require everyone's participation. Results: each nurse got an individual printer, saved money in wasted steps per day and per year, and were able to follow up orders and complete charts easier.
- Spreading phone calls across all the nurses, in addition to having a phone call nurse.

- Create standard orders: as one physician said, "Now I don't get calls at home or on the way into the hospital at 5:30 a.m."
  - Explain how the standard order form works and that the goal is to eliminate mistakes prior to anesthesia screening.
  - Standardize Pre-Op order form for medical clearance. The form needs to be designed to be simple check boxes that then dictate the necessary screening. The form also provides room for additional consults, which the surgeon or office staff can fill in or complete. There is room for the surgeon to add tests, orders, or consults they deem necessary. Again, it can replace, in some cases, dozens of existing surgeon forms or be used in conjunction with them.
- In the physician's office, the following was identified:
  - There is a need to have consent signed in the surgeon's office.
  - Establish and provide contact numbers for faxing and feedback.
  - There should be an agreement by offices that, if they send their patient to pre-testing, pre-testing will take care of everything for them.
  - If they send the patient to a family practitioner, separate laboratory, or radiology center, etc., then the doctor's office will be responsible to convey all the reports and furnish as a package to the pre-testing area.
  - There should be an explanation of how any "abnormals" will be handled.
  - During the office visit, provide the opportunity for any questions and a frequently asked questions (FAQ) sheet.

Results: *Hospital 1* was profiled in an article for their implementation of Lean principles while hospitals 2 and 3 utilized the Lean System Implementation method we propose in this book (Table 15.7). It can be clearly seen the BASICS approach resulted in greater productivity. Quality has maintained or improved with every implementation to date.*

Pre-Testing Model Calculations

Figure 15.14 is an example of sample value stream process boxes from a pre-testing area. Owing to the business model of this department, we had to implement in phases. We started with an Average Daily Demand (ADD) of 45 patients.

Available time = 12 hrs or 720 min (5:00 a.m. to 5:00 p.m. clinic)

Customer average daily demand = 45 patients.

To calculate our Takt time, we take the available time (12 hrs) and the customer demand at 45 patients per day. Our average Takt time is:

$$720 \div 45 = 16 \text{ min per patient.}$$

This means we have to devise a system that can get a patient in and out every 16 min on average. Utilizing the example box Step #3 of the process nurse review, we can calculate how many rooms and how much labor we need.

If we have the Takt time, we use the formula LOS ÷ Takt time = # rooms:

$$90 \text{ min} \div 16 \text{ min} = 5.63 \text{ rooms,}$$

and TLT ÷ Takt time = # persons required

$$25.5 \text{ min} \div 16 \text{ min} = 1.59 \text{ FTEs.}$$

assuming one can balance the work evenly across the employees, see Table 15.8.

Section III Pre-Op

An opportunity was identified post-VSM to improve the Pre-Op area (Figure 15.15). First, several patients were followed through the process. It was determined that patients would be categorized by the length of time it took to work up a patient. The specialties of orthopedics, general surgery, and cardiovascular were selected. Nurses, technicians, and physicians of each skill type were videotaped. Each video was then analyzed with the individual filmed present and the results were as follows.

The PPF analysis provided the cycle time or LOS for each process step. The full work analysis showed the Total Labor Time (TLT) equaled 60 min for 1 patient. Several of the Pre-Op nurses were filmed, caring for patients with different levels of acuity. As the videotapes were analyzed we asked the staff to document each step, determine if there were any issues, and identify problems and ideas that could lead to improvements. Outlined is a list of ideas from reviewing the videotape with the staff.

- Point of use materials and supplies
- Materials located in multiple areas (excessive travel for staff)
- Lidocaine not refrigerated
- IV cart needed to be relocated to be more accessible
- Standardize supplies at bedside
- IV bags more accessible
- Flow—consider team approach vs. non-team approach
- Determine appropriate skill level for task
- Need standard work (work standard)
- Trigger Pre-Op pull for next patient from OR charge nurse
- Flip rooms (what is the impact, positive or negative?)
- Free up storage space (5S the area)

---

* "Streamlining Care (Pre-testing)," *Advance For Nurse* (Vol. 10 No. 13, June 8, 2009, 8).

TABLE 15.7

Pre-testing Clinic Results From Three Different Hospitals Implementing Lean Pre-Testing Departments

	Hall Patients	Phone Calls	Total Patients and Calls	# Nurses	# Clerical	# Techs	Total Persons	Working Days	Working Hours (assumes 40 hrs per week)	Nursing Hours Per Patient Visit	Total Labor Hours Per Patient	Patients Seen Per Person Per Day	# Total FTEs	Hours Per FTE	Notes
Hospital #1	UK	UK	13,000	22	2	6	30	250	45,760	3.52	4.80	1.73	UK	UK	No data on change nurses
Hospital #2	10,534	3962	14,496	11	3	2	16	250	22,880	1.58	2.30	3.62	UK	UK	Secretaries also do scheduling
Hospital #3	12,314	6376	18,690	9.9	3	2	14.9	250	20,592	1.10	1.66	5.02	14.80	1.65	Does not include change nurse. 11 nurses but 9.9 FTEs. Actual productivity running 1.39 or less

Note: Hospital #1 was profiled in a paper as having streamlined their care compared to hospital #2 and #3, which conduced Lean system implementations. UK = unknown.

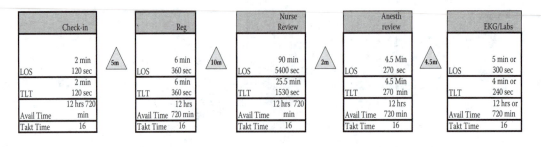

FIGURE 15.14   Pre-testing clinic VSM (value stream map) Base.

- Review charts the night prior to surgery for "abnormals," draw blood, MRI, CT
- Surgeon consult done ahead of time in consult room located near surgery
- Need nerve block room location
- Set up speed dial on phones
- Move Lidocaine and angiocaths to more accessible location
- Pre-testing to write consents
- Add check boxes to belongings sheet
- Make allergy sticker/contact/weight printable
- Combo sticker with standard allergy portion on bottom
- Pre-testing to fill out allergy, weight, contact on front of chart
- Property list filled out in waiting area
- Decrease supplies at bedside, combine supplies in bedside carts, correct supplies with par levels
- Charge Lidocaine at end of day for all patients
- Carts at bedside for all supplies (like PACU)
- Handheld printer scanners for blood draw
- Move ECG machine
- Dress stretcher with gown packet

PRE-OP TIME STUDY

Because there is so much variation in Pre-Op and there were no computerized tools to track cycle times, we manually tracked cycle times for several weeks (Figure 15.17). Over time, we found they averaged out per nurse and per

TABLE 15.8
Pre-Testing VSM Boxes Blown Up

Nurse Review	
Given	
LOS	90 min 5400 sec
TLT	25.5 min 1530 sec
Available time	12 hrs 720 min
Calculated	
Takt time	16
Rooms	5.6 or 6
FTE	1.59

technician. The results of the time study allowed us to create a predictive model (Figure 15.18). The model could perform "what ifs" based on patient and staff arrival times per hour or per morning or per day. If someone was out sick, we could predict our completion time and take the necessary countermeasures.

BENEFITS OF TEAM NURSING IN PRE-OP

The team nursing approach was suggested by several of the Pre-Op nurses who had worked with it before at other hospitals. The manager of the area was initially against the approach. We decided to create the standard work and settled on a "hands on" nurse and a "hands off" nurse. The "hands on" performed all the steps requiring patient contact, such as IV, and the "hands off" nurse took care of the computer system and paperwork, including consents. The system was very successful and reduced the cycle time from 51 to 21 min. While it is only a 9 min saving overall, because the nurses worked in teams, it gave the technicians' time to work with the patients, reducing the cycle time further to 19 min. In the past, the technicians spent much of their time wandering around looking for ways to help out, but since each nurse now took a patient, there was not much for them to do. The benefits of the team nursing were:

- Right skill level for tasks—technicians can see patients, now 100% efficient vs. 50% efficient.
- Patients get completed more quickly vs. many patients being worked on but not completed.
- Team nursing is 20%–25% more efficient than individual nursing.
- 90%–100% of patients completed by 7:15 a.m. most days.
- No longer interrupted by anesthesia, so blocks get done quicker.

LET'S EXAMINE PRE-OP ON THE DAY OF SURGERY

Hospital X has 60 patients scheduled for surgery, 20% come from the floors (admitted) and 80% or 48 of the patients arrive for surgery on the same day in the Pre-Op unit. Historically, the patients were not required to have any pre-testing or medical clearance evaluation for surgery; therefore, often patients had their surgery delayed on the day of surgery while waiting

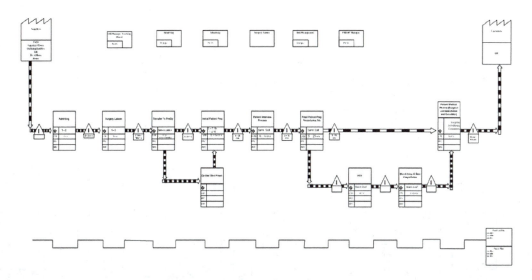

FIGURE 15.15 Pre-Op VSM (value stream map) in the making.

for laboratory results or investigation of potential medical problems. Because of this, the surgeons began requiring the patients to arrive in the Pre-Op area between 5:00 a.m. and 6:00 a.m., no matter what time their surgery was scheduled (Table 15.9). The Pre-Op unit would be inundated with patients, and the result was that many cases were delayed since the nurses had difficulty in preparing the first cases for surgery while simultaneously tending to patients who had surgery scheduled for later in the day. Figure 15.19 is a graph of how the patients arrive in the Pre-Op unit each morning.

The average length of stay (ALOS) in the Pre-Op unit was 150 min; the available time is 8 hrs or 480 min. The TLT to prepare a patient for surgery is 65 min. If we assume that we bring patients in 2.5 hrs early as the first cases begin at 7:30 a.m., we can calculate how many rooms and how much labor we need, given how the patients are currently being "asked to arrive," since patients do not have to be in the OR until 7:30 a.m. and we are asking the first set to arrive at 5:00 a.m. Let's determine the Takt time, which is

Available time from 5:00 a.m. to 7:30 a.m. of 150 min (2.5 hrs) ÷ 32 customers (customer demand for the first 2.5 hrs, 20 + 12) = 4.7 min per patient.

We use the formula LOS ÷ Takt time = # rooms

$$150 \text{ min} \div 4.7 \text{ min} = 32 \text{ rooms},$$

and TLT ÷ Takt time = # persons required

$$65 \text{ min} \div 4.7 \text{ min} = 13.8 \text{ FTEs},$$

this assumes one can balance the work evenly across the employees. The surgical services department performed a VSM and determined that surgeries were canceled owing to issues stemming from "patients not ready" for surgery when they arrived. A Lean initiative was undertaken, as described

above, and a dramatic improvement was seen in patients arriving "gift-wrapped" the day of surgery. If we assume we now bring down just the first 20 patients, since we only have 20 ORs, what will be the impact?

2.5 hrs ÷ 20 customers = 7.5 min per patient.

We use the formula LOS ÷ Takt time = # rooms

$$150 \text{ min} \div 7.5 \text{ min} = 20 \text{ rooms},$$

and TLT ÷ Takt time = # persons required

$$65 \text{ min} \div 7.5 \text{ min} = 8.7 \text{ FTE}.$$

There was a significant decrease in the number of rooms needed from 32 to 20 and the number of FTEs was reduced from 13.8 to 8.7. If the average nurse wage was $28/hr or

Idea Board

FIGURE 15.16 Pre-Op idea board.

Date:	Room	Time of Surgery	Patient Down	Tech start Prep	Tech End Prep	Tech In	Tech Out	Tech CT	Nurse 1 start Prep	Nurse 1 end Prep	Nurse 1 In	Nurse 1 Out	Nurse 1 CT	Nurse 2 start Prep	Nurse 2 end Prep	Nurse 2 In	Nurse 2 Out	Nurse 2 CT	Overall CT for PT	Total Labor Time	Anesthesia In	Surgeon In	Patient to Surgery	Nursing Team	Tech Name	Comments
Patient#1	B	7:30	5:45	6:01	6:07	6:08	6:12	0:11	5:48	5:48	5:59	6:03	0:15	5:59	5:59	5:59	6:03	0:04	0:20	0:24						
Patient#2	C	7:30	5:45	5:46	5:50	5:46	6:05	0:19	6:11	6:11	6:12	6:17	0:12	6:05	6:12	6:12	6:17	0:12	0:31	0:43						
Patient#3	H	7:30	5:48	6:23	6:23	6:24	6:27	0:04	5:48	5:48	5:48	6:01	0:13	5:48	5:48	5:48	6:01	0:13	0:17	0:30						
Patient#5	PACU 16	7:30	5:54						5:54	5:48	7:00	7:00	1:06						1:06	1:06						
Patient#4	PACU 21	7:30	5:48						5:48	5:48	7:00	7:00	1:12						1:12	1:12						
Patient#6	PACU 22	7:30	6:27						6:27	6:22	7:00	7:00	0:33						0:33	0:33						
Patient#7	D	7:30	6:06	6:08	6:08	6:08			6:22	6:22	6:22	6:32	0:10	6:22	6:22	6:22	6:32	0:10	0:25	0:35						
Patient#8	E	7:30	6:10		7:19	7:19	7:25	0:15	6:08	6:11	6:11	6:26	0:18													
Patient#9	A	7:30	6:06	6:12	6:25	6:12	6:23	0:11	6:19	6:11	6:27	6:43	0:24	6:19	6:11		6:43	0:24	0:29	0:29						
Patient#10	G	7:30	6:46	6:06	6:25	6:25	6:27	0:03	6:19	6:26	6:27	6:43	0:24						0:27	0:51	6:56					
Patient#11	PACU 17	7:30		6:50	7:07	7:07	7:12	0:22	6:27	6:32	7:10	7:10	0:43					0:13	1:05	1:05						
Patient#12	I	7:30	6:30	6:28	6:32	6:33	6:46	0:18	6:47	6:53	6:54	7:00	0:13	6:47	6:53	6:54	7:00	0:15	0:31	0:44						
Patient#13	F (floor)		6:30	6:27	6:31	6:31	6:33	0:06	6:33	6:33	6:33	6:48	0:15	6:33	6:33	6:33	6:48	0:09	0:21	0:36						
Patient#14	B		7:35	7:35	7:35	7:35	7:43	0:08	7:52	7:55	7:56	8:01	0:09	7:52	7:55	7:56	8:01		0:17	0:26						
Patient#15	D		7:56	7:57	8:00	8:00	8:14	0:17	8:05	8:05	8:05	8:21	0:16					0:25	0:33	0:33						
Patient#16	J		7:35	8:19	8:19	8:19	8:25	0:06	8:18	8:25	8:35	8:43	0:25	8:18	8:25	8:35	8:43	0:11	0:31	0:56						
Patient#17	I			7:56	7:56	7:56	8:07	0:11	8:02	8:04	8:04	8:13	0:11	8:02	8:04	8:04	8:13	0:37	0:22	0:33						
Patient#18	G		7:43	7:48	7:48	7:48	8:05	0:17	7:50	7:57	7:58	8:27	0:37	7:50	7:57	7:58	8:27		0:54	1:31			9:56			
Patient#19	H		8:17	8:30	8:33	8:47	8:47	0:17	8:30	8:53	8:54	9:09	0:39			8:54	9:05	0:21	0:56	0:56						
Patient#20	A		7:45	7:46	7:47	7:48	7:55	0:09	7:45	7:45	7:56	8:06	0:21	7:45	7:45	7:56	8:06	0:19	0:30	0:51						
Patient#21	F		8:20	8:21	8:26	8:26	8:35	0:14	8:26	8:35	8:35	8:45	0:19	8:26	8:35	8:35	8:45	0:13	0:33	0:52			9:39			
Patient#22	C		8:47						8:52	8:56	8:56	9:08	0:16	8:52	8:56	8:53	9:05		0:14	0:27			9:50			
Patient#23	A		8:56	8:56			9:07	0:11	8:56	9:08	9:08	9:35	0:39	8:56	9:08	9:08	9:35	0:39	0:50	1:29						
Patient#24	E (floor)		9:07						9:37	9:37	9:37	9:50	0:13	9:37	9:37	9:37	9:50	0:13	0:13	0:26			10:30			
Patient#25	I	10:40							9:29	9:36	9:36	9:52	0:23	9:29	9:36	9:36	10:13	0:44	0:51	1:35						
Patient#26	F		9:48	9:41	9:48	9:48	9:54	0:13	9:48	9:54	9:54	10:02	0:14	9:48	10:02	10:04	10:39	0:51	0:45	1:36						
Patient#27	J		9:43	9:44	9:51	9:51	9:58	0:14	9:44	9:57	9:57	10:06	0:22	9:44	9:57	9:57	10:06	0:22	0:36	0:58			10:45			
Patient#28	D		10:10	10:16			10:24	0:08	10:12	10:21	10:25	10:55	0:43	10:12	10:21	10:25	10:55	0:43	0:51	1:34						
Patient#29	B		10:59	10:59	11:02	11:02	11:22	0:23	11:22	11:37	11:37	11:47	0:25	11:22	11:37	11:37	11:47	0:25	0:48	1:13						
Patient#30	G (Floor)		10:49	10:50	10:50	10:58	10:59	0:09	10:55	11:07	11:08	11:30	0:35	10:55	11:07	11:08	11:30	0:35	0:44	1:19						
Patient#31	C		10:59	10:59	11:05	11:05	11:18	0:19	11:00	11:10	11:10	11:30	0:30	11:00	11:10	11:10	11:30	0:30	0:49	1:19						
Patient#32	E								10:56	11:09	11:09	11:24	0:28	10:56	11:09	11:09	11:35	0:39	0:33	1:12		11:24				
26-Jan																										
Patient#1	G	7:30	5:46	5:47	5:56	5:56	6:02	0:15	5:53	6:01	6:01	6:16	0:23	6:02	6:02	6:02	6:16	0:14	0:33	0:47						
Patient#2	A	7:30	5:47	6:03	6:08	6:08	6:14	0:11	6:16	6:20	6:20	6:24	0:08	6:16	6:20	6:16	6:24	0:08	0:19	0:27	7:10					
Patient#3	B	7:30	5:55	5:55					6:09	6:10	6:10	6:24	0:15	6:09	6:10	6:10	6:24	0:15	0:15	0:30						
Patient#7	E	7:30	6:04	6:15	6:18	6:18	6:23	0:08	6:26	6:29	6:29	6:35	0:09	6:26	6:29	6:29	6:35	0:09	0:17	0:26	7:09					
Patient#8	C	7:30	6:04	6:09	6:19	6:19	6:38	0:29	6:11	6:36	6:36	6:53	0:42	6:36	6:36	6:36	6:53	0:17	0:58	1:15						
Patient#9	F	7:30	6:12	6:27	6:32	6:32	6:40	0:13	6:24	6:40	6:40	6:40	0:16	6:24	6:24	6:24	6:40	0:16	0:16	0:32						
Patient#10	I	7:30	6:14						6:33	6:38	6:38	6:46	0:13	6:33	6:41	6:41	6:46	0:13	0:26	0:39						

FIGURE 15.17 Pre-Op time study. Note: (names have been whited out)

Notes: Need to look at when the shift ends

8 # nurses and techs

705

0:57 hours per nurse worked

76.86 minutes per patient

	Tech	CT	Minutes Per Shift (can be for 7:30 shift or all day)	# of shifts	Hours per shift	Patients Per Shift	Nurse1	CT	Minutes Per Shift (can be for 7:30 shift or all day)	# 60 min shifts	Patients Per Shift	Nurse2	CT	Minutes Per Shift (can be for 7:30 shift or all day)	# 60 min shifts	Patients Per Shift	Overall CT	Total (minutes converted to decimal)	PTs/ Hour	factor	# 60 min shifts	Patients Per Shift	Total Labor Time/ pt	Total Labor Time
team 1	1	0:14	60	1.00		4.29	1	0:19	60	1.00	3.16	1	0:19	60	1.00	3.16	0:33	33.00	3.16	2.00	1.00	3.16	0:53	2:48
Team 2	1	0:14	60	1.00		4.29	1	0:19	60	1.00	3.16	1	0:19	60	1.00	3.16	0:33	33.00	3.16	2.00	1.00	3.16	0:53	2:48
Team 3	0	0:00	60	-		-	1	0:21	60	1.00	2.86	1	0:21	60	1.00	2.86	0:21	21.00	2.86	2.00	1.00	2.86	0:42	2:02
	0	0:00	60	-		-	0	0:00		-		1	0:00		1.00	-	0:45	45.00	-	2.00	1.00	-	0:00	0:00
																			9.17			9.17		7:40

60.00 Clock Minutes

705 Clock Minutes

4.375

8.75

2

2.25

11.00 Total pts per 7:30 start with all 3 teams

13 Total pts per 7:30 start with all 3 teams and

	CT		
Team 1	33.00	min avg CT/ pt	
Team 2	33.00	min avg ct for both teams with tech	
Team 3	21.00	min avg ct / pt	
Team 4	-	min avg ct /pt for team without tech	
	268.4210526	weighted avg clockminutes	4.473684211
	29.26	min weighted avg cycle time per pt	3.58
	6.54	min weighted avg CT per patient per Team (divided by 4 teams)	5.77 Takt Time
	6.54	min weighted avg CT per Team w/o	

7:15 AM		
10	65.41	total clockminutes required
11	71.95	
12	78.49	
13	85.03	total clockminutes required
14	91.57	total clockminutes required w/o
15	98.11	total clockminutes required w/o
16	104.66	total clockminutes required w/o
17	111.20	total clockminutes required w/o
18	117.74	total clockminutes required w/o

2nd case starts

10 cases*

9.17 cases per hour possible

	CT 2 nurse w/Tech	CT 2 nurse No Tech	CT 1 Nurse
CT Tech			
0:14	0:19	0:21	0:45

FIGURE 15.18 Pre-Op predictive staffing model.

TABLE 15.9

Pre-Op Patients by Hour

Hour (a.m.)	# of Patients
5:00	20
6:00	12
7:00	8
8:00	5
9:00	3

$58,000 per year, the reduction of approximately five FTEs would yield $290,000.

The TLT in the Pre-Op unit was reduced from 65 to 40 min. The surgeons agreed to bring their first cases in 90 min prior to surgery instead of the 150 min that they historically required. The Takt time calculation was performed again using the available time, 90 min:

1.5 hrs ÷ 20 customers = 4.5 min per patient. We use the formula LOS ÷ Takt time = # rooms

$$90 \text{ min} \div 4.5 \text{ min} = 20 \text{ rooms},$$

and TLT ÷ Takt time = # persons required

$$40 \text{ min} \div 4.5 \text{ min} = 8.9 \text{ FTE}.$$

The number of rooms would still be 20, and the number of FTEs needed would be nine staff. Sixty (60) minutes of "in-room monitoring" time was saved per FTE because now the patients arrived at 6:00 a.m. instead of 5:00 a.m.

Once same-day patient readiness is completed, in order to achieve on time starts, inpatient readiness would need to be addressed. If only the same day patients were ready, the OR may not feel the entire impact if patients from the floor that were "not ready" were mixed throughout the schedule with patients who came "gift wrapped" from pre-testing.

HOSPITAL X PRE-OP LEAN IMPROVEMENTS

Once pre-testing and Pre-Op implemented the Lean initiatives, the "waste" was eliminated, clarity in "definition of

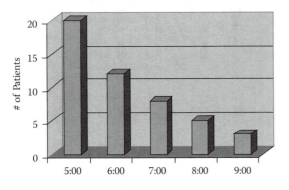

FIGURE 15.19 Pre-Op patients per hour graph.

patient readiness" was determined and standardized, and standard work was deployed. The next phase was to determine what it meant to be "ready for surgery" from the inpatient perspective. Several of the causes for delays to surgery on the inpatients included orders that were not completed when surgery called for the patient. The units were not always aware of when the patient was scheduled for surgery and there was no standard Pre-Op checklist. Some of the improvements made included creating standardized Pre-Op checklist for all surgery floor units, expectations related to "timing" on when to have the patient ready to go to surgery and a standardized distribution of the surgical schedule, including location and owner on the units, and streamlined handoff communication. Adjustments in process resulted in "on-time first-case starts" improving from 50% to 78%. To get to 90%–100% required interaction and collaboration between surgeon desires and scheduling. The goal was to "clean our house" first, meaning the internal hospital processes, and then address the surgeon and anesthesia-related opportunities.

SECTION IV GROUP TECH MATRIX

The goal of the group tech matrix (Figure 15.20) is to identify at what capacity the ORs are being utilized. It requires continually collecting data, which includes volume data (number of cases) by service line, by month, and average case time in hours by service line, see Figure 15.21. The average case time should be represented by "patient in to next patient in" times (if possible). The capacity of an OR is dictated by how long the room is tied up or unavailable for use, with or without a patient. Obviously, the room is tied up during the surgery, but it is also unavailable during a room turnover, as a patient cannot be moved into the room until it has been mopped and cleaned. So, capacity includes turnover time, hence we use the metric "patient in to next patient in".

It was discussed earlier that there are bottlenecks in the Post-Op recovery units owing to inpatient beds not being available for patients to move into; so what is the root cause? The root cause is that we are not level loading our schedules. Why are we not level loading?

- We've always done it this way.
- Surgeons all want 7:30 a.m. case starts and we have to keep them happy.
- That's how our block time is set up.
- The data have not been analyzed to optimize flow; therefore, the impact is not understood.

So, what would level loading look like? The operating hours for a routine scheduled case in surgery is from 7:00 a.m. to 5:00 p.m. If peak patient demand is 60 patients per day and a 108 min LOS (patient in to patient in), how many rooms are required?

Available time = 600 min or 10 hrs/day

Available Time Hours	141.5	1st floor rooms	2nd floor rooms	# Rooms	Room Hours	Avg Hours / Room	Total Hours	Percent	wt avg rooms / day
Available Time Per Room hours	12.4555	13		13	7:30 am - 3 pm	7.5	97.5	69%	8.96
Available Time Per Room min	747.331	9		9	3 pm - 7 pm	4	36	25%	2.29
Avg number of rooms scheduled (staffed)	11.3604	2		2	7 pm - 11 pm	4	8	6%	0.11
Working Days Per Month	21			20	Total Rooms		141.5	100%	11.36
Capacity based on Rooms Scheduled (staffed)		61.9%	Capacity based on overall # rooms						35.18%

Notes: ORMIS
Download File:

DEPARTMENT OF SURGERY

1ST AND 2ND FLOOR

Data Issues (Patient Out to Patient In) From File:_________			Patient in - Patient
Xtra patient in room			Patient In to Patient
schedule wrong			Patient out to Patient
scheduled >55			
Total Issues			

OR CASE SUMMARY - TOTAL HOURS PER CASE BY SERVICE LINE PER MONTH (Patient In to Patient In - Total Room Time)

Jul 2005 - Jun 2006

SERVICE	Oct-06	Nov-06	Dec-06	Jan-07	Feb-07	Mar-07	Apr-07	May-07	Jun-07	Jul-07	Aug-07	Sep-07	Totals	Average Hours per Month per Service Line	Std Dev	Daily Demand Hours Per Service Line	Avg hours / Case Patient In - Patient In	Avg Minutes Patient In - Patient In	No of Rooms per day Required based on time (avail time above)	No of Rooms per day Required based on time (9.5 hrs / day) Play with this column to figure out capacity by adjusting hours to get to total rooms	% of hours per case	Check Number (LOS /TT)
Anesthesia	1.53	2.12	0.42	0.72	0.00	0.38	0.42	2.02	0.00	0.45	1.60	1.27	11	0.9	0.8	0.04	0.52	31.2	0.00	0.005	0.05%	0.0035
Cardio-Thoracic	387.88	332.20	350.28	344.65	349.85	351.28	338.03	321.98	276.48	302.50	396.63	398.57	4150	345.9	36.6	16.47	3.23	194.1	1.32	1.734	20.41%	1.3223
ENT	64.53	106.07	99.38	102.97	102.38	82.80	76.38	119.15	130.23	73.22	101.12	128.90	1187	98.9	21.3	4.71	2.15	129.0	0.38	0.496	5.84%	0.3782
General Surgery	483.80	494.37	372.13	461.30	476.07	464.45	500.50	491.20	420.55	460.73	486.95	431.32	5543	461.9	37.4	22.00	2.07	123.9	1.77	2.316	27.26%	1.7661
Urology	99.75	62.05	90.52	73.23	111.67	93.95	84.82	88.57	86.05	86.13	88.43	58.75	1024	85.3	14.8	4.06	1.61	96.7	0.33	0.428	5.03%	0.3262
Gynecology	60.62	48.35	39.47	57.95	39.73	64.53	51.60	43.27	54.12	75.27	60.77	20.18	616	51.3	14.4	2.44	1.74	104.4	0.20	0.257	3.03%	0.1962
Neurosurgery	431.98	395.15	405.92	388.68	396.93	493.58	443.10	456.02	465.57	535.63	467.67	355.70	5236	436.3	50.8	20.78	3.39	203.3	1.67	2.187	25.74%	1.6681
Orthopedics	99.95	65.78	58.80	84.70	70.38	100.92	71.35	80.10	73.12	97.20	101.93	87.90	992	82.7	15.0	3.94	1.10	66.0	0.32	0.414	4.88%	0.3161
Ophthalmology	0.00	25.48	38.60	16.88	0.00	12.70	0.00	14.87	2.50	3.70	3.73	0.00	118	9.9	12.3	0.47	5.38	323.1	0.04	0.049	0.58%	0.0377
Oral Surgery	181.47	116.20	112.93	111.08	130.78	131.82	122.10	141.50	165.73	119.63	222.32	151.85	1707	142.3	33.4	6.78	2.56	153.4	0.54	0.713	8.40%	0.5440
Plastic Surgery	17.72	11.63	6.18	17.03	39.52	60.68	8.57	36.20	16.10	29.78	40.48	48.88	333	27.7	17.5	1.32	2.50	150.1	0.11	0.139	1.64%	0.1060
Transplant	97.37	86.73	100.68	94.62	76.43	114.68	110.65	83.00	104.22	124.15	95.37	79.03	1167	97.2	14.6	4.63	4.84	290.5	0.37	0.487	5.74%	0.3718
GRAND TOTALS	1927	1746	1675	1754	1794	1972	1808	1878	1795	1908	2067	1762	22085	1840.4	111.7	87.64	2.44	146.6	7.04	9.2	257	7.0362

Notes: Download (File Alldataver(2) - count of cases per month by specialty - not filtered and does not include outpatient surgery center

OR CASE VOLUME SUMMARY- CASES BY SERVICE

Jul 2005 - Jun 2006

SERVICE	Jul-05	Aug-05	Sep-05	Oct-05	Nov-05	Dec-05	Jan-06	Feb-06	Mar-06	Apr-06	May-06	Jun-06	Totals	Average Cases Per Month	Std Dev	Weekday Demand (24 working days)	Takt Time Min	Takt Time Based on 13.5 Ors (min)	Takt Time Based on 26 Ors (min)	Takt Time Based on 13.5 Ors (min)	Takt Time Based on 13.5 Ors (min)	
Anesthesia	3	5	1	1	0	1	2	3	0	1	3	1		1.8	1.5	0.08	8968.0	121,247	233,167.4			
Cardio-Thoracic	115	104	107	101	96	117	113	103	92	93	122	120		106.9	10.4	5.09	146.8	1,985	3,816.5			
ENT	37	47	43	45	48	38	36	54	58	37	51	58		46.0	8.1	2.19	341.2	4,613	8,870.5			
General Surgery	238	245	208	219	227	230	224	245	198	224	224	202		223.7	15.3	10.65	70.2	949	1,824.3			
Urology	58	45	55	48	61	54	51	64	52	50	55	42		52.9	6.3	2.52	296.6	4,010	7,711.0			
Gynecology	28	30	26	34	23	33	35	27	30	41	33	14		29.5	6.8	1.40	532.0	7,193	13,832.0			
Neurosurgery	126	117	109	124	114	151	123	145	151	146	131	108		128.8	15.9	6.13	121.9	1,648	3,169.3			
Orthopedics	97	64	61	81	69	88	69	81	64	81	80	67		75.2	11.1	3.58	208.8	2,823	5,428.5			
Ophthalmology	0	4	6	3	0	2	0	4	1	1	1	0		1.8	2.0	0.09	8560.3	115,736	222,568.8			
Oral Surgery	73	46	42	52	49	49	49	58	60	46	88	56		55.7	13.1	2.65	281.9	3,812	7,330.1			
Plastic Surgery	9	5	3	8	14	27	5	15	5	10	16	16		11.1	6.9	0.53	1416.0	19,144	36,815.9			
Transplant	22	17	20	19	18	28	21	18	22	24	17	15		20.1	3.6	0.96	781.4	10,565	20,317.5			
GRAND TOTALS	806	729	681	735	719	818	728	817	733	754	821	699	9,040	753.3	49.5	35.873	20.8	282	541.6			

FIGURE 15.20 OR group tech matrix example.

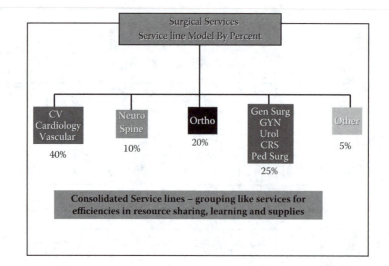

FIGURE 15.21   OR service line model.

60 patients with LOS of 108 min which equals a total of 6,480 min.

6,480 ÷ 600 min (available time per day per room) = 10.8 surgery rooms needed (not taking into account flip rooms or any other issues such as equipment failures, etc.)

Once the global number of rooms has been established to truly level load and have impact downstream (unit), the number of surgical rooms needed should be calculated by service line, the next step is to understand the number and type (if specialized equipment or use) of surgery rooms and hours of operation by service line. In addition, demand by service line should be calculated by day of week (which will can drive block times or scheduling). Typical service lines include: cardiac, vascular, thoracic, cardiothoracic or cardiovascular and thoracic (CVT), orthopedics, neurosurgery, general surgery, gynecology, urology, plastics, podiatry, ENT, ophthalmology, etc. Once the data are obtained, the average case time by service line and trends can be calculated.

Figure 15.20 is an example of a group tech matrix, in which one can adjust the number of rooms and available times determine utilization scenarios.

GROUP MATRIX BENEFITS

- Provides insight to case length by category
- Number of rooms needed by service line
- Utilization of ORs overall and by service line
- Assists in determining appropriate OR layout
- Materials strategy related to rooms, i.e., where to locate shared equipment

Once we determine the number of surgeries per service line/per room/per day, we create a spreadsheet template comparing how the rooms are currently utilized vs. dedicating certain rooms to certain surgeries based on geographic location (Figure 15.22). For instance, if we know we use 3 rooms every day for heart cases, then we would pick 3 rooms together and relocate our supplies and equipment for the heart cases in or near those rooms. Some hospitals do this by "feel" or intuition, but we find in most cases, there is a still a lot of opportunity to further dedicate and standardize rooms and then develop materials and equipment strategies to support the rooms. The big objection we hear is "what if we need that room for another case?" In the event you have to use the room for a different type of surgery, it is no problem. It just means the supplies and equipment for that surgery may be located in a different area.

Once the group tech matrix is created, it is critical to have someone maintain it, as the surgery mix and, therefore, dedicated rooms will change over time.

SECTION V OR LAYOUT/CAPACITY

How do we determine the capacity and what the new layout should look like? In most hospitals, there are limited data and, in many cases, the data are not accurate. In addition, experience has shown that accuracy and reliability of data, especially turnover time, is questionable, and assumptions may have to be made that may impact the final outcome. Generally, historical data are available to evaluate demand, but they are not always accurate. In many cases, future demand is only an estimate based on current demand, and sometimes we find marketing growth projections and planned business development initiatives are available. We also have to consider surgical case times and turnover times to determine if potential increases are needed in capacity (Table 15.10).

Other challenges lay in the unknown of what new technological advances will take place as surgery moves from open to minimally invasive or less invasive procedures migrating out of OR suites. When determining capacity, does one count on

Before (TOP) versus After rooms dedicated to service lines (Bottom)

Service Description	Room 1	Room 2	Room 3	Room 4	Room 5	Room 6	Room 7	Room 8	Room 9 (under Construction)	Room 10	Room 11	Room 12	Room 13	Room 14	Room 15	Room 16	Room 17	Room 18	Room 19	Room 20	Room 21
General Surgery	blue	blue	blue	blue	blue	blue			blue	blue			blue				blue	blue			
Gynecology	blue	blue	blue	blue	blue	blue			blue	blue		blue	blue		blue		blue	blue	blue		blue
Urology	blue	blue	blue	blue	blue	blue		blue	blue	blue	blue	blue	blue				blue				
Cardio Vascular		blue	blue		blue					blue							blue	blue			
Dental (Facial Max)	blue	blue	blue	blue	blue					blue							blue	blue			
Ear Nose Throat	blue	blue	blue	blue	blue	blue	blue			blue				blue							
Eye				blue	blue					blue											
Gastro intestinal	blue	blue	blue	blue	blue	blue				blue							blue				
Neurology	blue					blue				blue							blue	blue	blue		
Orthopedics	blue	blue	blue		blue	blue				blue							blue				
Plastics	blue	blue	blue	blue	blue																blue
Podiatry	blue	blue	blue	blue	blue	blue				blue		blue	blue							blue	blue
Primary Vascular	blue	blue	blue	blue	blue	blue				blue		blue		blue	blue	blue	blue	blue		blue	blue
Dedicated																					
Shared (service color)																					
Closed																					

Agreed Upon Room Utilzation Going Forward

Service Description	ROOM 1 (add on room)	ROOM 2	ROOM 3	ROOM 4	ROOM 5	ROOM 6 (laminar flow)	ROOM 7 (laminar flow) SPINE - requires remodel Ortho ADD ON room	ROOM 8 (Simple cystos only)	ROOM 9 (Under Construction)	ROOM 0 (PEDS)	ROOM 1 (CYSTO ONLY)	ROOM 2 (ROBOT)	ROOM 3 (ROBOT)	ROOM 4 (good for eyes, manipulations, bone marrow etc)	ROOM 5 (Ped Hearts and Hearts only)	ROOM 6 (Hearts and Vascular)	ROOM 7 (only other room that can be neuro)	ROOM 8 (Neuro only)	ROOM 9	ROOM 20 (laminar flow using as a flip)	OR21 (laminar flow)
General Surgery	1	1	1																		
Gynecology		1																			
Urology & Cysto								1			1										
Plastics				1	1																
Podiatry																					
Dental (Facial Max)																					
Gastrointestinal																					
Eye					1									1							
Ear Nose Throat																					
Cardio Vascular															1	0.33					
Primary Vascular																0.5	0.04				
Orthopedics / spine						1	1												1	1	1
Neurosurgery							0.11										0.11	1			
Demand Per Room	100%	100%	79%	25%	23%	100%	64%	26%	100%	low%	100%	100%	100%	22%	100%	100%	15%	100%	100%	100%	56%
Dedicated			21%	75%	77%	0%	36%	74%	100%	#VALUE!	0%	0%	0%	78%	0%	0%	85%	0%	0%	0%	44%

FIGURE 15.22 OR room allocation model.

TABLE 15.10

OR Group Tech Capacity Analysis

Available Time Hours	141.5	1st floor Rooms	2nd floor Rooms	# Rooms	Room Hours	Avg Hours/ Room	Total Hours	Percent	wt avg Rooms/day
Available Time Per Room hours	12.4555	13		13	7:30a - 3P	7.5	97.5	69%	8.96
Available Time Per Room min	747.331	9		9	3p - 7p	4	36	25%	2.29
Avg number of rooms scheduled (staffed)	11.3604	2		2	7p - 11p	4	8	6%	0.11
Working Days Per Month	21			19	Total Rooms		141.5	100%	11.36
Capacity based on Rooms Scheduled (staffed)		61.9%			Capacity based on overall # rooms				29.8%

an improvement or reduction in cycle time to calculate turnover time in the future? What is the percentage of time flip rooms will be utilized? When building for the future, will the case lengths remain the same, get longer or shorter? These are all inherent challenges when determining capacity and layouts.

Just because we are faced with these challenges does not mean that we should not try to make the best possible estimate of the rooms needed based on the information at hand, even if it is not complete. The goal would be to try to provide a sound analysis that provides a buffer for the best possible plan. In addition, Lean tools, such as process flow, point-to-point diagrams, and spaghetti diagramming, should be used to determine flow.

Lean Solution: *Leveraging PPFs, operator analysis, Takt time, customer demand and the group tech matrix will assist in providing the future capacity and new layout details. Remember that the decisions made today will impact the organization from a cost perspective and the lives of staff operationally in the future.*

OPERATING ROOM CALCULATIONS

When analyzing the utilization of data, one should look at types of surgeries done by day of week and opportunities to level load cases throughout the week. For example, if 20 orthopedic cases (each lasting 170 min, patient in to patient in) were performed on the same 2 days of the week, the average number of orthopedic cases per day is 10, total operating minutes per day

$$170 \text{ min/case} \times 10 \text{ cases} = 1700 \text{ min or } 28.3 \text{ hrs.}$$

If the operational hours of the OR were 7:30 a.m. to 3:30 p.m. = 8 hrs or 480 min of available time per room. The total rooms needed are $1700 \div 480$ min = 3.5 rooms per day.

This would mean that the OR would have to supply four orthopedic surgical teams in order to meet the demand for the two operating days. What happens to the staff the remaining 3 days? How many extra pieces of equipment would be needed to run 4 rooms simultaneously? What is the impact to the Post-Op recovery unit, intensive care units, and surgical

floors, as all the patients demand the same level of service on the same days? What if we level loaded the 20 orthopedic cases over 4 days?

$$20 \text{ cases} \div 4 \text{ days} = 5 \text{ cases per day}$$

$$170 \text{ min/case} \times 5 \text{ cases} = 850 \text{ min or } 14.2 \text{ hrs.}$$

The available time for each room is 480 min; therefore, the total rooms needed each day are $850 \div 480$ min = 1.8 rooms. Less equipment sets would be needed as only 2 rooms would be operating and "pulling" on equipment, two surgical teams would be needed and the likelihood that the surgeons could work with the same teams would increase. This would result in downstream leveling of demand in the Post-Op units and on the floors. Although a group tech matrix can assist in determining the number of rooms, helping to level case load in the ORs and assessing utilization, administration and area management must take into account customer preference and the use of flip rooms under certain conditions, which may reduce surgeon idle time between cases. This will be discussed in further detail in section VI. Remember, the primary customers of surgery (after patients) are surgeons and, as we often hear, "surgeons don't want more block time; they want more cases per day."

Lesson Learned: *Be careful with averages when using the group tech matrix. Until schedules can be level loaded, one must look at peak times by service line when apportioning rooms to service lines as well as future forecasted demand. In addition, someone must own and now maintain this matrix as hospitals live in a dynamic environment where technology and surgeon changes can greatly impact existing demand and room allocation. Recognize that changes in case mix and new technologies can provide challenges when predicting OR demand.*

SECTION VI OR ROOM TURNOVER

Traditional OR turnovers start when the patient leaves the room, i.e., "patient out or wheels out." It may be initiated by a staff member notifying a charge nurse station who communicates that the patient has exited the room and the room needs to be "turned over." This means that the room must be cleaned and prepared for the next patient.

All hospitals tend to vary as to what occurs at this point. The scrub nurse may start or have already started tearing down the case, as the patient is exiting the room accompanied by the circulating nurse and anesthesia doctor. Housekeeping or the OR technical staff may be paged; whether it is centralized or decentralized determines when they show up to assist.

Once the case is "broken down," the "dirty" items are taken to the "dirty" area where they are cleaned and then "flash" sterilized. If taken to the dirty elevator, they proceed to the sterile processing department where the instruments are cleaned and sterilized. The room is mopped or vacuumed and sanitized and a new "case cart" containing the surgical instrumentation and supplies for the next case is rolled into the room. The ideal scenario would be that all the items (supplies and instrumentation) on the surgeon's preference list (which lists all supplies and special instruments by case type) are "pulled" accurately, and the right instruments and supplies are at the right room, at the right time for the next case. In the event something is missing, the nurse or other staff member has to search and travel to get the needed supplies, either in the "core," hallway, or down in central supply. If the surgeon and team members are lucky, this is identified as the case is being set up. Yet, we have followed nurses searching for certain pieces of equipment and supplies for 20 min or more, delaying the start of the case. During this time, the anesthesiologists and the surgeon and, more importantly, the patient are left waiting! This waste all costs money in time (labor time of staff), excess anesthesia charges for the patient, potential delays to the next case, and physician dissatisfaction.

Yet most of this cost is hidden, as these costs are not tracked. Cases are delayed, cancelled, or rescheduled, and room utilization is not optimized.

Turnover is "midstream" in the surgical process; if one's goal is to improve turnover which is a big "Y" in Six Sigma terms for most OR metrics, then all the "x's" or causes that impact a successful turnover must be understood in order to achieve the desired turnover time.

Room turnovers do not occur in silos; thus many upstream processes, defects, and delays will impact one's goal. Reducing turnover times is important as they directly impact one of the internal/external customers in the surgical services area, the surgeon. For example, one can streamline the turnover, but if the patient is not ready at the time the case is scheduled and/or the anesthesiologist and surgeon hold up the patient to do necessary tasks such as have the consent signed or have the H&P ready, then the turnover time will still not decrease.

Figure 15.23 outlines "x's" or variables that impact turnover, which would be times collected for patient in to patient in.

- Inaccurate or missing supplies and equipment ready to set the case up (case picking or equipment availability—materials flow)
- Anesthesiology availability

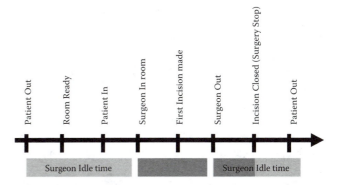

FIGURE 15.23 Surgeon idle time analysis.

- Support staff availability (transportation or anesthesia technicians)
- "Patient readiness" or medical clearance for surgical procedures
- Nurse/surgical technician team availability
- Level loading

Extended turnovers affect surgeon idle time and frustration. Surgeons provide services that are time dependent, thus creating revenue for both the hospital and themselves based on the time they can work, which is limited to the minutes and hours in a day (Table 15.11). If the surgeon's time is idle, then generally they are wasting money, as the only way surgery generates revenue is if the patients are in the ORs. This holds true for both surgeon and anesthesiologists. This is how the surgeons perceive turnover: Surgeons are only concerned with 'surgeon out to surgeon in,' which comprises their idle time.

HOW DO WE IMPROVE TURNOVER?

Our goal, like in manufacturing, is to obtain "single minute" turnovers. This means 9 min 59 sec or less for internal time (the time the room is down or does not have a patient utilizing it). At first glance, one may think this is impossible. Outpatient surgery centers can routinely hit these times, but it is much tougher in a hospital setting, although it has been

TABLE 15.11

Surgeon Efficiency Model Pivot Table

Example Surgery Efficiency by Service Line				
Week Ty	(Multiple lte)			
month ye	(All)			
Holiday T	(Multiple lte)			
Procedu	(All)			
Surgeon	(All)			
PV	353.0	117.88	68.4	44.45%
SP	94.0	128.28	63.3	46.11%
TH	142.0	130.96	66.5	38.19%
Grand T	14,364.0	113.54	77.8	42.70%

achieved. This is accomplished by putting together a multiple disciplinary team to analyze the tasks that are required to "turn a room over." Each individual involved in the turnover is videotaped at the same time. The films are reviewed with each person present and opportunities for improvement are identified.

We categorize time into two components; internal and external time. In car racing, internal times are things that can only be done when the car is in the pit, and external times are things that can be done while the car is going around the track.

Like car racing, the goal in healthcare is to improve the process using a "pit crew" approach. Each step is broken down into its components and determined whether the step is internal or external. In this case, internal work is work that can only be done when the OR is down, or being changed over. External work can be done while the patient is in the room (and parallel to other processes that may be occurring). The goal is to convert as much internal work to external work as possible. Internal work vs. external work can't be defined until you define the input and output boundaries of the setup.

It is not unusual to think that all work can't start until the patient leaves the room or after the patient enters the room, but this is not the case. Shingo's setup reduction process was called SMED (single minute exchange of dies) (Table 15.12). In hospitals, we call it SMER (single minute exchange of rooms) or SMEP (single minute exchange of patients). Prior to the start of the turnover, the pit crew (turnover dedicated staff) reviews the schedule to plan their attack. The charge nurse gives them 15 to 30 min notice. Everyone from nurses to doctors chip in to get the room turned over. A team was put together made up of a Lean specialist, surgical technician, circulating nurse, surgical assistant (role is to transport patients to, within, and from surgery, and room cleaning) and service line coordinator. Understanding that different service lines have varying setups, this organization opted to address turnover one service line at a time. The team started with general surgery.

Step 1: Videotaping each staff member as they performed the turnover at the same time. Findings were:

- No standard work.
- No specific standard work to tear down cases while the patient is still in the room.
- No role clarity (who is responsible for which task); some were not done and other tasks were duplicated.
- Surgeons were as much as 30 min late to surgery.
- Larger patients were hard to transfer and took longer.

TABLE 15.12

Die Explanation

A die in manufacturing is a tool that is changed over on a press. An analogy would be to think of play dough when you were a kid. You squeezed the play dough through a square form (die) and then changed the die over to a circle (die) and the squeezed it through the circle.

- Some patients took longer to intubate than others.
- Cases not picked correctly (inaccurate or missing supplies and equipment).
- Not a lot of parallel setup processing to patient entering room.
- Communication issues related to surgical assistance.
- Surgical assistants did not show up timely, when needed.
- Necessary room related equipment was missing from the room.
- Pre-Op delays related to patient communication.
- No clear definition of "room ready" and when to call for patient.

Step 2: Operator analysis of each member was performed to determine the value-added vs. non-value-added activities, the skill required to do each task, and what extended the turnover. In addition the rate limiting sequential step or tasks should be identified. These sequential tasks will drive the minimum turnover time. What was identified was that the circulating nurse was the rate limiting step he/she was responsible for

- Documenting the case
- Accompanying the patient to the Post-Op recovery unit
- Going to the Pre-Op unit to obtain information on the next patient scheduled
- Accompanying the patient to the room
- Assisting in counting the instrumentation

Lesson Learned: *Identify the critical tasks that need to be performed and who should perform them, and when they should be performed in an order to minimize "internal time."*

The circulator was performing most of the tasks sequentially during the turnover while no patient was in the room. The circulator nurse's assigned tasks were in the critical path of reducing room turnover. Each task that was critical was identified. Each task was analyzed to determine if it had to be internal or external, and who should do each task, and was there a need for them to be sequential. For instance, the surgical assistants spent time searching for a stretcher or bed, leaving everyone in the room waiting (including the patient).

Step 3: A surgical assistant checklist was created defining external work to be performed (while the case was still going on). It listed what needed to be ready outside each room, such as a bed with IV pole and cleaning cart. Since this happened when the team was in the room, there was no waiting for beds or IV poles, etc. All tasks were realigned across the team members.

Step 4: Standard work was created for each staff member so there was role clarity and responsibility for tasks. This alleviated tasks not getting performed or duplicated by the staff. In addition, since there was heavy circulating nurse activities required, the service line coordinator was assigned the responsibility to step in during critical components as fractional labor to aid as a "facilitating nurse in the turnover" to complete steps in parallel while the circulator was going to PACU and Pre-Op. The facilitator took on some of the sequential tasks that the circulator was doing, converting them to parallel tasks.

Example

As the circulator was accompanying the patient to the PACU, the facilitator could help unpack the next case with the surgical technician (which previously would have been the responsibility of the circulating nurse); this task could not be converted to external work (as one cannot unpack or setup the next case while the patient is still in the room). In some cases, anesthesiologists take the patient to PACU and also have the anesthesiologist and surgeon bring the patient from Pre-Op. This frees up the circulator for the room changeover. The anesthesiologist then gives a report to the PACU nurse.

Below is a sample of key process steps that occur in room turnover (these steps do not need to be in sequential order and many can and should be performed in parallel):

- Patient dressing on
- OR table breakdown
- Patient out of room
- Room cleaning and mopping
- Linen and trash removal
- Next case cart (supplies and equipment) in OR
- Linen on bed
- Next patient interview occurs
- Case documentation complete
- Patient called for—room is "ready for patient"
- Patient in room
- Patient on OR table
- Case supplies begin to be opened
- Case supplies complete
- Counting complete
- Patient induced
- Patient draped
- Pause for cause
- Incision made surgery start
- Having clean supplies and bed, IV poles, etc., ready

Step 5   Creating Standard Definitions, Expectations, and Role Clarity: One key finding was that there was no standard across the OR of "what constituted room ready" or the standard agreed-on time to bring the next patient in to the OR. There was great variability from circulating nurse to circulating nurse on timing and expectation of what needed to be accomplished prior to bringing the next patient into the room. This contributed to wide variability in turnover times.

This hospital determined that, owing to the culture within the OR and where they were on the Lean journey, it was best to work on activities that the hospital could control first, such as critical tasks, timing of tasks internal vs. external, standard work for staff, availability of supplies, and accuracy of case picking, thereby making improvements that impacted primarily patient out to patient in. They determined that they would address issues that related to physicians and anesthesia in subsequent initiatives.

LEAN RESULTS IMPACT OF TURNOVER PROJECTS

Our goal and typical result is to maximize the number of cases the surgeon can perform within the same amount of time. We find through turnover time reduction that we can normally get each surgeon 1 or 2 more cases per day; however, turnover time is impacted by many other hospital *processes, i.e., SPD, case picking, materials, suppliers, transport, housekeeping, etc. It is important to decentralize transport, registration, and housekeeping and have the staff report both to surgery operationally and, in the case of registration, have them matrix to the head of registration or billing.*

TURNOVER EXAMPLE

If the current average turnover time is 50 min and our average surgery time is 120 min (this assumes the turnover and surgery times are tracked; the average surgery time should be surgery start to surgery stop), turnover time can be expressed as patient out to patient in or can also be defined as surgery close to surgery cut. The latter definition will force more steps to come under scrutiny for improvement related to surgeon and team activities. If we can save 40 min of turnover time (patient out to patient in), then for every three surgeries, we pick up approximately one extra surgery case in capacity:

$$\frac{170 \text{ min (pt in to pt in)} \times 60 \text{ surgeries}}{130 \text{ min (pt in to pt in)}} = 78.46 \text{ cases.}$$

If we do 60 surgeries per day and have additional demand then this would translate into 18.5 extra cases per day in the same amount of time. This translates into millions of dollars of potential revenue and extremely happy surgeons. Most surgeons want to be able to do more cases per day in the same amount of time and eliminate all the waiting around.

Before implementing turnover improvements, one needs to make sure that Pre-Op can continue to supply at the new rate and that the Post-Op recovery unit can recover more patients with the number of beds they have, otherwise the turnover effort will fail.

Lesson Learned: *If we can introduce significantly more revenue per day, wouldn't this pay for additional people to support the dedicated turnover teams? The answer is an unequivocal "yes," but we have to get over the issue of finance wanting to cut our indirect FTEs and the issue of centralized transport, etc. We need to staff for growth and treat surgery as a profit center, not a cost center.*

Our experience is that surgeons have a built-in expectation of 30 min or less turnaround for medium to large cases and less than 15 min for short cases. But to a surgeon, this definition is based on their time, which is 'surgeon out to surgeon in'. This is drastically different from patient out to patient in.

As one analyzes turnover data, we have found that the data are inconsistent, organizations tend to categorize turnovers either globally such as 30 min for large cases and 10 min for small cases, or by service line grouping. The challenge is that there is wide variability in the tasks performed when viewing data globally as setup of equipment and amount of supplies can vary. Like cases don't necessarily follow one another. One surgeon may leave a room and he or she may have completed a large case (with significant cleanup); the following case may be with a different surgeon with a simple case, requiring fewer set-ups. This creates challenges in expectations of surgeons and scheduling times for cases following one another

OTHER TURNOVER/SETUP STRATEGIES

INDUCTION ROOMS

We first encountered induction rooms in the HBR video series Competing Against Time* with Tom Hout and George Stalk as they profiled Karolinska Hospital in Sweden. Karolinska utilizes induction rooms with added anesthesiologists in order to decrease turnover times. The patient was induced prior to surgery and rolled in when the OR was cleaned and set up. In many older hospitals, you will find induction rooms that are no longer utilized. After an Internet search, it was found that this is very common in European hospitals but not in the United States. It does seem to be used in some U.S. pediatric hospitals.

PROS FOR INDUCTION ROOM

The induction room addresses the internal time utilized by anesthesia that cannot be compensated by nursing, housekeeping, etc. We can decrease turnover time significantly to the point where the anesthesiologist puts the patient under and the patient is prepped. This is especially true for heart cases and orthopaedic cases where there can be up to 45 min turnovers while the patient is being prepped. Meanwhile, the surgeon is waiting (idle). Our experience is that 40%–60% or more surgeons spend their time waiting. We can't increase surgeries without increasing surgeon efficiency.

CONS FOR INDUCTION ROOMS

In order to support induction rooms, layouts may have to be changed and additional anesthesiologists, who may or may not be available, may be required. So the change can involve construction costs and anesthesiologists' costs. A cost benefit analysis has to be performed to see if it makes sense. One has to determine how many extra cases a day would offset the cost to hire an additional anesthesiologist. One should also consider what this would do for surgeon morale and the opportunity to grow the business with no need for expensive construction of additional ORs.

FLIP ROOMS

A flip room is providing 2 rooms for a surgeon who has cases that follow one after another with 2 staffs and 2 anesthesiologists. One would have a delayed start, ready and waiting so that the surgeon can literally go from the end of one case

(while the resident, fellow, or PA finishes the first case) to begin on the next or to follow the case where a second team composed of another anesthesiologist and a second surgical team (which might again include resident, fellow, or PA) has the patient prepped and ready to go. This is desired by many surgeons because their idle time is essentially eliminated. This makes sense in cases where the surgeon has a full team that surrounds him/her that can complete one case and start another. From the hospital perspective, this can reduce the time a room remains unused. If flip rooms were provided for every surgeon, it would be very costly for an organization, as the number of rooms, anesthesiologists, and staff resources would increase.

PROS FOR FLIP ROOMS

- Reduced surgeon turnover time to essentially zero.
- Increased surgeon satisfaction.
- Surgeons can do more cases in 1 day or end their day early as their day is compressed.

CONS FOR FLIP ROOMS

- Staff can be idle if the first case has a delay or complication.
- Anesthesiologist idle time (costly or requires robust anesthesiology scheduling practice).
- Could cause the organization to need additional space and rooms.

NEW ROOM FOR A "TO FOLLOW" CASE REFERRED TO AS "MOVE"

This approach includes staggering rooms and schedule times. When a surgeon has a "to follow case" (sequential cases) and completes the first case, a 'move' would be having the next case set up and ready to go in a new room. The anesthesiologist, surgeon, and staff would all move to the new room. The perception from the surgeon's view is a decrease in turnover time.

PROS FOR MOVE ROOMS

Move rooms minimize turnover time; however, in our experience this is sometimes only perceived, depending on the location of the available room and the availability of the anesthesiologist and staff. The same staff may still have to set up the new room, get the patient, etc., which can be done in less than 10 min. The old room can be changed over on "external time" and be ready for the next case. It is good for two or more "to follow" cases.

CONS FOR MOVE ROOMS

- Ties up an extra OR (which is only bad if there is no demand for them).

- OR/cases can change rooms, which then impacts the case cart, supplies, etc. (and supplies may not always end up at the right place and at the right time, eliminating any time savings).
- Cases can be cancelled, resulting in cost of opened items or re-sterilizing instruments, when communication fails.

Lessons Learned:

- *Room turnover improvements don't sustain unless driven by management.*
- *Much of room setup can occur while the patient is in the room.*
- *If we can get a changeover down to less than 10 min, do we still need flip rooms or move rooms?*

Family Waiting

Traditionally, surgeons have to walk to the surgery waiting area to consult with patients' family members. We can't tell you how many times we see surgeons hunting or searching for family members after long walks (sometimes upstairs and down) to the waiting room; families may not be aware that the surgery is near completion, and that they should be in the waiting room. More often than not, it is the one time they left the room, Murphy's Law. How might we improve this? Some organizations are creating an area near the OR where the surgeon can meet with family members, separate from the waiting room, similar to a "consult room." The room staff communicates with the waiting area to bring the family member to the surgeon in the "consult room." We have never found this to be a dissatisfier for patient families (i.e., having to walk to the consult room). This approach makes surgeons happy and saves them time and frustration.

Section VII Surgical Services Materials Readiness

Preference Cards

Preference cards or lists are a documented accounting, generally by a surgeon, by case type of the instruments and supplies required to perform a case (Figure 15.24). This helps to ensure that the right instruments and supplies are gathered for a surgeon ("his or her preference") for a scheduled procedure. This has been a challenge for most organizations, as preference cards end up being a project at every hospital. They can reach 10,000–20,000 or more, as they are made for each surgeon for each case performed. In many cases, the preference cards are the foundation for billing supplies used in the OR for each surgical procedure. They are difficult to keep updated or complete (unless a surgeon assigns one of his/her staff to be responsible). The root causes of inaccuracies normally center on the lack of ownership and accountability for the updating process. This can cause major opportunity costs in terms of billing costs, if there is not a good accounting of what has been "pulled" to setup the case. The number of preference cards and the difficulty in updating them emphasizes the problems most ORs face related to the lack of standardization by surgeons for

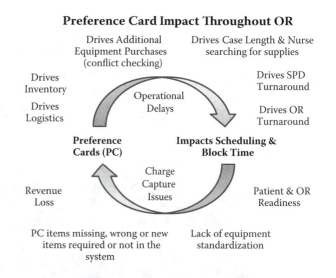

Preference Card Impact Throughout OR

FIGURE 15.24 Surgery preference card analysis.

supplies and instruments. We have found the most efficient surgeons standardize on materials and supplies. Historically, most healthcare organizations have had difficulty trying to get surgeons to standardize on supplies and equipment. Having non-standard supplies is costly as it creates increased inventory to order, track, and monitor, but does not enable the hospital to obtain volume discounts. More importantly, depending on the equipment, there may be safety issues surrounding the staff needed to keep proficiencies on multiple types of equipment. Standardization in the OR is a challenge for organizations as surgeons who come from different training institutions have established comfort with particular types of instruments, and they do not want to be forced to conform to other less familiar instruments. In addition, they may have alliances with companies that, for example, provide dinners for their offsite group meetings. What if we could reduce preference cards to only "A" or high inventory or high dollar items? This would mean expensing "B" and "C" items (low dollar items) and incorporating them into the overhead cost per case. This would decrease the number of picked items, assuming the B and C items were located in or adjacent to the OR. This would alleviate defects or inaccuracies in the "picking process." What if we could standardize and create more custom packs? While custom packs are kits (preassembled groups of supplies) and not truly Lean, it is difficult in many OR cores and halls to have enough room to pick cases with the number of supplies that are required for the different case types and variety in surgeon preferences. The cons of custom packs are how to treat items not used and how to handle ongoing maintenance of the packs. They also tend to be more costly than stocking materials separately. The pros are that they are easy to unpack and eliminate searching when setting up the sterile field. They also eliminate waste in the current "green" environment.

Case Picking

Case picking is the process of gathering supplies, instruments, and specialized equipment so that it is ready for the "surgical

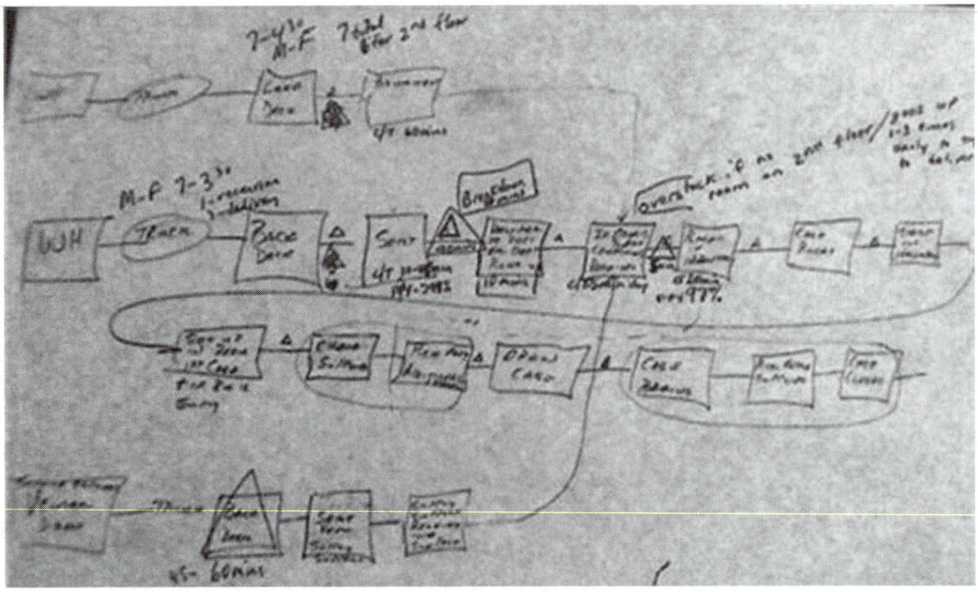

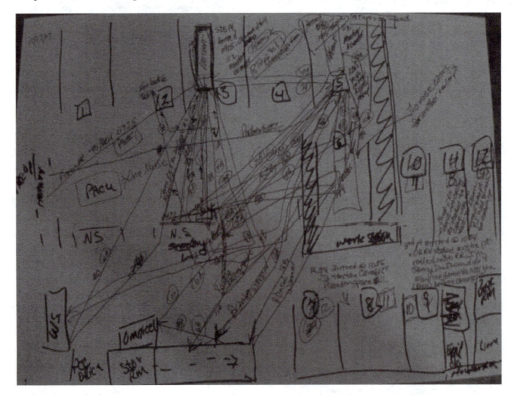

FIGURE 15.25   Case picking materials VSM from receiving dock to OR including returns after initial walkthrough.

team" to setup for the case, by what is documented on the preference cards (Figure 15.25). Traditional case picking involves knowledgeable workers who know where everything is located. When they pick a case, they place their cart in a centralized area and then make trips like "Supermarket Sweeps" back and forth, carrying as much as they can (Figure 15.26).

At Hospital X, we created a new process working with one of the case pickers. She liked the new process that was more than 50% faster and better. Yet, we could not get anyone else to follow the new process, and our operator was chastised

by her co-workers. To facilitate adoption and resistance to change, we opted to make the charge nurse responsible for the re-laying out of the supply core area, ignoring the conventional wisdom in which we would have changed it all over a weekend.

Note: It did not matter to us how the area was laid out since we could set up the preference cards to "pick by location."

The charge nurse was instructed to have a staff meeting to determine their optimal layout. After a couple of very heated

FIGURE 15.26   Case picking spaghetti map.

FIGURE 15.27 New configuration of surgical materials bin.

arguments, the staff reached a consensus. The entire materials core was moved around during the next week throughout the day and night shifts. While there was some chaos and confusion, the new configuration was set up bin by bin with the nurses (constantly rotating) by our sides guiding the order and location of supplies and assisting in the implementation. Everyone participated in the change (see Figure 15.27).

Once this was complete, the charge nurse insisted that the new case-picking process be utilized. The original team member now became the training coach for the others and was no longer chastised but respected for her participation.

Note: In many cases when re-organizing the supplies within the surgical cores, one will realize savings in inventory as supplies that historically might have been located throughout the OR will be consolidated, saving on redundant inventory; however, we have seen significant soft benefits in staff satisfaction as they are empowered to make changes that ultimately improve accessibility of supplies and in their environment, which make their daily life easier.

Lean Results: Case Picking

- 44% reduction in case picking time (32 min to 18 min) and 65% total walking distance reduction (928 ft. to 323 ft.)

Section VIII Post-Anesthesia Care Unit (PACU)

When we did the VSM, we discovered that the Post-Op recovery unit process cycle time is driven by the recovery time of the patient, which is directly influenced by the anesthesiologist caring for the patient (Figure 15.28). It was discovered through video analysis that the nurse's job was broken into pieces, including steps to be performed when the patient arrived and steps performed in what we termed "cycling" or re-evaluating the patient every 15 min, which was required at a minimum by the Association of Perioperative Registered Nurses (AORN)* standard and stipulates the nurse-to-patient

---
* http://www.aorn.org/PracticeResources/AORNStandardsAnd RecommendedPractices/

ratio based on patient recovery criteria outlined in the AORN guidelines.

What We Find

The first hour in PACU is the most critical and can require 1:1 nursing. In this case, the nurse is tied to the patient (Table 15.13). Some patients are more critical than others, yet we apply 1:1 or 2:1 standard to all patients, just in case. If we had better monitoring technology, maybe nurses would be able to watch more patients safely. When reviewing the FWA of the operator, we found the following problems:

- A lot of reaching for supplies.
- A lot of walking around beds.
- Computers take up too much space.
- Duplication of documentation.
- Too many pages for documentation.
- Trash can and linen containers are not readily accessible.
- Walking to the front desk to get the patient's printouts.
- Need hand washing between patients.
- Warm blankets were put on twice.
- It took 17 min after giving report to the floor nurse and yet no transporters responded to the PACU transport request, and the PACU technician had to take the patient to the floor.
- The layout is poor. The nurse station is in the south end of the area so the charge nurse cannot see all the patients. The area is not user-friendly or ergonomically correct. The head wall is set back due to the counter. You can't completely hook up a patient without walking from side to side.
- Can't get to the cabinet storage when there is a patient in the bay, and we don't need most of what is in storage.
- Nursing carts aren't standardized. Each nurse has their own cart.
- Nurses are doing work technicians could do (because they are transporting).
- When transport does not show up on time, patients may have to be given more pain medication. This can change their status from being ready to discharge from PACU to additional monitoring needed prior to transfer. So when the transporter finally shows up, the patient is no longer ready to leave.
- We normally hear we need more PACU beds, but this is almost never the root cause of the problem.

PACU Opportunities

The biggest opportunity in PACU is to reduce LOS while maintaining safety. What is driving our LOS in PACU? The answer should be recovery time, but this is not always the case. Many times, something as simple as lack of patient transportation can tie rooms up for hours. When all the

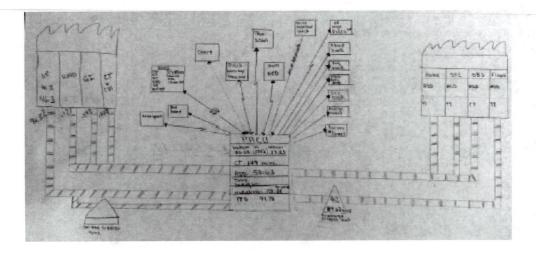

FIGURE 15.28   VSM (value stream map) hand-drawn PACU—copy.

rooms are tied up, we shut down the ORs, causing surgeons and staff to wait until the bottleneck is removed. This is extremely costly to the system and to physician satisfaction. The driver of recovery time is the anesthesia given to the patient. Sometimes, the patient is given a second "bump" due to a problem in surgery or a slow surgeon. This creates longer recovery times in PACU. There is quick-recovering anesthesia available, but it doesn't make sense to use them until such time as we can move the patients out of PACU. Lack of floor beds also creates PACU holds. We have found that 57% of the time we were delayed by lack of bed availability on the floors.

Other opportunities include Five S, point of use materials, standard work, workstation design, and overall layout. The Five S test: any nurse should be able to use any cart or find and reach everything at bedside setup within 3 seconds. Due to the critical nature of the patients, the Post-Op recovery units require nurse to patient ratios of 1:1 to 1:2 and that nurses are "tied" to patients in a similar manner to manufacturing, where operators are "tied" to machines (nurses don't like this comparison but the analogy is real). If we had better monitoring technology, nurses would not have to "watch" each patient.

Most hospitals have installed some type of fast track PACU process geared toward specific patients. The fast track includes a "step down" or "Phase II" recovery area with recliners and a nurse until the patient's family arrives. This area frees up PACU beds. The only problem with this type of system is that it can "mask" the real problem—we can't seem to get patients out of PACU. The organization had a centralized transportation service and the Post-Op recovery unit was listed seventh within the transport priority listing. Therefore, the Post-Op recovery unit nurses and technicians had to take the patients to the floor. In addition, this resulted in "boarding time" for the remaining patients and, at times, would back up cases and force patients to wait in the ORs for a Post-Op recovery bed. The VSM findings revealed that once patients had met the criteria to exit the Post-Op recovery unit, 99% of those patients were delayed by "waiting" for centralized transport. This represented the time it took from when transport received the call until a transporter was assigned, but it took another 30 min before transporters showed up and took patients to the floor. Because this area was given a low level of priority, transporters sometimes were not assigned for more than an hour. When the Post-Op recovery unit couldn't wait for transport to show up, the request would be cancelled, and the

TABLE 15.13

PACU Nurse Job Breakdown

Criteria Scale	
0 to 7	• Patient Arrival Tasks 15–20 min
	– Take Report, Hook up monitors and IV's Check dressings, SCD's, assess patient, review history, document, blankets etc.
	• Patient Monitoring Tasks
4 – 7	– Cycle every 15 min of which 3 to 5 min is checking vitals and charting, call liaison
	– Other tasks – meds, ice chips, Check Bed status etc.
	• Patient Discharge D/C Tasks
8 – 10	– 5 to 15 min (average 5.6 min)
	– Average Nurse had 2 patients

recovery unit staff would transport the patients to the floor. Interestingly enough, transport did not keep track of the number of cancellations and, when a request was cancelled, they totally removed the elapsed time from their database; therefore, the data reported were skewed and under-reported to management. Because of the bottlenecks that were created, management thought more capacity was needed. Capacity was determined by looking at the overall average time that patients spent in the Post-Op recovery unit, which was about 3 hrs (which we were told is all the hospital is reimbursed). The next step was to calculate available bed hours. There were 21 Post-Op recovery unit beds (one was isolation); however, only 16 beds were available based on staffing. The unit ran 12 hrs shifts, 9:00 a.m. to 9:00 p.m. This resulted in 12 hrs (of available time) × 16 (staff beds) = 192 bed hours of available time. This is then divided by a 3 hrs ALOS (which includes all the delays), yielding the ability to handle 64 patients in that 12 hrs period. They currently processed an average of 51 patients a day. If all the beds were utilized (staffed), the overall capacity would be 12 hrs × 20 beds = 240 bed hours, divided by 3 hrs (ALOS), yielding the ability to handle 80 patients in a 12 hrs shift. Once 64 patients is reached or if LOS rose above 3 hrs, then the Post-Op recovery unit would back up and result in a bottleneck for the OR and surgery would grind to a halt. To prevent this; either more staff would need to be brought in, Post-Op recovery beds opened, or more beds would need to be available on the units.

Result: *The answer was not to build another unit; they just needed to staff the beds they currently had and move patients to the floors in a more timely fashion.*

PACU Initial first month Lean results

- OR table hold hours per month reduced from 4.5 to 4.07
- Transport average delays 21 min to zero
- Productivity increased 4.66 to 4.41 worked hours per patient

SECTION IX LEAN LEADERSHIP AND STAFF READINESS IN THE OR

Staff readiness is the last component of a successful surgical system. Staff must arrive on time and be scheduled to demand. One can tell when the surgical schedule is not level loaded, as the "easy way out" is to schedule a full complement of staff every day and then "census manage" people home early. It makes it "easy" for the manager, but frustrating for employees. Traditional ORs operate with an anesthesiologist, surgeon(s), PA, surgeon nurse, circulator, and scrub nurse. Most surgeons want dedicated teams. Dedicated teams get to know the surgeon and the operations. For more on this, see the book, Complications.* Most

---

* Atul Gawande, *Complications: A surgeon's Notes on an Imperfect Science* (New York: Metropolitan Books) 2003.

OR directors will not allow surgeons to have the same team. There are pros and cons to this. The pros are that the surgeon's cases will go much faster with the same team and surgeries are probably safer and more efficient. The con is cross-training. The surgery director must make sure people can flex so they can fill their schedules properly and support weekend cases. Staff also needs ongoing Lean training in order to continue the pursuit of ongoing improvements. We have found that both of these wishes can live together, if scheduled properly.

When you are managing in the old OR batch environment, you probably spend most of your time fighting fires. In a Lean environment, the supervisor's role morphs into that of a coach or mentor. Most of the firefighting goes away and the leader's job is now to do the following: become a leader, explain, and teach. The leader must understand Lean principles, be willing to apply Lean, and practice as a Lean leader. Gemba walks are critical in the OR environment to go and see what is actually occurring in order to understand what waste can be eliminated and to identify opportunities to improve. The leader must have standard work and set the standard for acceptable behaviors and eliminate undesirable behaviors (Table 15.14). The leader must continue to videotape, do continuous process improvement activities ("Kaizen"), and create ways to generate ideas for continuous improvement from all employees. The leader must cross-train the employees so they can be flexible. An example of a Lean initiative in one hospital's Operating Room who wanted to ensure that patients are consistently ready when surgeons wish to begin a procedure, reduce patient wait and walking time during the OR preparation process, and reduce inventory carrying costs.

CULTURE

We would be remiss if we did not at least mention that culture plays a critical role in being able to implement any Lean initiatives across the surgical continuum. In order to achieve success it takes senior level executives to lead the charge, remove the barriers and provide support as the resistance to change surfaces. It is imperative executives play a visible role in the process improvement initiative and have a clear understanding of the challenges as they surface and the progress being made. Ensuring that area management and staff stay the course and maintain open lines of communication with physicians and frontline staff is critical as challenges within surgical services can play a significant role in the overall viability of the organization.

CONCLUSION

The surgical value stream creates some unique opportunities. Although we have not covered every opportunity to eliminate waste and streamline the processes, we hope that providing some examples as to what others have uncovered on their

TABLE 15.14
Leader Standard Work—Pre-Op—PACU—PASS Manager

Job Step #	Manager Description (what they do)	Hours	Items to Look For:
	Daily		
	Labor reports		
	HR issues		
	Gemba walking × 3 departments		
	Attending to daily issues		
	Assist with AM starts in Pre-Op		
	BiWeekly		
	Ordering supplies biweekly		
	Weekly		
	Lean team meeting (entire day)		
	Lean weekly checkout		
	6 S audits in each department		
	Weekly meeting with OR director		
	Lean weekly		
	Meeting with clinical leader		
	Sit in on weekly huddles in each dept		
	Update Five Ups for each department		
	Review metrics for each department		
	Make sure huddle boards are up to date		
	Review and update control plan		
	Review Leader Standard Work		
	Make sure action items are updated for each department		
	Follow up on standard order rollout		
	BiMonthly		
	Penimer data verification bimonthly × 3 departments		
	Managers meeting		
	Monthly		
	Monthly variance reports		
	Monthly licenses verification		
	Monthly anesthesia meeting		
	Monthly joint meeting		
	Monthly charge nurse meeting		
	monthly tollgate		
	Staff meeting		
	surgical services council meeting monthly		
	Quarterly		
	Quarterly LDI		
	Totals seconds		
	Totals minutes		

quests to improve the surgical experience for surgeons, staff, and patients helped you gain insight into the possibilities.

Section X Overarching Results*

- Average patient wait time dropped from 126 min to 75 min – a 40% improvement.
- The average distance walked by patients fell from 1,646 ft. to 326 ft. – an 80% reduction.
- Better inventory management saved $182,000 and eliminated a restocking procedure that was consuming 600 nursing hours a year.

Other Hospital Results—Surgery

- $2 million in cost savings.
- 7.8% decrease in labor expense per case.
- Improved pre-admission testing first pass yield from 5% to 80%.
- 48% reduction patient in to cut.
- 27% reduction – patient out to patient cut.
- Increased nurse satisfaction; improved flow of materials from SPD to OR room.
- Core Stock: Freed up over $100,000 of stock in multiple locations by standardizing each area and use of group tech matrix.
- CVT Service: Increased number of cases done each week by over 10%.
- Improved ordering process (simplified) for cultures taken during surgery to be sent for testing.
- Heart services videotaped. Opportunities identified.
- Identified opportunity to reduce inventory by over 80% and convert it to VMI.
- Reduced ED diversions from 26 hrs to 6 hrs (now 0 hr).
- Reduced surgery holds from 6 hrs per month to zero.
- Reduced PACU holds from 624 hrs to 157 hrs per month.

Pre-Testing Results

- Volume total visits 63.51 to 87.7
- # Completed charts 41% to 90%
- % Patients to pre-testing 46% to % 80%
- Productivity 1.80 to 1.35 hrs per patient
- Pre-testing FTE's 15.8 to 15.96
- Days ahead on telephone interviews from 0 to 5.5

Pre-Op

- % Charts completed with orders 80.3%
- Hours patients arrive prior to OR schedule 151 min to 120 min
- Pre-Op TLT Time/PT from 83 min to 45 min
- On time case starts (no buffer) 44.3% to 75%
- Productivity through from 1.58 to 1.49 hrs/patient

---

* These actual results are from various hospitals whose names are not mentioned because they were not written up in approved case studies. This is the reason some results appear duplicated with different result numbers.

- Arrival in Pre-Op prior to OR schedule 79.8 min to 60 min
- OR Table hold hours per month 4.5 to 4.07

Other Misc. Results

- Transport average Delays decreased 21 min to zero
- Productivity 4.66 to 4.41
- Implemented a process to reduce the number of lost OR Instruments

- Standardized operating room supply design and set-up
- Standardized supply par levels for operating room
- New instrument and supply location blueprint and process complete
- Visual management plan applied to operating room supply and equipment rooms
- Lean case picking process completed and implemented
- 5S the supply room with new shelving material, bin labels, min - max quantities

16 Nutritional Services

The Nutritional Service Department (NSD) provides patient food, retail food, and catering to ancillary support, administrative meetings, and clinical services within the hospital. The NSD may be operating the retail side of their services as a bottom-line profit center to help offset the cost of the NSD patient services. In most instances, the NSD may account for a small percentage of the total hospital expense budget and because of this, is not often one of the primary targets for Lean implementation; however, NSD areas in most hospitals are a great place to start and can really show the benefits of Lean more quickly because it is very straightforward and quite similar to implementing a Lean assembly in a factory. The following sections outline a few examples of Lean initiatives that were part of a nutritional services Lean program.

TRADITIONAL TRAY LINE ASSEMBLY

In a traditional NSD, one would find a tray line and an array of supporting equipment and processes (Figure 16.1). The tray line normally runs three times a day, corresponding to patient meals, and each meal has a different menu. There is both an informational component dealing with the menus and a physical assembly component to compiling the trays. Both support the regular and special diet meals and special orders from the floors. Other key processes are the inventory/ordering process, food preparation, and diet ordering process. The tray lines may take various forms but, overall, they are a conveyor, usually automated, with on/off buttons, which can stop the line at critical times. Operators normally stand on both sides of the line. One person starts the tray and it moves down the line from person to person. Each person adds a group of food items to the tray. There is normally one or more persons chasing missing items and restocking the line, while a person at the end is inspecting the trays to make sure they are correct. The cooks support the tray line with either fresh food or hot food that has been cooked in advance in a batch. Sometimes this food is prepared days in advance using a "cook chill" process. The food is cooked, put into plastic bags, quickly chilled and stored in a refrigerator until it is pulled to heat up and serve. You can always tell if the food has been through the "cook chill" process because it is very watery. With Lean we eliminate the cook chill process.

PROBLEMS WITH TRADITIONAL TRAY LINES

By using the 8 Wastes to analyze NSD processes, a significant amount of "waste" and opportunities for improvement were identified. If you stand and watch a tray line run for an hour, you will probably observe that the cycle time per tray, despite an automated tray line, is normally quite long. The employees workloads are usually not well balanced between stations, as some people will be really busy while others are idle. Restocking personnel are interrupting the operators as they restock the food. Operators are normally surrounded and "locked in" on two or three sides by racks, dishware, tray components, etc., in layouts with isolated islands where people are basically trapped and can't flex between positions. The inspector at the end of the line (or downstream) frequently stops the line to correct mistakes made by an earlier person in the process and, whenever the line stops, everyone else on the line is idle until the problem is resolved.

Some nutritional areas have "pod" layouts instead of tray lines, where, normally, there are people on both sides of the pod. The pod is an island with a person trapped inside who is handing food off to the people outside the pod. In order to restock the pod, the operator once again is interrupted.

Traditional NSD tray assembly and pod layouts do not meet Lean principles and standards. We always hear complaints from staff, and they want us to tell upper management there is not enough space and they need more room.

FIGURE 16.1 Nutritional tray line.

BATCHING SALADS AND SANDWICHES— COLD PRODUCTION EXAMPLE

Sandwiches and salads are normally made in large batches. Videotaping the salad making revealed a batch process where all the salad bowls were lined up, completely filling the tables. Next, a huge bowl of lettuce was rolled out and lettuce was placed in each bowl one at a time until all were filled. Then came the carrots, followed by all the other ingredients in like manner. Once the bowls were filled with the ingredients, all the lids were placed, then the labels and price tag.

A simple turkey sandwich is made the same way (Figure 16.2). Slices of bread are put down until they fill the tray(s) to make multiple sandwiches (twenty or more). Then a slice of turkey is put on each slice of bread one at a time, followed by two slices of bread stacked, so two sandwiches are made at a time, which, believe it or not, was a process improvement at the time—albeit not a Lean one. Next, another slice of turkey is put on and then the final slice of bread. From the analysis, we determined the baseline original process took more than 34 min to get to this point, and not even one sandwich was considered complete. Next, all the sandwiches are cut diagonally, then all are put into a container one at a time and stacked on trays. The trays are taken over to another area across the room, where the sealing machine is located and each is sealed. This was approximately 1 hr into the process, but we are not done yet. Now labels and the price stickers are placed on each one, they are loaded up on trays, and rolled into a cold storage unit. It is not until this point that we have one complete sandwich that could be given to a patient or sold to a patron.

Lesson Learned: *Batching is slow and takes up lots of space with food exposed to the elements for long periods of time. What happens to food quality and food safety in 1 hr of a batch process? Batch processes can increase food safety risks and decrease food quality.*

OVERPRODUCTION

Another problem is the huge waste of overproduction (Figure 16.3). How many meals are delivered only to find that the patient has been taken to radiology, therapy, or some other appointment? How many meals are uneaten because the patient is not hungry or the meal was cold or not what the patient ordered? Every hospital, we have found, wastes a tremendous amount of money in food that has to be discarded along with the labor that was required to produce it, deliver it, retrieve it, and then wash and store the dishes.

Lesson Learned: *Overproduction results in significant dollars of scrap and spoilage.*

STEPS TO IMPROVE THE PROCESS

The best place to start is to improve the tray line, and this was our pilot for the Lean initiative. First, we value stream mapped (VSM) the process. During the VSM process, we calculated our baseline metrics. These included number of operators, cycle time, output per operator, etc. Calculating cycle time is impossible in a batch environment, so we looked at cycle time based on the overall process. For example, if we produced 500 sandwiches in 125 min, then we are averaging

FIGURE 16.2 Nutritional batch sandwiches.

FIGURE 16.3   Nutritional batch sandwiches bread.

15 sec per sandwich. This is misleading because we don't see the sandwiches come out one at a time every 15 sec; we see them all get done at once. If we have 10 people assembling and sealing the sandwiches, then we are actually averaging 150 sec per sandwich or:

$$10 \text{ people} \times 15 \text{ sec} = 150 \text{ people/sec.}$$

Next, we followed the first food item on the tray from beginning to end. This is called Product Process Flow (PPF), the product being the "tray." We also drew a point-to-point diagram. Then each operator involved with the tray line assembly and line support was videotaped in order to conduct a full work analysis of the operator. This was a very eye-opening process. We observed a significant amount of idle time, and wasted motions by watching the video. One operator commented, "Wow! I didn't know I did that!" Most employees want to do a good job, but the process and layouts make it very difficult.

Lesson Learned: *Employees want to do a good job and will do the best job they can with the tools, space, and expectations we give them.*

Videotaping made staff uncomfortable at first, but then allowed everyone to voice their opinion as they were able to see the waste and inefficiency for what it was. We drew a spaghetti diagram to show the staff how much they traveled back and forth across the room.

Next, we brainstormed ideas with the team for improvement. The team included the supervisor and the tray line staff. After somewhat slightly heated discussions, it became

obvious we needed to change the system. We concluded that the entire tray line and pod system was extremely inefficient and needed to be replaced. The ironic part is that the equipment was originally purchased based on a return on investment (ROI) of increased equipment efficiency and improvements to the department.

Note: *Remember when we said that the product, operator, and setup give you different pieces of Lean? The tray line probably did produce a significant improvement (and ROI) over the original batch tray assembly process. This is because the tray line forced the implementation of the "product" piece of Lean, which normally yields a 20%–40% improvement. Our guess is that is what they realized here with the tray line implementation. The point-to-point diagram of the tray line, with a couple of exceptions, looks pretty good. The problem is that they were missing the operator piece. This is because it is virtually impossible to balance this type of line owing to the layout and the fact that the operators are trapped among the food and equipment, etc. Therefore, when assessing a tray line, we can always determine there is room for another 20%–40% improvement by eliminating the tray line and putting in a new Lean work "cell" layout.*

This means tearing out the tray line and setting up an assembly line Lean work cell (Figure 16.4). The significant level of re-education and change can be a source of stress to the staff and a large challenge for the leadership team to manage, as this seems counter-intuitive. This is a huge cultural change for everyone and may meet significant resistance from employees and management in and out of the area, but results in great benefits and makes the employee's job easier.

WORK CELLS VS. TRAY LINE

To set up the work cells, we put every step in order of the process and then figured out how long it would take to do each step. Flex zones were created in order to balance the line since every tray can be customized, based on the customer's request (VOC). The work cells can be set up in different ways (Figure 16.5). We have set them up in a straight line,

FIGURE 16.4   Lean nutritional sandwich line.

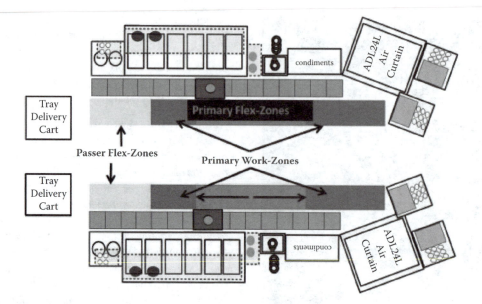

FIGURE 16.5   Lean nutritional line design.

U shape, L shape, and parallel lines. All operators work on the inside while materials are replenished via a *Kanban* process from outside so that the operators won't be interrupted on the line. Each operator was trained in the new process. Every employee was given a minimum of 8 hrs of Lean training prior to the rollout. A pilot line was set up while the "old" system was still in place in order to teach them how it would function. The employees came up with some great objections that spawned additional ideas on how to improve the line even more. It is critical to gain feedback from front-line staff and address all their concerns through communication and revisions as appropriate to the process. This is to improve the chances for acceptance and success. Standard work and scripting was created for the line and management employees up to the director level of the department (Figure 16.6). Visual controls were added in the form of a menu (information flow) process, which had to be completely revised, along with a day-by-the-hour chart. The transporters were taught how to flex into the line as they were available so they didn't have to stand idle and wait for their tray carts to be completed. They increased the number of trays made per day by more than 300. The amount of space needed for the tray line was reduced by 61% and the amount of time to complete one tray was reduced by more than 90% (Table 16.1).

Similar cells were added for making salads and sandwiches. They were able to reduce the number of staff needed by 50% and increase the number of units (salads and sandwiches) by 17%. We reduced the time to complete the first sandwich from the batch system, which took more than an hour, to 25 sec with Lean and increased productivity by more than 70% in 50% of the space we were originally using.

BENEFITS OF THE NEW LEAN SYSTEM

Every time we have implemented these work cells, we have seen a 50% improvement in productivity, and the employees (eventually) like it better than the old system; however, a stressful part for an employee in a Lean implementation is the employee now has nowhere to hide whether they are or are not contributing to the process. Employees who don't have the skill or competency or don't want to pull their weight, immediately stand out. It is now easier for management to see what is happening and make improvements. It is also a work equalizer and is seen as positive by employees who had previously carried the load.

BATCH VS. MAKE TO ORDER

The overall goal for the NSD should be to move to a "make-to-order" model. This can be accomplished by having a line(s) setup that can now react quickly to any type of order.

Diet Aide Script

Kock Kock,

Hello, My name is _____.
I am from the Foodservice Dept, may I have a moment of your time? Are you Mr. or Mrs. _____? (Verbally confirm if you can't check their wristband) (If possible sit with patient do not leave room to get a chair)

Would it be ok to get your ____ (meal) selections now?
Our chef is creating a special meal, the special entrée for (meal) is ------, how does that sound?

• Would you like an appetizer? We have _____.
• Our baker has created a special dessert—_____. What can I get for you?
• What would you like as beverage.

(Complete menu selections)

Is there anything else I can get for you off the menu before I leave? Thank you for your time Mr. or Mrs. _____

FIGURE 16.6   Lean nutritional cell—scripting example.

TABLE 16.1
Sandwich Line Results

Baseline Metrics Sandwich		
Operators	6	
Units per day	1050	
Units per operator	175	
Space	448 sq. ft.	
Lean Metrics Salad and Sandwich combined		
Operators	3	−50%
Units per day	1639	+56%
Units per operator	546	+212%
Space	375 sq. ft.	−17%

The menu size and item usage will determine the location of the item in the work cell. The menus are then filled by the work cell and delivered just in time (JIT).

Once the Lean line is put in place, we start to question the need for the advance preparation of meals in general. After all, isn't this batching as well? In the past, meals were made whether the patient wants them or not. This leads to the waste of food never eaten or food that is cold by the time the patients return to their rooms. Once we had created an efficient, rapid-response process, we started to wonder if we should change the system and transition to making meals on a strictly needed or JIT basis. This would create a "pull" system (Figure 16.7).

Lean Solutions: *Hospital X set up a make-to-order process in its kitchen. Two lines were created, one for an "on-demand" type menu where patients could call their request down at any time. This menu would include things like a salad or sandwich, milk, juice, etc. The other line supports breakfast, lunch, or dinner.*

Each line is set up similar to a Subway® shop, with all the items in order of how they are used. When an order is received, the operator walks down the line and fills the order. The operator is on the inside, and meals are replenished using a two-bin system from the outside. The empty bin goes back to the food preparation area, where it is refilled and returned to the line. The orders are then placed in tray carts (in some cases, heated) and delivered to the floor every 5–10 min.

The trigger to make a meal comes directly from the patients vs. just making the meals as before. Now the meals

FIGURE 16.7 Lean nutritional cell—make to order cell.

delivered are made fresh and hot when they reach the patient. It also eliminated the need to batch up so much food ahead of time, which meant the cook-chill process/retherm process was no longer required. This increased satisfaction almost immediately. The overall effort took a lot of cooperation from, and was supported by, the floor nurses.

HOT FOOD, COLD PREPARATION

The hot food, cold preparation area prepared and cooked the food for customers using the cafeteria in the hospital. A Lean initiative was performed in this area, which leveraged cycle time, throughput time, customer demand, PPFs, operator analysis, spaghetti diagrams, and point-to-point diagrams.

Prior to the Lean initiative, the menu for the next day's food was "prepared," meaning the ingredients were taken out of the freezer or storage area and placed on a cart, then transported to a preparation area. Multiple pans or containers would be placed on a table all at once; the food/ingredients needed were opened and, in batch, and emptied into pans in preparation for cooking the next day (up to 20 hrs later). The pans or containers would be covered, placed back on the cart, and transported to the freezer until needed the following day. The carts, while stored, would block the entrance and walkway within the freezer, making it difficult for staff to access food, taking up freezer space and contributing to an unsafe environment. The following day, the carts would be rolled out to the cook area, where the prepared trays of food would be taken out in batches and placed in ovens. Once cooked, in batch, they were then transported in small batches to the cafeteria, where they were placed in "hot boxes" waiting for customers' requests. This can impact the taste and nutritional qualities of the food. Videotaping revealed:

- Lots of holding/storing of food taking up freezer space (carts in walk areas).
- Searching for equipment (pans were not always stocked for food preparation).
- No standard operating procedures for food preparation, as different staff prepared food in different ways.
- Supplies were not at point of use.
- Ingredient locations were not labeled (lots of searching).
- Excess transport.

Not preparing and cooking to customer demand resulted in excess food that, in some cases, was overcooked and had to be scrapped. Food utilization was analyzed to "predict" how many trays would need to be prepared and cooked to begin the meal cycle, which was based on historical demand, preparation and cook time.

The goal was to eliminate the steps in the food preparation process so that the food could be directly prepped and given to the cook instead of going to overnight storage. After this, food would be replenished (prepared, cooked, and delivered) as trays were consumed. This would help free storage and freezer space, improve throughput (anticipate improved food taste/quality, not sitting in storage pans for lengthy duration), and ultimately help to eliminate unnecessary amounts of food prepared and cooked that would not be utilized.

The process resulted in improved workspace in the freezer and eliminated the need for multiple "hot boxes" to store food, and the food was cooked closer to customer demand levels, resulting in a 90% reduction in throughput time. There was an 80% reduction in distance traveled and the new process freed up the freezer as no "prepped" food was kept in the freezer overnight and fractional labor in food preparation was saved.

DISH ROOMS

Traditional dish rooms contain some of the most expensive food service equipment, batching systems for dumping and loading the machines. There is often a huge amount of custom stainless steel fabrication that links the conveyor into the machine. The dumping function is not always near the machine so extra distance must be covered to get the items into the machine.

Hospital X redesigned the layout and flow of the dish room, resulting in a parallel one-piece flow dump station perpendicular to the longer entry conveyor. The dump station was connected to the pulper. This design increased productivity and greatly reduced the space and removed many feet of counters and conveyors that supported the prior batch dumping process.

LEAN LESSONS LEARNED FROM A NUTRITIONAL SERVICES DIRECTOR

HUMILITY

Before you start your Lean journey, you may think you have exhausted all ideas for process improvement in your operation. After initial Lean training, the blinders are lifted as you begin to see the 8 Wastes everywhere you look, recognizing you had developed "boiled frog syndrome." It can be easy to become overwhelmed with the realization of how much waste removal is going to be needed. Every operation has a tremendous amount of waste and you need to put aside your ego to humbly accept the challenges that will come with eliminating all this waste. Once you realize waste is everywhere, you must make sure you don't convey this frustration to your staff in a negative way. Work to stay positive and future-state focused. Don't start changing things without really understanding the value stream, data, and impact on your area and others. It is very important to prioritize your changes since we all have limited resources. This is a marathon, not a sprint.

COMMUNICATION

Even if you think you are a good communicator, you will find during the Lean journey that you can't communicate enough.

We heard this until we were tired of hearing it in training, but it doesn't really sink in until you go through it and look at it in hindsight. All forms of communication become necessary. Written communication is important, but regular verbal communication in team meetings, visual signs, and pictures are necessary. Showing video clips to staff to help them see how they work in current state helps to ease fears and gives employees more understanding of what is going to change and how they can contribute to help make it better. Your body language and tone are critical because tensions can be high when you go from a pilot to live scenario. People can see right through you if you say one thing but your actions or body language say another.

CHANGE MANAGEMENT

It is very important to educate your management team and staff on handling change prior to making the Lean changes that will be identified in the Lean tools. Myers-Briggs Type Indicator (MBTI) styles training skills significantly helped us with the conflicts that arose as we worked through the changes.

Hospital X's food service proactively used the "Who Moved My Cheese"* change management video and tools to introduce the department-wide program for change. Employees and management found it very powerful in providing a common language and examples of dealing with change. "Are you moving my cheese?" was frequently heard throughout the department and began to embed in the culture of the department. Make sure that this aspect is considered and addressed prior to a Lean project so there is less reactivity to the fear of change.

EMPLOYEE RELATIONS

Human resources (HR) and employee health need to be brought into the discussions prior to the Lean project. They need to be prepared for the volume of employee issues that will develop, such as:

- Productivity improvements that may lead to staff being reassigned to new duties.
- Fear of layoffs.
- Competency evaluations because positions need to be work balanced and not all employees are of equal performance.
- More physical-related health complaints because employees who were used to being idle now have to become more active.
- Compensation may need to be changed to match a cross-trained workforce with fewer job classes.
- Discipline for active disengagement.
- Language fluency and reading/writing deficits.
- Shift changes that will change employees' current schedules.

---

* Spencer Johnson, *Who Moved My Cheese* (New York: GP Putnam and Sons) 1988.

- Employees may be on the wrong seat of the bus or on the wrong bus for the new Lean environment.
- Ergonomic demands that require support and special equipment or modifications to the physical area and equipment. This is a critical component, and one needs to be prepared to spend much time and energy, being proactive vs. reactive.

Your employees are essential to making and sustaining the changes. The management team needs to be aligned in its goals and commitment to Lean. We have seen some management staff that didn't really support the changes because they perceived them as a threat to their job security or were uncomfortable having to coach, mentor, and develop employees as much as Lean changes will require. Lean requires a significant change in the way you manage any environment. There is a need to prevent the old "batch system management," which is a hard concept to understand. Additionally, management is typically too involved with meetings and desk work, which keep them from being in the operation to observe the work and problems. This is a cultural change that needs to be driven from the top and take place within the organization.

TRAINING

Give adequate training to your management team prior to starting a project. They need to understand the principles and key tools prior to moving it into the employee arena. If you are launching a Lean implementation, it is a significant project that requires you select key employees (employees who you want to grow as part of your succession plan) and make them available full time to the project, reassigning their duties to others. If the people assigned to a team are still required to complete their day-to-day tasks, they become very stretched and tired even if they are excited to be part of the Lean team. Team members need to be positive and influential staff that employees and management respect, and they will help smooth the way as changes are rolled out because they know the operation and the staff. Key vendors need to be part of the training so they can see how their role in the value stream may need to be changed to help your Lean vision become a reality.

Hospital X involved external representatives from their prime vendor, secondary vendor, produce vendor, food service design consultant, and disposable vendor in its 5-day Lean training session because of the management focus on inventory and production Lean changes. This really helped the vendors be open to making changes that they normally would have resisted, such as frequent deliveries, pack size changes, and other improvements. An internal consultant from finance was on the team to assist with data collection, analysis, accountability metrics, and financial ROI measurements. The 5-day training was intriguing and logical but not totally convincing until hands-on, real-life Kaizen on the sandwich line proved the power of one-piece flow over batch production. It was then the lights went on for the team, and that was day four of five. If at all possible make sure you have a live demo as part of your training.

COMPUTER SKILLS

Microsoft Excel skills are critical to team success. Choose team members who have these skills or who will quickly learn them. IT requirements of laptops, projector, additional software such as Microsoft Visio® and dedicated meeting rooms have to be committed. It is critical that senior level administration approval and administrative support is received for the team before the project starts. Electronic file organization and huge numbers of pictures may require IT support or non-network drive storage. Don't skimp on picture taking of before-and-after changes. Keep these organized, as they help with presentations and training materials. The Lean team needs to be located very close to the project area in order to help with communication, quick access to operation, and dispel fear through positive presence. Prove early with pilots, small projects or areas that 5S and one-piece flow works.

FACILITIES AND ENGINEERING

This area quickly becomes critical to Lean improvements. When the new flow has been determined, usually there are many physical changes that need to be made:

- Equipment removal and disposal.
- Electrical and plumbing needs because of equipment changes or need for new equipment.
- Healthcare infection control risk assessment (ICRA) and other regulatory codes for work being done in the work area must be followed.
- Often, hospitals have limited electric and plumbing service available to an area, so additional services may be necessary, which sometimes significantly increases the costs that may be incurred to create a Lean layout and flow.
- Air conditioning needs to be evaluated and corrected if the heat generated in a work cell increases from the tightly positioned equipment.
- Detailed equipment specifications, layout drawings, building code compliance, etc., are critical to a successful implementation.

These types of changes take more time than desired because of the regulations in healthcare, design, costing, bidding, contracting, and phasing. The ROI needs to be sufficient to cause administration to approve the funds. There needs to be a clear expectation that there will be capital needs at the beginning of the project and a capital construction fund set up proactively, or one may find delays in the project between analysis and the ability to make some of the recommended structural changes. It needs to be clearly understood by administration that it is difficult to estimate these costs upfront. The flow and layout, which are an outcome of the project, need to be determined first. This will drive the capital required for renovations and building repairs. The layout and flow needs to be flexible and movable with quick disconnects (plug and play) in order to easily clean and allow for future Lean improvements to be made with minimal cost. Always remember to keep in mind creativity before capital.

EQUIPMENT

Food service equipment selection is very important. Standard equipment is preferred but there may be a need to customize equipment, which increases cost and creates a longer lead time for the implementation.

Hospital X used back fill refrigerators with open retail fronts in their work cells, and custom aluminum and stainless steel work was needed in all layouts.

Someone on the team needs to be good at drawing clear diagrams with enough detail so that the fabrication companies can clearly understand what they need to draw for approval, and then create. Also, it is hard to predict what equipment is going to be needed in a Lean project. Administration needs to understand that capital funds need to be provided and the cost and ROI will become clear once the team defines a layout and flow.

RECOGNITION AND INCENTIVES

In an inaugural Lean project, there are usually significant changes that lead to large improvements in productivity, space utilization, and inventory control. We realize huge financial improvements. The management team and staff who have provided this success need to be rewarded with celebrations, access to air time in presentations, approval for capital and renovation funding, and new equipment. Compensation incentives are very motivating, considering that employees see how the hard-won changes have led to savings for the organization. These need to be objectively tied to performance measures. HR and finance can help create a plan that administration can support.

EXPANSION PAINS: "WE DON'T HAVE ENOUGH SPACE!"

Most department management and staff will usually say they need more space to handle more volume. Their work areas are often crowded and cluttered. If they get more space, you can count on more crowding and clutter. Traditional master planning space standards are meant for traditional non-Lean operations. Architects will likely overestimate the space needed for the volumes projected in the master plan.

Hospital X food service master plan showed that the department was below the average for existing volumes. Hospital X was going to experience a 30% increase in volumes and the master plan for food service reflected a 50% space increase, necessitating expansion of the existing facility to a new excavation site since the current area could not accommodate that size of expansion. This created a level of cost that could not initially be approved. The Lean team was created with consultants to analyze exactly how much more space would be required if we moved to a Lean one-piece flow. Six months into this major Lean project, it was

determined that the new space excavation was not needed and, in addition, the expansion was reduced from 50% to 20% to meet the new volume projections. Instead of a major expansion involving new construction, a renovation in existing space was planned. This was a multi-million dollar savings for the hospital!

Lesson Learned: *Cost avoidance can be a huge driver of Lean initiatives in food service projects and, often, this is how Lean transformations enter organizations.*

When there is a belief that the food service needs to be expanded, I recommend first investing in a Lean project. The expansion may be needed, but a Lean project would help reduce the expansion and correct wasteful layouts and processes that will result in reduced capital costs through smaller renovation projects. This approach of Lean projects should be the first step prior to any new design or expansion planning, in any department.

FOOD SERVICE DESIGN

While there may be some features that are efficient in traditional food service design, that does not make it a Lean design. Most food service designers are interested in designing big kitchens with lots of space, equipment, counters, etc. In my experience, I have ripped out tray lines—some as long as 37 feet—removed countless counters and custom conveyors in dish rooms, moved walls, removed racks from crowded storerooms, and more because we changed layout, flow, inventory, and production processes that are typical in traditional food service design.

Hospital X knew that they had to make radical changes in their expansion design in order to bring it into budget and space constraints. A Lean project was conducted in each critical department area to determine layout and flow. Pilots in each area were conducted to prove the layout worked and fine tune it. Using this experience, layouts were shared with the design consultant who put them into CAD. My experienced and trusted food service design consultant was often outwardly doubtful and initially uncomfortable with this, but soon began to see the results in the pilots and became more open to Lean designs. Because the designer worked with us on this one multi-phased Lean project, they think they know Lean, but in reality they still have a lot to learn.

Hospital Y is a brand new 2009 facility designed by a well-known food service design company. Our initial Lean observations included:

- An entry door in the wrong place impeding the flow of supplies from the dock to the storeroom.
- The storeroom had wall-to-wall racks, vendor palettes could not get through to the freezer/refrigerator without road hazard insurance.
- There was a long custom stainless steel counter and sink opposite the four-door refrigerator walk-in, preventing easy flow of carts in/out of these main coolers and along the corridor.

- There are custom stainless steel counters where standard mobile counters would have worked well.
- There is too much cooking equipment, oversized steam kettles and floor mixer for a 245-bed hospital (contributing to overprocessing or lot delays).
- There are too many racks along the walls of the main traffic corridors that needed to be designed in a low traffic location closer to the work areas which need these products.
- There is a huge three-compartment power sink along the main corridor opposite the room service cooking area. This is a safety hazard and sanitation hazard. It needs to be moved into the dish room adjacent to where it is utilized.
- There are racks along every foot of wall space, too much custom stainless steel, and inefficient layouts in all areas.

These findings are all part of a brand new design. Why? Because they used a traditional design company, with no Lean knowledge, with the end results being excessive cost to the hospital and a less than efficient and effective layout and flow.

FOOD SERVICE LEADER

The department leader/director, although not likely a team member, will need to keep in very close communication with the Lean team about what is going on with the projects. Managers need to spend a significant amount of time engaged with the Lean team. If at all possible, consultants recommend that area management dedicate a portion of their time to the team (50% or greater). For senior level leaders this may not be realistic; however, you must make weekly visits to show encouragement and executive support validating the strategic importance to the organization. The leaders need to listen to the Lean consultants for insights and help to tie the pieces together so it is a well-balanced approach between tools and people. External and internal consultant agendas need to be managed. If you don't stay connected to them, you may be out of the loop, leaving you with situations to deal with after the fact, such as overly aggressive ROIs, which you could have influenced differently ahead of time. The leader needs to understand the data collection method and results because this drives the analysis of ROI.

Lesson Learned: *It is key that senior leaders be able to question and correct assumptions and data sources to balance the tension between aggressive ROI goals and pace of change. This can't easily be delegated to lower level management who may not have the full scope of financial and labor tracking knowledge, thus validating the importance of engaging with the team.*

LEARNING THROUGH LEAN

Many times, Lean initiatives may be started and scopes are determined because of the need to reduce full-time employees (FTEs) or potentially avoid a capital project. This can sometimes be misleading, as the number of FTEs or perceived area of square footage that can be reduced may not be the "root cause" of the problem. Project scopes need to be monitored and may need to be revised as the team learns through data and facts and analyzes the process.

Lesson Learned: *Cold Production for a Retherm System – Leaning out a tray line into a fast-producing work cell can be crippled if you haven't Leaned out the cold production that supports the cells. Our saying for this is, "You have to be able to feed the beast."*

Hospital X's Lean project didn't include cold production in the approved project list because there were too few FTEs in the work area. This is a case where FTE productivity improvement was the wrong item to focus on rather than the "pull" needs from assembly to the cold production product.

CHANGE MANAGEMENT

It is easy to determine a new layout and flow. The really hard part is the people management of the change process. Culture will eat strategy for breakfast every day. As senior administration and finance leaders get excited about the potential results from a good ROI, if not adequately addressed, the pace of change can't go as quickly as they hope to access the ROI benefits. There is tension between accessing ROI results and the pace of change that the department staff culture can effectively handle. Administration's verbal commitment to balancing these two issues must be backed up by support and realistic time frames. It is important that area managers work to keep senior leaders apprised of change management issues and have a plan to communicate to staff "what's in it for me."

Not all employees have to be on board with supporting Lean changes; however, identify the influencers (or informal leaders) early, to educate and support them. A majority will follow the informal/formal leader, and good communication keeps them from slipping into active disengagement. It is possible that, when efforts are employed to work cooperatively with employees, you will have a small number who actively create discontent and undermine the Lean changes. Unfortunately, once the changes are in place, there will be a small number of people who can't overcome their fear factor and will choose to leave voluntarily. There may be a small few who stay but wish they had left, which creates problems that will require discipline on management's part to overcome. Good communication with HR and employee health can help make sure that management has done due diligence prior to suspension or termination of dissenters or staff who can't meet the new Lean state competencies.

Executive-supported Lean initiatives in which there is an understanding of cultural changes that need to occur, along with proactive planning, will increase the likelihood that you will be successful.

17 Pharmacy

HOSPITAL PHARMACY—WHAT WE FIND

The hospital pharmacy consists of order receipt, fill, and distribution. Order receipt involves receiving the order and then filling the order. In general, in most pharmacies there are separate processes for STAT vs. routine requests. Once the order is received, the pharmacist must review (double check) the physician's orders to make sure that they are complete, have the right dosing range, and that there are no drug-to-drug interactions or allergies. Orders are normally batched up via paper, in which there may not be FIFO (first in, first out order), or queued on the computer for review. Once reviewed, the orders are normally queued up again and wait to be filled. The orders are then retrieved, filled, and sent to the floor via tube system, cart, or manually retrieved by unit personnel. Carts are normally processed in batches overnight for morning rounds. Some hospitals have robots that are utilized to improve the "picking" or filling operations.

Traditional pharmacies are stockrooms housing expensive inventory. Some pharmacies also spike solutions, that is an assembly-type task. When stock is received, it is inspected and then stored in a designated location on a shelf or in a robotic location. If there is a robot, it normally has to be shut down during the re-filling process.

Hospital X was performing a value stream map of the pharmacy process. Many members of the nursing staff on the Lean team were not happy with the pharmacy service, which caused strained relations between the pharmacy and nursing units. It was discovered that the feelings of dissatisfaction were mutual. The nurses constantly complained that the pharmacy was very poor at responding to both routine orders and STAT orders. This resulted in re-work, with double and triple ordering of drugs and numerous phone calls from the unit by nursing personnel looking for their patients' medications. The pharmacy insisted it was responding to the requests.

We explained the issues were not person dependent but process dependent, and the blame that was occurring was probably hiding the root cause of the problem. A Product Process Flow of a routine medication, order to fill, was performed to analyze the situation. Part of our team was stationed in the pharmacy and the other part of the team was on the nursing floor. The team documented the nurse placing the order in the computer. The pharmacy received the order and processed it as a routine order. They put it into the tube system, punched in the number of the floor and sent the tube on its way. 15 min passed and the team on the nursing unit had not received the tube. The team members on the unit called down to the pharmacy and

the team in the pharmacy assured us it had been sent. The team on the unit placed another order and the pharmacy sent it again. Another 15 min went by and the team on the unit still hadn't received it. The team proceeded to track the tubes down. Forty five min later, we found the tubes in the maintenance department on another floor! It turned out that the tube system could not be relied on to deliver the tube to the proper location and maintenance was engaged to repair the tube system. Once the tube system was repaired, it fixed the problem.

Next we analyzed a STAT medication order which turned out to be a different problem. The operator analysis showed the nurse needed to place a STAT label on the order and fax it to the pharmacy. In the pharmacy, a bar code reader would pick up and flag the "STAT" request in the system. The team sent down the STAT order with our Lean team in the pharmacy and found the STAT order did not register in the system as a STAT order. On investigating (at the Gemba), it was determined that the STAT label was not positioned correctly on the form (Figure 17.1). It was discovered that if the STAT label was even an eighth of an inch off, it would not be read. Apparently, this was communicated in a memo to all the floor nurses 6 months ago but, as new nurses arrived, they were not told of the precision required when affixing the STAT label. Our temporary counter measure was to re-educate the nurses and have the pharmacy double check all STAT orders as they were entered into the new system. The long-term solution was to change the process so that the STAT label could be placed without such precision.

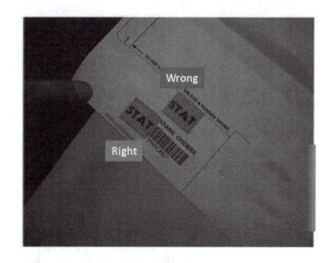

FIGURE 17.1 Pharmacy STAT label. The STAT label had to be placed within an 1/8 of an inch of the "right" location to be read by the bar code scanner.

STEPS WE FOLLOW AND TOOLS WE USE WITH LEAN

First, identify the problems the clinical area needs to solve, obtain baseline metrics, and then value stream map (VSM) the flow in order to identify opportunities and prioritize projects. The next step is to create several Product Process Flows. Normally, both the STAT process and the routine process is flowed because of the difference between delivery methods and robots if they exist. A videotape of the staff (operators) performing the tasks is performed and analyzed with the staff (operators) and supervisors to identify what can be eliminated, rearranged, simplified, and combined.

WHAT WE NORMALLY FIND

Through our analysis tools, we typically find that problems are different for different hospitals, but most pharmacies share one or all of the following problems:

- Trouble with STAT order delivery cycle times
- Trouble with routine order delivery cycle times
- Trouble with morning or evening runs
- Lots of batching, work not performed in single-piece flow
- Poor location markings, re-work
- Lots of inventory
- Slow and sometimes inaccurate IV processing
- Long queues waiting for approval, orders not processed in FIFO (first in, first out)
- Few metrics, metrics not posted, targets not communicated
- Lack of or no visual controls, people who seem very busy all the time
- Poor layouts, with sit-down order processing stations, divided labor (i.e., between processors and pickers etc.)
- Disruptive flow of medication fill within pharmacy
- No 5S—drawers and cabinets with doors and full of stuff
- Significant amount of work in process (WIP)

PROBLEM WITH DISPENSING ROBOTS

Robots were created to speed up the picking process, make it more efficient, but even more important, to correct the human mistakes of picking the wrong items. Robots, however, are only as good as the cycle time on which they work and the accuracy of the person re-filling medications inside the cage for the robot to pick. Lengthy processes are involved with re-filling robots—medication has to be packaged in special bags or containers so that the robot can find it and pick it up. At times, the robot can't keep up with the necessary cycle time and lags behind, so staff end up hand-picking stock anyway. In general, no investigation of robots cycle times, capacity or refilling time were performed prior to the acquisition. Robots also need maintenance (daily, weekly, monthly, etc.)

and can—and do—break down. Expensive labor is required to fix them.

The goals with Lean come in different levels for pharmacy. The first level is to improve the existing process. The second level to look at how the pharmacy interacts with the rest of the hospital system. The key with the pharmacy VSM is to step back and see the big picture.

FIRST LEVEL

The first level involves improving processes within the pharmacy (Figure 17.2). This involves order processing, picking, inventorying, IV processing, etc. We recommend implementing two-bin systems and Kanbans where it makes sense and streamlining the process by aligning the inventory with 80% of the most frequently used medication in the order that it is traditionally picked. It is recommended that you work with suppliers to improve packaging and containers to facilitate re-stocking cycle times. A plan for every part should be implemented that will help reduce inventory levels and free up space. Areas should be organized to assemble trays and other carts and the assembly flow should be in the order of how it is stocked in the trays and carts.

IV assembly should be analyzed along with daily demand, and Takt time in order to re-size the stock to only what is needed. Kanbans should be set up to trigger replenishment accordingly so that stock does not expire.

Re-stocking Pyxis® machines should be assessed and consideration should be given to share work or cross-train with the floor technicians who have idle time on the third shift. In many cases, technicians on the floors can be trained and certified by the pharmacy for the stocking process.

TYPICAL RESULTS

Inventory is reduced, space is freed up, and errors are reduced. Excess, obsolete, and expired material is virtually eliminated. Queues are reduced with one-piece flow

FIGURE 17.2 Pharmacy layout base.

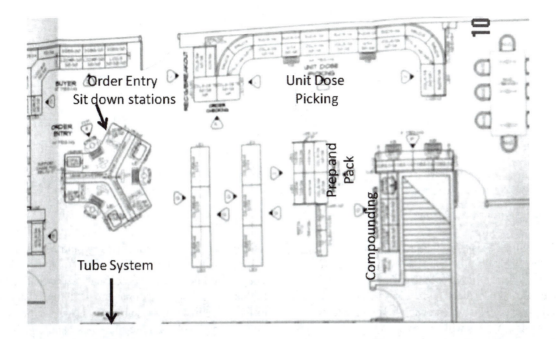

FIGURE 17.3 Pharmacy architect layout.

processing. Essentially, what used to be the STAT process becomes the routine process so orders don't have to be identified as STAT. Orders are processed in FIFO bases.

Lesson Learned: *The goal with Lean is to design the process to treat every order as a STAT order.*

PROPOSED PHARMACY LAYOUT

This was a layout presented to me by a pharmacy director at hospital X (Figure 17.3). This layout is from a leading architectural firm. The pharmacy director was very happy with it and thought it looked great. He asked me what I thought of it. What problems do you see with this layout? Try to answer before you read on.

This was my response to him.

Let's start with order entry (receiving area). First, it is an isolated island and it is sit-down (Figure 17.4). What are the chances that anyone is going to get up from their chairs flex and help each other out? What are the chances that anyone else in the department will help out order entry? This will result in people who are hired only to do order entry. When order entry has too many staff, they will be idle because they won't help anyone else out. When there are not enough staff, orders will

FIGURE 17.4 Pharmacy sit-down order entry.

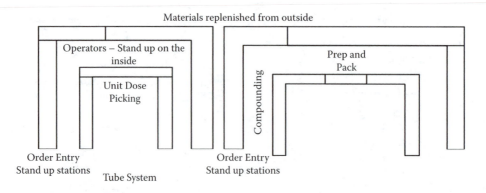

FIGURE 17.5   Pharmacy Lean conceptual layout.

back up. In Figure 17.3, notice the proximity of receiving to the tube system. That distance has to be walked by each order entry person. So what will happen? They are going to pick up a bunch of tubes and take them to their desk to receive because of the travel distance. This will probably result in batching the rest of the process. All this will lead to extra labor required by the department.

Once the order is entered, it has to be picked. Notice how far away the unit dose picking is from the receiving station. Again, the travel distance will force batching. Since the unit dose picking flows from left to right, where will the picked order be completed? It will be way over to the right, next to the new conference room. Notice the distance away from the tube system it has to travel once it is picked. Again, every order multiplied by this distance is going to drive extra labor.

The prep and pack and compounding areas are chock full of isolated islands back-to-back. Again, no flexing will drive extra labor and batching. Again, they are all quite far away from the tube system.

RECOMMENDATION

Create stand-up order entry, feeding each parallel unit dose pick lines (Figure 17.5). If the tube system cannot be moved, then set up U-shaped cells that start and end near the tube system. If the tube system can be moved, it might be best to centralize it with U-shaped cells feeding it from both sides. We now cross-train all personnel in order entry, and it becomes part of the standard work. This drawing (Figure 17.5) is conceptual and needs much detail work, but the idea is there. We need to create the layout so we can flex and minimize travel distance and labor.

SECOND LEVEL

In Lean, our goal is to reduce inventory and eliminate stockrooms, where possible, in favor of "point of use" or "point of floor," have medications on the unit. Many hospitals have installed Pyxis® machines that put the drugs at a centralized or multiple centralized locations. Where you can't move to point of use inventory, you should work to streamline the "order to delivery process." These should be considered interim solutions. The ideal state would be to have whatever routine medications, even narcotics, in the patient rooms. They would be in a locked cabinet with combination locks. If this could not be accomplished, the next step would be to have localized pharmacies on each floor or, serving two floors. This involves more materials handling, but takes the tube system and, in some cases, the need for Pyxis® systems out of the equation. The goal would be to have the pharmacies re-stocked by the supply chain and the medications owned by the supplier until they are distributed to the patient.

LEAN RESULTS: PHARMACY[*]

Serving a 341-bed hospital, the facility was filling 1300 orders per day and was staffed by 30 full-time employees (nine pharmacists, 16 technicians, and one secretary). The goals were to

- Relieve the congestion of a cramped workspace
- Reduce the frequency of Pyxis® station stockouts
- Reduce the work of re-stocking unused medications

The Lean team identified key causes of waste, including an inherently inefficient layout, lack of up-to-date information from the hospital floors, and poor inventory management. The team developed a more efficient layout, cleared out non-productive inventory, and instituted more frequent order processing and Pyxis® refills. After the Lean implementation:

- The number of Pyxis® stockouts fell by 81%.
- The number of returned doses fell by 10%.
- The pharmacy reduced its standing inventory.
- Staffing levels remained steady, even though the pharmacy added a dedicated customer service position.

The pharmacy has components of both a service organization and manufacturing company. The application of Lean concepts and tools across the value stream can provide significant benefits to the pharmacies internal operations and the clinical areas that it serves.

---

[*] ValuMetrix® Services consultants' Lean implementation at Riverside Medical Center Pharmacy in Kankakee, IL.

18 Emergency Department

THE TYPICAL EMERGENCY DEPARTMENT

LONG WAIT TIMES FOR OVERCROWDED EMERGENCY ROOMS ACROSS THE UNITED STATES

A new study reports on wait times in the nation's emergency rooms (ERs)[*]

Over 50: Percentage of all hospital visits in the United States that take place in ERs

243: Average number of minutes of wait time per visit for 2008

245: Average number of minutes of wait time per visit for 2007

27: Increase in minutes of wait time between 2002 and 2008

172: Average wait time in minutes in South Dakota for 2008, the lowest in the nation

408: Average wait time in minutes in Utah for 2008, the highest in the nation

TOTAL TIME SPENT IN THE EMERGENCY DEPARTMENT

The *Pulse Report* collects data from patients regarding their total time (door-to-door) spent in the emergency department (ED). According to the *2009 Pulse Report*, which analyzes data from 2008, patients spent an average of 243 min, or 4 hrs and 3 min, in the ED. When compared with data from 2002, that's an additional 27 min in the ED.

PATIENT SATISFACTION WITH THE EMERGENCY DEPARTMENT

We all know total time spent in EDs has increased in the past several years. During this same time, satisfaction is gradually improving as well. This slightly improved satisfaction may indicate that providers are doing a better job of focusing on improving quality and meeting patient needs.

Patients who spend more than 2 hrs in the ED report less overall satisfaction with their visit than those who are there less than 2 hrs. Since much of the time in the ED is spent waiting—in the waiting room, in the examination area, for tests or to be discharged—reducing total time and keeping patients more informed should have a positive impact on patient satisfaction. The best way to get patients treated and discharged from the ED is to address overcrowding in general and get the critical patients through the ED and to the appropriate floor faster. This frees up resources for the less critical patients to be cared for and discharged from the ED.

Patient experiences can vary based on many factors, including where patients receive care. One might assume that small EDs may experience less crowding and fewer wait time issues; however, larger facilities often take greater efforts to improve patient satisfaction, even if total time spent is higher on average. Regions with the highest mean scores are setting a new standard for excellence. Remaining competitive requires a concentrated focus on meeting patient needs and expectations.

Comments on ED visits from nearly 1.4 million patients in 2008 were predominantly positive. In particular, well over two-thirds of the comments about nurses, doctors, tests, and treatment of family and friends were positive.

EMERGENCY DEPARTMENT VISITS[†]

- Number of visits: 119.2 million
- Number of injury-related visits: 42.4 million
- Number of visits per 100 persons: 40.5
- Most commonly diagnosed condition: injury and poisoning
- Percentage of visits with patient seen in fewer than 15 min: 22%
- Median time spent in ED: 2.6 hrs
- Percentage of visits resulting in hospital admission: 13%
- Percentage of visits resulting in transfer to a different hospital: 1.9%

Overcrowding and long waits in EDs have been the focus of attention as the discussion continues on how best to provide high-quality care in an efficient, cost-effective manner. According to the *2009 Pulse Report,*[‡] which analyzes data from 2008 on total time spent in ED (door-to-door), it was reported that patients spent an additional 27 min in the ED, when compared to 2002, for an average length of stay (LOS) of 243 min, or 4 hrs and 3 min.

In addition, the Institute of Medicine (IOM) report of June 2006, "Hospital-Based Emergency Care: At the Breaking Point" underscores the importance of the critical challenges faced by EDs in the United States, including overcrowding,

---

[*] http://www.pressganey.com/cs/about_the_emergency_department_pulse_report, June 26, 2009.

[†] National Hospital Ambulatory Medical Care Survey: 2006 Emergency Department Summary, tables 1, 10, 12, 21, 25. Data is for United States only.

[‡] Press Ganey http://www.pressganey.com/cs/about_the_emergency_department_pulse_report & http://www.usnews.com/articles/opinion/2009/06/26/long-wait-times-for-overcrowded-emergency-rooms-across-the-us.html.

ambulance diversions, and inefficient patient flow and hospital operations. According to the report, "By smoothing the inherent peaks and valleys in patient flow, and eliminating the artificial variability that unnecessarily impair patient flow, hospitals can improve patient safety and quality while simultaneously reducing hospital waste and cost."* Anyone who has spent time in the ED with a loved one or friend has, for the most part, encountered long waits and frustration in trying to get through the process.

THE TRADITIONAL EMERGENCY DEPARTMENT MODEL

The traditional patient flow business model for an ED is driven on room availability and is "hurry up and wait" focused and designed (Table 18.1). In other words, capacity or bed availability dictates when the patient will be evaluated by either the physician or mid-level provider (MLP) or extender and, in most cases, bed availability plays a key determinant on when that will occur (Figure 18.1). The typical non-emergent patient will check in, have a brief encounter with a staff member (skill type may vary), and be asked to sit and wait. The patient will then be asked to complete the registration pages, and to return to the lobby to sit and wait. This may occur before or after the patient receives "full" triage performed by the triage nurse, who will assess the patient in greater detail and ask for their chief complaint and brief medical history. The triage nurse determines the severity of the patient's illness and then decides if the patient can wait or needs a critical care room immediately. If they are deemed non-urgent, i.e., stable patients, they will be told to go back to the lobby area or a hallway and wait. The patient may be called by another nurse who carries out secondary triage, depending on the process within a particular ER. Depending on the patient's symptoms, this may trigger "a protocol," which begins the evaluation/diagnosis process even before the patient is completely assessed by a doctor. If a patient is placed on a protocol, they may be sent to the laboratory or radiology department; in either case, the patient ultimately returns to the lobby to wait again. The patient still hasn't received what they came for—an evaluation by the physician. Some patient waits can extend beyond 10 hrs or more, in which case many decide to leave the ER and become a LWSD (left without seeing doctor) statistic. The reason for this is that patients are not necessarily seen by the physician in the order that they arrive or FIFO (first in, first out). Urgent and non-emergent patients are prioritized, and the remaining patients are continually "re-sorted" and sent to a room or hallway once all other higher acuity patients are treated. This is due, in part, to the fact that open rooms or "beds" drive the ability to see patients. If a bed does not open up (despite the fact that there may be a physician available), the patient remains in the waiting room. In most EDs, only when a room or

TABLE 18.1
ED Traditional Model

Traditional model
• Sequential processing
• Physician evaluation 5th step or later
• Bed dependent
• Nurse driven protocols to facilitate care
• Sorting No FIFO
• Physician productivity <2 patients per hour
• Staff to desire vs. hourly demand
• Patient remains in one room with same nurse caring for patient throughout most of ED stay

"hallway" slot opens up is the patient taken to the room. The typical scenario is that, once in the room, the patient waits again. Eventually, the physician will arrive, take a history and physical and evaluate the patient, order diagnostic testing, receive results and determine a disposition, and discharge to home or admit. Sometimes patients need more testing, as often the wrong protocol was chosen in triage or the patient's complaint changed or there are additional circumstances that complicated the original situation. This results in another round of waiting for results. The doctor or nurse will then return to provide updates throughout the patient's stay until a final disposition is attained and the patient is either admitted or discharged. If the patient is admitted, additional orders are written, consults obtained, and the "hunt" for an inpatient bed begins. If the patient is discharged, then discharge paperwork is completed by the physician and nurse, prescriptions and follow-up information are provided, and the patient is sent home.

This is a typical scenario that plays out in more EDs than we would like to believe, with extended waits to be seen by a physician, treated, and then disposed to the final destination.

ED throughput (Figure 18.2) is not just about the ED processes, but has tentacles that reach well into the rest of the hospital's bed availability and care process. This system, while inherent with waste, works as long as there are rooms available and patient demand is aligned with the provider's hours; however, this is typically the ideal vs. realistic scenario and not how the EDs or providers have staffed the department.

The traditional model, if executed well and capacity and staffing are available, can reach published world-class benchmarks of arrival to physician examination of 45 min and average outpatient LOS of 2 hrs (Figure 18.3). Typical average physician statistics are 1.8–2.1 patients per hour, based on data we have collected. Every hospital, however, has its unique patient population. Each ED also has its own level of acuity. Most hospitals don't measure door-to-physician, and those that do sometimes have a lot of validity issues with the metrics. Hospitals that report on door-to-physician often internally do not have a standard on what "door" means. Is it when the patient signs in, is it after the patient waits in line 4 patients deep to sign in, or whatever is on clock when the

---

* "Hospital-Based Emergency Care: At the Breaking Point," Institute of Medicine (IOM) report of June 2006.

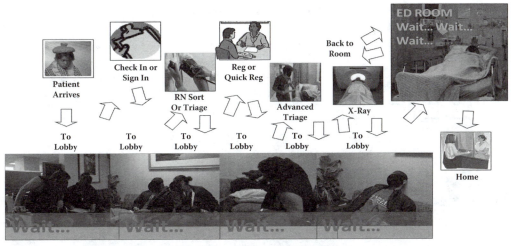

Traditional ED Models are patient to "Room" and "Hurry Up &
Wait" For Doctor and Treatment

FIGURE 18.1   ED traditional model.

time is finally captured? Other challenges include physician-related data capture.

In some EDs, the stated 30 min times to seen are very misleading. At some hospitals, "seen" means seen by a triage nurse or an initial provider "screening" and is not the full doctor exam. The true 30 min comes into question when physicians log into patients prior to seeing them so they can hit their times. In other hospitals, they forget to log in, so their times are better than what is reported. When physicians batch, they may enter their time the patient was seen way before they even enter the patient's room. For example, we find most ED physicians grab 3 charts or more at once (if they can find them), logging into the third person probably 20–30 min early. This gives the illusion their door-to-doctor time was better than it was. Although this may seem trivial, it

can skew the data by 15–30 min or more. When one reviews results from a "benchmark" hospital, one needs to be somewhat skeptical. While some hospitals may truly have benchmark results, not all organizations have the same definition of what it means to be "seen" by a physician, and the comparisons in reality are not comparable.

ED patients can average anywhere from a low acuity (level 1) to high acuity (level 5). Some ERs in tertiary settings attract higher acuity patients, thus appropriately increasing the LOS times. Trauma centers obviously have a very high acuity, and most have very different flow patterns.

Patients' arrival to the ED per hour and overall volume can vary significantly across EDs as well as patient types (i.e., psychiatric, pediatrics, etc.). As a result, the majority of hospitals with higher acuities or inpatient backlogs do not

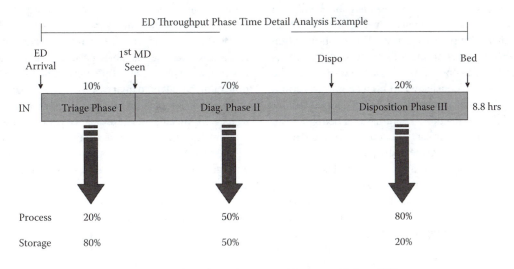

FIGURE 18.2   ED throughput example.

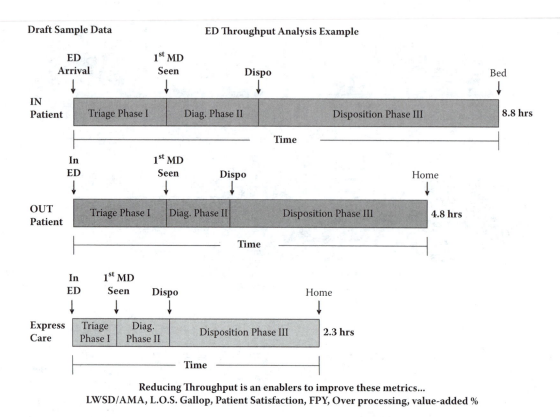

FIGURE 18.3 ED throughput detail example.

achieve these published world-class benchmarks. During certain times of the day, some of these hospitals have wait times exceeding 4–10 hrs or more for the patient to enter a room (or hallway) and see the provider. In addition, the current view of overcrowding in the ED limits initiatives to relieve the overcrowding within the ED itself. The industry at large has come to accept waits of 6–8 hrs in the lobby for less emergently ill patients as an unavoidable consequence of infrastructure overload.

ED charge nurses and physicians must negotiate with bed management and on-call physicians to get admission orders and bed assignments for patients. These ED patients are often in competition with direct admissions from provider offices and hospital operating rooms for the same bed. Because the ED patient is typically considered to be receiving care in a critical care environment, the priority is on placing the other patients first. This can lead to ED admissions being held in the ED for many hours, or days occupying limited treatment space and exacerbating the bottleneck for patients in the waiting room who are waiting to be seen. The industry as a whole has come to accept patients on stretchers in ED hallways, but has been much less willing to accept this same intervention on inpatient units to create inpatient capacity. To alleviate the ED overcrowding, some hospitals have created "code purple or red or other color" type plans, which means when a predetermined metric is triggered i.e., ED available slots (beds or hallway) down to two, the organization "must" respond to free up beds on the floors. But at many hospitals, these calls for code purple go unheeded. Some hospitals have adopted "pushing" patients to already filled units, and the

patients are moved from hallways in the ED to hallways in units. Although this does relieve some of the burden of the staff in the ED, it still does not address the root cause of the underlying problem.

The delay and flow problems in the ED are often exacerbated by a lack of inpatient bed capacity. This lack of capacity can be related to several major factors, including increased demand in the community beyond the actual physical capacity of the hospital, lack of appropriate nursing staff to keep all available beds in operation and, of course, the efficiency of their patient flow management.

Holding patients who are awaiting inpatient bed placement in the ER takes up valuable space and staff time. Caring for patients who may be awaiting a critical care bed or even step down unit care who demand a 1:2 or 1:3 patient-to-nurse ratio can place a significant burden on ER staff who may be staffed to care for much lower level acuity patients (1:4 or even 1:5), thus creating an unsafe environment for both patients and staff.

Furthermore, the hospital staff of an inpatient unit are entrenched in the traditional paradigm that the census on their unit is limited to the number of staffed beds they have available and their patients are only those on their unit. While the patient in the ED may have been assigned a bed on a unit, the patient is essentially "out of sight," thus "out of mind" and still considered an "ED" patient. This rationale would be accurate and not an issue except for two things: frequently the ED is holding inpatient admissions in as many as 60% of the available treatment spaces; and up to 60 untreated patients were routinely waiting in the ED lobby during our peak demand hours of 3:00 p.m. to midnight. Many staff members outside the ED do not understand or have not been exposed to the impact of delaying acceptance of a patient to their floor unit. The ED does not typically get credit in its budget for the inpatient services they supply when the floor forces the ED unit to hold patients.

THE CURRENT PROCESS IS BROKEN

At Hospital X we were told that they had done away with triage and all patients were screened within 20 min, and patients saw the doctor within 30 min. In addition, they abolished the waiting room. Does this sound too good to be true? In fact, the system they put in place was much better than the 8–10 hrs waits they used to have to see a doctor. Their new system replaced a traditional 6–8 min triage nurse with a 4 min screening by a paramedic and an adjacent area to screen chest pain patients immediately. They transformed the original waiting room to a small holding area on the critical care side and to hall chairs on the fast-track side. While it is true that all patients were screened within 20 min, they still did not necessarily see the doctor any faster. Once they were triaged and it was determined they needed the acute care side, a physician assistant (PA) initially screened ("first look") the patient, followed later by a doctor exam. On the fast-track side, 1–3 doctors worked 6 rooms and batched their patients. There were 4 procedure rooms staffed by 2 nurses, a technician, and a secretary. The secretary spent her time re-entering orders into two different systems, when the doctors had already entered the same orders into yet another system. While this may seem odd, it is quite common at most hospitals. When things got busy (more than 220 patient visits a day in a 37-bed ED) and inpatient beds became less available, the fast-track and the acute holding area would fill up and back up quickly. It was actually all very predictable. As their fast-track filled up, it basically ground to a halt owing to lack of available rooms in the ED. The physicians on the fast-track side would start screening patients in the hall. On the acute side, patients continued to be packed in. This holding area was the equivalent open space of maybe 3 examination rooms with 13 chairs, two rows back-to-back, 2 recliners and a bed. Patients were examined, history and blood samples obtained, and medication given as everyone else in the area was watching and listening. While this scenario sounds made up, it was the result of an ED physician-led improvement team based on another ED that they had "benchmarked" (visited). This shows that some physicians will go to any lengths to see and treat their patients, even if it means their patients have to congregate in medieval conditions. Interestingly enough, while the patients were obviously not happy vomiting in their chairs or being next to someone else vomiting in their chair, no one outwardly complained and most seemed happy that someone was trying to help them.

This ED had reduced their waiting time but at what cost! Some nurses and physicians refused to work the acute care holding area. Also, nurses refused to administer certain medications while their patients were sitting in chairs. In the

community, there were some urgent care clinics in the area; however, this was the only hospital in the region. One has to wonder, if they had closer competition, would they have survived. At another hospital, nurses and doctors actually thought a 2 hrs wait was just about right. They saw nothing wrong with longer waits; after all, it has always been that way! People expect to wait when they come to the ER. Obviously, there was no compelling need to change and the employees told us that they saw no reason to bring in a consultant to improve the process. Does this sound like the "boiled frog syndrome" we spoke of earlier in the book?

Some physicians are concerned standard work will force them to somehow standardize the diagnosis process. This is not the goal of Lean; however, Lean thinking would support computer-driven diagnosis if this were possible. The goal of standard work is to standardize what happens after the diagnosis is made, thereby driving best practice treatments and allowing patients to flow through the ED with a minimal of wait time. *One of the patients we followed had blood drawn by the nursing staff without orders. This was a standard unwritten protocol. The staff routinely drew "rainbows," which is drawing multiple tubes of blood in tubes of all colors (thus allowing multiple test types). While the staff said they did not do protocols, in essence, they were doing protocols, with the thinking that every patient was going to need blood drawn and testing so they drew these rainbows on every patient. This might seem to make sense to some, but the nurses complained to us that some patients' blood expired before they could even get the orders from the physicians to do the laboratory work. In some cases, the nurses did not mix the tubes properly, resulting in blood clotting and bad samples and the patients then had to be redrawn. In other cases, some tubes were not marked immediately, opening up the possibility of attaching the wrong patient label to the tube, which is very dangerous. It should also be noted that we have found some hospitals have initiatives to reduce the amount of "blood" taken from patients from a quality and safety perspective.*

A Lean team member was doing a patient process flow (PPF) at a hospital. The intention was to follow an ambulance patient to see how that process worked compared to someone arriving at the front door. The patient we picked came in by ambulance with chest pain to the ER. An electrocardiogram (EKG) done immediately on arrival was negative and, since there were no critical beds, she was put into the dreaded acute holding area described above with 13 other patients sitting in chairs. The team member sat down next to her with the video camera and notepad and waited with her to "experience her pain." After about 45 min, the team member noticed her reach up and start to turn the knob on the IV tubing. The nurse attending to the area was too busy to notice. The patient was asked how she knew to do that. The patient said she had been an emergency medical technician (EMT) for 5 years and she didn't want air from the IV going back into her veins. It took an hour and a half before the PA came to see us and more than 3 hrs before she saw the doctor. It wasn't until the doctor saw her that her blood orders were entered into the system. Since the wait was so long, she had to be redrawn. From that point it took more than an hour to get the results back and another 15 min before the doctor came back to give her the results. The patient almost left twice against medical advice (AMA). She told the team member that even though she still felt awful, she was going to tell the doctor she felt better so she could get out of there!

Lesson Learned: *If you want to see what your patients experience, accompany them during their entire stay. What a great way to get the true voice of the customer.*

CURRENT EMERGENCY DEPARTMENT IMPROVEMENT IDEAS

As stated earlier, the normal response to improve the ED is to build more beds. When they can't add beds, many hospitals are experimenting with different approaches to solve the wait time and throughput issues for their patients. Some:

- Build more triage rooms
- Build more ED rooms
- Create fast-tracks or express care areas
- Put a doctor in triage
- Providers see patients in the lobby
- Add staff
- Filter patients and send low acuity patients to an off-site urgent care
- Continually add or try to improve protocols

But most of the time, these approaches still yield suboptimal results, and each has its own set of pros and drawbacks.

BUILD MORE ROOMS

The obvious solution to inpatient capacity issues is more beds, more staff and/or better utilization of the available beds. Unfortunately, most of those interventions are time consuming and may not be immediately achievable. In addition, this obvious solution may not be the correct one.

Adding rooms is like adding inventory into a product-based value stream. The inventory (rooms) hides the underlying problems. In the short run, adding rooms helps, as there is a place to put the inpatient holds; however, in most EDs we have witnessed that this solution only lasts until the new rooms are filled up. Six months to a year later, the ED is in the same boat as before, but the problem is worse because of the additional rooms. The additional rooms also require more staff.

Lesson Learned: *Adding rooms is a short sighted and short-term solution unless the data backs up the need for them.*

The correct thought process is if one can reduce LOS throughout the hospital and eliminate wasted time in the process, then one may not need extra inpatient or ED beds. ED throughput requires study of not just the ED systems thinking by reviewing overall hospital patient throughput and bed management systems within the hospital.

PROBLEMS WITH EXPRESS CARE AND FAST-TRACK MODELS

Express care models, *in theory*, should be Lean models. Patients with very low acuity are directed to another area where they are typically seen by a physician extender. The drawback to this model is that patients can either stack up or demand can be zero, depending on how many rooms are available in the area, how patients arrive, how the area is staffed, and whether the physician gets pulled back to attend to a critical patient. Therefore, we have found wait times can vary significantly depending on time of day.

Our Lean team, composed of people from the ED, other support areas, and Lean practitioners, saw the need to re-evaluate the typically suggested express care/fast-track solution. However, at other hospitals we benchmarked, we found that patients were still waiting a long time for and in the express care process. Additional first pass yield issues are listed below:

- Express cares are typically open for peak demand hours, i.e., 10:00 a.m. or 11.00 a.m. to 5:00 p.m. or in some cases until 11:00 p.m. As a result, patients who arrived prior to 10:00 a.m. were asked to wait for express care track to open. Some of these patients arrived as early as 8:00 a.m. The nurse's thought process was that it was worth their time to wait because they would still get through express care faster than the main ED at that time. This resulted in the express care area starting the day with a backlog of several patients, which made it difficult for express care to ever get ahead of the patients walking in the door, thus everyone waited.
- Because patients were sorted at triage, some patients were inappropriately sent to express care, which required the patients to be moved back to the main ED, in some cases with the express care doctor still responsible for them since they did not handoff patients.
- Patients do not come to the ED one at a time. Typically, anywhere from 6 to 15 patients or more can arrive within a period of 1 hr. Sometimes, the express care track wouldn't have any patients and, at other times, they were overloaded. This created under-utilization or over-utilization for the provider and staff who could not easily flex back into the main ED so they would spend their time waiting around and chatting or reading during slow times.
- Normally express care tracks (also true with urgent care) depend on physician extenders as providers. As a result, the physician extender has to travel to and wait for the physician to be available (which could be a few feet or several hundred or even a thousand feet) to have a consultation and sign off their paperwork.

Lessons Learned: *Express Care and Fast track models work until all the rooms fill up. Then they result in idle staff. Many times they become holding areas for the inpatient floors.*

Our team's goal was to develop a new model and to eliminate the need for express care or fast-track and treat every patient as an express care patient in FIFO order and enable patients to be seen many times faster than a traditional express care or fast-track.

"Doctor in Triage" Model

In some hospital "doc in triage" models, only patients requiring a 10 min or less workup are sorted by the physician to stay in the track, while the rest are sent to the critical care area. This model is essentially a fast-track in triage supported by 2 or 3 rooms where nurses carry out the short 10 min or less workups and the patient is discharged. If the doctor examination is done in triage, it can hold up the incoming patients or force the need for more doctors than necessary to be staffed. When providers or physician extenders are in triage, they are typically still doing protocols but are normally unable to separate them from performing the patient examination and call it a "patient screen." Most doctors have trouble doing a "screening" and want to finish examining the patient. In some models, the patients are treated in triage. This model can work well in lower acuity hospitals, but the question of what we do with mid to higher acuities remains. They normally get sent to the more critical area. This means the doctor in triage has to "handoff" the patient to the doctor in critical care. In most cases, this means a PA or a nurse practitioner has to man the triage area unless the doctors have worked out the "handoff" liabilities. If a PA is in triage, it requires a physician signoff for each patient, which can slow the process down.

Providers See Patients in the Lobby

We have witnessed providers seeing patients in the lobby many times. This is because their patients aren't flowing because the ED rooms are backed up. The providers are serious about caring for their patients and this shows when the provider goes above and beyond to treat their patients anywhere they can. But this is by far a noble yet questionable solution and is not fair to the patients or the providers. By Leaning out the ED we can eliminate this option because patients will now flow through the process.

Adding Staff

Sometimes EDs are understaffed, and this is easily backed up by supporting data. If this is the case, it makes sense to add staff; however, we have found just adding staff is normally not the answer and again will hide the true problems facing the ED. The processes must be fixed.

Filter Patients and Send Low Acuity Patients to an Off-site Urgent Care

Some hospitals are filtering patients on their arrival and forcing them to leave the ED and go to an urgent care. While this method may relieve some of the overcrowding, it is not a patient-friendly model and has some inherent risk, especially where the triage nurse or paramedic misses a more serious complication.

The Problem with Protocols

Most ERs are trying to make improvements to their processes. The first place most start is working on improving their protocol systems. In the traditional system, standing orders or protocols are initiated by the nurses at triage. Protocols are developed by the doctors based on the patient's chief complaint (CO) and are not necessarily customized to each individual patient. Instead, they are based on the nurse's best clinical judgment at the time based on vital signs, patient complaints, patient appearance, and the triage nurse's experience or intuition.

The reason for development and utilization of protocols is two-fold. One is to have the preliminary tests completed and resulted by the time (theoretically) the provider sees the patient. This is an attempt to increase efficiency and reduce LOS. The other is because the patients don't see the doctor until late in the process. Many times, the protocols increase the door-to-doctor cycle times.

The problem we have found with protocols is that they are 50% correct the first time.[*] Protocols often end up being the waste of "over processing". Subsequent re-work via the need for additional orders ensues once the provider completes the patient examination. Many times, once a patient is placed on a protocol, it is difficult to retract or revise the orders and the patient continues on the protocol to completion. In reality, this results in longer wait times for patients, increasing LOS, sometimes more pain (additional sticks) for the patient, cost, and dissatisfaction. The patient may feel that they are getting care until the rework begins. So the patient experiences a two step process with protocols.

As overcrowding continues, and in an attempt to facilitate the evaluation process, many hospitals continue to convert to more protocol-based processes.

But when one thinks about it, the real reason for initiating protocols is that we can't get the patient in to see the doctor right away. Often the doctor examination is the sixth or seventh step in the VSM process. So we need to ask an important question: If the patient was able to see the provider within 30–45 min or sooner, would protocols be required? The answer is a resounding "NO!"

We have teams challenge this solution because protocols are actually inherently inefficient. The experience at every facility of organizations that had protocols was they actually created more problems than they solved. In 50%–60% of the cases, we experienced the following first pass yield issues:

- Patients were placed on the wrong protocol.
- Patients were placed on the right protocol but had other problems.

[*] Based on witnessing many hospital processes and interviews with ED physicians.

- The triage nurse ordered an x-ray that was not necessary, ordered the wrong x-ray, or did not get the right view.
- Patients tell the doctor different problems than they told the triage nurse.

In reality, the patient now waits longer, is subjected to more pain (additional sticks), and is more dissatisfied. Protocols put more work (rework) on the ancillary areas, i.e., laboratories that have to find and re-pull the specimen or an already backlogged x-ray department that has to take additional rework scans.

Lessons Learned: *Most of the solutions we have put in place in the past have caused the problems we have today. Most current ED improvement ideas, like protocols are geared to fix the symptoms but not the root causes of the problems. In order to fix the ED we must change the system and fix the underlying root cause which is getting the patient in to see the doctor as quickly as possible once they enter the ED.*

THE LEAN EMERGENCY DEPARTMENT SYSTEM APPROACH

Our first step was to value stream map and evaluate baseline metrics for the existing ED process. We met with the entire ED staff to let them know the process we would be following

and what to expect. We also did a 5-day training session with all the ED senior leadership, ED Lean team, and supporting staff for radiology, laboratory, pharmacy, bed management, and nursing floors.

VALUE STREAM MAP

The Lean team utilized Lean principles and tools to review and analyze the overall ED system to determine what a Lean transformation could impact (Figure 18.4). The Lean initiative began by value stream mapping (VSM) the ED patient flow, from arrival to disposition (bed or discharge), a separate VSM of the paper flow, and another VSM of the flow of the patient from the ED room to the unit, i.e., from the admission order until the patient reached the inpatient bed (including a look at bed management and the inpatient bed changeover process).

Through the process of BASICs (PDSA), which begins with baselining metrics and collecting data for the value stream maps, we discovered that the bulk of patients (60%–82%), depending on the average acuity of the hospital, enters the ED and leaves the ED the same day. This is substantiated throughout the United States, as most patients who visit the ED are not admitted to the hospital. Simply stated, the majority of ED patients are outpatients (depending on the type of community, trauma vs. tertiary care facility). After analyzing

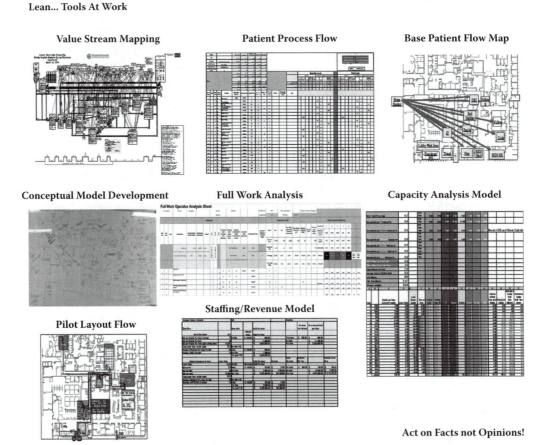

FIGURE 18.4 ED Lean tools at work.

the data collected through the VSM, the outpatient population was the focus of the Lean initiative for the following reasons:

- The majority of patients who present to the ED remain outpatients
- Outpatient solutions did not have to rely on improvements in inpatient capacity (to free beds), thus, there is an opportunity to produce change more quickly
- There were many more "x's" or patient satisfaction drivers if you include the inpatient stay (admissions)
- There was more opportunity to make radical change and impact on the acuity of levels that did not include "emergent, resuscitative, or equivalent" and, in general, the belief was that the high level acuity were treated "just in time" on arrival

Therefore, the focus on patients was all acuity levels except critical care. Although it was anticipated the majority of these patients would remain outpatients, it was recognized that there would be a subset of "admitted patients" which could be impacted by the initiative, as evaluation of patients is not "black and white." Note: this would NOT meet the definition of an express care or fast-track patient.

PRODUCT PROCESS FLOW: "THE PATIENT"

The Product Process Flow was performed with the "patient" as the "product." We looked at what was value-added to the patient. We followed patients with the three highest presenting diagnoses. The main activities that met the criteria of value-added was receiving the necessary care to correct the diagnosed patient problem, initial communication that the patient was going to be OK and eventual communication of results to the patient, and initiation of a subsequent treatment plan that included pain management. Therefore, receiving procedures (i.e., respiratory treatments) and medications, as well as peace of mind were considered to be value-added.

The rest of the patients' stay (LOS) was composed of transportation and waiting (or storage) time, which in some cases, might have been necessary. We did not consider the doctor examination, in and of itself, to be value-added from the patients' point of view since it is basically an inspection step; however, we did consider the initial communication between the physician and the patient to be value-added, as it reassured the patient that it was good that they came in and they are not dying and will be treated which was a contributor to increased patient satisfaction. It was labeled necessary but non-value-added.

OPERATOR FULL WORK ANALYSIS

Next, the work of the physicians, nurses, and staff was videotaped and analyzed with the ED Lean team, physician and staff we videotaped. The team was surprised to find 50% or more of the medical provider's time was waste and not value-added to the patient. In some cases, it was even higher for the nurses. The definition of value-added is based on meeting

three criteria (based loosely on the definition in the video *Time is the Next Dimension of Quality*),[*] which are:

1. The patient has to care and be willing to pay for the step
2. It has to physically or emotionally change the patient for the better
3. It has to be done right the first time

We found they were searching for a chart, checking on patient results, calling to find out why a result was not back, trying to determine what insurance the patient had in order to find a doctor to admit a patient, deciding which chart to pick next, socializing, and wandering around. Because the patients waited so long they were normally angry when they finally saw the doctor. As a result, some providers felt a need to give the patient their "money's worth" and would over-order diagnostic tests and spend more initial time examining the patient. This is equivalent to the waste of over-processing, waste of movement, and waste of idle time. The over-ordering of tests increases the LOS for the patient, cost to the healthcare system, and creates useless work for the nurses and support staff. It also puts unnecessary pressure on ancillary and support departments that are already backed up, such as laboratory, radiology (x-ray), imaging (CT), etc.

Let's look at what is really value-added for a provider (physician or physician extender). These processes include, examining and assessing the patient, writing out the orders for only *necessary* labs and x-rays to diagnose the patient's condition (until computerized physician order entry (CPOE) and electronic records are adopted), reviewing EKGs, pelvic examinations, sutures, lumbar punctures, etc.

Communications that were value-added were initial discussion with the patient or obtaining the patient's chief complaint and history, then discussing with the patient the physician evaluation, their possible diagnosis, and the findings of the diagnostics. Anything else the provider did was considered a necessary but not value-added activity. Because there was so much waste in the process for staff and patients, it was concluded that if processes were streamlined and waste was eliminated, provider productivity could potentially double and result in a significant reduction in LOS.

HYPOTHESIS

When we looked at our analysis data, we started to see the big picture. The doctor visit was late in the process 5th to 8th and as much as half of the doctor's time was spent doing activities that added no value for the patient. What if the process could be improved so that patients can get to see the doctor quicker? What difference would that make?

- Door-to-doctor time would decrease.
- Protocols would not be needed.

---

[*] *Time is the Next Dimension of Quality* video, American Management Association.

- LOS and LWSD would decrease.
- Physician and staff over-processing of patients would decrease.
- Patients would be happier (as they come to the emergency room to "see the doctor") and thus patient satisfaction would improve.
- Waiting rooms might be empty some of the time.

The problem statement was: excessive LOS and wait times to see the physician and treatment, results in a negative patient experience. The objective then became to improve the ED throughput time, door-to-provider time, patients per hour per doctor, and patient satisfaction.

We began by asking several questions:

1. Why do patients come to the ER?
2. How do we improve the patient experience and patient satisfaction?
3. How do we get outpatients to *flow* through the overall process, reduce bottlenecks and reduce LOS?
4. How do we get outpatients out of the ED when inpatient holds are taking up most of the rooms?
5. How do we capture registration for all patients?
6. How do we meet all of our clinical directed standards and objectives (i.e., 5 min EKG)?
7. How do we eliminate the need for protocols? (waste and rework)?
8. How do we improve on express care or fast-track solutions?
9. How do we set up a process that incorporates one-piece flow concepts, but is not considered an assembly line (any more than one might consider express care an assembly line)?
10. How would you design a new system if it was your company and you needed to make a profit?

This led to much interesting discussions which are summarized below:

1. Patients come to the ED (documented early through focus groups) to see the doctor.
2. In an ideal world, the provider would examine the patient on entering the ED; however, this is difficult to do because it requires more providers be available, and there are some steps that need to be carried out prior to the provider seeing the patient, such as pre-registration.
3. Patients can't flow or experience progress if they reside in a room with little or no outside communication and in many cases, no windows.
4. Protocols are really a workaround because they are driven by incomplete assessments, as patients don't see the doctor right away and are often more wrong than right.
5. Express care and fast-tracks can get low acuity patients through quickly, but leave other, more urgent patients dependent on capacity. These tracks also

frequently back up when the five or six rooms are filled. They also reduce overall patient satisfaction, as less urgent patients continued to watch patients who arrived after them going before them. The goal should be to get all patients through quickly.

6. Most patients are not admitted (62%–80%) and leave the ED the same day.
7. Physician scheduling should be driven by demand per hour, not by "bed capacity" in the ED.
8. We need an out-of-the-box solution that can work even with "in patient holds."

If one considers setting up an ED as if it were one's own new business and without any pre-conceived visions of how it works in most institutions today; what models already exist that one might leverage? This consideration led to discussions around how a typical family practitioner, or internist's office operates and what concepts could be leveraged. When you think about the office-based physician, the revenue they generate is based on services rendered in the most efficient way possible in order to stay in business. Time, in essence, is money. If their office is inefficient or patients are dissatisfied and time is wasted, then it will directly impact their ability to make a living and operate the business.

Consider the Family Physician Office Flow Model

Patients arrive, are registered and, in most offices, co-pays or money is collected upfront at the registration desk. A nurse takes patients back to a scale, where they are weighed. Then the nurse places them in an examination room, where he/she checks their vital signs, takes their chief complaint, and places their chart in a holder outside the room (a visual cue that the nurse has completed the patient). In some offices, there is a secondary visual cue of flags that are set outside each room to indicate patient status; the different colored flags communicate to the doctor the state of readiness.

The doctor typically has 3 or 4 rooms that are rotated through on a first in, first out basis unless there is an emergency. The number of rooms is probably not based on Takt times or cycle times, but in general, the number of rooms does reflect the time the doctor sees the patient and is able to move from room to room in an efficient manner without running into a patient who is not ready.

During the patient visit, the doctor evaluates the patient and completes notes on a chart (manually or on computer) and gives them a prescription or decides additional labs or x-rays are required to complete the diagnosis. If a lab is needed, the physician sends the patient to their laboratory (in a separate room or, depending on insurance, an outpatient center to which they have to drive; the same is true for radiology). Since the patient was moved to the laboratory, the next patient can be loaded into that examination room to keep the flow going. The first patient is then directed or escorted to the checkout desk with the disposition paperwork (as the chart stays in the back or is electronic), and the office staff takes care of any referrals or additional items required, completing the visit.

The examination and laboratory rooms are located in close proximity, and most offices have a physician desk close by to complete notes and make calls. This way the physician has access to what is needed and can move from room to room without traveling across the office, "similar to the kitchen triangle." While all of those who have visited a doctor's office know there are processes that could be improved, the fundamentals of the system are sound. If patients end up waiting a long time, it is normally because the office schedule is not being handled properly or there were several emergent cases that had to be "squeezed in."

Since we discovered that the majority of patients in the ED are not emergent, it was determined that applying the physician office concept of flow to the ED might provide the basis of a new model of evaluating non-emergent patients. We then worked on developing this model, since the ED is, in fact, different from the doctor's office.

THE NEW EMERGENCY DEPARTMENT MODEL

This model (Figure 18.5) does not directly address very high acuity patients determined to be either resuscitative or emergent. Most hospitals are still in the traditional "bringing everything to the patient" model; however, the new model has indirectly helped out the providers who work with these patients, as there is more capacity for emergent patients by removing patients that don't require beds/rooms during their stay and reducing overall LOS. The process allows staff to deal with patients who demand more immediate and emergent care rather than tying up staff with less acute patients. We have also explored and piloted application of Lean principles to improve care in the high acuity area.

The team began by questioning the current paradigm of the "availability of a patient room" driving the encounter with the physician. Then we asked the question, "Why do people come to an ED, to wait for a room?" The answer was "To see the doctor." This then became our driving force in developing a future state. How do we get the patient to see the provider sooner, independent of the "bed" capacity of the ED? Our initial goal was 30 min or less.

Since the nature of express care is Lean, it was decided that we should be able to study express care to begin developing a solution. We took it one step further and asked how we can create a process where everyone is treated as an express care patient, recognizing the inherent nature of "sorting" patients is inefficient and not fair to the other patients and results in wide variations in door to doctor time. Although most EDs have signs stating that patients presenting symptoms will drive the order evaluation, this does not really help the patient who has been sitting in the waiting room as they watch countless people triaged and treated while they are still left waiting.

GOAL

With our Lean project, we set out to create a new model with the following goals in mind:

1. Get the patient to the provider as fast as possible. After all, the number one thing a patient wants is to see the provider (and be told that they are not dying and everything is going to be all right, and/or receive pain control).
2. Maximize the provider's and nurse's time with the patients while maintaining continuity of care for the patient.
3. Improve overall patient satisfaction.
4. Reduce LOS.
5. Reduce left without seeing doctor (LWSD) or left without being seen (LWBS).

Our project charter specified we work with the patients who come in and leave the same day. Our objective was to create the "doctor's office" model within the ED.

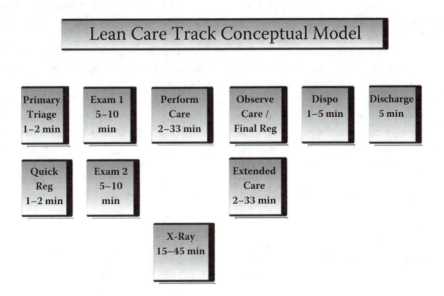

FIGURE 18.5 ED Lean care tracks.

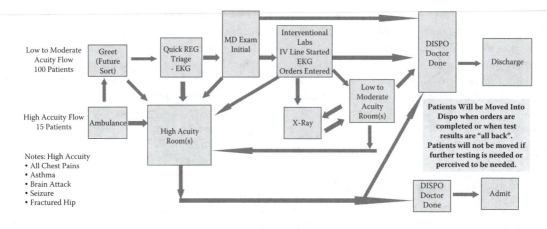

FIGURE 18.6   ED Lean care track model flow.

We created a model where the patient enters the ED and is primary triaged and pre-registered in parallel. (Note: due to regulations, insurance information and money is collected later in the process.) We take the patient's vital signs, if time allows, and move the patient to an examination room (not an ED room). We found most physicians only need a patient's weight. The physician is given 2 or 3 rooms to work, depending on the new flow, size of the area and ED volumes. The provider examines the patient, prepares a customized plan of care and writes the orders before going to the next patient. The provider must complete all the clinical documentation (plan of care) before moving on to the next patient. After the doctor examination, the patient is moved to a laboratory room where blood is drawn, medications given, and orders are entered. We call this "Perform Care". The orders are entered into the computer system in parallel with a nurse who is initiating the orders written by the provider and cares for the patient. Medications, if called for, are retrieved and given to the patient. We refer to this process as "single patient flow" (applying the concept of the Lean single piece flow) in the Lean "care tracks." The nursing assessment was moved to after the doctor examination, which then leads one to wonder if the nursing assessment is really needed. Many nurses would argue that it is, but we have not seen objective evidence to support it other than hospital policies that may require it still be completed. The patient is then directed to x-ray, if necessary, or an area we call observe care, where they wait for their results. Observe care is a new area filled with lounge chairs, TVs, and vending machines for the patient's family members. The area has a room where the patient can be reassessed or medications given. When we first implemented this model, we had to get approval for the new area from state agencies and the Joint Commission on Accreditation of Healthcare Organizations (JACHO). Nurses then reassess, monitor, and check the status of the patient's results. Once the results are completed ("all back") and ready for review, the nurse calls the flow technician or nurse who moves the patient, along with their chart back to one of the 2 or 3 examination rooms. The provider sees the patient and reviews their results and course of action or treatment. When the physician has dispositioned

of the patient, the nurse will come into the same room and discharge the patient or complete admission paperwork. Then a nurse discharges the patient, who goes to the registration desk to verify payment or the patient is admitted and waits for an inpatient bed. Most of the registration process and financial information is now done in parallel during the time the patient is waiting in observe care.

In some of our models, we have another area we call extended care, designed for treatments of 1 hr or less with observation. Three or four rooms are staffed by 1 nurse. We also use these rooms for sutures or splints, which are implemented by the doctor or the staff, depending on the hospital. Each ED room is set up so a pelvic examination can be easily performed. The rooms are loaded by a flow technician or flow nurse. If we use a flow nurse, she/he can also do discharges. The flow technician or nurse's job is to make sure the patient is always ready in time and undressed to the extent required for the physician examination. Generally, patients are moved into a Lean care track in FIFO order with limited sorting opportunity, depending on the number of patients presenting at the same time. In some cases, the acuity of a patient may give them precedence in continuing to the next step (safety and physician judgment prevails) (Figure 18.7).

This new model has been implemented in several hospitals starting back in early 2004. Implementing this model takes time. It is normally a 12–14-week process to bring up the first track with training, education, and coaching. Standard work is created and implemented, and we have found it works best if the physicians are trained in separate pilot rollouts of about 4 hrs each. The pilots work best with the physician spending 4–5 hrs in the Lean track, with 1–2 hrs to "clean up" or complete their patients. The Lean consultant's role is to coach the coaches.

DISCUSSION

This new model was based on creating a process that increases value-added steps for patients and physician while it minimizes waits and wastes (Table 18.2). This required the creation of a new patient care flow model for the ED.

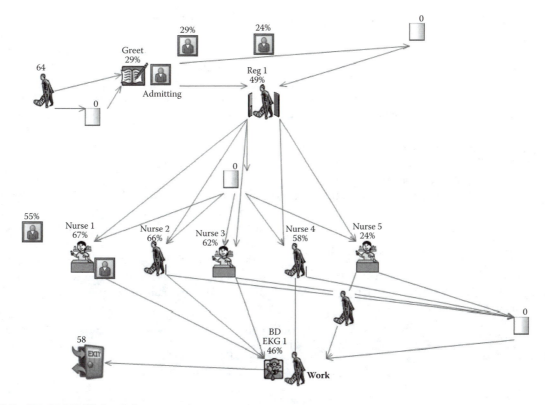

FIGURE 18.7 ED SIMUL8® simulation.

The emphasis was placed on doing things in parallel vs. sequential processing and moving the doctor examination as close to the front of the process as possible. Giving the provider the opportunity to see the patient in a timely manner provided an environment for customized individual patient care to be delivered (thus minimizing the use of protocols). When we first implemented the new model, physicians could not believe how we increased their efficiency

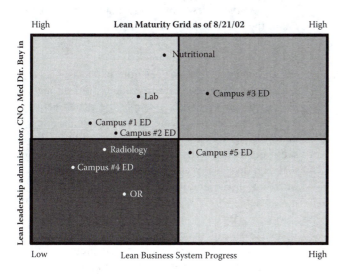

FIGURE 18.8 ED Lean maturity grid. This grid plots a Lean implementation based on "leadership buy in" vs. their Lean progress. The goal is to be in the upper right hand corner. Implementations in the lower left hand corner will have a difficult chance of sustaining.

and patients were happier so they no longer had a need to over-process.

The model also strives to bring everyone to the doctor and have everything the doctor needs at their fingertips in his or her "kitchen triangle." Eliminating the need to have the provider "travel," alleviated distractions and focused the provider on evaluating, treating, and dispositioning the patient. Movement of the patient through the process is critical to the patient's perception; providing the "feeling" of progression through the ED process ultimately drives satisfaction within the ED service.

We have developed statistical models that can reliably predict lobby volume by hour, number of rooms required based on LOS, staffing models for nursing and providers, as well as how many Lean care tracks are required and at what hours.

TABLE 18.2

ED Single-Piece (Patient) Flow

Single patient flow model
• Parallel processing
• Physician evaluation 3rd step
• Independent of Bed availability
• Provider driver protocols "customized" care
• FIFO driven (as appropriate)
• Physician productivity 3–4 per hour experienced
• Staff to patient actual demand
• Patient moves and may not have same nursing staff as he/she progress through the evaluation

We have also developed revenue models for the providers and the hospital. While this model is still technically in its infancy, we have seen dramatic results at some facilities. The single patient flow model allows for "customized care" by the provider specific to each patient. In the new model, we eliminate the need for protocols by moving the provider up front in the process. This results in reduced or zero lobby wait time for the patient.

Most hospitals have now recognized the ED is the front door to their hospital. The doctor's offices concept in the ED is a traditional yet non-traditional solution that gets results and allows us to take better care and spend more time with our patients.

Emergency Clinical Pathways/Evidence-based Medicine

The solution had to make sure it did not negatively impact or impede other initiatives the hospital might have in process related to critical clinical pathways such as:

- Code STEMI
- Stroke intervention
- CAP protocols
- Door to EKG
- Others

We found in most cases these metrics improved or stayed the same.

Physician Scheduling

One of the many challenges encountered when migrating from the traditional ED models to the single patient flow model was physician and staff scheduling. In most cases, physician hours typically do not match up with patient arrival hourly demand for the ED. This is for various reasons. In high-volume hospitals, physicians tend to schedule around projected availability of rooms vs. actual demand. This scheduling made sense in the traditional model since providers were not producing during the hours the ED was bottlenecked. Physicians also have to develop schedules with "work/life balance" in mind or traditional shifts that most hospitals used because that is what most are accustomed to, such as 7:00 a.m. to 7:00 p.m., 11:00 a.m. to 11:00 p.m. They may have been created because of the perceived "busy times."

In this new Lean model, however, it is imperative to align physician coverage with patient arrival demand of the actual facility. This may seem like common sense, but it is not usually the practice. Patients who leave prior to seeing the doctor (LWSD) directly correlate with door-to-doctor time. If demand begins at 8:00 a.m. and additional physician staff doesn't start until 9:00 a.m., then the arriving physician already starts the day behind. Thus, the sorting begins, as then the staff will take the higher acuity patients first (lost of FIFO), and the staff reverts back to the old way of doing business. If there is not enough physician coverage, patients will leave, presenting additional risk to the hospital and the providers. In order to staff the new Lean model, the organization needs to understand how the patients arrive in the ED by hour and how long it takes to perform each step in the process. We use demand models to assist the management in assessing the impact of demand, growth, and staffing needs on an hourly basis. This allows the ED to be able to adjust the opening and closing of the Lean care tracks and align with the patient arrival demand to maintain our metric goals of door to doctor in less than 30–45 min. This also allows physician, nursing, and ancillary departments to adjust staffing to meet demand in a more timely fashion. These models can be applied throughout the healthcare enterprise in radiology, laboratory, and surgical areas. We find, in many cases, healthcare organizations do not understand customer demand on an hourly and daily (day of week) basis and end up having to census staff according to patient or customer demand. Understanding customer demand and being able to offer services (and staff to support them) is critical as healthcare resources become more of a scarce and costly commodity.

Other Paradigms Challenged

- Patient satisfaction
  We found that the main drivers for patient satisfaction were:

  1. Being able to see the doctor quickly
  2. Ongoing and positive communication with the patient as they move through the process
  3. Attention to the patient needs. Most patients enjoyed going through an "efficient" process.
  4. Interaction with the doctor not just during the exam but also disposition

  Ninety-nine percent of patients really just want to know that they are OK and in a place that can provide appropriate care. Most patients want to receive relief from their presenting complaint and get in and out of the ED as quickly as possible.

- Patients don't mind being moved
  We discovered, through real-time patient surveys, that most patients don't mind being moved through the process and most see it as positive progression. In addition, in the old model most patients don't enjoy sitting in a room for hours waiting to finally see a doctor, who then only stays for 5 min or so and then, in some cases, doesn't come back for what turns into hours and sometimes they never see the doctor again.

- Patients want the same nurse throughout their care
  We found no evidence to support that patients were upset or complained because they did not have the same nurse throughout the process. Patients just want to be cared for and feel like someone is paying attention to their needs as they go through the process.

RESISTANCE

Initially, the new Lean model met with significant resistance. Most EDs feel the problem is not a result of their systems and that someone or something else is to blame. We typically hear: "We don't see any need to improve 2–3 hrs waits are normal! Our system works well, inpatient holds are the problem. Laboratory or radiology take too long." The ED providers felt that the problem could only be resolved by building more rooms and/or solving the inpatient problem. This resulted in everyone complaining about the problems but not fixing them. Even after implementation, we had employees calling the state regulatory bodies to review our process. **Each review of the process passed any and all scrutiny.**

This new model truly takes a paradigm shift in order for the organization to adapt and adopt. It requires clinical area staff, management, and physicians to really understand their "current state" value stream map, have a compelling need to change, executive level support and engagement, and removal of barriers in order to pave the path to make radical cultural change. Physician ED leadership and engagement is paramount, as many of the changes will impact how physicians provide care to patients. The ED physician is a key stakeholder to the clinical processes in the emergency department. Their input and buy-in can make or break the implementation.

Lesson Learned: *Our most successful implementation had a doctor and nursing director full time on the team with us. There is nothing like having the physician write the standard work and coach his/her peers in how to work effectively in the care track environment.*

To implement this model will mean changing physician schedules and potential reimbursement models within physician groups, depending on how revenue is currently allocated within the physician group. Staff members need to be completely engaged in the Lean initiative as they, too, will resist, as it will impact how the staff perceive they currently care for patients.

Through the elimination of wasted activities and applying the Lean tools (VSM, Product Process Flow, operator analysis, standard work, understanding cycle times, Takt times, and staffing), the journey and results will be both enlightening and gratifying.

SYSTEMS IMPACT OF IMPLEMENTATION

The model as described above focuses on changes that the ED could do "in a silo"; however, the ED does not deliver care in a silo. By starting in the ED, there is some impact to every ancillary or support service that the ED interacts with or depends on, such as radiology, laboratory, transportation, pharmacy, inpatient units, surgery, medical records, and others. There are many variables or "x's" that impact the "Y's" that were identified as goals and objectives to improve, the ED door-to-provider time, throughput time LOS, and patient satisfaction. Thinking Lean requires systems thinking because all processes are inter-related. For instance, LOS is directly impacted by many of the support services. It is dependent on the ability of radiology,

laboratory, pharmacy, and transportation to respond in a timely manner to the patients in the ED. When implementing the single patient flow model and having orders placed in "near real-time in the system," radiology and laboratory may experience changes in the demand by hour for services. If radiology and laboratory could not respond in a timely manner, it would impact the ability for the ED to "move" LOS and even patient satisfaction. By the very nature of changing the system, depending on what was outlined as improvement targets, all parts of the organization that impact the ability to improve would have to be examined and modified. This is the beginning of the systems thinking principles. Simply, system-type changes impact every process within the organization because all processes are inter-related. Therefore, as one embarks on Lean initiatives, the organization must recognize the limitations of each initiative that is done as a "silo" initiative and should adopt a systematic strategy to engage in subsequent inter-related Lean initiatives to achieve optimal results (Figure 18.8).

AMBULANCE PATIENTS

Ambulance patients are triaged the same as other arrival patients. If a patient is ambulatory, then they are placed in the track within FIFO order. In some models, patients are moved on their bed board directly to an open exam room.

TRIAGE SORTING CRITERIA

It is critical to the model that only track-appropriate patients are sent down the track. If a patient is too sick, they will end up pulling the doctor out of the track and the track will shut down. In the event that the track cannot be staffed or run properly and the wait exceeds 60–90 min or more, then we will revert back to protocols. The nursing director decides this criterion. One problem we experienced is if the critical care is tied up, the nurses will send the patients down the Lean track because that is the only place they can get them seen.

RESULTS

In many of the pilots we have conducted over the years, we have experienced 22 min average door-to-doctor examination times. Some hospitals are averaging 30–45 min or less door to doctor exam for the entire year across the whole ED. In each case, lobby wait times have been reduced by more than 50% and, in some cases, virtually eliminated and LWSD improved to <1% after a couple of years. In addition, providers range from 2.4 (very slow) to 6 or more patients (less acuity) per hour in the Lean care tracks, but average between 2.8 and 3.5. In every case, we have increased the number of patients per hour the providers see by 30%–50%. This makes sense when you consider that, in the traditional model, 50% or more of the time is wasted. On average, our providers see 3–4 patients per hour, including dispositions and procedures and more when the staff can do minor sutures, splints, etc. We have even had comments from provider groups stating that they could potentially earn the same revenue and work shorter hours (shifts). Now that is a value-added proposition for the physician.

Now the doctor sets the "protocol," and we get it right the first time. The patients are all processed through the Lean care track and none are moved back to the critical care area, unlike the doctor in the triage model. If the physician is ready, we will skip triage vitals. We have seen patients get through the entire process in a lower acuity hospital in less than 45 min.

PHYSICIAN BENEFITS OF THIS PROCESS

- Increase in patients seen per hour (normally doubles).
- Physicians are assigned rooms in close proximity to one another. Physicians are not traveling distances across EDs, moving from a patient in bed #1 to bed #15 that may be across the ED and getting stopped 2–3 times between each patient by staff.
- Everything is brought to the physician, including patient re-evaluations.
- Everything the physician needs is available when and where it is needed. There is no more searching for charts and supplies.
- Complete documentation for patient as they are evaluated.
- Physicians are no longer "batch documenting" or batching patients.
- True door-to-doctor examination times.
- Patients are happier when they see the doctor, and the need to over-process them, as in the past because they waited so long, is gone.
- The physician leaves with a sense of accomplishment as opposed to frustration. (One physician stated "I feel like I can actually be a doctor again)

PATIENT BENEFITS FROM THE NEW MODEL

- They find out quicker they are going to be ok and are told they did the right thing by coming to the ED.
- They are happier when they see the doctor.
- There is less waiting time.
- Less overall time is spent in the ER.
- There is a constant feeling of progress throughout the visit.
- There is less over-processing and less pain due to elimination of protocols.
- Real-time order processing—orders are being processed by staff right after they are transcribed by the physician in FIFO.

BENEFITS TO THE HOSPITAL

- Some patients going through this model are admitted to the hospital.
- Happier staff makes happier patients.
- Reduced LOS, door-to-doctor time.
- Increased registration capture percentage (100%, if layout is correct).
- Generally, an increase in volume as word of mouth spreads.
- Reduces need for new construction to add beds.
- Less supplies utilized (you can't possibly use as many supplies in a 45–60 min LOS as you can in 4–10 hrs).
- No negative clinical quality or safety impact.
- Reduced LWSD.
- Number of patients in the waiting room decreases or reduced to zero during what used to be peak times.

19 Laboratories

Laboratories are very similar to manufacturing. In fact, Lean has been widely accepted and often "enters" a healthcare organization through the laboratory.

Laboratories in hospital are traditionally made up of core laboratories and non-core laboratories. The core laboratory refers to the clinical functions of chemistry, hematology, urinalysis, coagulation, serology, immunology, phlebotomy, blood bank (transfusion), specimen receiving, billing and administrative support services. Non-core laboratory functions include anatomic pathology, histology, cytology, microbiology, and other special testing. Some laboratories may have patient draw stations attached and some may process blood for non-hospital clients. Many may have satellite laboratories in other areas or campuses as well. Sometimes the laboratory is run by the hospital and sometimes it is contracted out to a third-party supplier.

TRADITIONAL CORE LABORATORIES

The laboratory process is as follows: physicians order laboratory tests, which originate from the hospital inpatient or outpatient areas (including patient care units, surgery or procedural areas, and affiliated healthcare clinics). Some healthcare organizations act as a reference laboratory, performing specialty testing, from other entities through contracted arrangements.

START WITH A "GEMBA"

With each Lean initiative, it is important to start with a "*Gemba*" to see what is occurring. In most cases, you have met executive sponsors and area managers who have presented their business problem and what it is they are trying to accomplish through the Lean initiative. The *Gemba* provides another view into what is actually occurring in the clinical work area. No matter what area of the laboratory you go to, typical findings include:

- Staff/operators walking and searching
- Idle time, especially when employees are hidden from view
- Batching of specimens
- Large batch equipment, some with automated track systems
- Sit-down operations, wasted movements
- Lots of work in process (WIP) (racks of tubes)
- Long turnaround times
- Separate areas for machines that process specimens
- Clutter, dirty and unorganized areas with drawers, cabinets with doors, etc., with lots of supplies "stashed" in them

- Excess staffing with everyone busy or looking busy
- Lots of inventory, overfilled bins or empty bins
- Not a visual workplace

SPECIMEN COLLECTION

Specimens are collected and transported by the staff locally in the clinical areas, or there may be a team of phlebotomists who collect specimens. Specimens can also reach the laboratory via transport services within the organization, the tube system, or they can be dropped off by courier services, depending on the size and outreach of the laboratory.

WHAT WE FIND

- Phlebotomists collect from patients on half of one floor or the entire floor during morning rounds prior to tubing or delivering to the laboratory.
- Phlebotomists send specimens in batch to the laboratory via the tube system.
- Missing supplies in the phlebotomy cart.
- Phone calls interrupt the process.

This impacts collection to result times, disrupts the ability to process specimens in FIFO (first-in, first-out) order, batches the arrival of specimens to the laboratory, and contributes to the flow challenges within the laboratory.

SPECIMEN RECEIVING

In most instances, the specimen receiving area is located within the laboratory near a tube system (Figure 19.1). The methods of how specimens arrive into the laboratory can be broken down into tube systems (servicing the hospital units and/or emergency department (ED)-specific) or hand carried by personnel or couriers. In any case, the tubes or specimens arrive individually or in groups containing one to several bags of specimens. Each bag can contain from 1–6 tubes/specimens. Hand carried specimens, are dropped, time-stamped and placed into a large bin to wait to be checked in. The "receiver" will take the bag from the bin and remove all the tubes/specimens and "paperwork" that accompanies the specimens from the bags. The bags are thrown away and the information is either manually entered or scanned into the computer system. This begins specimen tracking within the laboratory. In most cases, only test tubes arrive via the tube system. As the tubes drop into the laboratory, depending on the demand cycles, the "transport tubes" may pile up at the base of the tube

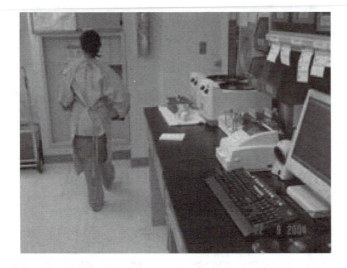

FIGURE 19.1   Laboratory order entry distance to tube.

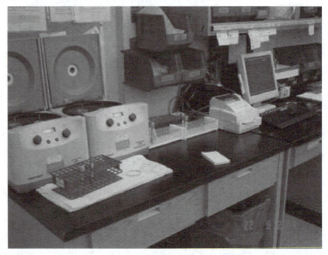

FIGURE 19.2   Laboratory batch centrifuge station.

system as receiving personnel unpack the transport tubes and sort the test tube specimens and paperwork. Each test tube (specimen) is then scanned into the system and placed in "unlabeled racks."

What We Find

- Tubes or specimens arrive into the laboratory in waves
- Tubes piled up waiting to be received (accessioning), are not "checking in" in FIFO order
- Other specimen types are hand carried in or sent via tube to the laboratory in batches
- Specimens are "checked in" in batches
- Sorting and matching of specimens to paperwork (increasing the chances of matching errors, wrong specimen to wrong order)
- Large travel distance from drop-off in the laboratory to where specimens are actually processed
- Idle time (at demand troughs)

Specimen Movement within the Laboratory

The specimens are placed in racks in preparation for processing. The specimens that do not need centrifuging are sorted into a rack and transported to the appropriate processing area in the laboratory, where they are again checked in to wait for processing. The racks with specimens that require centrifuging are eventually moved to the centrifuge area, (Figure 19.2) where they are stored until the large centrifuge comes to a stop. They wait until someone comes to unload and re-load the centrifuge. As many tubes as possible are loaded into the centrifuge; therefore, at times one will find tubes "waiting" to be centrifuged until a full batch can be run creating "lot delays". Once they are spun and removed, they are placed in new racks, and then moved to the next area to wait for processing. When they reach the clinical processing area, they are logged into the computer again for tracking

purposes. Is this process Lean? They are then moved to the appropriate processing area to a technician who will "split" or aliquot the specimens if multiple tests on different machines are ordered. Ultimately, they are loaded onto the appropriate machines and processed. Once processing is complete, the tubes are removed and placed into another set of racks. Lastly, they are transported to a storage area where they may wait to be logged into the computer again before being placed into storage in case additional tests are ordered. Then they are resulted electronically on the system at which point they are available to anyone with access to the Lab Information System (LIS).

What We Find

- Tubes piled up at the centrifuge and big 50-count centrifuges.
- Specimens waiting in up to 27 locations for the next step.
- Tubes wait for aliquoting.
- Lots of walking, searching, inventory, and rework.
- Specimens are difficult to locate when they are in transport waiting to be signed into the tracking system, denoting that they have reached the next stage of the process.
- Job classification impediments, i.e., processors cannot load machines.
- Machine maintenance issues and long changeover times for reagents.
- Slow turnaround times.
- The most frequently used machines are furthest away.
- Laboratory draw stations, if they exist, are slow and inefficient.
- Automated track machines constantly break down.
- Differential processing, which is slow and labor intensive.
- Lots of idle time.

- Constant back and forth on who draws the patients, phlebotomist or floor nurse?
- Lots of phone calls interrupting the process.
- Long turnaround times from collection to result.
- Difficult to find where specimens are located within the process as they may be waiting in between processes to be checked in at the next location, thus resulting in the perception of "lost specimens."
- Staffing not matched to demand.
- Low percentage of morning runs "resulted" by 7:30 a.m.
- Lots of inventory everywhere.

EVERY LABORATORY TEST SHOULD BE TREATED AS A "STAT"

In many laboratories, there are different processes for how stats are handled as opposed to how routine specimens are handled. Sometimes there are even different tube stations for areas such as the ED so that labs can be processed in a timely manner. The goal of Lean would be to design the system so that every order would be processed just as quickly or faster than a "STAT" order is today. If the processes are streamlined, and the equipment is appropriately sequenced, we can eliminate wastes and defects, re-work, errors, staff to demand, and engage in flex staffing the laboratory. The laboratory should be able to handle peaks and troughs to eliminate the need for STAT testing; however, when analyzing throughput of order to result, one will have to look at the value stream beyond the laboratory to the suppliers, such as patient care units, ED, and procedural units. So in essence every order is treated as if it was STAT

If we deconstruct the laboratory process, it goes something like this:

- Physician order to order receipt (joint ownership area and laboratory)
- Order receipt to collect (joint ownership area and laboratory)
- Collect to receipt in laboratory (joint ownership area and laboratory)
- Receipt in laboratory to processor (laboratory-owned process)

- Processor to result (laboratory-owned process)

There are many activities within the process that can contribute to achieving the throughput desired.

Consider this scenario: The laboratory needs to meet a turnaround time order to resulted of 45 min. The emergency room nurse does not notice for 10 min that the physician has written an order. The nurse performs the laboratory collection, which takes 6 min, and then gets stopped/distracted in the process of sending the specimen to the laboratory for another 10 min.

$$10 + 6 + 10 = 26 \text{ min.}$$

If the turnover time that we are trying to meet is 45 min, this leaves the remaining 19 min for the specimen to get transported to the laboratory (via tube system), "received," processed, and resulted. If the machine time of the processor is 20 min, this leaves little room for error on the part of the laboratory. In addition, we have seen tube system delays of several minutes during peak times or if they are not optimized. This becomes even more challenging if the target is 30 min. Remember, the by-products of delays result in.

PHLEBOTOMISTS' MORNING RUN

Consider the phlebotomists' "morning run." The phlebotomists go from room to room collecting blood. Each patient may have one to several test tubes of blood drawn, depending on the number and type of tests ordered by the physician. In most cases, phlebotomists draw half of the patients on the unit, depending on the location of the "tube" system station (utilized to transport specimens to the laboratory). They are sent in batch mode to the laboratory, where they land in the bottom of the tube station all at once. Sending multiple patients' specimens down to the laboratory in large batches can create difficulties for laboratories that are trying to meet turnaround time metrics, e.g., lab draw to result times (Table 19.1).

In this case, the phlebotomist arrived on the unit and began the first patient at 2:58 a.m. The phlebotomist was able to complete routine patients' blood draw within a 4–6 min

TABLE 19.1
Laboratory Phlebotomist Times

Patient	#1		#2		#3		#4		#5		#6		#7		At tube station
In room	2:58		3:03		3:08		3:21		3:28		3:38		3:46		
Out room	3:01		3:07		3:20		3:26		3:32		3:44		3:55		3:57
Travel (min)		2		1		1		2		6		2		2	
Draw time	0:03		0:04		0:12		0:05		0:04		0:06		0:09		
Delays					difficult blood draw				delayed by RN				difficult blood draw		
Total Process Time from drawing first patient to tube station on unit															0:59

TABLE 19.2

Laboratory Patient Times Base

Patient	Cumulative Time		Lab Cycle Time		Estimated TAT
1	0:56	+	20	=	76
2	0:50	+	20	=	70
3	0:37	+	20	=	57
4	0:31	+	20	=	51
5	0:25	+	20	=	45
6	0:13	+	20	=	33
7	0:02	+	20	=	22

time period and had 2 patients who were difficult to draw, taking 9 and 12 min. The phlebotomist took 59 min to complete 7 patients and all the blood was tubed to the laboratory at the same time.

What if the laboratory was trying to achieve an average turnaround time of 60 min? The actual time in minutes to the time the phlebotomist reached the tube system by patient is outlined in Table 19.2. If we assume that it would take a minimum of 20 min for each specimen to reach the laboratory by tube, be received, checked in, and have the test performed in the laboratory, then the first two specimens could not possibly meet the target of 60 min. The next two specimens would more than likely be at risk of not meeting the goal as well. Therefore, it would be a challenge for the laboratory to meet the 60 min turnaround time.

Let's apply the concepts of single-piece flow to the scenario. If all specimens were drawn one at a time and then immediately sent to the laboratory, the goal of a 60 min turnaround would be achieved; however, it probably does not make sense to expect a phlebotomist to perform a blood draw on a single patient and then travel to the tube station after each blood draw. Remember, travel distance forces us to batch! One can still apply the concept of single-piece or small-lot batching to this scenario and have the phlebotomist only draw 2–4 patients. This would not only increase the probability of achieving the turnaround time goal but would also level load the work in the laboratory (Table 19.3).

Results that are not received in a timely manner to the unit or ED can impact the physician's ability to make further treatment decisions or even delay the discharge process

TABLE 19.4

Laboratory Patients Times Small Lot

Patient					Estimated TAT
1	0:31	+	20	=	51
2	0:25	+	20	=	45
3	0:12	+	20	=	22
4	0:06	+	20	=	26

(Table 19.4). Therefore, it is important to look beyond the "laboratory proper" at the value stream when trying to achieve targets, as most processes are a series of interconnected activities.

TOOLS WE USE

BASELINE METRICS AND VALUE STREAM MAPPING

Baseline metrics help (to the extent possible) to see current state and be able to determine what future state could be, and gauge the improvement once the Lean initiative is in process. A value stream map of the "product" or specimen "test tube" through the overall process, helps to identify areas of opportunity, wastes, throughput times, and prioritize projects.

GROUP TECH MATRIX

A group tech matrix is performed which generally breaks the laboratory tubes into components

- Do they need to be aliquoted?
- Do they need to be centrifuged?
- What tests are performed by what machines?
- What is the demand for each test (and demand by test by machine)?

The group tech matrix helps to determine the most frequent tests performed and what pieces of equipment are most commonly used. This will assist in how the laboratory "cell" layout should be designed. In addition, tests that require centrifuges are also reviewed to determine placement of centrifuges within the cell. We analyze demand by hour and calculate the Takt times and cycle times for all key tests.

TABLE 19.3

Laboratory Phlebotomist Times Small Lot

Patient	#1		#2			#3		#4		At tube station
In room	2:58		3:03			3:08		3:21		
Out room	3:01		3:07			3:20		3:26		3:32
Travel (min)		2			1		1		6	
Draw time	0:03		0:04			0:12		0:05		
Delays					Difficult blood draw					Delayed by RN
Total process time from drawing first patient to tube station on										0:31

TABLE 19.5

PPCS Histology Example

Description	Part Production Capacity Sheet (PPCS)	Available Time (hrs/day)	Available Time (min/day)	Available Time (sec/day)	Customer Demand (units/day)	Takt Time: (sec)	Factory Demand (units/day + scrap)	Required Cycle Time	Total Labor Time	Number of People Required
Description	Histology	24.0	1,440.0	86400	990.0	87.3	990.0	87.3	245.0	2.8

Basic Time   ***Capacity***

Specimen / Work Sequence	Description of Process	Manual Operation Time (sec)	Machine Processing Time (sec)	Completion Time (sec)	Loads per Day Based on Completion Time	Max Container Batch Size	Machine Container Capacity per Hour	Max Machine Capacity per Day	SWIP	# of Machines Required
	Cumulative Times	245	33,302	33547						
	Percent Manual Op. & VA Time	0.7%	99.3%							
1	tissue prep	60.0	30,501.0	30,561.0	2.0	150.0	2.0	600.0	350.2	1.7
2	embed	10.0	21.0	31.0	2,787.0	1.0	1.0	2,787.0	0.4	0.4
3	cutting	60.0	80.0	140.0	617.0	1.0	1.0	617.0	1.6	1.6
4	staining	10.0	2,700.0	2,710.0	31.0	30.0	6.0	5,580.0	31.1	0.2
5	signout	105.0		105.0	822.0	1.0	1.0	822.0	1.2	1.2

PRODUCT PROCESS FLOWS

Product Process Flows (TIPS) are performed to identify "wastes" within the process, transport, inspection, value-added and non value-added processes, and storage and identifying, reducing, and managing WIP. Common wastes are excess storage of specimens, lot delays resulting from "batching" on the floors through the phlebotomy collection process of waiting for centrifuges, and having specimens waiting in storage racks because of the distance between processors.

OPERATOR ANALYSIS, STAFF TO DEMAND

Operator analyses are performed to determine operator wastes, including travel distances, the right tools to perform the task, idle time, skills required, wasted motion, disruptions (opportunities for errors), and mistake proofing.

We review the demand and compare it to the existing schedules, for both the laboratory staff and phlebotomists. We set initial improvement targets to reduce turnaround times by 50% or more, and we set a goal for 95% completion for morning rounds by the appropriate hour, i.e., 7:00 a.m. A part production process capacity sheet (PPCS) (Table 19.5) is completed for each area to determine proper staffing and output per shift. Staffing is revised to meet demand. Day-by-the-hour boards are put in place as visual controls. We recommend reviewing customer demand with relation to timing of draw times on the units and expected receipt of results, as this may help to level load phlebotomists' workloads and specimen receipt in the laboratory.

NEXT STEPS

LAYOUT, WORKSTATION DESIGN, AND FLOW

We develop a master block layout by studying adjacencies. Each area is studied to determine the square footage requirements assuming 50% growth, unless other projections are available.

The master layout cells for hematology and chemistry are driven by the findings of the group matrix to determine the appropriate sequence for the machines within the cell. In small laboratories, there may be a "mixed" laboratory cell with hematology and chemistry equipment within the same cell. In larger laboratories, there may be separate chemistry and hematology cells. Some specialty tests may be located adjacent but outside the "cell" so staff can flex. We analyze demand and develop the Takt time. We put all the processes in the correct order and "right size" the equipment, placing it as close together as possible, installing flexible utilities and re-designing the workstations with smaller centrifuges (smaller batches) and 5S (Figure 19.3). Depending on the equipment, the layout re-design in most laboratories is oval shape (two opposing "U" shape cells) or a modified "c" shape, with the technicians on the inside and material handlers replenishing from the outside. We design standup and walking lines, 5S and organize the areas for one piece flow (Figure 19.4). Once we finalize the layout spaghetti diagrams and point-to-point diagrams (Figure 19.5) are used to validate the flow within the cell.

FIGURE 19.3   Laboratory mini centrifuges.

The operators review how they perform the tests step-by-step, the supplies needed, in the order and quantity needed each day. This facilitates appropriate workstation design, as supplies will be in the order of use. Inventory management staff will review and understand demand and match demand with supplies needed. Using the PFEP we make sure the right quantity is at the workstation and determine appropriate replenishment strategies. Most importantly, engaging the frontline staff will facilitate ownership and foster change management and training in Lean concepts to encourage continuous improvement within the organization. The goal is to create flow and eliminate over processing.

In some cases, the operators refuse to believe that the machines are correct so they manually test the samples to verify and validate the machines. *In one laboratory, this manual testing had been going on since the machine was installed 2 years ago. When I asked why, the supervisor said it gives them a comfort level that the results are correct. We asked how often the machine was wrong. The answer was never. Sometimes when they thought the machine was wrong but they found it was something that occurred during the manual sample that caused the error. We eliminated the 100% auditing of the machine and went to a once-a-week validation.*

LEVERAGING CHANGEOVER REDUCTION AND "SETUP" IN THE CORE LABORATORY

In addition to operator analysis and Product Process Flow, it is important to perform setup analysis for loading, unloading,

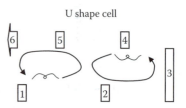

FIGURE 19.4   Laboratory U-shape cell.

cleaning, and washing equipment. This can reduce equipment downtime and increase capacity. *One of our favorite stories involves a laboratory technician at Hospital X. He wasn't on the Lean team but had some ideas on how to improve his operation. He made improvements on the changeover of cassettes and on the reagent changeover for the one of the machines (Table 19.6). The changes made were based on moving internal work to external work, and the end result was a reduction in the amount of downtime of the machine, thus creating additional capacity to run tests.*

Potential 5S projects that can be leveraged in the laboratory:

- Standardize phlebotomy carts
- 5S supply closet, workstations, remove doors from cabinets, remove drawers where possible
- Standardized workstation, right tools, right place, label, organize and label drawers that cannot be removed
- Red tag project to eliminate equipment that is no longer needed or used, to free up space
- Develop audits and standards
- Establish Visual Controls
- Develop a plan to handle phone calls

Laboratories have documented increased storage space, improved processing time, and varying amounts of cost savings related to 5S projects.

CHALLENGES

As in most Lean initiatives, the laboratory can present change-resistance challenges. Although laboratory staff tends to be more analytical, more accustomed to standard work, and has a better appreciation of the value of quality control and audits, there is still a significant "people" piece to implementing Lean. We have found most managers are not used to "staffing to demand." This is, in part, due to the limited availability of some of the highly skilled technicians required to work within the laboratory in certain areas of the country. The peaks and troughs experienced within the laboratory are sometimes difficult to change without reaching beyond the laboratory to get to the root cause. They also require short-time increments of fractional labor, which is often difficult to staff unless creative ways are identified to appropriate resource usage. For example, when you analyze the number of phlebotomists needed for morning runs, it may be double the staff required at any other time. Given this occurs between the hours of 2:00 a.m. and 7:00 a.m., it is often difficult to

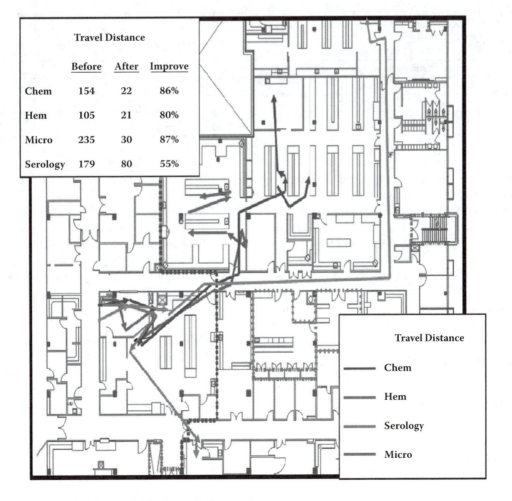

Travel Distance			
	Before	After	Improve
Chem	154	22	86%
Hem	105	21	80%
Micro	235	30	87%
Serology	179	80	55%

Travel Distance
— Chem
— Hem
— Serology
— Micro

FIGURE 19.5 Laboratory before layout with before and after metrics.

TABLE 19.6

Laboratory Standard Work After Improvements (True Kaizen)

Operator Standard Work Form						
See policy and procedures for more detail as necessary Rev None 11/3/04						
Standard Work: Change Reagents Sysmex Comparison						
Job Step No.	Operation Description	Quality/ Notes	Base Time	Projected Time	Actual Time	Percentage Saved
1	Heard alarm signaling reagent change needed—change displayed on screen		17	17	4	
2	Open cabinet for reagent access		2	2	2	
3	Locate empty container and verify that it is low		17	17	4	
4	Walk to supply closet to retrieve reagent		7	7	7	
5	Return to machine with reagent		13	13	12	
6	Open reagent container		22	22	23	
7	Transfer tubing from old container to new container, initial, and date		29	29	27	
8	Place in position in cabinet		6	6	6	
9	Replace cap on old reagent		6	6	6	
10	Locate logbook		2	0	0	
11	Open logbook to correct section		30	0	0	
12	Locate lot no. on container		10	10	16	
13	Removing labeling material that obscured the manufacturing label		52	0	0	
14	Log the lot no. etc. in logbook		72	0	0	
15	Close cabinet door		3	3	3	
16	Return logbook to top of machine		3	0		
17	Initiate reagent prime		9	9	21	
18	Take empty container to disposal spot		15	15	13	
19	Prime completed—ready for run		9	9	16	
	Total		324	165	160	51%

hire part-time workers. In addition, most of the skilled workers do not appreciate non-laboratory-trained staff coming into the laboratory and helping them to make improvements. To use this labor efficiently requires interdepartmental cooperation and coordination. Not an easy endeavor. Many laboratory managers have "grown up" in the laboratory and may not have received training to handle some of the difficulties associated with a Lean transformation. Others may have tried but have not received upper management support to engage in Lean and, when they do, laboratory staff often resists having external consultants or staff involved.

NON-CORE LABORATORIES

Non-core laboratories normally contain isolated islands within the layout and even within the areas. In some cases, this isolation may be necessary but normally it's not. We find:

- Lots of operator walking and searching
- Idle time, especially when employees are hidden from view
- Lots of batching of specimens

- Large batch equipment
- Sit-down operation
- Lots of WIP
- Long turnaround times
- Separate areas for machines that process specimens
- Dirty and unorganized areas within drawers, cabinets with doors, etc., with lots of stuff in them
- Excess staffing but everyone busy or looking busy

TOOLS WE USE

We baseline metrics, value stream map the process, follow the product (Table 19.7) and operator and, in some cases, perform setup analysis (Figure 19.6) for loading, unloading, cleaning, and washing equipment and machines.

NEXT STEPS

We develop a master block layout by studying adjacencies. Then we study each area to determine the square footage requirements, assuming 50% growth. We then analyze demand and develop the Takt time. We revise the layouts

TABLE 19.7
Laboratory Hematology Pilot PPF (Product Process Flow)

PRODUCT PROCESS FLOW DETAILED ANALYSIS				
Product: FLUIDS				
Input boundary	Receipt in laboratory			
Output boundary	Result			
	Initial	Pilot	Reduction	Reduction (%)
Total steps	125	48	77.00	62
Orig seconds	4327	1711	2616.00	60
Min	72.1	28.5	43.60	60
Hours	1.2	0.5	0.70	58
Days	0.1	0.02	0.08	80
Distance	633.5	50.7	582.80	92
Value-added	32.22%	64.12%	−0.32	99
Non-value-added	1.62%	0.76%	0.01	53
Storage	59.42%	9.92%	0.50	83
Inspect	0%	0.04%	0.00	
Transport	6.75%	1.98%	0.05	71

and workstation design. We "right size" the equipment and put the processes in the correct order. We design standup and walking lines, 5S, and organize the areas (Figure 19.7). We revise staffing to meet demand. We put day-by-the-hour boards in place and visual controls. We complete a part production capacity sheet for each area to determine proper staffing and output per shift.

RESULTS

Lean is also being leveraged in more areas of the laboratory and re-designs have been done in microbiology, cytology, histology, and anatomical pathology. This is gaining traction as there has been a greater emphasis to get pathology and histology results back to the customer in a more timely manner.

Reagent Changeover Reduction

Moved Internal Work = 324 sec
I.E. Writing the lot number, exp date on the reagent box

To External Work
Int. 89 sec Ext. 71 sec = Total 160 sec

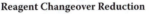

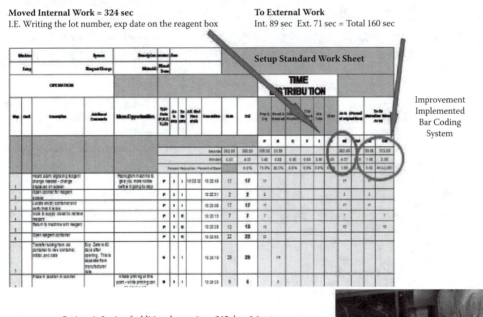

Improvement
Implemented
Bar Coding
System

Savings is 3 min of additional capacity = 365 days * 6 extra tubes per day = 2,190 extra tubes / yr. Plus supervisor no longer has to constantly follow up on log completion = admin savings

FIGURE 19.6 Laboratory reagent changeover reduction savings.

FIGURE 19.7 Laboratory laying out tools and supplies in order of use.

For example, setting up single-piece flow standing and walking layouts for embedding, cutting, and staining specimens is becoming widely accepted. Applying the same workflow ideas as was previously done in the core laboratory areas, creating layouts that provide proper adjacencies to facilitate movement and equipment in order of use, decrease transport among departments, facilitate sharing of common supplies, reducing inventory and storage.

- 50% or more reductions in turnaround cycle times.
- 90% reductions in WIP inventory.
- We normally free up and reassign labor roles and job descriptions.
- Sometimes, we get regulatory relief so processors can load the machines.
- Improved morale and eliminates the need for an internal tracking system, in most cases.
- Kanbans put in place to improve supply chain management within and outside the laboratory.
- Setup reduction and improved throughput on machines.
- Reductions in space requirements.

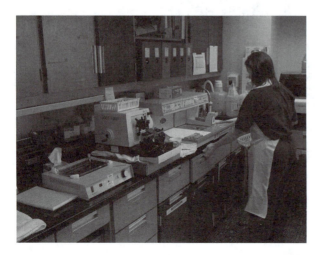

FIGURE 19.8 Example of "stand up" histology line (pilot).

TYPICAL RESULTS

Sometimes we get regulatory relief so the processor staff can load the machines. Improved morale and eliminating the need for an internal tracking system, in most cases Kanbans are put in place to improve supply chain management within and outside the laboratory setup reduction improved throughput on machines. Staffing levels are revised to meet demand. Cross-training phlebotomists should be considered in order to fully utilize them after morning rounds. Standard work is developed with the staff, who are trained, and put in place. Physician rounding times can also be analyzed and laboratory draws can be adjusted for physicians with later rounding times. This can help to level load the draw times. Water spiders should be considered to help "move" specimens and supplies throughout the laboratory.

Results obtained in a ValuMetrix® Services Lean initiative with West Tennessee Healthcare's Jackson-Madison Laboratory leveraging Lean Six Sigma yielded the following:

- Average turnaround time for phlebotomy fell from 20 min to just 6.5 min, a 62% improvement.
- Average turnaround time for inpatient specimens—from receipt to resulted improved from 64 min to 45 min, a 29% improvement.
- The laboratory was able to fit all its operations in 33% less space than the architect had projected, saving $1.2 million in construction avoidance.
- The labor and construction savings from this first project totaled more than $2.1 million.

Even more impressive, these turnaround time gains were achieved *after* the laboratory had automated its process.[*]

We have seen another facility that had funds available to build out additional laboratory space and decided to undergo a Lean initiative prior to construction. The Lean initiative revealed that the proposed laboratory space could be reduced by 40%, yielding a greater than $3.5 million dollar construction (cost avoidance) saving, which they were able to apply to re-designing the core laboratory and other renovations. This did not include the turnaround time results and the full-time employee (FTE) savings that were also recognized with a more efficient work cell.

Another hospital, engaged in a Lean initiative to root out wasteful processes, reduce space requirements, reduce headcount, and turnaround times before moving to a new facility. This resulted in an overall turnaround time reduction from 68 min to just 37 min—a 46% improvement. The laboratory reduced its FTE requirements by more than 12%. Their standing inventory was reduced by 30%; and they found that the laboratory could operate comfortably in a space that was 1000 square feet smaller, yielding a total savings exceeding $628,000.[†]

---

[*] Valumetrix Case Study at West Tennessee Healthcare's Jackson-Madison Laboratory.
[†] Valumetrix Laboratory Case Study at Avera McKennan Hospital and University Health Center, Sioux Falls, SD.

20 Inpatient Floors

WHAT A TRADITIONAL INPATIENT UNIT LOOKS LIKE

As hospitals grow they employ traditional methods of operations for inpatient units. When more beds are needed to care for patients, those beds are added to new floor units and divided into manageable unit-based areas. These units traditionally contain a central nursing station surrounded by rooms. This creates divisions and isolated areas of independent business units within an organization with different needs and performance expectations although they have the same patient goals.

Although these units operate independently, they depend on the services provided by the entire hospital to meet the needs of their patients. Services such as laboratory, radiology, hospitalists, physical therapy, care coordination, and social work have to be proliferated throughout the enterprise to meet the needs of patients located in each of the isolated pods.

TYPICAL PROBLEMS ENCOUNTERED

The problems encountered with the division of inpatient units include:

1. Continuity of care for patients: The patient's typical inpatient stay involves services from many departments within the organization. Patients with an unscheduled inpatient admission often start in the Emergency Room, are transferred to a telemetry level bed, then transferred to a general medical bed and discharged. Each of these areas is typically managed by an independent hierarchy management structure. The patient experience involves many handoffs to each of these areas. The ability to accept a patient on a unit is a domino effect of 1 patient getting discharged or transferred so that the next patient can be admitted. These units also have independent metrics and goals.
2. Increased complexity of communication between service areas: The patient movement between units increases the complexity of communication between these departments and the staff. Many large health systems have a department responsible for managing this communication and placement of patients between units (often called bed management or bed control). This department acts as a "third party" area that requires staff from one unit to communicate with this department, which in turn translates the information to the next unit. Just as the famous game

of "Telephone" results in a confused message, this additional communication often results in mistranslated or missing information. Additionally, service departments, such as care coordination, pharmacy, transport, and radiology, pass information about patients as they move throughout the organization and enter another's jurisdiction of control. This often results in more messages that get mistranslated.
3. Increased travel to and from patient locations: As patients transfer from unit to unit, so do some of the caregivers. A physician caring for his/her patients is required to travel throughout the hospital in order to see their patients. This may seem like a small issue, but physicians who see 20 patients located among seven different units, spend a minimum of 105 min in travel per day. Travel time for care coordinators, social workers, and many other departments is equally as complicated and wasteful.
4. Limited access to services when needed: The delivery of patient care is often random, based on the current condition of the patient. If a patient's condition worsens, a physician will need to be contacted, labs ordered, and x-rays performed. This requires multiple communications and delays that could be avoided if the staff was readily available, or if communication techniques were refined.
5. Increased patient length of stay (LOS): Hospitals throughout the nation look closely at their patient LOS. The Medicare and some insurance payers base the amount of payment for an inpatient stay on the expected LOS of the patient's illness. In other words, the payment is fixed based on the diagnosis no matter how long the patient stays. Other insurance payers base their pay on a per diem rate, or percent of charges.

Hospital X looked at an overall LOS, and then broke this down by unit to find the units that had lengths of stay greater than the expected. The units chosen for the Lean Six Sigma process improvement initiative had a baseline average LOS of 5.84 with a Lean expected LOS of 4.19.

LEAN BASICS AND SIX SIGMA TOOLS APPLIED—BASELINE

VALUE STREAM MAPPING

Value stream mapping (VSM) is a vital tool used to determine the current state of any process that is to undergo Lean transformation. This tool identifies the steps, communication, delays, quality, value-added and non-value-added time used to complete the patient process.

HOSPITALIST VALUE STREAM MAPPING

A value stream map can be performed on a specific group or service used to deliver care to a patient. Hospital X chose to look at the service value stream of physicians providing care to patients in the hospital. This involved admitting, discharging, and daily patient visits.

Breaking this process down revealed many opportunities for improvement. One group of hospitalists was responsible for admitting patients. Another group was responsible for daily patient visits and discharging patients. This division created a substantial delay in the care for the patient and had the potential to significantly increase the patient's LOS. The admitting group consisted of less than 3 physicians to admit approximately 35–40 patients a day. Because of the unequal distribution of patients that needed to be admitted each hour throughout the day, batching of admissions, and unequal distribution of work hours by the hospitalists, this created average patient wait times of over 3.5 hrs to see an admitting hospitalist. Compounding this problem was the assignment of the patient to the admitting physician for the first day of hospital admission until they could be assigned to the rounding team the next morning. With many patients already waiting to be admitted by the admitting physician, little, if any, care could be continued for the patient admitted. There are significant care issues created by the "handoff" of clinical information from one group of physicians to another even in the same group. Also, this wait to see the admitting physician could have significant quality and LOS implications. For many diseases, the sooner they get treated, the better the outcomes and the shorter the LOS.

INPATIENT VALUE STREAM MAPPING

An inpatient value stream map was developed that focused on the patient's experience and process through the hospital. This analysis revealed many opportunities to reduce transport, transfer, and improve communications.

Staff from all service and care-related groups want to provide the best care for their patients; yet, they are limited by the complexity of the systems. Simple understanding of a patient's condition and needs, for example, required communicating with several different groups. Caregivers do not have standard procedures, and work practices are inconsistent across inpatient units.

CARE COORDINATION VALUE STREAM MAPPING (INCLUDES CASE MANAGEMENT)

Another service-focused value stream map was done for the care coordination and the social work department. This analysis found that those providing social work and care coordination services were limited in the number of patients they

could see and the information they needed to perform their job. Communication from this service group to other caregivers was very limited. Care coordination worked independently on one information system to document care, while other caregivers documented on another. This communication method between the physician and care coordinator and then back from the care coordinator to the physician, resulted in significant delays in hours and days. Nurses were often unaware of the work being done for their patients by care coordination and social work.

EMERGENCY DEPARTMENT VALUE STREAM MAP

In Hospital X, a value stream map was done on the emergency department. This value stream map followed the patient through the process of treatment and discharge, or admission. The overlap of this department and the inpatient services was significant. Patients waiting for an inpatient bed created large bottlenecks in the ability of the emergency department staff to treat additional patients. With a high demand for services such as radiology and lab, delays in these inpatient service areas created significant impacts on the emergency department. All these delays created additional processes throughout the emergency department that had to be created as "patches" over the years to accommodate the regular flow of patients coming into the unit.

INPATIENT PROCESS IMPROVEMENT INITIATIVE

After evaluating each of the main value streams involving an inpatient admission, we recommended looking closely at an inpatient unit as a pilot to identify waste, opportunities for improvement, and to create a process that could address many of the problems identified through the value stream maps. Nursing staff, physicians, care coordinators, housekeeping, unit secretaries, and transport were all part of the initial Lean team. Others, such as home health, bed management, and pharmacy were brought in on an as-needed basis.

FINDINGS

The team found a general lack of knowledge among the various caregivers about the patient's overall care. Each group was unaware of the work being performed for the patient by the other groups. Since staff was often unaware of the patient's treatment plan, this information was seldom communicated with the patient. Communication among caregivers was delayed owing to the need to channel it through multiple systems and charting activities. Real-time knowledge and planning of patient care was virtually non-existent. Physician communication with the hospital team on the plans of care was also a significant challenge.

ANALYSIS

Lean Six Sigma tools were employed in the planning for the inpatient unit. We completed a Product Process Flow (PPF)

Housekeeping Room Clean Spaghetti diagram

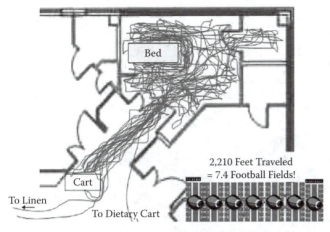

2,210 Feet Traveled
= 7.4 Football Fields!

FIGURE 20.1 Housekeeping spaghetti diagram.

analysis on patients processed through the pilot inpatient unit. The PPF identified multiple handoffs, communications, and delays created for the patients.

Full work/operator analysis was performed on nursing, physicians, unit secretaries, transport, housekeeping, social work, and care coordination. The value-added activities of these roles seldom reached above 15%. Travel time among these groups was greater than 45% of their daily activities. In one case, a housekeeper traveled the equivalent of 7 football fields during the cleaning of one room (Figure 20.1).

Although physicians attempted to minimize travel by seeing all their patients on each unit before traveling to the next, they often had 5–7 units in which their patients were located. This equates to 18% of their work day traveling from one unit to the next. In the same way, nurses were required to travel to and from central areas in the department to obtain linen, supplies, patient charting information, and medications for their patients.

SUGGEST SOLUTIONS

Understanding the current process through the tools of Lean Six Sigma was critical to establishing the need to make a change. Once the team understood the current process and could look at it with a new analytical way of breaking down the steps, they could move into a brainstorming session to come up with solutions. The problems at this point seemed to be self-evident, but the team went through a prioritization process to rank the most important problems to be addressed. Some of the key process problems identified were lack of communication among caregivers, extended LOS, unbalanced workload, and an increased amount of travel to perform the work. A benchmark analysis was done to research other hospitals and potential solutions that could work in Hospital X. The brainstorming efforts led the way to a future state value stream map. This map allowed the team to visualize an ideal model and address the barriers that kept them from attaining it. The solution identified, recommended, and approved was to create a unit-based model.

IMPLEMENTATION—UNIT-BASED MODEL (GEOGRAPHIC)

Two units were combined—a telemetry level care unit and a general medical unit. Patients that start in the higher-level telemetry unit are usually transferred to a general medical unit before discharge. Since this movement is fairly predictable, it made sense from a patient perspective to combine the units under one staffing management structure.

A whiteboard was created as a visual cue for the purpose of understanding the patient's condition and treatment plan. Many departments already had some form of a white board, but it was usually small and only met the needs of that department and the nursing staff. A group technology matrix was created to compare all the elements of the whiteboards throughout the system. This group tech matrix allowed the team to develop a standard whiteboard that would accommodate the needs of any unit (Figure 20.2).

Along with combining 2 units, the unit-based model also looked to combine the services the patients would need for recovery. Essentially, the thought was to bring the workers closer to the patient and open communication between these workers to coordinate patient care. This change resulted in locating physicians on the unit. All patients seen by those physicians would be limited to the unit-based model. The same change was made for care coordination, social work, housekeeping, and transport staff.

Getting the key caregivers located on one unit was only the first step in the process. The next step was to develop standard work among them so they could all communicate and manage the patient's recovery together. The whiteboard became the focal point of information transfer and communication. Physicians, nurses, and care coordination would meet at the whiteboard daily and discuss the plan of care for each individual patient. During these sessions, all primary caregivers were given an opportunity to discuss the patient's condition and needs while delegating the work that needed to be performed for that patient each day.

The unit-based model enabled caregivers to plan together the discharge of the patient on admission. An expected LOS was determined for each patient based on the patient's diagnosis and condition. Within 24 hrs of admission, an estimated date of discharge was determined. This date was documented on the white board and reviewed daily in the team rounding sessions. If changes to this date were required, the reasons were documented and tabulated so further process improvement activities could be identified and acted on. For example, delays in specialist consults were identified. This enabled staff to prioritize process improvement initiatives to ensure a rapid turnaround time for consults. In an effort to balance the workload among the staff, the rounding team would identify the next day discharges and schedule a discharge time for the patient. The work associated with a discharge was heavier than normal and the work that followed it with a new admission often doubled or tripled the amount of effort for the nursing and physician staff. By balancing the discharges throughout the available time in the day, the work could be spread among all caregivers.

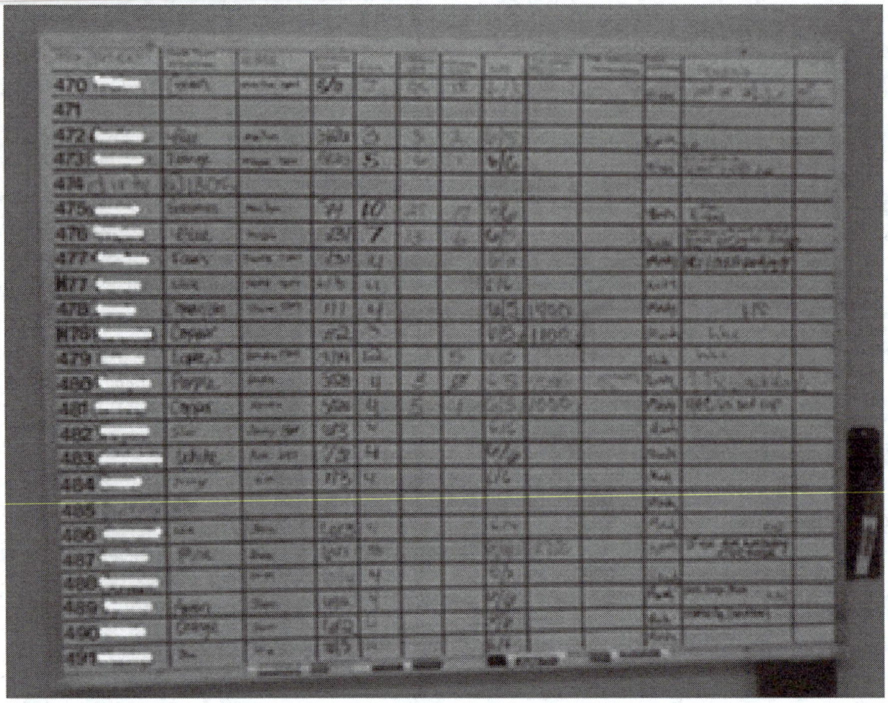

FIGURE 20.2   Unit-based white board example.

HOUSEKEEPING

In the traditional model, housekeeping and transport were located off the unit as part of a separate department. This creates multiple delays. For example, when a patient was discharged from the hospital, the unit secretary would put in a request to the transport department to move the patient. The transport department would then prioritize and assign a transporter to the job. When the transporter arrived to move the patient, they would notify bed management. Bed management would then notify housekeeping that the bed was dirty and needed to be cleaned. Housekeeping would prioritize and assign the job to a housekeeper. When the bed was clean, the housekeeper would notify bed management that the bed was ready. Bed management would then notify transport and the sending unit of the next patient to move the patient to the room. This process was riddled with too many communication steps, potential delays, and errors that resulted in an average bed turnaround time of 105 min.

With the unit-based model, these centralized resources were decentralized and assigned to the unit and worked to develop new work standards. Transport staff that normally had a lot of down time throughout the day were cross-trained to manage 5S areas, stock supplies, and round on patients.

Housekeepers worked with us to perform a changeover analysis. With their help during the videos and their subsequent input, we created a new proven work standard to clean a room that reduced the cleaning turnaround time from 30 to 17 min or over a 43% reduction.

The communication whiteboard allowed housekeeping and transport to plan their day. With scheduled discharge dates and times, housekeepers did not perform an "occupied" clean for rooms where the patient was scheduled to leave. The transport staff planned for the discharge and identified the location of the next patient to be put in the room. When transport took the patient for discharge, they would simply tell the unit housekeeper. The housekeeper would clean the room while he/she was away and the transporter would immediately get the next patient after taking the first patient out. On return, the housekeeper would have the bed ready for the new patient. By seeking input and having the staff work together as a team, they reduced the turnaround time from an average of 105 min to as little as 30 min, a 71% reduction.

5S

We implemented the Lean 5S tools to reduce the travel and non-value-added time by the unit nurses. All the nurses in the medication room, equipment room, and dirty utility room conducted 5S. Six supply stations were set up throughout the unit to move supplies closer to the patients. A Kanban card system was developed with these supplies to keep them adequately stocked.

RESISTANCE ENCOUNTERED

Resistance to change an existing process to a new one is inevitable. How we approach this resistance is the key to overcoming it. We welcome resistance. It is through resistance (or objections) that you will learn the reasons why the fear of change exists. With resistance comes knowledge of risks that should be identified and past experience that prevents current changes from moving forward. If the resistance is identified and analyzed, the root cause can be identified and dealt with before moving forward with any additional improvement initiatives.

In Hospital X, the hospitalist physician group leadership was very resistant to change to a unit-based model. The project team met with them on several occasions to work through this issue. In the initial meetings, the team obtained and prioritized the concerns that they had.

Once identified, these concerns were taken back to the leadership team to validate. Once validated, we performed benchmark and data analysis to address their concerns.

STAKEHOLDERS ANALYSIS

A stakeholder analysis was done with the majority of the physicians. In this stakeholder analysis, the new process was described and the physicians were asked for their level of support. The results of this analysis showed that the majority

of the physicians were highly supportive of the change. It was the leadership that was not. The results of the analysis, benchmarking, and stakeholder analysis was taken back to the physician leadership group. This was enough to convince them that this project was at least worthy of a trial.

The care coordination and social work department had to undergo many changes with the unit-based model. The work hours for this department usually started at 08:00 a.m. Monday through Friday. The new proposal was to assign unit-based employees and staff them starting at 07:00 a.m. 7 days a week. Resistance from this group was a result of staffing capacity. They simply did not have the staff to cover shifts for 7 days a week. The project team was fortunate to overcome this issue by obtaining approval to change a couple of part-time coordinators to full time to implement the pilot.

Transport staff was accustomed to a lot of downtime and some were not eager to be put in a place where work

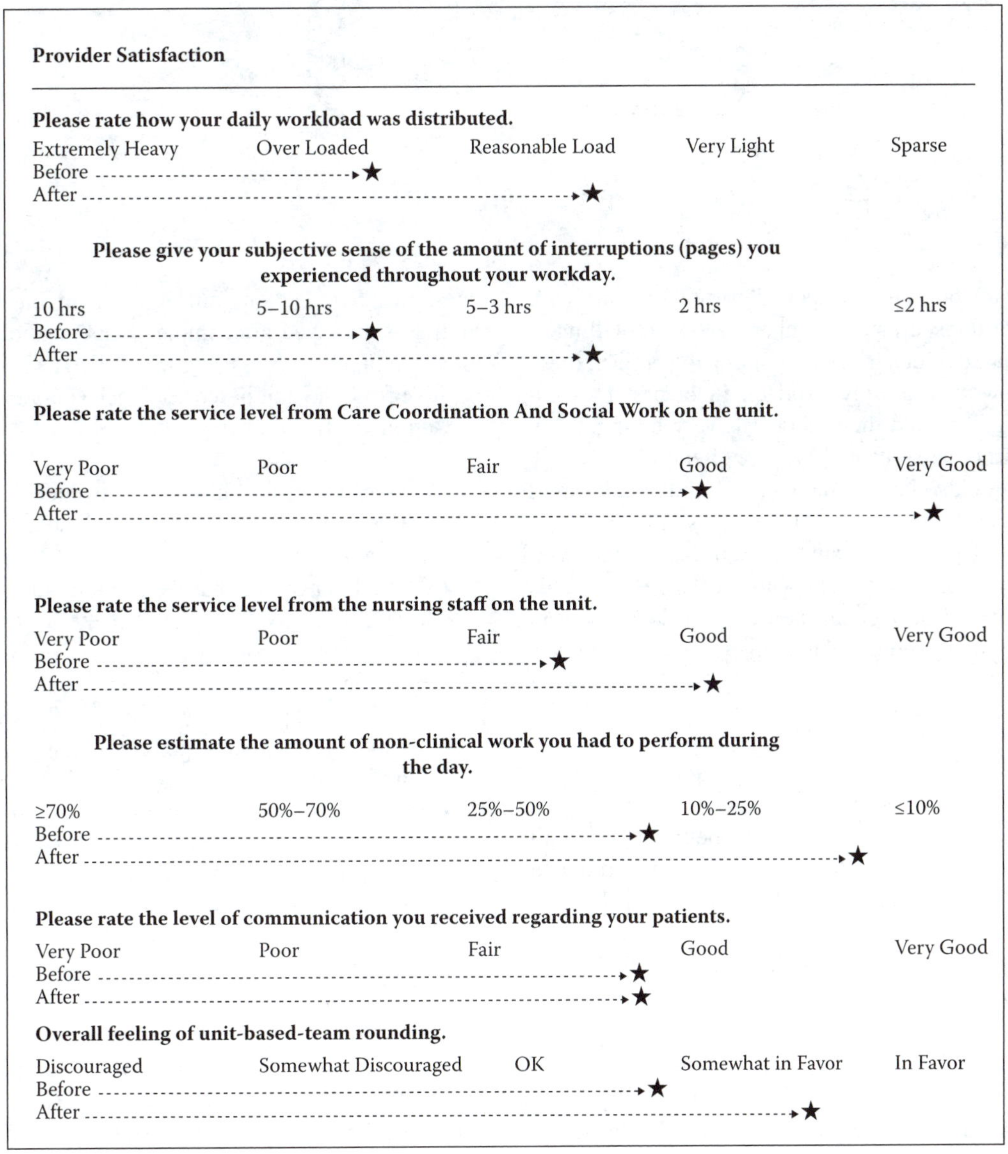

FIGURE 20.3 Provider satisfaction survey.

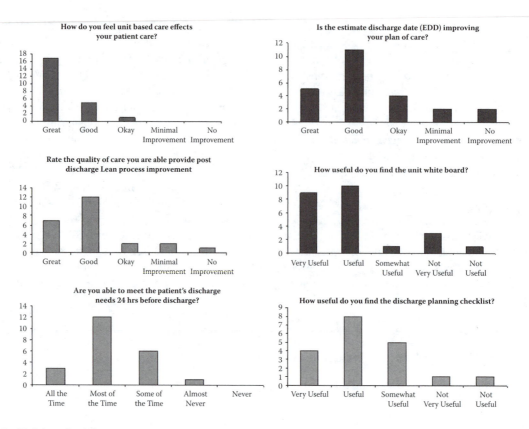

FIGURE 20.4 Unit-based results.

was readily available. The transport department identified a couple of eager transport staff members who were willing to give the unit-based pilot a try. After piloting the project, these staff members were pleasantly surprised. In the past, they felt the days dragged on and their work was very boring. They did not feel part of a team and they were often treated poorly because they "took so long to show up." With the unit-based model, they reported that they felt the days "flew by" and they actually felt part of a team. The unit-based staff welcomed them in and treated them with greater respect. This testimony resonated throughout the transport department in such a way that many requested to be part of the new model.

CHECK/SUSTAIN—RESULTS

LENGTH OF STAY

The inpatient unit-based model proved to be successful with its initial implementation. The average LOS was reduced from 5.84 to 4.89 days, a 16% reduction, within the first month. This reduction freed up additional capacity of 1068 available bed days per year and reduced the hospital's cost to care for those patients.

SATISFACTION

Physician and staff satisfaction was improved. Physicians were surveyed before and after the pilot using the same

questions. Satisfaction improved in all but one question. Staff was surveyed after implementation to determine their interpretation of success (Figure 20.3). The results were very positive from the unit based approach (Figure 20.4).

Comments from staff:

- "Since the project has been active the flow has been more consistent on the unit. Still stressful, but useful in prioritizing tasks."
- "The Lean system has tremendous advantages."
- "This Lean system should make it easier to handle patients than any system I've worked with previously."
- "Unit-based physicians are extremely helpful."
- "Unit-based would be perfect if all my patients were on the unit-based units."
- "The opportunity to dialogue with the MD and charge RN at beginning of the day is incredibly important."
- "Increases communication, expectations, and awareness."
- "I really appreciate the transporter, housekeeping and social worker/care coordinator!"

Lean/Sigma concepts and tools can be successfully applied to eliminate waste, increase value-added activities, and break down barriers, resulting in an overall improvement in the inpatient units.

21 Gastrointestinal Outpatient Clinic

The endoscopy procedural area is similar to outpatient surgery and outpatient cardiac procedural units. The patient is seen by the physician, who recommends an endoscopy, colonoscopy, or other specialized procedure and refers the patient to a specialist. The patient then calls to schedule an appointment, with a gastroenterologist who is participating in their insurance plan which unless urgent, can take several weeks. After visiting the gastroenterology specialist, the procedure is scheduled and the patient is either furnished or mailed a pre-admission packet explaining the procedure, preparations required by the patient, a past medical history questionnaire and medication list to complete and return, and where to purchase items that may be required prior to the procedure.

Imagine you are this patient. Prior to your visit, you may receive a phone call from the facility that will be performing the test, insurance verification is done, and a co-payment may be collected over the phone. On the day of the procedure, you show up and are greeted by a check-in person. You sign the log and are told to have a seat. Then you wait. You are called up to register and provide the contents of your pre-admission packet. Once registered, you wait (normally patients are told to come in 30–45 min early). Generally, the later your appointment, the longer you may wait, as procedures tend to get delayed. You are called by the intake nurse to review your pre-admission packet (medical history, reason for your visit, and any medication that you may be taking). Then, you wait again. You are called back to pre-operative area to get undressed and are assigned a gown and bed. A curtain is pulled and you wait for the nurse. The nurse again reviews your history and physical and any medications and you repeat it all again. The nurse then takes your vitals and starts an IV. Then you wait. Next, you are rolled to the procedure room, where the doctor may or may not greet you. There may be an anesthesiologist who again reviews your medical history and medications. Once the procedure is completed, you are rolled back to recovery, where you are awakened. While in recovery, the doctor will discuss with you and the person who accompanied you, your initial results. The nurse or the physician will provide your post-procedural instructions and advise you to contact your physician for the final report. Depending on the facility, you may be taken to a consult room (for the Health Insurance Portability and Accountability Act (HIPPA) reasons), where you could wait hours for the specialist to complete the discharge process.

HOSPITAL X OUTPATIENT GASTROINTESTINAL CLINIC

A tour of the endoscopy laboratory was provided at Hospital X. During the tour, they stated that they had a Lean consultant in the area several months ago and made several recommended changes to their layout; the consultant also told them they had enough rooms in each area.

Customer satisfaction was low. They were still experiencing backups and felt they needed more Pre-Op rooms. They had just added two recovery spaces, but they were still backing up in recovery, which meant holding patients in the procedure rooms, creating further delays and physician dissatisfaction. On top of the delays, they were being asked by their financial department to eliminate 3 full-time employees to meet budget. The manager said if they had to cut nurses they would have to close a procedure room, and drop cases each day. We found they had been experiencing delays averaging 2 hrs, but up to 3–4 hrs toward the end of the day and needed help from Lean. Recently, they installed digital signboards that showed each doctor's current delay time.

THE LEAN GEMBA ASSESSMENT WALK

The manager took us on a tour through the facility. We asked to follow the same path as if we were a patient. We constructed a combined product process flow (PPF) and a point-to-point diagram, as we toured (Figure 21.1). While we were walking around, we noticed a lot of nurse and registration idle time. They had 6 procedure rooms and the layout was sufficient in that the Pre-Op and recovery areas were adjacent to each other where nurses could flex between the two areas. Registration backed up in the morning and patients had to wait in line. We asked why, and the manager told us there was only one registration person at 5:30 a.m. when 10–12 people showed up at one time. We asked the manager for some data. She said she didn't have any hard data, but she could estimate. The data requested included hours of operations, hours for physicians, and how procedures were scheduled. After the tour, the information obtained was transcribed and additional information was requested from the clinic manager. During our walk, we asked why the patients saw the intake nurse. The reply was, to review and update their history and physical (H&P). We were told it was an in-house intake H&P form that the nurses reviewed with each patient. We inquired if the doctors did their own H&P. The reply was yes, but it was different information. We then asked why they used their form instead of the doctor's form. She said they had always done it that way. We asked why again. Because it is required. We asked, "Who owns the patient?" The answer was the doctor. We asked, "If the doctor does his own H&P and you are not using the intake H&P information for any particular reason, why are you still doing it?" On reflection, she agreed it was probably not value-added, as most of the

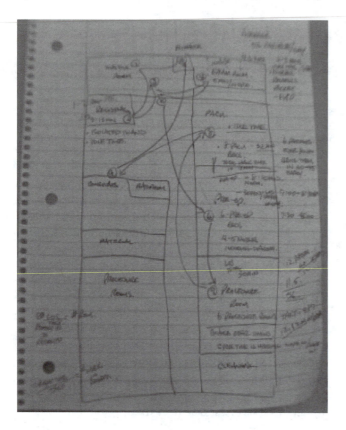

FIGURE 21.1   GI point-to-point diagram.

information was redundant and there was no hospital requirement for the form. This was discussed with the doctors, who agreed that it was not value-added, and it was eliminated. We asked how many nurses were doing the H&P intake form and were told 2–3 nurses, who could now be freed up to perform other tasks. Of course, the nurse manager wanted to hold on to them even though there was a shortage of nurses in the affiliated hospital. The following data was provided during the walk around.

- Registration time: 5 min with 2 registration people. One came in at 5:30 a.m. and the other at 7:00 a.m.
- Nurses worked 6:00 a.m. to 6:00 p.m.
- 56 patients per day.
- Available time = 11.5 hrs or 690 min.
- Patients spend on average 30 min in Pre-Op and recovery.
- Procedure time is scheduled in 30 min blocks.
- Delays average 1–2 hrs in late mornings and afternoons but can be up to 3–4 hrs.
- Patients are called to tell them when their appointment times have been delayed.

What would this system look like?

- Takt time would be 690 min divided by 56 patients = 12.32 min/patient
- 60 min/hr divided by 12.32 min/patient = 4.87 patients/hr

This means we need to design a process where a patient arrives, on average, every 12.32 min and leaves every 12.32 min. The problem was they did not schedule this way and daily demand varied, so we had to look at peak demand per hour. We were told that their peak demand is 12 patients per hour. This made sense because they schedule in half-hour blocks, have 6 rooms, and want to maximize their capacity. So their Takt time for peak demand is 60 min ÷ 12 patients, or 5 min. This means one has to design a system where a patient arrives and leaves every 5 min as opposed to every 12.32 min.

We then leveraged our Lean calculations to check the number of rooms and staffing.

Our formula for the number of rooms equals length of stay/Takt time (LOS/TT). The LOS for Pre-Op is 30 min, therefore:

$$30 \text{ min} \div 5 \text{ min (TT)} = 6 \text{ rooms.}$$

They needed 6 rooms to handle their capacity, which is exactly what they had. We asked about the total labor time (TLT) for Pre-Op and we were told it was 12–15 min per patient. Using our formula, TLT divided by TT, we know that Pre-Op staffing should have been one nurse based on average but 3 nurses based on peak demand.

We then looked at the recovery room where the LOS was 30 min:

$$30 \text{ min} \div 5 \text{ min} = 6 \text{ rooms.}$$

They had enough with 8 rooms because, they had just added 2 rooms even though they were told they did not need them by the last consultant. Staffing would equal 30 min TLT divided by average TT = 3 nurses and peak TT = 6 nurses.

Next, we discussed the procedural length and we were told they scheduled every 30 min, but some could take longer. Once again:

$$30 \text{ min} \div 5 \text{ min} = 6 \text{ rooms.}$$

There were 6 Pre-Op bays, 6 procedure rooms, and 8 recovery rooms, so why were there delays? Something did not add up because the data doesn't lie.

LEAN CAPACITY ANALYSIS (PEELING BACK THE ONION)

REGISTRATION

The problem with registration was the batching process. The registration cycle time is 5 min, which meets the Takt time. This means they can register a maximum of 12 patients an hour; however, the patients show up all at once. Think about the logic of this. We bring in all 12 patients at once. Only six can go to Pre-Op, so the other six are going to wait until at least until 7:00 a.m. when the first group of patients goes to the procedure rooms. Registration doesn't schedule its second staff person in until 7:00 a.m. By that time, the first wave of patients is registered, so they sit idle! But registration is centralized and does not report to clinic management. Therefore, the "GI (gastrointestinal) clinic" staff is unaware that the patients sit idle most of the day. The clinic nurse managers did not realize to what extent patients were being asked to arrive early and the length of time they sit waiting. One last thought: because they run from 5:30 a.m. to 6:00 p.m. and this is a 12.5 hrs shift, they needed additional labor or flex the staff to support the greater-than-12 hrs shift.

PRE-OP

The TLT for Pre-Op was 12–15 min. This means that approximately half of the 30 min LOS was unnecessary as 15 min of the LOS was because they could not move the patient out of Pre-Op until the procedure is done, the real LOS in Pre-Op should be 12–15 min. Therefore, the patient is "waiting" in Pre-Op a minimum of 15 min on average. This means Pre-Op does not pace the process, but the process paces Pre-Op.

CONSULT ROOM

We found the time patients waited varied significantly, depending on the physician in the consult area; however, there was plenty of room in the consult area and that did not prevent recovery from sending patients there.

RECOVERY

We asked if the LOS included getting the patient to the consult room and prepping for the next patient and were told, "No, that is another 5 min or so." This means LOS for recovery is really 35 min. Note: in reality, they were still experiencing delays in recovery, which meant it had to be longer than 35 min.

LENGTH OF STAY CONSIDERATIONS

In reviewing the procedural LOS, we asked if there were turnaround times for the procedure rooms and if they were included in the procedural times. They replied no and that each turnover averages 10–15 min.

Again, our initial data was incorrect. They were measuring the scheduled 30 min procedure time from when the physician started the endoscopic procedure to when it was complete, this part was correct; however, the real capacity per hour is driven by the procedure room turnover, in this case, physician end to physician start on next patient. Capacity should be based on when the patient is in the room to when the patient leaves, *plus* the turnover time, or patient in to patient in. The data that was missing was the patient in to procedure start, which we found was 3 min, procedure end to patient out of 2 min, and turnover time average of 12 min. Therefore, the *procedural LOS is really 30 min + 3 min + 2 min + 12 min or 47 min!*

From these data, we can deduce several things. This means the LOS in Pre-Op was not necessarily 30 min, but could have been up to 47 min.

$$47 \text{ min} \div 5 \text{ min peak TT} = 9.4 \text{ rooms, and they only had } 6 \text{ rooms.}$$

So they could flex into post-procedural recovery in the morning but not in the afternoon. This is why Pre-Op was backing up and they thought they needed more rooms.

So if procedure time averages 47 min and we have six rooms, how many patients can they see in 1 hr? With some simple algebra, we can determine:

LOS ÷ TT = # of rooms, which extrapolated means
rooms × TT = LOS or
$6X = 47$ min, which means $X = 47 \div 6$
so $X = 8$ min TT
TT = available time (AT) ÷ customer demand (CD)
TT = AT ÷ CD or TT × CD = AT
8 min × $X = 60$ min
$X = 60 \div 8 = 7.5$ patients/hr

So this means we can only see (maximum capacity) 7.5 patients per hour. But how many are we scheduled at the start of the day? 12 per hour. That was our "Ah ha" and why they had delays. They had even installed an electronic sign showing which doctors were delayed and for how long throughout the day (Figure 21.2).

It can then be calculated that, on average, 12 patients arriving per hour less the 7.5 that can be seen an hour means 5.5 patients are going to be waiting. How long will they be waiting? We do this by taking the 47 min procedure time minus 30 min scheduled time, which equals 17 min of waiting time per patient, but in reality some will wait shorter and

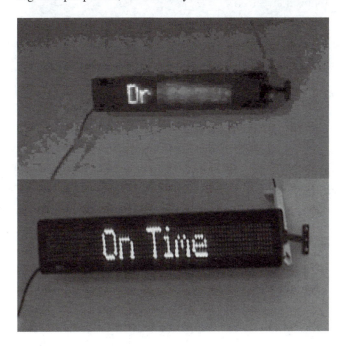

FIGURE 21.2 GI signboard.

some longer. If we multiply the 17 min wait time by the 5.5 patients, this equals a total of 93.5 min or 2 patients worth of time. This total delay time multiplies every cycle or hour they are doing procedures. Since procedure time is the bottleneck at 47 min and wait time per patient is 17 min, then 47 min procedure divided by 17 min wait time per patient equals 2.8 patients.

So for every 2.8 patients, over the 6 rooms or 7.5 patients per hour, we back up one more patient (Figure 21.3).

For years, prior to this analysis, the doctors flatly refused to change the 30 min appointments because they were afraid this would stretch out their day, patients would be late, and they would lose revenue. Does this make sense? No, in fact, by adjusting the appointment schedule to the real 47 min (plus walk-ins), we are level loading. We would need less staff, less waiting room space, less overtime, and still be able to see the same number of patients per day.

Physicians were actually scheduling their day from 7:30 a.m. to 5:00 p.m., with the last procedure scheduled at 4:00 p.m. The area had to be staffed from 5:30 a.m. to 6:00 p.m., but frequently ran over to 7:00 p.m., which meant overtime. If they averaged 56 procedures per day or 9+ procedures per room (56 ÷ 6 rooms), how many procedures should we schedule during the 7:00 a.m. to 4:00 p.m. physician procedure window?

The procedure window is 9 hrs. If we scheduled 7.5 patients per hour × 9 hrs, it would equal 67.5 procedures per day. So, the physicians would not be working longer and patient satisfaction will increase with the opportunity to do more procedures per day in the same amount of time.

The next problem we ran into was that the software only scheduled in 30 min increments!

So the real answer to the problem was not about more rooms; in fact, if we went to 7.5 patients per hour, how many rooms do we need?

$$TT = 60 \text{ min/hr} \div 7.5 \text{ pts/hr} = 8 \text{ min}$$
$$LOS = 47 \text{ min} \div 8 \text{ min} = 6 \text{ procedure rooms}$$
$$Pre\text{-}Op = 15 \text{ min LOS} \div 8 \text{ min TT} = 2 \text{ Pre-Op rooms.}$$

Notice, we should not be bringing patients to Pre-Op until there is a pull from the procedure room. In this case, there was a Pre-Op bay designated for each procedure room.

FIGURE 21.3   GI signboard delay.

Theoretically, the Pre-Op should have never backed up. But it was! When doing the analysis, it was easy to see that the only way Pre-Op could back up was if a patient was rescheduled but already in Pre-Op or if there were several consecutive very short procedures in one room.

$$Recovery = 35 \text{ min LOS} \div 8 \text{ min TT} = 5 \text{ rooms.}$$

So did we need to build 2 more recovery rooms? NO!!

STAFFING

Our formula for calculating staff is TLT ÷ TT.

TLT equals the touch labor time and any documentation time for 1 patient. Our TLT for Pre-Op is 10–15 min.

$$15 \text{ min TLT} \div 8 \text{ min TT} = 2 \text{ nurses.}$$

In reality, with a true pull system we shouldn't bring the patient to Pre-Op until 15 min before their procedure. If we calculated this correctly and appropriately staffed, we would only have a maximum of 7.5 patients per hour or 3.75 patients per half hour or 1.6 patients every 15 min, which would require a maximum of 2 Pre-Op rooms. Worst case, we would need 3–4 rooms if we continued to batch (47 min procedure time divided by 12–15 min Pre-Op preparation time). So the ratio would be a maximum of 1 nurse to 3 patients.

The argument we received was that the TLT should have been considered 47 min because we have to keep our eye on them the whole time. Was this a valid argument? No, if they are not in Pre-Op you don't have to keep an eye on them. The charge nurse's job was to keep an eye on the whole process, including the lobby. This means that patients would be waiting in the lobby until there was a "pull" or request from Pre-Op.

For recovery, we found that touch time (TLT) was actually 10–13 min. Let's take

$$13 \text{ min} \div 8 \text{ min TT} = 1.6 \text{ nurses}$$
$$Registration \text{ staffing} = TLT \text{ of } 5 \text{ min} \div 8 \text{ min}$$
$$TT = \text{less than 1 person.}$$

Again, this means 2–3 patients per nurse. Since the areas are adjacent, we only need 4 nurses plus the charge nurse.

They had 7 nurses with a charge nurse covering Pre-Op and one covering recovery and another 2 nurses covering intake. So with a 15 min walkthrough and 30 min of running some numbers, what did we learn?

SUMMARY

Within less than an hour, we were able to walk through the BASICS model tools. We completed a PPF, full work analysis, capacity and staffing analysis, found the root cause, and suggested modifications to the scheduling system. This is a very powerful system!

ROOT CAUSE

Their delays were caused by the way they were scheduling. They have plenty of rooms and staff. They did not need to spend the $50,000 to add the two additional recovery rooms. They did not need two more Pre-Op bays already approved for another $50,000. A 15 min pull system would only require 2 rooms and 2 nurses! Then, do we really need the charge nurse in Pre-Op?

If they eliminated the intake process, they could free up 2 or 3 more nurses. If we level load scheduling, delays go down and we can increase the number of procedures with less staff and get rid of the electronic wait status boards. We will also reduce overtime caused by delays. Now, we have eliminated our recovery room delays and freed up an extra room.

STAFFING

If we level load, we only need 2–3 nurses in Pre-Op and 2–3 nurses in recovery. This is why we saw so much idle time. We currently have 9 nurses plus the charge nurse; therefore, freeing up 3 nurses, which is what finance wanted, would not have been a problem. We only need 1 charge nurse for the overall area instead of 2 and 1 registration person. Worst case if we stayed at 12 per hour we should have 2 registration people for the first half hour and then free one up. There was a shortage of registration people in the hospital as well.

OTHER CONSIDERATIONS

What if we could reduce turnaround time by 5 min? What would happen if 50% of our patients recovered in 25 or 45 min instead of 35 min? Once we have data, we can figure all this out.

COMPARISON

BEFORE

Number of nurses: 11 (including two charge nurses)
OT: 25%
Average patient wait time: 1–4 hrs
Number of rooms:

- Pre-Op = 6 bays (with active construction request to add two more rooms)
- Recovery = 8 rooms

- Registration desks = 2
- Intake rooms = 3

Patient satisfaction: poor

PROPOSED AFTER

Number of nurses: 7 (including 1 charge nurse)—savings 4 nurses (note: redeploy to hospital)
OT: 0% savings 25%
Average patient wait time: 0–15 min
Number of rooms:

- Pre-Op = 6 bays (cancelled construction request to add two more rooms, for a cost avoidance of $50,000)
- Recovery = 8 rooms (stuck with 2 extra rooms)
- Registration desks = 2 (could be reduced to 1)
- Intake rooms = 3 (can all be eliminated)

Patient satisfaction: improvement by 100%

With all the potential changes we suggested, think about future layout changes. If they wanted to grow the business, we could now think about adding another procedure room. We challenged them at the end of our 2 hrs tour and discussion with the following:

- How would we grow the business?
- How do we improve materials?
- Can we reduce procedure time?
- Can we reduce turnover time?
- Can we flex labor?
- Can we improve the layout?
- Can we reduce TLT in Pre-Op and recovery?
- Do we need 2 nurses in every procedure room?
- What does registration do when they are idle? Because registration doesn't report to the GI clinic, their time is controlled by admitting. We cannot take advantage of their idle time. Shouldn't registration report to the clinic management and matrix to the registration director?

END RESULT

Once clinic administration and physician management saw this analysis, they saw the problem and agreed to revising the schedule.

22 Primary Care Clinics

OVERVIEW

Ambulatory medical care is the most widely utilized part of the American healthcare system. Physician offices comprised about four-fifths of all ambulatory medical care delivered in 2006.* Between 1996 and 2006, visit rates to medical specialty offices climbed by 29%; about 18.3% of all ambulatory care visits in 2006 were for non-illness or non-injury conditions, such as routine check-ups and pregnancy examinations. Because the ambulatory care setting plays a significant role in the healthcare delivery system, it is important to understand how Lean concepts and tools can be used to deliver high-quality, cost-effective care.†

Primary care clinics are one of the most important assets and often the first point of entry into the healthcare system. In many cases, unless a patient has open access, the primary care physician is the gatekeeper to accessing the next level of specialty care. Physician practice arrangements have become increasingly complex. They range from solo practitioners to large clinics that may provide primary care and sub-specialties. They may be owned and managed by the physician(s), a joint venture between a healthcare entity and physicians, or fully owned by a hospital system. The physician relation of employment varies as well, as they can be full or "partner" owners or "employees" of the physician-owned practice, clinic, healthcare entity, or hospital.

ACCESS TO THE CLINIC

From a customer value perspective, the process of accessing healthcare can be a challenge. Despite the fact that many practices are beginning to extend their operating hours, the majority offer typical "business hours" of 8:00 a.m. to 5:00 p.m. These hours are often inconvenient for patients who work or for family members who may have to accompany a child or aging parent to an office or clinic visit. If you are seeking a "routine" appointment for an annual examination, you may find you have to wait days or weeks to get an acceptable date and time to meet your schedule. In addition, they often close for extended lunch periods and shift the office phones to the answering service. This is often the most convenient time for patients to call, since it is their lunch hour as well.

The *Gemba* of the typical appointment begins with a phone call to the clinic, where the patient is usually greeted by a list of phone options. The requestor of the appointment selects the option to schedule an appointment; if you are lucky, you may then reach an appointment scheduler (normally after being on "hold"). During peak call hours, you may find you are updated by an automatic greeting that lets you know your approximate phone wait time or provides an option to leave a voice message so a staff member can call you back—"phone tag." Finally, you reach the scheduler who provides you with appointment options and your appointment is scheduled.

One of the key measures that is deployed across primary care clinics is a term called "third next available." This is a measure of patient access to the clinic. Access is a measure of the patient's ability to seek and receive care with the provider of their choice, at the time they choose, regardless of the reason for their visit. Counting the third next available appointment is the healthcare industry's standard measure of access to care and indicates how long a patient waits to be seen.

This measure is used to assess the average number of days to the third next available appointment for an office visit for each clinic and/or department. This measure does not differentiate between "new" and "established" patients.‡

When calling the clinic for an appointment, the metric considers the available appointment slots and selects the third available appointment as the standard to use. For many clinics, this can mean a wait of anywhere from 14 to 30 days. In reviewing the scheduling practices, wait times vary because clinics can vary widely in the number of physicians practicing in an office clinic location. For the most part, it is found that each of these physicians has his/her own way of handling available appointment slots. Some may choose to offer 15 min appointments for routine visits and 30 min slots for more involved patient requirements. Other physicians choose to offer 20 and 40 min slots. Some allow several 40 min slots to be scheduled back-to-back, while others make a rule never to offer two or three long appointments back-to-back. Some like all of their extended appointments in the morning, and others prefer these types of appointments late in the day. Thus, there is no standard way that appointments are scheduled across physicians. The customer service representatives (CSRs) are also expected to remember each one of the physician's scheduling patterns. The clinic staff members who are responsible for scheduling and managing patient/physician appointment slots are typically customer service members with limited medical knowledge to assess a patient's needs for a short or

---

* National Ambulatory Medical Care Survey 2006 Summary, "National Health Statistics Reports Number 3," August 6, 2008. http://www.qualitymeasures.ahrq.gov/summary/summary.aspx?ss=1&doc_id=10912.
† Ambulatory Medical Care Utilization Estimates for 2006, National Health Statistics Reports Number 8, August 6, 2008.

‡ Wisconsin Collaborative for Healthcare Quality, Inc., Access: time to third next available appointment. Madison (WI): Wisconsin Collaborative for Healthcare Quality, Inc.; July 11, 2006, 6.

long appointment slot. The CSRs may be provided with a standard script to follow, in order to schedule the prospective patient in the proper appointment slot. Clinics that have scripts typically do a very good job of standardizing the script that the CSRs follow; however, the lack of physician appointment standardization starts the patient appointment process on an uphill battle for success, since all these conditions contribute to errors in scheduling and cause delays in getting the patient into the clinic to visit their physician.

STANDARDIZE APPOINTMENT LENGTHS

One of the Lean principles that we apply to resolve this issue is a standard appointment template or times for all physicians. Through studies, we have found that the "actual" appointment duration for short visits has minimal variability, thus the 15 or 20 min slots can be standardized into "standard" or uniform 15 min appointment slots. Our analysis revealed the same result with the longer appointments, which could be standardized to 30 min.

EMERGENCY VISITS

One of the biggest challenges in scheduling is the urgent visit. How these are handled is critical to flow. Some offices leave slots open, others overbook, and some automatically send patients to the emergency department (ED). Some practices are even going to a totally open schedule each day. It is important to have a consistent way of dealing with these patients with some open spots available. The amount of urgent visits, much like ER volume, can be anticipated.

ARRIVAL TO PHYSICIAN

Once an appointment with the physician has been secured, the patient arrives at the clinic and registers or "signs in" at the reception desk. Sign-in takes a few minutes. The patient is then asked to be seated and, when the physician is ready, the staff will call the patient back. Additionally, the patient may be asked to update demographic and insurance information and, if they are a new patient, they may be asked to complete a health history form (this may be immediately at sign-in or while they are waiting to be seen). Now the wait begins! This delay in the patient care process is one of the biggest complaints that primary care clinics observe. It is not unusual for a patient to wait 30, 40, or even 60 min after a scheduled appointment time before being called back to an examining room.

Some clinic management have adopted the practice of 'taking the patients straight to the examination room'. This change, while having great intentions, almost always backfires because the delay in seeing the doctor hasn't changed at all. All this does is shift the "wait" from the reception area or waiting room to the examination room. The result is usually an even more upset patient, as once the medical assistant (MA) has taken the vitals and reason for the visit, the patient is now waiting behind a closed door with no contact

with staff or update as to the status of the visit. They are also cold (often in a gown), and forced to sit on an uncomfortable examination table with no reading materials!

So what are the reasons for the delays? Working with a Lean implementation team, we have observed some consistent non-value activities that delay the physician. Many times, the physician actually arrives late. They may be tied up in the hospital or have just not scheduled their activities correctly. There is often a non-patient focused attitude that physicians feel it's OK to have the patient wait for them. The physician often does not see the patient as a customer who has choices. Ironically, the later the physician walks into the room, the more the patient resents a short visit, and thus, the physician spends more time in the room and falls even further behind.

Physicians are observed searching for and, at times, must leave an examination room to

- Obtain supplies and instruments
- Obtain forms related to tests, prescriptions
- Retrieve results
- Answer phone calls

Often, test results that should be on the chart and ready to review with the patient are not in the medical file. This is extremely frustrating for both the patient and physician as, in many cases, this is the reason why the patient made the appointment and not only does this delay the "day" but also, if not found, can delay care or require the patient to return to the clinic for another appointment. Creating a standard process for following up on labs and x-rays is critical for patient satisfaction, Lean flow, and medical-legal protection.

Lack of standardization exists as to what should be in each room, supplies, equipment, and forms, and how many and where they are located. Physicians may travel from room to room with no consistency of what to expect in the room and where items are located. In addition, if the clinic does start with "standards," often these are not maintained and the labeling (visual identification) is not present. This environment causes a tremendous amount of wasted time and frustration as a result of this variation.

One of the foundations of Lean is the philosophy of 5S. The 5Ss stand for sort, set in order, shine, standardize, and sustain. When applying these principles, the results have a profound positive impact on the work that staff members perform each day. It usually eliminates the searching and sorting that is common in clinical practice. The 5S motto is a place for everything and everything in its place. Staff satisfaction levels improve dramatically after implementing 5S and, as a result, patient satisfaction levels also increase because the flow is much better. It is also one of the easiest and less controversial things to implement.

STAFFING

We have found that the staffing patterns that clinics employ contribute to patient delays. In many practices, the physician is assigned a dedicated MA and team. This has worked well in the past because each physician has his/her own way of handling certain things and having a dedicated person who understands or anticipates the physician's needs ensures a smooth patient flow. The result is some staff members are working steadily or are in an "overload" situation, while other staff members may have a slow day. Also, if a "critical" staff member takes a vacation or is sick, the substitute does not have standard work to follow. In one particular clinic, we observed four different physicians in a pod, and each had a designated MA who worked in different sequences. When a particular MA had some time available to assist another MA, they really couldn't help due to the lack of standardization.

In Lean, we implement a team-based model where it doesn't matter which physician or MA is working with the patient. They all know the standard work and, through visual management, can quickly pick up where someone else left off. One of the biggest challenges with this model is determining the proper amount of staff required to ensure smooth patient flow. During staff observation and interviews, we have learned there are a core set of tasks which happen during each appointment. By establishing times for these tasks and the number of patients scheduled, we can quickly determine the amount of staff needed. Prior to completing staffing, you must understand the patient demand—how the patients arrive throughout the day, if there are peaks and troughs, and if it is smooth or level throughout the day. In a manufacturing setting, we can quickly determine the number of staff members, the Takt time, and cycle times because demand is calculated on a daily or weekly basis and the formula is TLT time ÷ cycle time equals number of people needed; however, in a clinic setting, the demand fluctuates greatly throughout the day. This is in part because of patient cancellations; additionally, there are appointment times that are in demand, such as 8:00 a.m. or immediately after lunch. In order to properly determine the staffing, patient demand must be analyzed on an hourly basis.

For example, the patient demand for the 8:00 to 9:00 a.m. time slot is 16 appointments, and the time available to complete these appointments is 60 min. Using our formula of Takt time = time available/patient demand, we come up with

$$60 \text{ min} \div 16 = 3.8 \text{ min}.$$

This means that in order to see 16 patients within the hour time slot an appointment must be completed every 3.8 min. From this information, we can also determine the amount of rooms required to meet this demand. The formula is length of stay divided by Takt time. In our observations at this clinic, it was determined that the average length of stay for a patient was 53 min:

$$\text{LOS } 53 \text{ min} \div 3.8 \text{ min Takt time} = 13.95 \text{ rooms.}$$

Since we cannot use a partial room, we round this number up to 14. This means that in order to accomplish seeing 16 patients an hour with the current length of stay of 53 min, we need to be working out of 14 rooms throughout the hour. From this information, by simply using our formulas, we can also quickly determine the peak demand per day in order to determine the amount of rooms needed for the worst-case scenario. Now that we have established how many rooms we need, we need to determine how much staff is required to meet this demand.

CALCULATING STAFFING

Before we can do this, we need to know what "typical" tasks the staff performs for each patient visit. This can vary greatly based on each patient, and we have seen clinics get lost in trying to determine the required workload because of the variation. Through observations, we have noticed that around 80% of the patients' needs are routine, while the remaining 20% is actually where the variation comes in. If we look at typical MA duties, we find that they are performing tasks such as appointment preparation, patient intake, shot administration, documentation, retrieving and ordering supplies, and other tasks. The MAs perform many duties, and we could dedicate several chapters to discuss all the valuable work that these critical resources perform for our patients. To simplify our examples, we will concentrate on the above-mentioned tasks to illustrate how to calculate labor needs. Once we determine the amount of time required to perform these tasks, we can then determine staffing.

For example, it was determined that for each patient seen, the MAs had 16 min of task time per patient. Taking 16 min and combining this information with our 8:00 to 9:00 a.m. time slot Takt time of 3.8 min, we quickly determine that we need 4.21 or rounded to 5 MAs for this time slot:

$$16 \text{ min} \div 3.8 \text{ min} = 4.21 \text{ or } 5 \text{ MA.}^*$$

After obtaining this information, we can calculate the staffing needs for the remainder of the clinic by following the same steps of timing each task associated with a patient visit. An additional consideration is that certain tasks may require specific licensing or skill sets. Examples might be registered nurses, radiology technicians, and laboratory technicians. These must be considered in the skill mix.

Next, we look at patient medical records. In our example, the clinic is still using paper medical records. One of the deliverables for medical records is to ensure that the patient record is pulled and available for the medical staff to prepare for the patient appointment. There are many different tasks that happen in medical records in order to ensure that the patient chart arrives in the clinic by the desired time. The typical flow in medical records starts with a printed chart "pick list" 2–3 days ahead of the patient's scheduled appointment. This pick list is given to a "picker" who collects a batch of approximately 20 records on the list. This involves going up and down the storage shelves looking for the records in numerical order. This process of pulling each record in batches of 20 can take a couple of hours depending on the

---

* If we go with 5MA's, we may have to adjust the number of rooms by the new cycle time, which will now be 3.2 min vs. 3.8 min, assuming the work can be balanced across all 5 MAs.

number of staff available to perform as well as the number of patients seen per day. These records are hand-carried to a designated desk to be "cleaned." The picking process usually begins in the late afternoon and all the records are placed on the cleaner's desk by the end of the day. The next day, the cleaner would then begin working on purging the patient's file of unnecessary information as well as inserting new forms relating to their upcoming visit. This process varies greatly. One of the issues that causes this variation is the lack of a standard medical record. Often, notes are loosely placed in the record or are in the wrong section of the record. The cleaner's task is to make sure the record is organized properly, items are tacked down or two-hole punched into their proper location in the record. This process can take several minutes per patient record; we have witnessed a cleaner going back and forth through a patient's records multiple times in order to organize the file correctly. In our example, this process of cleaning and prepping the medical record took the entire day. The patient record that was cleaned at 8:00 a.m. sat on the desk awaiting all the other records to be cleaned. By the end of the day, all the records were ready to be delivered to the clinic floor. A medical records person typically delivers the records prior to the clinical staff starting their day. This happens so that once the clinical staff arrive, they have a batch of work waiting for them. One of the keys for the clinical workplace is maintaining a steady pace of work. Patients sometimes do not show for their appointments or cancel, and the staff will work on prepping the next day's appointments when time becomes available throughout the day. So, as a standard in the clinic we observed, they wanted to have the whole day's worth of appointments out and available to be worked on a day ahead of time. In addition, the staff needs time to follow up on required tests results, such as labs and x-rays. As stated earlier, it is critical that these get to the patient record and that there is an error-proof process to deal with abnormal test results should the patient not show up if the appointment is re-scheduled.

In the example above, we can quickly determine the amount of staff required to perform these different tasks in the medical records process by using the same formulas we did for the MAs. A typical finding observed in medical records is that staff workload is heavily imbalanced. The cleaners typically have a much larger and tedious workload. We try to work through this imbalance by cross-training staff and working on much smaller batches at a time.

Two solutions that can help with staffing are 5S and standard work. There are three basic components for standard work: (1) the work sequence, (2) the cycle time, and (3) the standard work in process (WIP). For the work sequence, we document the sequence of tasks that take place during a patient visit. Through direct observation, we have found that there is a tremendous amount of variation between medical staff in terms of when they perform tasks such as chart or room preparation. This variation causes the patient to wait for the MA or clinician to find the documents or tools to perform the task. For example, we measured the types of interruptions that the clinician had during a workday and the results were compelling. The two major categories for delays in the physician encounter were the lack of documentation or preparation work and the need for tools or paperwork to complete the visit. This causes frustration for both the staff and patient and adds to the patient throughput time. We can standardize the rooms to have the same instruments in the same location no matter what room the patient is visiting. Standardizing the location of the paperwork and data entry has been shown to dramatically reduce the non-value-added time associated with a patient visit. Another element of standardization is the sequence of patient intake. When the patient arrives in the room, the MA goes through a set of questions, such as height and weight, blood pressure and pulse checks and then the reason for the visit. Through observation, we have learned that each of the MAs has his/her own sequence for performing these tasks. By standardizing the process, we can remove many of the errors and variations associated with this task. In our implementations, we have noticed a significant reduction in re-work and non-value-added time due to standardizing the patient intake process.

Part two of standard work deals with cycle time. This is the standardized time associated with performing a task. We use a 10-cycle analysis form, an Excel© spreadsheet that documents the amount of time taken to perform a particular task. For taking a patient's height and weight, we can document how much time it took an MA to perform these tasks for 10 different patients. Based on this observation, we can then quickly determine the fastest repeatable cycle time observed and use that number as the standard.

OTHER CONSIDERATIONS

CASE STUDY—HUDDLE AND METRIC BOARDS

In one clinic where we implemented Lean, we observed communication and teamwork to be a significant issue that led to low morale and poor performance on critical clinic metrics. Staff didn't spend time discussing issues that happened throughout the day and, if they did share their problems, it was with their immediate supervisor, who would then become the hero of the day if he/she resolved the issue. Unfortunately, like most solutions, the problem recurred a few days later, and this pattern was repeated over and over again. The energy from solving the problem gets people through the day, but after observing some of the issues, it was clear that they were not getting to the root cause of the problem. After reviewing some of the recurring issues and discussing why these were happening, the team found a possible solution in the book entitled *Creating a Lean Culture* by David Mann.[*] The team spent several days reviewing the concepts and applying them to healthcare. The result was two separate boards that were posted in the work areas for everyone—including patients—to see. At first, there was a major concern about staff posting issues or problems in hallways and work areas where patients could review them, but after

---

[*] David Mann, *Creating a Lean Culture* (Productivity Press) 2005.

getting very positive feedback from patients, it was determined that it actually improved patient satisfaction because they felt that the staff was working on their issues. One board, called a metric board (Figure 22.1), posts data in real time or at least daily on how the team is performing in particular areas. For example, they tracked the time to answer a patient phone call and the amount of dropped calls. Goals are posted and individual performance is monitored hourly. By simply posting these metrics, the number of dropped calls decreased dramatically as staff knew who answered the phones and who did not. The remarkable thing was that it didn't require any management firefighting; the staff resolved the issue on their own.

The other board is called a huddle board (Figure 22.2). The board is divided into five sections consisting of "What is Going Well Today," "Ideas," "To Do," "Doing," and "Sustain". This board is placed on the wall right next to the metric board, and the team reviews this daily. After some discussion regarding when the team should get together to review the metrics and ideas, it was determined that they would meet every morning at 7:45 a.m. The supervisor initially leads the discussion about the staff adjustments necessary for the day, metric performance, and ideas for improvement to close the gaps. The focus for the group is to start the discussion with what is going well today. This creates a positive atmosphere and helps everyone to recognize the good work of others. The focus then turns toward metrics and ideas that can help improve the work environment.

Then the ideas are reviewed and staff members volunteer to take ownership of investigating the ideas further. The "doing" portion is for those ideas that have been supported by the team and are in the process of being implemented. "Sustain" is for those ideas that were implemented and are being monitored to ensure the expected benefits are realized and the new process becomes standardized.

This new process of getting the team together daily to discuss their issues as well as empowering staff to identify solutions for work issues is vital to sustaining a culture of ownership and accountability for the clinic.

Lessons Learned:

- *Clinic leadership is not aligned. Physician leadership has a separate reporting relationship from the nursing and clerical staff. Goals are not aligned and accountability is rare. It is important to have physicians and staff aligned and accountable to the same goals.*
- *Metrics drive behavior but most clinics do not have metrics. Establishing metrics and simply having a metric visible to staff provides staff with a goal. Recognizing positive results and brainstorming corrective actions provides a positive atmosphere for continuous improvement.*
- *Access to the clinic can be greatly improved by standardizing appointment templates and reviewing how appointment slots are allocated.*

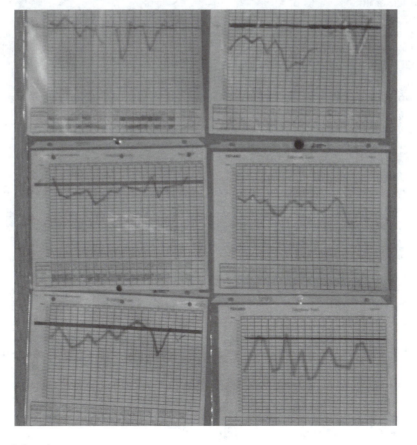

FIGURE 22.1 Clinic metric board.

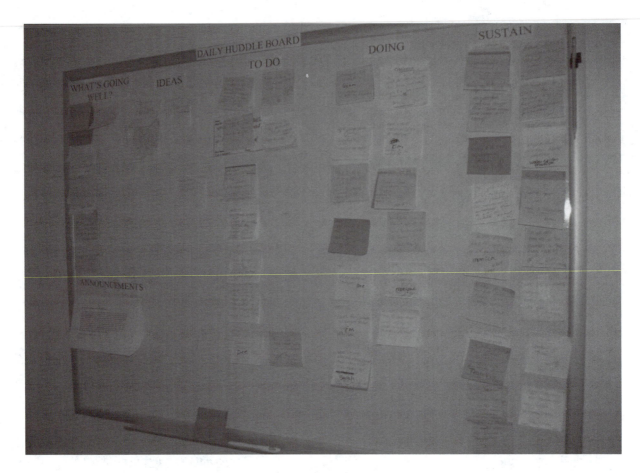

FIGURE 22.2   Clinic huddle board.

- *Patient rooms are not standardized, which causes delays in care. Creating set locations for materials and supplies in calculated quantities eliminates searching and delays.*
- *5S of work and storage areas dramatically improves productivity and staff morale.*
- *There are significant opportunities for increasing staff utilization. Working together as team-based care along with standardizing work allows staff to move from area to area without missing a step. Staff need and want to feel engaged.*
- *There are peaks and valleys with the often seemingly unpredictable patient flow. Understanding demand patterns and being able to move staff according to patient demand is critical to the success of the clinic. The clinic must also have a process to deal with urgent and emergent patient needs.*
- *Managers need to become more comfortable with cross-training staff and calculating the proper amount of staff required based on patient demand and time of day.*
- *The medical records staff plays a significant role in the success of the clinic. Determining the proper amount of staff, cycle times, and reducing the batch sizes allow the clinic to function with a smooth flow of information.*
- *Phone calls for information, test results, and refills are a significant part of any practice, and a process must be developed that does not affect current patient visits.*
- *Standardizing pick up and drop off times for medical records throughout the clinic must happen in order for the entire site to benefit from reduced batch sizes.*
- *Standard work needs to be deployed for staff to ensure that tasks are done related to patient preparation, i.e., results are obtained, medical records available for the patient visit. In addition, implementing standards helps cross-training and the ability to flex staff throughout the clinic.*
- *Teamwork is critical for the success of the clinic. Leadership needs to provide support and coaching for their staff rather than taking on all of the problem solving themselves.*
- *Training staff members in problem solving and providing recognition for a job well done establish the foundation for a successful clinic.*

In one clinic,* videotaping revealed a startling degree of waste. For example, only 10.4% of an MA's activity added value to

---

* ValuMetrix® Services Lean Case Study, San Mateo Clinic of Presbyterian Healthcare Services.

the process, while 80.3% went to moving things around and checking for errors, or was simply unnecessary. In addition, owing to inconsistent answering of calls, the delays began as soon as patients called for an appointment. Only 25%–40% of calls were answered within 1 min. The team began by measuring and posting how many calls each scheduler answered and how much they were contributing to the percentage of calls answered in less than 1 min. Posting these metrics also revealed disparities in productivity. Some schedulers were answering 100 calls a day, while others took just 20.

Additional changes included:

- Eliminating the sign-in sheet and having registrars enter arrivals directly into the computer system
- Adopting a standard procedure for prepping charts before a patient's arrival
- Handing paperwork back to arriving patients and having them carry it into the examination room themselves
- Installing racks so medical records can be processed from left to right instead of top to bottom
- Working with the staff to formulate and post the optimal way to perform each task, including prepping files for the doctor
- Delivering files as they arrive to doctors
- Establishing a permanent location for frequently needed instruments and supplies within each examination room

- Taking down walls between work areas to allow a clear field of vision of what is happening in each area

RESULTS ACHIEVED[*]

- The clinic is handling as many as 46 additional appointments each week.
- The percentage of calls answered within 1 min has risen from 40% to 80%–90%.
- Average patient cycle time has fallen from 128 min to just 20 min, an 84% improvement.
- Nearly all prescription refills are now completed the same day.
- The clinic reduced hours worked by the equivalent of 6.5 full-time employees, saving an estimated $201,500 per year.
- During flu shot season, the clinic reduced its use of overtime to save an additional $34,990.
- Employee turnover fell from 30% a quarter to less than 3%.

Lean concepts and tools can be applied to clinics to improve flow, reduce errors and re-work, eliminate waste, and add value to the patient clinic experience.

[*] ValuMetrix® Services Lean Case Study, San Mateo Clinic of Presbyterian Healthcare Services.

23 Radiology

TRADITIONAL FLOW

The traditional suppliers of radiology are:

- Outpatients
- Inpatients
- Emergency department (ED) patients to X-ray
- X-ray to ED patients

From the radiology perspective, the patient has to be scheduled, registered, insurance verified, documentation created, computer system updated, and X-ray or other diagnostic test performed. Outpatients are referred by their general practitioner or a specialist to either an outpatient radiology clinic or a radiology department within a hospital. Some radiology tests require pre-certification that may occur over the phone. X-rays (or tests), whether film or digital (PACS), may undergo a preliminary review by a physician if the radiologist is not available and are ultimately read and dictated by a radiologist. The process is generally as follows:

- Appointment made (prior to or at site)
- Prior to arrival ensure insurance coverage, if test pre-scheduled
- Arrive in department
- Sign in department and present the physician order unless it had been faxed or sent via another method
- Wait
- Insurance verification, co-pay may be collected and paperwork completed for registration
- Wait
- Called back and change into gown
- Test performed
- Change out of gown
- Check back with physician for results

Inpatient and ED patients follow similar processes. An order is written by the physician or the order is driven by physician protocols in the ED. The floors or ED then calls transport (which is centralized) to come and get the patient. The patient waits until transport shows up or, in some cases, nurses may transport the patient to the radiology department, depending on the patient's need. Note: all these delays add to overall length of stay (LOS).

Once the patient arrives, he or she is signed in (registered). The patient then waits for the X-ray procedure. Once the X-ray is completed and verified, transport is called to take the patient back to the ED or the floor. Again, the patient spends most of the time waiting.

STORY CHARLIE PROTZMAN'S JOURNAL

During a physical, the doctor told Charlie he needed an X-ray. They told him which facility his insurance would accept and that it was one of the best in the area. Charlie decided to keep this journal of his visit:

> *I looked at my watch and noticed I was behind but knew I could still make the appointment time (when I called, I was told I needed to be on time or they would reschedule me!) I rushed to the door right on time. When I walked up to the counter, I stood and waited for someone to acknowledge my presence. A couple of the people from behind the desk looked up at me but no one said a word, so I then looked around and saw the sign-in sheet. I signed in and walked back the 6 feet to the waiting area and sat down. I waited for 5.6 min until I was called by the front desk person to check in. I handed over my insurance information and co-pay. Then I was told to sit back down and wait until called to the back. Exactly 22.1 min went by until I was called to the back. I was escorted to a small dressing room where I was told to undress and put on a gown. Then I waited for another 12.6 min in this small room, with no magazine and nothing to do but look at the walls and listen to see if I could hear anything. Then I was called back to the X-ray room. I walked out, initially not sure which way to go, when I was taken to yet another small room for another 8.8 min while the current patient finished. Finally, I was called back and the X-ray tech escorted me to the X-ray room. The tech or radiologist positioned me and took the X-ray. I was then asked to wait until they verified the X-ray was good (10.3 min). I was then sent back to the changing room to get dressed (2.3 min). My last trip was to the counter to check out (1.2 min). Total time: 62.9 min, Value-added equaled none, or one could argue seconds for the X-ray and a couple of minutes once I heard the results from my doctor.*

The clinic and hospital processes are similar, although hospital-based systems seem to be more complex for some reason. Let's look at the clinics first.

HEALTH INSURANCE PORTABILITY AND ACCOUNTABILITY ACT AND LEAN

The patient shows up at the outpatient radiology clinic and goes to the check-in desk. They are told by a human or a sign, to sign in the Health Insurance Portability and Accountability Act (HIPPA)-protected sign-in sheet. They lift up the sheet to sign it and see everyone else's name! They think sarcastically, "Good thing the sheet is covered."

We have seen signs in radiology clinics that state to "wait here for patient privacy reasons," yet the whole lobby can hear everything being said.

Here is another example from Charlie Protzman's journal:

I had to go to a clinic for a drug test required by a client. It had to be done in a hurry since I was due to fly out the next day. The clinic was very gracious to schedule me; however, I ran into a problem because the fact my client required a drug test was not enough – I had to get it ordered by my doctor. So I was standing in the back ready for them to draw my blood when it was put on hold because the nurse had asked her supervisor this question. I was told to go back to the waiting room, where I tried to reach my client and get them in contact with my physician and the clinic. When I got my client (who was paying for the test) on my cell phone, I went back to the nurse at the reception desk and gave her the name of my client and contact on the phone. Meanwhile, a lady walked in and was standing next to me to check in. The nurse handed me the phone and said they now had what they needed for my drug test. The lady next to me told me, 'They just violated my HIPPA rights.' I told her that these folks had just bent over backward with very little notice late in the day to help me out and that because she now knew I was taking a drug test was not a concern to me.

Lesson Learned: *HIPPA, at times, becomes an excuse throughout the hospital environment to justify and not correct the red tape and bureaucracy that exists. This is, in part, because everyone has a different interpretation of HIPPA. There are varying opinions of what has to be done to meet the HIPPA or State rules. Processes are often put in place based on someone's belief of what should be done, which leads to the waste of over processing. We need to review how we implement processes that involve HIPPA compliance to make sure that it is value-added and doesn't add unnecessary waste.*

WHAT WE FIND IN RADIOLOGY

Regardless of the starting point, from the patient perspective, most of their time (90% or so) is spent waiting. We have been in many radiology departments that view and treat outpatients and inpatients differently and, unless it is an emergency, outpatients tend to get priority. What we have observed is that outpatients are more vocal if left waiting, and inpatients often don't know their appointment time and may not have a frame of reference from which to gauge their wait, or may be too ill to complain. Because inpatients tend to wait longer, their LOS expends costs on more materials and supplies. In some cases, the wait time means they miss the hospitalist rounding, which can delay their stay by another day.

This inpatient/outpatient priority presents a significant opportunity in many hospitals. Usually outpatients get scheduled in the early morning and afternoon, and the inpatients get slipped in late in the day when they run out of outpatient procedures. Why? Because the department is judged on how much revenue it brings in. They get paid for outpatients; inpatients do not add revenue to the radiology department. Inpatient revenues are often under global payments to the hospital, i.e., diagnosis-related groups (DRGs), so inpatients get the lowest priority.

This is, of course, completely illogical since a hospital day (LOS) is very expensive and the delay of an X-ray or CT/MRI can easily add a day to LOS. Forcing the radiology department to reprioritize the scheduling while looking at the big picture is an easy fix.

In addition, hospitals need to be more cognizant of the fact that the patient's experience begins when he/she enters the parking lot.

The radiology department in Hospital X had worked on eliminating internal wastes related to wait times and throughput, but despite their efforts, they continued to receive below average ratings for customer satisfaction. They decided to redo their value stream, this time starting it at scheduling instead of check-in and asking "why" five times for each step. They identified that patients had a difficult time finding not only a parking spot but also the radiology area within the hospital, creating an unsatisfactory perception of the radiology department before they even arrived. Insult was added to injury when they had to pay the parking attendant.

Lesson Learned: *There needs to be a greater awareness that customers don't view the hospital experience in silos. Perception starts at the point of entry or first contact. This could be scheduling an appointment or entering the parking garage. The customer value stream and the identification of value and satisfaction are NOT limited to the service provided by the clinical or non-clinical area. One must consider the entire value stream and ask why five times to get to the root of the waste and problems.*

TOOLS WE USE

We start with baselining metrics, looking at demand and available time, and calculating the Takt time. We then look at cycle times for the patient and turnaround times between patients. We also look at the cycle time of request to result for both X-ray and portable X-ray processes. Next, we value stream map (VSM) the process.

VALUE STREAM MAP—OUTPATIENTS, INPATIENTS, EMERGENCY DEPARTMENT PATIENTS TO X-RAY

In the VSMs shown, we normally find that most of the time the patient spends in the process is storage (Figure 23.1). In the information flow, there is normally a lengthy time between request for X-ray and presenting for X-ray and then another delay between X-ray taken and X-ray read. All these delays contribute to overall LOS delays in the ED or on the floors.

Current State Value Stream Map

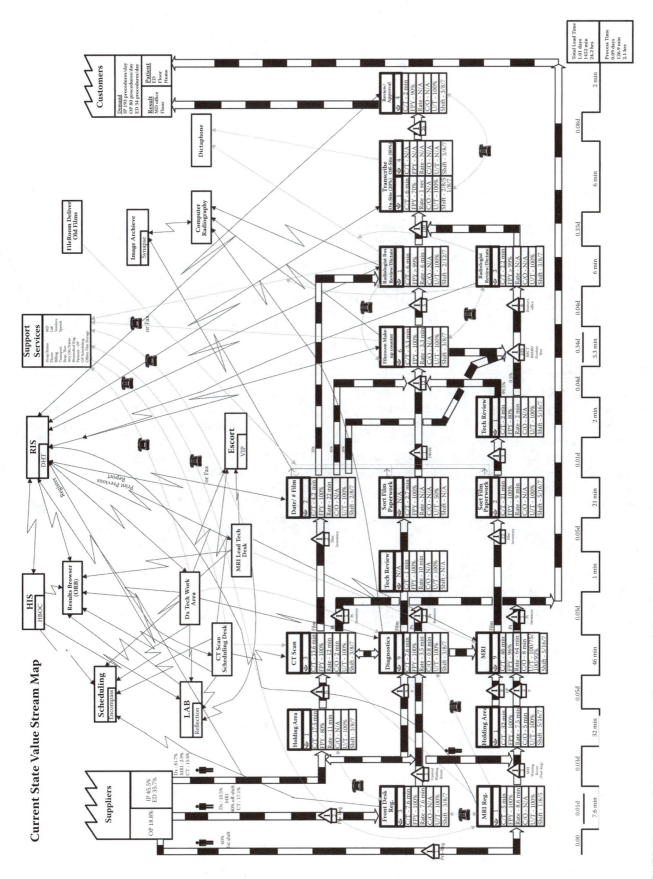

FIGURE 23.1 Radiology VSM. Note: Every triangle is storage!

PRODUCT PROCESS FLOW

What part of the flow is value-added for the patient? Since X-rays are a diagnostic tool, the answer, technically speaking, is none of it! X-ray is really inspection. We are trying to figure out whether or not something is wrong and, if so, where. So, the X-ray process, from the patient's point of view, is not considered value-added. We are not physically changing the patient and the X-rays are not always done right the first time and sometimes are not needed.

The results from the X-rays, once read, are not value-added until the physician turns them into a diagnosis and treatment if indicated or notification to the patient of their results. If we are following the X-ray process vs. the patient, one could argue the X-ray itself is value-added.

The product, which in this case is the patient is followed. We also follow the information flow, which is the request for X-ray to results. The radiology technicians, radiologists, and any support staff are videotaped during both the patient visit and changeover for the next patient, as they all play a significant contribution to throughput, capacity, and revenue.

OPERATOR FULL WORK ANALYSIS

We find that the technicians are normally busy most of the time, but are they performing value-added activities? If we are looking at the X-ray process itself, most of their time is non-value-added. One could argue, again following just the X-ray process, that only taking the X-ray is really value-added. Loading the patient onto a machine or positioning them on the machine is not value-added, but it is necessary.

STANDARD WORK

Once again, we film the X-ray technicians to understand their job and conduct a full work analysis. The videotapes are reviewed with the technicians, documenting their existing steps, and discussing improvements in the process steps. Next, the operator analysis will provide us with the total labor time (TLT), which we use to calculate staffing. Then we create their standard work. It is important to create and deploy (train) standard work and post it in the area.

TURNAROUND TIMES AND CALCULATIONS

This is normally the area that has the biggest opportunity for X-ray. By reducing the turnaround time between patients, we can immediately see an increase in available capacity. If we have enough demand, reduce our turnaround times, and revise our scheduling model, we can significantly increase our patient visits, asset utilization, and revenue.

Once again, all our formulas come into play. Here is an example of the relationship between the radiology department and the emergency room:

- Average daily demand for radiology, both inpatients and outpatients (including ED) = 204 patients
- Outpatients demand = 54
- Inpatients and ED demand = 150

The available time for radiology procedures related to ED and inpatient is 24 hrs (1440 min)

Outpatients are typically only performed from 8:00 a.m. to 5:00 p.m.; therefore, the available time is 9 hrs or 540 min

The LOS for all patients averages 25 min per patient
Turnover time = 10 min per patient
TLT = 25 min

We would calculate our Takt times as follows:

- Takt time for both the ED and inpatient radiology demand is

1440 min (available time) ÷ 150 (patient demand) = 9.6 min

- Takt time for just outpatient from 8:00 a.m. to 5:00 p.m. is

540 min (available time) ÷ 54 (customer demand) = 10 min

- Overall Takt time is

1440 min/day ÷ 204 patients/day or 7.059 min per patient

To calculate the number of radiology procedural rooms for outpatients, utilize the following:

- LOS divided by the TT or 25 min ÷ 10 min or 2.5 rooms

For the ED and inpatient:

- LOS/TT or 25 min ÷ 9.6 min = 2.6 rooms

Total number of rooms for inpatient, ED, and outpatient:

Total of 2.6 + 2.5 = 5.1 rooms or rounded up to 6 rooms during the hours of 8:00 a.m. and 5:00 p.m.

What portion of one room will be idle?

Answer: 6 rooms − 5.1 rooms = 0.9 rooms

If we only had 5 rooms available during the hours of 8:00 a.m. and 5:00 p.m., there would be times when patients would wait for their procedure. In order for the bottleneck not to occur, we would need to have the following:

0.1 of a room for either outpatient or inpatient

We often find, through analysis, that there is opportunity to eliminate waste in room turnover. If we could reduce turnover time by 1 min, how many rooms would we need?

- LOS/TT = 15 min procedure + 9 min turnover = 24 min LOS/9.6 TT = 2.59 rooms
- LOS/TT = 15 min procedure + 9 min turnover = 24 min LOS/10 min TT = 2.4 rooms

Total rooms needed with a 1 min reduction in turnover:

- 2.4 rooms + 2.59 rooms = 4.99 rooms

Another way to look at turnover time in this example is that turnover time is 40% (10 min /25 min) of procedure time. This means that for every 2.5 X-rays, we lose one full X-ray to changeover or setup time. What if we could get the setup time down from 10 to 5 min?

If the procedure time is 15 min, this means that for every 4 procedures ($20 \div 5 = 4$), we pick up capacity to do an additional X-ray procedure. If the demand is 54 procedures a day, this means we can pick up $54 \times 25 = 1350$ min $\div 20$ min = 67.5 procedures or 13.5 additional X-rays per day.

CREATING THE BENEFIT— INCREASING CAPACITY

If we could add the potential to do 13.5 additional X-rays per day, then we could conservatively quantify potential revenue for backfill as follows:

Assumptions: Monday through Friday operating 20.5 days per month, outpatients only
13.5 tests per day × 20.5 days per month = 277 additional radiology examinations per month
or
277 × 12 months = 3324 per year

If the net revenue per test was $35, this could yield an additional $116,340 per year (consider the revenue potential if this was applied to MRI or CT, where the potential revenue is significantly more).

As stated earlier, it is also important to include inpatient LOS as a financial benefit. If TAT for inpatients improves, this can have dramatic effects on LOS, but it is harder to qualitate financially.

Lesson Learned: *Hospital "X" performed a Lean Sigma project where they were able to show improvements that reduced throughput through the radiology department and the ability to do three more cases per day. However, the revenue was never achieved because a plan to "backfill" the freed-up capacity $20 \div 5 = 4$ was never put in place. Engaging marketing to create a plan to increase volume early in projects that create capacity is key to recognizing the benefits and return on investment.*

One can see the impact of turnover time on the number of rooms required and unleashing stored capacity. This same theory applies to procedure time. If procedure time can be reduced by 5 min, we get the same impact as reducing the turnover time by 5 min.

HOW DO WE IMPROVE TURNAROUND TIME?

Just like setup reduction in manufacturing, we film it. Normally we find 20–30 ideas for turnaround time improvement when watching a radiology video. The goal is converting internal time to external time, and we can reduce the internal time (the time no patient is in the room) by up to 50% or more.

This is achieved through a combination of converting internal to external work, standard work, 5S as the areas are cleaned up, and the right amount of supplies and "tools" are in the right place and labeled, so searching is reduced. In the case of the ED, we eliminate the need for the X-ray request and push the patients to X-ray. We reduce LOS for ED patients by the cycle time we free up for X-ray. Sometimes, this can result in full-time employee (FTE) reductions.

HOW DO WE CALCULATE STAFFING FOR RADIOLOGY?

The formula for staffing is as follows:

- TLT divided by Takt time or cycle time at which we have to run

Example:

- TLT for the example above was 25 min for 1 patient (keep in mind TLT = time required with patient in room as well as time required before and after a patient leaves, i.e., setup room with patient)
- The formula is 25 min ÷ 10 min = 2.5 or 3 people

Note that when calculating TLT, you must also add in other value-added tasks that may be required. If cleanup is 10 min, however, we would subtract this from available time, but note it in our staffing schedule.

In our example above, if we need 2.5 people, we either need a part-time person, which usually doesn't work out, so we schedule an FTE. Since we don't need them the whole day, they are not fully utilized. This creates "fractional" labor because 50% of one person's time will be idle time or the person will be assigned other tasks from another area. The idle time may be limited to one person or could be spread across all 3 people. For staffing purposes, we may also need a supervisor and a radiologist. The radiologist's job is to interpret the X-ray and dictate the X-ray findings/notes into the hospital system. This job is becoming increasingly more centralized and may even be performed remotely within the country or, in the future, read offshore with technology that exists today (if the regulatory agencies allow it). For example, some radiology groups are buying villas in Spain and other countries and have their radiologists take a 1 month working vacation reading nighttime scans (it is day there). There is no shortage of volunteers, and hospitals get real 24/7 coverage by their own group.

OTHER CONSIDERATIONS

STAT X-RAYS

STAT X-rays generally are X-rays where the equipment is taken to the room. We are often told the resolution of these portable X-rays is not as good, yet the paradox is that they are used on our sickest patients. In a truly Lean ED for example, we would have portable X-ray equipment in the doctor examination rooms. This would be too expensive for a traditional ED, but would be feasible in a Lean ED with Lean care tracks. The goal of any Lean process is, basically, to convert the STAT process to routine processes so everyone gets a STAT X-ray.

FIVE S

Five S is key for radiology, as it is for all areas. Having a place for everything and the support equipment we use most frequently near to us or at point of use can help speed up turnaround times.

BENEFITS OF APPLYING LEAN

Lean concepts and tools have been and can be readily applied in the radiology inpatient and outpatient settings. Eliminating wastes and increasing value-added activities can have an impact that reaches beyond the radiology department, reducing throughput in the ED and on the inpatient floors. In addition, reducing throughput and turnover within the radiology department offers the ability to do more examinations in less time, thus increasing capacity and creating the potential to add revenue. Staffing to demand and level loading work should help to reduce overtime and agency hours required by staff.

LEAN RESULTS: RADIOLOGY*

The Lean team identified numerous causes of delay, including pervasive batching, misused elevators, and frequent interruptions to radiologists. The department implemented hundreds of changes to address the various causes of waste and, as a result of the Lean implementation, achieved the following results:

- The volume of incoming calls, an indicator of effective problem resolution, decreased by 30%. The number of inquiries from outpatients fell by 90%.
- Average report turnaround time fell by 42% for inpatient X-rays and by 72% for inpatient CT scans.
- ER patients saw even greater improvement, with final reports ready more than 1.5 days sooner for both X-ray and CT examinations (72% and 82% improvements, respectively).
- Without adding staff or equipment, the department was able to schedule 15–16 more CT scans a day.
- The department freed up storage space, which was converted into a reporting area for residents.

---

* The Diagnostic Imaging Department of Kingston General Hospital in Ontario, Canada, called on ValuMetrix® services to improve patient access, reduce turnaround time from examination to report, and train in-house staff to drive continuous improvement in the department, which averaged 115,000 procedures a year.

Section IV

Appendices

Appendix 1   Lean Practitioner Quiz

- Name the two pieces of the Lean business system.
- What are the four things a product can do?
- What are the three types of storage?
- What are the three types of WIP?
- What is a world-class goal for value-added for the product?
- What are the two things an operator can do?
- What are the three types of non-value-added work for the operator?
- What are the three environments operators work in?
- What is world class for operators in each environment?
- Why is it important to separate the product from the operator?
- Why is it important to separate the product and operator from setups?
- What is a Product Process Flow analysis used for?
- What is a standard work sheet used for?
- What is a part production capacity sheet?
- What is TPM?
- What is OEE?
- What is Six Sigma?
- Name one Six Sigma tool.
- What is the difference between an error and a defect?
- What is *Poka Yoke?*
- What is the main thing you do not want to see in a layout?
- Draw examples of acceptable layouts.
- What are the four parts of a setup?
- What are the three components of SMED?
- What is world class for a setup?
- What is the difference between clock time and labor time?
- Define internal and external work. Where else does it apply?
- Who developed SMED?
- Who at Toyota was the first to try Kanban in the machine shop?
- What are the four major components of the Toyota Production System?
- What are the seven (eight) wastes in the TPS?
- What is a Product Process Flow analysis?
- What is a full work analysis sheet?
- What is a part production capacity sheet?
- What is a standard work combination sheet?
- What is a standard work sheet?
- What is *Jidoka?*
- What is Kaizen?
- What is a Kaizen event?
- When are good times to use Kaizen events?

- What are the Five S's? Briefly describe each one.
- What are visual displays? Give some examples.
- What are visual controls? Give some examples.
- What are examples of a visual management system?
- What are some of the benefits of Five S and visual controls?
- What is the linkage between visual controls and mistake proofing and TPM?
- What is the linkage between TPM, visual controls, and operator productivity?
- Name four of the Lean pieces the product gives you.
- Name four of the Lean pieces the operator gives you.
- What are the six things that force you to batch?
- What is the definition of standard work?
- Describe each of the three components of standard work.
- How do you calculate Takt time? Give an example.
- What is available time?
- What is completion time in a PPCS?
- How do you calculate the total number of operators required?
- Does Lean apply to an office environment?
- Do you implement Lean on the floor or in the office first? Why?
- What is WIP in an office?
- What kind of results can you expect in an office?
- What tool(s) are best to use in an office?
- How should on-time delivery be calculated?
- How should inventory turns be calculated?
- How do you calculate a day's worth of inventory?
- What are key metrics for a Lean environment?
- What are some of the problems with traditional cost accounting in a Lean environment?
- What problems does reducing inventory cause in a Lean environment?
- Can accounting processes be improved? Give examples.
- What is a value stream?
- What are the four components of a value stream map?
- What is the purpose of value stream mapping?
- What is the most important thing to do when creating a baseline or current state value stream map?
- What is the definition of Kanban—two types of usage?
- What is the formula to calculate Kanban?
- What is the benefit of Kanban?
- What is bad about Kanbans?
- When do you need a Kanban and what is its purpose?
- What impact do Kanbans have on cell layouts?
- What is the simplest form of Kanban?

- What are the two things you look for in a Lean line to see if it has problems?
- What is always the sign of a problem?
- When you're working on something you don't need… (finish sentence)
- Inventory hides… (finish sentence)
- What is the difference between a current state, ideal state, and future state value stream map?
- What are the major components of a project action list?
- How important is the "buy-in" from top management?
- What are four characteristics of a change agent?
- What are four things necessary for a change agent in an organization?
- What is the change equation?
- What do people want to know when making a major change?
- What is a paradigm?
- What is the difference between a breadman and a milkman system?
- Why are day-by-the-hour charts important?
- What are typical results one should expect from Lean when converting from batch to Lean?
- What are typical characteristics of a batch system?
- What are typical characteristics of a Lean system?
- What are three tools one can use to have more effective meetings?
- How do you tie value stream mapping to the strategic plan?
- How does the typical employee review and evaluation process need to be changed? How do you tie it into succession planning?
- Why is standard work important?
- What program from the early 1940s is standard work based on?
- What is the difference between standard work and a work instruction?

- Describe the Lean culture that is behind the TPS system.
- What is Hoshin planning?
- Where did the Japanese learn QC circles?
- What is total company-wide quality control?
- How does it differ from TQ in the United States?
- How did Toyota get 20 million ideas in 40 years?
- What is the primary component of the group leaders' main job at Toyota?
- How does Toyota use outside committees to help them out?
- What is one of the main criteria for advancement at Toyota?
- Why are standing walking operations necessary? How do they fit into Toyota's concept of respect for humanity?
- What is an A3 drawing used for at Toyota?
- How many suggestions per person per month does Toyota average? What is the implementation rate?
- Is Toyota's suggestion system voluntary?
- What do Toyota employees do with their money when they get paid for an improvement?
- How does Toyota get such a high implementation rate and participation rate with suggestions?
- What percentage of Toyota's improvements comes from Kaizen events?
- What role did Taylor's system have with Toyota's system?
- What role did Gilbreth's system have with Toyota's system?
- What roles did Gilbreth, Taylor, and Henry Ford play with Lean?
- What is the difference between Taylor's and Gilbreth's approaches?
- What is the difference between motion study and time study? Which is more user-friendly?
- What is a Therblig? Name four of the 18 Therbligs.
- When did Toyota benchmark Ford's plant?

Appendix 2   Lean Formulas

Available time = total time less breaks, meetings, etc. (weekly meetings are amortized across the days, i.e., 25 min meeting per week = 5 min per day)

Capacity = available time ÷ complete time

Complete time = labor value added + labor non-value added + machine value added + machine non-value added (note labor time has to be in addition to machine time, not done in parallel)

Cycle time = amount of labor each operator has assuming line is balanced (if there is no machine bottleneck)

Cycle time = available time ÷ factory demand

Cycle time = total labor time ÷ number of operators or staff (if there is no machine bottleneck)

Daily output = available time ÷ cycle time

Hourly output = 3600 sec/hr ÷ the cycle time in seconds

Interruptible work in process (WIP) = cycle time of the machine ÷ cycle time or Takt time of the line. If it is non-interruptible then double interruptible quantity

Kanban sizing = (total amount needed to cover replenishment time (includes production and delivery) + safety stock + buffer stock yield) ÷ container size

Number of operators required = total labor time ÷ cycle time

Takt time = available time ÷ customer demand

Total labor time = labor value-added + labor non-value-added time

Appendix 3   Bibliography and Suggested Readings and References

Category	Author	Publisher	Year
Lean Overview			
All I need to Know about Manufacturing I learned in Joe's Garage	Miller	Bayrock	1997
America's Best - Industry Week	Kinni, Theodore	John Wiley & Sons	1996
Andy and Me	Pascal Dennis	Productivity Press	2005
Applying Just in Time	Yashuhiro Monden	IIE Press	1986
Best Practices in Lean Six Sigma Process Improvement	Schonberger, Richard J.	John Wiley & Sons	2008
Breaking Through to Flow	Jones	Lean Enterprise Academy	2005
Built to Last	James C. Collins	Harper Business Press	1997
Competing Against Time	Stalk, George/Hout, Thomas	Macmillan	1990
Creating Continous Flow	Rother & Harris	Lean Enterprise Institute	2006
Creating Level Pull	Art Smalley	Lean Enterprise Institute	2004
Cycle Time Reduction	Habour	Quality Resources	1996
Design of a Period Batch Control Planning System for Cellular Manufacturing	Riezebos	Print Partners	2001
Execution	Larry Bossidy and Ram Charan	Crown Business Publishing	2002
Fast Track to Waste Free Manufacturing	Davis	Productivity Press	1999
Gung Ho	Blanchard, Ken & Bowles, Sheldon	Baker and Taylor	1995
How Toyota Became #1	Magee	Harper Collins	2007
Impressions From Our Most Worthy Competitor	McGuire Kenneth	APICS	1984
Improving The Extended Value Stream	Dolcemascolo	Productivity Press	2006
In Sam we Trust	Ortega	Random House	2000
Inside the Mind of Toyota	Hino	Productivity Press	2006
It's About Time	Guaspari, John	AMA	1992
It's Not Magic	Klein/Zawacki	Mich State University Press	1999
Japanese Manufacturing Techniques	Richard Schonberger	The Free Press	1982
JIT Factory Revolution	Hirano	Productivity Press	1988
Kaikaku	Bodek	PCS Press	2004
Kaizen	Massaaki Imai	McGraw Hill	1997
Kaizen - the Key to Japan's Competitive Success	Imai	McGraw Hill	1986
Key Strategies for Plant Improvement	Shingo, Shigeo	Productivity Press	1987
Knowledge Driven Work	Japan Business and Economic Series	Oxford University Press	1998
Leading Lean	Solomon	WCM Associates	2005
Leading the Revolution	Hamel	Harvard Business School Press	2000
Lean Company Making the Right Choices	Jordan	SME	2001
Lean Enterprise Conversion, Best Practice Guide	SAE	SAE	2000
Lean Enterprise Leader	Martin	Midpoint	2005
Lean Machines	Richard McCormack	Publishers & Producers	2002
Lean Manufacturing A Plant Floor Guide	Allen, John et al.	SME	2001
Lean Six Sigma for Service	George	McGraw Hill	2003
Lean Solutions	Womack, James P & Jones, Daniel T	Simon & Schuster	2005
Lean Thinking	Womack, James P & Jones, Daniel T	Simon & Schuster	1996
Lean Transformation	Henders/Larco	The Oaklea Press	1999
Less is More	Jennings	Penguin Group	2002
Managing in the Next Society	Peter Drucker	St. Martins Press	2002
Manufacturing Ideology	Tsui	Princenton Univ Press	2001

(continued)

(Continued)

Category	Author	Publisher	Year
Maverick	Ricardo Semler	Warner Books	1993
Million Dollar Turnaround	Monahan	Oakley Press	2005
Modern Approaches to Manufacturing Improvement	Robinson	Productivity Press	1990
New Manufacturing Challenge	Suzaki	Free Press Simon Schuster	1987
New Shopfloor Management	Suzaki	Free Press Simon Schuster	1993
Nuts	Freiberg	Broadway Books	1997
Orchestrating Success Improve Control With Sales and Operations Planning	Ling	John Wiley & Sons	1998
Plain Talk	Ken Iverson	John Wiley & Sons	1997
Powered by Honda	Nelson, Mayo, Moody	John Wiley & Sons	1998
Reinventing the Factory	Harmon	Free Press Simon Schuster	1992
Reorganizing the Factory	Hyer	Productivity Press	2002
Revolutionizng Product Development	Wheelwright	Free Press Simon Schuster	1992
Southwest Airlines Way	Gittell	McGraw Hill	2003
The Agenda	Michael Hammer	Crown Business	2001
The Elegant Solution	Matthew May	Free Press	2007
The Goal	Goldratt, Eliyahu & Cox, Jeff	North River Press	2004
The Gold Mine	Freddy and Michael Balle	Lean Enterprise Institute	2005
The Hitchhikers Guide to Lean	Flinchbaugh, Jamie & Carlino, Andy	SME	2005
The Hunters & The Hunted	Swartz, James	Productivity Press	1994
The Quantum Leap	Costanza	Costanza Inst. of Technology	1996
The Toyota Way Fieldbook	Liker	McGraw Hill	2005
The Toyota Way	Liker	McGraw Hill	2005
Toyota Management System	Monden, Yasuhiro	Productivity Press	1993
World Class Manufacturing	Schonberger, Richard J.	Free Press	1986
The Introduction of Group Technology	John L. Burbidge	Heinemann	1975
Lean Manufacturing / Tools			
5S for Operators	Productivity Press, Inc.	Productivity Press	1996
A Revolution in Manufacturing: The SMED System	Shingo, Shigeo	Productivity Press	1985
A Study of the TPS From an Industrial Engineering	Shingo, Shigeo	Productivity Press	1989
Applied Production & Operations Management	Evans, James	West Publishing	1984
Cellular Manufacturing	Productivity Press, Inc.	Productivity Press	1999
Continuous Improvement in Operations	Alan Robinson	Productivity Press	1991
Gemba Kaizen	Imai	McGraw Hill	1997
handbook of Advanced Motion Study	Sylvester	Funk & Wagnels	1950
Just in Time for Operators	Productivity Press, Inc.	Productivity Press	1998
Just in Time Manufacturing	TCE Cheng	Chapman & Hall	1993
Just-in-time for today and tomorrow	Ohno and Mito	Productivity Press	1986
Kanban for the Shop Floor	Productivity Press	Productivity Press	2002
Kaizen for Quick Changeover	Sekine, Kenichi & Arai, Keisuke	Productivity Press	2006
Kaizen and The Art of Creative Thinking	Shingo	PCS Press	2007
Lean Lexicon	Shook	Lean Enterprise Institute	2004
Lean Manufacturing Tools, Techniques and How to Use Them	Feld	The St. Lucie Press	2001
Lean Production Simplified	Pascal	Productivity Press	2002
Lean Six Sigma	Michael George	McGraw Hill	2002
Learning to See	Rother, Mike and John Shook	LEI	1999
Managing the Value Chain	Harvard Business Review Series	Harvard Business Review	2000
Managing To Learn	John Shook	LEI	2008
Motion and Time Study	Ralph M. Barnes	John Wiley & Sons	1937
Motion Study	Gilbreth	Hive Publishing	1911
Non Stock Production	Shingo, Shigeo	Productivity Press	1988
One Piece Flow - Cell Design	Sekine, Kenichi	Productivity Press	1992
Product Development for the Lean Enterprise	Kennedy	Oakley Press	2003
Productivity Through Motion Study	Kato	Productivity Press	1983

Category	Author	Publisher	Year
Productivity Through Process Analysis I.E. for the Shop Floor	Ishiwata	Productivity Press	1997
Putting 5S To Work	Hiroyuki Hirano	PHP Institute	1993
Quick Changeovers for Operators: The SMED System	Productivity Press, Inc.	Productivity Press	1996
Running Today's Factory	Standard and Davis	Hanser Gardner	1999
Seeing the Whole	Womack	LEI	2002
Standard Work for the Shopfloor	Team Editor	Productivity Press	2002
The Balanced Scorecard	Kaplan	HBR Press	1996
The Five S's	Osada	Asian Productivity Association	1991
The Five S for the Office User's Guide	MCS Media	MCS Media	2008
The Handbook of Advanced Time and Motion Study	Sylvester	Magazines of Industry	1950
The Improvement Guide	Langley, Nolan, Norman, Provost	Jossey-Bass Inc.	1996
The Lean Office Pocket Guide	MCS Media	MCS Media	2005
The Lean Pocket Guide	MCS Media	MCS Media	2003
The Kaizen Blitz	Laraia, Moody, Hall	AME	1999
The Machine That Changed the World	Womack & Jones	Productivity Press	1990
The New Lean Toolbox	Bicheno	PICSEI Books	2004
The New Shop Floor Management	Suzaki	The Free Press	1993
The Simply Lean Pocket Guide	MCS Media	MCS Media	2008
The Shingo Production Management System	Shingo, Shigeo	Productivity Press	1992
The Toyota Product Development System	Morgan and Liker	Productivity Press	2006
Time and Motion Study	Barnes	John Wiley & Sons	1937
Time Out - Visual Based system	Wayne Smith	John Wiley & Sons	1998
Tools for Team Excellence	Huszczo	Davies Black	1996
Toyota Production System 1st Edition	Monden, Yasuhiro	Institute of Industrial Eng.	1993
Toyota Production System 3rd Edition	Monden, Yasuhiro	Institute of Industrial Eng.	2002
Toyota Production System	Monden, Yasuhiro	Institute of Industrial Eng.	1993
Training Within Industry Manual	Dinero	Productivity Press	2005
Training Within Industry	Dinero	Productivity Press	2005
Value Stream Management for the Office	Tapping and Shuker	Productivity Press	2003
Visual Control Systems	Shimbun, Nikkan	Productivity Press	1995
Visual Systems	Galsworth	American Mgmt. Assoc.	1997
Winning Through Innovation	Tushman	Harvard Univ. Press	1997
Lean & Leadership, Teams, H.R. and Organizational Design			
Analyzing Performance Problems	Mager, Robert F & Pipe, Peter	Fearon-Pitman	1970
Benchmarking	Camp, Robert	Quality Press	1989
Bottom Up Management	Giben	Harper & Brothers	1949
Bringing Out The Best in People	Daniels, Aubrey	McGraw Hill	1994
Bullies, Tyrants & Impossible People	Shapiro & Jankowski	Crown Business Publishing	2005
Buried Alive, Digging Out of a Management Dumpster	Yount	Oakley Press	2004
Capitalizing on Conflict	Blackard	Davies Black	2002
Confronting Reality	Bossidy	Brown Business	2004
Control Your Destiny or Someone Else Will	Tischy, Noel/Sherman, Strattford	Doubleday	1993
Crucial Conversations	Patterson	McGraw Hill	2002
Death by Meeting	Lencioni	John Wiley & Sons	2004
Designing Organizations	Galbraith, Jay R	Jossey-Bass Inc.	1995
Developing a Lean Workforce	Harris	Productivity Press	2007
Flight of the Buffalo	Ralph Stayer	Warner Books	1993
Gainsharing	Carl Thor	Crisp Publications	1999
Gainsharing and Employee Involvement	Moore/ Ross	BNA Books	1995
Gainsharing, Boosting Productivity and Profit	William Jackson	Mascotte Publishing	1996
Good To Great	James C. Collins	Harper Business Press	2001
Hoshin Handbook	Pete Babich	TQE	1996
Hoshin Kanri for the Lean Enterprise	Jackson	Productivity Press	2006
Hoshin Kanri - Policy Deployment	Akao, Yoji	Productivity Press	1988

(continued)

(Continued)

Category	Author	Publisher	Year
How to Argue and Win Every Time	Spence, Gerry	St. Martins Press	1995
HR Scorecard	Becker	HBR Press	2001
Human Relations in Supervision	Parker, Willard & Kleemeier, R.	McGraw Hill	1951
It's Not Luck	Goldratt	The North River Press	1994
Leader Effectiveness Training	Gordon, Dr. Thomas	Wyden Books	1977
Light bulbs for Leaders	Glacel/ Robert	John Wiley & Sons	1996
Make It So	Roberts, Wess & Ross, Bill	Pocketbooks	1996
One Way	John Nora	Plymouth Proclamation Press	1990
Overcoming the FIVE Dysfunctions of a TEAM	Lencioni	Jossey-Bass Inc.	2005
Principals of Industrial Organizations	Kimball	McGraw Hill	1939
Rate Your Skills as a Manager	Crisp, Michael (Editor)	Crisp Publications	1991
Serious Play	Schrage	Harvard Business School Press	2000
Strategy & Structure	Chandler	MIT Press	1990
Strategy Formulation & Implementation	Thompson	Business Publications	1980
Stronger Than Steel	Alderson	Thomas Nelson Inc.	1994
Successful Managers Handbook	Davis, Brian L.	Personal Decisions	1996
Team Reconstruction	Prichett	Prichette & Assoc	1992
Team Toyota	Terry Besser	SUNY Press	1996
The 7 Habits of Highly Effective People	Covey, Stephen	Simon & Schuster	1989
The FIVE Dysfunctions of a TEAM	Lencioni	Jossey-Bass Inc.	2002
The FIVE Dysfunctions of a TEAM	Lencioni	Jossey-Bass Inc.	1965
The HR Scorecard	Becker, Huselid,Ulrich	Harvard Business School Press	2001
The Instructor The Man and The Job	Charles R. Allen	Lippincott Company	1919
The Leadership Road map	Baumgardner and Scaffede	North River Press	2008
The Lightening of Empowerment	Byham, William C.	Fawcett	1988
The Strategy Focused Organization	Kaplan Norton	Harvard Business School Press	2001
The Team Handbook	Schulties	Orielinc	2003
Theory R Management	Alderson	Thomas Nelson Inc	1994
Top Management Organization and Control	Holden	Stanford University Press	1926
Toyota Culture	Liker	McGraw Hill	2008
Toyota Talent	Liker	McGraw Hill	2007
Transforming Strategy Into Success	Shinkle, George et al.	Harvard Business School Press	2000
What the CEO Wants You to Know	Ram Charan	Random House	2001
Who Moved My Cheese	Johnson	G.P. Putnam's Sons	1998
Workplace Management	Taiichi Ohno	Productivity Press	1982
Zap the Lighting of Empowerment	Byham	Balatine Books	1988
Toyota Kata	Mike Rother	McGraw Hill	2009
Lean and Sales/ Marketing			
Customers For Life	Sewell, Carl	Pocketbooks	1990
Killer Customer Care	George Colombo	Entrepreneur Press	2003
Making Customer Satisfaction Happen	McNealy, Roderick	Kluwer Academic Pub	1996
Managing Customer Value	Bradley T. Gale	The Free Press	1994
Strategies for Growth	Harvard Business Review Series	Harvard Review Press	1994
The Alchemy of Growth	Baghai, Coley, White	Orion Publishing	1999
The Great Game of Business	Stack	Doubleday	1992
Lean Accounting and Finance			
Accounting for World Class Operations	Solomon	WCM Associates	2007
Cost Management in the New Manufacturing Age	Monden, Yasuhiro	Productivity Press	1992
Cost Reduction Systems	Monden, Yasuhiro	Productivity Press	1995
EVA & Value Based Management	Young	McGraw Hill	2001
Japanese Management Accounting	Monden, Yasuhiro	Productivity Press	1989
Making the Numbers Count	Maskell	Productivity Press	1996
Measuring Corporate Performance	Various Authors	HBR Press	1991
New Performance Measures	Maskell	Productivity Press	1994

Category	Author	Publisher	Year
Performance Measurement for World Class Manufacturing	Maskell	Productivity Press	1991
Practical Lean Accounting	Maskell	Productivity Press	2004
Real Numbers	Fiume	Managing Times Press	2003
Techniques of Financial Analysis	Helfert, Erich	Irwin Publishing	1997
The EVA Challenge	Stern	John Wiley & Sons	2001
Using ABM for Continuous Improvement	Pryor	ICMS	2000
Who's Counting	Jerrold Solomon	WCM Associates	2003
Lean and Maintenance			
Autonomous Maintenance in Seven Steps	Tajiri, Gotoh	Productivity Press	1999
Introduction To Total Productive Maintenance	Nakajima, Seiichi	Productivity Press	1988
TPM Development Program	Nakajima, Seiichi	Productivity Press	1989
Uptime	Campbell	Productivity Press	1995
Lean Design/Engineering			
Applied Imagination	Alex Osborn	Creative Education Press	1993
Design for Manufacturability	Anderson	CIM Press	1990
Design Team Revolution	Sekine, Kenichi/Arai Keisuke	Productivity Press	1994
Developing Products in Half the Time	Smith, Reinertsen	Thomson Publishing Inc.	1998
Experimenting for Breakthrough Improvement	M. Beauregard	Resource Engineering	2000
Product Design and Manufacture for Assembly	Boothroyd/Dewhurst	Marcel Dekker, Inc.	1994
The Development Factory - Lessons from Pharmaceuticals	Pisano	Harvard Business School Press	1997
The Structure of Scientific Revolutions, 3rd Ed.	Kuhn, Thomas	University of Chicago Press	1996
Tool and Manufacturing Engineers Handbook	Bakerjian	McGraw Hill	1976
Lean Quality/Six Sigma/Total Quality/Poka Yoke (Mistake Proofing)			
A Practical Guide to Statistical Process Control	M. Beauregard	Van Nostrand Reinhold	1992
Company Wide Quality Control	Kondo, Yoshio	JUSE Press	1993
Demystifying Six Sigma	Lorson, Alan	Amacom	2003
DOE Simplified	Anderson, Mark & Whitcomb, Patrick	Productivity Press	2007
Fast Focus on TQM	Derm Barrett	Productivity Press	1994
FMEA Reference Guide	Resource Engineering Inc.	Resource Eng	1998
Implementing Six Sigma	Breyfogle III, Forest	John Wiley & Sons	1999
ISO 9000 at the Frontline	Levinson	ASQ Quality Press	2000
ISO 9000 in 2000 Explained	West	ASQ Quality Press	2001
ISO Quality System Development Handbook	Hoyle	Butterworth Press	1998
ISO9001: 2000 Explained	Charles Cianfrani	ASQ Quality Press	2001
Leaning into SIX SIGMA	Wheat, Barbara	McGraw Hill	2003
Make No Mistakes	Hinckley	Productivity Press	2002
Poka Yoke	Nikkan Kogyo Shimbun	Productivity Press	1988
Practical Guide to SPC	Beaurgard	Vannostrand Rinholdt	1992
Six Sigma	Mikel Harry	Doubleday	2000
Six Sigma Simplified	Arthur, Jay	Biblio	2001
Six Sigma Team Dynamics	Eckes, George	John Wiley & Sons	2002
SPC Reference Guide	ASQ	Resource Eng	1996
Taguchi Methods & QFD	Ryan, Nancy (editor)	ASI Press	1990
The Basics of FMEA	Robin McDermott	Productivity Press	1996
The Deming Management Method	Mary Waltong	Putnam Publishing	1986
The Memory Jogger	Brassard, Michael & Ritter, Diane	GOAL/QPC	1994
The Six Sigma Instructors Guide	Jay Authur	LifeStar	2003
Total Quality Control for Managemnet	Nemoto	Princes Hall	1987
Understanding Variation	Wheeler, Donald J	SPC Press	2000
Zero Quality Control	Shingo, Shigeo	Productivity Press	1986

(continued)

(Continued)

Category	Author	Publisher	Year
Change Management/Systems Thinking			
Adhocracy	Waterman	Little Books	1990
Beyond Survival	Blaha, Robert	Air Academy Press	1995
Black Body Theory & the Quantum Discontinuity	Kuhn, Thomas	Oxford Press	1978
Changing Forever The Scanlon Principles	Carl Frost	Michigan State University Press	1996
Creating a Lean Culture	Mann	Productivity Press	2005
Death by Meeting	Lencioni	John Wiley & Sons	2004
Harvard Business Review on Culture and Change	Harvard Business Review	HBR Press	2002
Leading Change	Kotter	Harvard Business School Press	1996
Making Sense of Change	Cameron, Green	Stylus	2004
Managing at the Speed of Change	Conner, Daryl	Villard Books	1992
Managing the Change process	Carr, Hard, Trahont	McGraw Hill	1996
Meeting Change	Kotter	HBR Press	1996
Now Discover your Strength	Buckingham	The Free Press	2001
Reengineering Management	Champy, James	Harper Business	1996
Strategic Organizational Change	Beitler	Practitioner Press	2003
Systems Thinking and Learning	Haines	HDR Press	1998
The Change Agent Handbook	Hutton	ASQ Quality Press	1994
The Change Agent's Guide to Radical Improvement	Miller, Ken	ASQ Press	2002
The Fifth Discipline Field Book	Peter Senge	Doubleday	1994
The Fifth Discipline	Peter Senge	Doubleday	1994
The Five Temptations of a CEO	Lencioni	Jossey-Bass Inc.	1998
The Set-Up-To-Fail Syndrome	Manzoni	Harvard Business School Press	2002
The Systems Thinking Playbook	Sweeney and Meadows	0	1995
The Tipping Point	Gladwell	First Back Bay	2002
History/Key People with Lean			
An Inquiry into the Nature of the Wealth of Nations	Adam Smith	Liberty Fund	1976
Fatigue Study	Gilbreth	Sturgis and Walton	1916
Ford Methods & the Ford Shops	Arnold	Ayer Co. Publishers	2002
Frederick W. Taylor	Wrege, Charles D.	Irwin Publishing	1991
Fredrick Taylor - Authorized Biography	Copley	Harper and Brothers	1923
Henry Ford, A Pictorial Biography	Henry Ford Museum	University Lithoprinters	1990
Henry Ford's Lean Vision	William Levinson	Productivity Press	2002
Henry's Lietenants	Ford Bryan	Wayne State Univ. Press	1993
I'm a Lucky Guy	Gilbredth	Browerl	1951
Introduction to Industrial Management	Folts	McGraw Hill	1932
Manufacturing Knowledge	Gillespie	Cambride Univ. Press	1991
My 40 Years at Ford	Sorenson	Norton	1956
My Life & My Work Henry Ford	Charles Allen	Lippincott	1919
Principles of Scientific Management	Taylor	Dover Publ.	1998
Scientific Management	Taylor	Harper	1911
Self Help	Smiles	Oxford Press	2002
Stealing Time Colapse of AOL Time Warner	Klien	Simon and Shuster	2003
Telephone The First Hundred Years	Brooks	Harper and Row	1975
The 12 Principles of Efficiency	Emerson Harrington	Engineering Magazine Co.	1911
The Capitalist Philosophers	Gabor	Random House	2000
The CCS Industrial Management Manual	Protzman, Sarasohn	Unpublished	1949
The Copernicun Revelotion	Kuhn, Thomas	HBR Press	1957
The End of Detroit	Maynard	Doubleday	2003
The Essential Tension	Kuhn, Thomas	University of Chicago	1977
The Evolution of the Manufacturing System at Toyota	Takahiro Fujimoto	Oxford University Press	1999
The Man Who Discovered Quality	Gabor	Penquin Books	1990

Category	Author	Publisher	Year
The One Best Way	Kanigel	Penguin Books	1999
The Principles of Scientific Management	Frederick Taylor	Dover Publications	1998
The Puritan Gift	Hopper, Hopper	I B Tauris	2007
The Quest of the One Best Way	Gilbreth, Lilan	Society of Women Eng	1990
The Company, A Short History of a Revolutionary Idea	Micklethwait and Wooldridge	Modern Library	2003
The Visible Hand	Alfred Chandler	Harvard Univ. Press	1977
The Witch Doctor's	John Micklethwait	Random House	1996
Today & Tomorrow	Henry Ford	Doubleday	1926
Wealth of Nations	Smith, Adams	Oxford Press	1976
Willow Run	Kidder	Kidder, Warren	1995
Lean and MBTI® Styles			
I'm Not Crazy—I'm Just Not You	Pearman	Davies Black	1996
Jung's Function-Attitudes Explained	Thompson	Wormhole Publishing	1996
Memories, Dreams, Reflections	C.G. Jung	Vintage Books	1989
Sixteen Ways to Love Your Lover (MBTI)	Kroeger and Thuesen	Tilden Press	1994
The Character of Organizations	Bridges	CPP Books	1992
The Nine Ways of Working	Goldberg	Marlowe & Company	1999
What Jung Really Said (MBTI)	E.A. Bennet	Schocken Books, NY	1983
Work it Out	Sandra Hirsh	Davies Black Publishing	1996
Working Together	Isachsen	CPP	1988
Lean Materials / Supply Chain			
Custom Kanban	Louis	Productivity Press	2006
Implementing Mixed Model Kanban	Vatalaro Taylor	Productivity Press	2003
Integrating Kanban with MRP II	Louis	Productivity Press	1997
Kanban for the Shop Floor	Productivity Press	Productivity Press	2002
Kanban for the Supply Chain	Cimorelli	Productivity Press	2005
Kanban Just-In-Time At Toyota	Japan Management Assoc.	Productivity Press	1989
Kanban Made Simple	Gross, McInnis	Amacom	2003
Lean Supply Chain (Practices & Cases)	Taylor	Productivity Press	2004
Lean Supply Chain Management	Wincel	Productivity Press	2004
Making Materials Flow	Harris, Rick	Lean Enterprise Institute	2006
Managing the Value Chain	Harvard Business Review Series	Harvard Business Review	2000
Manufacturing Operations and Supply Chain Management	Taylor and Brunt	Thomson learning	2001
Lean Machining and Group Technology			
2006 POLCA Implementation Workshop	SURI	University of Wisconsin	2006
Build To Order	Larco	Oakley Press	2008
Creating Mixed Model Value Streams	Duggan	Productivity Press	2002
Handbook of Cellular Manufacturing Systems	Irani	John Wiley & Sons	1999
Hybrid Cellular Layouts	Irani	Ohio State	2005
Lean Advisory Tools for Jobshops	Ohio State University	Zip Publishing	2007
Planning Manufacturing Cells	Hales and Andersen	SME	2002
Quick Response Manufacturing	SURI	Productivity Press	1998
Simplified Systematic Layout Planning - 3rd Edition	Muther and Wheeler	Management and Industrial Research Publications	1994
Trade Analysis & Course Organization	Bollinger	Pitman Publishing	1955
Lean Suggestion System and Problem Solving			
40 years, 20 million ideas: Toyota suggestion system	Yasuda	Productivity Press	1990
8D Structured Problem Solving	Rambaud	PHRED Solutions	2007
Employee Driven Quality	McDermott	Resource Eng	2000
Gainsharing & Power	Collins	Cornell University Press	1998

(continued)

(Continued)

Category	Author	Publisher	Year
Lean Software and IT			
Lean Software Strategies	Middleton	Productivity Press	2005
Easier, Simpler, Faster	Cunningham	Productivity Press	2007
Lean Healthcare and Healthcare Related			
A3 Problem Solving For Healthcare	Jimmerson	Productivity Press	2007
Building Type Basics for Healthcare Facilities	Kobus	John Wiley & Sons	2000
Demanding Medical Excellence	Millenson	University of Chicago Press	1996
Discharge Planning Handbook	Birjandi and Bragg	CRC Press	2009
How Doctors Think	Groopman	Houghton Mifflin	2007
If Disney Ran Your Hospital	Lee	Second River Health Care	2004
Improving Healthcare Using Toyota Lean Production Methods	Chalice	ASQ Quality Press	2007
Lean Hospitals	Grayban	CRC Press	2009
Management Lessons From the Mayo Clinic	Berry and Seltaman	McGraw Hill	2008
Paradox and Imperatives in Health Care	Bauer and Hagland	Productivity Press	2008
Reducing Delays and Waiting Times	Nolan	IHI	2006
Spacemed Guidelines	Hayward	Spacemed	2006
Stop Rising Healthcare Cost using Toyota Lean Production Methods	Chalice	ASQ Quality Press	2005
The Baptist Healthcare Journey To Excellence	Al Stubblefield	John Wiley & Sons	2005
The Best Practice, How The New Quality Movement Is Transforming Medicine	Kenney	Perseus Book Group	2008
The Lean Healthcare Pocket Guide	Hadfield	MCS Media	2006
The Nun and The Beaurcrat	Savary	CC-M Productions	2006
The Pittsburgh Way	Grunden	CRC Press	2008
Self Help / Communication / Conflict Mgmt Books			
What Clients Love	Beckwith, Harry	Warner Business Books	2003
The Other 90%: How to Unlock Your Vast Untapped Potential for Leadership and Life	Cooper, Robert	Three Rivers Press	2002
The One Thing You Need to Know	Buckingham, Marcus	Free Press	2005
Management Compass	Bechtel, Michele	Blackhall Publishing	2002
The Facilitative Way	Pricilla H. Wilson	Bookworks Publishing	2003
The Art of Thinking	Allen F. Harrison and Robert M Bramson	Berkley Publishing	2002
Styles of Thinking	Allen F. Harrison	Random House	1982
The Acheivers	Dr. Dan Leimann	Great Quotations	1998
Bringing Out the Best in Others	Connellan, Thomas	National Book Network	2003
Effective Communication	Harvard Business Review Series	HBR Press	2001
Fierce Conversations	Susan Scott	Berkley Publishing	2004
Fish Sticks	Lundin, Stephen et al.	Sports Pub	2003
Fourth Generation Management	Joiner, Brian	McGraw Hill	1993
Get It, Set It, Move It, Prove It: 60 Ways to Get Real Results in Your Organization	Brown, Mark Graham	Productivity Press	1994
Invisible Leadership	Rabbin, Robert	Devorss	1998
Leading on the Edge of Chaos	Murphy, Emmett & Murphy, Mark	Penguin	2002
Managing Projects Well	Bender, Stephen	Butterworth-Heinemann	1998
Never Check E-Mail in the Morning	Julie Morgenstern	Harper Audio	2004
Never Wrestle with a Pig	McCormack, Mark	Audio	2002
Reducing Stress	Hindle, Tim	DK Pub	1999
Synchronicity the Inner Path of Leadership	Jaworski, Joseph	Group West	1996

Appendix 4 Glossary

Activity-based Costing: Developed in the late 1980s by Robert Kaplan and Robin Cooper of Harvard Business School, it is primarily concerned with the cost of indirect activities within a company and their relationships to the manufacture of specific products. The basic technique of activity-based costing is to analyze the indirect costs within an organization and to discover the activities that cause those costs.

Andon: Andon means management by sight—visual management. The Japanese translation means "light." A flashing light or display in an area to communicate a given condition.

A3: A3 refers to an A3 (11" × 17") piece of paper Toyota uses to convey the problem solving story.

Batch Manufacturing: A production strategy that is commonly employed in "job-shops" and other instances where there is discrete manufacturing of a non-repetitive nature. In batch manufacturing, order lots are maintained throughout the production process to minimize changeovers and achieve economies of scale. In batch manufacturing environments, resources are usually departmentalized by specialty and are very seldom dedicated to any particular product family.

Benchmarking: Method of establishing internal expectations for excellence based on direct comparison to "the very best at what they do." It is not necessarily a comparison with a direct competitor.

Cause and Effect Diagram: A problem-solving statistical tool that indicates effects and causes and how they interrelate. This diagram is normally in the shape of a fish bone with the head being the effect and the scales being the causes.

Checkpoint: Control item with a means. A checkpoint requires immediate judgment and handling. It must be checked on a daily basis.

Chaku-Chaku: Japanese term for "load-load." Refers to a production line that has been raised to a level of efficiency that simply requires the loading of parts by the operator without any effort required for unloading or transporting material.

Continuous Improvement (Kaizen): A philosophy by which individuals within an organization look for ways to always do things better, usually based on an understanding and control of variation. A pledge to every day, do or make something better than it was before.

Control Chart: A problem-solving statistical tool that indicates whether the system is in, or out, of control and whether the problem is a result of special causes or common system problems.

Control Item: An item selected as a subject of control for maintenance of a desired condition. It is a yardstick that measures or judges the setting of a target level, the content of the work, the process, and the result of each stage of breakthrough and improvement in control during management activity.

Control Point: Control item with a target. A control point is used to analyze data and take action accordingly.

Cp Process Capability: The measured, inherent reproducibility of the product turned out by a process. The most widely adopted formula for process capability (Cp) is

Cpk > 1.33 = more than adequate

Cpk ≤ 1.33 but > 1.00 = adequate, but must be monitored as it approaches 1.00

Cpk ≤ 1.00 but > 0.67 = not adequate for the job

Cpk ≤ 0.67 = totally inadequate

Cross-Functional Management: The overseeing of horizontal interdivisional activities. It is used so that all aspects of the organization are well managed and have consistent, integrated, quality efforts pertaining to scheduling, delivery, plans, etc.

Customer Relations: A realization of the role that the customer plays in the continuation of your business. A conscious decision to listen to and provide products and services for those who make your business an ongoing concern.

Cycle Time: Available time divided by the factory demand, or the time each unit is coming off the end of the assembly line, or the time each operator must hit, or the total labor time divided by the number of operators.

Eight Dimensions on Quality: Critical dimensions or categories of quality identified by David Garvin of the Harvard Business School that can serve as a framework for strategic analysis. They are: performance, features, reliability, conformance, durability, serviceability, aesthetics, and perceived quality.

Elimination of Waste: A philosophy that states that all activities undertaken need to be evaluated to determine if they are necessary, enhancing the value of the goods and services being provided and what the customer wants. Determining if the systems that have been established are serving their users, or are the users serving the system.

Five Whys: Method of evaluating a problem or question by asking "why" five times. The purpose is to get to the root cause of the problem and not to address the symptoms. By asking why and answering each time, the root cause becomes more evident.

5S's: Method of creating a self-sustaining culture that perpetuates a neat, clean, efficient workplace. The Five S's are Sort, Store, Shine, Standardize, Sustain.

Flow Chart: A problem-solving tool that illustrates a process. It shows the way things actually go through a process, the way they should go, and the difference.

Flow Production: Describes how goods, services, or information are processed. It is, at its best, one piece at a time. This can be a part, a document, invoice, or customer order. It rejects the concept of batch, lot, or mass producing. It vertically integrates all operations or functions as operationally or sequentially performed. It also encompasses pull or demand processing. Goods are not pushed through the process, but pulled or demanded by succeeding operations from preceding operations. Often referred to as "one-piece flow."

FMEA (Failure Mode and Effects Analysis): A structured approach to assess the magnitude of potential failures and identify the sources of each potential failure. Each potential failure is studied to identify the most effective corrective action.

Full Work Analysis (AKA Operator Analysis or Job Breakdown): 2nd tool used for analysis which follows the operator (or staff person) through the process. Each step is captured to the second and assigned a code for value-added, necessary work, unnecessary work or pure waste (idle time).

Hoshin Planning: Hoshin Planning is the involvement of all employees in obtaining the strategic goals of the company. It is a comprehensive goal deployment strategy which involves intense follow up and everyone in the organization knows exactly how they are contributing to the strategic plan.

Interrelationship Diagram: A tool that assists in general planning. This tool takes a central idea, issue, or problem and maps out the logical or sequential links among related items. It is a creative process that shows every idea can be logically linked with more than one other idea at a time. It allows for "multidirectional" rather than "linear" thinking to be used.

Jidoka: English equivalent is autonomation. The 2nd pillars of the Toyota House. Autonomation means automating with a human touch or mind. Automatic machinery that will operate itself but always incorporates the following devices: a mechanism to detect abnormalities or defects and a mechanism to stop the machine or line when defects or abnormalities occur.

Just-In-Time Manufacturing: The 1st pillar of the Toyota house. A strategy that exposes waste in an operation, makes continuous improvement a reality and provides the opportunity to promote total employee involvement. Concentrates on making what is needed, when it is needed, no sooner, no later. The goal is to reduce inventory to highlight problems.

Kaikaku: Transformational change.

Kaizen: (kai = change; zen = good). Process improvement that involves a series of continual improvements over time. These improvements may take the form of a process innovation (event) or small incremental improvements.

Kakushin: Revolutionary change.

Kanban: Japanese for a signboard. Designates a pull production means of communicating need for a product or service. Originally developed as a means to communicate between operations in different locations. It was intended to communicate a change in demand or supply. In application, it is generally used to trigger the movement of material to or through a process.

Lead Time: The time to manufacture and deliver a product or service. This term is used in many (often contradictory) contexts. To avoid confusion, lead time is defined as the average total lapse time for execution of the product delivery process from order receipt to delivery to the customer under normal operating conditions. In industries that operate in a build to order environment, lead times flex based on the influences of seasonal demand loads. In environments where production is scheduled in repeating, fixed-time segments or cycles, the lead time is usually determined by the length of the production cycle (i.e., days, weeks, months, etc.).

Lean Production: The activity of creating processes that are highly responsive and flexible to customer demand requirements. Successful Lean production is evident when processes are capable of consistently delivering the highest quality products and services, at the right location, at the right time, in response to customer demand and doing this in the most cost effective manner possible.

Manufacturing Resources Planning (MRP II): A second generation MRP system that provides additional control linkages, such as automatic purchase order generation, capacity planning, and accounts payable transactions.

Materials Requirements Planning (MRP): A computerized information system that calculates materials requirements based on a master production schedule. This system may only be used for materials procurement or to execute the material plan through shop floor control.

Means (measure): A way to accomplish a target.

Monthly Audit: The self-evaluation of performance against targets. An examination of things that helped or hindered performance in meeting the targets, and the corrective actions that will be taken.

Multi Process: Multi Process means the person is capable of running multiple processes or machines.

Multi-Skilled Workers: Description of individuals at any level of the organization who are diverse in skill and training. Capable of performing a number of different tasks, providing the organization with additional flexibility.

Not Value-Added but Necessary: Meets one or two of the three criteria for value-added.

Objective: What you are trying to achieve with a given plan. The desired end result. The reason for employing a strategy and developing targets.

One-Year Plan: A statement of objective of an organizational event for a year.

Operation: A series of tasks grouped together such that the sum of the individual task times is equal to the Takt time (cycle time to meet product demand requirements). It is important to distinguish between operations and activities. Operations are used to balance work content in a flow manufacturing process in order to achieve a particular daily output rate equal to customer demand. An operation defines the amount of work content performed by each operator in order to achieve a balanced flow and linear output rate.

Operator: Generic description of the person doing the job whether in manufacturing, service industry or healthcare. This person can be staff or executive level.

Organization Structure: The fashion in which resources are assigned to tasks. Includes cross-functional management and vertical work teams. Also includes the development of multi-skilled workers through the assignment of technical and administrative personnel to non-traditional roles.

Organizational Tools: These provide a team approach in which people get together to work on problems and also get better at what they are doing. Organizational tools include work groups and quality circles.

Pareto Chart: A vertical bar graph showing the bars in order of size from left to right. Helps focus on the vital few problems rather than the trivial many. An extension of the Pareto Principle, which suggests that the significant items in a given group normally constitute a relatively small portion of the items in the total group. Conversely, a majority of the items in the total, even in aggregate, will be relatively minor in significance (i.e., the 80/20 rule.).

PDCA Cycle (Plan-Do-Check-Act): Sometimes referred to as the Deming cycle, this system is the most important item for control in policy deployment. In this cycle, you make a plan that is based on policy (plan); you take action accordingly (do); you check the result (check); and if the plan is not fulfilled, you analyze the cause and take further action by going back to the plan (action).

PDSA (Plan-Do-Study-Act): PDSA developed by Shewart - and later changed to PDCA.

Physical Layout: A means of impacting workflow and productivity through the physical placement of machinery or furniture. Production machinery should be grouped in a cellular arrangement based on product requirements, not process type. In addition to this, in most instances there is an advantage in having the work flow in a counter-clockwise fashion. Similarly, in an office environment, furniture should be arranged such that there is an efficient flow of information or services rather than strictly defined departments.

Plan: The means to achieve a target.

Poka yoke: Japanese expression meaning "common or simple, mistake proof." A method of designing processes, either production or administrative, that by their nature will prevent errors. This may involve designing fixtures that will not accept a defective part or something as simple as having a credit memo in a different color to a debit memo. It requires that thought be put into the design of any system to anticipate *what* can go wrong and build in measures to prevent them.

Policy: The company objectives that are to be achieved through the cooperation of all levels of managers and employees. A policy consists of targets, plans, and target values.

Policy Deployment: Orchestrates continuous improvement in a way that fosters individual initiative and alignment. It is a process of implementing the policies of an organization directly through line managers and indirectly through cross-functional organization. It is a means of internalizing company policies throughout the organization, from highest to lowest level. Top managers will articulate its annual goals, which are then "deployed" down through lower levels of management. The abstract goals of top management become more concrete and specific as they are deployed down through the organization. Policy deployment is process oriented. It is concerned with developing a process by which results become predictable. If the goal is not realized, it is necessary to review and see if the implementation was faulty. It is most important to determine what went wrong in the process that prevented the goal from being realized. The Japanese name for policy deployment is Hoshin Kanri. In Japanese, Hoshin means "shining metal," "compass," or "pointing in the direction." Kanri means "control." Hoshin Kanri is a method devised to capture and concretize strategic goals as well as flashes of insight about the future and develop the means to bring these into reality. It is one of the major systems that makes world-class quality management possible. It helps control the direction of the company by orchestrating change within a company. The system includes tools for continuous improvement, breakthroughs, and implementation. The key to Hoshin planning is that it brings the total organization into the strategic planning process, both top down and bottom up. It ensures that the direction, goals, and objectives of the company are rationally developed, well defined, clearly communicated, monitored, and adapted based on system feedback. It provides *focus for the organization*.

Prioritization Matrices: This tool prioritizes tasks, issues, product/service characteristics, etc., based on known weighted criteria using a combination of tree and matrix diagram techniques. Above all, they are tools for decision making.

Problem-Solving Tools: These tools find the root cause of problems. They are tools for thinking about problems, *managing by fact*, and documenting hunches. The tools include: check sheet, line chart, Pareto chart, flow chart, histogram, control chart, and scatter diagram. In Japan, these are referred to as the seven QC tools.

Process: A series of activities that collectively accomplish a distinct objective. Processes are cross-functional and cut across departmental responsibility boundaries.

Process Decision Program Chart: A method of mapping out conceivable events and contingencies that can occur in any implementation plan. In time, it identifies feasible countermeasures in response to these problems. This tool is used to plan each possible chain of events that need to occur when the problem or goal is an unfamiliar one.

Process Hierarchy: A hierarchical decomposition from core business processes to the task level. The number of levels in a hierarchy is determined by the breadth and size of the organization. A large enterprise process hierarchy may include: core business processes, processes, sub-processes, process segments, activities, and tasks.

Process Management: This involves focusing on the process rather than the results. A variety of tools may be used for process management, including the seven QC tools.

Process Segment: A series of activities that define a subset of a process.

Product Delivery Process: The stream of activities required to produce a product or service. This activity stream encompasses both planning and execution activities to include demand planning, order management, materials procurement, production, and distribution.

Product Process Flow: 1st tool used for analysis which follows the product (or patient) through the process. The object is to become the thing going through the process. It assigns a code to each step based on the acronym TIPS (transport, inspect, process, store).

"Pull" Production: In a pull process, materials are staged at the point of consumption. As these materials are consumed, signals are sent back to previous steps in the production process to pull forward sufficient materials to replenish only those materials that have been consumed.

"Push" Production: In a push process, production is initiated by the issuance of production orders that are offset in time from the actual demand to allow time for production and delivery. The idea is to maintain zero inventory and to have materials complete each step of the production process just as they are needed at subsequent (downstream) activities.

Quality Circles: An organizational tool that provides a team approach in which people get together to work on problems and improve productivity. Their primary objective is to foster teamwork and encourage employee involvement.

Quality Function Deployment: A product development system that identifies the wants of a customer and gets that information to all the right people so that the organization can *effectively exceed competition in meeting the customers' most important wants*. It translates customer wants into appropriate technical requirements for each stage of product development and production.

Quality Management: The systems, organizations, and tools that make it possible to plan, manufacture, and deliver a quality product or service. This does not imply inspection or even traditional quality control. Rather, it involves the entire process involved in bringing goods and services to the customer.

Quick Changeover: Method of increasing the amount of productive time available for a piece of machinery by minimizing the time needed to change from one model to another. This greatly increases the flexibility of the operation and allows it to respond more quickly to changes in demand. It also has the benefit of allowing an organization to greatly reduce the amount of inventory that it must carry because of improved response time.

Rate-based Order Management: This order management system employs a finite capacity loading scheme to promise orders based on the agreed demand bound limits. These minimum and maximum demand bounds reflect potential response capacity limits for production and materials procurement.

Rate-based Planning: A procedure that establishes a controlled level of flexibility in the product delivery process in order to be robust to anticipated variations in demand. This flexibility is achieved by establishing minimum and maximum bounds around future demand forecasts. The idea is that both the production facility and the materials supply channels will echelon sufficient capacity to accommodate demand swings that do not exceed the established demand bounds. As future demand forecasts move closer to the production window, updated demand bounds are periodically broadcasted to the materials suppliers. At the point of order receipt and delivery promising (within sales or customer service), demand bounding limits are enforced to ensure the rate-based production plan remains feasible.

RONA: Return on net assets.

Root Cause: The ultimate reason for an event or condition.

Run Chart: A statistical problem-solving tool that shows whether key indicators are going up or down and whether that's good or bad.

Scatter Diagram: One of the seven QC tools. The scatter diagram shows the relationship between two variables.

Self-Diagnosis: As a basis for continuous improvement, each manager uses problem-solving activity to see why he or she is succeeding or failing to meet targets. This diagnosis should focus on identifying personal and organizational obstacles to the planned performance and on the development of alternate approaches based on this new information.

Seven New Tools: Sometimes called the seven management tools. These are affinity and relationship diagrams for general planning; tree systems, matrix and prioritization matrices for intermediate planning; and activity network diagrams and process decision program charts for detailed planning.

Seven QC Tools: Problem-solving statistical tools needed for customer-driven master plan. They are: cause and effect diagram, flow chart, Pareto chart, run chart, histogram, control chart, and scatter diagram.

Seven Wastes: Toyota Seven types of waste have been identified for business. They are as follows:

1. Waste from over production of goods or services
2. Waste from waiting or idle time
3. Waste from transportation (unnecessary)
4. Waste from the process itself (inefficiency)
5. Waste of unnecessary stock on hand
6. Waste of motion and effort
7. Waste from producing defective goods

The eighth waste—waste of talent

Shine: Keep things clean. Floors swept, machines and furniture clean, all areas neat and tidy.

Simultaneous/Concurrent Engineering: The practice of designing a product (or service), its production process, and its delivery mechanism all at the same time. The process requires considerable up-front planning as well as the dedication of resources early in the development cycle. The pay-off comes in the form of shorter development time from concept to market, lower overall development cost, and lower product or service cost based on higher accuracy at introduction and less potential for redesign. Examples of this include the Toyota Lexus 200 and the Ford Taurus.

Sort: Clearly distinguish between what is needed and kept, and what is unneeded and thrown out.

Standard Deviation: Statistical measurement of process variation (σ). It measures the dispersion of sample observations around a process mean.

Standard Work: Standard work is a tool that defines the interaction of man and his environment when processing something. In producing a part, it is the interaction of man and machine, in processing an invoice, it is the interaction of man and the supplier and the accounting system. It details the motion of the operator and the sequence of action. It provides a routine for consistency of an operation and a basis for improvement. Further, the concept of standard work is that it is a verb, not a noun. It details the best process we currently know and understand. Tomorrow it should be better (continuous improvement) and the standard work should be revised to incorporate the improvement. There can be no improvement without a basis (standard work).

Standard work has three central elements: cycle time, standard sequence of operations, and standard work in process. Standard work (as a tool) establishes a routine/habit/pattern for repetitive tasks, makes managing (scheduling, resource allocation) easier, establishes the relationship between man and environment, provides a basis for improvement by defining the normal and highlighting the abnormal, and it prohibits backsliding.

Standard Work in Process: The amount of material or a given product that must be in process at any time to ensure maximum efficiency of the operation.

Standardize: Maintain and improve the first three "S's" in addition to personal orderliness and neatness.

Standardization: The system of documenting and updating procedures to make sure everyone knows clearly and simply what is expected of them (measured by daily control). Essential for application of PDCA cycle.

Standardized Work: When the process actually meets the standard work.

Statistical Methods/Tools: Statistical methods allow employees to manage by facts and analyze problems through understanding variability and data. The seven QC tools are examples of statistical tools.

Store: Organize the way that necessary things are kept, making it easier for anyone to find, use, and return them to their proper location.

Strategy: A means to an objective.

Sub-Process: A series of interrelated process segments that forms a subset of a total process.

Supplier Partnerships: An acknowledgment that suppliers are an integral part of any business. A partnership implies a long-term relationship that involves the supplier in both product development and process development. It also requires a commitment on the part of the supplier to pursue continuous improvement and world-class quality.

Sustain: Achieve the discipline or habit of properly maintaining the correct procedures.

System: The infrastructure that enables the processes to provide customer value. Business systems are comprised of market, customer, competition, organizational culture, environmental and technological influences, regulatory issues, physical resources, procedures, information flows, and knowledge sets. It is through physical processes that business systems transform inputs to outputs, thereby delivering products and services of value in the marketplace.

Systems Thinking: Systems Thinking is the process of looking at things from the "Big Picture", understanding how they interact and inter-relate.

Takt Time: The frequency with which the customer wants a product, how frequently a sold unit must be produced. The number is derived by taking the amount of time available in a day and dividing it by the number of sold units that need to be produced. Takt time is usually expressed in seconds.

Target: The desired goal that serves as a yardstick for evaluating the degree to which a "policy" is achieved. It is controlled by a "control point," "control item," or "target item."

Target Costing: Method for establishing the cost objective for a product or service during the design phase. The target cost is determined by the following formula:

Sales price – target profit = target cost.

This becomes one of the measures of success for the design team. It also recognizes that the majority (70%) of the cost of a given product or service is determined in the design phase. By the time the product is in production, it is too late to greatly reduce cost without a redesign. The tools used to develop target costs are cross-functional work teams, cost management during the design process, quality management, value adding vs. non-value adding, JIT, space minimization, and total productive maintenance. Target costing is the *fundamental* cost management technique (as prices fall costs must come down).

Target Value: Normally a numeric definition of successful target attainment. (It is not always possible to have a numeric target.) You must never separate the target from the plan.

Throughput Time: A measure of the actual throughput time for a product to move through a flow process from Raw Material to Finished Goods (or recycling).

Total Employee Involvement: A philosophy that advocates the harnessing of the collective knowledge of an organization through the involvement of its people. When supported by management, it is a means of improving quality, delivery, profitability, and morale in an organization. It provides all employees with a greater sense of ownership in the success of the company and provides them with more control in addressing issues that face the organization. TEI does not allow top management to abdicate

its obligation to properly plan and set objectives. However, it does provide more resources and flexibility in meeting those objectives.

Total Labor Time: The sum of labor value-added and labor non-value-added times.

Total Productive Maintenance: TPM is productive maintenance carried out by all employees. It is equipment maintenance performed on a company-wide basis. It has five goals:

1. Maximize equipment effectiveness (improve overall efficiency)
2. Develop a system of productive maintenance for the life of the equipment
3. Involve all departments that plan, design, use, or maintain equipment in implementing TPM (engineering and design, production and maintenance)
4. Actively involve all employees—from top management to shop-floor workers
5. Promote TPM through motivational management (autonomous small group activities)

The word total in "total productive maintenance" has three meanings related to three important features of TPM: total effectiveness (pursuit of economic efficiency or profitability); total PM (maintenance prevention and activity to improve maintainability as well as preventative maintenance); total participation (autonomous maintenance by operators and small group activities in every department and at every level).

Tree Diagram: Diagram that systematically breaks down plans into component parts. It systematically maps out the full range of tasks/methods needed to achieve a goal. It can be used as either a cause-finding problem solver or a task-generating planning tool.

Value-Added: To be value-added a step must meet all three criteria: if the customer cares about it, it physically changes the product or emotionally changes the patient for the better and it is done right the first time. Even value-added steps can be eliminated, rearranged, simplified or combined.

Value-Added Work Content Ratio: Steps that actually transform and increase the value of the product or test requirements that are legislated by industrial licensing agencies. The value-added work content ratio is formed by simply dividing the sum of all value-added work steps by the product lead time for the total process. This ratio can also be used to evaluate waste only in the manufacturing process segment by dividing the numerator by the manufacturing flow time.

Value Stream Map: Follows the overall flows or subsets of a product or information. The map contains process and data boxes, information systems interactions with process boxes, materials flow, and a time line with a results or summary box.

Vertical Teams: Groups of people who come together to meet problems or challenges. These teams are made up of the most appropriate people for the issue, regardless of their levels or jobs within the organization.

Vision: A long-term plan or direction that is based on a careful assessment of the most important directions for the organization.

Visual Control: Causes or compels someone to action i.e., red light. It may not necessarily force the action but is generally a reminder.

Visual Control Mechanism: Visual Control Mechanism that supplies, feedback to an area.

Visual Display: Displays information.

Visual Display Mechanism: Visual Display Mechanism that relates information and data to employees in the area through a display.

Visual Management: The use of visual media in the organization and general administration of a business. This would include the use of color, signs, and a clear span of sight in a work area. These visuals should clearly designate what things are and where they belong. They should provide immediate feedback as to the work being done and its pace. The other function served by visual management is to provide access to information needed in the operation of a business. This would include charts and graphs that allow the business status to be determined through their review. This review should be capable of being performed at a glance. In order to facilitate this it is necessary to be able to manage *by fact and let the data speak for itself.*

Water Spider: New role for the material handler. Water Spider can be a low skill or high skill job. Water Spider's job is to replenish empty bins on the line daily, plays vital role in mixed model parts sequencing, should stay 15 min or more ahead of the line, can be utilized as a floater, can be utilized to release parts orders from suppliers, should have standard work and walk patterns/milk runs.

Work Groups AKA Quality Circles: An organizational tool that provides a team approach in which people get together to work on problems to improve productivity.

Work Standard: A one off process or process that cannot be totally standardized.

World-Class Quality Management: The commitment by all employees. It is a philosophy/operating methodology totally committed to quality and customer satisfaction. It focuses on continuous process improvement in all processes. It advocates the use of analytical tools, and scientific methods and data. It *establishes priorities and manages by fact.* World-class quality management *has perfection (world class) as its goal.* We should benchmark to be better than the competition by a large margin, *the best.* To obtain this status, all employees must be involved, everyone, everywhere, at all times. The result will be products and services that consistently *meet or exceed the customers' expectations* both internal and external.

Yokoten: Yokoten is "knowledge sharing" across the organization

Index